OXFORD EARLY CHRISTIAN STUDIES

General Editors
Gillian Clark   Andrew Louth

THE OXFORD EARLY CHRISTIAN STUDIES series includes scholarly volumes on the thought and history of the early Christian centuries. Covering a wide range of Greek, Latin, and Oriental sources, the books are of interest to theologians, ancient historians, and specialists in the classical and Jewish worlds.

AMBROSE
De officiis

Edited with an Introduction,
Translation, and Commentary by
IVOR J. DAVIDSON

Volume II
Commentary

OXFORD
UNIVERSITY PRESS

OXFORD
UNIVERSITY PRESS

Great Clarendon Street, Oxford OX2 6DP

Oxford University Press is a department of the University of Oxford.
It furthers the University's objective of excellence in research, scholarship,
and education by publishing worldwide in

Oxford New York

Athens Auckland Bangkok Bogotá Bombay Buenos Aires Calcutta
Cape Town Chennai Dar es Salaam Delhi Florence Hong Kong Istanbul
Karachi Kuala Lumpur Madrid Melbourne Mexico City Mumbai
Nairobi Paris São Paulo Singapore Taipei Tokyo Toronto Warsaw

with associated companies in Berlin Ibadan

Oxford is a registered trade mark of Oxford University Press
in the UK and in certain other countries

Published in the United States
by Oxford University Press Inc., New York

© Ivor J. Davidson 2001

The moral rights of the author have been asserted
Database right Oxford University Press (maker)

First published 2001

British Library Cataloguing in Publication Data

Data available

Library of Congress Cataloging in Publication Data

Data applied for

Set ISBN 0-19-924578-9
Volume 1 ISBN 0-19-827023-2
Volume 2 ISBN 0-19-827024-0

1 3 5 7 9 10 8 6 4 2

Typeset in Imprint
by Joshua Associates Ltd., Oxford
Printed in Great Britain
on acid-free paper by
Biddles Ltd., Guildford & King's Lynn

CONTENTS

Book 1

The introduction covers 1.1–22. A. begins modestly: conscious of his inadequate preparation to take on the role of teacher, he confesses that his concern is simply to pay diligent attention to the Scriptures, and thus to learn himself as he fulfils his pastoral obligation to instruct others (1.1–4). In 1.5–22 he goes on to argue that the first lesson to learn is how to keep silent; by practising self-control, people discover when it is right to speak and when it is best to say nothing. Too many rush to speak because they do not know how to keep quiet (1.5). Silence is both meditative, an opportunity to listen for divine instruction or to direct one's words secretly to God (1.5–9), and ascetic, a refusal to give vent to passion or to respond to provocation (1.13–22). Humility and modesty are indispensable to Christian virtue (cf. 1.1–2, 13–14, 19–20). 1.5–22 is loosely structured around some verses from Ps. 38, a passage to which A. returns in 1.233–45; both sections draw on Origen's *Hom. Ps. 38*.1–2, which is also inspirational for A.'s *Expl. Ps. 38*.

These paragraphs have caused scholars a number of problems, focused in three areas. The first is the degree of diffidence A. expresses. Self-depreciation at the commencement of a work was a classical convention (see T. Janson, *Latin Prose Prefaces: Studies in Literary Conventions* (Stockholm, 1964), 116–61, especially 124 ff.), but the language of 1.1–4 has been thought to go beyond the usual confessions of intellectual inadequacy or artistic inability. The circumstances of A.'s election seem fresh in his memory, and his unpreparedness for the *sacerdotii necessitudo* (1.2) appears to be an enduring concern rather than just an unpleasant memory. Similar sentiments can be found in *Virg.* 1.1–4; 2.1–5 (especially 2.2), a work published in the late summer or autumn of 377, when A. had not yet been three years in the episcopate (*Virg.* 2.39). The second question surrounds the references in 1.13 and 1.15 to liturgical readings which have been heard *hodie*: these have been thought to imply that the section stems from a sermon. Finally, there is traditionally assumed to be no evocation of Cic. in 1.1–22.

On the basis of these three points, it has often been assumed that 1.1–22 must derive from a homily preached in the early days of A.'s episcopate, on the virtues of silence before speech, which has been crudely attached to the treatise (Emeneau, 49–50; Palanque, 453–4, 527; Homes Dudden ii. 694). On a somewhat different reading, 1.1–4 does stem from the late 380s, but it reflects A.'s enduring sensitivity to the criticism that he was elected bishop in unusual circumstances, without adequate theological preparation, while 1.5–22 incorporates material from a homily on Ps. 38, upon which A. also draws in 1.233–45 (Testard, 'Etude', 155–6, 164, 171–2; 'Recherches', 88–9, 96; Testard i. 273 n. 12; 'Observations', 22–5). The assumption is still that the *praefatio* mostly lacks Ciceronian inspiration, and that A. does not formally launch into his topic until 1.23.

Such theories are mistaken. There is no reason to assume on the basis of the two brief phrases in 1.13 and 1.15 that either the whole of 1.1–22 or 1.5–22 as it stands is sermonic [Introduction V]. Nor is it plausible that the A. of the late 380s was still haunted by the circumstances of his election, or that he had somehow had to wait tactically for this moment before daring to offer extensive advice to his clergy. Most importantly of all, 1.1–22 actually evokes Cic. *Off.* 1.1–6 to a significant degree, and the exceptional modesty which A. evinces is strategic (Savon, 'Intentions'). A. builds up a deliberate contrast between Cic.'s confidence, as he sets out to instruct Marcus, and his own self-effacing approach as a spiritual teacher. The *adrogantia* which A. disclaims (1.1) is spoken of by Cic. in *Off.* 1.2. A. hails the example of the *magister humilitatis*, David (1.1), and of Christ, the *unus . . . verus magister* (1.3); Cic. also speaks of a *magister*, Marcus' philosophical mentor, the Peripatetic Cratippus (*Off.* 1.1). A. refers to learning (*discere*) and teaching (*docere*) (1.1–4), and to 'passing on' (*tradere*) counsel (1.3; cf. 1.2); Cic. uses similar language in *Off.* 1.1–2, and of 'passing on' precepts on duty (*Off.* 1.4 and 1.6). A. speaks of the fear of the Lord as something *qui communis videtur esse omnibus* (1.1); Cic. refers to the *quaestio* of duties, *communis est omnium philosophorum* (*Off.* 1.5). A.'s references to *officium/officia* in 1.2–3 seem to pick up Cic.'s frequent use of the words throughout *Off.* 1.1–6, and there are other close verbal associations which suggest that Cic.'s early paragraphs are in A.'s mind (see on *inter filios* (1.1); *arbitror* (1.1); *praeceptorem* (1.1); *exemplo* (1.2); *non vacavit* (1.4)). Further reminiscences of other passages of Cic. can be traced in 1.14, 18, and 20, which preclude any sharp distinction between 1.1–4 and 1.5–22.

Unlike Cic., with all his boasts about his literary prowess and his aspirations to add his own contribution to a philosophical tradition, A., obliged to offer instruction to his spiritual 'sons' by virtue of an office which he did not seek and for which he feels morally unworthy, takes the lowliest teaching role as a fellow-student with his pupils of Scripture's wisdom. Instead of bragging about his rhetorical gifts, he seeks to imitate the humility of spiritual giants like David and Paul—indeed to advocate the silence, meditation, and self-mastery epitomized by Christ himself. 1.1–22 is an integral part of the text which follows: A. signals many of the emphases that will be crucial when he comes to specify the content of virtue in detail—humility, modesty, chastity, true wisdom, genuine happiness, disciplined speech, the right kind of activity (the *silentium* must be *negotiosum*: 1.9), resistance to anger, mastery of passion, and forgiveness of insults (Savon, 'Intentions', 166; Steidle, 'Beobachtungen', 23, 28).

See further I. J. Davidson, 'A Tale of Two Approaches: Ambrose, *De officiis* 1.1–22 and Cicero, *De officiis* 1.1–6', *JThS* NS 52 (2001), 61–83. Savon, 'Intentions' (especially 160 ff.), points out some features of A.'s contrast with Cic. but by no means all; Testard's diffuse response to Savon in 'Observations' largely misses the point by continuing to ignore the Ciceronian evocation in 1.1–22 and exaggerating the constraints within which A. operated in the late 380s.

CHAPTER 1: THE UNWORTHY (UNSCHOOLED)
TEACHER

1.   **Non adrogans videri arbitror:** Cf. Cic. *Off.* 1.2: *Nec vero hoc adroganter dictum existimari velim.* Cic. *Off.* 1.1 also has *se arbitrentur.* On avoiding arrogance, a *mala ruina* (*Expos. Ps 118.*3.35), cf. 1.70; 2.119, 122, 124, 134; 3.28, 36. For similarly modest beginnings, cf. *Virg.* 1.1–5; 2.1–5 (especially 2.2); and, among many examples, Sulp. Sev.*VM*, ep. dedic.; Jer. *Epp.* 60.1.1; 130.1.1–2; Paul. *VA* 1; Max. Taur. *Serm.* 78.1; Ps.-Aug. *Vita Chr.*, praef.

inter filios: A.'s clergy; see on 1.24. Cf. Cic.'s address in *Off.* 1.1: *Marce fili.*

humilitatis magister: David, a favourite exemplar in *Off.*, and the central one in 1.1–22; cf. *Apol.*, *passim*, and see Pizzolato, 117–29. A. establishes at once the pattern he will follow throughout the work: biblical figures, especially from the OT, are to be his moral and spiritual guides. But David is also a personal model for a bishop who feels inadequate: humility and teaching can go together. On David as *magister*, cf. 1.7, 96 (cf. Mary as *magistra humilitatis* in *Luc.* 2.22); on his *humilitas*, cf. 1.21, 236–8; 2.34; *Ep. extra coll.* 11 [51].9; Aug. *En. Ps. 131.*2; on his significance to the theme of *officia*, cf. 1.31; also 3.1. David is effectively a substitute for Cic.'s references to Cratippus (*Off.* 1.1–2); the self-depreciation which A. goes on to express is consonant with David's example, and contrasts with Cic.'s effort to add his own authority to that of Cratippus in the estimation of Marcus. Humility, a Christian antithesis to the classical *gloria*, is one of the main emphases of the clerical image A. seeks to cultivate (cf. 1.13, 19, 65, 237; 2.34, 67, 87, 119, 122–4; 134; 3.36, 133); on the juxtaposition with *adrogantia*, cf. *Cain* 1.27. Pride is regarded as the greatest sin: *Expos. Ps. 118.*7.8. Priestly humility is patterned upon the example of the Jesus who washed feet (e.g. *Sacr.* 3.4–7; *Myst.* 33; *Spir.* 1.15; *Virgt.* 57–9; *Expl. Ps. 48.*8–9; *Luc.* 6.67) and wept at the tomb of Lazarus (*Paen.* 2.66–79); see Sauer, 140–2; Dassmann, 240–4; Gryson, *Prêtre*, 311–17; on the background, A. Dihle, 'Demut', *RAC* iii. 735–78; K. Wengst, *Humility:*

Solidarity of the Humiliated (London, 1988). The author's own example (highlighted by Paul. *VA* 16) is signalled right from the start with a self-conscious appeal to distinguished spiritual precedent; cf. *Iac.* 1.12; *Myst.* 33; *Paen.* 1.1–3.

***Venite, filii . . . docebo vos*:** Ps. 33: 12.

verecundiae: Another key ethical principle, to be developed at length in 1.65–97, especially 1.65–89; see on 1.65.

***timorem Domini*, qui communis videtur esse omnibus:** Cf. Cic. *Off.* 1.5: *Atque haec quidem quaestio communis est omnium philosophorum.* For Cic. it is the subject of duties that is of universal interest among philosophers; for A. it is an innate fear of the Lord that is basic to the human race. In the Wisdom tradition, fear of the Lord is the state of heart that epitomizes a right relationship to God (G. Wanke, *TDNT* ix. 201–3); A. treats it as an essential human instinct. The apparently subtle substitution of the biblical idea for Cicero's thought is essential to the perspective with which A. is setting out: his implication is that the working out of this fear constitutes the heart of all duty. The fear which Stoicism counted as an irrational passion and Epicureanism derided as an obstacle to happiness is for A. the indispensable first stage in moral virtue: cf. *Ex.* 1.12; *Expos. Ps. 118*.8.55–6; *Iac.* 1.9. On faith as fundamental, cf. 1.117, 124, 126, 142, 252–3; 2.7

cum ipse timor initium sapientiae sit: Ps. 110: 10; Eccli. 1: 16 (also Prov. 1: 7; 9: 10).

beatitudinis: The ingredients of this outcome of morality are explored at length in 2.1–21.

timentes Deum beati sunt: Ps. 127: 1; cf. *Expos. Ps. 118*.8.1: *Ergo qui timentes Deum, sapientes; qui autem sapientes beati . . . Hi quoque, qui timent Deum, beati sunt.* All *beatitudo* comes from God: *Expos. Ps. 118*.5.33; *Fug.* 36.

praeceptorem: Cic. *Off.* 1.1, 4, 6 uses various cognates of this word (cf. also *Off.* 1.60).

2. Spiritus . . . sapientiae: Cf. Is. 11: 2.

usu . . . atque exemplo: VC's **usu** makes greater sense than the better-attested *visu*, as it gives a pairing of similar words: cf. 2.25: *usu atque institutione.* Cic. *Off.* 1.1 speaks of *exempla*.

quasi liberis: See on 1.24.

tradimus: Cic. uses this verb several times in *Off.* 1.4–7
(also *Off* 1.60), and it is equally used in the NT for the
handing on of early Christian teaching (Lk. 1: 2; 1 Cor. 11: 2,
23; 15: 3; also Rom. 6: 17; 2 Pt. 2: 21; Jd. 3): on παραδίδωμι
and παράδοσις as technical terms, see F. Buchsel, *TDNT* ii.
169–73. See further on 1.3.

**cum iam effugere non possimus . . . sacerdotii neces-
situdo:** This could be read as an indication that A. is in the
early days of his episcopate, but it could equally reflect a
sensitivity to continuing swipes by his opponents at his
fitness to teach. Testard, 'Aveu', 227–30; 'Observations',
13–22, argues that A. remained all too aware that his
ordination had breached the principle of 1 Tim. 3: 6 that a
bishop should not be a novice, and he suggests that the
irregularity of his elevation continued to be cited against him
by his enemies. Jer. *Ep.* 69.9, speaks of *adrogantia* and
humilitas in the context of 1 Tim. 3: 6. A. does seem to be
sensitive about 1 Tim. 3: 6: he omits it when he quotes
extensively from the surrounding passage in 1.246. But the
main note here is a contrast with Cic.'s assured confidence as
instructor. On A.'s reluctance to be ordained, see on 1.4.
Dedit enim *Deus quosdam quidem . . . doctores*: Eph.
4: 11.

3. **quos ipse Filius elegit Dei:** Cf. Jn. 15: 16, 19.
**intentionem et diligentiam circa scripturas divinas
opto adsequi:** Having disclaimed any right to the status of
apostle, prophet, evangelist, or even pastor, A. also refuses to
call himself a *doctor*. He is content to take the humblest role:
by quietly attending to the Scriptures, he will be able to learn
as he teaches. The Bible is inspired by the Holy Spirit (cf.
3.14; *Ep.* 55 [8].1; *Spir.* 3.112; *Parad.* 38; *Expos. Ps.*
118.18.37; *Ep. extra coll.* 14 [63].78) and is thus uniquely
normative, for it is the true revelation of God's will for
human behaviour. It is the supreme source of A.'s authority
(1.102), and is to be diligently studied by clerics (1.88, 165).
On the formative role of Scripture here for one without
adequate preparation to serve, cf. *Expos. Ps. 118*.8.59; 12.28;
also, in particular, Aug. *Ep.* 21.3–6. For A.'s insistence upon
a proper approach to a careful understanding of the Scriptures, see Pizzolato, 269–301.

quam ultimam posuit apostolus inter officia sanctorum: A. may be thinking of more than Eph. 4: 11. 1 Cor. 15: 9–10 may well be in his mind: *Ego enim sum minimus apostolorum, qui non sum dignus vocari apostolus* (Savon, 'Intentions', 163–4). He evokes the latter passage in a similar context in *Paen.* 2.73; see on 1.4 below.

et hanc ipsam ut docendi studio possim discere: Cic. *Off.* 1.1–2 has similar language (*doctoris . . . docti . . . disces*), which A. is probably echoing; see also on 1.4.

Unus enim verae magister est: Cf. Mt. 23: 8, 10; also *Expos. Ps. 118*.8.59; *Ep.* 65 [75].5.

ab illo accipiunt: Cf. Cic. *Off.* 1.4: *Nam cum multa sint in philosophia et gravia et utilia accurate copioseque a philosophis disputata, latissime patere videntur ea quae de officiis tradita ab illis et praecepta sunt*; and 1 Cor. 11: 23: *Ego enim accepi a Domino quod et tradidi vobis.* A. evokes Ciceronian language; but he also echoes Scripture. Just as David is the Christian's *magister* in place of the young Cic.'s Cratippus in 1.1, so here Christ is the ultimate *magister* and the supreme source of whatever true teaching people pass on. The philosophers are out: Christ is in. By humble devotion to the Scriptures, A. will learn from Christ, and so his teaching will carry authority, for all his inherent inadequacy. He may shy away from claiming the glory of the apostles; but at the same time he hints that submission to the Christ of the Scriptures will afford him a quasi-apostolic *persona*: like Paul, he will be teaching as one whose material comes from the Lord. If 1 Cor. 15: 9–10 is also in his mind, he is suggesting that however unworthy his past may have been, it makes him no less fit for his task than Paul was himself: by the grace of God, the unworthy are given the qualifications they need. On Paul's didactic example, cf. 2.87.

4. Ego enim raptus de tribunalibus . . . quod ipse non didici: A vivid picture of the unwillingness of A. to be consecrated as bishop. There are very similar descriptions in *Paen.* 2.67:

qui de forensium strepitu iurgiorum et a publicae terrore administrationis ad sacerdotium vocatus sim; 2.72–3: Dicetur enim: 'Ecce ille non in ecclesiae nutritus sinu, non edomatus a puero, sed raptus de tribunalibus, abductus vanitatibus saeculi huius, a praeconis voce ad psalmistae adsuefactus canticum, in sacerdotio manet non virtute sua, sed Christi gratia, et inter convivas mensae caelestis recumbit.' Serva, Domine, munus tuum, custodi donum, quod contulisti etiam refugienti. Ego enim sciebam, quod non eram dignus vocari episcopus, quoniam dederam me saeculo huic. Sed gratia tua sum quod sum, et sum quidem minimus omnium episcoporum et infimus merito [cf. 1 Cor. 15: 9–10]; tamen quia et ego laborem aliquem pro sancta ecclesia tua suscepi, hunc fructum tuere, ne, quem perditum vocasti ad sacerdotium, cum sacerdotem perire patiaris.

The milieu of A.'s former life would certainly have offered scant preparation for any conventional understanding of the role of spiritual instructor: on the unavoidably harsh duties of a *consularis* of Aemilia-Liguria (not to be identified, however, as A. himself), cf. Jer. *Ep.* 1.3–15: interrogation under torture and severe measures to maintain public order were standard practice, despite Paulinus' rather unlikely claim that A. had been more lenient: *VA* 7. On A.'s consistently negative later assessment of his secular career, see A. Lenox-Conyngham, 'The Judgement of Ambrose the Bishop on Ambrose the Roman Governor', *SP* 17 (1982), 62–5. Cf. also *Ep. extra coll.* 14 [63].65: *Quam resistebam ne ordinarer! Postremo cum cogerer saltem ordinatio protelaretur! Sed non valuit praescriptio, praevaluit impressio. Tamen ordinationem meam Occidentales episcopi iudicio, Orientales etiam exemplo probaverunt* [cf. Con. Nic. *can.* 2]. *Et tamen neophytas prohibetur ordinari ne extollatur superbia* [cf. 1 Tim. 3: 6]. *Si dilatio ordinationi defuit, vis cogentis est, si non deest humilitas competens sacerdotio, ubi causa non haeret, vitium non imputatur.* The story of his attempts to resist ordination is famously told by Rufin. *HE* 2.11 and, with elaboration, by Paul. *VA* 7–9; on his leaving the secular world behind, cf. Bas. *Ep.* 197.1. See Y.-M. Duval, 'Ambroise, de son élection à sa consécration', in *AmbrEpisc* ii. 243–83. It was standard practice in late antiquity formally to decline high office, pleading one's unworthiness and unwillingness, before humbly consenting to be appointed (C. Roueché, 'Acclamations in the Later Roman Empire: New Evidence from Aphrodisias', *JRS* 74 (1984), 181–99), and the same custom became part of the etiquette of

Christian ordination processes, where the *humilitas* ideal lent an additional impetus to the formality: e.g. Pont. *Vita Cypr.* 5; Paul. Nol. *Epp.* 1.10; 4.3; Sulp. Sev. *VM* 5; Gaud. Brix. *Tract.* 16.2; Greg. Naz. *Or.* 2.1–9; John Chrys. *Sacerd.* 1.6; Jer. *Ep.* 60.10.3–4; Aug. *Ep.* 21.1; *Serm.* 355.2; Possid. *Vita Aug.* 4: see P. H. Lafontaine, *Les Conditions positives de l'accession aux ordres dans la première législation ecclésiastique (300–492)* (Ottawa, 1963), 72–91. But A. was not only faced with being translated directly from imperial service to the ecclesiastical life; he was also confronted with the task of leading a church deeply riven by doctrinal tensions: his reluctance was very likely genuine enough, *pace* H. von Campenhausen, *Ambrosius von Mailand als Kirchenpolitiker* (Berlin and Leipzig, 1929), 26–9. A. was not *chosen* as bishop purely as a result of democratic popularity (on which see R. Gryson, 'Les Elections épiscopales en Occident au IVe siècle', *RHE* 75 (1980), 257–83, especially 269–73), nor was he directly imposed as an imperial candidate, *pace* C. Corbellini, 'Sesto Petronio Probo e l'elezione episcopale di Ambrogio', *RIL* 109 (1975), 181–9. Rather, by intervening in the election of a homoian successor to Auxentius, he had implicitly demonstrated his support for the cause of the Nicene dissidents, which had little chance of carrying the day without such official endorsement; the Nicene party had seized the opportunity and succeeded in persuading Valentinian I to sanction the choice (McLynn, 1–52; cf. Ramsey, 19–21).

ut prius docere inciperem quam discere: The collocation of *docere . . . discere* is quite common, even quasi-proverbial: e.g. Sen. *Ep.* 7.8; Petr. *Sat.* 88.6; Serg. in Donat. 4.486.11; and especially Cic. *Off.* 1.1–2 (*TLL*, 5.1.1331, 1748). In A., cf. *Sacr.* 6.26: *Docuimus pro captu nostro forsitan quod non didicimus*; also *Ex.* 5.10; *Parad.* 56, 58; *Abr.* 1.68; *Iac.* 2.12; *Exc. fr.* 1.9: *Non omnes ad docendum idonei, utinam omnes ad discendum habiles!* It occurs in Jerome a number of times (*Epp.* 52.7.1–8.2; 53.3.1; 10.1–2, 6.2–7.2; 58.8.3; 69.9.1; 84.3.1; 108.26.1). It has been suggested that in these passages Jerome is taking one of his many anonymous swipes at A.'s incompetence (Testard, 'Aveu', 238–9), but this is rightly challenged as a general assumption by N. Adkin, 'Jerome, Ambrose and Gregory Nazianzen (Jerome, *Epist.* 52, 7–8)', *Vichiana*, 4 (1993), 294–300. Adkin does not consider the other possible grounds for inferring some connection between Jer.'s *Ep.* 52 and *Off.*: see I. J. Davidson, 'Pastoral Theology at the End of the Fourth Century: Ambrose and Jerome', *SP* 33 (1997), 295–301 (but I now withdraw my comment there about *discere–docere*).

quoniam non vacavit ante discere: Cic. uses the verb *vacare* in *Off.* 1.4. A. had come from a Christian family; he had not been baptized as a child, though this was not at all unusual in Christian families of the time: the same was true of, *inter alia*, Basil, Gregory of Nazianzus, John Chrysostom, Jerome, and Augustine (A. would in time strongly advocate infant baptism: *Abr.* 2.81, 84; *Elia* 84–5). He had spent his teenage years at Rome, in an environment where the family received regular clerical visits (Paul. *VA* 4), and would certainly have heard news of major developments such as the goings-on at the Council of Milan in 355. By the time of his election A. was already a catechumen (Paul. *VA* 7). His sense of theological or spiritual inadequacy thus needs to be measured against a background of Christian influences. Novice he may have been, but he had not been entirely deprived of spiritual nurture. Self-taught clerics were not unusual at this time, either; all that distinguished A.'s case was the abruptness of his initiation. Few leaders had at the time of consecration passed through what we should deem a formal seminary programme; it was normal to do much of the learning on the job. A. never went on to write a series of theological *retractiones* after the manner of Augustine, who could express himself in some similar terms: *En. Ps. 126.*3: *tamquam vobis ex hoc loco doctores sumus; sed sub illo uno magistro in hac schola vobiscum condiscipuli sumus*; see further Madec in BA vi. 545–8. In the present context, the humility is a deliberate contrast with Cic.'s approach, rather than a heartfelt confession by one in the early days of his ministry: as the work proceeds, there is little other than assurance in A.'s style.

CHAPTER 2: SILENCE AND SPEECH

1.5–22 is on the theme of silence and the restraint of speech in situations of provocation; cf. 1.31–5, 68, 234. At first glance, there seems to be little direct inspiration from Cic. but in fact 1.18 is almost certainly suggested by *Off.* 1.137; 1.17 may well evoke *Off.* 1.34; and there is language from *Off.* 1.134 in 1.14 and *Off.* 1.108 in 1.18. Silence was regarded as a virtue in Stoicism (e.g. Epict. *Ench.* 33.2; see also on 1.202; also Plu. *Mor.* 502b–515a, especially 504a), and for A. this particular focus on self-control provides a useful bridge into his topic. We learn by humbly listening to God (1.5, 7); just as wisdom begins with the fear of the Lord (1.1), sin begins with hasty speech (1.5–8). Silence is, then, the very first thing which the believer needs to learn (1.5, 7; cf. 1.35); it is the product of a well-guarded heart (1.6–14), and the evidence of the *humilitas* A. is so keen to commend (1.13, 19). It is a poignant index of the inner self (1.11) when confronted by the temptation to sin, whether the temptation comes subtly from Satan (1.15–16) or openly from a *peccator* (1.17–20). A. offers a series of biblical *exempla*, not least the model of Christ himself (1.9; cf. 1.20), but he does evince a certain spiritual realism: it takes divine protection, ultimately, for a person to avoid sinning with his tongue (1.6); and anger, the urge to respond in kind, is a natural emotion (1.13). He is not advocating perpetual silence or dumbness (1.9; cf. 1.31–4), but a careful weighing of words (1.11–14). A Stoic ideal of the mastery of passion is combined with the Christian picture of the godly sufferer who prefers to commit his case to God (1.9, 14–22; cf. 2.19–21). It is a *negotiosum silentium* that A. commends, in which communion with God is possible, and where the testimony of a good conscience is considered eloquent enough in itself (1.9; cf. 1.6, 18, 21; also 1.35, 68).

Silence is an indispensable part of Ambrosian spirituality, then, but it is the silence which facilitates an appropriate fulfilment of duty in the workaday world of sinful realities. This section is not a somewhat spiritualized digression from the pragmatic theme of *officia*, but the first step towards spelling out what it means, in A.'s mind, to serve God in society. It encapsulates at the start of the work the author's preoccupation with the overall image of self-mastery, and the attendant motifs of humility, modesty, chastity, and restraint (Savon, 'Intentions', 166). It is intriguing to speculate on whether A.'s stress on silence is in part a response to criticism of his own failure to confront his homoian opponents in his early years; such silence had of course been a strategic necessity as much as a sign of particular spiritual grace. On some of the other (numerous) places where A. praises silence, e.g. *Virgt.* 80–1; *Inst. virg.* 4–5; *Exh. virg.* 84–90; *Expl. Ps. 37*.42; *Expl. Ps. 38.* 3–13; *Interp.* 2.3–10; *Luc.* 1.39–42, see M. Pellegrino, '"Mutus . . . loquar Christum." Pensieri di sant'Ambrogio su parola e silenzio', in R. Cantalamessa and L. F. Pizzolato (eds.), *Paradoxos Politeia. Studi patristici in onore di Giuseppe Lazzati* (Milan, 1979), 447–57, especially 449–54; A. M. Piredda, 'Il tema dell'ascolto negli scritti di Ambrogio di Milano', in *Dizionario di spiritualità biblica e patristica* v (Rome, 1993), 292–9; also Jacob, 121–38.

In 1.23, A. claims that it was meditating on Ps. 38 that led him to write on duties, and 1.5–22 is loosely structured around Ps. 38: 1–3, verses which are treated as useful introductory principles for the morality to follow (1.231). In 1.232, A. says that he chose to restrict his attention to the opening verses of the Ps. so as not to prolong the *praefatio*; in 2.233–45 he goes on to exploit further verses (Ps. 38: 4–8, 12) in the context of *temperantia*; see further ad loc. Both 1.5–22 and 1.233–45 draw on Origen, *Hom. Ps. 38*.1–2 (preserved in Rufinus' Latin version: see *Origène, Homélies sur les psaumes 36 à 38*, ed. E. Prinzivalli, with notes by H. Crouzel and L. Brésard (SCh 411, Paris, 1995)). Both 1.5–22 and 1.233–45 are very similar to A.'s exegesis in *Expl. Ps. 38*.1–27, written in the same period as *Off*. On A.'s debts to Origen on the Ps., see L. F. Pizzolato, *La 'Explanatio Psalmorum XII'. Studio letterario sulla esegesi di sant'Ambrogio* (Milan, 1965), 36–40; H. J. Auf der Maur, *Das Psalmenverständnis des Ambrosius von Mailand. Ein Beitrag zum Deutungshintergrund der Psalmenverwendung im Gottesdienst der alten Kirche* (Leiden, 1977), 91–8, 257–8. In both 1.5–22 and 1.233–45 A. may be drawing upon familiar expository themes, indebted to Origen, but, for all the rhetorical texture of aspects of both sections, there is no reason to suppose that he has simply adapted an earlier sermon on the Ps. (*pace* the unpublished paper by F. Claus, 'L'origine du De officiis de saint Ambroise: un nouveau compte rendu "tachygraphie"', cited in Testard i. 273 n. 12; 'Recherches', 88 n. 66 [Introduction V]. For all the inspiration of Ps. 38 (1.23), its significance to A.'s argument should not be exaggerated: Steidle, 'Beobachtungen', 49–54, goes too far when he argues that the Ps. acts as a unifying device for book 1 as a whole, and C. Riggi, 'L' "Auxesis" del salmo XXXVIII nel "De officiis" di s. Ambrogio', *Salesianum* 29 (1967), 623–68, fancifully tries to argue that A. finds the three 'theological' virtues in the Ps. and makes these central to his whole exposition of duties.

5. **Quid autem . . . debemus discere . . .?:** Picking up the repetition of *discere* in 1.4.
    ne prius me vox condemnet mea: Cf. Job 9: 20; 15: 6.
    Ex verbis tuis condemnaberis: Mt. 12: 37; cf. the similar association of the words with the need for modesty in *Virg.* 1.1.
    Scio loqui . . . nihil prosit: Possibly evoking an old saying with Greek roots (Epich. fr. 272 [Kaibel]; Democr. *fr. Phil. Gr.* 178), *Qui cum loqui non posset, tacere non potuit*; cf. Gell. *NA* 1.15.15–16; Jer. *Epp.* 130.17; 69.2; Ps.-Aus. *Sap.* 247; Ps.-Sen. *Mor.* 132. A. repeats the words almost verbatim in 1.35.
    sapientia Dei: This identification of the personified Wisdom of the OT with Jesus evokes a major strand of NT Christology, especially in Mt., Jn., Col.; see J. D. G. Dunn, *Christology in the Making*, 2nd edn. (London, 1989), 163–212.
    Dominus dedit mihi . . . dicere: Is. 50: 4. On the equation of Christ with the Isaianic Servant of Yahweh, cf. e.g. 1 Pt. 2: 21–5.
    Homo sapiens tacebit usque ad tempus: Eccli. 20: 7.
6. **sancti Domini:** Cf. Pss. 29: 5; 30: 24; etc.
    initium erroris humani: Speech is the exact antithesis of the humble fear of the Lord, which is the beginning of wisdom (1.1); on the dangers of speaking too much cf. *Expl. Ps. 1.20*.
    sanctus Domini: David.

***Dixi: custodiam vias meas . . . in lingua mea*: Ps. 38: 2.**
The treatment of Ps. 38 in the following paragraphs is
noticeably close to the exposition given in *Expl. Ps. 38*,
drawing on Origen: the chief references are cited below.
There are also a few parallels with Didym. *Fr. Ps. 38*, as
Testard i. 25–6 n. 2 points out: both authors cite Mt. 12.37
(as does Orig. *Hom. Ps. 38*.1.3); Rom. 7: 22; and Eph. 3: 16,
and both dramatize the role of Satan. We can glimpse the
typical pastiche of influences on A.'s OT interpretation.
legerat: A. seems to believe that David had read the book of
Job.
divinae . . . protectionis: Cf. *Ex*. 6.60; on the principle of
being kept by divine grace, cf. e.g. *Iac*. 1.16; *Paen*. 2.11;
Interp. 3.1; *Ob. Theod*. 25; *Fug*. 2.
ut homo a flagello linguae suae absconderetur: Job 5:
21; the context there is the description by Eliphaz the
Temanite of the *beatus homo* who is corrected by the Lord
(Job 5: 17–27). Cf. Orig. *Hom. Ps. 38*.2.7, evoking Eccli. 23:
2; also A. *Exh. virg*. 84–90; *Ep*. 29 [43].16.
a conscientiae suae testimonio: For the phrase, cf. 2 Cor.
1: 12 (also Rom. 2: 15; 9: 1). David set a guard on his mouth
so that his tongue would not prove a scourge to him by being
an instrument of evil, and to ensure that his conscience
would remain clear; it is God who provides the necessary
grace to achieve this. This is A.'s first mention of conscience,
which turns out to be a recurring motif throughout the work.
Testard's investigation (Testard, '*Conscientia*') concludes
that A.'s view of conscience is more classical than biblical,
and that his language makes conscience sound like the kind
of internal norm which regulates the choices of the autono-
mous Stoic sage rather than the Christian notion of an innate
awareness of one's accountability to a creator deity. It is
unnecessary, however, to think purely in terms of alternatives here, for the NT (especially Pauline) idea of conscience
clearly evokes and overlaps with elements of the Stoic legacy
(on which see Stelzenberger, 186–216). It is better to say that
(typically) A. *combines* perspectives from classical philosophy
and from Scripture. Elsewhere, he can speak of the natural
law of God as a standard impressed upon the heart of those
created in the image of God: see Löpfe, 72–7. The scriptural

side is certainly significant in the present passage: the opposite of silence and a good conscience is idle speech and the pollution of sin. The *viae meae* of which the Psalmist speaks are to be determined by the *viae Domini* in 1.7.

Quis autem est qui mundum cor . . . aut non delinquat in lingua sua?: Cf. Prov. 20: 9: *Quis potest dicere: Mundus est cor meum, purus sum a peccato?*

7. **cautionis magistrum:** Cf. 1.1 on David as *humilitatis magister*.

vias Domini: Probably A. thinks of Ps. 127: 1, the first part of which he has echoed in 1.1: *Beati omnes qui timent Dominum, qui ambulant in viis eius.* On the different *viae*, cf. *Expl. Ps. 1.24–6; Expos. Ps. 118.2.2.*

Audi, Israel, Dominum Deum tuum: Dt. 6: 4, the opening of the *Shema*, traditionally recited along with Dt. 11: 13–21 and Num. 15: 37–41 as a Jewish daily prayer.

Ideo Eva lapsa est . . . a Domino Deo suo: Ironically, Gen. 3 does not actually describe Eve speaking to her husband, only Adam listening to her (Gen. 3: 17); but obviously the inference that she told him what the serpent had said is legitimate in the light of Gen. 3: 6, 12. The main point is that she voiced a proposal which was at variance with God's word. A. gives a similar explanation for the Fall in *Expl. Ps. 38.3*: *vixissemus, si Eva tacuisset. . . . Atque utinam aut Adam surdus fuisset aut Eva obmutuisset*; and also in *Virgt.* 81. Elsewhere, he pictures Eve as the sensual corrupter of the rational Adam (cf. *Parad.* 54; *Ep.* 34 [45].17; *Ep. extra coll.* 14 [63].14), though in *Inst. virgt.* 25–31 he concedes that Eve's guilt was less serious than Adam's: Adam ought not to have listened to his wife. In 1.169, her fault seems to be her gullibility: in her innocence she trusted the serpent, not realizing that there could be such a thing as *malevolentia*.

Prima vox Dei dicit tibi: *Audi.* **Si audias . . . cito corrigis:** The injunction to silence in Dt. 6: 4 sums up God's primary requirement. By listening to God's word, sin is avoided; and if a slip does occur, God's word also brings correction. The Christian perspective contrasts interestingly with the conception of silence in Graeco-Roman ritual: whereas in classical religion an ill-omened word may ruin

everything (e.g. Hor. *Od*. 3.1.2; 14.11–12; Verg. *Aen*. 5.71), in A.'s understanding the necessity is to be silent in order to receive and act upon the word of God. Cf. *Expos. Ps. 118*.15.3: *In officio igitur audiendi omnium firmamentum est.*
In quo enim corrigit iuvenior . . . verba Domini?: Ps. 118: 9.

8. **ore suo condemnetur:** See on 1.5 (cf. also Lk. 19: 22).
turpitudinis: The Ciceronian antithesis to *honestas* (*Off*. 1.9); cf. 1.220 below.
si pro otioso verbo reddet unusquisque rationem: Cf. Mt. 12: 36. For a similar argument, cf. *Expl. Ps. 38*.5; and Orig. *Hom. Ps. 38*.1.3.
verba praecipitationis: Cf. Ps. 51: 6: *Dilexisti omnia verba praecipitationis.*

CHAPTER 3: THE RIGHT KIND OF SILENCE

9. *Est enim tempus tacendi et est tempus loquendi:* Eccl. 3: 7.
pro otioso silentio: On avoiding the silence of complicity in evil, for example, cf. 3.35; cf. also Max. Taur. *Serm*. 91.2; 107.1; and 106, 108. On the contrast of *otiosus . . . negotiosus,* cf. 3.2–7.
ut erat Susannae . . . quam si esset locuta: On the silence of Susanna at her trial, when falsely accused of adultery by two elders whose designs on her had been frustrated, see Dan. 13, especially 13: 28–64. Instead of attempting to defend herself, she prayed to God, who brought her deliverance from death through Daniel. There is in fact no particular emphasis on her silence in the narrative of Dan. 13, though her silent innocence became a standard Christian model: cf. e.g. 1.68; 3.90; *Fug*. 53; *Ios*. 26; *Exh. virg*. 87; *Expl. Ps. 37*.45 (note also 46–7 on David); Zen. Ver. *Tract*. 1.40 (2.16); Jer. *Comm. Dan*. 13.42; Aug. *Serm*. 318.2. In A. see A. M. Piredda, 'Susanna e il silenzio: l'interpretazione di Ambrogio', *Sandalion* 14 (1991), 169–92. The idea of an eloquent silence has strong classical precedents: e.g. Cic. *Sest*. 40; *Div. in Caecil*. 21; *Cat*. 1.16, 18, 20, and especially 21: *cum quiescunt, probant, cum patiuntur, decernunt, cum*

tacent, clamant; for further examples, see Testard, 'Conscientia', 221–2 n. 2. Cf. further 3.2; *Expos. Ps. 118.*17.9 (on Anna, in 1 Ki. 1: 13); *Ios.* 26; and Jer. *Ep.* 24.5.2.

suae castitatis: Purity within marriage, not strict chastity, in Susanna's case; cf. *Vid.* 23–4; Aug. *Serm.* 343.1–8; and see on 1.68.

Conscientia loquebatur: The slant of the conscience theme here is obviously Christian: the witness of Susanna's conscience is related to her innocence in God's sight.

quae habebat Domini testimonium: Like Enoch; cf. Heb. 11: 5: *testimonium habebat placuisse Deo.*

Ipse Dominus in evangelio tacens operabatur salutem omnium: Christ was silent before the high priest (Mt. 26: 63; Mk. 14: 61), before Herod (Lk. 23: 9), and before Pilate (Mt. 27: 12, 14; Mk. 15: 5; Jn. 19: 9); cf. Cypr. *Pat.* 23. For other references to Susanna and Christ, cf. *Luc.* 10.97–9; *Expl. Ps. 38.*7; *Nab.* 46; Max. Taur. *Serm.* 57 (drawing on *Luc.*); Ps.-Aug. *Serm.* 112.1–3. On Christ's self-effacement as an example, cf. 3.36; *Expl. Ps. 37.*45; *Interp.* 2.9; *Fid.* 3.52; 5.106–9.

ergo: A loose connective, to bring us back to Ps. 38: 2, cited in 1.6; Susanna and Christ observed a fruitful silence at a crucial time.

10.   *Omni custodia serva cor tuum*: Prov. 4: 23.
      O miser ego . . . immunda labia habeam: Is. 6: 5.

11.   *Saepi possessionem tuam . . . et verbis tuis iugum et stateram*: Eccli. 28: 28–9.

Possessio tua mens tua est . . . argentum tuum eloquium tuum est: A typical attempt to interpret Scripture spiritually, which continues below; see Introduction IV.5.

Eloquia Domini . . . examinatum: Ps. 11: 7.

homo mundus: One who is pure in the sense of Ps. 50: 9 or Mt. 5: 8.

It is worth noting the military terminology which A. uses: **circumvallato** (cf. Hil. *In Ps. 140.*5); **munito . . . irruant . . . captivam ducant . . . incursent . . . diripiant** suggest that he visualizes the heart as a territory to be defended against the besieging forces of the vicious passions and emotions (cf. the soul as a *civitas* in 1.245). Partly under Philonic influence, he assumes an essentially Platonist struggle between the rational mind and the **irrationabiles corporis passiones** (Seibel, 129–45; A. Loiselle, *'Nature' de l'homme et histoire du salut. Etude sur l'anthropologie d'Ambroise de Milan*, Diss. (Lyons, 1970), 27–53). This anthropology also coexists with a middle Stoic view of both reason and appetite as *motus* of the soul (1.98, 228–30).

munito sollicitudinibus: [*munito spinis sollicitudinibus* VM¹, W, Maurists, Testard: *spinis sollicitudinis* M², E, Krabinger: *spinis sollicitudinum* A, Zell; with Winterbottom, 559, I delete *spinis* altogether; COB and Monte Alto's *piis sollicitudinibus* perhaps makes the *sollicitudines* too precise at this point] The allegorical link for A. clearly lies in the parable of the sower (Mt. 13: 22; Lk. 8: 14); cf. *Expl. Ps. 38.5.*

ne diripiant vindemiam eius transeuntes viam: Cf. Pss. 79: 13; 88: 42. The vine or vineyard is frequently a symbol for God's chosen people (Ps. 79: 9–17; Is. 5: 1–7; Jer. 2: 21; cf. the church as a vine in *Ex.* 3.49–52; *Luc.* 9.29–33, with Toscani, 156–62), but here it stands for the precious inner being of those who are God's; cf. *Expl. Ps. 38.5*; also *Sacr.* 5.16.

interiorem hominem: Cf. Rom. 7: 22; Eph. 3: 16. This NT preoccupation with an inner nature is a favourite emphasis of A.'s, and, in conjunction with a pronounced Platonism, is basic to much of his mystical and ascetic teaching. The 'outer' or 'old' man is for him equated with the body of sin which must perish; the 'inner' man is the soul imprinted with the divine image, which is redeemed, and so made 'new', by Christ. The old man perishes in baptism (cf. 3.108), and the image of God is then progressively restored in the inner man. See Seibel, 161–94; G. Madec, 'L'Homme intérieur selon saint Ambroise', in *Ambroise de Milan*, 283–308.

cuius fructus non caducus . . . salutis est: Again following the parable of the sower (Mt. 13: 23; Mk. 4: 20; Lk. 8: 14–15; cf. also Jn. 4: 36).

12. *Non est malagma . . . adligaturam*: Is. 1: 6. On the rare scriptural word *adligatura* and its use in A. see I. Gualandri, 'Il lessico di Ambrogio: problemi e prospettive di ricerca', in *Nec timeo mori*, 267–311, at 301–3.

habenas mentis: One is reminded irresistibly of Horace's celebrated lines: *ira furor brevis est: animum rege, qui nisi paret, | imperat; huiuc frenis, hunc tu compesce catena (Ep.* 1.2.62–3). Cf. also Sen. *Ira* 3.1.1: *iram refrenare*; and see on 1.229, on 'the reins of reason'.

sobrietas: Cf. generally 1.70, 211, 256; 2.7, 65, 76. On the *sobrietas mentis* of the spiritual person, frequently equated, oxymoronically, with the overflowing abundance of the Holy Spirit's power, see J. Pépin in *AmbrEpisc* i. 461–2 nn. 121–4; H. Lewy, *Sobria ebrietas: Untersuchungen zur Geschichte der antiken Mystik* (Giessen, 1929), especially 146–57; E. Dassmann, *La sobria ebrezza dello Spirito: la spiritualità di sant'Ambrogio vescovo di Milano* (Varese, 1975).

13. Sit ori tuo ostium: Cf. Ps. 140: 3: *Pone, Domine, custodiam ori tuo, et ostium circumstantiae labiis meis.*

iracundiam: A. does not distinguish, as classical Latin generally does, between *iracundia* (the temperament prone to anger) and *ira* (the expression of anger); he treats the words as synonyms.

Audisti hodie lectum: On this apparent vestige of a sermonic exegesis, cf. 1.15, *sicut audisti hodie legi*, and see Introduction V. The Psalms were part of the daily office at Milan; see on 1.67.

***Irascimini et nolite peccare*:** Ps. 4: 5. The verse is quoted in Eph. 4: 26, where the context, especially in 4: 29 (*Omnis sermo malus ex ore vestro non procedat*) is similar to that in the present passage: Eph. 4 is probably in A.'s mind here.

This paragraph begins the slanting of the silence theme to the injunction to keep silent when provoked to anger (1.13–22); the same point is made in 1.90–7 (quoting Ps. 4: 5 again in 1.96) and in 1.231–8 (1.90–7, unlike the other two sections, does not draw on Ps. 38); cf. also *Luc.* 5.54. On the necessary patience involved in such a controlled stance, cf. Lact. *Inst.* 6.18.10–35.

adfectus naturae est non ⟨nostrae⟩ potestatis: ⟨nostrae⟩ seems a necessary addition; cf. Cic. *Fin.* 4.15 (Winterbottom, 559). The implication is that anger is a passion over which there may (at least sometimes) be no control; since it is so much a part of nature, it cannot be extirpated (cf. 1.90). It is to be checked by reason, if possible, but it is not invariably an evil; the main necessity is to moderate the expression of anger. A. retains the Stoic emphasis on the restraint of anger by reason, tempered with middle Stoicism's realism. But the subject is related to the biblical idea of being tempted to sin: A. speaks of provocation from Satan and from *peccatores*.

The variety of imagery used throughout these paragraphs is noteworthy, and illustrates the richness of A.'s diction: there are images from horticulture (11); warfare (11); rivers (12); bits, bridles, and reins (12–13); doors and locks (13; cf. Plu. *Mor.* 503c–d); and weights and measures (13); the scriptural verses also supply language from metal-refining (11) and medicine (12).

Restringatur habenae vinculis: On the bridling of the tongue, cf. Jas. 3: 2–11 (and 1: 26), though the warning is blunt: *linguam autem nullus hominum domare potest* (3: 8).
sermones proferat libra examinatos iustitiae, ut sit gravitas . . . pondus . . . modus: Continues the language of weights and measures, from **iugum . . . et statera . . . mensura** above.

CHAPTER 4: TEMPTATION BY SATAN

14. mitis mansuetus modestus: The lack of a cognate noun to describe the state of being **mitis** prevents a perfect chiastic and alliterative balance in the following sentence; A. has to make do with **patientia** (on which see Sauer, 150–4).
non alicuius passionis indicium det . . . vitium aliquod esse in moribus aperiat et prodat: Cf. Cic. *Off.* 1.134: *In primisque provideat ne sermo vitium aliquod indicet inesse in moribus; quod maxime tum solet evenire cum studiose de absentibus detrahendi causa aut per ridiculum aut severe maledice contumelioseque dicitur.* On the idea that one's *sermo* indicates the quality of one's heart, cf. 1.71, 89; Cic. *Off.* 1.131. An obvious inspiration is Lk. 6: 45: *Bonus homo de bono thesauro cordis sui profert bonum; et malus homo de*

malo profert malum: ex abundantia enim cordis os loquitur (cf. Mt. 12: 34).

ardorem libidinis: A. broadens the scope of the passions (cf. **alicuius passionis indicium**) to include other evils which may be revealed in hasty, immoderate speech; cf. Cic. *Off.* 1.14: *tum in omnibus et opinionibus et factis ne quid libidinose aut faciat aut cogitet.*

interiora: See on 1.11.

15. adversarius: Satan (1 Tim. 5: 14–15; 1 Pt. 5: 8), the enemy of humanity (*Expl. Ps. 43*.33). On the portrayal of Satan in A.'s corpus generally, see Homes Dudden ii. 589–91; on the exegetical works in particular, M. P. McHugh, 'Satan and Saint Ambrose', *Classical Folia* 26/1 (1972), 94–106 (and id. 'The Demonology of Saint Ambrose in Light of the Tradition', *WS* 91 (1978), 205–31); on the terminology, G. J. M. Bartelink, 'Quelques observations sur les dénominations du diable et des démons chez Ambroise et Jérôme', in Bartelink *et al.* (eds.), *Eulogia: Mélanges offerts à Antoon A. R. Bastiaensen* (The Hague, 1991), 1–10. *Pace* Testard i. 226 n. 2, the identity of the *adversarius* here is clear at once; we do not need to wait for the biblical allusion at the end of 1.16: A. can assume that his addressees will identify this NT name for the devil, and the mention of *laqueos* below clearly evokes 2 Tim. 2: 26: *diaboli laquei.*

tunc fomites movet, laqueos parat: Images from Roman hunting techniques. The prey is frightened into the snares with the use of fire, usually by setting fire to the brush; see J. Aymard, *Essai sur les chasses romains, des origines à la fin du siècle des Antonins (Cynégetica)* (Paris, 1951), 228–33, on fire; 207–18, on nets/snares. On the devil's snares and nets, cf. *Paen.* 1.73; his ways need to be studied in order for one to defend oneself properly (*Parad.* 58).

sicut audisti hodie legi: Cf. 1.13, *Audisti hodie lectum,* and see Introduction V.

propheta: David.

Quia ipse liberavit me . . . a verbo aspero: Ps. 90: 3.

Symmachus: Translator of the OT into Greek, *fl.* late second century BC (Jer. *Vir. ill.* 54). Almost nothing is known of his life. He is said by Euseb. Caes. (*HE* 6.17.1) to have been a member of the Jewish-Christian sect, the

Ebionites; the Ebionites were sometimes known as 'Symmachians' (Mar. Vict. *Comm. in Gal.* 1.19; Aug. *C. Faust. Man.* 19.4, 17; Cresc. *Don.* 1.36; Ambros. *Comm. in Gal.*, prol. 1). Epiph. *Mens. et pond.* 16, speaks of him as a Samaritan who became a Jewish proselyte. His version of the OT appears in the fourth column of Origen's *Hexapla*, after Aquila's and before the LXX and Theodotion's text (F. Field, *Origenis Hexaplorum quae supersunt; sive Veterum Interpretum Graecorum in totum Vetus Testamentum Fragmenta*, 2 vols., 2nd edn. (Oxford, 1874)); the extant fragments reveal a clear Greek style and an effort to tone down many of the scriptural anthropomorphisms: see S. Jellicoe, *The Septuagint and Modern Study* (Oxford, 1966), 94–9. A. did not know Hebrew (cf. *Expl. Ps. 40*.36: *ut adseruerunt qui librum legerunt in Hebraicis litteris scriptum*), but preferred to study the OT in Greek, which he believed conveyed a greater sense of power and mystery (*Expos. Ps. 118*.12.45). He clearly had access to a copy of part (though almost certainly not all) of Origen's *Hexapla*, from which his information here is derived. For other such references to alternative readings, cf. *Ep.* 18 [70].14; *Expl. Ps. 1*.29, 31, 39, 43–4; *Expl. Ps. 35*.18; *Expl. Ps. 36*.11, 70; *Expl. Ps. 37*.33; *Expl. Ps. 38*.21; *Expl. Ps. 40*.21; *Expl. Ps. 43*.23, 33, 36, 44, 54, 64, 67, 73, 79, 94; *Expos. Ps. 118*. 9.20; 15.12; 22.36, 41, 45.

irritationis verbum dixit, alii perturbationis: On Ps. 90: 3, Symmachus reads ἀπὸ λόγου ἐπηρείας (*a verbo nocumenti*) for the Vulg.'s *a vero aspero*, while the LXX has ἀπὸ λόγου ταραχώδους *(a verbo turbulento)*. **alii** presumably refers to Aquila and/or Theodotion, neither of whose renderings of the verse is extant. A.'s mention of these variants is of no particular value to the elucidation of his argument: it is simply a display of learning—and one which puts the claims of ignorance in 1.1–4 in a certain perspective.

inimicus: Another scriptural term for Satan, from the parable of the wheat and the tares (Mt. 13: 25, 28, 39; cf. also Lk. 10: 18–19).

Quanto tolerabilius . . . perire!: On perishing with one's own sword, cf. Cic. *Caecin.* 82; Lact. *Inst.* 3.28.20; also Ter. *Ad.* 958; Pub. Syr. 79.

16. nostra arma: Cf. Eph. 6: 11: *Induite vos arma Dei, ut possitis stare adversus insidias diaboli* (cf. 6: 13). A. evokes yet another NT image of Satan, this time as a military adversary, spying out the believer's armour to find a chink where he may drive in his *tela ignea* (Eph. 6: 16). The moment of anger provides just such an opportunity for this foe: Eph. 4: 26–7 (4: 27 is echoed below). For similar rhetoric, cf. Cypr. *Zel.* 1–3; Didym. *In Ps. 36*.14; on the Christian life as a daily struggle against the devil's darts and weapons, cf. Cypr. *Mort.* 4.

quasi escam . . . vindictae possibilitatem: The imagery changes back to hunting or fishing: the possibility of revenge is like bait on Satan's hook. On the evils of revenge, cf. 1.131; 3.59.

custodiam adhibere debet ori suo: Harks back to Ps. 38: 2; cf. also Ps. 140: 3.

ne det locum adversario: Cf. Eph. 4: 27.

sed non multi hunc vident: By implication, it seems, only the spiritually mature are sufficiently prudent and alert to discern the tempter's presence; cf. *Expos. Ps. 118*.7.11. On the differentiation of the few from the many, cf. 1.218; 3.10.

CHAPTER 5: THE PROVOCATION OF A SINNER

17. Sed etiam ille cavendus est qui videri potest: A visible enemy, no less than the invisible devil, presents danger. On foes visible and invisible, cf. Aug. *Pat.* 8–9; also *Agon. Chr.* 1–2.

luxuriae aut libidinis: As in 1.14, A. considers other excesses besides anger.

Peccator: Suggested by Ps. 38: 2: *Posui ori meo custodiam cum consisteret peccator adversum me.* Cf. *Expl. Ps. 38*.13; and Orig. *Hom. Ps. 38*.1.4.

qui iniuriam facit: Cic. *Off.* 1.34 speaks of responsibilities towards those from whom ones receives *iniuria.*

similes: An echo of Prov. 26: 4: *Ne respondeas stulto iuxta stultitiam suam ne efficiaris ei similis.*

A. builds up to the dramatic picture of the sinner's challenge, the assessment of the onlookers, and the sinner's inner reaction, which follows in 1.18–19: note the series of short clauses; the anaphora of *quicumque*, *tunc*, *ad*, and *qui*; the homoioteleuton of *exerceamus* and *erubescamus*; and the alliterative congeries of *luxuriae aut libidinis*. The translation attempts to convey something of the briskness of the style.

18. si taceas, si dissimules: Cf. Cic. *Off.* 1.108 (on differences in personality types): *Callidum Hannibalem ex Poenorum, ex nostris ducibus Q. Maximum accepimus, facile celare tacere dissimulare insidiari, praeripere hostium consilia.* One thinks of Horace vainly trying in vain to ignore the bore who accosted him on the Sacred Way (*Sat.* 1.9.8–16). Juvenal complains that the street bully will beat up the poor man anyway, whether he attempts to answer or not (*Sat.* 3.278–301, especially 297 ff.). In A.'s picture, the encounter will have a happier outcome, provided the righteous person resists the temptation to respond, and quietly reflects on the innocence of his own conscience. But he uses humour to make a serious point, as he describes the absurd frustration experienced by the *peccator*.

superiorem se factum arbitratur quia parem invenit: The rhetoric tumbles out: the sinner cannot literally have 'found an equal' if he has 'become superior'; A. obviously means that the sinner believes he has gained 'one up' on the just man if he has goaded him into responding.

dicetur: The judgement of onlookers.

bonorum iudicio . . . gravitate morum suorum: The reference to the onlookers, and to the need to maintain dignity in the face of provocation from an enemy, is evocative of Cic. *Off.* 1.137: *Rectum est autem etiam in illis contentionibus quae cum inimicissimis fiunt, etiam si nobis indigna audiamus, tamen gravitatem retinere, iracundiam pellere; quae enim cum aliqua perturbatione fiunt, ea nec constanter fieri possunt neque iis qui adsunt probari.* A.'s respect for the judgement of *boni* and his pride in *gravitas* of character reflects his own background. As one who had had to work hard to earn his acceptance among an élite (McLynn, 31–5), he remained sensitive about proving the sort of studied self-mastery essential to social respectability. A concern to promote a similar finesse among his clergy is a powerful element in the vision behind *Off.*: clerics are to care

about what the best people think; on **bonorum iudicio**, cf.
1.227. The ideal of humility and restraint not only manages
to coexist with a deliberate aspiration to grandeur (cf. *Ep.* 6
[28].2): it is in fact partly grounded in an appeal to social
approval. On Roman *gravitas*, see J. Ferguson, *Moral Values
in the Ancient World* (London, 1958), 172–8; for NT reference to such a principle, cf. Tit. 2: 7, quoted in 2.86 below.
On the combination of biblical and classical nuancing of the
ideal of dignity and obvious self-control in *Off.*, see Sauer,
146–7.

silere a bonis: Cf. Ps. 38: 3: *silui a bonis*, also evoked in
1.236 and *Expl. Ps. 38.*13 as meaning 'I kept quiet about my
good deeds, relying on my conscience's testimony to them'.
The Latin version imitates the LXX's ἐσίγησα ἐξ ἀγαθῶν.
The righteous man refrains from defending himself by
parading his virtues.

19. **humilior:** 'Too humble', not (as Testard) 'sufficiently
humble'.
On the problem, cf. Lact. *Inst.* 6.18.25: *Qui enim referre
iniuriam nititur, eum ipsum a quo laesus est gestit imitari.*

maestificare: A favourite Ambrosian verb: cf. e.g. *Expos.
Ps. 118.*7.17; 22.29; *Iac.* 1.31 (*TLL* viii. 44).

graviora in eum: CO: *graviora in eo* VM, Testard: *in eo
graviora* E.

20. *mitis atque humilis*: Such a man is not behaving in a
Christlike fashion: Mt. 11: 29. As in 1.9, the humility of
Christ is again the ultimate model.

nequam spiritus: Cf. 1 Ki. 16: 14: *exagitabat eum spiritus
nequam* (though there the evil spirit troubling Saul is said to
come from the Lord). In Mt. 13: 38, Satan is the *nequam*, and
in Eph. 6: 16 he is the *nequissimus*, against whose *spiritalia
nequitiae in caelestibus* (Eph. 6: 12) believers must fight. The
return to military language (last found in 1.16) below
suggests that the Eph. 6 passage is in A.'s thoughts.

in petra: The obvious place of stability: cf. e.g. Pss. 26: 6;
39: 3; Mt. 7: 24–5; Lk. 6: 48.

Etsi servus . . . etsi infirmus . . . etsi pauper: Cf. Cic. *Off.*
1.113, on enduring *contumelias servorum ancillarumque* (alluding to Hom. *Od.* 17.204–53; 18.320–39; 19.65–88); cf. also
Orig. *Hom. Ps. 38.*1.4; it is also important to maintain justice

with even the lowest, including slaves, according to Cic. *Off.* 1.41. Abuse from such social inferiors is borne patiently by the just man; cf. *Interp.* 2.5: *Propterea ergo sanctus tacet etsi servus proteruit; etsi pauper conviciatur, tacet iustus; etsi peccator opprobria iacit, iustus ridet: etsi infirmus maledicit, iustus benedicit.* Indeed servile patience should be shown (cf. 1.237; *Expl. Ps. 38*.9). The mention of inferiors signposts the celebrated case of the abuse of David by Shimei in the next paragraph (though not a slave, Shimei was David's subject). On the proper treatment of slaves, cf. *Ep.* 36 [2].31. On A.'s attitude to slavery in general, see Klein, 9–51; on slavery as a dishonourable state, Klein, 27–32; also Faust, 52–61.

cedendo vincat: Cf. Ov. *AA* 2.197 (of the wooing lover): *cede repugnanti: cedendo victor abibis.*

sicut periti iaculandi cedentes solent vincere . . . vulnerare ictibus: On the tactic of feigning retreat in order to dupe the enemy into a false sense of security and so to overcome them unexpectedly, cf. Veg. *Epit. rei milit.* 3.22, and the examples documented by his major source, Front. *Strat.* 2.3, 5 (so Testard i. 227 n. 5; on the strategy outlined by Veg. *Epit. rei mil.* 3.11–22, see G. Webster, *The Roman Imperial Army*, 3rd edn. (London, 1985), 231–4). A. offers an illustration (though not with **periti iaculandi**) in *Ep.* 57 (61).12.

CHAPTER 6: THE SILENCE OF DAVID

21. dicentem: David.

Obmutui et humiliatus sum et silui a bonis: Ps. 38: 3.
Nam cum ei conviciaretur Semei filius . . . non permiserit: The story of David's meekness when cursed by Shimei (2 Ki. 16: 5–14; cf. 3 Ki. 2: 8–9) is an apt illustration of patient silence; A. returns to it in the related section, 1.236–8. For some reason, A. gets the name of David's accuser wrong: he is Shimei, son of Gera, not Shimei's *son*; the error is repeated in 1.236, though not in *Expl. Ps. 38*.7; *Expos. Ps. 118*.7.23; 10.4; *Apol.* 30; *Interp.* 2.6. The text given by the Maurists in PL, *Semei filius Iemini*, is a gloss to explain that Shimei was a Benjamite

(cf. 2 Ki. 16: 11; 19: 16; 3 Ki. 2: 8). It is interesting that
A. does not name **Sarviae filio** (Abishai), either: the mistake
about Shimei is perhaps produced by a desire to balance
Semei filius and **Sarviae filio**: one *filius* hurls abuse, the
other *filius* urges David to take revenge; David, in his
humility, is superior to both. On David's behaviour, cf.
Expl. Ps. 37.42–51; 38.3 ff; *Expos. Ps. 118.7.23*; 10.4; *Apol.*
30–2; *Interp.* 2.5–6.

cum vir appellaretur sanguinis: 2 Ki. 16: 7–8.

cui abundabat bonorum operum conscientia: There is
no mention of conscience in the OT narrative.

22. **qui autem dolet quasi senserit . . . :** One or two words
have dropped out of the text after **senserit.** E² and Amerbach supply *torquetur*, reproduced by the Maurists and
Krabinger–Banterle; the idea may have come from *Interp.*
2.9: *Tacere ergo debet qui recognoscit obiectum: ne vulnus
exasperet et scindatur cicatrix, tacere et qui non recognoscit
audit enim alterius, non suum crimen; quod si referat, suum
facit: si tacet, retorquet, et conviciantem vulnerat.* Another
possibility might be to supply something like *ipse despicitur*,
to complete the parallelism with the previous clause and to
pick up the sense of **facit se dignum videri contumelia** in
the preceding sentence.

1.23–9 sets out the formal *propositio* for the work, introducing
the theme of *officia* proper (several MSS register a scribal mark
to this effect at the start of 1.23: Testard, 'Etude', 155–6 n. 3),
and setting out the scope of the discussion to come. 1.23 seeks
to connect the subject with the reference to Ps. 38 in 1.1–22;
1.24 explains the suitability of the *personae* involved, the bishop
and his 'sons'; 1.25–6 justifies the relevance of *res ipsa* from
Scripture and from reason (a significant pairing of authorities);
and 1.27–9 compares the approaches of the philosophers with
the one to be taken in a Christian treatment.

CHAPTER 7: THE THEME OF DUTIES

23. **Neque improvide . . . usus sum:** A. seeks to justify the
relevance of his introductory material on Ps. 38; cf. *pulchre* in

1.231, when material from Ps. 38 is again inserted. **ad vos filios meos:** A.'s clergy; see on 1.24. **scribens:** See Introduction V. In referring to the process of writing here (and in 1.25 and 1.29), A. is very probably thinking of Cic. *Off.* 1.4: *Sed cum statuissem scribere ad te aliquid hoc tempore.* Cic.'s inspiration to write comes from his desire to add his own contribution to the distinguished tradition of moral philosophy from which his son (and others) might benefit; A.'s comes from meditating on Scripture. The two introductions reveal these quite different foci. There are other apparent linguistic echoes of Cic. *Off.* 1.4 below as well, which support the view that that passage is in A.'s thoughts: **tenendum**—*tenuisset*; **delectatus**—*delectatus*; **contemptum** - *contempsit*.

sancto Idithun canendum: Jeduthun is the recipient of Ps. 38 (Ps. 38: 1). He is listed as one of David's musicians in 1 Chr. 16: 41–2; 2 Chr. 5: 12; his sons are also said to be musicians in 1 Chr. 25: 1, 3, 6. In 2 Chr. 35: 15 he is listed as one of David's seers. Also the recipient of Pss. 61 and 76, Jeduthun's task would have been to set these compositions to music. Cf. *Expl. Ps. 38*.1; *Expl. Ps. 61*.3.

in posterioribus contemptum divitiarum: Cf. Ps. 38: 6–8, 12. A. will expand on the contempt for riches suggested by these verses in 1.241–5. On the theme, cf. 1.182, 184–5, 192–3, 242–6; 2.66, 128.

maxima virtutum fundamenta . . . hoc psalmo doceri: The chief bases of virtue (patient silence, timely speech, and contempt for riches) are laid down in Ps. 38, so the Psalm is relevant to the ensuing exposition of virtue. On **virtutum fundamenta**, see also on 1.126.

successit animo de officiis scribere: See above on Cic. *Off.* 1.4.

24. **De quibus . . . scripserint:** Cf. Cic. *Off.* 1.4: *Nam cum multa sint in philosophia et gravia et utilia accurate copioseque a philosophis disputata, latissime patere videntur ea quae de officiis tradita ab illis et praecepta sunt;* 1.5: *Atque haec quidem quaestio communis est omnium philosophorum. Quis est enim qui nullis officii praeceptis tradendis philosophum se audeat dictum?* (also 1.6).

Panaetius: Panaetius of Rhodes (*c*.180–109 BC). After introducing Stoicism to Rome during his stay there (*c*.146–131 BC), he became head of the Athenian Stoa in 129 BC. An eclectic, Panaetius introduced changes into Stoicism (some of them anticipated by his predecessors, especially Chrysippus), among which were new psychological and ethical emphases: he imported from the Platonist–Aristotelian tradition a distinction between the rational and the irrational parts of the soul, and between theoretical and practical virtue, thus offering a casuistical treatment of duties which made Stoicism seem less severe and more appealing as a moral code. Panaetius was interested more in the ethical efforts of the ordinary person trying to progress towards virtue than in the rather theoretical ideal of the Stoic sage. See M. van Straaten, *Panétius, sa vie, ses écrits, et sa doctrine, avec une édition des fragments* (Amsterdam and Paris, 1946); J. M. Rist, *Stoic Philosophy* (Cambridge, 1969), 173–200; A. A. Long, *Hellenistic Philosophy* (London, 1974), 114, 211–16. On his περὶ τοῦ καθήκοντος, Cic.'s essential source for *Off.* 1–2, see Introduction III (i), and Dyck, 17–29; A. knows of it only through Cic.'s reference to it.

filius eius: Posidonius of Apamea (135–50 BC). He studied under Panaetius at Athens (*c*.125–114 BC), hence his designation by A. as Panaetius' 'son'. He established himself thereafter in Rhodes, where he taught Cic. in 78–77 BC. A polymath of prodigious literary activity, he was particularly interested in natural science. He brought a number of innovations to Stoic thought, and in particular went further than Panaetius in developing its psychological reflection in a Platonist direction. His concern for empiricism probably accounts for his breaking with orthodox doctrines which he believed did not help the Stoic cause. See M. Laffranque, *Poseidonios d'Apamée* (Paris, 1964); Rist, *Stoic Philosophy*, 201–18; Long, *Hellenistic Philosophy*, 115, 216–22; Colish i. 10–12, 22–60. On Cic.'s reading of his work on ethics, see Introduction III (i); once again, A.'s knowledge of Posidonius' contribution to the subject is dependent on Cic.

Tullius: The first mention of (M. Tullius) Cic.; others will follow in 1.43, 82, 180.

apud Graecos . . . apud Latinos: The pairing is probably evocative of Cic. *Off.* 1.1, where Cic. counsels Marcus to follow his father's habit of combining things Latin with things Greek, and speaks of the service he has performed in rendering Greek philosophy and rhetoric into Latin.

non alienum duxi . . . scriberem: In *Off.* 1 4, Cic. says that he is going to expound a subject which is very much suited (*aptissimum*) to Marcus' age and to his own *auctoritas* (cf. also *Att.* 15.13.2); for A. too, it is appropriate to his ecclesiastical *munus* to deal with the theme, as part of his teaching to his charges. The implicit criterion is that of *decorum*, or what is seemly (see on 1.30); cf. *conveniunt . . . conveniat* in 1.25. A.'s style is also faintly reminiscent of Lk. 1: 1–4: *Quoniam quidem multi conati sunt ordinare narrationem quae in nobis completae sunt rerum, sicut tradiderunt nobis* [cf. on 1.2 above], *visum est et mihi, adsecuto a principio omnibus, diligenter ex ordine tibi scribere, optime Theophile, ut cognoscas eorum verborum, de quibus eruditus es, veritatem.*

Et sicut Tullius . . . ita ego quoque ad vos . . . filios meos: As Cic. wrote for his son Marcus (Introduction III (i)), so A. (now approaching the age of fifty) writes for his spiritual 'sons', members of the Milanese clergy, and especially younger men. Both Cic. and A., of course, aim at a much wider readership. Note the link between the *filii* mentioned in this paragraph: Panaetius and his *filius*, Posidonius; Cic. and his *filius*, Marcus; A. and his *filii*, the Milanese clergy. A. has already made clear his fatherly attitude towards his addressees in 1.1–2 and 1.23; here, he underlines the suitability of the Christian idea of spiritual paternity to the parallelism with his philosophical predecessors (see generally Gryson, *Prêtre*, 145–7; note also the bishop's reception of his guest Augustine *paterne* in *Conf.* 5.13.23). So far from hiding his debt to Cic.'s text, A. highlights his continuity with the classical tradition, but he is determined to validate his position biblically at every turn: he is setting out to take over and transform the same territory. As a spiritual 'father' by grace, he has every right to do so for his sons:

quos in evangelio genui: 1 Cor. 4: 15; for other references to spiritual paternity, cf. 2 Cor. 6: 13; 1 Thess. 2: 11; Phil. 2: 22; 1 Tim. 1: 2; 2 Tim. 2: 1; Tit. 1: 4; Philm. 10; 1 Pt. 5: 13; 3 Jn. 4.

natura . . . gratia: A classic NT antithesis (cf. espccially Eph. 2; Rom. 11), which has precipitated endless theological wrangling, above all in the Augustinian–Pelagian disputes and their numerous long-range echoes; on A. see briefly Maes, 60–4. On the relationships established by grace within the church, cf. 1.170.

vos ante elegimus: 'Grace' does not preclude episcopal judgement (White, 123–4): on choosing friends, cf. Cic. *Amic.* 62, 78, and especially 85 (from Thphr. fr. 74); on the choosing of spiritual disciples, cf. Jesus' words in Jn. 15: 16, 19 (also Jn. 13: 18), to which A. alludes in 1.3. If the rhetoric here is to be believed (cf. also 2.25), A.'s initial problems with inherited clergy (cf. 1.72) have apparently now subsided considerably: he can count on the loyalty of men whom he has personally selected for service.

magnum caritatis pondus: It is easier to love adopted sons, selected by choice for their good character, than natural sons, who may turn out bad. On A.'s love, and the importance of unity, love, and peace in the ecclesiastical family, cf. 2.155; also 1.170, 247; 3.19, 125–38.

CHAPTER 8: THE SUITABILITY OF THE THEME

25. Ergo quoniam . . . reperiatur divinis: Having 'proved' from Scripture that the father–son approach of the classical tradition is legitimate—the respective 'roles' (**personae**) of giving and receiving instruction are appropriate—A. now seeks biblical authority for adopting the subject-matter of the classical tradition as well. On **conveniunt . . . conveniat**, see on *decorum* in 1.30.

Pulchre itaque: Cf. 1.23, *neque improvide*, and **quasi adhortaretur . . . sanctus Spiritus**, below. A. wants the whole project to be seen as divinely inspired.

dum legimus hodie evangelium: Not a liturgical allusion (*pace* Moorhead, 157 n. 1), but a private reading by A. on the day of composition.

in nobis: Winterbottom, 559, suggests *a nobis*, to make the words at the end of the paragraph into a reprise, but the parallelism of the two clauses perhaps need not be so precise.

Nam cum Zacharias . . . non posset: See Lk. 1: 5–25,57–80. On Zacharias' silence, cf. *Virg.* 1.4; *Luc.* 1.39–42. See also Hahn, 20–3.

Factum est . . . in domum suam: Lk. 1: 23.

Legimus igitur officium dici a nobis posse: In Lk. 1: 23, *officium* translates λειτουργία, the usual term for the week of service performed twice yearly (in NT times) by the twenty-four divisions of priests (cf. 1 Chr. 24: 1–19). In Cic., however, the word is used as the best Latin equivalent of the Stoics' καθῆκον, signifying 'appropriate action' (Cic. *Off.* 1.8; *Fin.* 3.20; *Att.* 16.11.4; 16.14.3): see Introduction III (i); Dyck, 3–8. A. conflates the functional and the philosophical senses of the word in a contrived attempt to authenticate his theme from the Scriptures. It is interesting that both Cic. and A. are sensitive about the use of the word *officium*, albeit for very different reasons: Cic. worries that it does not do full justice to καθῆκον; A. is anxious to justify a philosophical theme as biblically legitimate.

26.　**Nec ratio ipsa abhorret:** It is not just scriptural to talk of duties: it is also rational. This is a determined effort to show that the Christian approach is no less intellectually credible than the classical ones, for Cic. speaks of the importance of reason in *Off.* 1.7: *omnis enim quae [a] ratione suscipitur de aliqua re institutio debet a definitione proficisci, ut intellegatur quid sit id de quo disputetur.* By applying this idea to the area of etymology in particular, A. assumes (in Stoic fashion) that the basis of language lies in nature rather than in convention; revelation and reason are mutually corroborative.

officium ab efficiendo dictum putamus quasi efficium: This etymology, which may well come from Varro, is found also in Donat. *ad* Ter. *Andr.* 236 (1.5.1); and *ad Ad.* 69 (1.1.69); schol. Gronov. *ad* Cic. *Verr.* 1.28; Paul. *Fest.*, s.v. *officiosus*; Isid. *Orig.* 6.19.1 (*TLL* ix/2.518). The correct derivation of the word is from *op(i)ficium*: A. Ernout and A. Meillet, *Dictionnaire étymologique de la langue latine: histoire des mots*, 4th edn. (Paris, 1959), s.v. *officium*. On A.'s interest in etymology, see Introduction IX.

quae nulli officiant, prosint omnibus: On the word-play of *officium–officere*, cf. Lucr. 1.336–7; and especially Cic. *Off.*

1.43 (of the kind of *liberalitas* which benefits some by depriving others): *Id autem tantum abest ⟨ab⟩ officio ut nihil magis officio possit esse contrarium*; one should pursue kindness *quae prosit amicis, noceat nemini*; cf. 1.20: *ut ne cui quis noceat, nisi lacessitus iniuria*; 3.64: *sive vir bonus est is qui prodest quibus potest, nocet nemini*; 3.76: *iam se ipse doceat eum virum bonum esse qui prosit quibus possit, noceat nemini nisi lacessitus iniuria* (on which cf. 1.131; 1.177 below, and see ad locc.); cf. also 3.58–9 below.

CHAPTER 9: PHILOSOPHICAL AND CHRISTIAN
CONCEPTIONS OF DUTY CONTRASTED

27. Officia autem ab honesto et utili . . . quid praestet: The subject must be understood to be the *philosophiae studentes* of 1.24. A. is drawing on Cic. *Off.* 1.9, where Cic. relates how Panaetius considers that doing one's duty involves asking three questions: (i) is an action *honestum* (καλόν)? (ii) is it *utile* (συμφέρον)? (iii) what should one do when the *honestum* and the *utile* seem to conflict? See Introduction III (i); Sauer, 16–20, 21–5. For **officia . . . duci**, cf. Cic. *Off.* 1.100, 152–3; 2.1; 3.96.

deinde incidere . . . quid utilius: In *Off.* 1.10, Cic. argues (probably on the basis of Academic assumptions) that Panaetius' division is inadequate, and that it is necessary to consider two additional questions: is one course *more* honourable than another, and is one course *more* beneficial than another? The three themes thus become five.

in duo honesta . . . iudicium: Cf. Cic. *Off.* 2.9: *Quinque igitur rationibus propositis officii persequendi, quarum duae ad decus honestatemque pertinerent, duae ad commoda vitae, copias opes facultates, quinta ad eligendi iudicium, si quando ea quae dixi pugnare inter se viderentur* ; cf. also Cic. *Off.* 1.9, 25, 29. However, A.'s summary of this passage effectively reduces Cic.'s five categories to three again, probably on the basis of Cic.'s retention of a three-book structure from Panaetius (Panaetius himself had left untackled the question of the apparent conflict between virtue and expediency).

A. is therefore giving a résumé of the treatment of *officia*

by Panaetius and by Cic. without naming the philosophers:
Panaetius and Cic. are bracketed together as **illi** (note,
however, that Cic. himself uses some vague plurals in *Off.*
1.9). He gives no indication that he will in fact follow any of
the philosophers' arrangements (a fact seldom borne in mind
by scholars analysing the composition of the work: Steidle,
'Beobachtungen', 31), though in the end he is closer to the
threefold rather than the fivefold structure. He goes on to
distance himself from the pagan definitions of the *honestum*
and the *utile*.

28.   **Nos autem:** A sharp antithesis with *haec illi* at the end of
1.27.

   quod deceat: The words are Cic.'s, in *Off.* 1.14; on the
principle, see on 1.30.

   **futurorum magis quam praesentium metimur for-
mula:** A. is anxious to emphasize the distinction in his
perspective from that of the philosophers: they consider
duties only with regard to this world; he measures them by
their significance for the world to come. This eschatological
reference-point is crucial to the ethic as it unfolds.

   nihilque utile nisi . . . ad delectationem praesentis: Cf.
2.23–7 (and 2.8 ff. in general); 3.9, 12, 63. The secular or
popular conception of the *utile* is rejected; the only thing that
is truly beneficial is that which contributes to the attainment
of eternal life. Worldly advantage is an impediment to
eternal *beatitudo*; hardship can actually be an advantage
(2.10–21, especially 2.16).

   eaque oneri . . . cum erogantur: A. probably thinks of the
case of the rich young man, to which he refers in 1.36–7 (Mt.
19: 16–29; Mk. 10: 17–30; Lk. 18: 18–30).

   cum adsunt: An indicative mood is necessary to match
cum erogantur in the parallel clause that follows, and
changing the *sint* of the MSS to *sunt* seems too weak:
adsunt captures the sense best (Winterbottom, 560).

29.   **Non superfluum . . . illi aestimaverunt:** Cic. sets out
his claims to write (*Off.* 1.1–6), and asserts that he will be
following the Stoics, albeit with discretion (*Off.* 1.6). He
does not hesitate to state the omissions in Panaetius'
arrangement (*Off.* 1.9–10). His contribution is worthy, he
suggests, because the Stoics have not told the whole story.

A.'s authority is Scripture, which compels him to say something quite different from all the philosophers: the Christian definition of duty is utterly distinct, because its criterion lies beyond the present life. This reference to the **diversa . . . regula** is thus A.'s version of Cic.'s opening *definitio* in *Off.* 1.7(–10) (cf. *Off.* 1.101). His contribution is **non superfluum**, because the classical story is not just inadequate: it is wrong.

Illi saeculi commoda in bonis ducunt: Those things which early Stoicism had termed 'preferable', Panaetius called 'beneficial', but they were still not intrinsically 'good' unless they were virtuous. Cic. is closer to the Peripatetics (cf. *Off.* 1.2; 3.20) in regarding the advantages of this life as goods in themselves, albeit limited when compared with virtue (a view which A. repudiates in 2.1–21). A. seems to have other philosophical positions in mind here besides middle Stoicism; he mentions Aristotle in 1.31.

non haec etiam in detrimentis: Probably suggested by Phil. 3: 7–8: *Sed quae mihi fuerunt lucra, haec arbitratus sum propter Christum detrimenta. Verumtamen existimo omnia detrimentum esse propter eminentem scientiam Iesu Christi Domini mei, propter quem omnia detrimentum feci.*

ut ille dives . . . et Lazarus . . . invenit: See Lk. 16: 19–31; cf. 1.57 below. On **hic . . . illic**, cf. 1.58, 103, 147, 238–40; 3.11, 36.

qui illa non legunt, nostra legent si volent: Cf. Cic. *Off.* 1.2: *Quam ob rem disces tu quidem a principe huius aetatis philosophorum, et disces quam diu voles; sed tamen nostra legens non multum a Peripateticis dissidentia . . ., de rebus ipsis utere tuo iudicio . . . orationem autem Latinam efficies profecto legendis nostris pleniorem*; 1.3: *Quam ob rem magnopere te hortor, mi Cicero, ut non solum orationes meas sed hos etiam de philosophia libros . . ., studiose legas.* Cic. commends his work not least for its stylistic value; A. echoes his language, but goes on to disavow literary pretentions: **qui non sermonum supellectilem neque artem dicendi sed simplicem rerum exquirunt gratiam.** He wishes his text to be read by those who do not read the pagan treatment of duties; in other words, he aspires to replace Cic.'s work for Christian readers. The rejection of style is more than mere

conventional modesty, or just a Christian *topos* about the
simplicity of biblical language over against the sophistries of
classical literature or philosophy (e.g. Min. Fel. *Oct.* 16.6;
Cypr. *Ad Don.* 2; Arnob. *Adv. Nat.* 1.58–9; 2.6, 11; Lact.
Inst. 5.1; Paul. *VA* 1; in A. especially *Ep.* 55 [8].1; *Luc.* prol.
1; 7.218; 8.13, 70; *Inc.* 89; *Expos. Ps. 118*.22.10): it is a
deliberate contrast with his classical predecessor (cf. 1.116;
3.139; note also 2.49). Cic. offers style; he offers plain truth.

CHAPTER 10: 'SEEMLINESS' AND MEASURED
SPEECH

1.30–5 begins with an attempt to prove that the philosophical
idea of the *decorum* (1.27–8) is scriptural. A. argues that the
philosophers came after the OT, and so, implicitly, they stole
its ideas. He focuses on one example, Pythagoras' rule of
silence for his novices, and compares it with David's determination to control his speech (1.31). This leads to some
further reflections on the need to practise restraint of language,
and on the virtues of silence (1.32–5). The series of thoughts on
the value of practice (1.31–3) evokes a shorter reference to the
same idea in Cic. *Off.* 1.60. There is some repetition of points
made earlier (cf. 1.34 and 1.9, 21; and 1.35 and 1.5). A. is
deliberately reinforcing his opening stress on the primacy of
silence (1.5–22, especially 1.5, 7): control of the tongue is the
primum officium (1.35). It is a basic evidence of what the
decorum is all about, because it is a sign of spiritual sensitivity
(1.35). Care of the inner self, which is reflected in carefully
measured speech, is bound up with a right relationship to God.
Just as A. has not rushed to voice his instruction, but has been
seeking to listen to God's voice in Scripture (1.1–4), so his
charges must learn to show reverence for divine authority
(1.35). A. thus underscores the principle established already
in 1.1, 5, 7, 9, 28–9: progress in duty depends upon practice of
the right kind—the practice of submission to God.

30. Decorum: Picking up the reference to *quod deceat* from
Cic. in 1.28 above.

in nostris scripturis: Continues the antithesis of *illi . . . nos* from 1.27–9.

quod Graece πρέπον **dicitur:** Cf. Cic. *Off.* 1.93: *Hoc loco continetur id quod dici Latine decorum potest, Graece enim* πρέπον *dicitur.* Cic. treats the *decorum* (or *quod decet*) as part of his discussion of the fourth cardinal virtue (*Off.* 1.93–151), having signposted this in *Off.* 1.17, but he mentions it also in *Off.* 1.14 and 1.66. A. similarly discusses it as part of his exposition of the fourth virtue (1.211, 213, 219–25). He there makes a fine distinction between the *decorum* and the *honestum* (1.219–21), but in 1.28 (echoing Cic. *Off.* 1.14), 122, 140, 182, and 202 he uses it more or less as a synonym for the *honestum*; modesty is so significant that it effectively epitomizes virtue. The Panaetian emphasis on seemliness as an aesthetic norm is crucial to Cic. and no less so to A. Doing what is seemly means being *seen* to do the appropriate thing with one's particular gifts in each particular situation, and to do so consistently; cf. especially 1.219–25. It is a mean that visibly avoids extremes. See Sauer, 25–30; further on the Ciceronian background, see M. Thurmair, 'Das Decorum als zentraler Begriff in Ciceros Schrift de Officiis', in E. Hora and E. Kessler (eds.), *Studia humanitatis: Ernesto Grassi zum 70. Geburtstag* (Munich, 1973), 63–78. Both Cic. and A. assume the *decorum* principle in their respective introductory remarks about suitability of theme, author, and recipients.

Te decet hymnus, Deus, in Sion: Ps. 64: 2. A. adds the LXX version to underline the equivalence of *decorum* and πρέπον, but also to air his knowledge of the Greek OT; for the display of learning, cf. 1.15 and see ad loc.

apostolus: Paul, as standard in Christian writers.

Loquere quae decent sanam doctrinam: Tit. 2: 1.

Decebat autem . . . per passionem consummari: Heb. 2: 10. The ascription of Heb. to Paul is common in the Fathers (cf. Aug. *CD* 16.22), though doubt had already been expressed by Tertullian, who considered Barnabas a likelier author (*Pudic.* 20), and by Origen, who believed that while the epistle was fully Pauline in content, it could have been written by Clement or Luke (Euseb. Caes. *HE* 6.25.11–13); Eusebius says that there were already several people at Rome during the third and fourth centuries who rejected Pauline authorship (*HE* 3.3.5; 6.20.3).

A.'s attempt to substantiate *decorum* from these three verses is clearly less forced than his effort to justify *officium* in 1.25.

31. Numquid prior . . . quam David . . .?: David's reign, at the beginning of the first millennium BC, pre-dated the Greek philosophers. The anteriority of biblical truth to the insights of the philosophers, and the latter's consequent plagiarism of it, is a frequent theme in *Off.*, picked up from the Alexandrian and Apologetic traditions: e.g. Tert. *Apol.* 19; 47; *Test. anim.* 5; *Anim.* 2; Min. Fel. *Oct.* 34.5; Aug. *Doctr. Chr.* 2.28.107–8; cf. *CD* 8.11; 18.37; *Retract.* 2.30.2: see P. Pilhofer, *Presbyteron Kreitton. Der Altersbeweis der jüdischen und christlichen Apologeten und seine Vorgeschichte* (Tübingen, 1990); also A. J. Droge, *Homer or Moses? Early Christian Interpretations of the History of Culture* (Tübingen, 1989); D. Ridings, *The Attic Moses: The Dependency Theme in Some Early Christian Writers* (Gothenburg, 1995). For subsequent examples in *Off.*, see Introduction IV.2; cf. also *Noe* 24; *Abr.* 1.82; 2.54; *Bon. mort.* 45; 51; *Exc. fr.* 1.42; *Expos. Ps. 118.*2.13; 18.4; *Ep.* 7 [37].28. The reference to David here is to his observance of silence to avoid sinning (cf. 1.5–22). David's *lex silentii* amounted to a prescription for *officium*, hence, once again, the relevance of the introductory section.

Panaetius: See on 1.24.

Aristoteles: The great Aristotle of Stageira (384–322 BC), disciple then critic of Plato, and founder of the Lyceum at Athens in 355 BC, which, with its interest in scientific research, became a rival to the mathematically oriented Academy; see Guthrie vi, *passim*.

qui et ipse disputavit de officio: Rather than thinking of a particular work, such as the *Nicomachean Ethics*, A. probably alludes to Aristotle's *corpus* generally (Madec, 133 n. 236, *pace* Testard i. 229 n. 5). However, duty in the sense implied in A.'s context originates with the Stoics, and is not an Aristotelian theme; Aristotle's ethics are concerned with the realization of εὐδαιμονία by living rationally and avoiding extremes. A.'s reference to Aristotle is not suggested by Cic.'s *Off.*; it is indicative of his own (mostly second-hand) knowledge of a philosophical tradition, and his tendency to lump pagan thinkers together as a group: see Homes Dudden i. 14; Madec, 133–7. He elsewhere associates Aristotelianism with Arianism (*Expos. Ps. 118*.22.10; as do many others, e.g. Jer. *Adv. Lucif.* 11), which implies nothing if not hostility.

ipse Pythagoras: The philosopher-mathematician who migrated from his native Samos on the advent of the tyrant Polycrates in the late 530s or early 520s BC and went to Croton in Magna Graecia, where he founded a religious community which practised Orphic-style asceticism and self-examination; see Guthrie i. 146–340. After a three-year probationary period, novices were bound by a five-year rule of silence before becoming initiates: the idea was that the tongue was the hardest thing for a person to control. Strict control, rather than complete silence, was probably the requirement. A. mentions it also in *Expos. Ps. 118*.2.5. For references, cf. Timae. *FGrHist* 566F13 = DL, 8.10; Isoc. *Bus.* 29; Alex. fr. 197.6 [Kock]; Iamb. *VP* 71–4; Lucian, 27. 3; Epiph. *Dox. Gr.* [Diels] 587.6–7; 590.13–14; Clem. Alex. *Strom.* 5.67.3; Euseb. Caes. *HE* 4.7.7; Greg. Naz. *Or.* 27.10; cf. also Gell. *NA* 1.9.3–6; Apul. *Flor.* 15.22–7; Theod. *Graec. aff. cur.* 1.55, says that the novices kept quiet so that they could hear their master's words. See further P. Gorman, *Pythagoras: A Life* (London and Boston, 1979), 113–32, especially 122–4. A specific source for A. is hard to determine, but clearly a Greek Christian author is his likeliest informant. In common with several Greek authors, both Jewish and Christian, A. believes that Pythagoras was of Jewish descent and had studied the books of Moses (*Ep.* 6 [28].1), and he follows Cic. (*Tusc.* 5.10) in attributing to Pythagoras the invention of the word 'philosophy' (*Abr.* 2.37; cf. *Virg.* 3.19; also Aug. *CD* 8.2; 18.37) (Madec, 106–8); see A. M. Piredda, 'Aspetti del βίος pitagorico nell'etica cristiana di Ambrogio', in *L'etica cristiana nei secoli III e IV: eredità e confronti* (Rome, 1996), 305–16 (somewhat overstating A.'s originality).

Socrate: The great Athenian philosopher (*c.*469–399 BC); see Guthrie iii. 322–507. A. calls him *philosophiae summus magister* (*Expos. Ps. 118*.16.11), knows that Plato and Xenophon were his disciples (*Abr.* 1.2), and asserts that Plato or

Socrates himself read and borrowed from the OT (*Noe* 24; *Bon. mort.* 51).

The point being made here is that Pythagoras, though earlier than the esteemed Socrates (cf. Aug. *Doctr. Chr.* 2.28.108), was still later than David.

ut loquendo ⟨minus⟩ magis disceremus loqui: The addition of **minus** makes the point clearer (Winterbottom, 560).

sine exercitio . . . sine usu: Cf. Cic. *Off.* 1.60: *Sed ut nec medici nec imperatores nec oratores, quamvis artis praecepta perceperint, quicquam magna laude dignum sine usu et exercitatione consequi possunt, sic officii conservandi praecepta traduntur illa quidem, ut facimus ipsi, sed rei magnitudo usum quoque exercitationemque desiderat.*

profectus: On the importance of progress in a general moral sense, see on 1.233–4.

32.   **tamquam in procinctu:** For the metaphor, cf. e.g. Sen. *Dial.* 4.1.4; 11.11.3; *Ep.* 74.30; Quint. *Inst.* 10.1.2; 12.9.21; Aus. *Grat. act.* 42; Jer. *Ep.* 112.1.2; Sid. *Ep.* 2.9.10; in A. cf. *Fid.* 3.1; *Is.* 16.

iaculandi: Cf. 1.20.

vigilanti exit obtutu: Cf. Verg. *Aen.* 5.438: *oculis vigilantibus exit.* A. also echoes the phrase in *Ex.* 6.50; *Tob.* 27. On his knowledge of Vergil in general, see Introduction IX.

Qui navem . . . laborem adsuescunt: As in seafaring, singing, and wrestling, so in speaking, the practice of patient effort is necessary, if speech is to be uttered at the right time and in the right measure. On the imagery of gradual practice in seafaring (and in children's learning of words, as below in 1.33), cf. *Abr.* 1.30: *nec potest mare quisquam navigare intrepidus nisi qui ante in fluminibus navigaverit.* On practising on calm waters first, cf. Jer. *Vita Malch.* 1. Seafaring and fighting are mentioned by Cic. in a different connection in *Off.* 1.87 (alluding to Plato in the first case); cf. also Xen. *Mem.* 1.7.3; Vell. 2.79.1–2; Col. *Agr.*, praef. 3–4; Cypr. *Mort.* 12. On seafaring, cf. also *Cain* 2.9; *Ep. extra coll.* 14 [63].92; Greg. Naz. *Or.* 43.26 (first the oars, then the helm).

vocem excitant: Cic. *Or.* 55–8, speaks of quasi-singing (modulating speech); cf. also Quint. *Inst.* 11.3.19–29. A. *Elia* 47, refers to actors exercising their voices.

33. Haec ipsa natura nos . . . docet: [Haec V², E, Zcll: *nec*
V¹ MA, C¹ NB: *nam* W, C², Testard: *nec non* Amerbach] Cf.
1 Cor. 11: 14: *Nec ipsa natura docet vos.*
exercitatio: The reading of CN, retained by the Maurists
and Krabinger, seems more plausible than VM, E's *excitatio*,
preferred by Banterle and Testard: see A. V. Nazzaro,
'Ambrosiana I. Note di critica testuale ed esegesi', in
R. Cantalamessa and L. F. Pizzolato (eds.), *Paradoxos
Politeia. Studi patristici in onore di Giuseppe Lazzati*
(Milan, 1979), 436–9. *excitatio* could have crept in under
the influence of *excitant* in 1.32, and **quaedam** looks more
appropriate to *exercitatio* than to *excitatio*. In 1.32, the voice
is roused or stimulated by singing gradually or softly
(*sensim*); here, children make sounds as a kind of practice
for proper speech; cf. the imitation spoken of by Quint. *Inst.*
1.1.4–5; also Aug. *Conf.* 1.8.13; 1.14.23. The idea of practice
rather than arousal here is further supported by **exerceant**
and **exercitiis** below. For the use of *exercitatio* in this
context, cf. Cic. *Off.* 1.60 (see on 1.31 above), 133; in A.
Cain 2.22; *Abr.* 2.8 (also Cic. *De Or.* 1.156; *Brut.* 240; *Div.*
2.96; Auct. ad Her. 3.15.27; Quint. *Inst.* 11.3.19–29). On
palaestra, cf. Cic. *De Or.* 1.81; *Brut.* 37; *Or.* 186; in A.
*Expos. Ps. 118.*12.28. On the need to practise virtue, cf. *Cain*
2.8; *Expl. Ps. 36.*51.

34. peccatori: Suggested by Ps. 38: 2 (cf. 1.17); the obvious
allusion is to Shimei: cf. 1.21. On not keeping perpetual
silence, cf. 1.9.
Et, sicut alibi ait, . . . non aperiebat illis os suum: Ps. 37:
13–14.
Noli respondere . . . ne similis illi fias: Prov. 26: 4 (cf.
1.17).

35. Primum igitur officium est loquendi modus: Cf. 1.5
and 1.7, on the primacy of control here.
sacrificium laudis Deo: For the phrase, cf. Ps. 49: 14 (also
Ps. 115: 17; Heb. 13: 15).
cum scripturae divinae leguntur: The problem of keeping congregations quiet during the liturgy was common in
the early church; there are regular complaints about chatter
and noise: *Virg.* 3.11–14 (cf. Athan. *Virg.* 23); *Expl. Ps. 1.*9
(also *Expos. Ps. 118.*7.25 on wandering attention); cf. *Apost.*

Const. 2.57.8; Caes. Arel. *Serm.* 13.3; 19.3; Jer. *Ep.* 22.35.2–3; on a deacon's call for silence, cf. Greg. Tur. *Hist. Franc.* 7.8; also Aug. *CD* 22.8. See N. Adkin, 'A Problem in the Early Church: Noise during Sermon and Lesson', *Mnemosyne* 38 (1985), 161–3. A.'s introduction of congregational hymn-singing was partly designed to promote a corporate unity which would overwhelm such distractions. On silence in approach to holy mysteries, cf. 3.108.

hoc honorantur parentes: On the honouring of parents, cf. e.g. Ex. 20: 12; Mt. 15: 4; 19: 19; Eph. 6: 2. Children show deference to the wisdom and maturity of their parents when they do not answer back.

Scio loqui . . . non prosit loqui: Repeated almost verbatim from 1.5 (N omits both sentences here); see ad loc.

quid dicat, et cui dicat, quo in loco et tempore: For further advice on similar such standard concerns of rhetorical teachers, cf. 1.99–104 and see ad loc.

modus . . . modus . . . mensuram: This Aristotelian emphasis on moderation is suggested by Cic. *Off.* 1.15, 17, 93, 102, 104, 135, 140, 142, etc.; cf. A.'s derivation of *modestia* from *modus* in 1.78 (also Ciceronian).

est etiam factis modus: This is not obviously implied by the preceding section, but A. is just rounding off the passage on modesty. Perhaps he thinks of the silent response to provocation as the alternative to sinful acts of vengeance.

officii: Again, as with **officium** above, integrating this section with the theme.

CHAPTER 11: 'MIDDLE' DUTIES AND 'PERFECT' DUTIES

1.36–9 gives the formal division of the theme of duties into *media officia* and *perfecta officia*. A. seeks to find both in the NT, and naturally commends perfect duty to his spiritually minded addressees, equating it with self-sacrificial *misericordia*. Such a standard constitutes an ethic of perfection because it is rooted in the imitation of the God who is perfect (1.37–8) and reflects a due awareness of one's accountability to him (1.39).

36. Officium autem omne aut medium aut perfectum est: Cf. Cic. *Off.* 1.8: *nam et medium quoddam officium dicitur et perfectum*. *Perfectum officium rectum, opinor, vocemus, quoniam Graeci* κατόρθωμα, *hoc autem commune officium* ⟨μέσον⟩ *vocant. Atque ea sic definiunt, ut rectum quod sit, id officium perfectum esse definiant; medium autem officium id esse dicunt quod cur factum sit ratio probabilis reddi possit* (also Cic. *Off.* 3.14–16). It is not entirely clear how Cic. understands the distinction between the two kinds of duty. In *Fin.* 3.59, he implies that *commune officium* is so named because it is common to both the sage and others (the correct view: *SVF* 3.136.6); in *Off.* 3.14–15, he says that such actions are so called because they are within the reach of ordinary people. In *Off.* 1.8, he does not specify. On the language and its roots, see Dyck, 2–8, 78–81. A. takes over the middle-Stoic schema, but goes on to try to justify it **scripturarum auctoritate** (on which see Ring, 183–96), and thus to give it a new slant: perfect duty is the relevant norm for the clergy.

Si vis in vitam aeternam venire . . . sicut te ipsum: Mt. 19: 17–19.

quibus aliquid deest: This anticipates the rich young man's question in Mt. 19: 20, which A. goes on to quote in 1.37. *Media officia* involve the keeping of the commandments of the Decalogue (and so they are inevitably common to both ordinary people and those who pursue perfection), but there is something missing: they fall short of the ultimate standard of Christ. On perfection as the state in which nothing is lacking, cf. *Fid.* 2.10; *Iac.* 2.21.

37.   *Dicit illi adulescens . . . sequere me:* Mt. 19: 20–1. Perfect duty is complete obedience to the dominical injunction to sacrifice all for the kingdom. A. picks up the emphasis of the Sermon on the Mount (to which he turns below), that the morality of keeping the OT law is inferior to obeying Christ's more demanding norms. For a quite similar distinction between legal or imposed *praeceptum* and suggested or proposed *consilium*, cf. *Vid.* 72–4. The idea that the perfect or Christlike way is attained only by a few (3.10–11; cf. also 1.16, 125, 184, 246, 249) is basic to A.'s view of spiritual devotion and asceticism as a higher path of morality, a vocation for a select group who have consecrated themselves completely to the service of God's church. The Panaetian–Ciceronian casuistry is turned into a Christian ethic of a two-tier spiritual calling; A. thus gives seminal expression to an assumption that is essential to much subsequent Western moral theology. There is a special vocation to ecclesiastical service, and, implicitly, the virtues of those who respond to this call superabound for believers of a more ordinary kind; cf. in detail *Ep.* 6 [28]. The later idea of spiritual *opera supererogatoria* can be traced to such a principle; see A. Harnack, *History of Dogma* v, ET (London, 1898), 49 n. 3; Stelzenberger, 234–42; Homes Dudden ii. 521–2. On the difference between A.'s approach and Cic.'s, see on 3.8–28.

supra habes scriptum: Earlier in Mt.

diligendos inimicos . . . maledicentes: Mt. 5: 44–5.

si volumus perfecti esse sicut Pater noster: Mt. 5: 48.

qui super bonos . . . pinguescere: Mt. 5: 45.

pluviae rore: Dew is not mentioned in Mt. 5: 45; A. is probably thinking also of a verse such as Gen. 27: 39 or Gen. 27: 28 (Testard i. 230–1 n. 5); certainly, dew and rain are often linked in the OT (e.g. Dt. 32: 2), and the bestowing or withholding of both is a sign of God's favour or displeasure (Dt. 33: 13, 28; Zech. 8: 12; also 2 Ki. 1: 21; 3 Ki. 17: 1).

qui corriguntur omnia . . . habere: Evoking the root meaning of κατόρθωμα, literally 'that which is set right'.

lapsus: The word obviously carries theological overtones: the failure to attain perfection is inevitably attributable to sin.

38. misericordia: By showing mercy, the believer imitates his perfect heavenly Father, who shows mercy to all. 'Mercy' (*plenitudo virtutum: Luc.* 2.77) of course = almsgiving: see H. Pétré, '"Misericordia". Histoire du mot et de l'idée du paganisme au Christianisme', *REL* 12 (1934), 376–89.

quia imitatur perfectum Patrem: Cf. Mt. 5: 48 and especially Lk. 6: 36: *Estote ergo misericordes, sicut et Pater vester misericors est.*

ut communes iudices partus naturae . . . fructus terrarum: On this fundamental Stoic doctrine that the earth's produce is given for all in common, cf. Cic. *Off.*

1.22, and especially *Off.* 1.51: *In qua omnium rerum quas ad communem hominum usum natura genuit est servanda communitas.* A. develops the theme in 1.132; cf. also 1.118; 3.16, 45–9. He synthesizes the Christian virtue of mercy with the Stoic principle: the just person gives to the poor because the poor are his fellow-creatures and are no less entitled to the fruits of the earth; by showing such a spirit, he mirrors the mercy of God the provident creator, who gives to all without discrimination.

nummum: A trifling sum, or coin of little value.

denarius: A copper coin, at this time (cf. Macr. *Sat.* 1.7.22), so cash in the sense of 'small change'. The three pithy clauses of the last sentence drive home the point: to you, mercy is only the disbursement of a small coin, or 'loose change'; to the poor man, it amounts to the gift of life, substance, and wealth. Cf. *Nab.* 56, challenging the rich man: *Totius vitam populi poterat anuli tui gemma servare.*

39. Ad haec plus ille tibi confert cum sit debitor salutis: There is a weighty spin-off: you give the poor the means of temporal, physical salvation, and it will have eternal, spiritual benefit for you. For the poor person, the *salus* is earthly; for the giver, it is eternal. Cf. *Elia* 76: *vilis pecunia, sed pretiosa est misericordia*; *Expl. Ps.* 37.24: *Vilis est pecunia, sed fit pretiosa per fidem; vilis est cum conditur, pretiosa cum dispergitur*; also *Nab.* 36. Almsgiving is a *negotiatio*, an exchange of small things for great, the storing of treasures in heaven: cf. e.g. Max. Taur. *Serm.* 27.1; 96; Aug. *Serm.* 60.7; *En Ps. 121.*11. The merciful man heals his own wounds while he helps others (*Ob. Theod.* 16).

Si nudum vestias: A. is thinking of Mt. 25: 36–40 (cf. the whole section 25: 31–46): to be kind to the needy believer is to show unselfconscious kindness to Christ himself, which has eternal reward. Cf. *Vid.* 54: *Ministra pauperi, et ministrati Christo*; also e.g. Jer. *Ep.* 130.14.8: *Christum vestire in pauperibus*; Pet. Chrys. *Serm.* 8.4; 14.4.

te ipsum induis iustitiam: Cf. Job 29: 14: *Iustitia indutus sum, et vestivi me, sicut vestimento et diademate, iudicio meo.*

si peregrinum sub tectum inducas tuum: On the importance of hospitality, cf. 1.86, 167; especially 2.103–8; and see on 2.103.

ille tibi acquirit sanctorum amicitias et aeterna tabernacula: Cf. Lk. 16: 9: *Et ego vobis dico: facite vobis amicos de mamona iniquitatis, ut cum defeceritis recipiant vos in aeterna tabernacula.* A. believes that the departed saints (particularly the apostles and martyrs) have power both to intercede with God on behalf of the needy (*Vid.* 54–6; *Exc. fr.* 2.135) and to dispense blessings to the faithful in this world (e.g. *Virgt.* 130; *Exc. fr.* 1.17; *Exh. virg.* 15; cf. also Aug. *CD* 22.8–10; Caes. Arel. *Serm.* 26). In their position *in sinu Abrahae* (Lk. 16: 22; cf. 1.57 below), they have a privileged place of influence with God (Niederhuber, *Reiche Gottes*, 219–32). The poor pray for their benefactors, and will intercede for them on the day of judgement (cf. Max. Taur. *Serm.* 27.1). Augustine pictures such saints as *laturarii* of almsgivers on the way to heaven (*Serm.* 18.4; 38.9; 25A, 4; 60.8).

corporalia seminas et recipis spiritalia: Reminiscent of Paul's language about the resurrection of the dead in 1 Cor. 15: 35–49, especially 15: 42–4, 46, where the contrast is between the earthly body, subject to decay, which is 'sown' in burial, and the 'spiritual' body, incorruptible, which is resurrected at the last day. A. likewise applies the terminology to the contrast of present material gift and future spiritual reward.

Miraris iudicium Domini de sancto Iob?: For similar commendation of Job in such a context, cf. *Nab.* 57.

eius qui: Job himself.

Oculus eram caecorum . . . . Ego eram infirmorum pater: Job 29: 15–16.

velleribus agnorum meorum calefacti sunt humeri eorum: Job 31: 20.

Foris non habitabat peregrinus: Job 31: 32.

magis beatus quam . . . suae debitorem misericordiae: Cf. Ps. 40: 2: *Beatus qui intellegit super egenum et pauperem; in die mala liberabit eum Dominus.* The idea of **quem habebit suae debitorem misericordiae** is suggested by Prov. 19: 17, *Faeneratur Domino qui miseretur pauperis,* a verse which A. quotes in *Tob.* 55 (*ecce usura laudabilis . . .*); *Exc. fr.* 1.60; cf. also Prov. 13: 8; Eccli. 3: 30; Lk. 11: 41. On obtaining redemption as a reward for almsgiving, cf. e.g. 1.150; 2.126; *Nab.* 36, 58–60; *Elia* 76; *Expl. Ps. 37.24; Expl. Ps. 38.27;*

Expos. Ps. 118. 8.41; *Paen.* 2.83; *Luc.* 7.245; *Ep. extra coll.* 14 [63].92. On the twin emphases of Christ's identification with the poor and the atoning value of almsgiving (classically expressed in Cypr. *Op. et el.*), see B. Ramsey, 'Almsgiving in the Latin Church: The Late Fourth and Early Fifth Centuries', *ThS* 43 (1982), 226–59; also R. Garrison, *Redemptive Almsgiving in Early Christianity* (Sheffield, 1993).

CHAPTER 12: GOD'S CARE FOR HUMAN AFFAIRS, AND AN EXCURSUS ON JOB

1.40–64 deals with divine providence, with an *excursus* (A.'s own word: 1.47) on the sufferings of Job (1.41–6). The section is not inspired by Cic. and the theme of duties is not mentioned after 1.40 until 1.65. This has led to speculation that the piece derives from a separate source—even from two sources, if 1.41–6 is taken to belong to a separate development from the paragraphs which surround it (Testard, 'Etude', 165; 'Recherches', 90). There are some similarities between the passage from the end of 1.40 to 1.46 and *Interp.* 2 (Testard, '*Conscientia*', 228 n. 1; 'Recherches', 90 n. 76). However, it is just as likely that A. is developing various familiar expository themes, not least on the stock character of Job, the godly sufferer; the section can still be seen as part of a conscious plan (and there is in fact a brief echo of Cic. in 1.46). The absence of a similar section in Cic. is beside the point, for Cic. had already discussed the ramifications of the *summum bonum* in *Fin.* and had no need to explore these issues again in *Off.* For A. on the other hand, it is entirely logical to offer an outline of his foundational assumptions on the human lot *vis-à-vis* divine justice and the problems of good, evil, and suffering, and to defend his assumptions about the rationality and purposive character of the moral universe indwelt by his addressees. Having laid such emphasis on the fact that *officium* is both offered to God and rewarded by God, he seeks to deal with a number of commonplace objections to this theology before proceeding to his substantive treatment of duties as such. The arguments to which he responds were doubtless common enough in his pastoral experience (note the force of *plerique revocantur* at the start of 1.40). He may also be seeking to anticipate the challenges of pagan readers (especially those with sympathies for hedonist corruptions of Epicurean logic: cf. 1.47, 50) to his basic premise of a just, benevolent God who ultimately punishes the evil and rewards the good. See Steidle, 'Beobachtungen', 31–2.

The subject of God's awareness of evil, and divine justice, a central theme of the Wisdom literature (above all, of course, in Job) and the Psalms (e.g. Pss. 9, 36, 49, 72) is explored by A. in several places, particularly in *Interp.* 1–2, on Job, and *Interp.* 3 on Ps. 72; cf. also e.g. *Expos. Ps. 118* 7.10 ff.; 9.7 ff.; 14.15 ff. It is a topic which crops up frequently in patristic preaching: notable treatments include John Chrys. *Prov.* (especially 12); Aug. *CD* 1.8 ff.; 20.2; Nemes. Emes. *Nat. hom.* 42–4; Theod. *Prov.*; Salvian, *Gub. Dei*, especially 1–3; Ps.-Prosp. Aquit. *Carm. div. prov.*; see the collection of some important texts in J. Walsh and P. G. Walsh, *Divine Providence and Human Suffering* (Wilmington, DE, 1985). Christian writers frequently exploit Stoic arguments on theodicy to defend the benevolence of God's ways (e.g. Just. *Dial.* 1; Athen. *Leg.* 19.3; Iren. *Adv. Haer.* 3.25; Min. Fel. *Oct.* 12.2; 17–18; 36.3–5; Tert. *Anim.* 20.5; Novat. *Trin.* 8.4–6; Clem. Alex. *Strom.* 6–7; Lact. *Opif. Dei* 2–8, 10–14; *Ira* 9–13, 17; *Inst.* 1.2–8; 2.10; 3.17; 7.1–8; Bas. *Hom.* 9); or merge Stoic assumptions on πρόνοια with Neoplatonist ideas that suffering is intended as spiritual purification (e.g. Aug. *Ord.*; *Conf.* 7.12–8; *CD* 22.22–4; Boeth. *Consol.*). For A. the rationale is simple: the Bible speaks of a God who is good, omniscient, and just, and there will be eschatological justice and reward for those who suffer in the present life. The 'theodicy', such as it is, is close to a classical 'Irenaean' approach: the world is a vale of soul-making, and in God's design there is ultimate redemptive value to be gained through temporal struggle and privation. There is thus a fairly typical fourth–fifth-century pastoral synthesis of biblical themes with notions which have general roots in both Stoic and Platonist thinking; but the key concern of A. is to establish the fact that God sees and rewards moral behaviour, despite all the challenges of practical despair or intellectual scepticism.

40. dispensatricis misericordiae: Mercy is personified (*dispensatrix* is a very rare feminine form); cf. *ratio* as a *domitrix* in 1.228.

dum putant . . . luctu frequenti: This *divisio* (1.47) lists three objections to the assertion of divine interest in human affairs: (i) the Epicurean (1.47) and Aristotelian (1.48, 50) belief that God is uninterested in humanity; (ii) the view of *flagitiosi* (1.47), that God has no knowledge of human actions; (iii) the view of other *flagitiosi* (cf. 1.47), that God knows but is unjust in his judgement, since the righteous are seen to suffer while the wicked flourish. The division is repeated in 1.47, after the digression on Job (1.41–6), and (i) is dealt with in 1.48–50; (ii) in 1.51–6; and (iii) in 1.57–64. **Dominum:** VA, EW: *Deum* M, CNB.

quid teneat nostra conscientia: Conscience here is in a clearly Christian context: these people imagine that God is ignorant of the secret deeds to which conscience testifies. On the absurdity of the creator knowing less than the creature, cf. 1.51–6.

quando peccatores divitiis abundare vident: Cf. Ps. 72: 12: *Ecce ipsi peccatores et abundantes in saeculo obtinuerunt divitias.* Ps. 72 is a *locus classicus* on the prosperity of the wicked and the suffering of the righteous; A. expounds it in *Interp.* 3. **sanitate** may be suggested by the references to the health of the wicked in Ps. 72: 4; though the antithesis with the needy, dishonoured, childless, weak, and grieving righteous points particularly to the case of Job, the pre-eminent model of patience and fortitude (cf. 1.113, 195), whose godly character was proved by his sufferings (2.20): see generally J. R. Baskin, 'Job as Moral Exemplar in Ambrose', *VChr* 35 (1981), 222–31.

41. tres illi reges amici Iob: Eliphaz the Temanite, Bildad the Shuhite, and Zophar the Naamathite (Job 2: 11–13). The designation of them as **reges** comes from the LXX, which in Job 2: 11 calls both Eliphaz and Zophar βασιλεῖς, and Bildad τύραννος (cf. *Expl. Ps.* 37.51; *Interp.* 2.2); the Hebrew text makes no mention of their status in this verse (they are simply said to be *seniores* in Job 32: 4, as compared with the young man Elihu); cf. 3.138.

inopem factum . . . ad pedes videbant: Cf. Job 1: 1–3,
13–19; 2: 7–8, 12; 7: 5; 19: 19–20; 30: 17, 30.
*Cur impii vivunt? Inveteraverunt autem . . . non est in
ipsis:* Job 21: 7–9.

42.   **infirmus corde:** One whose faith is weak (cf. Rom. 14; 1
Cor. 8: 7–13), who cannot see that God has a benevolent
purpose in allowing the just to suffer.
Portate me . . . onus sermonum meorum: Job 21: 3–4.
The version of the second verse which A. quotes (*Nam etsi
arguor, quasi homo arguor*) is not what the biblical text
says, and *Portate ergo onus sermonum meorum* is not
in the passage at all. Doubtless he paraphrases from memory.
He apparently realizes his inaccuracy (**aut certe quia ita est
versus**), and proceeds to give a rendering of Job 21: 4 that at
least begins more faithfully, with *Numquid . . .?*. However,
this quotation also goes astray: having first said that Job is
criticized *as* a man, A. now has him criticized *by* a man,
whereas the point of the verse is that Job is complaining to
God, not man, since he thinks God is responsible for his
condition. He is not being criticized *as* a man for his foolish
words, or *by* a man for the sins which have brought his
misfortunes upon him. On the moral, cf. Cypr. *Pat.* 18.
*Discede a me, vias tuas scire nolo . . . opera autem
impiorum non videt:* Job 21: 14–16. A. makes the first
clause singular, to agree with his subject, **infirmus**; in the
biblical text, the whole of the passage is in the plural, with
the subject as *impii* (Job 21: 7). Quite boldly, A. equates the
infirmus with the wicked (hardly the NT import of 'weakness'), who see no purpose in serving God; cf. *Interp.* 2.17.

43.   **Laudatur in Platone . . . personam dicere:** A reference to Glaucon, who claims that his task of speaking against
justice (restating Socrates' version of Thrasymachus' case) is
imposed on him simply for the purposes of the dialogue and
in order to investigate the truth: Plat. *Rep.* 357a ff., especially
358c–d (cf. 361e).
Quod eo usque Tullius . . . dicendum putaverit: Cic.
adopts the idea **in libris quos scripsit de Republica**
(*Rep.*) 3.8, making Laelius' interlocutor Philus say that he
is prepared to state the case against justice only because it is
his custom to get at the truth by playing devil's advocate,

and in order to humour Laelius (cf. also Sen. *Ep.* 108.30). Several pages are missing from our text of Cic.'s *Rep.* on either side of the passage, but presumably A.'s text did include the information. If not, we must assume that he has read the Plato for himself, which seems fairly unlikely, given the paucity of evidence for *direct* debts elsewhere: Madec, 111–13. W. Wilbrand, 'Ambrosius und Plato', *RQA* 25 (1911), 42*–49*, and, to a lesser extent, Madec, 109–32, argue that A.'s knowledge of Plato generally derives from intermediaries such as Cic., Apuleius, Plotinus, Porphyry, and Origen, not from a reading of Plato himself. The only other certain reference to Plato's *Rep.*, in *Abr.* 1.2, seems indebted to Cic. On Plato, cf. *Abr.* 1.2; 2.37; *Expl. Ps.* 35.1.

44. Quanto antiquior illis Iob . . . aestimavit!: See on 1.31. The book of Job is variously dated from the tenth to the third century BC, with the sixth century being the most popular estimate; we do not know when A. thought Job lived. Plato's dates are 428–347 BC; *Rep.* was written *c.*375 BC. Cic. lived 106–43 BC, and wrote his *Rep.* in the late 50s. But, chronology aside, the connection between Job and Plato/Cic. is in any case highly tenuous. Job does not say in Job 21 that he is going to propound an argument of which he is not fully convinced, as Glaucon and Philus do. Rather, resigned to the fact that his friends will criticize him anyhow, he merely asks indulgence of his complaint against God's injustice—a complaint that for him *is* genuine, in his state of misery. After an inaccurate quotation and explanation of the text of Job 21 in 1.42, A. is here drawing an illegitimate parallel between Job's address and the classical dialogues. Behind it all is his obsession with showing the superiority of biblical truth to philosophical insight.

exstinguatur . . . eversio: Job 21: 17.

Deum doctorem . . . veritatis iudicem: Cf. Job 21: 22.

non secundum forensem abundantiam . . . arbitra: On the contrast of outward prosperity with true, spiritual *beatitudo*, cf. 2.8–21, and especially 2.1–2, 10, 12, 19, 21 on the worth of a good conscience. The judgement of God is associated with the self-judgement of human beings: the person who knows that he cannot evade God (cf. *Expl. Ps.*

*36.*63) and so keeps himself from sin finds that his good conscience mirrors God's positive judgement of him. Happiness, both in this life and in the life to come, lies in knowing that one is innocent before and approved by God, regardless of outward circumstances. Conscience and divine approval are co-ordinate norms of conduct and criteria of blessedness, since conscience is a divine endowment; cf. e.g. *Parad.* 39; *Iac.* 1.20; *Paen.* 2.103; *Expl. Ps. 38.*13; *Epp.* 7 [37].18, 32; 58 [60].5; 63 [73].2–3.

Moritur innocens . . . gerens: Cf. Job 21: 23–4.

quamvis foris abundet . . . odoribus fragret: Cf. *Nab.* 3; *Luc.* 6.27; 8.14.

in amaritudine animae suae . . . claudit: Cf. Job 21: 25.

nihil secum auferens: Cf. Job 27: 19: *Dives cum dormierit nihil secum auferet: aperit oculos suos et nihil inveniet.*

45. This and the following paragraph are a rhetorical challenge to consider the ultimate plight of the ungodly man as compared with the faithful sufferer; cf. the picture in 1.29.

Dicite, inquit, *mihi ubi est protectio tabernaculorum eius?*: Cf. Job 21: 28.

Signum eius non invenitur: Cf. Wisd. 5: 11.

Vita etenim . . . evanuit delectatio: Cf. Job 27: 19, quoted on 1.44 above. (The demise of the wicked is compared to a dream by Zophar in Job 20: 8 also.) Testard punctuates with a question mark after **oculos**, but this must be wrong: there is no question in Job 27: 19, and it is much better to treat as one the entire phrase from **vita** down to **delectatio**, with a tricolon after **somnium**.

etiam dum vivunt, impiorum requies in inferno sit: Cf. Num. 16: 30, 33; Ps. 54: 16. On the argument that the wicked who prosper are punished while they live by becoming more and more estranged from virtue, cf. generally Boeth. *Consol.* 4.6.

46. Nonne gravius omnibus foetet sepulcris?: Cf. *Ex.* 6.51: *Nulla discretio inter cadavera mortuorum, nisi forte quia gravius foetent divitum corpora distenta luxurie.*

introspice ulcera . . . cordis maestitudinem: Cf. Cic. *Off.* 3.85: *Hunc tu quas conscientiae labes in animo censes habuisse, quae vulnera?*

Quia non in abundantia est vita eius: Lk. 12: 15.

Nulla enim hereditas peccatoris: A. probably thinks of Ps. 36 (especially 36: 10–11, 18, 20, 22), where the fate of the *peccator* is that he will be left desolate in the end, while the righteous inherit the earth; cf. *Interp.* 2.22.

CHAPTER 13: REFUTATION OF THE FIRST OBJECTION

47. **Sed revertamur ad propositum:** A. returns to the subject announced in 1.40 and interrupted by the *excursus* on Job.

Epicurei: Disciples of the school founded by Epicurus (*c*.341–270 BC). In Epicurus' physics, the gods take no interest in human affairs but live a life of detached quietism in the *intermundia*, where they enjoy one another's friendship and speak Greek. There is, for Epicurus, no eternal human destiny (the soul is mortal) and no divine providence, so fear of the gods is absurd (cf. the exposition of Epicurean theology in Cic. *ND* 1.18–56; Lucr. especially 1.150–8; 2.167–83, 646–51, 1090–1104; 4.1233–9; 5.64–90, 110–234, 1161–1240; 6.58–91, 379–422); in A. cf. *Noe* 100: *ut primum excludamus philosophorum quorundam opiniones, qui negant Deum curam habere super homines.* See A. J. Festugière, *Epicurus and his Gods*, ET (Oxford, 1955), especially 51–93; A. A. Long, *Hellenistic Philosophy* (London, 1974), 14–74, especially 41–9. On the hostility of Christian spokesmen towards Epicurean ethics in particular, see on 1.50.

Nec superfluus . . . cum ipsi se miseros putent: The presentation of the integrity of Job's faith in the midst of his sufferings makes the objections easier to deal with. The logic is not quite right, though: Job's case is, strictly, relevant only to the third objection, and ought to be placed with the answer to it in 1.57–64. For another apology for an *excursus*, cf. 3.110 on 3.103–10. **iudicamus** must be preferable to the MSS' *iudicant*: it provides the necessary contrast between the assessment of others that the wicked are happy and their own secret unhappiness; and it points to **nobis** in the next sentence (Winterbottom, 560).

48. **proclive:** Cf. Cic. *Off.* 2.69: *dictu quidem est proclive*; the

word also occurs several times elsewhere in Cic.: e.g. *Rep.*
1.11; 2.17.

cetera: Cf. 1.40.

qui Deum putant curam mundi nequaquam habere:
There seems to be little or no distinction between divine care
for *hominis actus* (1.40), or *de nobis* (1.47), and divine care for
the world in general: the picture is anthropocentric (cf.
1.132; also *Noe* 10; *Inst. virg.* 17; *Ep.* 29 [43].1; *Ex.* 5.25;
Luc. 7.125–30). This makes the Aristotelian error which
follows no better than the Epicurean one, since both divorce
the divine from direct involvement with human affairs, even
if their theologies differ in other respects: cf. e.g. Orig. *Cels.*
1.21; 3.75, and see Madec, 134–5, citing A. J. Festugière,
L'Idéal réligieux des Grecs et l'Evangile (Paris, 1932), 253–4.
**sicut Aristoteles adserit usque ad lunam eius descen-
dere providentiam:** A standard claim in 'doxographies'
(e.g. DL, 5.32), frequently denounced explicitly or implicitly
by Christian authors: e.g. Tat. *Or.* 2; Athen. *Leg.* 25.2;
Clem. Alex. *Protr.* 5.66.4; *Strom.* 5.90.3; Orig. *Sel. in Ps.*
*35.*6; *In Ep. ad Rom.* 3.1; Euseb. Caes. *PE* 15.5.1; Greg. Naz.
Or. 27.9; Theod. *Graec. aff. cur.* 5.47; 6.7; *Haer. fab.* 5.10;
Prov. 1.8; Cyr. Alex. *In Ps. 35.*6; Nemes. Emes. *Nat. hom.*
44.127–8. It has not been identified in Aristotle's extant
works; Aristotle did however posit a division of the universe
into supra- and sub-lunar regions, and his Prime/Unmoved
Mover did not actively interfere in the world of human
beings (cf. Ps.-Arist. *Mund.* 397^{b}20–400^{b}15); J. Pépin, *Théologie cosmique et théologie chrétienne (Ambroise, Exam. 1,1,1–
4)* (Paris, 1964), 135–72, 472–92; cf. also 1.50 below.
Courcelle, *Recherches*, 20, suggests that Calcidius, *In Tim.*
250 (which he dates to 380), provides a source for A. here
(since Orig. *In Ep. ad Rom.* 3.1, which is otherwise a
probable reference-point, does not actually mention
Aristotle's name), but it is equally likely that the charge
was simply proverbial in Christian rhetoric. Throughout
1.47–50, A. uses **ipsi** to refer to the pagans as a group,
regardless of their differences: all of them together are to be
contrasted with the truth of the Christian revelation (I am
indebted to Madec, 136–7, for his comments on this section).
Si iniuria est neglegere: neglegere makes much better

sense than the MSS' *regere*, in view of **neglegat** above, and the whole context (Winterbottom, 560–1).

49. **de illis:** The Epicureans. The denial of divine creation is Epicurean, as is the idea to which A. alludes, that humans and beasts are no different metaphysically, since they are all made of the same atoms. However, the doctrine of divine immanence in the world (**Per omnia ire Deum . . . terras caelum maria**) is Stoic, though *horum*, at the start of 1.50, meaning Epicurus' disciples, must surely there refer to the **ipsi** who have just been mentioned. Epicurean and Stoic ideas seem to get confused. A. should logically have little reason to quarrel with the Stoics in this context, since they believed strongly in deterministic providence, and espoused a cosmic anthropocentrism not dissimilar to his own (though Cic. himself remained very opposed to any such idea; see J.-P. Martin, *Providentia deorum* (Paris, 1982), 19–65). He implicitly commends their derision of Epicureanism in 1.50. There is a blurring of the edges between the philosophical schools: A.'s main target is Epicurean thought, but he conflates Epicurean and Stoic ideas in his concern to contrast pagan tenets with Christian belief.

Per omnia ire Deum ipsi adserunt: A clear echo of Verg. *Georg.* 4.221–2: *deum namque ire per omnis | terrasque tractusque maris caelumque profundum* (222 = *Ecl.* 4.51; cf. also *Aen.* 1.58, 280). For other use of these lines, cf. e.g. Apul. *Mund.* 374; Min. Fel. *Oct.* 19.2; Lact. *Inst.* 1.5.12; Jer. *In Eph.* 2.4.6; Aug. *CD* 4.11; *Conf.* 7.1.2; Salv. *Gub. Dei* 1.1.4; Calcid. *Comm.* 100 (see P. Courcelle, 'Virgile et l'immanence divine chez Minucius Felix', in A. Stuiber and A. Hermann (eds.), *Mullus: Festschrift Theodor Klauser* (Münster, 1964), 34–42). On divine immanence/omnipresence/omniscience, cf. e.g. *Ex.* 6.21; *Cain* 1.32; *Abr.* 1.7; *Expl. Ps. 35*.11; *Expl. Ps. 36*.63; *Expos. Ps. 118*.19.36, 38; *Fid.* 1.106; 2.60; *Spir.* 2.35–6; *Ep.* 29 [43].15.

scientia: The reasoning here is more appropriate to the refutation of the second objection (1.51–6), where A. is arguing against the charge that God has no knowledge of humans; in this first section, the subject is supposed to be that God has knowledge of but does not care for humans (cf. Testard, 'Etude', 166 n. 18).

50. magistrum: Epicurus.

velut ebrium et voluptatis patronum: Epicurus' ethic proposed that the highest good was the attainment of *voluptas* and the avoidance of *dolor*. This was not in the first place the debased hedonism which later became associated with his name, but a largely negative ideal of a life of quietism and freedom from passion, the enjoyment of friendship, and the contemplation of the universe. Cic., however, viewed the *voluptas* ideal with extreme suspicion (especially *Fin.* 2; also *Tusc.* 3.36–51), and his hostility was passed on to Christian writers, who invariably assume that Epicurus was an advocate of unrestrained sensuality: e.g. Lact. *Inst.* 3.17.35; Pet. Chrys. *Serm.* 5. A. calls Epicurus *adsertor voluptatis* (*Ep. extra coll.* 14 [63].13); *defensor voluptatis* (*Ep. extra coll.* 14 [63].19); *patronus luxuriae* (*ibid.*); and his disciples *adsertores voluptatis* (*Ep. extra coll.* 14 [63].17); he does concede, though, that Epicurus' own morals were better than his logic suggested they might have been (*Ep. extra coll.* 14 [63].19). Cf. also 2.4 below; *Abr.* 2.3, 85. See further W. Schmid, 'Epikur', *RAC* v. 681–819, especially 774 ff., 792–6; H. Jones, *The Epicurean Tradition* (London and New York, 1989), 94–116; on A., see Madec, 87–8, 138–9.

ipsi qui putantur sobrii . . . philosophi: The Stoics and Cic. On other philosophy's disowning of the Epicurean ideal, cf. *Ep. extra coll.* 14 [63].19–20.

qui putat Deum . . . modo degere: Aristotle's god lives as a king self-sufficient and content in his own lofty realm, delegating his power over the regions of the lower world but taking no concern for them himself (cf. Ps.-Arist. *Mund.* 398b).

ut poetarum loquuntur fabulae . . . inter se bellum excitent: A reference to the story of the division of the world between Zeus, Poseidon, and Hades (Hom. *Il.* 15.187–99); Courcelle, *Recherches*, 19 n. 1, points out similarities in Lact. *Inst.* 1.11.30; Ps.-Serv. (Serv. Dan.), *In Aen.* 1.139; also 6.287; 10.40. The myth is brought in to make Aristotle's view of a deity who is only interested in the supra-lunar realm (like Zeus in heaven) seem ridiculous: the philosopher merely follows the poets.

Et quomodo ipsi excludunt quos sequuntur poetas?: In several passages, Aristotle quotes myths with some approval: e.g. *Metaph.* 1074^b1–14 (and cf. the philosophical 'myth-lover' at 982^b18–19); *Polit.* 1269^b27–31; 1341^b2–7; see further J. Pépin, *Mythe et Allégorie. Les origines grecques et les contestations judéo-chrétiennes*, 2nd edn. (Paris, 1976), 121–4. Elsewhere, however, he calls the poets liars (*Metaph.* 983^a3–4). **ipsi** once again refers to the philosophers in general, not just Aristotle.

CHAPTER 14: REFUTATION OF THE SECOND OBJECTION

51. cura non praeterit: E² CO's **cura** is preferable to the at-first-tempting *curam* of PVM, E¹, in order to retain the chiastic structure of **cura non praeterit, praetereat scientia.**
Qui plantavit aurem . . . non considerat?: Ps. 93: 9.
52. Non praeteriit haec vana opinio sanctos prophetas: Again, truth was first delineated, and error first refuted, by scriptural characters. **Non praeteriit** [*praeterit* V, E] picks up the language of the previous paragraph. On **vana**, cf. generally 1.242–5.
David inducit eos . . . inflatos adserit: In Ps. 93.
sub peccato: A Pauline motif: Rom. 3: 9; 7: 14; Gal. 3: 22.
Usquequo peccatores, Domine . . . gloriabuntur?: Ps. 93: 3. A. is confused here: in Ps. 93, it is David who asks the question, not the proud sinners (who might be less likely to say *Domine*?). He fails to remember the obvious sense of the verse, yet he is able to quote several parts of the psalm very accurately in this paragraph.
Et dixerunt: Non videbit Dominus . . . Deus Iacob: Ps. 93: 7. This time, David *is* quoting the words of the proud, though they are not criticizing others, as his apparent linking of this statement with the previous quotation seems to suggest.
Intellegite nunc insipientes . . . quoniam vanae sunt: Ps. 93: 8–11.
Potest opus suum ignorare artifex?: The *reductio ad*

absurdum: the creator cannot be ignorant of his own creation; cf. *Fid.* 5.196–9. The argument has parallels in the Stoic doctrine of the providential government of the world: cf. Cic. *ND* 2.73–156. Augustine's defence of providence in *Gen. ad litt.* 5.42–6 covers some of the same ground.

Haec illi: V: *haec illis* MSS, Testard; cf. 1.27.

53. **Ceterum nobis:** Contrasts sharply with *Haec illi* at the end of 1.52; another antithesis of ungodly and Christian views.

Ego sum scrutans corda et renes: Jer. 17: 10.

Quid cogitatis mala in cordibus vestris?: Lk. 5: 22.

evangelista: Luke.

Sciebat enim Iesus cogitationes eorum: Lk. 6: 8. For A. Christ's knowledge is of course God's knowledge; cf. e.g. *Fid.* 5.188–226; *Spir.* 2.114–29; *Luc.* 8.33–6.

54. **satis ⟨nos⟩ movere:** The addition of **nos** seems essential (Winterbottom, 561).

iudicem . . . occultorum scientiam: Perhaps reminiscent of Rom. 2: 16: *in die cum iudicabit Deus occulta hominum*; cf. also Ps. 43: 22; and *Expl. Ps. 40.7*; *Ep.* 63 [73].3.

sciens opera eorum: Cf. Apoc. 2: 2, 19; 3: 1, 8, 15.

tradidit eos in tenebras: On God 'handing over' sinners, that is, allowing their judgement to run its course, cf. Rom. 1: 24, 26, 28 (also Acts 7: 42).

In nocte . . . posuit suae: Job 24: 14–15. C's *servavit* [*servabit* MSS, Testard] and VM, O²'s *considerabit* [*consideravit* P, E, CO¹] are faithful to the tenses in the biblical passage.

Omnis enim qui lucem fugit, diligit tenebras: Cf. Jn. 3: 19–21. Light and darkness are favourite images in A.'s Christological and soteriological expression; consult Morgan, *passim*.

qui intra profundum abyssi . . . volvenda cognoscit: Cf. Eccli. 23: 28.

Quis me videt? . . . quem vereor?: Eccli. 23: 25–6.

in lecto suo positus haec cogitet: On the evil man plotting evilly upon his bed, cf. Ps. 35: 5.

Et erit . . . timorem Dei: Eccli. 23: 31.

55. Nature illustrates the penetrating knowledge of God. The argument is from lesser to greater: if the sun's warmth and

light, created by God, can reach through physical obstacles, how much more can God's own knowledge penetrate the minds and hearts of human beings (1.56)? On the sun's warmth, cf. *Ex.* 3.27; also 2.16; 4.21, 25–7. The language is reminiscent of Lucretius' descriptions of atomic force: e.g. Lucr. 1.354–5, 489–97; 6.951–4, and especially 6.962–4: *principio terram sol excoquit et facit are, | at glaciem dissolvit et altis montibus altas | exstructas⟨que⟩ nives radiis tabescere cogit.*

varios terra se fundit in fructus: Cf. Verg. *Ecl.* 9.40–1: *varios hic flumina circum | fundit humus flores.* A.'s **se fundit** and **in fructus** give slightly curious twists to the more logical Vergilian language.

56. Si igitur radius solis fundit lumen suum . . . impeditur: Also quite Lucretian: cf. Lucr. 2.114–15: *contemplator enim, cum solis lumina cumque | inserti fundunt radii per opaca domorum.* For similar language, cf. *Expos. Ps. 118.*8.57.

in cogitationes hominum et corda: Cf. Eccli. 23: 28. Rather ironically, in view of 1.48 and 1.50, the argument goes back to Aristotle: God cannot have made a creature with the potential to be greater than himself.

CHAPTER 15: REFUTATION OF THE THIRD
OBJECTION

57. Tertium genus: The third objection mentioned in 1.40 and 1.47; this time, doubt is not cast on God's providence or his knowledge, but on his justice.

cur peccatores abundent . . . aut liberorum: Cf. Ps. 72: 12.

illa evangelii parabola: Lk. 16: 19–31.

in sinu Abrahae: Cf. Lk. 16: 22, and see Niederhuber, *Eschatologie*, 62–4.

Nonne evidens est . . . post mortem manere?: The answer to those who question God's justice is eschatological: there will be a great reversal of fortunes in the life to come.

58. *Certamen,* inquit, *bonum certavi . . . qui diligunt adventum eius*: 2 Tim. 4: 7–8.

In illa, **inquit,** *die reddet*, **non hic:** Cf. 1.29, 103, 147, 238–40; 3.11, 36.

Hic autem in laboribus, in periculis, in naufragiis: Cf. 2 Cor. 11: 21–33, where Paul lists his sufferings.

per multas tribulationibus . . . in regnum Dei: Cf. Acts 14: 22.

non potest quis praemium accipere nisi legitime certaverit: Cf. 2 Tim. 2: 5.

For similar rhetoric, cf. e.g. *Cain* 1.17; *Interp.* 2.7; *Expos. Ps. 118.*10.30; 18.5; *Expl. Ps. 36.*17.

CHAPTER 16: RICHES AND POVERTY IN TRUE PERSPECTIVE

59. *Beati pauperes spiritu . . . regnum caelorum*: Mt. 5: 3. A résumé of six of the Matthaean Beatitudes follows, though not in the scriptural order. The Beatitudes were often recited in the morning office at Milan (cf. *Expos. Ps. 118.*19.32), and are frequently quoted by A. Elsewhere, he follows Greek exegetes like Gregory of Nyssa in visualizing them as a series of stages in the Christian soul's progress towards perfect blessedness, thus endorsing a distinctly Platonist synthesis: see B. In-San Tschang, *Octo Beatitudines. Die Acht Seligpreisungen als Stufenleiter der Seele bei Ambrosius*, Diss. (Bonn, 1986). This idea is not explicit in *Off.*, but it is significant that A. can hold up the ideal of eschatological *beatitudo* in the context of an appeal to persevere in the labour of the *athleta Christi*: the equation of perfect duty, asceticism, with the ascent motif is not too far away; cf. the progress image in 1.233–9.

Non dixit: *Beati divites*, **sed** *pauperes*: A. equates poverty of spirit with material poverty (cf. the version of the Beatitude in Lk. 6: 20; and especially Tert. *Adv. Marc.* 4.14.9–13); he takes a similar position in 2.15–16; *Luc.* 5.49–53; *Apol. alt.* 57; *Nab.* 40; *Expl. Ps. 36.*24; *Expl. Ps. 43.*93; cf. the focus on spiritual poverty in *Expl. Ps. 40.*5; *Exc. fr.* 1.56 (see generally Vasey, 183 ff.). The materially poor have the advantage of not being encumbered with the dangers of wealth, and in the realization of their physical need they look to God for salvation. In the present context, the godly poor are those who suffer in this world and do not appear to be blessed, but who in the world to come will inherit eternal riches, while the evil rich will be punished.

Beati qui esuriunt quia ipsi saturabuntur: Mt. 5: 6.
Beati qui lugent . . . consolationem habebunt: Mt. 5: 5.
Beati misericordes . . . miserebitur Deus: Mt. 5: 7.
Beati mundo corde . . . Deum videbunt: Mt. 5: 8.
Beati qui persecutionem patiuntur . . . merces vestra copiosa est in caelo: Mt. 5: 10–12.

Quid alibi poscis . . . et tu iam otium petis?: The section which follows to the end of 1.63 contains two rhetorical flourishes. First, there is a challenge to the individual to continue in the Christian struggle. Note the series of short rhetorical questions with anaphora, and the dramatic evocation of a wrestling-contest, with the imagined exchange of words between athletes and spectators, using devices such as rhetorical anticipation of objections (1.60, *Sed forte dicas . . .*) (1.59–60). Secondly, we have a judgement-day scene, as the rich person is rebuked for failing to help the needy (1.63). The use of imagery from athletics and the gymnasium to describe the Christian life is of course very common in the NT (e.g. 1 Cor. 9: 24–7; Phil. 3: 13–14; 1 Tim. 4: 7–10; 2 Tim. 2: 5; 4: 7–8; Heb. 12: 1–3; see V. C. Pfitzner, *Paul and the Agon Motif: Traditional Athletic Imagery in the Pauline Literature* (Leiden, 1967)), and although by this time the gymnasium was for Christian writers generally associated with pagan culture and values, A.'s exploitation of the language gives his argument an enduring biblical flavour: cf. 1.183; and e.g. *Elia* 78–81; *Ex.* 6.50; *Parad.* 55; *Cain* 1.17; 2.9; *Interp.* 2.7–8; *Sacr.* 1.4; *Ep.* 29 [43].4–6; *Ep.* 75a [*C. Aux.*].6; *Luc.*, prol. 6; some other references are listed at Vasey, 154 n. 81. See I. Gualandri, 'Il lessico di Ambrogio: problemi e prospettive di ricerca', in *Nec timeo mori*, 267–311, at 303–8.

coronam . . . pulverem: One is reminded of Hor. *Ep.* 1.1.51: *cui sit condicio dulcis sine pulvere palmae.* Cf. *Elia* 79: *Nemo stadium pulverulentos ingreditur, sed pulverulentum reddunt certamina: ibi colligitur pulvis, ubi palma proponitur. Nemo iterum nitidus coronatur, pulverulentum decet victoria;*

Expos. Ps. 118.18.5: *Non decet redimitos floribus corona, sed pulverulentos; nec molles deliciis, sed labore exercitatos ornat victoria*; also Cypr. *Mort.* 12; Aug. *Agon. Chr.* 1. On the crowning of the righteous, cf. e.g. *Expl. Ps. 40.7*; *Expos. Ps. 118.7.17*.

scammate: A late word, directly from the Greek; cf. *Elia* 79.

60. **qui non subscripserint ad coronam:** Those who do not enter their names in the competition; cf. *Elia* 79.

non se perfundunt oleo, non oblinunt pulvere: Wrestlers anointed themselves with olive oil before entering the *conisterium* (Vitruv. 5.11.2; Lucian, 37.2, 24, 29; Gal. *Gymn.* 37). Cf. *Expos. Ps. 118.12.28*; 14.16; 18.5; *Luc.*, praef. 6; also John Chrys. *Hom. Stat.* 1.18; 3.7; *Hom. Tim.* 8. On the procedure at a typical wrestling-bout, see H. A. Harris, *Greek Athletes and Athletics* (London, 1964), 102–5.

61. **Habent lucrum laboris:** The rich have the benefit of others' effort; they are like spectators, at ease while the contestants labour to entertain them. A. hints at the exploitation of the poor by the rich, a frequent theme of denunciation (e.g. *Nab.* 2 ff.).

Horum requies in infernis: See on 1.45.

tua in paradiso: Cf. Lk. 23: 43. On the fate of the wicked and the reward of the blessed, see Niederhuber, *Eschatologie*, 23–46, 64–126.

Unde pulchre vigilare eos in tumulo Iob dixit: Cf. Job 21: 32. As in 1.41–6, the story of Job (again from Job 21) almost inevitably reappears in the context of theodicy.

soporem quietis . . . quem ille dormivit qui resurrexit: A. relates Job 21: 32 to the resurrection of the just in *Interp.* 2.19; here, he seems also to be thinking of Ps. 3: 6, which was often read messianically: *Ego dormivi et soporatus sum; exsurrexi quia Dominus suscipiet me*; cf. *Expl Ps. 36.67*.

62. **Noli igitur ut parvulus sapere . . . ut parvulus cogitare:** Cf. 1 Cor. 13: 11. The reward of eternal life is only for the mature, who have progressed beyond the spiritual education of this world (on Christian maturity, cf. e.g. 1 Cor. 3; 14: 20; Eph. 4: 14–15).

Exspecta ut 'veniat quod perfectum est': Cf. 1 Cor. 13: 10; on perfection, cf. 1.235–9 below.

quando non *per speciem in aenigmate,* **sed** *facie ad faciem*: 1 Cor. 13: 12.

formam ipsam redopertae veritatis: Cf. Cic. *Off.* 1.15: *Formam quidem ipsam . . . et tamquam faciem honesti vides* (drawing on the famous image of Plat. *Phaedr.* 250d); cf. also Cic. *Fin.* 2.48; 4.19. On the tradition of beauty or truth imparting a likeness to those who love her, which, via Plotinus, influences A. *Is.* 78–9, see P. Courcelle, 'Le visage de Philosophie', *REA* 70 (1968), 110–20.

63. Typically, A. urges the rich to recognize their duties to the needy; wealth provides an opportunity for virtue if it is correctly used. Although there is doubtless *some* suggestion here of contemporary social ills, for all his rhetoric A. gives no direct application of his polemic; he simply inveighs against stock evils which are denounced in the Scriptures. On the *potens*, cf. 2.102. For the imaginary judgement-day scene, cf. 2.137–8.

Fortasse dicatur: The MSS have *ut* after **fortasse**, but this is superfluous; the other subjunctives below which depend on **fortasse** (**Dicatur . . . Dicatur**) stand alone (Winterbottom, 561).

ut excusationem habere non possis: On being without excuse in the face of God's judgement, cf. Rom. 2: 1. Conscience is the most terrifying accuser on judgement day: *Expl. Ps. 1.*52; *Nab.* 45; *Apol. alt.* 66–7.

viduae, orphanis: The standard types of the needy, frequently mentioned in Scripture: e.g. Ex. 22: 21; Pss. 67: 6; 81: 3–4; 145: 9; Eccli. 35: 17; Is. 1: 17; Jer. 22: 3; Jas. 1: 27. See Biondi ii. 209–23, 229–38.

Eripe iniuriam accipientem: Eccli. 4: 9.

Eripite pauperem et egenum . . . liberate: Ps. 81: 4.

Liberis et honoribus: A, O², Maurists, Testard: *Liberis honoribus* PVM, EW, CO¹ B, Zell.

Famulus meus: Probably A. has in mind the master/servant parables, such as Mt. 18: 23–35; 24: 45–51 (Lk. 12: 42–6); 25: 14–30 (Lk. 19: 12–26).

quid feci tibi aut quid contristavi te?: Mic. 6: 3.

despiciebas mandata mea: Cf. e.g Lev. 26: 15, 43; Ezek. 20: 13, 16, 24.

64. **de Iuda proditore . . . qui et apostolus inter**

duodecim electus est: See Mt. 10: 2–4; Mk. 3: 14–19; Lk. 6: 13–16; Jn. 6: 71–2.

et loculos pecuniarum . . . commissos habebat: Cf. Jn. 12: 6; 13: 29; Judas was a dishonest keeper of the purse.

quasi praevaricatus gratiam: The verb is used of Judas in Acts 1: 25: the sense of 'sin against' (possibly with an even stronger force than *peccare*) is Christian (cf. *praevaricatio* in Rom. 4: 15; Heb. 9: 15); on the development of the word, see Barry, 230 n. 8. With Judas' increased privilege came increased responsibility. On sinning against grace, cf. Rom. 6.

CHAPTER 17: MODESTY: BEFITTING FOR YOUNG MEN

In 1.65, A. commences the heart of his theme of duties (**de officiis adgrediamur dicere**). Some of the medieval copyists mark this point as the start of book 1 proper, with all that has gone before serving merely as an introduction; see Testard, 'Etude', 155–6 n. 3, for details. A. has however been laying significant theological foundations in the preceding sections, especially in pointing to the realities of eschatological reward and punishment (1.65; cf. 1.28–9, 37–9, 44–6, 59–64), and he has dropped strong clues about the kind of themes on which he will be dwelling as the subject unfolds.

The treatment of *officia* opens with a discourse on the virtue of *verecundia*. This covers 1.65–97; A. appears in 1.81 to have finished with the topic, but this turns out not be the case—an interesting indication of the informality of his style—though *verecundia* is not actually mentioned after 1.85. 1.85–97 warns of possible dangers to modesty, and 1.98–114 goes on to expound the theme of the *decorum*. There is a significant amount of Ciceronian evocation throughout 1.65–114. Cic., however, covers both *verecundia* and the *decorum* under temperance, following the Panaetian innovation of equating τὸ πρέπον (the *decorum*) with the fourth cardinal virtue (*Off.* 1.93–151). Why, then, does A. fragment his discussion of temperance, which begins properly at 1.210 and deals with the *decorum* in 1.219–25, by spending so much of the earlier part of book 1 on related themes (cf. also the *decorum* material already in 1.30–5)? Do 1.65–114 and 1.210–51 stem from different stages of composition, or separate sermonic strands? No such drastic conclusion is necessary. Two things need to be said. First, A. has nowhere promised to adhere rigidly to the Ciceronian layout in every detail; his entire pattern of evocation is piecemeal and discursive. We should not be surprised to find Ciceronian material on modesty and temperance scattered around book 1, whatever that says about the relative thematic clarity of A.'s work compared with Cic.'s. Secondly, A. surely has a deliberate point in commencing the main *officia* section with this lengthy discussion of modesty. It should already be clear that it is a favourite emphasis. Modesty, and all that it entails, is for A. the epitome of spiritual duty, and the hallmark of a ministry which is beyond reproach. He has already sign-posted this in several ways (1.1–22, 31–5); he now begins to spell out in detail how the ideal applies to his clerics, talking about, for example, chastity (1.68–9); prayer (1.70, 88); Bible-study (1.88); and the appropriate ecclesiastical practices in matters like gesture and gait (1.71–5), tone of voice (1.67, 84), social company (1.86–8). He draws on Cic.'s use (*Off.* 1.105–25) of the Panaetian theory of four *personae* and on the ways in which specific circumstances affect what is appropriate for a given individual (*Off.* 1.126–40; cf. 1.211–30 below, especially 1.212–18) (on Cic. and his sources, see M. Fuhrmann, 'Persona, ein römischer Rollenbegriff', in O. Marquard and K. Stierle (eds.), *Identität* (Munich, 1979), 83–106; C. Gill, 'Personhood and Personality: The Four-*Personae* Theory in Cicero, *De Officiis* I', *OSAPh* 6 (1988), 169–99; Dyck, 238–319).

It is perfectly understandable, then, that A. covers motifs from the fourth virtue here, and then returns to some of them in 1.210–51, while saying far more than Cic. does on the glories of *verecundia*. Since the *honestum* is for A. synonymous with the *decorum*, pictured first as devotion to God and then as appropriate conduct in the public realm (cf. 1.253), exposition of the qualities which cluster around the *decorum* naturally dominates book 1. For an overview of the *verecundia* material, majoring firmly (if rather uncritically) on the Christian dimension which A. gives to the Ciceronian framework, see

J. Janssens, 'La verecundia nel comportamento dei chierici secondo il De officiis ministrorum di sant'Ambrogio', in F. Sergio (ed.), *La formazione al sacerdozio ministeriale nella catechesi e nella testimonianza di vita dei Padri* (Rome, 1992), 133–43.

65. quae nobis ab adulescentia spectanda sunt . . . quae ornamento sunt minori aetati: Cf. Cic. *Off.* 1.122: *Et quoniam officia non eadem disparibus aetatibus tribuuntur aliaque sunt iuvenum, alia seniorum, aliquid etiam de hac distinctione dicendum est. Est igitur adulescentis maiores natu vereri, exque iis deligere optimos et probatissimos quorum consilio atque auctoritate nitatur.* A. (whose interest in the young extended in some circumstances to the care of friends' children in his residence (*Epp.* 26, 38 [54–5]) is addressing, in the first instance, young clerics, a point rightly stressed with regard to this section by Steidle, 'Beobachtungen', 20; cf. generally 34 ff. He takes over some of Cic.'s points on the obligations of youth (*Off.* 1.122), but adds some specifically Christian features. Fear of God comes first in the list of obligations; then, as well as respect for elders generally, we have deference to parents; **castitatem tueri** goes rather further than Cic.'s warnings against *libidines* and *intemperantia* (*Off.* 1.122); **humilitatem** of course evokes a core Christian virtue for A. (see on 1.1); and **clementiam** probably implies godly compassion (though cf. Cic. *Off.* 1.88).

iuvenibus . . . adulescentibus: The latter are youths in their late teens or early twenties; the former are young men in their late twenties and especially early thirties. Cf. *Ep.* 31 [44].12: *infans, puer, adulescens, iuvenis, vir, veteranus, senex* (and generally 12–19, evoking the celebrated Hippocratic sequence, *via* Philo); on classical and Christian schemata for distinguishing the different stages of life (e.g. Isid. *Orig.* 11.2), see J. A. Burrow, *The Ages of Man: A Study in Medieval Writing and Thought* (Oxford, 1986). Those in their late teens are probably readers (though the lectorate was frequently held by mere *pueri*); see E. Peterson, 'Das jugendliche Alter der Lektoren', *EphLiturg* 48 (1934), 437–42; cf. *Exc. fr.* 1.61 (referring to a *parvulus*); also *Exh. virg.*

55; Horontianus, one identifiable cleric who had been brought up in the church of Milan (*Ep.* 18 [70].25), had probably served as a reader in his boyhood. Junior or subdeacons were generally aged 20–25, and deacons 25–30. Thirty was widely regarded as the *aetas perfecta* for the priesthood, the age of maturity at which Christ was said to have been baptized and commenced his public ministry, and, in antiquity, the age at which youth was deemed to end and the *cursus honorum* began. For a useful survey, see E. Eyben, 'Young Priests in Early Christianity', in M. Wacht (ed.), *Panchaia: Festschrift für Klaus Thraede* (Münster, 1995), 102–20.

alacritas: Cf. 1.218.

velut quadam dote commendatur naturae: On the importance of nature as a norm for modesty, a core Stoic principle also exploited by Paul, cf. 1.77–8, 84, 223, and see on 1.77, on the tensions between this assumption and the idea that nature is fallen.

66. Erat Isaac Dominum timens . . . nec mortem recusaret: See Gen. 22: 1–19. Contrary to what A. implies, Isaac was unaware that he was about to be sacrificed—at least, we may assume, until he was tied to the altar.

Ioseph quoque . . . deferebat patri: See Gen. 37: 9–11.

castus ita . . . nisi pudicum: A reference to Joseph's resistance of the seductive wiles of Potiphar's wife: Gen. 39: 6–20.

humilis usque ad servitutem: He was sold into slavery by his brothers (Gen. 37: 28), and also by the Midianites/ Ishmaelites (Gen. 37: 36; 39: 1).

verecundus usque ad fugam: His flight from Potiphar's wife: Gen. 39: 11–12.

patiens usque ad carcerem: His imprisonment for allegedly attempting to rape her: Gen. 39: 20.

remissor iniuriae usque ad remunerationem: Joseph forgave and showed generosity to his brothers: Gen. 45–7. Note the rhetorical rhythm of the string of **usque ad** clauses.

comprehensus a muliere . . . quam verecundiam deponere: With Potiphar's wife: Gen. 39: 12; *mulier* here carries a pejorative force, as often.

Moyses quoque: See Ex. 3: 1–4: 17, especially 3: 11. On Moses's modesty, cf. also Num. 12: 3.

Ieremias: Jer. 1: 4–19, especially 1: 6.

The exemplars in this paragraph illustrate the virtues of young men which are specified in 1.65: Isaac, fear of God and deference to his father; Joseph, deference to his father, chastity, humility, modesty, mercy; Moses and Jeremiah, modesty.

CHAPTER 18: MODESTY OF SPEECH AND PHYSICAL DEPORTMENT

67. Pulchra igitur virtus . . . in ipsis spectatur sermonibus: Modesty is beautiful: it *looks* good.

ne ⟨ultra⟩ modum: The addition of **ultra** is logically necessary; cf. e.g. Cic. *Tusc.* 4.38 (Winterbottom, 561).

ne quid indecorum sermo resonet tuus: Cf. Cic. *Off.* 1.134: *In primisque provideat ne sermo vitium aliquod indicet inesse in moribus.*

Speculum enim mentis plerumque in verbis refulget: On speech reflecting the state of the heart, cf. Cic. *De Or.* 3.221–3, and see on 1.14 above.

Ipsum vocis sonum librat modestia: This appropriate tone of voice is explained further in 1.84 and 104.

in ipso canendi genere: Cf. 1.32, on gradual development of the voice in singing.

psallere: Singing or intoning a psalm (cf. 1.203; 3.100), regularly the task of a boy-reader (*Exc. fr.* 1.61); cf. 1.216. On psalmody in the Milanese liturgy, see H. Leeb, *Die Psalmodie bei Ambrosius* (Vienna, 1967), 24–89 (37–40 on *psallere*); also Monachino, 139–51.

sensim . . . incipiat: As part of a *captatio benevolentiae*, Cic. *De Or.* 2.182–3 (cf. in general *De Or.* 2.178 ff.) suggests that an impression of *lenitas* should be given by restraint of voice (and, he adds, of facial expression). For the orator, this is to gain a positive hearing. A. implies that his interest is simply in the psalm-leader, singer, or speaker showing suitable modesty; but his goal is not far removed from Cic.'s: if the clergy show this modesty, then they too, like the orator, will gain respect. (Banterle, 67 n. 2 compares Hor. *Sat.* 1.10.13–14, where it is said that the clever orator keeps his strength in reserve by carefully rationing it out; but this is simply for practical purposes, not as a *captatio*.)

68. Silentium quoque ipsum . . . maximus actus verecundiae est: On the virtues of silence, cf. 1.5–22 and see ad loc.; 1.31–5.

si aut infantiae putatur aut superbiae: Care must be taken not to give the wrong impression as to the reasons for silence; it must be clear that it stems from modesty, and not from a fit of childishness or arrogance.

Tacebat in periculis Susanna: See on 1.9.

gravius verecundiae . . . tuendam salutem: The threat of having her chastity violated was more serious to her than the threat to her life; cf. 2.20, 136; also Ps.-Cypr. [Novat.], *Bon. pud.* 9.

ora . . . virum: virum PM¹, O¹B, Testard: *viri* O²: *virorum* VM²A, EW, C. A. uses an archaic genitive plural with **ora**; cf. e.g. Verg. *Aen.* 8.197.

videre . . . videri: Susanna exemplifies a certain classical ideal of feminine self-effacement: cf. Ov. *AA* 1.99–100; and Tert. *Spect.* 25.3: *Nemo denique in spectaculo ineundo prius cogitat nisi videri et videre* (Testard i. 238 n. 7).

69. Est enim verecundia pudicitiae comes: Modesty has a particular connection with sexual purity, as the case of Susanna exemplifies. Cf. *Virg.* 2.14: . . . *in virgine comes singularum virtutum est pudor* (on *comes*, cf. 1.177 below); *Ios.* 2; also Tert. *Cult. fem.* 2.8: *Nam ubi Deus, ibi pudicitia, ⟨ubi pudicitia⟩ ibi gravitas, adiutrix et socia eius.* A. assumes the standard patristic hierarchy (e.g. Tert. *Exh. cast.* 1) of three grades of chastity, in ascending order of virtue: purity in marriage, widowhood, and virginity: 3.84; *Vid.* 23–6, 83; *Virgt.* 34; *Ep.* 14 [63].40). Here, *pudicitia* means virginity (A. goes on to speak about the Virgin Mary); *pudor* is effectively a synonym for *verecundia* in a sexual context, and is said to protect virginity no less than it protects *castitas*, which is purity in marriage, like Susanna's (see W. J. Dooley, *Marriage according to St Ambrose* (Washington, DC, 1948), 43–56). On *pudor* and *pudicitia*, see V. D'Agostino, 'I concetti di "pudore" e "pudicizia" negli

scrittori antichi', *RISC* 17 (1969), 320–9. The crucial
importance of priestly chastity is stressed in 1.248–9. The
literature on A.'s teaching on virginity is vast; much of the
theological assessment is lovingly uncritical, and fails to set
his activity in its social context: e.g. Homes Dudden i. 144–
59; R. D'Izarny, 'La Virginité selon saint Ambroise', Th.D.
thesis, 2 vols. (Institut Catholique de Lyon, 1952); for more
socially anchored analyses, see Brown, *Body*, 259–84;
McLynn, 60–8.

praetendat: [PV²MA, EW, OB, Zell, Testard: *praetendant*
V¹: *praetendet* C: *praeteneat* Erasmus-Gelen] Modesty is like
a sentry keeping watch over a camp. The military imagery is
continued appropriately in the conjectural insertion of **prae-
caveat** after (and to explain) **et** (the latter is removed by E²)
(Winterbottom, 561).

Domini matrem commendat legentibus: Readers of the
Annunciation scene in Lk. 1: 26–38 are struck by the
modesty of the Virgin Mary, who is for A. the *imago* or
the *magistra virginitatis* (*Virg.* 2.6–15), the supreme exemplar of ascetic perfection; J. Huhn, *Das Geheimnis der
Jungfrau-Mutter Maria nach dem Kirchenvater Ambrosius*
(Würzburg, 1954); C. W. Neumann, *The Virgin Mary in
the Works of Saint Ambrose* (Fribourg, 1962), especially 35–
66. The description of the Annunciation scene here is similar
to (though naturally more compressed than) those in *Virg.*
2.11 and *Luc.* 2.8–9. *Virg.* 2.11 draws on Athan. *Ep. virg.*:
Y.-M. Duval, 'L'Originalité du De virginibus dans le mouvement ascétique occidental: Ambroise, Cyprien, Athanase', in
Ambroise de Milan, 9–66, at 46. What we have is very much a
stylized portrait of Mary as the ideal spiritual woman, who
spends her time meditating alone in her chamber, away from
male company, responding only with the minimum of words
when given her (divine) orders: to A., Mary knew her place.

testis locuples: The words may be suggested by Cic. *Off.*
3.10; they are found elsewhere in Cic. as well: e.g. *Div.* 1.37;
on *locuples*, cf. *Div.* 2.119; *Brut.* 47; *Rep.* 1.16; in A. cf. e.g.
Expos. Ps. 118.10.6; 20.47.

peregrinatur: EW, CB, Testard: *peregrinantur* O: *peregri-
natus* PVMA: *peregrinam turbatur* Maurists, Krabinger,
other editors. The use of the verb to mean 'consider it

strange' (and so here, with **aspectus**, 'blushes') is biblical (1
Pt. 4: 4, 12); emendation to *peregrinam turbatur*, resorted to
by many editors, is unnecessary; cf. *Exh. virg.* 71; *Virg.* 2.11;
also *Ep.* 11 [29].13.

proferret: P, VA, EW's *praeferret* [*referret* C: *refelleret* OB:
referleret M²: *ferret* ?M¹] retained by Testard, hardly makes
sense: the idea is not that Mary avoided 'prolonging' the
conversation, but that she did not talk for the sake of it
(Winterbottom, 561).

70. **In ipsa oratione nostra:** A. moves from the model of
Mary's encounter with the divine spokesman to outline the
kind of attitude that is appropriate in prayer to God today.
multum conciliat gratiae apud Deum nostrum: A. is
still thinking of the Annunciation scene, where Gabriel says
to Mary: *invenisti enim gratiam apud Deum . . .* (Lk. 1: 30).
**Nonne haec praetulit publicanum . . . quem deforma-
vit praesumptio:** See Lk. 18: 9–14.
in incorruptione quieti . . . ante Deum locuples: 1 Pt.
3: 4. In context, though, the verse is talking about the chaste
adornment of Christian wives, not about prayer.
nihil sibi usurpans, nihil vindicans: The vocabulary is
reminiscent of 1.1–4, on the author's own modesty; cf. 2.124.
apud quem nemo dives: By nature, all human beings as
sinners are paupers in God's sight. For a striking appeal to
charity based on this principle, cf. Aug. *Serm.* 61.6–7.
Dei portio est: Cf. Pss. 118: 57; 141: 6; also 1.246 on the
Levites.
cum verecundia et sobrietate: 1 Tim. 2: 9. 1 Tim. 2: 8
speaks of men praying; 1 Tim. 2: 9 continues on the theme of
prayer, though the argument is broadened out to cover
women's deportment generally. On *sobrietas* as a Christian
virtue, cf. 1.12 (and see ad loc.), 211, 256; 2.7, 65, 76.
⟨**et**⟩ **quo plus defert verecundiae:** A connective is necessary; E² adds *qui*.

71. **Est etiam in ipso motu gestu incessu tenenda verecundia:** Topics covered in Cic. *Off.* 1.126–32: cf. especially
Off. 1.126: *Sed quoniam decorum illud in omnibus factis dictis,
in corporis denique motu et statu cernitur*; *Off.* 1.128: *status
incessus sessio accubitio vultus oculi manuum motus teneat illud
decorum.*

Habitus enim mentis in corporis statu cernitur: The interpreting of body language was a very popular activity throughout antiquity. Nor was it just a speculative pastime: it was seen as a vital way of gauging the moral character of the public figure. See R. Förster, *Scriptores physiognomici Graeci et Latini*, 2 vols. (Leipzig, 1893); E. C. Evans, *Physiognomics in the Ancient World* (Philadelphia, 1969); on A. see Introduction VII (ii), with literature cited there. In Cic., of the orator's gestures, cf. *De Or.* 3.220–3, especially 222: *est enim actio quasi sermo corporis* . . . ; *Or.* 55; and Cic. *Off.* 1.102 (a passage echoed by A. in 1.229): . . . *a quibus* [sc. *appetitus*] *non modo animi perturbantur, sed etiam corpora. Licet ora ipsa cernere iratorum aut eorum qui aut libidine aliqua aut metu commoti sunt aut voluptate nimia gestiunt; quorum omnium vultus voces motus statusque mutantur*; *Fin.* 5.35–6. Christian interest was encouraged by passages such as Eccli. 19: 26–8.

homo cordis nostri absconditus: 1 Pt. 3: 4; see also on 1.11.

aut levior aut iactantior aut turbidior: These faults are all condemned by A. at different points: levity in 1.72, 102–3; boasting in 1.147; 2.76, 102, 122; 3.133; and irritability or anger in 1.13–22, 90–7, 231–8 (on anger, cf. Sen. *Ira* 1.1.7; 2.35.3, 36.1; 3.4.1–2).

72. **Meministis, filii, quemdam amicum . . . oculos feriret meos:** An illustration from the experience of the Milanese clergy (for a similar *meministis*, cf. 2.150–1); the translation uses an idiomatic future tense, though of course the Latin is in the present. We have no other information on the two men mentioned here. The author of the Carolingian *vita Ambrosii* mentions the story (69–70), on the basis of the present passage. A.'s standards are high: the visual impression of the church is all-important. The first man was rejected as a candidate for the clergy solely because of his undignified deportment, **cum sedulis se videretur commendare officiis**: the judgement had nothing to do with his doctrinal position or his apparent devotion to his duties. A. evidently had no shortage of applicants, if he could refuse a man simply because of his gait. The second individual was among the clergy inherited by A. from Auxentius' time

(**cum in clero repperissem**). A. had initially endeavoured not to create alienation by directly replacing those of homoian sympathies with his own pro-Nicene candidates, but perhaps he found some subtler ways of altering his retinue. We have no indication that the kind of rejection described here was typical, but even an isolated case or two would have contributed indirectly to the end-result of ensuring that the bishop's ranks were filled with the 'right' men; see M. Meslin, *Les Ariens d'Occident, 335–430* (Paris, 1967), 45; M. Simonetti, *La crisi Ariana nel IV secolo* (Rome, 1975), 438; Y.-M. Duval, 'Ambroise, de son élection a sa consécration', in *AmbrEpisc* i. 243–83, at 254. This particular cleric was forbidden to walk in front of the bishop in a formal procession (primarily in a liturgical context, but also perhaps on official visits to the imperial palace: for clerical accompaniment there, cf. Paul. *VA* 35) because his gait was offensive to A.'s eyes (**quia velut quodam insolentis incessus verbere oculos feriret meos**; on **insolentis**, cf. 1.208). Soz. *HE* 8.6.3–8, provides us with another example of A.'s strict code of discipline. He tells of one Gerontius, a gifted deacon of the Milanese church, who was given a year's penance by A. for spreading stories of private religious experiences; Gerontius refused the imposition, and left to become bishop of Nicomedia (an office in which he proved popular, to A.'s enduring chagrin). Gerontius' individualism too had presumably violated A.'s personal notions of *humilitas* (cf. 2.119–23). **iubere me:** PVMA, EW, O¹B, Zell, Testard: *iuberem* C: *iussisse me* O² Erasmus-Gelen, mg. Erasmus-Gelen-Coster: *iussisse* O³. **oculos feriret meos:** The words are probably suggested by Cic. *Off.* 1.128: . . . *ab omni quod abhorret ab oculorum auriumque approbatione fugiamus.*

cum redderetur post offensam muneri: The allusion is unclear; the implication seems to be that the man had also committed some other misdemeanour for which he had been temporarily removed from his clerical duties.

alter Arianae infestationis tempore fidem deseruit: A reference to the notorious crisis of 385–6, and especially its climax in the spring of 386, when A. refused to surrender a basilica to his enemies; see Introduction VII (i). On *infestatio*

as an attack on believers, cf. Cypr. *Ad Dem.* 12; *Ep.* 17.1;
Tert. *Apol.* 1.1; Hil. *In Ps. 118*.11; *Coll. Avent.* 2.79; 2.119
(*TLL* viii/1. 1403–4). On 'deserting the faith', cf. 1 Tim. 4: 1;
for A. this true faith is naturally the Nicene position; cf. also
1.188, 256; 3.126. The layman had not been rejected because
of his doctrinal allegiances, but he showed his true character
by apparently going over to the homoian camp. Williams,
121–2, is right to say that this passage does not imply that
A. took steps to remove or exclude homoian sympathizers
from the ranks of the clergy in the immediate aftermath of
his consecration; but (if A. is to be relied upon here) he is
wrong to say that this layman was rejected *because* he
deserted the faith: the desertion came afterwards, and was
the confirmation of the bishop's suspicions. On the strength
of homoian opposition in the early years of A.'s episcopate,
and its particular impetus from *c*.384 (when Auxentius of
Durostorum evidently enticed a number of defectors from
the official church and rebaptized them (*Ep.* 75a
[*C. Aux.*].37)), see Williams, 202–17; Humphries, 168–9.
P. I. Kaufman, 'Diehard Homoians and the Election of
Ambrose', *JECS* 5 (1997), 421–40 challenges the evidence
for a serious homoian opposition to A. from the first, but his
analysis is unconvincing, and involves a misreading of
infestationis tempore here to mean a general 'disturbance'
(which Kaufman, 438, dates to 'soon after 378'), rather than
'a specific bout of organized persecution'; see the responses
by D. H. Williams, 'Politically Correct in Milan: A Reply to
"Diehard Homoians and the Election of Ambrose"', *JECS*
5 (1997), 441–6; and N. B. McLynn, 'Diehards: A
Response', *JECS* 5 (1997), 446–50. The first readers of
Off. could hardly identify these words as anything other
than an allusion to 386.

**alter pecuniae studio, ne iudicium subiret sacer-
dotale, se nostrum negavit:** Apparently the man had
been involved in some illicit deal for his own profit and
resigned his charge in order to escape being arraigned before
the bishop's tribunal. On the bishop's powers of judgement,
see on 2.124–5; 3.59; and Gryson, *Prêtre*, 251–3.

scurrarum percursantium: Wandering jesters employed
to 'clown around' to entertain at dinner-parties; on the *scurra*

as both jester and stereotypical social pest, see P. Corbett, *The Scurra* (Edinburgh, 1986).

73. qui sensim ambulando imitantur histrionicos gestus: Cf. Cic. *Off.* 1.130: *histrionum nonnulli gestus ineptiis non vacant* . . . ; also *De Or.* 3.213–23, especially 214, 220. Artificially slow or stagey movements are no less offensive than the uncouth haste mentioned in 1.72; cf. generally *Ep.* 27 [58].5; *Ex.* 3.5; *Elia* 66; *Expos. Ps. 118*.7.26; *Luc.* 6.5, 8; *Paen.* 2.42. For all the effort required to sustain an appropriate public image by a 'correct' bodily carriage, it is crucial that the gestures of the convincing public figure *look* natural, not 'put on'; obvious contrivance is synonymous with the artificiality of the stage and its perceived moral depravity. 1.104 contains a similar condemnation of histrionics in the context of the voice. On the evils of the theatre in Christian polemic, see e.g. H. Jürgens, *Pompa Diaboli. Die lateinischen Kirchenväter und das antike Theater* (Stuttgart, 1972); W. Weismann, *Kirche und Schauspiele. Die Schauspiele im Urteil der lateinischen Kirchenväter unter besonderer Berücksichtigung von Augustin* (Würzburg, 1972); C. Schnusenberg, *Das Verhältnis von Kirche und Theater. Dargestellt an ausgewählten Schriften der Kirchenväter und liturgischen Texte bis auf Amalarius von Metz (a.d. 775–852)* (Frankfurt, 1981); K. Sallmann, 'Christen von dem Theater', in J. Blänsdorf (ed.), *Theater und Gesellschaft im Imperium Romanum* (Tübingen, 1990), 243–60.

quasi quaedam fercula pomparum et statuarum motus nutantium: Cf. Cic. *Off.* 1.131: *Cavendum autem est ne aut tarditatibus utamur ⟨in⟩ ingressu mollioribus, ut pomparum ferculis similes esse videamur* . . . ; Jerome echoes Cic. in *Ep.* 125.16.2; cf. also Hor. *Sat.* 1.3.9–11. **fercula** are litters used to carry spoils or sacred images in public processions. Those who bear them move with slow, measured paces, as if marking time; e.g. Hor. *Sat.* 2.8.13; also Liv. 27.37.14. On the use of *nutare*, cf. Juv. 3.254–6; also Ov. *Am.* 3.2.58 (*adnuit*).

74. Nec . . . honestum arbitror: A significant note of personal authority; cf. 1.102–4 (*arbitror . . . arbitror . . . arbitror*); also 1.208, *reor*; cf. **Nec . . . probo**, below; also 1.84, *non probo*; 1.75; 3.125, *probabilis*; 1.144, *non . . .*

probabilis; 1.150, *probanda*; 3.45, *nequaquam probandi*. As the incidents in 1.72 illustrate, it is what the bishop thinks that matters.

Nam plerumque festinantes . . . naevus iustae offensionis est: Cf. Cic. *Off.* 1.131: [sc. *cavendum est ne*] *aut in festinationibus suscipiamus nimias celeritates, quae cum fiunt anhelitus moventur, vultus mutantur, ora torquentur*; also *Off.* 1.102 and 1.146.

excursorum ruinas: The MSS' *excussorum ruinas* is very peculiar. Testard thinks the words should be translated 'the tumblings of acrobats' (Testard i. 240–1 n. 28, with acknowledgement to R. Braun), but in none of the passages he cites is *excussor* found as a noun, nor is there evidence that the perfect participle, *excussus*, is ever used with substantival force in this sense; there is therefore little support for the notion that the word can *of itself* mean 'acrobats'. *Excussus* is used of riders thrown from horses (e.g. Verg. *Aen.* 11.615, 640; cf. *excussit* in Livy, 8.7.10; etc.), but a substantival use would be exceptional. The best suggestion may be that offered in *TLL* v/2. 1295 (s.v. *excursor*), that the text should be emended to **excursorum ruinas**, which will then mean, literally, 'the stumblings of those who rush forward'. The translation attempts to convey this more freely: 'people virtually tripping over themselves in a mad rush to dash about their business'. Both 1.73 and 1.74 reflect an observant humour: people who walk either too fast or too slow look equally ridiculous. The humour, however, must have its proper place: Paul. *VA* 35 narrates how on one occasion A. rebuked his deacon Theodulus for laughing at someone who tripped when walking to or through the imperial palace.

75. probabilis: See on 1.74.

motus sit purus ac simplex: Similar qualities are commended for language (1.101); the voice (1.104); and, naturally, the heart (1.93); the same basic features of modesty must be evident in every dimension of behaviour. Cf. generally 2.112–20; 3.76.

fucatum: A favourite Ciceronian word in this sense: e.g. *Amic.* 95; *Brut.* 36; *Planc.* 29; *Mur.* 26.

Motum natura informet: On the significance of following nature's norm, see on 1.77.

76. **hoc enim graviter coinquinat hominem . . . sed verborum obscenitas:** Cf. Mt. 15: 10–20; Mk. 7: 14–23. The words *verborum obscenitas* occur in Cic. *Off.* 1.104 (cf. *De Or.* 2.252; and Isid. *Eccl. Off.* 2.2.2); cf. also *Off.* 1.127–8, on the *obscenitas* of speaking about bodily parts or functions which nature has intended to be kept private; on the Stoic background there (cf. Jer. *In Is.* 47.3), see Dyck, 300–1, 303; and cf. Eph. 5: 12, on evildoers: *quae enim in occulto fiunt ab ipsis turpe est et dicere.*

In nostro vero officio nullum ⟨sit⟩ verbum quod inhoneste cadat aut incutiat verecundiam: The majority reading, *In nostro vero officio nullum verbum quod inhoneste cadat, non incutit* [PV¹M, E¹, C] *verecundiam* makes for somewhat odd Latin, as several correctors have noticed: I suspect that O²'s addition of ⟨sit⟩ may be right, and that V², E², O's **incutiat** makes for better sense; O²'s *non quod* for *non* seems less helpful, and I opt for E²'s **aut** (*au* E¹).

ne aurem quidem debemus huiusmodi praebere dictis: Cf. Cic. *Off.* 1.128: *ab omni quod abhorret ab oculorum auriumque approbatione fugiamus.*

sicut Ioseph . . . veste fugit relicta: See on 1.66.

77. **Intellegere quoque . . . . Spectare vero:** It is bad enough to know about something that is *turpis*; actually to show interest in such a thing is quite appalling.

Nec ipsa natura nos docet. . .?: Cf. 1 Cor. 11: 14: *Nec ipsa natura docet vos . . .?*; cf. 1.223. A. finds a striking affinity throughout this section between the language of 1 Cor. 11–12 and the argument of Cic. in *Off.* 1.126–37: the Stoic conviction about following nature (e.g. *Off.* 1.128: *Nos autem naturam sequamur*) is shared by the NT, which for A. of course lends it proper sanction; cf. e.g. *Abr.* 2.93; *Exc. fr.* 1.45; *Ep. extra coll. 14* [63].27. To live according to nature is, for A., to live in accordance with one's design as a creature made in the image of God, though there remains something of a tension between the Stoic principle and the Christian view that nature is fallen and in need of divine grace in order to realize moral virtue; see Maes, 123–38. The Panaetian idea that nature possesses aesthetic sensitivity does however overlap with a contention that the human body is designed teleologically, to teach people modesty: e.g. Min. Fel. *Oct.*

17.1–2, 11; Lact. *Opif. Dei, passim*; *Inst.* 3.17; Greg. Nyss. *Hom. Opif.* 8–9; Aug. *CD* 22.24 (cf. also parallels in Arist. *PA* 681ᵇ26–8; Xen. *Mem.* 1.4.5–12). The key Ciceronian passage is *Off.* 1.126–7:

Principio corporis nostri magnam natura ipsa videtur habuisse rationem, quae formam nostram reliquamque figuram, in qua esset species honesta, eam posuit in promptu, quae partes autem corporis ad naturae necessitatem datae aspectum essent deformem habiturae atque turpem, eas contexit atque abdidit. Hanc naturae tam diligentem fabricam imitata est hominum verecundia. Quae enim natura occcultavit, eadem omnes qui sana mente sunt removent ab oculis, ipsique necessitati dant operam ut quam occultissime pareant.

quasi in arce quadam locatus: This phrase, together with **amandavit**, evokes the Stoic description of providence's design in the structure of the human body in Cic. *ND* 2.140–1. A. exploits Cic. *ND* 2.133–53 in other passages on the body (*Ex.* 6.54–74; *Noe* 13–30), especially *Ex.* 6.55, 60; *Noe* 17; cf. also Plin. *NH* 11.135; Min. Fel. *Oct.* 17.11; Lact. *Opif. Dei* 16.4; Macr. *Somn. Scip.* 1.6; John Chrys. *Fat. prov.* 1; Isid. *Diff. rer.* 2.17.49. W. Gossel, *Quibus ex fontibus Ambrosius in describendo corpore humano hauserit (Ambros. Exaem. VI.54–74)*, Diss. (Leipzig, 1908), 30–67, points out the Platonist influences in *Ex.*, on the tension of body and soul (cf. also J. Pépin, *Théologie cosmique et théologie chrétienne* (Paris, 1964), especially 113–17), but the Stoic input is also strong in the Ambrosian synthesis, there as here. On the subject in general, see F. Bottomley, *Attitudes to the Body in Western Christendom* (London, 1979), 65–72; D. M. Foley, 'The Religious Significance of the Human Body in the Writings of Ambrose of Milan', Ph.D. Diss. (University of Saint Paul, Ottawa, 1996).

78. **Nonne igitur ipsa natura est magistra verecundiae?:** Cf. Cic. *Off.* 1.129: *Retinenda igitur est huius generis verecundia, praesertim natura ipsa magistra et duce.*
  modestia . . . quam a modo scientiae quid deceret appellatam arbitror: The etymology comes directly from Cic. *Off.* 1.142: *Haec autem scientia continentur ea quam Graeci εὐταξίαν nominant, non hanc quam interpretamur mod-*

estiam, quo in verbo modus inest. The derivation of *modestia* from *modus*, to mean 'keeping measure', is correct; cf. Paul. *Fest.* p. 127M; Non. p. 30M (with reference to Cic.); Tert. *Exh. cast.* 9; Aug. *Beat. vit.* 32.

id quod in hac nostri corporis fabrica abditum repperit, operuit et texit: Cf. Cic. *Off.* 1.127, quoted on 1.77 above.

ut ostium illud quod ex transverso faciendum in arca illa Noe iusto dictum est: See Gen. 6: 14–16.

in qua vel ecclesiae vel nostri figura est corporis: On the ark as a type of the church, a very common image (in A., cf. e.g. *Luc.* 2.92; 3.48), see H. Rahner, *Symbole der Kirche. Die Ekklesiologie der Väter* (Salzburg, 1964), 504–47. The ark as a figure of the human body is classically found in Philo, *Quaest. Gen.* 2.1 ff. especially 2.5–6; and cf. e.g. Orig. *Hom. Gen.* 2.6; Aug. *CD* 15.26; *C. Faust.* 12.14; in A., cf. *Noe* 13–30, alluded to below; also *Ex.* 6.71–2. On A.'s allegorical and typological technique, see generally Introduction IV.5; on the ark, see J. P. Lewis, *A Study of the Interpretation of Noah and the Flood in Jewish and Christian Literature* (Leiden, 1968).

Ergo naturae opifex . . . ne purgatio ventris visum oculorum offenderet: Cf. Cic. *Off.* 1.127, quoted on 1.77 above. A. changes the ultimate agency: it is not just nature's work, but that of nature's **opifex**, God. On the hiding of the back passages in particular, cf. e.g. Xen. *Mem.* 1.4.6; Theod. *Prov.* 4.11. On the magnificence of the body as a work of divine art, cf. *Ex.* 6.47; *Expos. Ps. 118*.10.6; 16.6.

Quae videntur . . . honestatem abundantiorem habent: 1 Cor. 12: 22–3.

Quod alio loco etiam altius interpretati sumus: See *Noe* 13–30.

eorum indicia ususque membrorum suis appellationibus nuncupare indecorum putemus: Cf. Cic. *Off.* 1.127: *quarumque partium corporis usus sunt necessarii, eas neque partes neque earum usus suis nominibus appellant, quodque facere non turpe est, modo occulte, id dicere obscenum est* (cf. also *Off.* 1.128).

79. **Denique si casu aperiantur hae partes . . . impudentia aestimatur:** Cf. Cic. *Off.* 1.129, on the *vetus*

disciplina verecundiae of actors, who never step on to the stage without wearing a breech-cloth (*subligaculum*, a loin-cloth worn under the toga): *verentur enim ne, si quo casu evenerit ut corporis partes quaedam aperiantur, aspiciantur non decore*; see Daremberg–Saglio iv/2. 1550.

Unde et filius Noe Cham offensam retulit . . . acceperunt benedictionis gratiam: See Gen. 9: 20–7.

Ex quo mos vetus . . . auctoritas minueretur: Cf. Cic. *Off.* 1.129: *Nostro quidem more cum parentibus puberes filii, cum soceris generi non lavantur.* The Ciceronian phrase justifies the insertion of **cum soceris** [so Monte Alto] before **non lavarent** in A.'s allusion, obviating recourse to Testard's awkward parenthesizing of **puberes vel generi**. The story, also mentioned by A. in *Noe* 116, is found equally in Cic. *De Or.* 2.224; Plu. *Cat. Ma.* 20.7–8; Val. Max. 2.1.7; cf. also *Hist. Aug. Gord. tres* 6. A. suggests that the custom was plagiarized from Gen. Augustine's father was not an observer of the practice: *Conf.* 2.3.6; it was inevitably long gone in Rome, too; indeed, part of Cic.'s lament in his own context is to do with the demise of Rome's good old customs. On Christian perspectives on bathing, see F. K. Yegül, *Baths and Bathing in Classical Antiquity* (New York, 1992), 314–20; on Cic. and A. here, see E. W. Merten, *Bäder und Badegepflogenheiten in der Darstellung der Historia Augusta* (Bonn, 1983), 80–1.

80. **Sacerdotes quoque veteri more . . . *et non inducent super se peccatum ne moriantur*:** See Ex. 28: 42–3. A. appears to give the neuter *ea* [PVMA, E^1 W, CB: *eas* E^2, O] after the feminine **bracas lineas** because he uses the latter as a replacement for the biblical text's *femoralia linea*, and inadvertently leaves the pronoun unchanged (Testard i. 242 n. 44). This biblical *vetus mos* is implicitly added to the case of Gen. 9: 20–7 in 1.79 as further evidence of OT precedent for the *mos* that Cic. cites.

Quod nonnulli nostrum servare adhuc feruntur: Many clerics in A.'s day consider the wearing of linen under-garments to be still obligatory. He himself is inclined to interpret the text spiritually: the important thing is to maintain modesty and chastity; the OT is not prescribing an enduring rule about clerical dress. On wearing special garments for ministry at the altar, cf. Jer. *Comm. Ezech.*

13.44.17; on the significance of linen in particular as symbolic of purity, see W. J. Burghardt, 'Cyril of Alexandria on "Wool and Linen"', *Traditio* 2 (1944), 484–6; M. P. McHugh, 'Linen, Wool and Colour—Their Appearance in Saint Ambrose', *BICS* 23 (1976), 99–101. On clothing generally, cf. 1.83.

spiritali interpretatione: Cf. *Expl. Ps. 36*.1: *Omnis Scriptura divina vel naturalis vel mystica vel moralis est*; see generally Introduction IV.5.

CHAPTER 19: MODESTY OF THE BODY AND
THE VOICE

81. Delectavit me diutius in partibus demorari verecundiae: This suggests that the treatment of *verecundia* is now at an end, but in fact the discussion continues in 1.85, and 1.81–4 is itself on the same lines (*verecundia* appears in 1.83).

ad vos loquebar: See Introduction V–VI.

qui aut bona eius ex vobis recognoscitis aut damna ignoratis: Not simply flattery: A. is training clerical candidates from an early age, thus preserving them from the corrupting influences of the *saeculum*, and ensuring that they conform to his specific ideals; cf. 1.65–6 (though 1.145 assumes other addressees who have converted from paganism after having had opportunity to commit *gentilitatis vitia*).

Quae cum sit omnibus aetatibus . . . annos maxime decet: Cf. Cic. *Off.* 1.125: *Ita fere officia reperientur cum quaeretur quid deceat et quid aptum sit personis temporibus aetatibus*, a summary of the Panaetian principle that there are different roles for different ages and situations (see on 1.65 above).

82. quadret sibi: For the metaphor, cf. 1.224.

ordo vitae tuae: *ordo* is one of Cic.'s designations of temperance (*Off.* 1.14, 17, 98, 126, 142, 144): it is the maintenance of order (in Stoicism, εὐταξία) in the conduct of life; Dyck, 320–1. A. assumes the same principle; cf. 1.211, 219.

Unde Tullius etiam ordinem putat . . . et ideo satis esse

intellegi: Cf. Cic. *Off.* 1.126: *Sed quoniam decorum illud in omnibus factis dictis, in corporis denique motu et statu cernitur, idque positum est in tribus rebus, formositate, ordine, ornatu ad actionem apto, difficilibus ad eloquendum, sed satis erit intellegi.* This is the only occasion in the work where A. names Cic. and then quotes him (the reference in 1.180 comes after an allusion, not a direct quotation). According to the start of 1.83, he is struck by Cic.'s reference to *formositas*; the word occurs only here in all of Cic.'s extant works (otherwise in Apul. *Met.* 4.28; 6.16; 9.17; 10.31; and late authors). A. singles out this category of seemliness in particular for disagreement (Testard i. 243 n. 2; 'Recherches', 87). Perhaps he is also keen to ensure that his earlier comments on physiognomy are not misconstrued as an appeal to cultivate an undue level of physical elegance. At any rate, a direct contrast between the Ciceronian and the Christian views follows.

83. quamvis etiam ille vires corporis laudet: Cic. does not in fact extol physical strength as a part of the *decorum* at this point; he mentions it in connection with courage in *Off.* 1.79 (where he says it is less significant than strength of spirit), and as an advantage to be weighed against external advantages such as wealth in *Off.* 2.88. A.'s charge is somewhat overstated. (Cic. speaks of *pulchritudo* in *Off.* 1.14, where he also mentions *ordo* and propriety, but the context is different from *Off.* 1.126.). The antithesis of **ille . . . nos certe** is typical.

in pulchritudine corporis locum virtutis non ponimus: Cic. does not locate virtue in the body, however; he merely says that physical attractiveness, which is a part of nature's wise design of the body, intended to protect modesty, is connected with outward propriety (cf. also *Off.* 1.98). A. has himself stressed the importance of physical *decorum* in 1.71–2. An instinctive suspicion of conceding too much to the physical now produces a contrast with Cic. which is unreasonable. On physical beauty as a spiritual snare, cf. *Bon. mort.* 16.

in ipso quoque corporis decore . . . decor corporis: A. uses the masculine *decor*, 'attractiveness'; in 1.82, evoking the reference to *decorum* in Cic. *Off.* 1.126, *in illo decore* employs the neuter *decus*, 'propriety'; but the root of both words is the same.

sed naturalis simplex . . . nihil accedat nitori: Cic. *Off.*
1.130 urges the observance of *mediocritas* in clothing and
outward appearance; **vestimentis** here is doubtless suggested by Cic.'s *vestitus.* The need to avoid preoccupation
with or extravagance of dress is a pervasive classical and
Christian *topos*: e.g. Mt. 6: 25; 1 Tim. 2: 9–10; Sen. *Ep.*
5.1–3; *Const. Apost.* 1.2; Clem. Alex. *Paid.* 2.11; 3.11; Bas.
Reg. 22; *Ep.* 2.6; Amm. 30.8.10; Greg. Naz. *Orat.* 18.23; Jer.
Epp. 22.27–8; 52.9.1; 60.10.2; 66.5.1; 107.10.1; 127.3.4; Paul.
Nol. *Ep.* 29.12; Cass. *Inst.* 1. A. often condemns the
ostentatious attire of the wealthy (*Ex.* 5.77; *Nab.* 3; *Tob.*
19; *Luc.* 5.107). People sometimes confused him and his
brother Satyrus (*Exc. fr.* 1.38), which may suggest that the
two dressed similarly as well as looked alike; perhaps the
bishop's ordinary clothing was similar to that of an important layman. Functional simplicity was meant to mark the
servus Dei: Cyprian conformed nicely (Pont. *Vita Cypr.* 6),
and Augustine was conspicuous in his plain black *birrus* (cf.
En. Ps. 147.8), maintaining that expensive silk clothing was
inappropriate for him (*Serm.* 356.13; cf. also Possid. *Vita
Aug.* 22.1). Not all of A.'s garb could be described as
simplex, all the same: he also possessed some decidedly
grand robes for special occasions: see G. Granger Taylor,
'The Two Dalmatics of Saint Ambrose', *Bulletin de Liaison,
Centre International d'Etude des Textiles Anciens* 57–8 (1983),
127–73.

84. Vox ipsa: The tone of the voice is a particularly important gauge of modesty: cf. 1.67, 104. On the voice generally,
cf. *Ex.* 6.67. Significantly, A. himself apparently suffered
from a weak voice (Aug. *Conf.* 6.3.3; cf. A. *Sacr.* 1.24),
despite (or maybe because of?) his prowess as an orator. For
similar advice about control and clarity of voice, cf. e.g.
Clem. Alex. *Paid.* 2.5–7; Basil, *Ep.* 2.5.

sucum virilem: *Sucus* is used classically of the spirit of a
discourse (e.g. Cic. *De Or.* 2.93; 3.96; *Brut.* 36; *Or.* 76).
A. repeats this emphasis on manly vigour of voice in 1.104;
for the language, cf. also *Ex.* 4.21. The natural distinction
between men's and women's voices (*Ep.* 69 [2].2–3) should
not be blurred; on genuineness, cf. Jer. *Ep.* 22.27.6. On the
background, see A. Rousselle, 'Parole et inspiration: le

travail de la voix dans le monde romain', *History and Philosophy of the Life Sciences* 5 (1983), 129–57; M. W. Gleason, *Making Men: Sophists and Self-Presentation in Ancient Rome* (Princeton, 1995), 103–30.

ordo . . . ornatus . . . actionem: Picks up the language of Cic. *Off.* 1.126, quoted on 1.82 above.

Sed, ut molliculum et infractum . . . ita neque agrestem ac rusticum: [**rusticum:** Milan Trivulz. 399 Milan Ambros. B 54 inf. Zell, Testard (on the MSS, see Testard i. 78): *rusticam* PVMA, EW, COB] Cf. Cic. *Off.* 1.129: *Quibus in rebus duo maxime sunt fugienda, ne quid effeminatum aut molle et ne quid durum aut rusticum sit* (on effeminacy, cf. also *Off.* 1.14). On the concern to show an appropriate 'manly' *persona* in order to win secular respect (cf. 1.85, 138; 2.9) see generally Introduction VII (ii); cf. also Cic. *Fin.* 2.47. For **molliculum et infractum**, cf. Cic. *Tusc.* 4.64: *nam videndum est . . . ne quid humile, submissum, molle, effeminatum, fractum, abiectumque faciamus*; in A. cf. 2.9, and e.g. *Ep. extra coll.* 14 [63].97: *Nihil molliculum, nihil infractum ad laudem pervenit.* On **non probo**, see on 1.74.

Naturam imitemur: Cf. Cic. *Off.* 1.128: *Nos autem naturam sequamur*; of the voice, cf. *Or.* 58–9; Quint. *Inst.* 11.3.30, 32.

CHAPTER 20: MODESTY AND UNSEEMLY
COMPANY

85. Habet sane suos scopulos verecundia: A favourite Ciceronian image: e.g. *De Or.* 2.154; 3.163; *Pis.* 41; *Cael.* 51; *Rab. Perd.* 25; *Rosc. Am.* 79. For similar imagery, cf. e.g. *Fid.* 1.46–7; 3.4; *Expos. Ps. 118*.8.36; *Luc.* 4.3. 1.85–97 documents the dangers: *voluptas/cupiditas* (1.85–8), and *iracundia* (1.90–7). On the senses, cf. *Ep.* 34 [45].17.

intemperantium . . . consortia, qui sub specie iucunditatis venenum infundunt bonis: The standard principle of avoiding bad company: e.g. Prov. 13: 20; 22: 24–5; 1 Cor. 15: 33 (= Men. *Thais* fr. 218 [Kock]); 2 Cor. 6: 14–18; Eph. 5: 1–20; cf. 1.212; 2.97 below; *Ep.* 27 [8]; Clem. Alex. *Paid.* 3.4; Jer. *Epp.* 22.29; 52.5; 130.18.

ludo ac ioco: Cf Cic. *Off.* 1.103: *Neque enim ita generati a natura sumus ut ad ludum et iocum facti esse videamur, ad severitatem potius et ad quaedam studia graviora atque maiora. Ludo autem et ioco uti illo quidem licet, sed sicut somno et quietibus ceteris, tum cum gravibus seriisque rebus satisfecerimus.*

enervant gravitatem illam virilem: The masculine classicism surfaces again: for an example of such weakened moral capacity through debauchery, cf. the depiction of Herod in 3.77; on *gravitas*, see on 1.18.

Caveamus itaque ne dum relaxare animum volumus . . . quasi concentum quemdam bonorum operum: Cf. Cic. *Off.* 1.122: *Atque etiam cum relaxare animos et dare se iucunditati volent, caveant intemperantiam, meminerint verecundiae.* A.'s musical image is reminiscent of an emphasis common to many ancient philosophies, that virtue lies in harmony of body and soul, attained by rational control: cf. Cic. *Off.* 1.145 (and *Off.* 1.111, evoked in 1.222 below); *Tusc.* 1.19, 41 (on Aristoxenus); DL 6.27, 65; Lucr. 3.100, 118, 131; Sen. *Ep.* 88.9; Lact. *Opif. Dei* 16.13–18; *Inst.* 7.13.9; Bas. *Hom.* 14.1; Aug. *CD* 22.24, 30; *Serm.* 243.4. But the reference to *bona opera* slants the language to a Christian context.

86. ecclesiasticis, et maxime ministrorum officiis: *Minister* is frequently used by A. to refer to a cleric generally, though often it designates a deacon in particular (as probably in 1.247; 2.121–2, 134; 3.58). Here it probably refers to priests and deacons generally, as distinct from lesser ecclesiastics like readers, exorcists, and doorkeepers; see R. Gryson, 'Les Degrés du clergé et leurs dénominations chez saint Ambroise de Milan', *RBén* 66 (1966), 119–27. On **ministrorum officiis** here as inadequate evidence for the longer title for the work, see Introduction I.

declinare extraneorum convivia: Clerics (like virgins: *Virg.* 3.8, 25–31; *Exh. virg.* 71–2; cf. *Luc.* 2.21) must avoid secular dinner-parties, with their temptations to over-indulgence and lewd talk. A. elsewhere pictures the excessive drinking, erotic dancing and singing, coarse joking, even brawling among intoxicated guests at such functions (*Elia* 46–68); his language is paralleled in the colourful sketches of

Ammianus (e.g. 14.6.16, 18; 28.4.12–13, 21, 34) and Jerome (e.g. *Adv. Helv.* 22; *Ep.* 52.11). Christian writers exploit the language of satire and comedy to berate the worst social excesses of their time; the reality was probably hardly so ugly, though there is doubtless a core of truth to some of the descriptions. Clement of Alexandria warns of the dangers of party-going (*Paid.* 2.1 ff.); and Jerome advises Nepotian against attendance at dinners (*Ep.* 52.11; 52.15.2); for conciliar prohibitions on clerics taking part in banquets, see Gaudemet, 155; cf. also Isid. *Eccl. Off.* 2.2.2. Augustine is said to have followed A.'s rule on the matter, and stayed away from such gatherings (Possid. *Vita Aug.* 27.4). On fleeing excess eating, cf. *Elia* 81; on general extravagance at table, cf. 2.109; 3.10 below, and *Cain* 1.14; *Expl. Ps.* 37.30; *Luc.*, prol. 6; *Tob.* 17, 19). The force of **extraneorum** is noteworthy: the church is a community surrounded by a hostile world, a group of faithful believers who are 'inside' and who need to maintain significant moral barriers between themselves and the temptations of the ungodly realm outside; cf. 1.251–2 (also, on 'outsiders', 1.247). A. can concede that the Lord does not always forbid 'eating with sinners': it is permitted if there is good cause (*Luc.* 5.18). The reality for the bishop himself, at any rate, was straightforward: he could dine with the great and the good by inviting them to his own table, thus neatly establishing his episcopal residence as a centre of hospitality and social influence without necessarily having to venture abroad himself (cf. the references to his hospitality in Sulp. Sev. *Dial.* 1.25.6; Paul. *VA* 30.1, and on his imposing domestic space, see Humphries, 200–1; Jerome may well have A. in mind when he comments to Nepotian on the disgraceful sight of a consul's lictors waiting outside an episcopal residence, and of provincial governors dining with ascetics: *Ep.* 52.11). A. was also free to visit or lodge with Christian *clarissimi* and *clarissimae* when he travelled (Paul. *VA* 10.1; 28.1; cf. McLynn, 257), and there is no evidence that he incurred the charges of inaccessibility levelled at John Chrysostom for his solitary dining (cf. Phot. *Bibl.* 59, with defence in Pallad. *Dial.* 39–45, and see J. H. W. G. Liebeschuetz, *Barbarians and Bishops: Army, Church and State in the Age of Arcadius and Chrysostom* (Oxford, 1990), 208–22).

ut ipsi hospitales sitis peregrinantibus: On the import-ance of hospitality, cf. 1.39, 167; and especially 2.103–8; see on 2.103. Possibly A. is thinking here of Cic.'s advice in *Off.* 1.139 that a house must be appropriate to the business of entertaining guests, and that it must be used accordingly.

Subrepunt etiam fabulae frequenter de saeculo ac voluptatibus: claudere aures non potes: The world's ways are like Siren voices (Hom. *Od.* 12.173–7); cf. *Expl. Ps. 43.*75 and esp. 80: [*Ideo adfligimur*] *deinde quia voluptas et delectatio mundi frequenter inrepit. Unde non vinculis hominis illius ligare nos atque vincire debemus nec cera aures claudere, sed avertere aurem, quotienscumque aliena a fide et contraria vel adversa utilitati nostrae aliquis existimat obloquenda, ne in eo sermone operiat umbra nos mortis*; also *Fid.* 3.4–5; *Ep. extra coll.* 11 [51].3; *Luc.* 4.2–3 (and see P. Courcelle, *Connais-toi toi-même de Socrate à saint Bernard*, 2 vols. (Paris, 1974), 1.415–33, especially 420–1 and n. 40; J. Doignon, 'La Tradition latine (Cicéron, Sénèque) de l'episode des Sirènes entre les mains d'Ambroise de Milan', in *Hommages à Jean Cousin: Rencontres avec l'antiquité classique* (Paris, 1983), 271–8; N. Pace, 'Il canto delle Sirene in Ambrogio, Ger-olamo e altri Padri della Chiesa', in *Nec timeo mori*, 673–95, especially 681–95). On *fabulae*, cf. *Exh. virg.* 72; on the *salsior dicacitas* typical in such situations, cf. *Ep.* 62 [19].15. Clem. Alex. *Paid.* 2.6.49–52. Stories of course found their way to the episcopal table as well: Augustine forbade them, according to Possid. *Vita Aug.* 22.

condemnari non debet praesentia tua: The emphasis, typically, is on image: the faithful cleric must be beyond reproach (cf. 1 Tim. 4: 12).

87. **Viduarum ac virginum domos . . . cum presbyteris:** The visitation of widows in need is a NT injunction (Jas. 1: 27), but A. is anxious to warn of the obvious dangers involved in younger clerics frequenting the homes of single women. Even where there is no risk of sexual temptation (**illecebra**), it is still necessary to give no cause for idle gossip and innuendo (**locum et dederunt suspicioni**). The priest lives with the eyes of the world upon him (cf. 1.229; *Ep. extra coll.* 14 [63].71–2), and female company is just too

great a danger (cf. also 1.256). Jerome notoriously accuses elements of the Roman clergy in the early 380s of having sought the priesthood or diaconate simply in order to see women more freely (*Ep.* 22.28.3–4), and he warns virgins to keep away from the homes of extravagant widows, which flatterers, including ecclesiastics, are prone to visit (*Ep.* 22.16.3; 22.28.4–6). Nepotian is counselled against visiting women alone or without the company of venerable elders (*Ep.* 52.5.4–6; cf. *Ep.* 60.10.7). The importance of avoiding potentially compromising situations crops up again and again in ecclesiastical texts from this period, presumably in response to questionable behaviour. Numerous conciliar enactments forbade women other than blood-relations from living under the same roof as clergy (e.g. Con. Elv. *can.* 27; Con. Nic. *can.* 3; Con. Carth. 3 (397), *can.* 17, 25; cf. also Con. Tol. 1 (400), *can.* 9; *CTh* 16.2.44 (420); *Nov.* 123 c. 29; Isid. *Eccl. Off.* 2.2.3; Amal. Metz, *Reg. Can.* 1.94). Augustine would not let even his immediate female relatives lodge with him; and he never met with or visited women unchaperoned, according to Possid. *Vita Aug.* 26–7. He expelled a deacon who had been seen speaking with a nun at an inappropriate hour of the day (Aug. *Ep.* 20*.5.1); however, manpower shortages in rural North Africa made it impracticable to insist that clergy travelled in pairs to avoid compromising situations (*Ep.* 13*.1.2; 3.3). A. suffered from no such staffing problems, and so can insist on a strict rule of no unaccompanied visiting.

vel si gravior est causa: Most likely for group-prayer with the sick; cf. Jas. 5: 14–15; also *Const. Apost.* 3.15; Commod. *Instr.* 71; Cass. *Conf.* 20.8.

cum presbyteris: On *presbyteri*, see Gryson, *Prêtre*, 137–42. On the importance of older company generally, cf. 1.212; 2.97–101.

Quid si aliqua illarum forte labatur?: The women are the weak party, apparently. On women as a source of temptation, cf. *Expos. Ps. 118*.8.34; 15.18; 16.3.

88. There is a certain resemblance in this passage to Cypr. *Ad Don.* 15: *Sit tibi vel oratio assidua vel lectio. Nunc cum Deo loquere, nunc Deus tecum* (Y.-M. Duval, 'Sur une page de saint Cyprien chez saint Ambroise. Hexameron 6, 8, 47 et De habitu virginum 15–17', *REAug* 16 (1970), 25–34, at 34 n. 43); A.'s style is considerably more rhetorical.

Cur non illa tempora . . . lectioni impendas?: Cf. 1 Tim. 4: 13: *Dum venio, attende lectioni . . .* (probably, *pace* A., a reference to public rather than private reading of the Scriptures). On staying at home to read, cf. *Const. Apost.* 1.4–5; on the importance of meditative reading, cf. *Expos. Ps. 118*.7.25; 10.39; *Ep.* 14 [63].82; Jer. *Ep.* 52.7.1; 60.10.8–11.3; Caes. Arel. *Serm.* 7; and see on 1.3; 1.165. Augustine testifies to the diligence of A.'s own reading habits (*Conf.* 6.3.3), which invested his preaching with such a synthesis of scriptural knowledge and philosophico-exegetical learning; cf. also Paul. *VA* 38. The reading of Scripture here is contrasted with the attention to the *fabulae* of the world mentioned in 1.86; cf. below.

Cur non Christum revisas . . . Christum audias?: The cleric ought to keep visiting Christ in prayer rather than visiting the homes of pagans or unmarried women.

Illud adloquimur cum oramus: On prayer, cf. e.g. *Expl. Ps. 36*.65–7; *Fid.* 1.132–7; *Spir.*, prol. 13–14; *Virg.* 3.18–20; *Virgt.* 80; *Cain* 2.22; *Expos. Ps. 118*.7.32; see further K. Baus, *Das Gebet zu Christus beim hl. Ambrosius: Eine frömmigkeitsgeschichtliche Untersuchung* (Trier, 1952).

Quid nobis cum alienis domibus?: Unlike Cic., who expects a man's reputation to be enhanced by the kind of house he has and the hospitality he extends in it (*Off.* 1.139), the clergy should have no interest in other people's homes: they have a special home of their own:

Una est domus quae omnes capit: Cf. Cic. *Off.* 1.54: Cic. speaks of the fellowship that exists between people in *una domus*, and the bonds between those *qui cum una domo iam capi non possint, in alias domus tamquam in colonias exeunt*. On the church as a household, cf. Gal. 6: 10; Eph. 2: 19; 1 Pt. 4: 17. The *domus* of the church is the cleric's proper home, not the *domus* of 1.86–7; on the unity of the church, see Homes Dudden ii. 638 and n. 6.

Illi potius ad nos veniant, qui nos requirunt: As of course people did to A. in their throngs, according to Aug. *Conf.* 6.1.3; 6.3.12. The demand that people must come to the clergy rather than have the clergy come to them was of course a subtle way of reinforcing an image of ecclesiastical authority as well; though A. insists that churchmen certainly need to be approachable (2.61). The prescription requires a delicate balancing act between creating an impression of sanctified otherness and dignity on the one hand and being available to people on the other. On spiritual activity, the right use of *otium*, as the way to impress, cf. 3.1–7.

Quid nobis cum fabulis?: Cf. 1 Tim. 1: 4; 4: 7 (also 6: 20; 2 Tim. 2: 16, 23; 4: 4; Tit. 1: 14; 3: 9; 2 Pt. 1: 16). This makes clear the antithesis between the worldly *fabulae* of 1.86 and the **divina oracula** of the Scriptures mentioned above.

Ministerium . . . recepimus: Cf. Col. 4: 17: *Vide ministerium quod accepisti in Domino, ut illud impleas.* On **ministerium altaribus Christi**, cf. 1.247. On avoiding the praise (**obsequium**) of men, cf. the warnings against seeking flattery in 1.209, 226 (also 2.66). The ministry must be identifiably distinct. The cleric is not to retreat into a monastic detachment; but he must abjure the *mores* of a corrupt world and devote himself to Christ in such a way that his higher vocation is obvious to all.

89. A summary of some of the essential features of modesty, synthesizing biblical and Ciceronian language (cf. 1.13–22, 35, 71–2), though the subject is far from closed: advice on how to deal with anger is yet to come (1.90–7).

mansuetos . . . patientes: Cf. 2 Tim. 2: 24: *Servum autem Domini . . . oportet . . . mansuetum esse ad omnes, docibilem, patientem . . .* ; on the need for *mansuetudo*, cf. also Cic. *Off.* 1.88.

ut nullum vitium esse in moribus . . . sermo adnuntiet: Cf. Cic. *Off.* 1.134: *In primisque provideat ne sermo vitium aliquod indicet inesse in moribus*; also 1.10 above, and see on 1.14.

CHAPTER 21: ANGER

1.90–7 is on the avoidance of anger, another of the *scopuli* (1.85) into which *verecundia* can run, and the one to which A. devotes most attention. The subject has already been raised in 1.13–22, and it is touched on again in 1.231–8. The idea comes chiefly from Cic.'s discussion of anger in the case of rebukes and personal disputes in *Off.* 1.136–7 (cf. also *Off.* 1.69, 88–9, 102), though the illustrations are biblical (including a contrast with a Ciceronian exemplar (not from *Off.*) in 1.92). Despite reservations in some quarters about how well the section fits into the argument here (Testard, 'Recherches', 91–2), the relevance of the Ciceronian background should not be minimized. Nor should the overlaps with 1.13–22 be exaggerated. A. does pick up points from 1.13–22 (Steidle, 'Beobachtungen', 39), but the treatment of anger here is broader: it is not just about keeping silence when provoked, but about the larger question of how to control one's emotions rationally (especially in 1.97), a theme which continues in 1.98. 1.90–7 is not a thematic doublet with 1.13–22 or 1.231–8. The passage has its own point where it stands: it rounds off the modesty section, and leads appropriately into the general account of the *decorum*. The absence of the word *verecundia* after 1.85 misleads Testard, who concludes that the *verecundia* topic is over in 1.89, and thus has a problem integrating 1.90–7 into the flow of the argument. In A.'s discursive style, however, the absence of the word does not mean that the discussion is at an end (after all, *verecundia* is not mentioned in 1.86–9 either). The whole of 1.85–97 is explaining a related series of challenges to *verecundia*. See generally Sauer, 143–54.

Anger was a standard area of concern for the responsible public figure of antiquity: outbursts of rage and excessive cruelty were thought to betray a weakness of character in men who dealt with dependants every day (cf. Gal. *Cogn. an. morb.* 1.4; generally Plu. *Mor.* 452f–464d). Stoic treatments can be found in Cic. *Tusc.* 4.77–81 (cf. 4.16, 20–1, 27); Sen. *Tranq. an.* and of course *Ira*; anger is subsumed under desire as a passion to be conquered by reason. Biblical writers issue several warnings (e.g. Ps. 36: 9; Prov. 14: 17; 15: 18; 16: 32; 27: 4; Eccl. 7: 9; Eph. 4: 26–32; Col. 3: 8; 1 Tim. 2: 8; Tit. 1: 7; Jas. 1: 19), which shape early Christian perspectives: e.g. Lact. *Ira*; Bas. *Hom.* 10, *Adv. Irat.*; Aug. *En. Ps. 38.2*; Nemes. Emes. *Nat. hom.* 16, 21. A. goes part-way with the Stoics: anger, like every other passion (*Noe* 30; *Abr.* 2.20, 28) ought to be restrained and tempered by reason. But (unlike Posidonius at least) he assumes that it need not be stamped out entirely. He

argues on biblical grounds that anger is permissible if there is
good cause and if it cannot be contained, so long as it is
carefully moderated (1.90, 96; cf. *Iac.* 1.1–2; *Ep. extra coll.*
14 [63].60–1, 100; *Ios.* 78; *Expl. Ps. 36.*18; *Expos. Ps. 118.*12.18;
Luc. 5.54; 7.28; *Ob. Theod.* 14; *Exh. virg.* 77; *Sacr.* 6.19). We
should be angry with ourselves if we have been disturbed
(1.96), and have succumbed to this 'illness' (1.194); if the
spirit cannot be pacified, the tongue at least should be checked
(1.92). 'Regulation, not total suppression, is what is wanted'
(Homes Dudden ii. 509; see further Sauer, 147–50). In the end,
the scriptural input places A. closer to the Aristotelian/Peri-
patetic position than to the Stoics: anger is a mean between
irascibility (*iracundia*) and complete detachment. It may be
right to be angry on occasion and in due measure (cf. Cic. *Tusc.*
4.43). Cic. prefers the classical Stoic ideal of complete ἀπάθεια
(though he nods to the Peripatetic view in deference to
Marcus' current position as a student of Cratippus: *Off.*
1.89). For a perhaps more obviously Stoic stance by A. on
resisting emotional pressures engendered by circumstances,
cf. 1.182–4.

90. tranquillitas: Cic. contrasts this with *iracundia* in *Off.*
1.69 (cf. also 1.72, 102), though in the context of *fortitudo*.
A. links it with temperance as well (cf. 1.95, 98, 185, 210);
Sauer, 176–7. In Panaetian perspective, the aim is for an
inner calm produced by rational detachment from passion
and external circumstances (εὐθυμία).
ratione reprimatur: Typically Stoic; cf. 1.97–8, 106–14,
228–9.
**ita plerumque motus infixus est . . . ratione reprima-
tur:** Elsewhere, A. often adopts Philo's exegesis of the Fall:
Adam represents reason, which is tempted by Eve, who
stands for sensuality (e.g. *Ep.* 34 [45].17; *Ep. extra coll.* 14
[63].14; *Parad.* 52–4; *Fug.* 3); as a result of the Fall, the flesh
is no longer subject to reason (*Luc.* 4.62–7; *Ep.* 34 [45].17)
and so passion is constantly scoring victories over our higher
nature: Seibel, 129–45. Note the typical fondness for military
imagery: **si provideri potuerit, ratione reprimatur. . .
occupatus . . . consilio prospici ac provideri potuerit ne
occuparetur . . . vincas . . . . Resiste . . . cede . . .** (cf

1.92, 97; and Sen. *Ira* 1.9.4, who pictures the passions as disobedient soldiers). This vocabulary comes hard on the heels of the quasi-horticultural language of **infixus est . . . evelli. . . .**

Date locum irae: Rom. 12: 19. In context, Paul urges his readers to leave God's anger to be worked out for their vindication, rather than seeking to avenge themselves. A. understands the verse thus in *Abr.* 2.30 and *Ios.* 78. Here, however, he takes it to mean that one ought to yield to an angry opponent: draw back rather than fight (as Jacob drew back from Esau: 1.91–2); cf. *Ep. extra coll.* 14 [63].100; *Iac.* 2.14.

91. Iacob fratri indignanti . . . cum fratrem mitigatum putaret: Jacob was advised by his mother Rebecca to flee to her brother Laban to escape the anger of Esau, when Esau realized that Jacob had usurped his blessing from their father Isaac: Gen. 27: 1–45, especially 27: 41–5. On A.'s predilection for such 'two-brothers theology', see Hahn, 149–63.

Rebeccae, id est patientiae: A standard explanation of Rebecca's name: e.g. Philo *Leg. Alleg.* 3.88–9; *Sac.* 4; *Det.* 30–1, 45, 51; *Plant.* 169–70; *Mig.* 208–9; *Congr.* 37; *Fug.* 24, 39, 45, 194–5; *Somn.* 1.46; *Cher.* 41, 47; Orig. *Hom. Gen.* 10.4; Jer. *Interpr. Hebr. nom.* 9.23; 74.29; 81.16; Isid. *Orig.* 6.35. A. also mentions it in *Is.* 1 (cf. 18); *Iac.* 2.14; *Ep.* 4 [27].17; *Ep. extra coll.* 14 [63].100 (cf. also *Fug.* 20–2); his likeliest source is Philo. On his interest in names, see D. H. Müller, 'Die Deutungen der hebräischen Buchstaben bei Ambrosius', *Sitzungsberichte der Kaiserlichen Akademie der Wissenschaften in Wien, Phil.-hist. Klasse* 167/2 (1911); W. Wilbrand, 'Die Deutungen der biblischen Eigennamen beim hl. Ambrosius', *BiblZeit* 10 (1912), 337–50.

apud Deum invenit gratiam: A common biblical phrase: e.g. Gen. 6: 8; 18: 3; Ex. 33: 12–13; Prov. 3: 4; Lk. 1: 30; Acts 7: 46.

quantis muneribus . . . meminisset delatae satisfactionis: Jacob appeased Esau with gifts of livestock and servants: Gen. 32: 3–33: 17.

92. Ergo si praevenerit . . . non relinquas locum tuum: Cf. Eccl. 10: 4: *Si spiritus potestatem habentis ascenderit super* *te, locum tuum ne demiseris; quia curatio cessare faciet peccata maxima*; A. also continues the military note from 1.90.

Locus tuus patientia est . . . sedatio indignationis est: The point is driven home rhetorically with the aid of epanaphora and chiasmus.

Aut si te contumacia respondentis moverit . . . reprime linguam tuam: Cf. 1.17–22, especially 1.13.

Cohibe linguam tuam a malo . . . ne loquantur dolum: Ps. 33: 14.

Inquire pacem et sequere eam: Ps. 33: 15. The verses are quoted together in 1 Pt. 3: 10–11.

frenos linguae impone tuae: Cf. Jas. 3: 2–12 (and Jas. 1: 26); cf. also 1.12–13 above.

Haec oratores saeculi de nostris usurpata . . . sed ille sensus huius habet gratiam qui prior dixit: A. is of course thinking of Cic., who insists that reproofs should be moderate and clearly designed to benefit rather than antagonize the recipient, warning that anger is a dangerous emotion in this context (*Off.* 1.136–7). Once again, we have the accusation of pagan plagiarism from the Scriptures; the psalmist David (**ille . . . qui prior dixit**) is to be credited as the first to teach this restraint of anger.

A. engages in some special pleading in his presentation of Jacob in 1.91–2 (cf. *Ep. extra coll.* 14 [63].100–3). According to the Gen. narrative, Jacob did not go abroad because he personally considered that it was a dutiful thing to allow Esau to calm down, but because he recognized the prudence of his mother's advice to flee for his life. Similarly, his gifts of reparation were prepared in fear of Esau's revenge, and we read of him pleading with Esau to accept them. The story hardly illustrates the mastery of passion by reason, as A. would have us believe.

93. in laudibus . . . in vitiis: The words are found in Cic. *Off.* 1.71.

naturae illud: Cic. *Off.* 1.89 criticizes the Peripatetics for 'praising' *iracundia* as a gift of nature, *utiliter a natura data[m]* (in other words, as an emotion that is right on some occasions and in appropriate measure).

commotiones in pueris innoxiae . . . quam amaritudinis: Children's squabbles are more endearing to the adult onlooker than they are serious to the participants; children soon calm down and are reconciled to one another. They deserve to be imitated. Cf. Sen. *Ira* 2.19.4, who claims that a predominance of humours in women and children makes their anger more vehement in expression than it is serious in nature. On children's fickleness, cf. 3.128 below.

Nisi conversi fueritis . . . in regnum caelorum: Mt. 18: 3.

ipse Dominus, hoc est *Dei virtus*: Cf. 1 Cor. 1: 24; cf. 1.18.

cum malediceretur, non remaledixit: 1 Pt. 2: 23, part of a passage which echoes the servant-song of Is. 53, interpreting it messianically.

non exerceas: Cic. uses the verb in *Off.* 1.88.

Locum tuum serva: See on 1.92.

simplicitatem et puritatem: Cf. 1.75, 101, 104; 2.112–20; 3.76.

Noli respondere . . . imprudenti ad imprudentiam: Prov. 26: 4; cf. *Fug.* 56: *Bene fugis si non respondeas*.

Cito culpa culpam excutit; si lapides teras, nonne ignis erumpit?: Typical of A.'s ability to fashion short, pithy *sententiae*; see generally Introduction IX.

94. **Ferunt gentiles:** A reference to the pagans in general, but A. owes his knowledge of the anecdote to Cic.

ut in maius omnia verbis extollere solent: The pagans habitually exaggerate their praise of notable exemplars (unlike A. of course).

Archytae Tarentini dictum philosophi . . .: *O te infelicem, quam adflictarem nisi iratus essem!*: Archytas of Tarentum (*fl. c.*400–350 BC) was a distinguished philosopher of the Pythagorean school, Sicilian politician, acquaintance of Plato, and the reputed founder of mechanics. He was famed for his wisdom (e.g. Cic. *Tusc.* 5.64; *Sen.* 39–41; *Amic.* 88), though little of it survives. He is the addressee of Hor. *Od.* 1.28, where it is suggested that he perished at sea on some military exploit. See Guthrie i. 333–6. The saying to which A. refers is quoted by Cic. in *Rep.* 1.59–60 and *Tusc.* 4.78; it is also found in Val. Max. 4.1. ext. 1. For other Christian references, cf. e.g. Lact. *Ira* 18.12; Jer. *Ep.* 79.9.4, *In Ioel* 1.5.

Sed iam David . . . Abigail deprecatione revocaverat: Inevitably, David got there before Archytas—and excelled him, not only heeding a plea to desist from anger, but issuing a blessing to the one who had dissuaded him from his desire for revenge. A. refers to the encounter of David with Nabal and Abigail: 1 Ki. 25: 2–42. Abigail appeased David when he and his men were about to wreak vengeance on her foolish husband Nabal for insulting them; Nabal died shortly afterwards, and Abigail became one of David's wives.

tempestivis: Cic. *Off.* 1.88 says it is unhealthy to develop a habit of getting angry with people for approaching one *intempestive*.

95. **de inimicis:** Cic. *Off.* 1.88 speaks of those who think it right to be angry with *inimici*.

Quoniam declinaverunt . . . molesti erant mihi: Ps. 54: 4.

Quis dabit mihi pennas . . . et requiescam?: Ps. 54: 7.

Illi ad iracundiam provocabant, hic eligebat tranquillitatem: See on 1.90, on Cic. *Off.* 1.69.

96. *Irascimini et nolite peccare*: Ps. 4: 5; cf. 1.13 above, and *Luc*. 5.54; also Aug. *En. Ps. 4.6*. There is some similarity between this paragraph and Origen's comments in *Hom. Ps. 4.5* (Testard i. 245 n. 19), though Origen differs from A. in insisting that ὀργίζεσθε (**irascimini**) is an indicative, not an imperative, which seems a strange idea in view of the prohibition that follows ('do not sin').

Moralis magister: David, similarly described in *Expos. Ps. 118*. prol. 1 (*moralium magnus magister*); and cf. 1.1 above, *humilitatis magister*; 1.7, *cautionis magister*.

qui naturalem adfectum inflectendum . . . exstirpandum noverit: Cf. Lucr. 3.307–13, on the inability of *doctrina* to eradicate from human nature tendencies to evils like anger. For other quasi-Lucretian language, cf. 1.55–6. On anger as an *adfectus naturae*, cf. 1.13.

moralia docet: Winterbottom, 561, proposes deleting these words after **moralis magister**, but this may be unnecessary. The style is informal: 'Here is a (real) master of morality . . . —he is the one to give us (real) moral instruction.'

Melior est . . . quam qui urbem capit: Prov. 16: 32.

97. Cavere igitur debemus . . . improviso percellit ictu:
Cf. Cic. *Off.* 1.131: *quod adsequemur si cavebimus ne in
perturbationes atque exanimationes incidamus et si attentos
animos ad decoris conservationem tenebimus.* The *perturbationes animi* were fourfold in classical Stoic thought: desire
(including anger), fear, grief, and pleasure (Cic. *Tusc.*
3.24–5; 4.11–14; Verg. *Aen.* 6.733; Hor. *Ep.* 1.6.12; in A.,
Virgt. 95); middle Stoicism, following Platonist influence,
treated anger as a separate force (cf. Cic. *Off.* 1.69).

Ideo praevenire pulchrum est . . . adstricta mitescat:
The remedy for passion here anticipates the function of
courage of spirit in 1.188–92. Temperance and courage
tend to elide in A.'s thinking, perhaps in part because his
memory of Cic.'s text is patchy. On **iugo . . . habenis**, cf.
1.12–13; **improviso percellit ictu . . . praevenire** extends
the military language of 1.90, 92.

CHAPTER 22: THE TWIN 'MOTIONS' OF THE
SOUL, AND SEEMLY SPEECH

1.98 acts as a bridge between the discussion of anger in 1.90–7
and the commencement of the section on the *decorum* in 1.99.
1.97 has referred to other passions besides anger; this leads
naturally to an explanation of the relationship between the
rational and the irrational, inspired by Cic. *Off.* 1.132. The
decorum is all about reason mastering appetite. 1.99–114 goes
on to explore the implications of the *decorum* (though the
vocabulary of seemliness is used only in 1.99 and 1.105).
There are two stages: first, seemliness as it applies to speech,
language, and the voice (1.99–104; the transition from the twin
motus of the soul in 1.98 to propriety of speech mirrors Cic.'s
sequence); second, seemliness as it applies to action (1.105–14).
The categories are supplied by Cic. but 1.99–114 does not
closely adhere to the Ciceronian order. A. takes points at
random, following his memory of Cic.'s account of the fourth
virtue. The substance of 1.98 reappears in 1.228–9: the repetition is another product of A.'s twofold treatment of the
modesty theme (see on 1.65). In 1.99–104, the combination
of precepts about the voice (1.104; cf. 1.84); language and

length of delivery (1.101); and subject-matter (1.100–1), almost amounts to a kind of outline *institutio oratoria* for the cleric (cf. 1.35, on the basic concern of rhetoric: what to say, to whom to say it, and when to say it; also 1.14), anticipating in very rudimentary form elements of the territory covered by August-ine in *Doctr. Chr.* 4, and merging Ciceronian motifs with practical injunctions drawn from the Pastoral Epistles. A. promotes a model of Christian speech which observes the proportions of rhetorical convention, but which is above all infused with the language of the Scriptures: right discourse, whether informal or (especially) formal, is about simultan-eously maintaining due measure and sounding biblical. See Graumann, 224–30; id. 'St Ambrose on the Art of Preaching', in *Vescovi e pastori* ii. 587–600.

98.   Sunt autem gemini motus . . . alteri appetitus: Cf. Cic. *Off.* 1.132: *Motus autem animorum duplices sunt: alteri cogitationis, alteri appetitus*; also *Off.* 1.101–2.
Cogitationes verum exquirere . . . impellit atque excitat: Cf. Cic. *Off.* 1.132: *Cogitatio in vero exquirendo maxime versatur, appetitus impellit ad agendum.* The notion that reason controls the passions is classically Stoic, but only with the middle Stoa did the idea emerge that the soul comprises competing rational and irrational faculties. Under the influence of Plato (cf. the charioteer and horses image of *Phaedr.* 246a–247c) and Aristotle, Panaetius and Posidonius accounted for the passions by attributing them to the irrational powers of the soul rather than to errors of judgement about what is right. These passions must be controlled by the discipline of reason. For Panaetius, there are six parts to the soul (fr. 85); one of them, the ἡγεμονικόν comprises the faculties of both passion and reason. It is this middle Stoic thinking that A. takes over from Cic. (Cic. uses the image of horse-taming in *Off.* 1.90, and then, strikingly, in *Off.* 1.102–3; A. follows him in 1.228–9; cf. too the language of 1.12–13, 97). In several other places, A. speaks of the control of the passions by reason (e.g. *Noe* 5, 30; *Iac.* 1.1 ff.), and mentions Platonist psychological categories (e.g. *Abr.* 2.54; *Is.* 65–7; *Virgt.* 93–7, 111–19). The inspiration in these other passages is often partly from the amalgam of

Stoic and Platonist doctrine to be found in Philo; here, though, the debt is clearly to Cic. 1.228–9 is similar to 1.98, but if we speak of doublets or blame A. for poor composition we need to censure Cic. as well, for he too mentions the twofold power of the spirit twice (*Off.* 1.101–3 and 1.132).

emolere: The metaphorical use of this rare word to describe the 'grinding down' of truth is very unusual; cf. *Ep.* 54 [64].3–4 (of faith, with allegorical reference to Mt. 24: 41) (*TLL* v/2. 519–20, at 520).

Itaque ipso genere naturae suae . . . motum agendi excutit: The language is evocative of Cic. *Off.* 1.102–3.

Ita ergo informati sumus ut . . . obtemperet: Cf. Cic. *Off.* 1.101: *Ita fit ut ratio praesit, appetitus obtemperet*; also *Off.* 1.102, 132.

99. **ad conservationem decoris . . . in factis dictisque qui modus:** Cf. Cic. *Off.* 1.131: *et si attentos animos ad decoris conservationem tenebimus*; *Off.* 1.14: *Nec vero illa parva vis naturae est rationisque, quod unum hoc animal sentit quid sit ordo, quid sit quod deceat, in factis dictisque qui modus.*

sermo in duo dividitur . . . fidei atque iustitiae: Cf. Cic. *Off.* 1.132: *Et quoniam magna vis orationis est eaque duplex, altera contentionis, altera sermonis, contentio disceptationibus tribuatur iudiciorum contionum senatus, sermo in circulis, disputationibus, congressionibus familiarium versetur, sequatur etiam convivia.* Cic. distinguishes oratory (*contentio*) from conversation (*sermo*); A. uses *sermo* for both informal discourse and more formal *tractatus disceptatioque*, so the translation adopts a more general rendering of *sermo* as 'speech'. Cic. considers oratory in terms of judicial and political speeches; A. relates it to exposition and discussion of *fides atque iustitia*. He goes on to prescribe a Christian content for both formal discourse/preaching (*tractatus* is the usual word for preaching) and informal conversation: Scripture and the doctrines and morals of the faith are to be the subject of both; on the association of *fides* and *iustitia*, cf. e.g. Rom. 3: 22; 4: 11, 13; 9: 30; 10: 6; Phil. 3: 9; 2 Pt. 1: 1; and see on 1.110.

In the present paragraph, the focus, in the case of conversation, is on psychological qualities in particular (the need to avoid conveying or evoking wrong emotions through one's speech); the importance of choosing the right themes and of not going on for too long follows in 1.100. In 1.101, on *tractatus*, the underlying principles are, naturally, slightly more technical: A. offers brief advice on themes, on format (following the suggestion of a *lectio*), length, style, diction, and tone. Other 'secular' rules about jokes are said to be irrelevant for those governed by the *ecclesiastica regula* in 1.102–3, but some fairly traditional-sounding advice follows on the voice in 1.104 (though the context of the correct, 'natural' tone now is not so much the political forum or the lawcourt but the church: the voice must be appropriate for the conducting of divine mysteries). On the vocabulary of speech, see generally Mohrmann ii. 63–72; M. Pellegrino, '"Mutus . . . loquar Christum." Pensieri di sant'Ambrogio su parola e silenzio', in R. Cantalamessa and L. F. Pizzolato (eds.), *Paradoxos Politeia. Studi patristici in onore di Giuseppe Lazzati* (Milan, 1979), 447–57, at 455–7; Biermann, 211–16.

contumelia: Cic. *Off.* 1.134 mentions the harm done by someone who speaks *maledice contumelioseque*; cf. also *Off.* 1.89 and 1.137.

Absit pertinax in familiari sermone contentio: *Contentio* is used by Cic. in *Off.* 1.132 as a neutral word for formal discourse; A., however, uses it pejoratively (as Cic. does in *Off.* 1.133 and 137), and excludes it from conversation. He may also be thinking of verses like 1 Tim. 6: 4; 2 Tim. 2: 14; Tit. 3: 9. On **absit**, cf. Cic. *Off.* 1.136: *sed tamen ira procul absit*; on **pertinax**, cf. Cic. *Off.* 1.134: *Sit ergo hic sermo . . . lenis minimeque pertinax*. On the advantages of *suavis sermo*, cf. 1.67, 226; and 2.29–30, 96.

quaestiones enim magis excitare inanes . . . adferre solet: On the necessity of avoiding such *quaestiones*, cf. 1 Tim. 1: 4; 6: 4; 2 Tim. 2: 23; Tit. 3: 9.

sine ira . . . sine amaritudine . . . sine asperitate . . . sine offensione: Cf. Cic. *Off.* 1.136–7 on avoiding *ira* and *iracundia* in reproofs, and on making it clear that the *acerbitas* of a rebuke is for the good of the recipient; cf. too *Off.* 1.134. **severitas** in place of the MSS' *suavitas* (which in any case makes no sense at all in the context) is supported by Cic.'s use of the word in *Off.* 1.137 (Winterbottom, 561).

**Et sicut in omni actu vitae id cavere debemus . . .
aliqua exprimamus indicia:** Cf. Cic. *Off.* 1.136: *Sed
quomodo in omni vita rectissime praecipitur ut perturbationes
fugiamus, id est motus animi nimios rationi non obtemperantes,
sic eiusmodi motibus sermo debet vacare, ne aut ira exsistat aut
cupiditas aliqua aut pigritia aut ignavia aut tale aliquid
appareat.*

100. **Sit igitur sermo huiusmodi de scripturis maxime:**
This contrasts sharply with the topics which Cic. mentions
in *Off.* 1.135: domestic business, public affairs, and the study
and teaching of the arts. On forming one's speech by
attention to Scripture generally, cf. *Ep.* 36 [2].3–11; also
Aug. *Doctr. Chr.* 4.5.19 ff.

**Magis nos oportet loqui de conversatione optima . . .
disciplinae custodia:** Cf. Cic. *Off.* 1.132: *Curandum est
igitur ut cogitatione ad res quam optimas utamur.* For A., the
best subjects are of course those of spiritual value, which are
rooted in the Scriptures.

Habeat caput eius rationem et finis modum: Cf. Cic.
Off. 1.135: *Animadvertendum est etiam quatenus sermo delectationem habeat, et ut incipiendi ratio fuerit, ita sit desinendi
modus.*

Sermo enim taediosus iram excitat: Cf. Prov. 15: 1:
Responsio mollis frangit iram; sermo durus suscitat furorem;
scriptural allusion is appended to Ciceronian advice.

101. **Tractatus quoque de doctrina fidei:** Cf. the regular
exhortations in the Pastoral Epistles: 1 Tim. 4: 13, 16; 2
Tim. 4: 2; Tit. 2: 1 (cf. 1: 9).

de magisterio continentiae: A. of course seeks to show
the way in his own promotion of asceticism.

non unus semper: Cf. Cic. *Off.* 1.135: *neque enim isdem de
rebus nec omni tempore nec similiter delectamur.*

ut se dederit lectio: The practice A. seems to follow
himself in 1.23 and 1.25, and more loosely in his exposition
of scriptural verses throughout his work; the decisive motivation is the *ad hoc* inspiration of a scriptural passage. For
Cic., the important thing is to tailor the treatment of the
theme according to the company (*Off.* 1.135).

**neque nimium prolixus . . . desidiam prodat atque
incuriam:** Cf. Cic. *Off.* 1.135: *Danda igitur opera est ut,*

etiamsi aberrare ad alia coeperit, ad haec revocetur oratio. On
striking a balance between making things clear to an audience and boring people by labouring a point, cf. Aug. *Doctr.*
Chr. 4.11.67–71.

oratio pura simplex dilucida . . . sed non intermissa
gratia: Purity, simplicity, clarity, and dignity must characterize one's language; cf. 2.112–20; 3.76; especially *Ep.* 36
[2]; *Virg.* 1.41; cf. also *Luc.* 2.42. According to Cic. *Off.*
1.132, the same basic rules about *verba sententiaeque* apply to
both oratory and conversation; on using everyday language,
cf. Cic. *Off.* 1.111; on pure and clear diction (not specified in
Cic. *Off.*), cf. Cic. *De Or.* 3.38–51; *Or.* 99; Quint. *Inst.*
11.3.30. On keeping vocabulary clear and simple (albeit
with stylistic variation), cf. Aug. *Doctr. Chr.* 4.10.64–11.73.

CHAPTER 23: ON AVOIDING JOKES, AND THE
CORRECT TONE OF VOICE

102.   Multa praeterea de ratione dicendi dant praecepta
saeculares viri . . . ut de iocandi disciplina: An oblique
reference to Cic., who speaks of *praecepta* of speech in *Off.*
1.132, and deals with *ratio dicendi* in *Off.* 1.132–7. Cic.
discusses joking in *Off.* 1.103–4, though in connection with
the *decorum* and human nature, not the *decorum* and speech.
The subject is clearly congenial to Cic. as an orator (cf. *De*
Or. 2.216–90; *Or.* 87–90; also Quint. *Inst.* 6.3). He advocates
moderation in the use of humour, and advises that where
jokes are used they need to be indicative of good character—
i.e. be in good taste—and genuinely witty. In *Off.* 1.134, Cic.
asserts that *lepos* should be applied if conversation is *de rebus*
iocosis; but he also warns of the dangers of insulting people in
order to raise a laugh. A. maintains that joking is unbecoming for clerics: **quae nobis praetereunda arbitror . . . ab**
ecclesiastica abhorrent regula. For Christian warnings
about laughter and joking, cf. e.g. Eph. 5: 4; Clem. Alex.
Paid. 2.5–6; Bas. *Ep.* 2.2; *Reg. Brev.* 31; *Const. Monach.* 12;
Salv. *Gub. Dei* 7.1.6; Bened. *Reg.* 6.8; see also T. Baconsky,
Le Rire des Pères. Essai sur le rire dans la patristique grecque
(Paris, 1996). For all the pastoral intimacy of his preaching

style, A. strikes most modern readers as a fairly serious character himself, though he allows himself the orator's luxury of making regular verbal puns: cf. *Exc. fr.* 1.10; *Ep.* 75a [*C. Aux.*].33; *Epp.* 43 [3].2; 12 [30].15; 26 [54].1; 58 [60].1; 24 [82].12; 42 [88].1; *Ep. extra coll.* 14 [63].107 (Homes Dudden i. 115 n. 3). On **arbitror** here and in 1.103–4, cf. 1.74.

Nam licet interdum honesta ioca ac suavia sint: Cf. Cic., *Off.* 1.103, on keeping jokes compatible with *honestas*. Quint. *Inst.* 6.3.20 alludes to Horace's prescription that comment must be *molle atque facetum* (*Sat.* 1.10.44–5) (on which see M. B. Ogle in *AJPh* 37 (1916), 327–32).

quae in scripturis non repperimus, ea quemadmodum usurpare possumus?: A major key to A.'s perspective. Scripture is the supreme source of his teaching: if a principle cannot be found outlined or illustrated there, he claims, it cannot be utilized. The **ecclesiastica regula** is determined by the parameters of Scripture (Toscani, 94–146); cf. 1.3, and, for the strategy in action, 1.25, 30, 36–7, 221, 223–4; 2.23–7. The Ciceronian material which remains is thus implicitly validated by this authority.

103. in fabulis: Anecdotes which illustrate a moral point; *fabulae* of an improper kind are condemned in 1.86, 88.

gravitatem severioris: Reminiscent of Cic.'s language in *Off.* 1.103, 134, 136–7.

Vae vobis qui ridetis, quia flebitis!: Lk. 6: 25.

illic fleamus: The wicked will weep with anguish in hell (Mt. 8: 12; 22: 13; 24: 51; 25: 30; Lk. 13: 28). On **hic . . . illic**, cf. 1.29, 58, 147, 238–40; 3.11, 36.

Non solum profusos sed omnes etiam iocos declinandos arbitror: A. goes further than Cic. who says: *Ipsumque genus iocandi non profusum nec immodestum . . . esse debet* (*Off.* 1.103), but allows joking that is *ingenuus et facetus*; on the classical background, see S. Halliwell, 'The Uses of Laughter in Greek Culture', *CQ* 85 (1991), 279–96; E. S. Ramage, *Urbanitas: Ancient Sophistication and Refinement* (Norman, OK, 1973), 53–64, especially 56–8.

nisi forte plenum urbanitatis . . . non indecorum est: [**urbanitatis:** in support of this conjecture in place of the equally implausible *gravitatis*, followed by Testard, or CO's *suavitatis*, Cic. has *urbanum* in *Off.* 1.104 (Winterbottom, 562)] Although jokes in general are to be avoided, a certain refined pleasantry is nevertheless desirable in clerical discourse; on *urbanitas*, cf. generally Quint. *Inst.* 6.3.17 (and 11.3.30).

104. Nam de voce quid loquar?: Cf. already 1.67, 84

simplicem et puram: Cf. 1.75, 93, 101; 2.112–20; 3.76.

canoram: In Cic. *Off.* 1.133, *canora* is used pejoratively of the voice (cf. Quint. *Inst.* 11.3.170; A. *Ep.* 15 [69].3), whereas here (as in Cic. *Brut.* 234, 247, 268, 303; *De Or.* 3.28; Tac. *Ann.* 4.61) it is not; cf. *Ex.* 6.67. A. implies that this sonorous quality is a gift of nature which some possess and others do not, rather than something which can be worked up.

naturae est, non industriae: Cic. says in *Off.* 1.133 that clarity and attractiveness of voice are natural gifts, but he also maintains that *exercitatio* can improve the first of them, while the second will develop by imitating people who speak distinctly and gently; cf. *Or.* 58–9. A.'s memory of Cic. is not too clear, and he implies a distinction between pleasantness of voice, which is purely natural, and clarity and simplicity of voice, which can be practised. Earlier, he does commend the application of *industria*, in connection with bodily movement (1.75), and he speaks of the need for practice or exercise to restrain our natural tendency to speak out (1.32–3).

et plena suci virilis, ut agrestem ac subrusticum fugiat sonum: Cf. Cic. *Off.* 1.129: *Quibus in rebus duo maxime sunt fugienda, ne quid effeminatum aut molle et ne quid durum aut rusticum sit.* On **suci virilis**, see on 1.84; also Introduction VII (ii). Cic. also uses *sonus* in *Off.* 1.133.

rhythmum . . . scaenicum: An affected kind of delivery, appropriate to the stage; cf. the condemnation of histrionic gait in 1.73; and see ad loc. The condemnation of theatricality is perhaps a swipe at Cic. who commends the modesty of *scaenicorum mos* in *Off.* 1.129.

mysticum: A tone of voice which is appropriate to a solemn approach to the mysteries of the faith—the Scriptures and the sacraments (cf. generally 1.251).

CHAPTER 24: SEEMLINESS OF ACTION;
INTRODUCTION TO THE CARDINAL VIRTUES

105. De ratione dicendi satis dictum puto; nunc de actione vitae . . . . Tria autem in hoc genere spectanda cernimus: Having completed his remarks about the *decorum* in speech (1.99–104), A. moves on to discuss the *decorum* in *actio* (1.105–14). This new section is inspired by Cic. *Off.* 1.141–2 (**cernimus** points the allusion), where Cic. summarizes the criteria to be observed to ensure the *decorum* in action, as he has outlined them in *Off.* 1.126–40. A., however, treats Cic.'s summary as a *divisio* of material to be dealt with in the paragraphs which follow, and he attempts to illustrate Cic.'s points with biblical *exempla*. Cf. Cic. *Off.* 1.141: *In omni autem actione suscipienda tria sunt tenenda, primum ut appetitus rationi pareat, quo nihil est ad officia conservanda accommodatius, deinde ut animadvertatur quanta illa res sit quam efficere velimus, ut neve maior neve minor cura et opera suscipiatur quam causa postulet. Tertium est ut caveamus ut ea quae pertinent ad liberalem speciem et dignitatem moderata sint.* A. retains Cic.'s first two points more or less as they are, but rephrases the third point, replacing the classical concern for moderation in the appearance and status of a gentleman with the general theme of moderation of *studia operaque*. In 1.106, he explains that Cic.'s third feature (which he does not mention there) is irrelevant *apud nos*. The *dignitas* of which Cic. speaks had already taken on pejorative overtones by the time of Augustan Latin (the shift in the connotations of *dignitas* is the exact reverse of the change in the meaning of *humilitas* between classical and Christian Latin); A. equates it with a haughty demeanour which is unbecoming for the Christian. **De ordine quoque rerum . . . non dissimulandum puto:** Cf. Cic. *Off.* 1.142: *Deinceps de ordine rerum et de opportunitate temporum dicendum est.*

106. Sed primum illud quasi fundamentum est omnium, ut appetitus rationi pareat: A. agrees with Cic. on the prime importance of impulse obeying reason:

cf. Cic. *Off.* 1.141: *Horum tamen trium praestantissimum est appetitum obtemperare rationi*; also *Off.* 1.102.

Secundum et tertium idem est, hoc est in utroque moderatio: A reasonable simplification of Cic.'s third and fourth points: the observance of measure is the essential note in both cases.

Vacat enim apud nos . . . dignitatis contemplatio: The standard antithesis of the Ciceronian principle and the attitude that is appropriate **apud nos**; for the point, see on 1.105. De Romestin erroneously translates **Vacat . . . apud nos** as 'There is room with us' (a common meaning of this originally poetic construction), but this gives the opposite sense to what A. intends; an aspect of the third Ciceronian point is being dismissed rather than acknowledged to be possible for Christians.

Sequitur de ordine rerum . . . in aliquo sanctorum consummata possimus docere: A misunderstanding, presumably because A.'s memory of the classical text is faulty. Cic. lists three points in *Off.* 1.141, as outlined in 1.105 above. At the start of *Off.* 1.142, Cic. has *de ordine rerum et de opportunitate temporum*, but he does not make this a fourth point: instead, he introduces the phrase with a disjunctive, *deinceps*. At the end of 1.105, A. introduces *de ordine . . . rerum* with a *quoque*, without suggesting that it is supplementary to the scheme of the *tria* mentioned above. Here, though, it is clear that he does conceive of it as a separate point. Having merged Cic.'s second and third points, he still manages to have three in all. The contrived attempt to illustrate these points with scriptural *exempla* turns out to be pretty haphazard. 1.110 appears to return to a four-point scheme, as in 1.105 (and perhaps also alludes to the tetrad of the cardinal virtues); 1.111 has three points, 1.112 and 1.114 allude to two, and 1.113 has none at all (I expand on the feature noted by Testard, 'Etude', 167–8 n. 22).

107. pater Abraham: A standard designation of the patriarch, based, of course, on the root of his name ('father'): e.g. Josh. 24: 3; Is. 51: 2; Lk. 1: 73; Jn. 8: 39–58; Acts 7: 2; Rom. 4: 1–25; Jas. 2: 21.

qui ad magisterium futurae successionis informatus

et instructus est: The role of the patriarch is exemplary; God dealt with him as he did in order to instruct the faithful of later times (cf. Rom. 4: 16–25; Gal. 3: 6–29). On **informatus et instructus est,** cf. 1.246, *informatus atque institutus est.* On Abraham as practical exemplar in *Off.*, see generally R. Berton, 'Abraham dans le *De officiis ministrorum* d'Ambroise', *RSR* 54 (1980), 311–22.

iussus exire de terra sua . . . et de domo patris sui: See Gen. 12: 1–5, especially 12: 1.

Quem enim terrae suae . . . non delectaret?: On A.'s patriotism, see on 1.144.

uxorem: Sarai.

Deinde cum descenderet . . . non uxorem ipsius: See Gen. 12: 10–20. The deception was an act of self-preservation on Abraham's (Abram's) part: if Pharaoh was to add Sarai to his harem as Abram's wife, he would have to kill Abram first (cf. also Gen. 20).

108. Note the series of perfect tenses (**praevaluit . . . consideravit . . . vicit . . . praestitit**) after the imperfects (**timebat . . . timebat . . . habebat**): A. presents Abraham's wise decision to obey reason as an instinctive response in the midst of his continuing problems. Abraham is pictured almost as a prototypical *pius Aeneas*, setting out faithfully in pursuit of his own and his people's destiny, checking sexual passion (though not his own) and facing great dangers in obedience to a divine command.

ratio exsequendae devotionis: The basis of Abraham's rationality is his obedience to God; the Stoic *ratio* of which Cic. speaks is reformulated as an attitude of faith. Elsewhere, A. can commend Abraham for exercising faith *instead of* looking at his circumstances rationally (*Abr.* 1.21).

Dei favore ubique tutus esse potest: He who follows God is always safe: cf. *Abr.* 1.9.

109. Capto nepote . . . recusavit: [**repetit:** PVMA, EW, O: *repetiit* Testard: *recepit* CB] The seizure of Lot by Kedorlaomer and his confederates led to a revenge-attack by Abraham to recover Lot and his possessions (Gen. 14: 8–24).

Promisso quoque sibi filio . . . contra usum naturae Deo credidit: God's promise of Isaac (Gen. 15: 1–6; 17: 15–22; 18: 1–15), despite Sarai's age/sterility (Gen. 11: 30; 16: 1;

17: 17; 18: 11–15) and Abraham's centenarianism (Gen. 17: 17). A. omits any mention of Sarai's and Abraham's scheme to have a son by the servant-girl Hagar (Gen. 16), and of their laughter at the promise of a second son in their old age (Gen. 17: 17; 18: 12–15): only the positive side is highlighted. **Deo credidit** is emphatically placed at the end of the sentence, after the mention of all the obstacles to Abraham's faith; cf. Gen. 15: 6; Rom. 4: 3–25; Gal. 3: 6–29; Jas. 2: 23.

110. **Adverte convenire omnia:** All the points of 1.105.

nec magna pro vilibus nec minora pro magnis duceret: Abraham's belief in God's great promises, on the one hand, and his leaving home and father's house (Gen. 12: 1–5) and rejecting material gain (Gen. 14: 21–4), on the other.

Fide primus, iustitia praecipuus: Abraham's faith was 'credited to him as *iustitia*' (Gen. 15: 6; Rom. 4: 3, 9, 22; Gal. 3: 6; Jas. 2: 23). Biblically, *iustitia* embraces not only 'justice' but 'righteousness', the condition of moral rectitude which is indispensable to a right standing with God: the two are linked both semantically and theologically, in both OT and NT (G. Schrenk in *TDNT* ii. 192–210). A. repeatedly elides this biblical framework with the Ciceronian sense of *iustitia*, especially in 1.126–9 (and thus helps to strengthen Western theology's already firm preoccupation with justification as a juridical phenomenon).

in proelio strenuus, in victoria non avarus: See Gen. 14: 15–24.

domi hospitalis: See Gen. 18: 1–15.

uxori sedulus: Perhaps A. thinks that the deceptions about Sarai's status were an act of care on Abraham's part (Gen. 12: 10–20; Gen. 20); or possibly he has in mind Abraham's acquiescence in Sarai's plan for her husband to have a son by Hagar (Gen. 16: 2—but given the silence about this in 1.109, it seems less likely).

Overall, he appears to hint at the four cardinal virtues here, in anticipation of the introductory summary in 1.115: the reference to Abraham's faith implies that he showed prudence; *iustitia* is mentioned explicitly; **in proelio strenuus** suggests courage; and **in victoria non avarus** points to temperance (Steidle, 'Beobachtungen', 42); see further on 1.115.

111. Sanctum quoque . . . fraternae iracundiae locum: See Gen. 27: 1–45, and on 1.91 above.

Acceptus domi parentibus . . . alter amore pio propenderet: See Gen. 27: 1–40.

fraterno quoque iudicio praelatus . . . secundum pietatem cessit petito: See Gen. 25: 29–34, for the famous account of Esau selling his birthright for 'a mess of pottage'. But A. garnishes the story considerably: Jacob made Esau swear to give him his birthright before he handed over the food; there is not much evidence of Esau's *pietas* in that. The chronology presented here is also not faithful to the Gen. narrative: Jacob usurped the blessing before he left home. A. cites at random various incidents from Jacob's life, to build up a case.

Pastor domino gregis fidus . . . in labore impiger: See Gen. 29: 1–30, on Jacob's hard service for his uncle Laban, by whom he was duped into working for fourteen years rather than the originally agreed seven to earn Rachel as his wife.

in convivio parcus: The allusion is uncertain. Jacob was evidently none too sparing in his drinking habits, at least: on his first wedding-night he managed not to notice that he had been given Leah, not Rachel, as his wife (Gen. 29: 21–5).

in satisfactione praevius, in remuneratione largus: Jacob's reparations to Esau: Gen. 32: 3–21; 33: 1–17.

cuius verebatur inimicitias: A reality not mentioned by A. in his portrayal of the story in 1.91.

adipisceretur gratiam: Cf. Gen. 33: 8, 10, 15.

The Ciceronian language is again worked in: **Vicit appetitum . . . mensuram . . . temporibus opportunitatem**: this time, A. appears to have just the three points of 1.106, as compared with the four of 1.105 as applied in 1.110.

112. Quid de Ioseph loquar . . . officii sui moderatione dispensans: Here the sequence does follow the chronology of Gen. (Testard i. 247–8 n. 11). For Joseph's servitude, chastity, incarceration, wise interpretation of dreams, rise to political power, and prudent management of grain harvests, see Gen. 37; 39–50, *passim*.

virtute constans: Perhaps a reference to Joseph's chastity, and so A. thinks of reason governing appetite (the first point of 1.105–6), though he does not say so.

moderatus . . . ordinem rebus . . . et opportunitatem temporibus . . . moderatione: [The MSS have *laudis* between **ordinem** and **rebus**, but the word is both redundant in the context and ruled out by the Ciceronian evocation (Winterbottom, 562)] An attempt to bring in the third and fourth points of 1.105, or the second and third points of 1.106.

113. **Iob quoque . . . se consolabatur:** This time, no reference at all is made to the Ciceronian points; A. simply summarizes Job's virtues as those of another biblical hero; see e.g. Job 1: 1–2: 10.

114. **David etiam fortis in bello:** See e.g. 1 Ki. 17; 2 Ki. 8: 1–14; 1 Chr. 18: 1–13.

patiens in adversis: Such as when pursued by Saul (1 Ki. 19 ff.); during the conspiracy of Absalom (2 Ki. 15 ff.); and when abused by Shimei (2 Ki. 16: 5–14).

in peccato dolens: Especially in the aftermath of his sin with Bathsheba (2 Ki. 11: 2–12: 23, especially 12: 13–23; Ps. 50); also after taking the census in Israel (2 Ki. 24, especially 24: 10, 17; 1 Chr. 21, especially 21: 8, 17).

rerum modos, vices temporum: Alluding to two of the points of 1.105–6. David observed the particular duties of each phase of his life. A. evokes the Panaetian principle of different ages and circumstances requiring different manifestations of virtue; see on 1.65, 213–16. Note the deliberate use of a musical image (**sonos**, and probably **temporum** as well) here with reference to the psalmist David (**canendi suavitate . . . sui fudisse meriti cantilenam**); David also met the Ciceronian criteria for the voice: cf. *Off.* 1.133.

115. **Quod his viris virtutum principalium officium defuit?:** The scheme of the four cardinal virtues, prudence, justice, courage, and temperance: A. at last comes to the real philosophical meat of book 1. 1.115–21 seeks to exemplify the virtues from a series of OT *exempla maiorum*; for a related synthesis, cf. 1.251. This is done partly in order to justify the scheme from Scripture, and partly because the author realizes he has taken a long time to reach this point

(1.116). He wants to show the relevance of the foregoing chapters by demonstrating that the OT exemplars of the *decorum* also show us the four virtues in action.

primo loco constituerunt prudentiam . . . infundit cupiditatem: Cf. Cic. *Off.* 1.15: *Sed omne quod est honestum, id quattuor partium oritur ex aliqua. Aut enim in perspicientia veri sollertiaque versatur . . . velut ex ea parte quae prima descripta est, in qua sapientiam et prudentiam ponimus, inest indagatio atque inventio veri, eiusque virtutis hoc munus est proprium*; 1.16: *Quocirca huic quasi materia quam tractet et in qua versetur subiecta est veritas*; 1.18: *primus ille, qui in veri cognitione consistit, maxime naturam attingit humanam. Omnes enim trahimur et ducimur ad cognitionis et scientiae cupiditatem*; 1.19: *quae omnes artes in veri investigatione versantur. . . . Omnis autem cogitatio motusque animi aut . . . aut in studiis scientiae cognitionisque versabitur.*

secundo iustitiam . . . communem aequitatem custodiat: Cf. Cic. *Off.* 1.15: *aut in hominum societate tuenda tribuendoque suum cuique et rerum contractarum fide*; 1.20: *latissime patet ea ratio qua societas hominum inter ipsos et vitae quasi communitas continetur*; *Sed iustitiae primum munus est ut ne cui quis noceat, nisi lacessitus iniuria, deinde ut communibus pro communibus utatur, privatis ut suis.*

tertio fortitudinem . . . corporisque praestat viribus: Cf. Cic. *Off.* 1.15: *aut in animi excelsi atque invicti magnitudine ac robore*; 1.79: *Omnino illud honestum quod ex animo excelso magnificoque quaerimus animi efficitur, non corporis viribus. Exercendum tamen corpus et ita adficiendum est ut oboedire consilio rationique possit.*

quarto temperantiam . . . quae vel agenda vel dicenda arbitramur: Cf. Cic. *Off.* 1.15: *aut in omnium quae fiunt quaeque dicuntur ordine et modo, in quo inest modestia et temperantia*; 1.17: *Iis enim rebus quae tractantur in vita modum quendam et ordinem adhibentes, honestatem et decus conservabimus.*

A. thus gives a résumé of Cic.'s definitions of the cardinal virtues from *Off.* 1.15 ff. The first definition is, however, somewhat oversimplified. Cic. in fact stresses that prudence is the investigation of the truth with a view to action, and he condemns dogmatism and the study of abstruse subjects—

doubtless anxious to ensure that Marcus and his peers do not
lose sight of the importance of their public careers by paying
too much attention to the wrong kind of intellectual pursuits
(*Off.* 1.18–19). Also, Cic. does not, unlike A., rank prudence
primo loco (he allocates that place to justice): he asserts
only that prudence is the virtue that touches human nature
most closely (*Off.* 1.18), and says that it is first in his
description of the virtues (*Off.* 1.15) and the first *officii fons*
(*Off.* 1.19). A. goes on to exceed Cic.'s definitions of the
virtues in at least the first two cases: for him, prudence is the
knowledge of God by faith (1.122–9), and justice is more
than the Platonist–Aristotelian–Stoic *suum cuique* formula: it
is Christian charity, above all, in which the significance of
intention is crucial (1.130–74). Courage and temperance
(especially the latter) remain more obviously Stoic than the
first two virtues, but A. gives biblical orientation to them,
and, in the case of courage, seeks to downplay the military
side as irrelevant to his clerical addressees (1.175–9; though
cf. 1.196–201).

A canon of four principal virtues can be traced back to the
fifth century BC at least. The first definitive formulation
comes, possibly under Pythagorean-Orphic influence, in
Plat. *Rep.* 427eff. where the ideal State is said to require
the four qualities of wisdom, courage, self-control, and
justice. Ultimately rejected by Aristotle, the Socratic tetrad
was revived above all by the Stoics: Zeno linked the scheme
to his conviction that virtue is a unified whole; to be inclined
towards virtue *per se* is to be inclined towards all its aspects
(e.g. DL 7.92). By A.'s time, the Greek church had an
established tradition of exploiting the scheme, particularly
in Platonist form, to conceptualize the ideals of asceticism
and the ascent of the soul; the influence of Philo's work in
this process was significant, as was an allusion to the tetrad in
Wisd. 8: 7 (part of which A. quotes in 2.65), which doubtless
helped to convince Christians of its enduring validity. See
e.g. C. J. Classen, 'Der platonisch-stoische Kanon der
Kardinaltugenden bei Philon, Clemens Alexandrinus und
Origenes', in A. M. Ritter (ed.), *Kerygma und Logos:
Festschrift Carl Andresen* (Göttingen, 1979), 68–88.

A., one of the great pioneers of the scheme in the West,

draws heavily on Cic.'s extensive use of the virtues in his philosophical writings, but elsewhere he also assimilates ideas from Philo and from Greek Christian authorities. It is in fact A. who first gives the four their conventional name: *virtutes cardinales* (*Exc. fr.* 1.57; *Luc.* 5.49, 62; *Sacr.* 3.9). For him, there is great significance in the Stoic premiss that there is an essential unity and interconnection between the virtues (1.115, 119–21, 126–9, 176, 251; 2.43, 49, 65–6, 84; 3.14; cf. *Parad.* 14, 22; *Expos. Ps. 118.11.11*; *Exc. fr.* 1.57; *Virgt.* 113–14; *Luc.* 3.47; 5.63). In *Parad.* 14–23 (cf. *Expl. Ps. 35.21*; *Expl. Ps. 45.12*; *Abr.* 2.68), he follows Philo's exegesis (e.g. *Leg. Alleg.* 1.63 ff.; *Quaest. Gen.* 1.12) that the four rivers of paradise in Gen. 2 are symbolic: Phison represents prudence, Gihon temperance, Tigris fortitude, and Euphrates justice; the tetrad also signifies the four ages of the world: from creation to the flood is the age of prudence, the time of the patriarchs is that of temperance, the age of Moses and the prophets is that of fortitude, and the era of the gospel is that of justice. In *Luc.* 5.49–50, 62–8, he argues that the four Beatitudes of Lk. 6: 20–2 signify temperance, justice, prudence, and fortitude, respectively (borrowing from Greg. Nyss. *Beat.*); while in *Sacr.* 3.8–10 (at 3.9) he describes the seven gifts of the Spirit in Is. 11: 2 as *istae quasi cardinales . . . quasi principales* (cf. *Ep.* 31[44].3; *Spir.* 1.179). In *Abr.* 2.53–4; *Is.* 65; and *Virgt.* 94–7, 113–14, there is a fusion of the tetrad with images such as those of the four celestial creatures of Ezek. 1, Plato's notion of the chariot of the soul (known to A. from Apuleius, if not from Plato himself), and the chariot mentioned in Ct. 6: 11; a similar synthesis can be found in Origen and Jerome (J. Préaux, 'Les Quatres vertus païennes et chrétiennes. Apothéose et ascension', in J. Bibauw (ed.), *Hommages à Marcel Renard* (Brussels, 1969), i. 639–57). In *Exc. fr.* 1.42–62, A. seeks to demonstrate how Satyrus exemplified each of the cardinal virtues (see Biermann, 67–81); for other references, cf. *Cain* 2.21; *Iac.* 2.43; *Expos. Ps. 118.11.11*. The synthesis of scriptural teaching with the cardinal virtues remains prominent in numerous passages of Jerome and Augustine (especially *Mor. Eccl.* 25–47), and in a succession of medieval writers, who increasingly aspire to merge the tetrad with the three 'theological virtues' of faith, hope, and charity (1 Cor. 13: 13): Dante celebrates the victory of the triad (*Purg.* 8.88–93), though later he pictures both schemes together (*Purg.* 29.121–32).

From a mass of literature, see e.g. J. Ferguson, *Moral Values in the Ancient World* (London, 1958), 24–52; H. North, *Sophrosyne: Self-Knowledge and Self-Restraint in Greek Literature* (Ithaca, NY, 1966), *passim*; ead. 'Canons and Hierarchies of the Cardinal Virtues in Greek and Latin Literature', in L. Wallach (ed.), *The Classical Tradition: Literary and Historical Studies in Honor of Harry Caplan* (Ithaca, NY, 1966), 165–83; J. Pieper, *Das Vier-gespann. Klugheit, Gerechtigkeit, Tapferkeit, Mass* (Munich, 1964); further Western patristic references can be traced in PL 120 (index 3), 630–8. On A., see generally Biermann, 60–7; Löpfe, 129–46; on *Off.*, Becker, 15–212, supersedes all previous studies, such as V. T. Tanzola, 'A Comparative Study of the Cardinal Virtues in Cicero's De Officiis and in St Ambrose's De Officiis Ministrorum', Ph.D. Diss. (Catholic University of America, 1975)—a dry and sometimes inaccurate analysis; P. Circis, *The Ennoblement of the Pagan Virtues: A Comparative Treatise on Virtues in Cicero's Book De Officiis and in St Ambrose's Book De Officiis Ministrorum* (Rome, 1955)—a highly tendentious account; Colish ii. 62–70.

CHAPTER 25: THE CARDINAL VIRTUES IN THE
LIVES OF THE SAINTS

116. Haec forsitan aliquis dicat . . . nascuntur officiorum genera: Any reader with a passing knowledge of Cic. will realize how different the structure of A.'s argument so far in book 1 has been. In *Off.* 1.7, Cic. says it is necessary to define duty (*Placet igitur, quoniam omnis disputatio de officio futura est, ante definire quid sit officium*), but what he proceeds to offer is a breakdown of the ways in which the topic has been dealt with, and an explanation of the route that he will take himself (*Off.* 1.7–10). He goes on to assert the connection between the *honestum* and human nature (*Off.* 1.11–17), and then launches straight into the exposition of the cardinal virtues (*Off.* 1.18 ff.), which he has already introduced in *Off.* 1.15–17. Duty is not 'defined' as such until *Off.* 1.101, and then only in rough terms: *Omnis autem actio vacare debet temeritate et neglegentia, nec vero agere quicquam cuius non possit causam probabilem reddere; haec est enim fere descriptio officii*; many editors regard these sentences as an interpolation, echoing *Fin.* 3.58 (Dyck, 261–3). A. too has nowhere 'defined' duty; but he has made it clear that a right relationship with God is pivotal to right behaviour (1.1; cf. 1.28–9, 36–9), and he has gone to some lengths to show how closely God is involved in the sphere of human activity (1.40–64). The thematic division of Cic. *Off.* 1.7–10, has been sandwiched in the midst of all this, in 1.27, followed by A.'s dissent from the classical conceptions of the *honestum* and the *utile* in 1.28. The present passage does not directly evoke Cic. *Off.* 1.101 (but cf. 1.229 below); A. is thinking more of Cic. *Off.* 1.7, since he has just taken the scheme of the cardinal virtues from this introductory section of Cic. No definition follows (1.26, evoking Cic. *Off.* 1.7 on *ratio*, gives a capsule explanation of the word *officium*: *ut ea agas quae nulli officiant, prosint omnibus* (cf. Cic. *Off.* 1.43), but this hardly contains all that A. would mean by 'defining' duty). To seek philosophical definitions is to be preoccupied with an *ars* in which A. affects to have no interest. The course followed so far is better, A. suggests, because it has been centred on the practical examples of Scripture, which demonstrate duty in action— true duty, founded on faith in God. Perhaps he does implicitly admit that his own structure is less clear than Cic.'s, as Testard, 'Etude', 168, 190–1 n. 79, thinks: but the main point is that he knows it may *look* less clear, or disappointing, to those who expect close adherence to the Ciceronian lines, so he endeavours to explain why he has taken a different path, and to show the relevance of his focus on Scripture thus far.

Nos autem artem fugimus: For the typical antithesis of **nos autem** after the allusion to Cic. cf. 1.27–9; on the disavowal of *ars*, cf. 1.29.

exempla maiorum proponimus: Cf. 3.139; *Ios.* 1: *Sanctorum vita ceteris norma vivendi est*; and see Introduction IV.4. On **speculum**, cf. *Ios.* 2, of Joseph as *tamquam speculum castitatis.*

A string of pejoratives emphasizes the simplicity and the superior spiritual worth of the biblical illustrations to the pagan approach: **obscuritatem . . . ad intellegendum . . . ad tractandum versutias . . . calliditatis commentarium . . . disputandi astutia.** Cf. 2.8, 49; and generally *Ex.* 1.9; *Ep.* 55 [8].1.

117. primo loco: As in 1.115, A. alludes to Cic.'s description of prudence as 'first' (*Off.* 1.15, 18, 19), but A. means 'first in importance' (as in 1.126), whereas Cic. means 'first in order of treatment', as Hagendahl, 351 n. 1, rightly says. (*Primo loco* in 1.116 seems to be just a coincidental use of the same phrase, without the connotations carried by the words in 1.115 and 1.117.)

Credidit Abraham Deo . . . ad iustitiam: Gen. 15: 6.

Nemo enim prudens qui Dominum nescit: The knowledge of God is the key to wisdom; cf. 1.1; 2.46–7; *Ep.* 7 [37].29. This formulation of prudence cuts across the learned research prized by classical thinkers (cf. 1.122–5). Cic. plays down the relevance of speculative wisdom (*sapientia*—σοφία), in accordance with his emphasis on practical good sense (*prudentia*—φρόνησις) (*Off.* 1.18–19; cf. 1.153). He consistently ranks justice above speculative wisdom; though *sapientia* is, strictly, the most important virtue, justice is the most important duty (*Off.* 1.153). A. does not observe this distinction between *sapientia* and *prudentia*, as the present paragraph indicates (cf. also 1.118–21; 1.123–4 with 1.126, 129). He draws on the Wisdom tradition, where *sapientia* predominates but *prudentia* is also used (cf. e.g. the combination of the two in Prov. 3: 13; 5: 1). He shares Cic.'s regard for practical *prudentia*, but he uses the term synonymously with *sapientia* under the influence of the Bible; Sauer, 67–74. The wisdom reflected in spiritual faith gives a person instinctive good sense in the affairs of life.

Denique insipiens dixit quia *non est Deus*: The atheist cf. Pss. 13: 1; 52: 1.

qui dicit lapidi: *Pater meus es tu*: The pagan idol-worshipper: cf. Jer. 2: 27. See also on 1.122.

qui dicit diabolo ut Manichaeus: 'Auctor meus es tu': Manichaeism, founded by the Syro-Persian Mani (216–76), assumed a dualist cosmic system. In a primordial battle, the Kingdom of Light had been invaded by the Kingdom of Darkness, but Darkness had then been duped into swallowing particles of Light, which are now imprisoned in all living things. By a process of *gnosis*, the soul can be awakened as to its divine origins, and released from its place in a corrupt and evil body (see M. Tardieu, *Le Manichéisme* (Paris, 1983), especially 94–112; S. N. C. Lieu, *Manichaeism in the Later Roman Empire and Medieval China: A Historical Survey*, 2nd edn. (Tübingen, 1992)). The Manichee who says that his body is evil, or 'the demon', is, in A.'s eyes, claiming that the devil, not God, is his *auctor*. In reality, God is the creator of matter (*Ex.* 1.5), but he is not responsible for evil (*Ex.* 1.30–1), despite all the problems the flesh causes the spirit. For further hostile references to Manichaeism, cf. *Ex.* 3.32; *Apol. alt.* 72; *Luc.* 8.13; *Fid.* 1.57; 2.44; 3.57; 5.104; *Inc.* 8; *Ep.* 69 [72].10; and see F. De Capitani, 'Studi su sant'Ambrogio e il Manichei: I. Occasioni di un incontro', *RFN* 74 (1982), 596–610; 'II. Spunti antimanichei nell' Exameron ambrosiano', *RFN* 75 (1983), 3–29.

ut Arianus . . . verum atque perfectum: Arius, presbyter of Alexandria (*c*.256–*c*.336), had taught that God was uniquely divine and eternal in essence whereas Christ, though the special servant of the Father, was a creature with a beginning, whose dignity was derivative and dependent upon the Father's will (R. Williams, *Arius: Heresy and Tradition* (London, 1987)). A. tends to blur the distinctions between Arius himself and the numerous 'Arianisms' which emerged in the course of the fourth century; like Athanasius in the East and Hilary of Poitiers in the West before him, he deliberately associates the theology of his opponents with the name of a figure who had been notoriously condemned (see M. R. Barnes and D. H. Williams (eds.), *Arianism after Arius: Essays on the Development of the Fourth-Century Trinitarian Conflicts* (Edinburgh, 1993), especially part I). To A., the 'Arians' may be divided among themselves (a mark of their confusion), but all alike are heretics, propagating an erroneous and blasphemous view of Christ; cf. *Fid.* 1.44. The real target of his polemic, of course, is on the whole the 'homoian' view that though Christ was not true and perfect God, he was 'like' God the Father, since he owed his being wholly to the Father's will (*Fid.* 1.43 ff.; 2.15 ff.). On Christ as the 'true' God, cf. *Fid.* 5.16 ff.; as the 'good' God, *Fid.* 2.15 ff. (on the context, see R. P. C. Hanson, *The Search for the Christian Doctrine of God* (Edinburgh, 1988), especially 557–97, 667–75; Williams, 128–52; Markschies, 165–212). The abuse here is typical: homoian Christology is plain foolish, because it reduces the creator to an imperfect being.

Marcion: Marcion, from Sinope in Pontus (*c*.80–*c*.160), best known for his views on the canon of Scripture: he rejected the OT as sub-Christian and established the earliest extant list of NT books, comprising a shortened version of Lk. and an edition of ten Pauline epistles. He apparently held that the God of the OT, the creator of the material universe, was a completely different being from the Father of Jesus Christ: the one was a *Demiourgos* God of law and justice, the other a God of mercy and compassion. Marcion's depreciation of the created world is indicative of Gnostic influence; he seems to have moved gradually towards the view that the universe was created not merely by an inferior deity but by Evil itself, out of pre-existent matter. See E. C. Blackman, *Marcion and his Influence* (London, 1948), especially 66–97; for other negative references in A. cf. *Ex.* 1.30; *Expos. Ps. 118*.13.4; *Luc.* 8.13; *Fid.* 2.44; 3.57; 5.104, 162; *Inc.* 8; *Ep.* 69 [72].10.

Eunomius: Eunomius (*c*.330–*c*.394), bishop of Cyzicus, and former pupil of the 'neo-Arian' Aetius of Alexandria, taught that God was uniquely uncaused, ingenerate essence, and that Christ the Son was not generated within the divine nature but immediately produced by the Father: the Son was therefore 'unlike' (ἀνόμοιος) the Father in substance, and only resembled him in so far as he was given creative power to initiate everything else that is. To A., this makes Eunomius' view no better than the Marcionite dualist idea of a perfect deity who stood over against an evil material world. Eunomianism (along with Manichaeism and Photinianism, which denied the pre-existence of Christ) was excluded from the right of free assembly granted by Gratian in 378 (*CTh* 16.5.5; Socr. *HE* 5.2.1; Soz. *HE* 7.1.3; Theod. *HE* 5.2; *Haer. fab.* 4.3), and was condemned several times under Theodosius (*CTh* 16.5.6, 8, 11–13); it was in any case never so popular in the West as in the East. See T. A. Kopecek, *A History of Neo-Arianism*, 2 vols. (Cambridge, MA, 1979), ii. *passim*; R. P. Vaggione, *Eunomius: The Extant Works* (Oxford, 1987); R. P. C. Hanson, *The Search for the Christian Doctrine of God* (Edinburgh, 1988), 611–36; for a reassessment, M. Wiles, 'Eunomius: Hair-Splitting Dialectician or Defender of the Accessibility of Salvation?', in R. Williams (ed.), *The Making of Orthodoxy: Essays in Honour of Henry Chadwick* (Cambridge, 1989), 157–72. For other negative references in A., cf. *Ex.* 2.20; 3.32; *Apol. alt.* 72; *Fid.* 1.44–5, 57; *Inc.* 7.

The list of villains here is typical: cf. *Luc.* 8.13, where the Manichee, Marcion, Arius, and other heretics are pictured as (with the Jews) an evil brotherhood.

Initium enim sapientiae timor Domini: See on 1.1.

Sapientes non declinant . . . in confessionibus suis: Prov. 24: 7 (VL).

Reputatum est ei ad iustitiam: Gen. 15: 6, as above.

alterius virtutis: *iustitia*: Abraham's prudence, evidenced in his faith in God, ensured that he was credited with the second cardinal virtue; see on 1.110.

118. Primi igitur nostri definierunt: The habitual claim that biblical exemplars delineated truth earlier than the classical thinkers: Introduction IV.2.

prudentiam in veri consistere cognitione: Cf. Cic. *Off.* 1.18: *primus ille, qui in veri cognitione consistit* (cf. also *Off.* 1.15); Cic.'s *primus* refers to the sequence of the cardinal virtues.

Abraham, David, Salomonem: Abraham is the main exemplar in these paragraphs. By David, A. means the author of the quotations from Pss.; by Solomon, the author of those from Prov.

iustitiam spectare ad societatem generis humani: [**spectare**: EW, COB: *exspectare* PVMA] Cf. Cic. *Off.*

1.15: *aut in hominum societate tuenda*; *Off.* 1.20: *qua societas hominum inter ipsos et vitae quasi communitas continetur*.

Dispersit, dedit pauperibus, iustitia eius manet in aeternum: Ps. 111: 9.

Iustus miseretur, iustus commodat: Ps. 111: 5.

Sapienti et iusto totus mundus divitiarum est: Prov. 17: 6 (VL). This is one of A.'s favourite verses: cf. 2.66; 3.7; *Abr.* 2.37; *Iac.* 1.37; *Expl. Ps. 48.*17; *Epp.* 10 [38].4; 36 [2].11; *Ep. extra coll.* 14 [63].86–95. He elides the ideal of the Stoic sage who possesses all things with the biblical image of the truly wise person as the one who inherits everlasting treasure through the wisdom of faith and the charitable disposal of possessions in this world; V. R. Vasey, 'Proverbs 17.6b (LXX) and St Ambrose's Man of Faith', *Augustinianum* 14 (1974), 259–76.

Iustus communia pro suis habet, sua pro communibus: A. is echoing, and disagreeing with, Cic. *Off.* 1.20: *deinde ut communibus pro communibus utatur, privatis ut suis*; cf. 1.132–8 below.

Susceperat in senectute filium per repromissionem: Probably evoking Rom. 4: 20, of Abraham's trust in God's promise of a son: *In repromissione etiam Dei non haesitavit diffidentia*. For the Gen. texts, see on 1.109.

reposcenti Domino negandum ad sacificium, quamvis unicum, non putavit: See Gen. 22: 1–19 on the sacrifice of Isaac; cf. also *Abr.* 1.66–79.

119.   **Adverte hic omnes virtutes quattuor in uno facto:** The single incident of the sacrifice of Isaac demonstrates all four virtues.

appetitum ratione cohibere: See on 1.98.

Ducebat hostiam pater . . . meruit ut filium reservaret: The rhetorical build-up of tension and pathos is marked: note the string of short clauses, largely in asyndeton, the use of the imperfect tense, and the climax of the series of **dum** clauses in the decisive **meruit**: Isaac is saved in the nick of time; Abraham's faith is rewarded.

devotionem: On Abraham's *devotio*, cf. *Parad.* 9.

120.   **qui Deum vidit *facie ad faciem*:** Gen. 32: 30, when Jacob wrestled with God in human form at the place he afterwards named *Peniel*, 'face of God' (Gen. 32: 22–32).

qui ea quae acquisierat . . . cum fratre divisit: See on
1.91, 111.

qui cum Deo luctatus est: See Gen. 32: 22–32.

**ut filiae iniuriam mallet praetexere coniugio . . . odia
conligenda censebat:** Jacob's daughter Dinah was raped
by the Hivite, Shechem, but Jacob was prepared to let the
man have her in marriage rather than incur the hatred of the
neighbouring Canaanites and Perizzites by avenging the
outrage (Gen. 34). A. conveniently ignores the sequel:
Shechem and all his fellow-citizens were slaughtered by
Jacob's sons, who took a more direct approach to such
matters. On **praetexere coniugio**, cf. Verg. *Aen.* 4.172
(of Dido): *coniugium vocat, hoc praetexit nomine culpam.*

121.   **qui tantam fabricavit arcam:** See Gen. 6: 9–22; on
the flood, see generally Gen. 6: 1–8: 22.

solus ex omnibus . . . est factus: Not strictly true: Noah's
wife, his three sons, and their wives were also saved in the
ark; cf. *Expos. Ps. 118*.7.15. On Noah's *iustitia*, cf. Gen. 6: 9;
7: 1; 2 Pt. 2: 5.

mundo potius et universis magis quam sibi natus: See
on 1.136.

quando corvum . . . agnoverit: See Gen. 8: 6–12; on its
last excursion, of course, the dove did not return at all. The
MSS' *agnosceret* makes no sense next to **captaret**, and the
quando clauses must be dependent upon a verb of recogni-
tion parallel to **toleraverit**: hence the emendation to **agnoverit** (Winterbottom, 562).

CHAPTER 26: PRUDENCE: THE KNOWLEDGE
OF GOD

The effort to demonstrate the four cardinal virtues together in
the lives of *maiores* (1.116–21) is now over, and A. goes on to
explore each of the virtues in turn. Prudence is covered in
1.122–9. Like Cic. (*Off.* 1.18–19), A. devotes less space to it
than to the other virtues, but unlike Cic. he makes prudence
the source of the other three, in keeping with the perspective
signalled in 1.1. The focus is God-centred: true wisdom comes
from spiritual faith. Yet it is also, typically for A., practical

rather than speculative: the knowledge of God is worked out in good works, in forms of activity which are pleasing to God and which mirror his own character. Do not waste time in abstruse enquiries, the argument goes: know God, and let this higher level of *pietas* be seen to control your immediate *pietas* towards your neighbour. The argument is well summed up by Becker, 38–40.

122. Itaque: Picks up the thread from 1.115, and the plural verbs (**tractant . . . ipsi faciunt . . . probant**) again allude to Cic. and his treatment of the first virtue in *Off.* 1.18–19.

in veri investigatione: The phrase appears in Cic. *Off.* 1.19.

ut summo studio requiramus . . . occupare animum: Cic. warns of two errors in the pursuit of knowledge: *unum ne incognita pro cognitis habeamus hisque temere adsentiamur* (*Off.* 1.18); *Alterum est vitium, quod quidam nimis magnum studium multamque operam in res obscuras atque difficiles conferunt easdemque non necessarias* (*Off.* 1.19). A. evokes Cic.'s first point more closely in 1.123; in the present passage, he replaces *incognita pro cognitis* with **falsa pro veris**, thus instilling a Christian nuance: the findings of human study may be falsehood, as compared with the revealed truths of God; science can be equated with impiety. On the revealed knowledge of God versus speculation, cf. *Ex.* 2.3; 5.86; *Spir.* 3.164; *Paen.* 1.21; *Ep.* 73 [18].7. Cic. is advancing the Stoic view that intellectual enquiry is legitimate only if it contributes to progress in virtue. Excessive inquisitiveness may lead away from the virtuous life; it is practical rather than theoretical knowledge that we need to pursue. The dangers of idle *curiositas* are highlighted in the Platonist tradition as well: Socrates himself shunned irrelevant speculation in favour of practical morality (Xen. *Mem.* 1.1.11–16; Cic. *Tusc.* 5.10–11), and Apuleius repeatedly associates curiosity with sacrilege, an equation which significantly influences Tertullian and, above all, Augustine: A. Labhart, 'Curiositas. Notes sur l'histoire d'un mot et d'une notion', *MH* 17 (1960), 206–24; P. Courcelle, *Les Confessions de saint Augustin dans la tradition littéraire. Antécédents et postérité* (Paris, 1963), 101–9; J. M. Rist,

Augustine: Ancient Thought Baptized (Cambridge, 1994), 140–5; more generally, see P. G. Walsh, 'The Rights and Wrongs of Curiosity (Plutarch to Augustine)', *G&R* 35 (1988), 73–85. Intellectual enquiry needs to be kept within the parameters of a life that is pleasing to God. A. endorses this perspective of both philosophical streams (cf. *Interp.* 1.29; *Paen.* 1.68). The believer should be content to marvel at God's ways in creation, and should not seek to know the inscrutable (on knowing God from creation, cf. *Ex.* 1.9, 17; 2.15; *Fug.* 10; *Luc.* 1.7). But more than this: the believer must not pursue legitimate ends by illegitimate means; even natural science runs the risk of impiety. O'Donnell ii. 150 suggests that the present passage could be an important influence on Augustine (cf. *Conf.* 10.35.54; also 3.2.2). On *curiosius* in the context of prying into holy things, cf. 3.102 below; also 1.251 and see ad loc.

venerari ligna: On the futility of worshipping wooden images carved by one's own hands, cf. e.g. Is. 44: 13–20; 45: 20; Jer. 10: 3–5. The condemnation of idolatry is of course widespread in Christian authors: e.g. Tert. *Apol.* 10– 16.; *Idol.*; Arnob. *Adv. Nat.* 6; Athan. *C. Gent.*; Aug. *Doctr. Chr.* 2.20.74; 2.23.89–90. A.'s hostility is exemplified vividly in his rhetoric over the proposed restoration of the Altar of Victory to the Roman senate-house in 384 (though that *contretemps* and its enduring echoes were about much more than theology; see R. Klein, *Der Streit um den Victoriaaltar: Die dritte Relatio des Symmachus und die Briefe 17 18 und 57 des Mailänder Bischofs Ambrosius* (Darmstadt, 1972); with qualifications by J. J. O'Donnell, 'The Demise of Paganism', *Traditio* 35 (1979), 45–88 at 73–6; K. Rosen, 'Fides contra dissimulationem: Ambrosius und Symmachus im Kampf um den Victoriaaltar', *JbAC* 37 (1994), 29–36: cf. especially *Ep.* 73 [18].2, 9). For other related polemic, cf. 1.240–5 below; also *Ex.* 2.16; *Expl. Ps. 36.28*; *Expos. Ps. 118.8.23*; 10.25; 13.5; *Luc.* 2.75. Cic., who is implicitly the object of the attack here (**quod ipsi faciunt**), was actually opposed to the excesses of *superstitio* (cf. especially *Div.* 2), though he had been pragmatic enough to serve as an augur in 53 BC. Still, for all Cic.'s personal scepticism about aspects of traditional Roman rites, veneration of images was of course a standard element of Roman religion, so A.'s shaft is not without reason.

astronomia et geometria: Cic., *Off.* 1.19, mentions *astrologia* and *geometria*, along with dialectics and civil law (astronomy tended to be seen as at best rather pointless and at worst synonymous with astrology; the terms are used interchangeably: W. Hübner, *Die Begriff 'Astrologie' und 'Astronomie' in der Antike. Wortgeschichte und Wissenschaftssytematik mit einer Hypothese zum Terminus 'Quadrivium'* (Stuttgart and Wiesbaden, 1990); e.g. Cic. *Div.* 2.146; *Verr.* 2.2.129: cf. Aug. *Doctr. Chr.* 2.29.112–14; also Tert. *Idol.* 9; Aug. *Conf.* 4.3.4; 7.6.8; *Doctr. Chr.* 2.21.78–24.95; *Gen. ad litt.* 12.46; *Div. qu.* 45.1; *CD* 5.1–6; *Ev. Ioh.* 7.7. See W. Gundel, 'Astrologie', *RAC* i. 817–31, especially 828–9; M. L. W. Laistner, 'The Western Church and Astrology during the Early Middle Ages', *HThR* 34 (1941), 251–75). In A., cf. *Ex.* 4.12–19; 5.24 (the errors of the Chaldeans: cf. *Abr.* 2.39, 49); *Abr.* 2.9; *Expl. Ps. 36.*28; *Ep.* 69 [72].5. On the inadequacies/errors/reductionism of geometry, cf. A. *Ex.* 2.5; 6.7–8; *Abr.* 2.80; *Expl. Ps. 36.*28; *Ep.* 69 [72].5 (mathematics and geography likewise: *Ex.* 5.24; cf. *Ex.* 1.22; *Expos. Ps. 118.*12.20; *Exc. fr.* 2.86). The tension which remained in the educated mind between the desire to confess the worth of the natural sciences and the obligation to adhere to a Christian *simplicitas* is summed up best by Augustine's pilgrimage. At Cassiciacum, he could conceive of a classical formation as a preparation of the mind to receive higher truth (cf. especially *Ord.* 2). In later years, on the other hand, his view is that there is value in a judicious study of history, geography, natural science, mathematics, logic, and rhetoric, but as a means towards furthering one's understanding of the Scriptures; pagan learning contained plenty of falsehood and superstition, and often involved pointless effort, but had its uses—so long as it was applied to the hermeneutical task of rightly hearing and teaching God's word (*Doctr. Chr.* 2; H. I Marrou's influential work, *Saint Augustin et la fin de la culture antique*, 2nd edn. (Paris, 1949), 331–540, is wrong to see Augustine as evolving here a self-consciously distinct ive Christian 'culture': the *doctrina* Augustine has in mind i essentially the task of teaching Christian wisdom: see R. P. H

Green (ed.), *Augustine, De Doctrina Christiana* (Oxford, 1995), pp. ix–x). But although A. is almost certainly regarded by Augustine as one who rightly despoiled secular learning for higher ends (cf. *Doctr. Chr.* 2.40.146), he himself remains sceptical about the value of such pursuits:

relinquere causas salutis, errores quaerere: The study of the sciences leads away from the most crucial knowledge of all, the knowledge of God himself, and brings one into the **errores** of theories which conflict with Scripture.

123. eruditus in omni sapientia Aegyptiorum Moyses: Acts 7: 22; cf. *Ex.* 1.6; 6.8; *Abr.* 2.73; *Expl. Ps.* 47.21; also *Virgt.* 133 (Madec, 102 n. 14).

detrimentum et stultitiam iudicavit: A conflation of Phil. 3: 8, *existimo omnia detrimentum esse*, and 1 Cor. 3: 19, *sapientia enim huius mundi stultitia est apud Deum*; cf. 2.13.

Deum quaesivit . . . audivit loquentem: Moses saw and conversed with the Lord at the burning bush (Ex. 3: 1–4: 17); on Mt. Sinai (Ex. 19: 1–32: 16; Dt. 5: 4); and in the tent of meeting (Ex. 33: 7–11); the Lord knew him *facie ad faciem* (Dt. 34: 10).

qui omnem Aegyptiorum sapientiam . . . operis sui virtute vacuavit: Moses and Aaron performed certain miracles which the Egyptian magicians could equal (turning staffs into serpents: Ex. 7: 8–13—though Aaron's staff swallowed up the others; changing the waters of Egypt into blood: Ex. 7: 14–24; and bringing a plague of frogs: Ex. 7: 2–8: 15), but the Egyptians could not rival the subsequent plagues that they initiated: Ex. 8: 16–11: 10, especially 8: 16–19; 9: 8–11.

incognita pro cognitis: See on 1.122, on Cic. *Off.* 1.18.

quae duo in hoc maxime naturali atque honesto loco vitanda: Very close to Cic. *Off.* 1.18: *In hoc genere et naturali et honesto duo vitia vitanda sunt.* But A. takes the two clauses of Cic.'s first point as constituting both points one and two.

Non hic incognita pro cognitis habebat hisque temere adsentiebatur: His memory of the Ciceronian text is not clear (Testard, 'Recherches', 93 n. 87). Cic.'s *hisque temere adsentiamur* (*Off.* 1.18) betrays a typically Academic perspective: cf. *Acad.* 1.45.

turpe: Cic. has the word in *Off.* 1.18; *turpitudo* is of course the antithesis of *honestas*.

saxa adorare . . . quae nihil sentiant: See on 1.122 for the biblical texts on idolatry.

124. **Quanto igitur excelsior virtus est sapientia:** On the loftiness of **sapientia**, cf. Cic. *Off.* 1.153. On striving to attain it, cf. especially Prov. 4: 5, 7.

duo haec . . . conferre debemus: Cf. Cic. *Off.* 1.18: *quod vitium effugere qui volet (omnes autem velle debent) adhibebit ad considerandas res et tempus et diligentiam.* As in 1.123, A. is mistaken over the *duo* of Cic. *Off.* 1.18–19, dogmatism and obscurantism; this time he confuses them with a twofold devotion of **et tempus et diligentiam** to enquiry.

Nihil est enim magis quo homo ceteris animantibus praestet . . . causas rerum requirit: [quo: MA, CNB: *quod* PV, EW, Testard] Cf. Cic. *Off.* 1.11: *Sed inter hominem et beluam hoc maxime interest. . . . Homo autem, quod rationis est particeps, per quam consequentia cernit, causas rerum videt* (cf. also *Off.* 1.107; *Leg.* 1.22; Sen. *Ira* 1.3.7 (*prudentia*); A. *Ep.* 29 [43].14; on the human habit of giving, not shared by the animals—presumably to do with reason?—cf. 3.21). But A. adds a Christian phrase at once: **generis sui auctorem investigandum putat**: humans are endowed with reason in order to search after their Maker.

in cuius potestate vitae necisque nostrae potestas sit: On the divine sovereign power and will, cf. Dan. 5: 23; and *Ex.* 1.22; 2.4, 8–10; 3.8, 26.

cui sciamus rationem esse reddendam nostrorum actuum: Cf. Rom. 14: 12: *Itaque unusquisque nostrum pro se rationem reddet Deo* (also 2 Cor. 5: 10; 1 Pt. 4: 5).

Nihil est enim quod magis proficiat ad vitam honestam . . . et honesta delectent: Once again, A. emphasizes the eschatological reference-point which dominates his logic: right conduct is motivated in particular by the knowledge that God is to be our judge; cf. 1.28–9, 39, 40–64, 188; 2.96; 3.33. The need for careful and lengthy weighing of evidence (Cic. *Off.* 1.18) is related to the need to reflect on one's relationship with God. The prudence of recognizing that God is creator, sustainer, and judge is the primary prerequisite for the honourable life.

125. Omnibus igitur hominibus inest secundum naturam humanam verum investigare . . . et inquirendi infundit cupiditatem: Cf. Cic. *Off.* 1.18: *primus ille, qui in veri cognitione consistit, maxime naturam attingit humanam. Omnes enim trahimur et ducimur ad cognitionis et scientiae cupiditatem.* Cic. is alluding to the Aristotelian maxim (famously expressed in the opening words of *Metaph.*) that the universal human quest for knowledge is implanted by nature (cf. also *Off.* 1.13 and 1.105). The search is natural, but some areas of study may prove dangerous, because they sidetrack the enquirer from practical virtue.

In quo excellere universis pulchrum videtur: Cf. Cic. *Off.* 1.18: *in qua excellere pulchrum putamus.*

sed paucorum est adsequi: Cf. 3.10–11 (also 1.16, 36–7, 184, 246, 249): this is the path of the select few.

cogitationes, consilia: Cic. *Off.* 1.19 has *cogitatio* and *consiliis.* On intellectual effort, cf. 2.42; on the connection with courage here as well, cf. 1.188–92.

ut ad illud beate honesteque vivendum pervenire possint: Cf. Cic. *Off.* 1.19: *Omnis autem cogitatio motusque animi aut in consiliis capiendis de rebus honestis et pertinentibus ad bene beateque vivendum aut in studiis scientiae cognitionis versabitur.*

operibus: Cic. *Off.* 1.19 has *sine opera.* Cic. is thinking of how ceaseless mental activity maintains a natural pursuit of learning even without great effort on the part of the student; A. is referring to Christian good works as essential to attaining the eschatological *vita beata*; cf. 2.1–21.

***Non enim qui dixerit,* inquit, *mihi: Domine, Domine . . . sed qui fecerit ea quae dico*:** A mélange of the Matthean and Lukan versions of this saying, Mt. 7: 21, *Non omnis qui dicit mihi, Domine, Domine, intrabit in regnum caelorum, sed qui facit voluntatem Patris mei qui in caelis est,* and Lk. 6: 46, *Quid autem vocatis me, Domine, Domine, et non facitis quae dico?*

studia scientiae: Cic. *Off.* 1.19 has *in studiis scientiae.*

Throughout this paragraph, then, A. pieces together a mosaic of words from Cic. *Off.* 1.19. But the underlying thought is quite different. While Cic. warns of an excessive intellectualism where learning is pursued at the expense of *actio*, A. is thinking of the quest for knowledge as the search after God by faith, which must not be undertaken without a corresponding display of good works (cf. Jas. 2: 26). The happy and honourable life is attained by a combination of faith and good works; it is not, as it is in Cic. *Off.* 1.19, merely one possible focus for mental activity, with learning as an alternative.

CHAPTER 27: PRUDENCE AND JUSTICE

126. Primus igitur officii fons prudentia est: Cf. Cic. *Off.* 1.19: *Ac de primo quidem officii fonte diximus*; but see on 1.117: Cic. is referring to the traditional order of the virtues, while A. is classifying their importance.

Qui tamen fons et in virtutes derivatur ceteras: There have been suggestions that the image here, as in *Parad.* 13–18, is indebted to Philo, *Leg. Alleg.* 1.63–76 (Zelzer, 'Beurteilung', 185, followed by Testard i. 26 n. 1, 251 n. 2). A far likelier inspiration is Cic.'s use of the word *fons* in *Off.* 1.19. In the present passage, prudence is the *fons* from which the other virtues flow, whereas in *Parad.* 13–18 prudence is one of the four rivers which spring from the divine *fons* of paradise or the soul.

neque enim potest iustitia sine prudentia esse: In *Off.* 2.35, Cic., having suggested in *Off.* 2.33–4 that prudence without justice will be of no avail while justice without prudence will be able to do much, claims that he is not genuinely making a division between the virtues, since the person who is prudent must also be just (on the interconnection of the virtues generally, cf. *Fin.* 5.66–7). On the Stoic conviction that the virtues are a unity, see on 1.115. The key to A.'s association of prudence and justice lies, however, in the biblical legacy of wisdom–faith–righteousness, and especially in the example of Abraham, which he has cited in 1.117; Ciceronian 'justice' is elided with biblical 'righteousness' (see on 1.110). On the link between the first two virtues, cf. 1.252–3; 2.41–55; 3.14.

Qui enim iustum iudicat iniustum . . . exsecrabilis apud Deum: Prov. 17: 15–16 (VL).

Commentary 567

pietas enim in Deum initium intellectus: See on 1.1.
The introduction of **pietas** begins the transition to the
treatment of the second virtue: cf. 1.127. Though he draws
on Cic. below, A.'s formulation of *pietas* carries more
Christian than classical significance: Sauer, 75–80.

Quo advertimus: A², E²W², CNB: *quod advertimus*
PVMA¹, E¹W¹, Testard.

**illud ab huius saeculi translatum magis quam inven-
tum sapientibus:** An oblique reference to Cic. in particular:
pietas fundamentum est virtutum omnium: Cic.
Planc. 29, also quoted in *Expos. Ps. 118*.21.7. Cic. expresses
a similar sentiment in *ND* 1.4: without *pietas adversus deos*,
justice, the most excellent virtue, could not exist; cf. too, the
view of the Academic Cotta in *ND* 1.116: *Est enim pietas
iustitia adversum deos*. The theme is famously treated in
Plato, *Euth.* 12a ff. On faith as the beginning of the Christian
life, cf. *Expos. Ps. 118*.20.57.

127. **prima in Deum, secunda in patriam, tertia in
parentes, item in omnes:** In *Off.* 1.57–8, Cic., possibly
following Panaetius, ranks responsibility to country, parents,
children, household, and relatives in that order; he omits the
gods altogether. In *Off.* 1.160, however, perhaps drawing on
Posidonius or reflecting traditional Roman views, his
sequence is closer to A.'s: *prima diis immortalibus, secunda
patriae, tertia parentibus, deinceps gradatim reliquis.* A.'s
equation of *prudentia* with *pietas* facilitates the synthesis of
biblical and classical principles. The knowledge of God is the
basis of all the virtues, as the Wisdom literature declares, but
a concern for country and family is proper to true *Romanitas.*
A. endorses the traditional Stoic conception that there are
degrees of οἰκείωσις. There are concentric circles to human
society (cf. 1.169); the belief in the cosmopolis, and the
corresponding obligation to fulfil our responsibilities to
humanity as a whole (3.13–28), do not preclude a particular
concern for our native land and for our nearest and dearest.
God must come first (cf. *Abr.* 1.9; *Expos. Ps. 118*.7.34; *Ob.
Val.* 20), but patriotism and love of family are not only
legitimate but essential (cf. *Luc.* 4.47); see on 1.144. Wisdom
works at two levels, with two practical kinds of devotion. See
P. Keseling, 'Familiensinn und Vaterlandsliebe in der

Pflichtenlehre des hl. Ambrosius (Max Pohlenz zum 80. Geburtstag)', *ZRG* 5 (1953), 367–72.

quae et ipsa secundum naturae est magisterium: Cf. Cic. *Off.* 1.22, on people's responsibility to help one another: *in hoc naturam debemus ducem sequi* (also 1.100, 129; 2.73; *Leg.* 1.20).

Hinc caritas nascitur . . . in quo est principatus iustitiae: Cf. 1 Cor. 13: 5: [*caritas*] *non est ambitiosa, non quaerit quae sua sunt.* A. combines the Platonist–Stoic sentiment of Cic. *Off.* 1.22, with the pre-eminent NT ideal of charity. He is here anticipating the exposition of justice which begins at 1.130, in which altruism or charity is the key note, the attitude which epitomizes what just treatment of others is all about.

128. **Omnibus quoque animantibus innascitur . . . quod est prudentiae:** Cf. Cic. *Off.* 1.11: *Principio generi animantium omni est a natura tributum ut se vitam corpusque tueatur, declinet ea quae nocitura videantur, omniaque quae sint ad vivendum necessaria anquirat et paret, ut pastum, ut latibula, ut alia generis eiusdem.*

congregabilia natura sint: An exact echo of Cic. *Off.* 1.157, where Cic. is reciting the familiar argument that bees illustrate the gregarious tendency of humans (cf. Arist. *Pol.* 1253^{a}1–3, 7–9; *Hist. an.* 487^{b}33–488^{a}13, where the political character of humans nevertheless sets them apart from bees and other social animals); *congregabilis* is a Ciceronian coinage in that passage. Cf. also 3.21 below, and *Ex.* 6.22.

et maxime pares paribus delectari: Cf. Cic. *Sen.* 7: *Pares autem vetere proverbio cum paribus facillime congregantur.* On animals loving their own kind, cf. e.g. *Nab.* 12; *Expos. Ps. 118*.13.5.

cervos quoque cervis et plerumque hominibus adiungi: On the *cervus* as a friendly animal, cf. Ov. *Met.* 10.109–32, especially 117–19. In A., cf. *Interp.* 4.1–5, on the guilelessness of stags, which are prepared to attach themselves to the very people who are leading them into traps (A. seems to be thinking in that passage of the pagan New Year custom of people disguising themselves as stags (and other animals), a traditional habit often denounced by Christian spokesmen: H. Leclercq, 'Janvier (Calendes de)'

DACL vii/2 (1927), 2147–53). On *cervi* generally, cf. *Ex.* 3.37, 40; *Expos. Ps. 118.2.2; Ep.* 15 [69].3.

Iam de procreandi studio et subole . . . in quo est iustitiae forma praecipua: Cf. Cic. *Off.* 1.54: *Nam cum sit hoc natura commune animantium, ut habeant libidinem procreandi. . . quae propagatio et suboles origo est rerum publicarum. Sanguinis autem coniunctio et benevolentia devincit homines ⟨et⟩ caritate.* On the natural desire to procreate, and the appropriate fulfilment of this desire in marriage, see W. J. Dooley, *Marriage according to St Ambrose* (Washington, DC, 1948), especially 1–15.

129. cognatas: E²W², CNB, most editors: *cognitas* PVMA, E¹W¹.

fortitudo, quae vel in bello . . . vel domi . . . plena iustitiae sit: This is Cic.'s distinction of military and civil courage; see on 1.115.

captare etiam temporum et locorum opportunitates, prudentiae ac modestiae sit: Cf. Cic. *Off.* 1.142: *Deinceps de ordine rerum et de opportunitate temporum dicendum est.* Cic. goes on to talk of *loci* and of *modestia.*

magnanimitas: Cic. calls the third virtue by this name in *Off.* 1.152.

CHAPTER 28: JUSTICE—PAGAN AND CHRISTIAN
IDEAS CONTRASTED

Having shown the inseparability of prudence and justice, A. moves on to explore the second virtue itself (1.130–74).

130. Iustitia igitur ad societatem generis humani . . . illa censuram tenet, ista bonitatem: Cf. Cic. *Off.* 1.20: *de tribus autem reliquis latissime patet ea ratio qua societas hominum inter ipsos et vitae quasi communitas continetur. Cuius partes duae: iustitia, in qua virtutis splendor est maximus, . . . et huic coniuncta beneficentia, quam eandem vel benignitatem vel liberalitatem appellari licet.* Here, unlike in 1.127, A. omits the dimension of responsibility to God; he follows the Stoic emphasis on human society. Ancient Stoicism had treated justice *simpliciter* as the second

virtue; Panaetius had emphasized the purposive dimension
by differentiating the negative obligations imposed by strict
justice (*iustitia*/δικαιοσύνη) from the positive acts of kindness
(*liberalitas*/*beneficentia*/the Aristotelian ἐλευθεριότης) which
promote the kind of society that justice naturally demands.
Cic. follows him, treating strict justice in *Off.* 1.20–41 and
kindness in *Off.* 1.42–60. A. reiterates Cic.'s ranking (*Off.*
1.20) of the first as higher than the second (**iustitia mihi
excelsior videtur**), but he spends longer on kindness in
the end (1.131–42 covers strict justice; 1.143–74 discusses
kindness), focusing the argument on an appeal to Christian
charity. On justice as the source of the other virtues, cf.
Parad. 18, 22.

censuram: Translators have generally taken this as a
pejorative: *Strenge* (Niederhuber); *severità* (Cavasin; Banterle); 'strictness' (De Romestin); *sévérité* (Testard), but the
context hardly supports this. 'Sober judgement' is nearer the
mark (cf. 1.230; 2.67; and e.g. Sen. *Benef.* 4.28.5): justice
exercises a proper assessment of what is right, while liberality shows goodness to others with concrete gestures of
beneficence.

131. Sed primum ipsum . . . nisi lacessitus iniuria: An
allusion to Cic. *Off.* 1.20: *Sed iustitiae primum munus est ut ne
cui quis noceat, nisi lacessitus iniuria* (cf. also *Off.* 3.76: *iam se
ipse doceat eum virum bonum esse qui prosit quibus possit, noceat
nemini nisi lacessitus iniuria*; and A. 1.26; 3.58–9). **Sed
primum ipsum** intensifies the contrast between the secular
and the Christian perspectives: the very first thing which the
pagan philosophers reckon to be a duty of justice is un-
acceptable to those imbued with the gospel spirit.

quod evangelii auctoritate vacuatur: Cf. Mt. 5: 43–8;
Lk. 6: 27–38 (also Lk. 9: 51–6; Mt. 26: 51–4; Lk. 22: 49–51;
Jn. 18: 10–11). Although A. goes on to articulate a Christian
ethic of a just war under Cic.'s influence (1.139; especially
1.176–7; cf. 2.33; 3.86–7), in the personal sphere he is a
pacifist (3.27, 59; note also 1.16, 233; 3.23–4), sharing with
other Christian authors (e.g. Lact. *Inst.* 6.18.15–35) the
conviction that the believer when insulted should turn the
other cheek: cf. *Ep. extra coll.* 14 [63].84; *Ios.* 3; *Abr.* 2.29–
30; *Expl. Ps. 38*.10; *Expl Ps. 39*.3; and see L. J. Swift, 'S

Ambrose on Violence and War', *TAPhA* 101 (1970), 533–43; for parallels, cf. DL 6.33, 89; Basil *Ad adulesc.* 7 (Dyck, 109). Testard, 'Aveu', 253–4; 'Observations', 22, reminds us that A. seems never to have responded to the caustic verbal attacks that rained upon him from Jerome, so perhaps the advice is not *just* rhetoric. See, however, on 1.177, on *nisi lacessitus.*

vult enim scriptura ut sit in nobis spiritus filii hominis: In addition to the passages cited above, cf. Phil. 2: 5–11: *Hoc enim sentite in vobis, quod et in Christo Iesu*; Christians are to emulate the spirit of the one *qui cum malediceretur, non maledicebat; cum pateretur, non comminabatur: tradebat autem iudicanti se iniuste* (1 Pt. 2: 23).

conferre gratiam: Cf. Jn. 1: 17: *gratia . . . per Iesum Christum facta est.*

132. **Deinde formam iustitiae putaverunt . . . privata pro suis:** [Winterbottom, 562, suggests **Deinde** ⟨*alteram*⟩ **formam** to clarify the move to the second type, but perhaps **Deinde** on its own does enough to mark the transition. The addition of *pro communibus* after **communia** (Winterbottom, 562 n. 5) is also unnecessary] Cf. Cic. *Off.* 1.20: *deinde ut communibus pro communibus utatur, privatis ut suis.* A. has already disagreed with this Ciceronian insistence upon the legitimacy of distinguishing between private and public property in 1.118.

Ne hoc quidem secundum naturam . . . in commune profudit: This is the basic Stoic tenet (Cic. *Off.* 1.22; cf. *ND* 2.37, 154–62; *Fin.* 3.67) that the earth's produce is for all, and thus should never be hoarded for purely private advantage (1.38; 3.37–52); cf. 3.16, 45.

Natura igitur ius commune generavit, usurpatio ius fecit privatum: An enormous amount of scholarly ink has been spilt over these words. The debate turns on the sense of **usurpatio**: does it mean simply 'use' or 'custom', or is there a negative force: 'usurpation' or 'unjust acquisition'? Supporters of the first interpretation point to Cic. *Off.* 1.21: *Sunt autem privata nulla natura, sed aut vetere occupatione, ut qui quondam in vacua venerunt, aut victoria, ut qui bello potiti sunt, aut lege pactione condicione sorte.* A.'s **usurpatio** is said to be the equivalent of Cic.'s *vetus occupatio.* This view has found some significant support: e.g. J. A. Ryan, *Alleged Socialism of the Church Fathers* (St Louis, MO, 1913), 61–2; G. Squitieri, *Il preteso communismo di s. Ambrogio* (Sarno, 1946), 102; L. Orabona, 'L'"usurpatio" in un passo di s. Ambrogio (De off., 1, 28) parallelo a Cicerone (De off., 1, 7) su "ius commune" e "ius privatum"', *Aevum* 33 (1959), 495–504; P. Christophe, *L'Usage chrétien du droit de propriété dans l'Ecriture et la tradition patristique* (Paris, 1964), 172; Maes, 26; Vasey, 131–6; Testard i. 252–3 n. 7. A larger number, however, take the word as pejorative: Thamin, 281; A. Amati, 'Nuovi studi su s. Ambrogio: La proprietà', *RIL* ser. 2, 30 (1897), 764–85, at 781; I. Seipel, *Die wirtschaftsethischen Lehren der Kirchenväter* (Vienna, 1907), 109; O. Schilling, *Reichtum und Eigentum in der altchristlichen Literatur* (Freiburg, 1908), 142; Niederhuber, 74; Homes Dudden ii. 546; A. O. Lovejoy, 'The Communism of Saint Ambrose', *JHI* 3 (1942), 458–68, at 459 and n. 6 [= *Essays in the History of Ideas* (Baltimore, MD, 1948), ch. 15]; F. Flückiger, *Geschichte des Naturrechts* i: *Altertum und Frühmittelalter* (Zurich, 1954), 335; S. Calafato, *La proprietà privata in s. Ambrogio* (Turin, 1958), 75–101, especially 85–91; E. Frattini, 'Proprietà e ricchezza nel pensiero di s. Ambrogio', *RIFD* 39 (1962), 745–66, at 754; L. Ndolela, 'Original Communism in the "De Officiis" of Ambrose of Milan', *World Justice* 12 (1970), 216–37, at 220–1 n. 10, 224–5; M. Hengel, *Property and Riches in the Early Church: Aspects of a Social History of Early Christianity* (London, 1974), 3–4; G. E. M. de Ste Croix, 'Early Christian Attitudes to Property and Slavery', in D. Baker (ed.), *Church, Society and Politics* (Oxford, 1975), 1–38, at 30 n. 104; Banterle, 105 n. 5; C. Avila, *Ownership: Early Christian Teaching* (Maryknoll, NY & London, 1983), 73–6; B. Gordon, *The Economic Problem in Biblical and Patristic Thought* (Leiden, 1989), 113; J. L. González, *Faith and Wealth: A History of Early Christian Ideas on the Origin, Significance and Use of Money* (San Francisco, 1990), 191; Becker, 47 n. 33. (S. Giet, 'La Doctrine de l'appropriation des biens chez quelques-uns des Pères. Peut-on parler de communisme?', *RSR* 35 (1948), 55–91, at 63–4 n. 4 translates **usurpatio** as *usage* but interprets it as pejorative in the context of A.'s disagreement with Cic.;

Cavasin translates it as *usurpazione*, but says (129 n. 4) that it corresponds to Cic.'s *vetere occupatione*).

Usurpare, *usurpator*, and *usurpatio* are found in neutral senses classically, but in later writers the force is commonly (though not always—cf. e.g. 1.102 above; *Expos. Ps. 118*.7.8) negative. The two most thorough studies of the passage rightly opt for the pejorative interpretation here: L. J. Swift, '*Iustitia* and *Ius Privatum*: Ambrose on Private Property', *AJPh* 100 (1979), 176–87, at 179–80; M. Wacht, 'Privateigentum bei Cicero und Ambrosius', *JbAC* 25 (1982), 28–64, at 51–2. The decisive point in favour of it is the context. In 1.131, A. disagrees with Cic.'s 'first office of justice' (*Off.* 1.20): revenge is forbidden to the Christian, even after severe provocation. In 1.132, he goes on to disagree with the second 'office' of Cic. *Off.* 1.20: all property, not just that which is common, is to be treated as common. **Ne hoc quidem secundum naturam** clearly dissents from Cic.'s second proposition (*pace* e.g. Orabona, 'L' "usurpatio" in un passo di s. Ambrogio', 500–1), especially since in 1.118 A. has already altered Cic.'s wording to **communia pro suis . . . sua pro communibus**. Cic. says in *Off.* 1.21 that by nature there are no private possessions, but long-standing occupancy entitles people to call territory their own. Cic. certainly does not propose a revolution in existing property relations: private goods are not wrong in principle; each person should zealously defend whatever has fallen to his lot (cf. also *Off.* 1.51). All he is doing is seeking to explain and justify the enduring distinction between the public and the private. He commends the essential Stoic axiom that people should help one another (*Off.* 1.22), but he by no means calls for a return to some primitive state in which all things were held in common; *sunt . . . privata nulla natura* cannot overturn the actual state of affairs that history has produced. A. makes no mention of protecting one's own possessions, but moves straight from the **natura . . . usurpatio** antithesis to the Stoic belief, which he claims (1.133–6) is lifted from scriptural teaching; then, in 1.136, he evokes the Ciceronian quotation (*Off.* 1.22) of Plato's sentiment about being 'born for others rather than for oneself'. In 1.137 he suggests that this design of nature for justice is undermined by *prima avaritia*: it is the primal greed of original sin that has destroyed nature's (or God's; cf. 1.78) intention that justice should hold all things as common.

Taking 1.132 in this whole context, then, private property is being attributed not to long-standing possession but to the Fall, to the greed which first brought about the loss of paradise and which continues in a sinful world. Whereas Cic. brings in self-interest, A. maintains a self-denying and altruistic perspective on justice: the evolution of private property, obtained through greed, is in conflict with God's original design. The asyndeton of **generavit, usurpatio** is adversative. This interpretation accords perfectly with what A. says in passages such as *Expos. Ps. 118*.8.22: *cum praesertim Dominus Deus noster terram hanc possessionem omnium hominum voluerit esse communem et fructus omnium ministrare; sed avaritia possessionum iura distribuit*; and *Ex.* 5.2: *Haec* [i.e. *natura*] *communia dedit, ne tibi aliqua velut propria vindicares. Tibi suos fructus terra producit, tibi scaros et acipenseres et omnes fetus suos generant aquae: et his non contentus interdicta tibi alimenta gustasti. Ad invidiam tuam omnia congeruntur, ut praevaricatio tuae aviditatis oneretur*; cf. also *Off.* 2.108, 132. On the usurpation of the common produce of the earth by greed, cf. *Ex.* 6.52; *Nab.* 2, 11–12, 52 ff.; *Luc.* 7.124, 247; *Vid.* 4–5 (and *Off.* 1.38; 2.128–33, especially 2.133; 3.16, 37–52); the just person treats his property as common: *Iac.* 1.37. The derivation of private property from the Fall is found in other patristic authors (e.g. Greg. Naz. *Hom.* 14.25). There are parallels with Stoic–Cynic condemnations of *avaritia*, and with the classical *topos* of a Golden Age in which possessions were common; see Calafato, *La proprietà privata in s. Ambrogio*, 96–101; J. A. Mara, *The Notion of Solidarity in St Ambrose's Teaching on Creation, Sin, and Redemption* (Rome, 1970), 18–26. Such images could be connected in the patristic mind with the early Christian practice of holding property in common (Acts 2: 44; 4: 32) to promote the ideal of the perfect society as a community of sharers: see R. M. Grant, *Early Christianity and Society* (London, 1978), 96–123.

This logic places A. closer to early Stoicism than to Cic. or Panaetius: Zeno had argued for the communal life of men and women, and for the abolition of coinage (cf. DL 7.33), whereas the middle Stoa, influencing Cic., had taken a positive view of the acquisition of property. In practice, however, A. is of course no more of a revolutionary than Cic. Marxist interpretations of his thought (e.g. de Ste Croix; Ndolela) are seriously misjudged: he is not interested in proposing primitive communism or any such political programme (Homes Dudden ii. 550). There is abundant evidence that A. does recognize the right of property: an inherited estate must not be lightly surrendered or sold (2.17; 3.63; *Nab.* 5 ff.), and a private house, still less a house of God, must not be unjustly taken away (*Ep.* 76 [20].19); violations of property rights are *adversus naturam* (3.28). It is part of justice's role to defend such rights (2.49), and special kindness must be shown to those who have lost their patrimony through no fault of their own (2.69). A. himself certainly held on to his property, albeit indirectly (see on 1.185), and he allows his clergy to do likewise (1.152, 184). The truth is simply that his perspective on the excesses of contemporary society is informed by assumptions shaped by orthodox Stoic and Cynic thought and Christian priorities, and he exploits this rhetoric in an appeal to Christian charity. Like other fourth-century churchmen, he consistently presents charity and almsgiving as the means by which people can emulate God's original purpose of universal *iustitia* in creation. *Iustitia* prior to the Fall spelt an altruism with which private property was incompatible; after the Fall, this altruism and its effects are relative principles in an imperfect world (Swift, '*Iustitia* and *Ius Privatum*', 185). In a sinful society, property is not entirely to be renounced, but it needs to be properly employed for charitable purposes. Wealth is not inherently an evil; what matters is the use to which it is put—selfish gain on the one hand, or, on the other, the imitation of a divine purpose in nature and God's ongoing determination to show compassion for the needy. Property may have a social function if self-interest is subjugated to the good of others. For other arguments in these areas, see P. C. Phan (ed.), *Social Thought* (Wilmington, DE, 1984); Avila, *Ownership*, especially 59–80 on A.

Quo in loco aiunt placuisse Stoicis . . . ut ipsi inter se

aliis alii prodesse possint: aiunt means Cic.: cf. *Off.* 1.22: *ut placet Stoicis, quae in terris gignantur ad usum hominum omnia creari, homines autem hominum causa esse generatos, ut ipsi inter se aliis alii prodesse possent.*

133. Unde hoc nisi de scripturis nostris dicendum adsumpserunt?: The allusion here (and in **didicerunt** and **censent**, below) is to the Stoics rather than Cic.

Moyses enim scripsit: A. has of course no worries over the Mosaic authorship of the Pentateuch.

Faciamus hominem ad imaginem nostram . . . super terram: Gen. 1: 26.

Omnia subiecisti sub pedes eius . . . et pisces maris: [**sub pedes** PMA, Testard: *sub pedibus* V, EW, COB, most editors] Ps. 8: 7–9.

134. *Non est bonum hominem esse solum . . . similem sibi:* [The masculine *similem* (PV, E¹W: *simile* MA, E², COB) is defensible since the VL treats *adiutorium* in a personal sense (Testard i. 253 n. 12)] Gen. 2: 18.

Ad adiumentum ergo mulier data est viro . . . adiumento foret: A.'s view of women, though scarcely congenial to a feminist, is actually often fairly positive for his time, perhaps partly owing to the influence of Stoic assumptions that the sexes have the same capacity for virtue. Here, he stays close to Gen. in stressing the role of woman as helper to man, without any mention of corresponding responsibilities for man; cf. *Parad.* 48–9.

Non est inventus adiutor similis illi: Gen. 2: 20.

135. Ergo secundum Dei voluntatem vel naturae copulam: The will of God revealed in Scripture and the purpose of God revealed in human nature are complementary authorities. The Stoic view, reproduced by Cic. (*Off.* 1.22, 51 ff.) mentions only the norm of nature; for A., nature's design is indicative of God's purpose (cf. 1.77–8; 3.15 ff.). The divine will and the impulse of nature are co-ordinate norms because God is creator; Maes, 65–120, 123–38.

ut verbo scripturae utar, adiumentum: A. alludes to Gen. 2: 18 and 2: 20, which he cites in 1.134; neither text, however, uses this word (they have *adiutorium* and *adiutor*, respectively).

ut inter nos societatis augeatur gratia: On *societas*, cf. Cic. *Off.* 1.50–7.

vel periculi terrore: On the role of courage here, cf. 1.186–95.

omnia sua ducat vel adversa vel prospera: Cf. Cic. *Off.* 1.30: *Est enim difficilis cura rerum alienarum . . . sed tamen, quia magis ea percipimus atque sentimus quae nobis ipsis aut prospera aut adversa eveniunt quam illa quae ceteris, quae quasi longo intervallo interiecto videmus, aliter de illis ac de nobis iudicamus.*

sanctus Moyses pro populo patriae bella suscipere gravia non reformidavit: e.g. the war with the Amalekites, in Ex. 17: 8–16.

nec regis potentissimi trepidavit arma nec barbaricae immanitatis expavit ferociam: Cf. Heb. 11: 27, *non veritus animositatem regis*, referring to Moses' boldness before Pharaoh (Ex. 5: 1–12: 33; cf. also Ex. 14: 10–31).

abiecit salutem suam: Cf. Cic. *Planc.* 79: *sed me dius fidius multo citius meam salutem pro te abiecero quam Cn. Planci salutem tradidero contentioni tuae.*

136. Magnus itaque iustitiae splendor: Cf. Cic. *Off.* 1.20: *iustitia, in qua virtutis splendor est maximus.*

quae aliis potius nata quam sibi: A celebrated phrase of Plato (*Ep.* 9.358a), suggested here by Cic. *Off.* 1.22: *non nobis solum nati sumus*; the version which A. quotes is, though, closer to that given in Cic. *Rep.* 3.12: [*iustitia*] . . . *quae omnis magis quam sepse diligit, alius nata potius quam sibi.* The idea is found also in Cic. *Fin.* 2.45 (and cf. Cic. *Mur.* 83; *Luc.* 2.383; Sen. *Clem.* 2.3). A. alludes to it in many places: e.g. 1.121; 2.28; 3.12, 14; *Parad.* 18; *Noe* 2; *Virgt.* 114; *Expl. Ps. 35*.7; *Expos. Ps. 118*.8.3 (God rather than self); 10.7; 16.14; *Ep.* 51 [15].3; see M. L. Ricci, 'Fortuna di una formula ciceroniana presso sant'Ambrogio (a proposito di *iustitia*)', *SIFC* 43 (1971), 222–45, who points out the similarity to 1 Cor. 10: 24, evoked in a similar context in 3.12–15.

communitatem et societatem: Cf. Cic.'s use of these words in *Off.* 1.20, 50 ff.

excelsitatem tenet, ut suo iudicio omnia subiecta habeat: Cic. has the words *excelsitas animi* in *Off.* 3.24;

omnia subiecta habeat picks up the language of Ps. 8: 7–8, quoted in 1.133.

A. is partly anticipating his treatment of courage (cf. especially 1.182–95), which serves to underscore the interconnectedness of the virtues.

137. hanc virtutis arcem: See on 1.192.

prima avaritia: See on *usurpatio* in 1.132; and 2.108. Cic. also mentions—though obviously without the theological overtones—the pernicious role of *avaritia* in injustice (*Off.* 1.24).

exuimus . . . amisimus: Reminiscent of Pauline language: cf. Rom. 13: 12, 14; Gal. 3: 27; Eph. 4: 22–4; Col. 3: 9–14.

138. Potentiae . . . cupiditas: Cf. Cic. *Off.* 1.26, where Cic. warns of the dangers of slipping *in imperiorum honorum gloriae cupiditatem*, adding that *honoris imperii potentiae gloriae cupiditates* are generally found in the most able men; he mentions the obvious example of his *bête noire*, Julius Caesar. Cic. also speaks of those who are *potentiae cupidi* in *Off.* 1.70.

virilem effeminat: Cf. Sall. *Cat.* 11.3: *Avaritia pecuniae studium habet, quam nemo sapiens concupivit; ea quasi venenis malis imbuta corpus animumque virilem effeminat*; also Gell. *NA* 3.1. Cf. 1.193; and see on 1.84.

Quomodo enim potest pro aliis intervenire . . . qui ipse gravem libertati adfectat potentiam?: On moral impediment to duty, cf. 1.248; on **pro aliis intervenire**, cf. 2.102; 3.59, and see ad locc.

CHAPTER 29: JUSTICE TOWARDS ENEMIES;
FAITH AS THE FOUNDATION OF JUSTICE

139. quod nec locis nec personis nec temporibus excipitur: Justice must be upheld in every situation without exception.

quae etiam hostibus reservatur: The idea is suggested by Cic.'s discussion of justice in war, in *Off.* 1.34–40 (cf. also *Off.* 3.107–15). On the fidelity of enemies to their word, cf. Aug. *Ep.* 129.11. Despite the high sense of principle spoken of here, A. apparently considered it acceptable for the

Romans to get their barbarian enemies drunk in order to rout them (*Elia* 54).

superiore gratia: Some divine overruling to grant victory to the right side (as happened in the Israelite encounter with the Syrians, below).

vehementior refertur ultio: This is what happens in war; compare A.'s exclusion of private revenge in 1.131.

ut de Madianitis . . . iracundia effusa est: Midianite women seduced the Israelites into sexual immorality and the worship of their god, the Baal of Peor, and 24,000 Israelites were struck dead with a plague. God then instructed Moses to take full vengeance on the enemy (Num. 25: 1–18). Having killed all the Midianite men, the Israelites were instructed by Moses to slaughter all the women involved in the sin, together with all male children; only virgins were saved (Num. 31: 1–24).

populum patrum: A frequent designation of the OT saints; see Introduction IV.4.

Gabaonitas autem . . . adficeret iniuria: See Josh. 9: 1–27; and cf. 3.67–9 below.

Syros vero Eliseus . . . venire piratae Syriae destiterunt: See 4 Ki. 6: 8–23; and cf. 3.86–7, 119 below.

regi Israel: Probably Joram.

Non percuties quos non captivasti . . . et eant ad dominum suum: 4 Ki. 6: 22. 'Their master' is the Syrian king, probably Ben-Hadad II.

140.   propheta: Still Elisha.

Noli timere . . . cum illis: 4 Ki. 6: 16.

Percutiat Dominus caecitate exercitum Syriae: [**Dominus** PVMA, EW: *Deus* CNB] 4 Ki. 6: 18.

Venite post me . . . quem quaeritis: 4 Ki. 6: 19.

Testard i. 254–5 n. 10, is troubled by various details of the account of the biblical story in this paragraph. A. omits to say that the horses and chariots which surrounded Elisha were fiery; **quibus descendentibus** is vague (it refers in fact to the Syrians); the servant Gehazi is named here, although his name does not appear in 4 Ki. 6 (but is in 4 Ki. 5); and no mention is made of the fact that the entire Syrian army besieged Samaria again. All of these features can readily be explained by the supposition that A. is simply recounting the story from memory. What *is* slightly bumpy is the way in which the first two sentences of the paragraph introduce the account which follows. A. begins by suggesting that he is going to talk about justice in peacetime, and implies (**et hanc gratiam**) that the story of 4 Ki. 6 illustrates this; yet the story clearly relates to a time of war, as the last sentence (**etiam in bello**) recognizes. Possibly the beginning of the paragraph is inspired by Cic.'s references to *pax* in *Off.* 1.35, but A. then continues with the same narrative as in 1.139, where Elisha's non-violent victory is a sort of triumph by pacifist means.

fidem . . . fides: Here in the Ciceronian sense of 'good faith' (*Off.* 1.23, 39–40), but in 1.142 in the biblical sense of faith in God.

141. Denique etiam adversarios molli veteres appellatione nominabant . . . peregrini dicebantur: Cf. Cic. *Off.* 1.37: *Equidem etiam illud animadverto, quod, qui proprio nomine perduellis esset, is hostis vocaretur, lenitate verbi rei tristitiam mitigatam. Hostis enim apud maiores nostros is dicebatur quem nunc peregrinum dicimus*; Cic. also has *tam molli nomine appellare*. Cic.'s point is that *hostis* has changed its meaning (cf. Varr. *LL* 5.3; also Paul. *Fest.* p. 102M; Serv. auct. *In Aen.* 4.424; Macr. *Sat.* 1.16.14–15): traditionally, *hostis* was used to describe a *peregrinus* ('stranger'); in Cic.'s time, *hostis* had taken on a harsher meaning, referring to a *perduellis* or 'foe'. The ancients thus gave their foes a 'gentler' name (as various scholars have noted, however, the semantic shift can be read another way as well: if the early Romans called all foreigners 'enemies', this suggests that their attitude towards strangers in general was hardly friendly; Dyck, 145–6). A. gets Cic.'s point the wrong way round, and says that the ancients actually called their adversaries *peregrini*, while their *hostes* were known as *peregrini*.

de nostris adsumptum: The usual charge of plagiarism: Introduction IV.2.

adversarios enim . . . appellabant vocabulo: ἀλλόφυλοι is often used in the LXX to describe the Philistines (though not in the Pentateuch or Joshua): the idea is that the Philistines were a non-Semitic race, and so 'foreign' to the

Israelites; cf. *Elia* 17; *Expos. Ps. 118*.17.25; 18.24; *Apol.* 1.16, 26; *Spir.* 2.13 (A. does not know Hebrew: see on 1.15). The word is not found transliterated into Latin prior to the Christian era (*TLL* i. 1692), when it is regularly used as a synonym of *alienigenae*.

in libro Regnorum: 1 and 2 'Kingdoms' is the LXX's name for 1 and 2 Ki. (= 1 and 2 Sam.); the use of this name here further hints that A. is relying on the LXX; cf. 3.118.

Et factum est . . . in pugnam ad Israel: 1 Ki. 4: 1. The sentence is missing from the Hebrew text, and is found only in the LXX and Latin versions (though some scholars believe that it is missing from the Hebrew through scribal haplography, the verb for 'went out' occurring in both 4: 1a and 4: 1b; the Jerusalem Bible retains the phrase). The reference is to the Philistines.

A.'s attempt to find earlier biblical evidence for Cic.'s history of the word *hostis* is thus decidedly flawed: (i) he misquotes Cic.; (ii) he tries to substantiate the usage of ἀλλόφυλοι from a verse which is not in the Hebrew text, while referring to **Hebraei**; and (iii) in his actual authority, the LXX, the word is used not to refer to enemies in general but to the Philistines in particular.

142. Fundamentum ergo est iustitiae fides: Cf. Cic. *Off.* 1.23: *Fundamentum autem est iustitiae fides, id est dictorum conventorumque constantia et veritas.* But it is immediately clear from what follows that A. refers to faith in the biblical, not the Ciceronian, sense (contrast 1.140): the ambivalence testifies to the twin influences at work in his mind; Sauer, 113–18; G. Freyburger, *Fides. Etude sémantique et religieuse depuis les origines jusqu'à l'époque augustéenne* (Paris, 1986), 134–5; J. Herrmann, '"Fundamentum est iustitiae fides." Vergleichende Betrachtung zu Cicero (De officiis 1,20 ff.) und Ambrosius (De officiis ministrorum 1,139 ff.)', in G. Schiemann (ed.), *Kleine Schriften zur Rechtsgeschichte* (Munich, 1990), 315–20.

iustorum enim corda meditantur fidem: Prov. 15: 28 (VL); cf. also Ps. 36: 30.

qui se iustus accusat: Cf. Prov. 18: 17.

Ecce, inquit, *mitto lapidem in fundamentum Sion:* Is. 28: 16. The formula **Dominus per Isaiam . . . inquit** is reminiscent of Acts 28: 25: *Spiritus Sanctus locutus est per Esaiam prophetam* (see Pizzolato, 114, especially n. 98). On the inspiration of Scripture, see on 1.3.

id est Christum in fundamenta ecclesiae: On the identification of the stone of Is. 28: 16/Is. 8: 16 with Christ and faith, cf. Rom. 9: 33; 1 Pt. 2: 6–8 (cf. also Ps. 117: 22–3 and Mt. 21: 42; Mk. 12: 10; Lk. 20: 17–18; Acts 4: 11). Cf. too, 1 Cor. 3: 11: *Fundamentum enim aliud nemo potest ponere praeter id quod positum est, qui est Christus Iesus*; and in A. cf. e.g. *Luc.* 6.97–8; *Inc.* 33–4. On faith as the foundation of the church, see Toscani, 386–91.

Fides enim omnium Christus: On the one faith, cf. Eph. 4: 5; Tit. 1: 4; and 1.72 above; see generally Löpfe, 102–13.

ecclesia autem quaedam forma iustitiae est . . . in commune temptatur: This sentence focuses A.'s conception of justice. In an imperfect world, the ideal of common rights and possessions is far from realized, but the nearest approximation is found in the church, which is one in its prayer, works, and affliction, and which testifies to the equality of its members by sharing all things and caring for *commune* rather than private *ius*. As such, the church is the model of justice for the world; cf. 2.124; also 2.96 (of the clergy); 3.19 (and 2.133, where contempt for money is the *iustitiae forma*); *Expos. Ps. 118*.8.26. 'A. substitutes the Christian church as a visible community grounded in faith for Cic.'s ideal republic and for the Stoic cosmopolis ruled by natural law' (Colish ii. 64). The whole thrust of his teaching on justice is aimed at making this ecclesial model all that he believes it must be in the eyes of the watching *saeculum*. On **commune**, cf. Cic. *Off.* 1.50–8.

qui seipsum sibi abnegat: Cf. Jesus's words in Lk. 9: 23: *Si quis vult post me venire, abneget se ipsum, et tollat crucem suam cotidie et sequatur me* (Mt. 16: 24; Mk. 8: 34).

ipse dignus est Christo: Cf. Mt. 10: 37–8.

Ideo et Paulus . . . aut malis iniquitas aut bonis iustitia est: Cf. 1 Cor. 3: 10–15, especially 3: 10–11. Christ is the foundation of the edifice of the church, with its good works; faith in him is essential for justice (cf. 1.126, 252; 2.7; *Cain* 2.28). The intrinsic association of faith with *iustitia* also indicates the biblical nuancing of *iustitia* (as righteousness) which accompanies the classical inspiration for A.

CHAPTER 30: KINDNESS: GOODWILL AND GENEROSITY

143. beneficentia . . . quae dividitur etiam ipsa in benevolentiam et liberalitatem: A. comes now to the second part of justice, **beneficentia**, according to the division of 1.130. In 1.130, he follows Cic. *Off.* 1.20 in giving *liberalitas* and *benignitas* as synonyms for *beneficentia* (cf. also *Off.* 1.42, where *beneficentia* and *liberalitas* constitute the second part of justice). Here, the subdivision of *beneficentia* into *benevolentia* and *liberalitas* is not strictly Ciceronian, but it is suggested by Cic.'s mention of *benevolentia* in *Off.* 1.47. A.'s memory of Cic.'s precise arrangement may be poor, but it is also likely that he deliberately places stress on *benevolentia* in his desire to emphasize motivation in giving. The conviction that right intent is vital to virtuous action is of course fundamental to Stoicism as well. Goodwill is not just a stage in the process of giving; it is constitutive of human society as a whole (1.167–74), and so it deserves special emphasis in the exposition of the altruism which is to characterize the Christian life in society. This second section of justice covers 1.143–74. See Becker, 111–14; A. Swoboda, 'Pojęcie beneficentia i benevolentia w "De officiis ministrorum" św. Ambrożego i w "De officiis" Cycerona', *VoxP* 8 (1988), 767–85.

Ex his igitur duobus constat beneficentia . . . proficiscatur: Both goodwill and generosity are necessary for perfection (1.151), though goodwill, the essential motive in kindness, may exist on its own where the means for liberality are lacking (1.167). Cf. *Paen.* 2.82–3 on faith commending a gift.

Hilarem enim datorem diligit Deus: 2 Cor. 9: 7.

Nam si invitus facias, quae tibi merces est?: Reminiscent of Mt. 5: 46, *Si enim diligatis eos qui vos diligunt, quam mercedem habebitis?*, as well as of 1 Cor. 9: 17, which A. goes on to quote next.

generaliter: The quotation is not about kindness as such, but about fulfilling the duty of preaching the gospel.

Si volens hoc ago . . . mihi credita est: 1 Cor. 9: 17.

In evangelio quoque . . . iustae liberalitatis: e.g. the story of the widow's mite, mentioned in 1.149; or the Good Samaritan (Lk. 10: 25–37); or Zacchaeus' reparations, mentioned in 1.145.

144. et eo largiri consilio ut prosis, non ut noceas: Cf. Cic. *Off.* 1.43: *Videndum est igitur ut ea liberalitate utamur quae prosit amicis, noceat nemini* (also *Off.* 1.42); and Cic. has *largiantur* in *Off.* 1.43.

Nam si luxurioso . . . ubi nulla est benevolentia: Kindness must not promote sinful extravagance.

prodesse: Cic. has this infinitive in *Off.* 1.42.

qui conspiret adversus patriam . . . qui impugnent ecclesiam: We have already glimpsed A.'s patriotism in 1.127 (cf. 1.254, evoking Cic. *Off.* 3.95; also 3.23, 127 below). Here we find a typical equation of political stability with the security of the church; cf. *Fid.* 2.136–43; *Expl. Ps.* 45.21. Heresies (and homoian theology above all) are synonymous with barbarism; the success of imperial government is contingent upon its maintenance of orthodoxy. By extension, the person who plots against his country, when that country stands for the defence and propagation of orthodox Christianity, is also attacking the church. Heresy and treason are all of a piece; there is a potent equation of Nicene fidelity with imperial security. The church embodies the ideal society, and all other social cohesion is ultimately contingent upon its well-being. On the political vision, see Palanque, 325–35; Morino, 53–5; M. Meslin, 'Nationalisme, état, et religions à la fin du IVe siècle', *Archives de sociologie des religions* 18 (1964), 3–20; M. Sordi, 'La concezione politica di Ambrogio', in *I Cristiani e l'Impero nel IV secolo. Atti del convegno di Macerata (17–18 decembro 1987)* (Macerata, 1988), 143–54; H. Inglebert, *Les Romains chrétiens face à l'histoire de Rome. Histoire, christianisme et romanités en Occident dans l'Antiquité tardive (IIIe–Ve siècles)* (Paris, 1996), 297–309. Naturally, A. is insistent that the church must come first where there is any possible conflict of interests (*Tob.* 51; *Expl. Ps.* 37.24). On gathering together *perditi*, cf. Cic.'s picture of Catiline in e.g. *Cat.* 1.23; *Sull.* 33. If A. has any specific target in mind here, it could be his old adversary Iulianus Valens, who had caused such trouble throughout northern Italy in 381 that A. had to beseech Gratian to have him removed from Milan: cf. *Ep. extra coll.* 4 [10].10: *qui nunc illicitis ordinationibus consimiles sui sociat sibi et seminarium quaerit suae impietatis atque perfidiae per quosque perditos derelinquere . . . is nunc Mediolani post eversionem patriae ne dicamus proditionem inequitavit.* The anti-pope Ursinus is linked in an unholy alliance with Valens in *Ep. extra coll.* 5 [11].3, and he too is said to have dealt with *perditi* (*Ep. extra coll.* 5 [11].5). (Ursinus was not himself a homoian, however; he probably sided with the extreme Nicenes of Milan, who felt that A. had not done enough to reform his predecessor's clerical body (McLynn, 58–9); Ursinus' main objective was probably to cause trouble for his real enemy, Damasus, back in Rome; A.'s tactic of associating him with the Milanese homoians is designed to smear him (Williams, 137–8).) On Arianism (like a hydra, rearing itself in many forms, whose representatives cannot agree among themselves) as a conspiracy against the church, cf. *Fid.* 1.46 (with criticism from Pallad., *Apol.* 87).

viduam et pupillos: See on 1.63.

eripere: Cic. *Off.* 1.43 has *eripiunt*.

145. si quod alteri largitur . . . iuste dispensandum putet: Cf. Cic. *Off.* 1.42: *et qui aliis nocent ut in alios liberales sint in eadem sunt iniustitia ut si in suam rem aliena convertant*; *Off.* 1.43: *Sunt autem multi . . . qui eripiunt aliis quod aliis largiantur . . . nihil est enim liberale quod non idem iustum.* A. continues to echo some of Cic.'s language on the universality of *iustitia* (Dyck, 158–9), but he goes on to exemplify the themes from Scripture. On the principle of the just acquisition of funds for alms, cf. Aug. *Serm.* 113.2; *Quaest. Hept.* 2.88; *Enchir.* 22.

ut ille Zachaeus, reddas prius ei quadruplum quem fraudaveris: See Lk. 19: 1–10, especially 19: 8; cf. also e.g. *Luc.* 8.80–90; Max. Taur. *Serm.* 95–6.

gentilitatis vitia fidei studio et credentis operatione compenses: On compensating for sins by good works, cf. *Luc.* 7.156; *Paen.* 1.10; 2.35, 83; *Apol.* 24, 39–40, 49; *Noe*

117; *Ep.* 36 [2].14, 16; Aug. *Ep.* 153.24; on almsgiving, see
on 1.39; on faith, cf. *Expos. Ps. 118.22.26.* The NT *locus
classicus* is Jas. 2: 14–26. A. here assumes readers who have
not been brought up in the church, but have lived as 'pagans'
in former days; contrast 1.81.

Fundamentum igitur habeat liberalitas tua: Cic. *Off.*
1.42 speaks of the *iustitiae fundamentum* that giving should
be in accordance with the worth of the recipient. But the
reference to the faith of Zacchaeus suggests that A. probably
harks back to the idea of Christian *fides* as the basis of justice
in 1.142. Both types of *iustitia*, strict justice and kindness or
generosity, have Christian belief as their foundation. Zacchaeus gave because he believed; his work was the sign of his
faith.

146. cum fide: Reverts to the classical sense of 'good faith'.
Quid enim opus est dicere?: There is no need to say
anything at all; keep quiet about your good deeds; cf. 1.147;
2.2–3; 3.36.

in tua potestate est largiri quod velles: [velles: P¹VMA,
W¹: *velis* P², EW², CNB] What you give is at your own
discretion; you do not have to pretend to give more than you
wish.

Fraus fundamentum solvit et opus corruit: Deception
vitiates an act of kindness. Although A. is thinking of good
faith, he continues to allude to the **fundamentum** and the
opus of Christian belief, from 1.145.

Numquid Petrus . . . vel uxorem eius?: See Acts 5: 1–11.
Ananias' and Sapphira's crime was not in keeping some of
the money, but in claiming that they had donated the full
revenue from the sale of their property.

Sed exemplo eorum noluit perire ceteros: Their deaths
were a deterrent to others (Acts 5: 5, 11).

**147. si iactantiae causa magis quam misericordiae
largiaris . . . quomodo a te proficiscitur sic aestimatur:**
Cf. Cic. *Off.* 1.44: *Videre etiam licet plerosque, non tam natura
liberales quam quadam gloria ductos, ut benefici videantur
facere multa quae proficisci ab ostentatione magis quam a
voluntate videantur. Talis autem simulatio vanitati est con-
iunctior quam aut liberalitati aut honestati.* A. gives a Christian slant to Cic.'s idea: the Stoic *voluntas* (βούλησις: cf. Cic

Tusc. 4.12) becomes *misericordia,* and A. goes on to stress the role of conscience in examining motive, and the eternal consequences of deceit. On the evils of giving for the sake of show, cf. 2.2–3, 76, 102, 109–11; *Paen.* 2.84; *Luc.* 1.18; and, strikingly, Aug. *In ep. Ioh.* 8.9, where charity and pride are pictured as alternative charioteers, either one of which may be driving an act of generosity. **Adfectus tuus nomen imponit operi tuo:** On the importance of motive, cf. 1.149; *Paen.* 2.83; *Vid.* 27: *liberalitas non cumulo patrimonii, sed largitatis definitur adfectu.* This interiority is crucial to A.'s ethic (Hill, 203–4).

moralem iudicem: There is always someone watching you, examining your motives in giving. Conscience, too, can function as a *iudex,* cf. 2.2; 3.24 (cf. also 3.29, 31).

Nesciat, **inquit,** *sinistra tua quod facit dextera tua*: Mt. 6: 3.

Non de corpore loquitur . . . frater tuus quod facis nesciat: Typical of A.'s search for deeper meanings in the scriptural text (Introduction IV.5). For other uses of this verse in similar contexts, cf. Jer. *In Ps. 133.*103–204; *In Isaiam* 13.2; Aug. *De Serm. Dom. in Mont.* 2.6–9; Max. Taur. *Serm.* 43.4; Pet. Chrys. *Serm.* 9.5.

ne dum hic mercedem quaeris iactantiae, illic remu-nerationis fructum amittas: There is no point in seeking a reward (human praise) in this world, if you lose your soul in the next; cf. 2.2–3; 3.36. On **hic . . . illic,** cf. 1.29, 58, 103, 238–40; 3.11, 36.

quem laudat os pauperis et non labia sua: Cf. Prov. 27: 2: *Laudet te alienus, et non os tuum; extraneus, et non labia tua.* On the gratitude shown by the poor recipient, cf. 1.38–9; 2.126–7; Paul. Nol. *Ep.* 34.10.

148. fide causa loco tempore: Reminiscent of the Panae-tian–Ciceronian casuistry which argues for different duties in different situations (cf. especially 1.174). Though A. believes that mercy is owed to all, various criteria need to be applied so that fellow-believers and those most in need receive the most liberality, and resources are not wasted on the unworthy. In this way, generosity is 'perfect'. **Fide** here is in the Christian sense again (*pace* Banterle, 113 and n. 6), in view of what follows.

ut primum opereris circa domesticos fidei: Cf. Gal. 6: 10: *Ergo dum tempus habemus, operemur bonum ad omnes, maxime autem ad domesticos fidei.* On showing priority to believers, cf. 2.107; and *Luc.* 8.79: *Da ergo prius parenti, da etiam pauperi, da illi presbytero quod tibi abundat terrenum.* On the church as a family, see on 1.24; *Vid.* 4.

Grandis culpa si sciente te fidelis egeat: For NT language to this effect, cf. 1 Jn. 3: 17–18; also Jas. 2: 15–16. On the needs of hunger and imprisonment in particular, cf. Mt. 25: 31–46.

qui praesertim egere erubescat: In the MSS, these words come after **aerumnam perpeti**, but this renders the relative clause without an immediate anchor (since **eum** picks up **fidelis**). Winterbottom, 563, persuasively suggests transposing the clause to follow **egeat**, which has the additional advantage of giving a rhetorical echo in **egeat . . . egere**. The entire sentence is notably complex; the translation attempts to convey the informality of the string of rhetorical protases. A. is thinking particularly of people of higher social standing who may fall on hard times; on being ashamed to beg, cf. the steward in Christ's story in Lk. 16: 3. On showing compassion to those who become needy through no fault of their own, cf. 1.158; 2.69, 77; *Expos. Ps. 118.*17.4: *Et omnibus quidem misericordia inopibus iure debetur, sed maior quidam, cum ex divitibus atque nobilibus in ultimum statum atque egestatis necessitatem aliquos aerumna deiecit, miserationis pulsat adfectus.* Paulinus of Pella (*c.*376–460) is an obvious example of a grandee who found himself in greatly reduced circumstances when he lost his estates to barbarians; his autobiographical poem, the *Eucharisticos*, narrates the details as the meditation of an octogenarian on his personal experience of divine providence. It says a great deal about A.'s social preferences that the plight of individuals of this type is specifically highlighted for concern.

Benedictio perituri in me veniat: Job 29: 13.

149. Personarum quidem Deus acceptor non est: Cf. Acts 10: 34 (also Jas. 2: 1–9); and 2.125 below.

plerique fraude eam quaerunt et adfingunt aerumnam: Spurious or professional begging was a significan problem; on the need to test the genuineness of pleas for mercy, cf. 2.76–7 and see ad loc.

Non enim avarus Dominus est, ut plurimum quaerat: On the correlation between giving to the poor and giving to the Lord, see on 1.39.

qui dimittit omnia et sequitur eum: As Peter claimed that the disciples had done: Mk. 10: 28; cf. Mt. 19: 27.

⟨secundum⟩ quod habet: The addition of **secundum** lends a specificity to an otherwise vague **quod habet** (Winterbottom, 563).

Denique duo aera viduae illius . . . partem exiguam contulerunt: See Mk. 12: 41–4; Lk. 21: 1–4. On this example, cf. e.g. *Vid.* 27–32; *Paen.* 2.82; *Ep.* 68 [26].4–6.

Adfectus . . . pretium rebus imponit: Cf. 1.147.

Dominus non vult simul effundi opes, sed dispensari: Cf. 2.76–84, 109–11; giving should, however, be to the point of sacrifice (2.136). Cic. says that giving should be within one's means (*Off.* 1.44).

ut Eliseus boves suos occidit . . . in disciplinam se propheticam daret: See 3 Ki. 19: 19–21.

150. **ut proximos seminis tui non despicias si egere cognoscas:** Cf. Is. 58: 7. Cic. says that responsibility to parents, children, household, and relatives comes first after obligation to country (*Off.* 1.58); in *Off.* 1.54, he specifies the order of bonds within a family: (i) husband and wife; (ii) parents and children; (iii) brothers; (iv) first cousins and second cousins; (v) relations by marriage. In A., cf. 1.127, 169.

quibus pudor est . . . postulare subsidium necessitati: It is disgraceful for relations to have to ask others for help when their own family ought to come to their aid; cf. *Luc.* 8.79.

pretio miserationis peccata redimas tua: Cf. Dan. 4: 24: *et peccata tua elemosynis redime, et iniquitates tuas misericordiis pauperum: forsitan ignoscet delictis tuis*; and 1.39, 145 above; see ad locc.

pretium tuum quaerunt, vitae fructum adimere contendunt!: Relatives who seek enrichment are depleting your resources to help others, and so are threatening your ability to redeem your soul by your good works. Some clerics evidently had families who pestered them to share their income with them. Such relations were interested more in enriching themselves than in the needs of other deserving claimants, and they were also depriving these men of the chance to build up merit by true charity. Relatives in need are to be helped because they are relatives, A. says, but they are not to be enriched if this means that you lose the ability to earn divine favour yourself. The works element in the soteriology here is strong indeed.

151. Consilium prompsimus: auctoritatem petamus: The authority of Scripture is invoked to validate the preceding advice; cf. 2.65. On the Pauline distinction between counsel and precept, cf. *Vid.* 72–85.

Primum neminem debet pudere . . . dum largitur pauperi: It is no disgrace to impoverish oneself materially through helping others; this is, of course, not the same point as is implicit in the reference in 1.148 to people of means being reduced to shameful need through some calamity.

pauper factus est, cum dives esset: 2 Cor. 8: 9; on A.'s citations of this verse elsewhere (e.g. 2.14), see M. Poirier, '"Christus pauper factus est" chez saint Ambroise', *RSLR* 15 (1979), 250–7.

ut bona ratio sit exinaniti patrimonii: Cic. forbids the exhaustion of an inheritance through indiscriminate giving (*Off.* 2.54, 64), and A. later seems to agree (2.109), but here he urges giving to the point of complete self-sacrifice. The pattern, crucially, is the incarnational kenosis of Christ (on which cf. 3.15; *Expl. Ps. 40*.1; *Expos. Ps. 118*.20.57): Christ willingly laid aside his riches and identified himself with the needy in order to enrich all by his redemptive work; Löpfe, 152–70, especially 163–8; Vasey, 190–5.

et consilium in hoc do, **apostolus dicit:** *hoc enim vobis utile est*: 2 Cor. 8: 10.

non tantum facere . . . ab anno praeterito: 2 Cor. 8: 10. **Perfectorum utrumque est, non pars:** The verse neatly illustrates A.'s division of kindness into generosity and goodwill, both of which are necessary for perfection. On the drive towards perfectionism, shaped by divine example, cf. 1.36–8, 233–9; 3.10–11. The ambition of the perfect is to do the maximum possible good to others (*Iac.* 2.21).

Nunc ergo et facere consummate . . . et qui modicum

non minoravit: 2 Cor. 8: 11–15. In 2 Cor. 8: 15, Paul is quoting Ex. 16: 18, on the gathering of the manna, when distribution ensured that the differing needs of all were fully met.

152. non enim patiuntur angustias nisi imperfecti: A somewhat astonishing sentiment at first sight, but one that is shaped by Stoic assumptions: the truly wise (or 'perfect') person (cf. 3.10–14)—for A., the one who fears God and follows Christ's example—rises above suffering and does not feel it, hence it is only those who are not in this category who experience difficulties. Cf. 1.188–95; 2.21; *Iac.* 1.27–39.

Sed et si quis ecclesiam nolens gravare in sacerdotio aliquo constitutus aut ministerio: *ministerium* often refers to the diaconate in particular, and *sacerdotium* describes the priesthood, the office of either bishop or presbyter (on which, see on 1.87). Clergy who have independent means and who do not wish to be a burden to the church are not obliged to give up all their wealth and receive an ecclesiastical benefice; they may retain what will provide them with an adequate income, and give the remainder of their money to the needy. See on 1.185.

153. *Ut vestra abundantia sit . . . ad vestram inopiam*: 2 Cor. 8: 14.

id est, ut populi abundantia sit . . . et conferat ei gratiam: Paul urges the Corinthians to complete the work which they had begun the previous year, of collecting money for needy Christians at Jerusalem; he contrasts the Corinthians' slowness with the selfless generosity of the Macedonians. He advocates wise giving to the poor by the better-off, not that the better-off should reduce themselves to poverty; giving and receiving are to produce equality. The Jerusalem Christians will be able to help the Corinthians if ever their positions should be reversed. The suggestion of *spiritual* wealth or poverty is not made in 2 Cor. 8. A., however, sees the Corinthian *populus* or *plebs* as rich materially but poor spiritually, whereas *illi,* the believers at Jerusalem, have material needs but enjoy spiritual prosperity. This is typical of his belief that there is a connection between outward poverty and spiritual wealth (cf. 1.59; 2.12–16). The renunciation of earthly wealth is the way to spiritual riches.

(Jer. *Ep*. 108.15, says that he used these verses to try to urge Paula not to overdo her material kindness.)

154. ***Qui multum non abundavit et qui modicum, non minuit***: 2 Cor. 8: 15, quoting Ex. 16: 18.

quia nihil est quidquid in saeculo est: Very much the other-worldly rationale of A.'s asceticism; cf. 1.242–5; 2.1–21; *Abr*. 1.4; *Is*. 78; *Fug*., *passim*.

qui exiguum habet non minuit, quia nihil est quod amittit: Not really what Paul means by citing Ex. 16: 18. The principle in the gathering of the manna was that those who had gathered much distributed to the less fortunate what was surplus to their requirements; caring distribution brought about equality. But A. argues that the rich person does not have much because earthly riches are worthless, while the poor person, by the same token, does not lack anything of any importance.

155. **eget semper qui plus concupiscit:** The rich person's wants are insatiable; cf. *Cain* 1.21; *Abr*. 1.12; *Nab*. 4–15. On the evils of avarice, cf. 2.108, 128–33. Christians should be content with what they have (2.89).

Similiter ergo . . . sed adlevat mentem: The lack of wealth is not a burden: he who gives spiritual blessings in return for material gifts has a heart lightened by grace.

156. **o homo:** For the address, cf. 2.52; also 3.16 (*homo*).

Iohannes: John the Baptist.

quo nemo maior est inter natos mulierum . . . in regno caelorum: Cf. Mt. 11: 11; Lk. 7: 28.

157. **Quis eius potest aut magnitudinem aut latitudinem comprehendere?:** Cf. Eph. 3: 18–19.

Fides si fuerit sicut granum sinapis, montes transferre potest: Cf. Mt. 17: 20.

et non tibi datur ultra granum sinapis: i.e. simple faith, pictured as a tiny grain of mustard seed, is all that you have; you do not have worldly goods. But this spiritual wealth is all that you require.

quia multi sunt . . . quam si nullam habuissent Domini gratiam: Possibly A. is thinking not just of people but also of the fallen angels (cf. Job 4: 18; Is. 14: 12–21; Ezek. 28: 12–19; Mt. 25: 41; 2 Pt. 2: 4; Jd. 6; Apoc. 12: 9), who fell through pride (*Expos. Ps. 118*.7.8) and lust (*Virg*. 1.53; *Expos. Ps. 118*.8.58; *Apol*. 4).

et quod parum videtur habenti, plurimum est cui nihil deest: The materially poor person does not consider his grace to be much, but it is a great deal to the rich person who has no spiritual treasure.

158. nonnumquam etiam verecundia quae ingenuos prodit natales: See on 1.148. This aside also gives a clue as to why *verecundia* is so important to A.: the virtue is a hallmark of good breeding and social respectability.

latrociniis: A major problem, both in Cic.'s context (*Off.* 2.40; cf. *Off.* 3.107) and in the fourth century: cf. e.g. 1.243; 2.77; 3.27; *Expos. Ps. 118*.8.25; 15.7; 19.7; *Luc.* 6.48; *Ex.* 6.59; *Expl. Ps. 36*.15; *Interp.* 4.21; for a useful survey, see R. MacMullen, *Enemies of the Roman Order: Treason, Unrest and Alienation in the Empire* (Cambridge, MA, 1966), 255–68.

159. Nam et Dominus ait . . . propter importunitatem: See Lk. 11: 5–13, especially 11: 8, about persistence in prayer. A. does not in fact draw a clear inference from the biblical illustration. He implicitly agrees with the objection that it is unjust for the blind man to be ignored while the healthy young man's *importunitas* brings him undeserved reward; the gift is the result of *taedium*, not *iudicium* (Cic. commends the use of *iudicium* in kindness in *Off.* 1.49). But we are left wondering whether we are supposed to beware of depriving the needy by being too ready to heed the persistent pleas of the less deserving (the interpretation which 1.158 might lead us to expect, given the emphasis on examining the needs of the potential recipient), or whether the *importunitas* is in fact a good thing (as the persistence is in the gospel story). The first conclusion is clearly more likely (cf. also 2.68, 77), but it is strange that A. does not make his point more obvious.

CHAPTER 31: REPAYING WITH GREATER
MEASURE

60. beneficium: Cic. has the word in *Off.* 1.48–9.

Quid enim tam contra officium quam non reddere quod acceperis?: Cic. *Off.* 1.47 argues for the careful repayment of kindnesses: *Sin erunt merita, ut non ineunda sed referenda sit gratia, maior quaedam cura adhibenda est; nullum enim officium referenda gratia magis necessarium est.* There are roots in Aristotle: e.g. *EN* 1164ᵇ31–2; cf. also Aug. *Ep.* 153.25. See generally C. Feuvrier-Prévotat, 'Donner et recevoir: remarques sur les pratiques d'échanges dans le De officiis de Cicéron', *DHA* 11 (1985), 257–90. Gratitude is the greatest duty: cf. *Exc. fr.* 1.44.

Nec mensura pari sed uberiore reddendum arbitror: [**mensura** V²A, EW, CNB: *mensuram* PV¹M, most editors; **pari:** VMA, EW, CNB, most editors: *parem* P, Testard] Cf. Cic. *Off.* 1.48: *Quod si ea quae utenda acceperis maiore mensura, si modo possis, iubet reddere Hesiodus* [*Op.* 349–51]; also *Brut.* 15; *Att.* 13.12.3.

A. places more emphasis than Cic. on repaying someone who is in need: **si ipse in necessitatem incidit . . . eius aerumnam . . . humanitate**. The Christian must be particularly concerned to help a former benefactor who is now suffering hardship (though Cic. does say that the neediest should be helped first: *Off.* 1.49).

161. Unde imitanda nobis est . . . reddere quam acceperit: Cf. Cic. *Off.* 1.48: *An imitari* [sc. *debemus*] *agros fertiles, qui multo plus efferunt quam acceperunt?*; *Sen.* 51: *quae* [sc. *terra*] *numquam recusat imperium nec umquam sine usura reddit quod accepit, sed alias minore, plerumque maiore cum faenore*; also Plin. *Paneg.* 32.3. On the idea of the earth repaying with interest the seed which has been 'invested' in it, cf. 3.40; *Ex.* 3.33–5; *Exc. fr.* 1.45; 2.56; *Ep.* 73 [18].20–1.

Sicut agricultura est homo insipiens . . . desolabitur Prov. 24: 30–1 (LXX).

aut spontaneos . . . aut creditos: Two types of generosity: spontaneous giving, and repayment of kindness in larger measure; cf. Cic. *Off.* 1.48.

quodam hereditario usu parentis: Somewhat obscure on first reading, but the *parens* is the earth (cf. 3.45), and **quodam** apologizes for the metaphor; cf. *Virg.* 2.2: *hereditario quodam paternae virtutis usu.*

Esto tamen ut aliquis excusare possit quod non dederi . . . non reddere vero non licet: Cf. Cic. *Off.* 1.48: *demu*

necne in nostra potestate est, non reddere viro bono non licet,
modo id facere possit sine iniuria.

162. Si sederis cenare ad mensam potentis . . . haec
enim obtinent vitam falsam: Prov. 23: 1–3 (LXX). The
use of these verses here is not immediately clear. In themselves, they urge us to think carefully before we eat the
delicacies of a rich man's table, considering the temptations
to excess. But A. seems to think that they tell us to consider
carefully how much we eat at his table, since we have to
repay his generosity (**te talia praeparare** [**te talia**: V,
CNB: *talia* PMA, EW, Testard] must convey the idea of
appropriate repayment, after **ideo** at the beginning of the
sentence). Different interpretations follow in 1.163–5; cf.
also 2.52.

scripsimus: See Introduction V.

in Proverbiis quoque habes . . . consuevit valere: In the
Wisdom literature, not in the book of Prov. specifically; the
allusion is to Eccli. 3: 31.

ut etiam in die ruinae inveniat gratiam quando pos-
sunt praeponderare peccata: The divine judge weighs up
sins and good works in a great balance: the sins are naturally
expected to preponderate, but may be forgiven by grace
where the good deeds adequately compensate: cf. *Apol.* 24;
Expos. Ps. 118.7.17; esp. 20.40; *Ep.* 36 [2].14–16; see generally Niederhuber, *Eschatologie*, 210–54.

cum Dominus ipse remunerationem uberiorem sanc-
torum meritis in evangelio polliceatur: On differing
rewards according to merit, cf. 1.233–8; *Luc.*, prol. 6;
5.60–1; on reward as incentive, cf. *Paen.* 1.89; *Expl. Ps.*
1.13; *Ep.* 16 [76].2.

Dimitte et dimittemini . . . dabunt in sinum vestrum:
Lk. 6: 37–8.

163. non de cibis sed de operibus est bonis: A. typically
looks for a spiritual meaning in Prov. 23: 1–3 [see generally
Introduction IV.5]. There does not seem to be an obvious
precedent for the interpretation which follows, though there
are a few similarities with the later stages of the development
of Origen in *Expl. Prov.* 23, where the ruler is first pictured
as Satan, and the courses as his false or evil attractions; then
the hand is seen as the mind, which is to receive the spiritual

food of the Scriptures, which will sustain the judgement of
God. A. first seems to have the *potens* as a human benefactor
who must be paid back for his hospitality (1.162); then as the
Lord himself, whose 'food' is good works (1.163), or the
wisdom of the Scriptures (1.164–5). In his enthusiasm to
show a versatile range of interpretations of these scriptural
verses, he moves steadily further away from the Ciceronian
point with which he begins in 1.160–1.

Meus cibus est . . . qui in caelo est: Jn. 4: 34, *Meus cibus
est ut faciam voluntatem eius qui misit me*, with the last part
influenced by Mt. 7: 21, *qui facit voluntatem Patris mei qui in
caelis est*, or Mt. 12: 50, *quicumque enim fecerit voluntatem
Patris mei qui in caelis est.*

164.   propheta: David.

Delectare in Domino: Ps. 36: 4.

Edamus ergo panes sapientiae: Cf. Prov. 9: 5, where
Wisdom says: *Venite, comedite panem meum.*

**non in solo pane sed in omni verbo Dei vita est
hominis:** Cf. Dt. 8: 3, quoted by Jesus in Mt. 4: 4; Lk. 4: 4.

facti ad imaginem Dei: Cf. Gen. 1: 26–7; on A.'s anthropology, see S.-E. Szydzik, *Ad imaginem Dei: Die Lehre von
der Gottebenbildlichkeit des Menschen bei Ambrosius von Mailand* (Diss., Free University, Berlin, 1961), especially 24–33,
34–75; id. 'Die geistigen Ursprünge der Imago-Dei-Lehre
bei Ambrosius von Mailand', *ThG* 53 (1963), 161–76.

De poculo vero: The cup of wisdom; in the context of the
quotation which follows, Job is talking about his wise
counsel which was eagerly sought.

Sicut terra exspectans pluviam . . . sermones meos:
Job 29: 23.

CHAPTER 32: SCRIPTURE AS A FEAST OF
WISDOM; GOODWILL IS ESSENTIAL TO
KINDNESS

165.   quasi ros sic in nos Dei verba descendant: Cf. Dt
32: 2: (Moses speaks) *Concrescat in pluvia doctrina mea, flua
ut ros eloquium meum, quasi imber super herbam et quasi stilla
super gramina*; cf. also Ps. 71: 6.

in paradiso delectationis positus atque in convivio sapientiae locatus: Scripture is a feast of wisdom at which Christ presides (cf. 2.52); the pleasure of this feast is associated with the delight of paradise (cf. *Cain* 1.19). Communion with Christ in the Scriptures (cf. 1.88) is the highest privilege of the soul: it recalls the paradise of the unfallen state, where humanity could have uninhibited fellowship with God, and it anticipates the bliss which awaits the godly in the world to come (cf. *Bon. mort.* 45–57). On the necessity of feeding upon or drinking in God's Word, cf. *Expl. Ps.* *1*.30–4; *Expos. Ps.* *118*.7.25; 12.28; 14.2–5; *Ep.* 36 [2].3; also *Cain* 2.22. On the feast of wisdom, see Pizzolato, 30.

prius quae: *prius quid* CO.

operibus exsequaris . . . repraesentes: This seems to explain the identification of the food at the feast with good works in 1.163: by feeding on the Scriptures, the faithful come to know God's will, and are enabled then to demonstrate that they have received grace by doing good deeds.

largitori muneris: God himself. The 'gift' is divine grace.

ut possint singuli dicere: Though the following words are Paul's.

Gratia autem Dei sum quod sum . . . abundantius illis omnibus laboravi: 1 Cor. 15: 10.

166. This paragraph brings us back to kindness, after the extended exegesis of Prov. 23: 1–3 in 1.163–5.

haud scio an etiam locupletius: Affection might be more generously repaid than material kindness. Cic. *Off.* 2.69 has *locupletes*, and A. is thinking of that passage here:

Gratia enim in eo ipso quod habetur refertur: Cf. Cic. *Off.* 2.69: *Nimirum enim inops ille, si bonus est vir, etiam si referre gratiam non potest, habere certe potest. Commode autem quicumque dixit pecuniam qui habeat, non reddidisse, qui reddiderit, non habere, gratiam autem et qui rettulerit habere et qui habeat rettulisse*; also *Red. Quir.* 23 (if the text is sound); *Planc.* 68; Gell. *NA* 1.4.2–8.

praestat benevolentia supra ipsam liberalitatem: The stress which A. places on goodwill or grateful affection as the superior element in kindness, though suggested in part by

Cic., is taken further under the influence of biblical teaching
(cf. 1.149); cf. 2.126–7.

167. quae amicitiam connectit et copulat: Cic. supplies
this Aristotelian and Stoic view that friendship stems from
goodwill: see below (and *Amic.* 19, 23); *copulatius* appears in
Cic. *Off.* 1.56. On friendship, cf. 1.171–4.

**ut David, cum esset prudentior, Ionathae tamen
iunioris consiliis acquiescebat:** When Jonathan's father
Saul was seeking to kill David, Jonathan advised his friend to
go into hiding while he sought to dissuade Saul (1 Ki. 18: 1–
20: 42, especially 19: 1 ff.). A. can scarcely forbear to mention
David and Jonathan when he thinks of *amicitia*.

**Tolle ex usu hominum benevolentiam: tamquam
solem e mundo tuleris ita erit:** A. waxes eloquent on
the practical glories of goodwill (Becker, 103, speaks of a
'hymn' to *benevolentia*); cf. Cic. *Amic.* 47: *Solem enim e
mundo tollere videntur qui amicitiam e vita tollunt, qua nihil
a dis immortalibus melius habemus, nihil iucundius* (alluding to
the Epicureans and Cyrenaics); also *Att.* 9.10.3.

**ut peregrinanti monstrare viam . . . lumen de lumine
accendere:** Cf. Cic. *Off.* 1.51, quoting Ennius (*Scen.* 398–
400 = *Trag.* 366–8 = 313–15 Jocelyn) on showing kindness to
strangers: *homo qui erranti comiter monstrat viam, | quasi
lumen de suo lumine accendat facit: | nihilo minus ipsi lucet,
cum illi accenderit*. Cf. also Cic. *Off.* 3.54; *Balb.* 36; and, on
lumen de lumine, cf. Ov. *AA* 3.93, and the Nicene creed's
description of Christ's divinity, quoted by A. in *Fid.* 1.118;
Spir. 3.82; *Exh. virg.* 81.

deferre hospitium: Cf. 1.39, 86; 2.103–7; and see on 2.103.
Foris autem . . . omni venienti patebat: Job 31: 32.

aquam de aqua profluenti dare: Cic., *Off.* 1.52, quotes
the maxim *non prohibere aqua profluente*.

tamquam fons aquae reficiens sitientem: A. may well be
thinking of verses such as Jn. 4: 13–14; Apoc. 21: 6.

tamquam lumen quod etiam aliis luceat: Again, perhaps reminiscent of verses like Jn. 1: 4–5, 8–9; 8: 12; 9: 5; 12:
46; 1 Jn. 2: 8–11; and especially Mt. 5: 14–16. The Ennian
Ciceronian language seems to be blended with scriptural
terminology in A.'s mind. The MSS' *in* between **etiam** and
aliis is redundant (Winterbottom, 563).

168. debitoris chirographum: A personal bond, or I.O.U. A. rails against the injustice inflicted on bankrupt debtors (e.g. *Nab.* 21–5—the stock story of a poor man contemplating selling his child to pay his debt), and urges the ready cancellation of debts (*Nab.* 57; *Ep.* 7 [37].44; cf. *Iac.* 1.10).

Iob sanctus admonet . . . non liberat syngrapham: Cf. Job 31: 35–6 (LXX).

Quid igitur, etiam si ipse non exigas . . . sine damno pecuniae repraesentare?: There is no point in deferring the recall of the debt yourself, only to pass it on to your heirs, since this will be of no advantage to *you*; write off the debt here and now: you will earn praise for your goodwill, and you will be no worse off personally than you would be if you left the matter to your heirs. On **exigas,** cf. *Epp.* 62 [19].4; 76 [20].6; also Aug. *Conf.* 1.4.4 (evoking Mt. 25: 14–30). On the greed of heirs, cf. 1.244.

169. benevolentiam: a domesticis primum profecta personis . . . per coniunctionum gradus in civitatum pervenit ambitum: An allusion to the argument of Cic. *Off.* 1.53–4, based on the Stoic οἰκείωσις doctrine, that the bonds of human society proceed outwards from family relationships; see on 1.150 above (for something similar, cf. also Cic. *Off.* 3.69; *ND* 3.38 (justice born in community); and *Amic.* 19). In that passage, Cic. has the words *coniunguntur . . . coniunctiones . . . coniunctio . . . gradus . . . civitatis . . . fratrum . . . benevolentia. Necessitudinum gradus* occurs in *Off.* 1.59. A.'s Latin is compressed, but his aim is clear: he wants to depict the triumphant advance of *benevolentia* from primordial family relations to the complex web of social ties which binds together the urban unit: **in civitatum pervenit ambitum.**

et de paradiso egressa mundum replevit: The divine command to man and woman in paradise is *replete terram* (Gen. 1: 28); after the flood, Noah and his sons are told: *implete terram* (Gen. 9: 1, 7). On paradise, cf. *Parad., passim; Ep.* 34 [45]; *Expos. Ps. 118.*4.2; 7.8; etc.

Erunt ambo in una carne: Gen. 2: 24. The addition of **et in uno spiritu** may be under the influence of Phil. 1: 27.

Unde se Eva serpenti credidit, quoniam . . . esse malevolentiam non opinabatur: See Gen. 3: 1–7.

A. offers a sophistic explanation for the Fall, bringing in
benevolentia/malevolentia to suit his argument; there is little
obvious support in Gen. 3 for this interpretation. For other
angles on the Fall, cf. 1.7 and see ad loc.; 1.137.

The convergence of influences in this paragraph is striking. A. adopts Cic.'s point that human society originates in
domestic relationships, and adds to this the biblical narrative
of the union of Adam and Eve in paradise, their fall from
grace, and the subsequent expansion of the human race to
replenish the earth. In so doing, he visualizes *benevolentia* as
part of God's design in creation, a principle which has bound
the human race together from its earliest, unfallen state. Just
as the first part of *iustitia*, strict justice, originates in the
community of goods and rights in the pristine state
(1.132–7), so *benevolentia*, the main constituent of the other
side of *iustitia*, kindness, likewise goes back to the divine
ideal in paradise. A specific framework of creation theology
underpins an essentially Stoic argument on the significance
of human relationships.

CHAPTER 33: GOODWILL AND THE CHURCH;
GOODWILL PRODUCES LIKENESS OF CHARACTER

170. Augetur benevolentia coetu ecclesiae: Once again,
the ecclesial community is the model, the epitome of virtue
at work: just as the church is the *forma iustitiae* (1.142), so it
is also the place where *benevolentia* is particularly fostered
(1.170). A. moves from the natural ties of 1.169 to a level of
relationship that is still more profound: the spiritual family.
'The long-lost solidarity of all humanity [is] regained
through the church' (Brown, *Body*, 364).

fidei consortio: Partnership in the one faith; cf. Eph. 4: 13;
Tit. 1: 4. On the church as constituted by faith, cf. *Ep.* 75
[21].24, and Toscani, 386–91.

initiandi societate: The fellowship of those who have
shared in the baptismal initiation rite. Cic. uses *societas* in
Off. 1.50–6; he also speaks of the bond between those who
share the same sacred rites (*Off.* 1.55). The slanting of these

ideas to the contemporary spiritual context of the addressees is subtle.

percipiendae: Cic. *Off.* 1.59 has *percipiendis*.

mysteriorum communione: Participation in the mysteries of the sacraments, pre-eminently the eucharist, the privilege of the initiates who have been cleansed by the water of baptism. There is a sharing of communion with Christ and with one another. On this very important dimension of A.'s ecclesiology, see Johanny, 161–236.

necessitudinum: Cic. *Off.* 1.59 has the word.

filiorum . . . patrum . . . necessitudo gratiae: The relations of the spiritual family (natural bonds having been mentioned in 1.169); cf. 1.24 and see ad loc. **germanitatem fratrum:** A frequent NT image for the church (Acts, *passim*; 1 Pt. 2: 17; etc.); cf. 2.155. Pétré, 129–33 (in general, 104–40), speaks of the Stoic influence on A.'s view of universal brotherhood, but in passages like this one the scriptural idea is clearly dominant: the application of the ecclesial ideal is quite specific.

171. Adiuvant etiam parium studia virtutum . . . morum facit similitudinem: Cf. Cic. *Off.* 1.55–6:

Sed omnium societatum nulla praestantior est, nulla firmior, quam cum viri boni moribus similes sunt familiaritate coniuncti [55]; et quamquam omnis virtus nos ad se adlicit facitque ut eos diligamus in quibus ipsa inesse videatur, tamen iustitia et liberalitas id maxime efficit. Nihil autem est amabilius nec copulatius quam morum similitudo bonorum; in quibus enim eadem studia sunt, eaedem voluntates, in iis fit ut aeque quisque altero delectetur ac se ipso [56].

Cf. also *Off.* 1.58: *estque ea iucundissima amicitia quam similitudo morum coniugavit*; and *Clu.* 46; Nep. 25.5.3.

Denique Ionathae filius regis imitabatur sancti David mansuetudinem: See 1 Ki. 19: 1–7; the king is of course Saul.

quod diligebat eum: Cf. 1 Ki. 18: 1; 19: 1, and Cic.'s reference to love in *Off.* 1.56.

Cum sancto sanctus eris: Ps. 17: 26.

filii Noe simul habitabant et non erat in his morum concordia: See Gen. 9: 18–27: Ham broadcast the nakedness of his drunken father; Shem and Japheth modestly covered it.

Habitabant etiam in domo patria Esau et Iacob: See Gen. 25: 19–34; 27: 1–45; A. may also be picking up Cic.'s references to living in *una domus* in *Off.* 1.54 (language he has already evoked in 1.88 above).

quae praeriperet benedictionem: See Gen. 27: 1–45 on Jacob's usurpation of Esau's blessing from Isaac.

alter praedurus, alter mansuetus: This presumably alludes to the different lifestyles of Esau and Jacob: Esau was a skilled hunter and farmer, Jacob a peaceful tent-dweller (Gen. 25: 27).

sanctus Iacob paternae degenerem domus virtuti praeferre non poterat: In his esteem for Jacob, A. implies that Esau *was* the weaker brother morally (he was 'unworthy to be called his father's son'), not just that Jacob thought it—though it was Jacob who was guilty of trickery. The Latin is again quite compressed; the translation attempts to bring out the apparent sense.

172.   **Nihil autem tam consociabile . . . quos pares nobis credimus, diligamus:** See on 1.171, on Cic. *Off.* 1.56.

Habet autem in se benevolentia fortitudinem: This underlines the interconnection of the virtues and signposts the discussion of courage which commences in 1.175.

cum amicitia ex benevolentiae fonte procedat: Cf. 1.167, and see especially on 3.125.

Et si mala, inquit, *mihi evenerint per illum, sustineo:* Eccli. 22: 26 (Vulg.: 22: 31).

CHAPTER 34: THE ADVANTAGES OF GOODWILL
IN FRIENDSHIP

173.   **gladium iracundiae:** On anger, see on 1.90.

ut amici vulnera utilia quam voluntaria inimici oscula sint: Cf. Prov. 27: 6.

ut unus fiat ex pluribus: This was Pythagoras' ideal in friendship, according to Cic. *Off.* 1.56; also *Amic.* 92 (and 23); *Leg.* 1.33; *Att.* 3.15.4; *Fam.* 7.5.1; cf. Arist. *EN* 1168[b]7

MM 2.19; DL 5.20; Quint. *Decl.* 16.6; Ov. *Trist.* 4.4.72. In A., cf. *Spir.* 2.154; see also on 3.134.

Simul advertimus etiam correptiones . . . dolores non habent: Cf. Cic. *Off.* 1.58: *interdum etiam obiurgationes in amicitiis vigent maxime*; Cic. also has *grata* in *Off.* 1.56.

Compungimur enim censoriis sermonibus sed benevolentiae delectamur sedulitate: The censures of a friend may sound irksome, but are in fact pleasant and something for which to be thankful, because they show his depth of concern. Cf. 3.128, 133–4; also Plaut. *Trin.* 23 ff.

174. Ad summam, non omnibus eadem semper officia debentur . . . ut plerumque pignora vincat naturae: The treatment of the second virtue closes here in the same way as in Cic. *Off.* 1.59, by introducing the middle Stoic casuistry: duty varies according to circumstance. There are numerous linguistic echoes of *Off.* 1.59:

Sed in his omnibus officiis tribuendis videndum erit quid cuique maxime necesse sit et quid quisque vel sine nobis aut possit consequi aut non possit. Ita non idem erunt necessitudinem gradus qui temporum, suntque officia quae aliis magis quam aliis debeantur, ut vicinum citius adiuveris in fructibus percipiendis quam aut fratrem aut familiarem, at, si lis in iudicio sit, propinquum potius et amicum quam vicinum defenderis [etc.].

For similar arguments, cf. 1.213–16, 258.

Melius est vicinus in proximo quam frater longe habitans: Prov. 27: 10.

ut plerumque pignora vincat naturae: Under Cic.'s influence, A. argues that friends or neighbours may sometimes come before blood-relations (cf. however, 1.150). Already he has stressed the significance of the spiritual family, the relationships brought about by grace rather than by nature (1.170).

CHAPTER 35: COURAGE—MILITARY AND CIVIL

A. now moves on to explore courage (1.175–209). He distinguishes military courage from courage in a civilian context, or, in more general terms, physical courage from spiritual courage

(1.175). The basic distinction is Ciceronian, though Cic.'s categories are not preserved entirely accurately (see on 1.175). Although A. argues that military courage is really irrelevant to his clerical addressees, he manages to say a good deal about the military glories of the saints (1.175–7; 196–201), and about the physical as well as the spiritual valour of the martyrs in the face of death (1.202–7). His main focus, though, is bravery of spirit, a moral disposition where the passions are kept under control and externals are despised (1.178–95). Under Ciceronian influence, the thrust is decidedly Stoic, even if the exemplars, and many of the vices or challenges, are biblical. Panaetius, following Aristotle, had reinstated an intellectual or spiritual μεγαλοψυχία as more significant than the kind of 'animal' bravery implied by ἀνδρεία. A. can however combine the Stoic ideal of rational triumph over πάθη with the scriptural images of the godly sufferer (cf. Job in 1.180, 192, 195); the *Christi athleta* (1.183); the *Dei miles* (1.185–7); and the faithful martyr (1.198–9, 202–7). For Cic., courage is the political virtue *par excellence*; for A., it is at the deepest level the ability by faith to overcome in the struggle against the evil within and the forces of darkness and opposition without. The supreme test is martyrdom (for martyrdom as a triumph over Satan's forces, cf. e.g. Tert. *Scorp.* 12.9; Cypr. *Epp.* 39.3.1; 58.3.1; this dimension is pointed out well by Becker, 157–60). The target of winning eschatological divine approval remains essential (1.188, 191). As ever, the ecclesiastical image must be seen to be at least as noble as the secular standard (1.184–6). Like Cic., A. is preoccupied with the public realm; it is as the church lives before the world that the Christian contempt for adversity and danger will be displayed to best effect.

175. Satis copiose . . . tractavimus: Cf. Cic. *Off.* 1.60: *Atque ab iis rebus quae sunt in iure societatis humanae quemadmodum ducatur honestum, ex quo aptum est officium, satis fere diximus*; 1.18: *Ex quattuor autem locis, in quos honesti naturam vimque divisimus.*

quae velut excelsior ceteris: Cf. Cic. *Off.* 1.61: *Intelle-gendum autem est . . . splendidissimum videri quod animo magno elatoque humanasque res despiciente factum sit.* Neither Cic. nor A. in fact ranks courage as the highest of the virtues in practice (Cic. gives the first place to justice (*Off.* 1.20, 153), and A. to prudence). Cic. says that the third virtue *appears* to be the most exalted and it thus elicits the greatest amount of popular praise. Its value lies, according to Stoic thinking, in the fact that it fights on behalf of justice (*Off.* 1.62). Cic.'s concern is mainly to point up the significance of the section which is to follow (*Off.* 1.61–92), rather than to classify in any strict sense. It is under this influence that A. here also says that courage is **velut excelsior** (cf. again in 1.176).

dividitur in res bellicas et domesticas: Cic. speaks of courage in the respective spheres of *res bellicae* and *res urbanae* (*Off.* 1.74), and compares *domesticae fortitudines* to *militares fortitudines* (*Off.* 1.78).

Sed bellicarum rerum studium a nostro officio iam alienum videtur: Cf. Cic. *Off.* 1.61: *studium bellicae gloriae*. Cic. maintains that courage in civil affairs can often be even greater than military bravery; the achievements of statesmen have often provided the necessary basis for the exploits of the military leaders (*Off.* 1.74–8). War must be waged only for the sake of peace, and temperance must be observed in the conduct of war; he illustrates this principle with warnings of men who made great mistakes thanks to their rash desires for martial glory (*Off.* 1.79–84). In general, Cic. puts a premium on the courage of the statesman rather than that of the military leader (*Off.* 1.85–92). A. follows Cic.'s preoccupation with civil courage (substituting cleric for statesman), but he does so on the grounds that military affairs are largely irrelevant to ecclesiastics. The force of **iam** here (and in **nec ad arma iam spectat usus noster**, below) is significant: A. contrasts the Christian priesthood with the age of **Maiores . . . nostri**, when the heroes of the OT narratives won glory for their victories in battle. The Christian warfare is primarily a spiritual one (cf. Eph. 6: 10–20, especially 6: 12; also Jn. 18: 36). However, A. is no pacifist at a national level (contrast the private realm, in 1.131): he recognizes the principle of a just war (1.176), and expresses admiration for the military achievements of the OT saints. In fact, he ends up extolling martial courage with greater enthusiasm than Cic., for all his pious insistence on

pacis negotia. On the Christian gospel as a message of peace, cf. e.g. Acts 10: 36; Rom. 10: 15; 14: 17; Eph. 2: 17; 6: 15.

quia animi magis quam corporis officio intendimus: Cf. Cic. *Off.* 1.79: *Omnino illud honestum quod ex animo excelso magnificoque quaerimus animi efficitur, non corporis viribus*; *Off.* 2.46: *Ut igitur in reliquis rebus multo maiora opera sunt animi quam corporis.* Cic. differentiates moral and physical courage (moral, *Off.* 1.67–78; physical, *Off.* 1.79–91). A. seems to equate this division with the distinction between civil and military courage, mentioned above, though this is not the case in Cic. (Testard, 'Etude', 170 n. 28).

Iesus Nave: For Joshua's military exploits, see especially Josh. 5: 13–12: 24. **Nave** for the Vulg.'s *filius Nun* is common in the Latin Fathers; it derives from the LXX's Ναυη (and provides a typology of the OT Jesus as the pointer to the NT Jesus, the ship of salvation; see J. Daniélou, *Sacramentum Futuri. Etudes sur les origines de la typologie biblique* (Paris, 1950), 203–16).

Ierobaal: Better known as Gideon (Jdg. 6: 32; 7: 1; 8: 35); see Jdg. 6: 11–8: 32.

Samson: See Jdg. 14: 19; 15: 1–20.

David: See on 1.114.

176. velut excelsior ceteris: See on 1.175 above.

sed numquam incomitata virtus: Evoking the essential Stoic premiss that the virtues are interconnected; see on 1.115. Ovid has the quite rare adjective *incomitata* with *virtus* in *Pont.* 2.3.35–6 (for *incomitatus* without *virtus*, cf. Ps.-Quint. *Decl.* 7.9; Aug. *Serm.* 161.9.9 (*TLL* vii/1. 984)).

fortitudo sine iustitia iniquitatis materia est: Cf. Cic. *Off.* 1.62: *Sed ea animi elatio quae cernitur in periculis et laboribus, si iustitia vacat pugnatque non pro salute communi sed pro suis commodis, in vitio est*; Cic. then goes on to approve the Stoic definition of courage as the virtue which fights for *aequitas*.

cum in ipsis rebus bellicis iusta bella an iniusta sint spectandum putetur: Cic. discusses justice in war in *Off.* 1.34–40, 80; 2.26–7; 3.99–111 (also in *Rep.* 3.34–5; *Leg.* 2.34). His concern is to show that Rome's ancient wars were all justified in the interests of peace, and inevitably he tends to whitewash the facts of history (A. Michel, 'Les Lois de la guerre et les problèmes de l'impérialisme romain dans la philosophie de Cicéron', in J.-P. Brisson (ed.), *Problèmes de la guerre à Rome* (Paris, 1969), 171–83). By A.'s time, the pacifism of most pre-Constantinian Western Christianity had of course well and truly subsided. A. is the first Western churchman to articulate the concept of a just war (*Tob.* 51: *ius belli*), and since he identifies the well-being of the Roman empire with the prosperity of the Nicene cause (cf. 1.144), he can pray for the success of the imperial forces against heathen enemies (e.g. *Fid.* 2.136–43), while holding Stoic and Christian views of a universal human brotherhood. The just war theory is elaborated most fully and acutely by Augustine, e.g. *CD* 15.4; 19.7, 12; 22.6. See L. J. Swift, *The Early Fathers on War and Military Service* (Wilmington, DE, 1983), especially 96–110; id. 'St Ambrose on Violence and War', *TAPhA* 101 (1970), 533–43; Homes Dudden ii. 538–9; Morino, 55–7.

177. nisi lacessitus: An intriguing concession to Cic.'s point in *Off.* 1.20, *ut ne cui quis noceat, nisi lacessitus iniuria*, from which A. explicitly dissented in 1.131; with 1.131, cf. 3.59, disagreeing with Cic. *Off.* 3.76. That which is wrong for the individual may be legitimate for the community and its leadership. A. never asks how we might establish the overall justice of a particular war. On going to war for the right reasons, cf. Cic. *Off.* 1.79–81.

Itaque prudentiam fortitudinis comitem habuit in proelio: Itaque implies that waging war only when provoked (and so fighting a just war, presumably) is a matter of *prudentia*. The first virtue, as well as the second, is linked to courage. (On the association of prudence and justice, cf. 1.126–9.) For **comitem**, cf. 1.69. On the glories of David's example, cf. 2.32–8 and, more generally, 3.23; on his courage against Goliath, cf. *Bon. mort.* 8.

adversus Goliam: See 1 Ki. 17: 1–54.

immanem mole corporis: Cf. Verg. *Aen.* 9.516, 542, with A., *Apol.* 26; *Apol. alt.* 15; also *Aen.* 3.656; 5.118, 223; 6.232, with A. *Ex.* 6.31.

numquam nisi consulto Domino bellum adorsus: See e.g. 1 Ki. 23: 1–5; 2 Ki. 5: 17–25/1 Chr. 14: 8–17.

manu promptus: The phrase appears in Sall. *Cat.* 43.4.

bello adversus Titanas suscepto: A reference to a battle with the Philistines (2 Ki. 21: 15–17). The biblical narrative lays stress on the formidable size of the opponents of David and his men: they are said to be of the line of Arapha (2 Ki. 21: 16, and 21: 18, 20, 22) or Rapha (1 Chr. 20: 4, 6, 7), identified as giants; cf. also the readings of the LXX and the Vulg. in Gen. 14: 5; 15: 20; Dt. 2: 10–11, 20–1; 3: 11; Num. 13: 33 (the etymology of Arapha/Rapha remains uncertain, as the variety of renderings in modern translations reflects). A. highlights their gigantic status by calling them 'Titans', referring to the mythological children of Uranus and Ge, who were often associated or confused with the Giants who challenged Jupiter for sovereignty in heaven and were hurled to Tartarus by his thunderbolt (e.g. Hor. *Od.* 3.4.42–80); *P-W* 6.A.2, 1491–1508. He does the same in *Fid.* 3.4; *Apol.* 33–4, perhaps pandering to a penchant among literate readers for mythological imagery (McLynn, 104 n. 93; cf. Moorhead, 167).

gloriae cupidus, incuriosus salutis: A strikingly traditional Roman Stoic admiration for the military courage of one who scorns death in pursuit of glory; cf. 1.200; 3.56; also 3.82–4. Such an attitude contrasts with the view expressed so forcefully by Tertullian two centuries earlier, that all profane glory is to be spurned (Vermeulen, 43–7). On this occasion, David's bravery almost cost him his life; having been rescued by Abishai, he was made to swear that he would not risk his life in battle with his men again.

178. non haec sola: Military courage.

qui per fidem magnitudine animi *obstruxerunt leonum ora . . . de infirmitate fortes*: Heb. 11: 33–4. In context, these verses extol the faith which inspired the courage. The first two allusions are probably to (i) Daniel (Dan. 6; 14: 23–42) and perhaps Samson (Jdg. 14: 5–6) and David (1 Ki. 17: 34–7); (ii) the three Hebrew youths (Dan. 3). The third reference is more general, evoking a common OT phrase, 'the edge of the sword' (Ex. 17: 13; Num. 21: 24; etc.). The wording of the fourth clause is strange, however. The VL and Vulg. punctuate with a comma after **infirmitate**, and **fortes** belongs to the next clause (*fortes facti in bello*). Though A. can quote the verses accurately elsewhere

(*Parad.* 21; *Ep. extra coll.* 14 [63].67), he conflates the last stages of the verse both here and in 2.20, presumably because his memory fails him. The mistake is unfortunate, since **de infirmitate** in Heb. probably refers to physical debility rather than moral cowardice (perhaps alluding to the case of Hezekiah in Is. 38), and **fortes** applies to war in the next clause. The inner courage of which A. speaks is not there in the verse as he cites it. E² adds *exstiterunt* after **fortes** here.

The association of *magnitudo animi* (cf. Cic. *Off.* 1.15, 17: see on 1.115) with *fides* is an important—if unsurprising—clue to A.'s approach to the subject of moral courage. True courage depends on faith in God; where this is exercised, God is with the sufferer, and speaks through the exploits of the spiritual hero, validating the person's piety.

succincti: EW, COB: *subiecti* PVMA, Testard.

nuda virtute: A classical collocation: e.g. Luc. 9. 594–5; Petr. *Sat.* 88.2.

Quam insuperabilis Daniel . . . et ille epulabatur: [**rudentes:** PV¹M, E¹, Testard: *rugientes* V², E², CO] See Dan. 14: 23–42; Daniel feasts on food brought by Habakkuk.

CHAPTER 36: COURAGE OF SPIRIT

179. Non igitur in viribus corporis et lacertis . . . sed magis in virtute animi: Cf. Cic. *Off.* 1.79: *Omnino illud honestum quod ex animo excelso magnificoque quaerimus animi efficitur, non corporis viribus.*

neque in inferenda sed depellenda iniuria lex virtutis est: Cf. Cic. *Off.* 1.23: *Sed iniustitiae genera duo sunt, unum eorum qui inferunt, alterum eorum qui ab iis quibus infertur, si possunt, non propulsant iniuriam* (cf. also *Off.* 3.74).

Qui enim non repellit a socio iniuriam . . . tam est in vitio quam ille qui facit: Cf. Cic. *Off.* 1.23: *qui autem non defendit nec obsistit, si potest, iniuriae, tam est in vitio quam si parentes aut amicos aut patriam deserat* (Cic. also mentions, just previously, a *socius*). A. urges pacifism at the level of response to personal injustice (1.131), but assumes that the individual also has a moral obligation to defend his neighbour against aggression (cf. 2.102). He manages to substantiate this Ciceronian point with OT authority:

Nam cum vidisset Hebraeum . . . in arena absconderet: See Ex. 2: 11–12.

Eripe eum qui ducitur ad mortem: Prov. 24: 11.

180.   Unde igitur hoc . . . transtulerint: Pagan plagiarism from the Scriptures: Introduction IV.2.

vel Tullius vel etiam Panaetius: The final mention of Cic. in the work; the allusion is to *Off.* 1.23, as echoed above, and A. takes it that Cic. draws on Panaetius: **vel . . . vel etiam** pairs them over against (**aut**) Aristotle; see on 1.24.

aut ipse Aristoteles: See on 1.31. Aristotle discusses courage particularly in *EN* 1115^{a}6–1117^{b}22, advocating a mean between fear and confidence, but without mentioning the point made in 1.179; see Gauthier, 65–118. But Aristotle stands here for just another pagan philosopher; A. is probably not thinking of a particular passage or text. On the development of and distinctions between the Aristotelian and the Stoic conceptions of magnanimity, see Gauthier, 119–64, especially 137–41 on Panaetius and Cic.

etiam his duobus: Panaetius and Aristotle, who lived earlier than Cic. but later than Job (**antiquior**).

Salvum feci pauperem . . . . Benedictio perituri in me veniat: Job 29: 12–13.

Accinge sicut vir lumbos tuos . . . omnem autem iniuriosum humiliato: Job 40: 2, 5–6. *altitudinem* implies that the verse is suggested to A. by Cic.'s reference to *altitudo animi* in *Off.* 1.88; likewise, *iniuriosum* evokes *iniuria* in *Off.* 1.23, echoed in 1.179.

Habetis fortissimam consolationem: Heb. 6: 18. The verse offers tenuous support for *fortitudo*, but clearly occurs to A. because it includes the word *fortissimam*. In context, the verse is part of an exhortation to recognize the encouragement that Christians should have in knowing that God fulfilled his promise to Abraham; Abraham's faith was prospective, while the faith of Christians is retrospective. On **Apostolus** with reference to Heb. see on 1.30.

181.   quando unusquisque se ipsum vincit . . . non adversis perturbatur, non extollitur secundis: This all sounds thoroughly Stoic: courage means the control of passions such as anger (it overlaps here with temperance), indifference to outward allurements, and superiority to external circumstances; cf. Cic. *Off.* 1.66–9. Nevertheless, A. goes on to synthesize this language with some of the NT's teaching on self-mastery and endurance. The contrast of **adversis . . . secundis** appears in Cic. *Off.* 1.90–1.

quasi vento quodam: On the effect of the wind as an image of instability, cf. Job 13: 25; 21: 18; 30: 15, 22; Eph. 4: 14; Jas. 1: 6; etc. Cic. has the metaphor of the storm of danger in *Off.* 1.83.

variarum rerum circumfertur mutatione: Perhaps an echo of Cic. *Off.* 1.67: *quae multa et varia in hominum vita fortunaque versantur.*

magnificentius: Cic. has the word in *Off.* 1.68.

adficere carnem: On the evils of the flesh, cf. Rom. 7–8; Gal. 5: 16–26; 6: 8; Eph. 2: 3; Col. 2: 20–3; 1 Pt. 4: 1–6; 2 Pt. 2: 10.

in servitutem redigere: Cf. 1 Cor. 9: 27: *sed castigo corpus meum, et in servitudinem redigo.* The Stoic–Ciceronian teaching on passivity with regard to *perturbationes* and externals is related to an active Christian asceticism, as the mind is exercised and the flesh reduced to submission; on the flesh/spirit antithesis, see generally Seibel, 129–37.

ut oboediat imperio: On *imperium* of the self, cf. e.g. Xen. *Mem.* 1.6; Plaut. *Trin.* 309–10; Cic. *Parad.* 5.1; Liv. 30.14.7; Val. Max. 4.1.2; Sen. *Epp.* 71.36; 90.35; 113.30; Ps.-Sen. *Mor.* 82. Note Sall. *Cat.* 1.2: *Sed nostra omnis vis animo et corpore sita est: animi imperio, corporis servitio magis utimur.*

propositum animi ac voluntatem: The intellectualism of the scheme is strong, following Panaetius–Cic.; cf. generally *Parad.* 17; *Is.* 60. On virtue (and vice) as a determination of the will, cf. *Iac.* 1.1–4, 10; *Ex.* 1.31; *Paen.* 1.68–77; *Expos. Ps. 118*.8.36; though debilitated by the Fall, the will remains free and capable of responding to divine grace, which enables it to overcome passion.

182. quoniam in duobus generibus fortitudo spectatur animi . . . usque ad effectum persequatur: Cf. Cic. *Off.* 1.66:

Omnino fortis animus et magnus duabus rebus maxime cernitur,
quarum una in rerum externarum despicientia ponitur, cum
persuasum est nihil hominem nisi quod honestum decorumque
sit aut admirari aut optare aut expetere oportere, nullique neque
homini neque perturbationi animi nec fortunae succumbere. Altera
est res, ut . . . res geras magnas illas quidem et maxime utiles, sed
[ut] vehementer arduas plenasque laborum et periculorum cum
vitae, tum multarum rerum quae ad vitam pertinent.

A. thus gives Cic.'s first point a particular slant: *res externae*
in general (health, wealth, nobility, high position) become
externa corporis, looking back to the idea of the flesh being
ruled by the mind in 1.181 (this is the **prima vis fortitudinis** at the start of 1.182). In the second of Cic.'s points,
A. simplifies and confuses the classical language: Cic. refers
to the *honestum* and the *decorum* in point one, not point two,
and he specifies difficult and dangerous deeds as the aim of
courage, while A. speaks simply of everything that is
honourable and seemly. On **despicienda**, see on 1.192.
On **honestas et illud** πρεπόν, cf. 1.27, 30 and see ad locc.
neque divitias nec voluptates neque honores: Cic. *Off.*
1.68 mentions *voluptas, divitiae,* and *gloriae cupiditas.*
Quod cum ita adfectus animo fueris: Cf. Cic. *Off.* 1.66:
ut, cum ita sis adfectus animo ut supra dixi.
**ut, quidquid acciderit quo frangi animi solent . . . pro
iustitia suscepta non moveant:** Cic. uses *frangi* similarly
in connection with fear and desire in *Off.* 1.68 (cf. also *Off.*
1.71).
The first two examples of misfortune, **patrimonii amissio**
and **honoris imminutio**, are typically classical; the third,
obtrectatio infidelium, is Christian (the disparagement of
the ungodly). So too is the fourth, enduring **pericula pro
iustitia** (cf. Mt. 5: 10; 1 Pt. 3: 14), though it also evokes Cic.
Off. 1.66, on *pericula.*
quasi superior non sentias: Cic. advocates the despising of
externals in *Off.* 1.66–8; cf. also 1.192 below. On the superiority of internal virtue over external fortune, cf. Cic.
Amic. 7.
    A. is effectively preaching Stoic ἀπάθεια in all but name,
though he gives Christian nuances to the Ciceronian argument, and goes on to justify this teaching from the Scriptures

in the following paragraphs, introducing the *Christi athleta*
(1.183), those who have 'died with Christ' (1.184), and the
militia Dei (1.185–7). On the Christian application of the
philosophical ideal of detachment, see generally Gauthier,
223 ff.

183. Christi athleta: Cf. 1.58–64 and see on 1.59; on the
soldier and the athlete, cf. e.g. *Ex.* 6.50.
nisi legitime certaverit non coronatur: 2 Tim. 2: 5.
*Tribulatio patientiam operatur . . . probatio autem
spem*: Rom. 5: 3–4.
Vide quot certamina, et una corona!: Cf. 1 Cor. 9: 24:
*Nescitis quod hii qui in stadio currunt, omnes quidem currunt,
sed unus accipit bravium? Sic currite ut comprehendatis.*
non dat nisi qui est confortatus in Christo Iesu: Cf. Phil.
4: 13; 2 Tim. 4: 17; the subject is of course Paul.
cuius caro requiem non habebat: Perhaps a reference to
Paul's *stimulus carnis* (2 Cor. 12: 1–10, especially 12: 7–9),
since the relevant passage is in A.'s mind below.
foris pugnae, intus timores: 2 Cor. 7: 5.
Et quamvis in periculis . . . in mortibus positus: Cf. 2
Cor. 11: 23–33.
ut potentior suis fieret infirmitatibus: Cf. 2 Cor. 12: 9–
10.

184. despicientiam rerum humanarum habere: Cf. Cic.
Off. 1.72: *Capessentibus autem rempublicam nihilo minus quam
philosophis, haud scio an magis etiam, et magnificentia et
despicientia adhibenda est rerum humanarum* (and *Off.* 1.66:
in rerum externarum despicientia). A. typically applies Cic.'s
advice to aspiring statesmen to **eos qui ad officia ecclesiae
accedunt**, the men who are in the public eye in a higher
service.
*Si ergo mortui estis cum Christo . . . ad corruptelam
ipso usu*: Col. 2: 20–2.
*Si ergo consurrexistis cum Christo, quae sursum sunt
quaerite*: Col. 3: 1.
*Mortificate ergo membra vestra quae sunt super
terram*: Col. 3: 5.
Cf. generally *Paen.* 2.97; *Bon. mort.* 10; *Ep.* 11 [29].13; also
Expl. Ps. 1.28.
Et haec quidem adhuc omnibus fidelibus; tibi autem,

fili: This distinction between the injunctions to 'all the faithful' (cf. Eph. 1: 1; Col. 1: 2) and the singular address to a spiritual 'son' (reminiscent of 2 Tim. 2: 1) is significant. A. envisages one level of teaching for believers in general, and another for the cleric (highlighting the different destinations of Col. and the Pastoral Epistles). The most exacting standards are prescribed for those in ecclesiastical office. The vocation to asceticism and the leadership of the church is a higher path of spirituality; cf. 1.36–8, 246, 249; 3.10–11; and especially the developed argument along these lines in *Ep.* 6 [28]. See also on 1.37. On the bishop's teaching as conformity to the Pauline pattern, cf. 1.3–4; 2.87; 3.139.

contemptum divitiarum: Cf. 1 Tim. 6: 6–11; see also on 1.23.

profanarum quoque et anilium fabularum suadet declinationem: Cf. 1 Tim. 4: 7; 6: 20; 2 Tim. 2: 16.

nisi quod te exerceat ad pietatem . . . *pietas autem ad omnia utilis*: Cf. 1 Tim. 4: 7–8.

185.　**ad iustitiam, continentiam, mansuetudinem:** Cf. 1 Tim. 6: 11.

ut fugias iuvenilia opera: Cf. 2 Tim. 2: 22.

confirmatus et radicatus in gratia: Cf. Eph. 3: 17; Col. 2: 7.

bonum fidei subeas certamen: Cf. 1 Tim. 6: 12; also 2 Tim. 4: 7.

non te implices negotiis saecularibus: Cf. 2 Tim. 2: 4.

si hi qui imperatori militant, susceptionibus litium, actu negotiorum forensium, venditione mercium prohibentur humanis legibus: *Militare* covers civil as well as military service, and the prohibitions which A. mentions here applied equally to civil officials, especially *curiales*. But A. is probably thinking of the soldiers or *viri militares* of the imperial court, since he evokes 2 Tim. 2: 4 just above, which speaks of a person *militans* as a *bonus miles Christi Iesu* (2 Tim. 2: 3). Three prohibitions are mentioned: undertaking lawsuits; taking part in judicial procedures; and engaging in commerce. For third-century texts, cf. *Dig.* 3.3.54; *CJ* 2.12 [13].7 (*a.* 223); 2.12 [13].9; 2.12 [13].13 (*a.* 239); 4.6.5 (*a.* 290). For similar bans in the fifth century, cf. Theod. *Nov.* 9 (*a.* 439); *CJ* 1.14.5 (*a.* 439); 4.65.30 (*a.* 439); 4.65.31 (*a.* 439);

12.35.15 (*a*. 458); *Inst*. 4.15.11. The fifth-century collections are obviously too late to be a relevant source, but *can*. 6 of the first Council of Carthage (345–8) had already applied similar legislation to the church, so the principles were doubtless well known. On the matter of involvement in legal business, the *audientia episcopalis* (2.124–5) constitutes an obvious exception to the rule. On avoiding lawsuits, cf. also 2.106. I am indebted to J. Gaudemet, 'Droit séculier et droit de l'église chez saint Ambroise', in *AmbrEpisc* i. 286–315, at 296–9; id. *Le Droit romain dans la littérature chrétienne occidentale du IIIe au Ve siècle* (Milan, 1978), 83–5; M. Sargenti and R. B. Bruno Siola, *Normativa imperiale e diritto Romano negli scritti di s. Ambrogio* (Milan, 1991), 77–9.

quanto magis qui fidei exercet militiam: A typical *a fortiori* argument: if these standards are prescribed for those who serve the emperor, how much more are they necessary for those who serve *noster imperator* (1.186; cf. *Expos. Ps. 118*.22.14; *Ob. Val.* 58) in the cause of the faith? The logic continues in 1.186, below. A. elsewhere asserts (cf. Job 7: 1) that *omnes qui sunt in ecclesia Deo militant* (*Ep.* 4 [27].15; cf. *Ep. extra coll.* 1a [40].29; also Sulp. Sev. *VM* 4), but here he clearly considers that clerics have a special calling. Their position must be carefully defined, however: they withdraw from the affairs of the *saeculum*, yet they are not monastic quietists. On the contrast of *militiae*, cf. 1.218; *Ep.* 77 [22].10; also *Epp.* 62 [19].3; 36 [2].12 (Christians as God's mercenaries). A.'s own intense involvement in business which could only be described as secular makes the rhetoric seem decidedly disingenuous, but the idea is that the clergy, to make an impression, must be seen to behave even better than the prominent officials at the palace—not least when they accompany their bishop on his business (cf. Paul. *VA* 35). On the *militia* of the cleric, see A. Harnack, *Militia Christi: The Christian Religion and the Military in the First Three Centuries* (Philadelphia, 1981), 27–64, especially 59 ff.; on A.: Gryson, *Prêtre*, 131–3; C. Corbellini, 'Il problema della militia in sant'Ambrogio', *Historia* 27 (1978), 630–6; F. Heim, *La Théologie de la victoire, de Constantin à Théodose* (Paris, 1992), 135–98, especially 137–41.

ab omni usu negotiationis abstinere debet: The psychology is revealing. Trade was traditionally considered to be
beneath the dignity of senators. Cic. believes that small-scale
trade is vulgar, though larger enterprise is not to be condemned (*Off.* 1.151; cf. generally Posidonius' classification of
artes according to Sen. *Ep.* 88.21–3), and the import–export
business is admittedly advantageous to society (*Off.* 2.13).
A. condemns the greed and foolhardiness of merchants
(1.243; 2.25–6, 67; 3.37–44, 57, 65), and forbids his clergy
to engage in the sordid pursuit of selfish gain via commerce;
cf. Tert. *Idol.* 11; Jer. *Ep.* 52.5.3; on clerical greed, cf. Paul.
VA 41. Yet they may have private means:

agelluli sui contentus fructibus si habet: Some members
of the clergy retained farms which they had inherited (cf. *Ep.*
17 [81].2), and were free to live off private income rather
than a church benefice (1.152). As far as A. is concerned,
clerics are entitled to keep their farms if they have them, for
they will thus save the church money, but they should
remain content with a modest income from their property,
and not seek to engage in larger-scale trade for the sake of
serious financial gain. On contentment with one's lot, cf. 3.28
and see ad loc. On his accession to the see, A. is said to have
donated his property to the church and the poor (Paul. *VA*
38.4; cf. A. *Ep.* 76 [20].8; and the similar actions of Cyprian,
according to Pont. *Vita Cypr.* 2.7; 15.1; Jer. *Vir. ill.* 67;
and—with much greater assets—Paulinus of Nola and his
wife Therasia, according to A. *Ep.* 27 [58].1–2). What this
meant was that he invested in Milan the income he derived
from the family estates that he held jointly with his brother
and sister: it did not imply that he liquidated his assets. Most
of the property was in Africa (*Exc. fr.* 1.17), probably in
Mauretania. The family home at Rome was retained to
provide a base for Marcellina (Paul. *VA* 9.4); there also
seems to have been land in Sicily (*Exc. fr.* 1.17; for later
evidence of Milanese holdings there, Cassiod. *Var.* 2.29;
Greg. Magn. *Regist.* 1.80; 11.6). For references to the
bishop's property, cf. *Ep.* 76 [20].8; *Ep.* 75a [*C. Aux.*].5.
Marcellina gave up her right to any claim in exchange for an
annual income or usufruct, which ensured her financial
independence in her ascetic life (Paul. *VA* 38.5). Satyrus

at considerable cost to himself in social terms, abandoned his personal right to marry or to make a will, and devoted himself to the supervision of the estates in order to relieve his brother of financial concerns (*Exc. fr.* 1.20, 40, 59); it was on one of his trips to Africa that he contracted his fatal illness in the autumn of 378. He and A. probably made a deliberate effort to maximize the income from the estates, not least to fund the bishop's church-building programme, which was already under way in 378 (*Exc. fr.* 1.20) (McLynn, 69–71).

Augustine, for his part, initially sought to insist on a communistic state among his clergy, but in later years had to concede that some of them could retain their *agelluli* (*Serm.* 355–6), though he gave up his own meagre patrimony (*Ep.* 126.7). For the practice of a bishop living in a simple community with his clergy, pioneered in the West, according to A., by Eusebius of Vercelli (*Ep. extra coll.* 14 [63].66, 71), cf. Hilary of Poitiers (Sulp. Sev. *VM* 6–7); Martin of Tours (Sulp. Sev. *VM* 10); Paulinus of Nola (*Ep.* 5.15–19); Victricius of Rouen (Paul. Nol. *Ep.* 23.8); and Aug. *Serm.* 355; Possid. *Vita Aug.* 3, 5, 11.

si habet, si non habet: Reminiscent of Cic. *Off.* 1.68: *si non habeas, si habeas.*

stipendiorum suorum fructu: As the application of the word *militia* had been extended to cover civil and ecclesiastical as well as military service, *stipendium* correspondingly came to be used for the pay of administrative and ecclesiastical officials (Gaudemet, 165–6).

bonus testis: The psalmist David.

Iuvenis fui et senui . . . nec semen eius quaerens panem: Ps. 36: 25.

tranquillitas animi: Cf. Cic. *Off.* 1.69, 72, 102; on A.'s association of the idea with **temperantia** as well as with courage, see on 1.90.

metu: Cic. mentions this in *Off.* 1.68–9.

CHAPTER 37: MAINTAINING AN EVEN TEMPER

186. Ea est etiam quae dicitur vacuitas animi ab angoribus: dicitur is an oblique reference to Cic.; cf. *Off.* 1.73:

Quocirca non sine causa maiores motus animorum concitantur maioraque efficiendi rempublicam gerentibus quam quietis; quo magis iis et magnitudo est animi adhibenda et vacuitas ab angoribus (cf. also *Off.* 1.69).

ut neque in doloribus molliores simus: Cf. Cic. *Off.* 1.71: *Sunt enim qui . . . in dolore sint molliores.* An equable temperament is required.

neque in prosperis elatiores: Cf. Cic. *Off.* 1.90: *Atque etiam in rebus prosperis et ad voluntatem nostram fluentibus superbiam magnopere, fastidium adrogantiamque fugiamus. Nam ut adversas res, sic secundas immoderate ferre levitatis est.*

Quod si hi qui ad capessendam rem publicam adhortantur aliquos, haec praecepta dant: Another vague reference to Cic.: *rempublicam capessentibus* occurs in *Off.* 1.71–2. In *Off.* 1.69–73, Cic. argues that public service is superior to a life of leisure (*contra* Epicurean quietism in particular); in *Off.* 1.74–8, he claims that civil administration is more important than military command; and in *Off.* 1.79–91 (especially 1.85–91) he discusses the qualities required in the statesman.

quanto magis nos qui ad officium ecclesiae vocamur: See on 1.184.

quae placeant Deo: Cf. Jn. 8: 29.

ut praetendat in nobis virtus Christi: Cf. 2 Cor. 12: 9: *ut inhabitet in me virtus Christi.* A.'s verb is stronger, and fits the military context: the power of Christ should be 'arrayed within us'.

nostro . . . imperatori: Contrasts with the secular emperor of 1.185; see *TLL* vii/1, 560, for the usage.

ut membra nostra arma iustitiae sint: Cf. Rom. 6: 13.

arma non carnalia in quibus peccatum regnet: A conflation of 2 Cor. 10: 4 and Rom. 6: 12.

quibus peccatum destruatur: Cf. Rom. 6: 6: *ut destruatur corpus peccati.*

Moriatur caro nostra: Cf. Rom. 8: 13; Col. 3: 5.

quasi ex mortuis viventes: Rom. 6: 13.

novis resurgamus operibus ac moribus: Cf. 2 Cor. 5: 17; Gal. 6: 15; Eph. 4: 24; Col. 3: 10. On **resurgamus**, cf. Rom. 6: 4–5; 1 Cor. 6: 14–20; Eph. 2: 5–6; Col. 2: 12–13; etc. The Stoic teaching on the subduing of the passions is thus

validated by the NT''s injunctions to mortify the flesh, while
the service of the state is replaced by the service of Christ,
and the waging of spiritual war with good deeds and with
bodies dedicated to *iustitia*.

187. honesti et decori: See on 1.182.

stipendia: See on 1.185.

**Sed quia in omnibus quae agimus . . . quid possibile sit
quaerimus:** Cf. Cic. *Off.* 1.73: *Ad rem gerendam autem qui
accedit, caveat ne id modo consideret, quam illa res honesta sit,
sed etiam ut habeat efficiendi facultatem* (also *Off.* 1.110).
A. endorses the Panaetian realism transmitted by Cic.; cf.
1.213–16; 2.134.

**unde nos tempore persecutionis . . . *fugere* vult Domi-
nus:** Cf. Mt. 10: 23: *Cum autem persequentur vos in civitate
ista, fugite in aliam*; cf. *Fug.* 17 for a spiritual reading of the
injunction.

**ne temere aliquis, dum martyrii desiderat gloriam . . .
ferre ac tolerare non queat:** Cic. has *temere* in *Off.* 1.73,
81, 103 (and *temeritate* in 1.101); cf. too *Off.* 1.83: *sed
fugiendum illud etiam, ne offeramus nos periculis sine causa.*
Cic.'s point is Aristotelian: courage is a mean between
cowardice and foolhardiness. A. applies this to Christian
persecution and martyrdom. Martyrdom was of course
traditionally seen as the ultimate test of Christian virtue
and the highest level of dedication to Christ; Vermeulen, 53–
96; on the martyr-confessor, see H. Delehaye, *Sanctus: Essai
sur le culte des saints dans l'antiquité* (Brussels, 1927), 74–121;
see also on 1.202. It was an unlikely fate for A.'s immediate
addressees (*pace* Vermeulen, 77–8; though see on 1.208), but
this naturally does not prevent him from using it as a potent
symbol of supreme spiritual obedience (cf. 1.202–7; 2.40–1;
3.89). The glory of martyrdom serves as a rhetorical device:
it underlines the idea that courage is all about overcoming in
the struggle against the dark forces of the devil and the
saeculum that he controls. A. advocates caution, however:
martyrdom should not be provoked out of a rash desire for
personal glory (cf. e.g. Cypr. *Epp.* 5; 7.1; *Mort.* 17); cf. 1.208.
The opportunity for such a glorious death should be seized if
it presents itself (2.141; it had been denied to A. himself in
386: cf. *Ep.* 23 [36].4, though he had skilfully exploited the

rhetoric of persecution and the martyr's crown at the height
of the drama: cf. especially *Ep.* 75a [*C. Aux.*]), but a reckless
courting of danger is wrong.

caro infirmior: On the weakness of the flesh, cf. Mt. 26: 41;
Mk. 14: 38.

CHAPTER 38: ANTICIPATING TROUBLES

188. propter ignaviam: Cf. Cic. *Off.* 1.73: *in quo ipso
considerandum est ne aut temere desperet propter ignaviam aut.*
deserere fidem: Cic. speaks of the extra challenges to
courage in public life; A. thinks of people deserting the
true faith. In particular, he may be thinking (cf. 1.72) of
clergy deserting to the ranks of his enemies; cf. 1.256; 3.126.
On courage in the face of danger, cf. 1.196–209; 3.82–5.
praeparandus est animus: Cf. Cic. *Off.* 1.73: *In omnibus
autem negotiis, priusquam adgrediare, adhibenda est praepara-
tio diligens.* The intellectualism is again sustained; cf. 1.189
below. Courage is tied to prudence; cf. 1.124–5; 2.42.
**stabilienda ad constantiam, ut nullis perturbari
animus possit terroribus:** Cf. Cic. *Off.* 1.80: *Fortis vero
animi et constantis est non perturbari in rebus asperis*; *Off.* 1.67:
*Nam et ea quae eximia plerisque et praeclara videntur parva
ducere eaque ratione stabili firmaque contemnere fortis animi
magnique ducendum est, et ea quae videntur acerba, quae multa
et varia in hominum vita fortunaque versantur, ita ferre ut nihil
a statu naturae discedas, nihil a dignitate sapientis, robusti
animi est magnaeque constantiae.* On *constantia*, a particularly
Roman virtue, cf. 1.112, 225, 229–30; 2.66, 125; 3.7.
frangi: See on 1.182.
**si consilio firmes animum tuum nec a ratione disce-
dendum putes:** [E, C omit **a**; **discedendum:** V², E², CO²:
descendendum P²V¹, Testard: *descendum* E¹: *discedendum*
P¹M, O¹] Cf. Cic. *Off.* 1.80: *sed praesenti animo uti et consilio
nec a ratione discedere*; also *Off.* 1.67.
**proponas divini iudicii metum . . . potes animi subire
tolerantiam:** The controlling factor is not just reason or
will-power; the fear of divine judgement is inspirational,
concentrating the mind wonderfully; cf. 1.124; 2.96.

189. diligentiae: Cf. *diligens* in Cic. *Off.* 1.73.
illud ingenii si quis . . . intellegat profuturos: Cf. Cic.
Off. 1.81: *illud etiam ingenii magni est, praecipere cogitatione futura et aliquanto ante constituere quid accidere possit in utramque partem, et quid agendum sit cum quid evenerit.*

190. tamquam explorare de specula quadam mentis:
On this *topos*, see P. Courcelle, *La Consolation de la philosophie* (Paris, 1967), 355–62; cf also *speculator* in 1.229; on keeping watch, cf. *Ex.* 1.31; also 6.55. See also on 1.192, on the mind as *arx*.

ne forte dicat postea: 'Ideo ista incidi, quia non arbitrabar posse evenire': Cf. Cic. *Off.* 1.81: *nec committere ut aliquando dicendum sit: 'Non putaram'*; also Cic. *Lig.* 30; *Att.* 6.1.2; Val. Max. 7.2.2; Sen. *Dial.* 4.31.4 (Holden, 207). The background lies in the Stoic notion of προλαμβά-νειν, the need to anticipate all possibilities and thus to be forearmed: cf. e.g. Sen. *Ep.* 24; see further Dyck, 213–14. The wisdom of strategic foresight in military (and, to Cic. political) affairs appeals to A. no less than to his Stoic sources: any eventuality, including death itself, can be faced squarely, provided one has sufficient foresight to prepare for its arrival.

191. In his igitur duobus . . . nullis cupiditatibus fluctuet: Cf. Cic. *Off.* 1.67: *si et solum id quod honestum sit bonum iudices et ab omni animi perturbatione liber sis.*
animi excellentia: Cf. Cic. *Off.* 1.17.
ut primum animus tuus . . . quod verum et honestum est videat: A Christian slant is given to the classical idea: while in 1.189–90 A. follows Cic.'s admiration for foresight and careful planning for eventualities, here he thinks not of plans but of good and pure thoughts, i.e. spiritual evaluation of externals; cf. 1.192.
Beati, enim, mundo corde quia ipsi etiam Deum videbunt: Mt. 5: 8.
atque id quod honestum est solum bonum iudicet: See above on Cic. *Off.* 1.67. The point is thoroughly Stoic, but the association with Mt. 5: 8 equates the **verum et honestum** and the **solum bonum** with God himself. The knowledge of God lies at the heart of courage, as it does with prudence and justice.

deinde nullis perturbetur occupationibus, nullis cupiditatibus fluctuet: Cf. Cic. *Off.* 1.67–9, 73; the second point remains Ciceronian–Stoic.

192. **Quid enim tam difficile quam despicere . . . quae plerisque videntur magna et praecelsa?:** [despicere: V, E², CO²B: *dispicere* PMA, E¹W, O¹, Testard] The idea of looking down from a citadel of wisdom, like the *specula* image in 1.190, is a common classical notion (e.g. Stat. *Silv.* 2.2.131–2; especially Lucr. 2.7–19); and Cic. uses *despicere* or *despicientia* in connection with courage in *Off.* 1.17, 61, 66, 72 (cf. also *Off.* 2.37; 3.100). A. has the phrase *velut ex arce quadam despiciat* in 2.66 (cf. also *hanc virtutis arcem* in 1.137); on contempt for riches, see on 1.23. See generally Gauthier, 223 ff.; for Ambrosian parallels, see Madec, 315 n. 207. On **quae plerisque videntur magna et praecelsa**, cf. Cic. *Off.* 1.67: *Nam et ea quae eximia plerisque et praeclara videntur*. As ever, A. demands a standard that elevates his clergy above the crowd.

stabili ratione confirmes: Cf. Cic. *Off.* 1.67: *Nam et ea quae eximia plerisque et praeclara videntur parva ducere eaque ratione stabili firmaque contemnere fortis animi magnique ducendum est.*

contemnas: Cf. Cic. *Off.* 1.67–8, 70–1.

idque grave et acerbum putetur, ita feras ut: Cf. Cic. *Off.* 1.67: *et ea quae videntur acerba . . . ita ferre ut.*

Nudus sum natus . . . Dominus abstulit: Job 1: 21.

et utique et filios amiserat et facultates: See on 1.41.

personam sapientis et iusti, sicut ille: Job equates to the Stoic sage.

Sicut Domino placuit . . . sit nomen Domini benedictum: Job 1: 21.

Sicut una insipientium mulierum . . . quae mala sunt non sustinemus: Job 2: 10.

CHAPTER 39: COURAGE WAGES WAR ON THE
PASSIONS

193. **nec discreta a ceteris:** See on 1.115.

quae bellum cum virtutibus gerat . . . adversus omnia

vitia decernat: On courage fighting for justice, cf. Cic. *Off.* 1.62–3; the military imagery endures. Cic. uses the word *vitium* in *Off.* 1.62.

invicta ad labores, fortis ad pericula, rigidior adversus voluptates: Cic. mentions *labores* and *pericula* in *Off.* 1.65–6; and cf. *Off.* 1.68: *Non est autem consentaneum . . . qui invictum se a labore praestiterit, vinci a voluptate* (*voluptas* is condemned in *Off.* 1.69).

nec, ut dicitur, 'Ave' dicat: Cf. 2 Jn. 10–11: (of the visitor who professes allegiance to different teaching) *nec 'Ave' ei dixeritis. Qui enim dicit illi 'Ave', communicat operibus illius malignis.*

pecuniam neglegat, avaritiam fugiat . . . quae virtutem effeminet. Nihil enim tam contrarium fortitudini quam lucro vinci: Cf. Cic. *Off.* 1.68: *et pecuniae fugienda cupiditas; nihil enim est tam angusti animi tamque parvi quam amare divitias, nihil honestius magnificentiusque quam pecuniam contemnere.* On **effeminet**, see on 1.138.

Frequenter pulsis hostibus . . . hostem in se revocaverunt, qui fugerat: Cf. e.g. Polyb. 10.17.4; Tac. *Ann.* 1.68 (PL 16, 86–7 n. 8).

194. **tam immanem pestem:** *avaritia*, stigmatized as the disease of the Fall in 1.137.

nec temptetur cupiditatibus nec frangatur metu: Cf. Cic. *Off.* 1.68: *Non est autem consentaneum qui metu non frangatur, eum frangi cupiditate*; *Off.* 1.69: *Vacandum autem omni est animi perturbatione, cum cupiditate et metu.*

iracundiam . . . aegritudinem: Both words are used by Cic. *Off.* 1.69; cf. the *aegrotationes animi* in *Tusc.* 4.79, 83 (and generally *Tusc.* 3). On anger as a passion particularly to be mastered by the courageous person, cf. Cic. *Off.* 1.88–9. Cic. also uses a medical illustration in *Off.* 1.83.

propulset: Cic. *Off.* 1.65 has *propulsant*.

consilium: Cic. mentions this in *Off.* 1.79–81.

gloriae quoque caveat appetentiam: Cf. Cic. *Off.* 1.68: *Cavenda etiam est gloriae cupiditatis, ut supra dixi* [*Off.* 1.65] (cf. also *Off.* 1.83–4); and A. 1.187, 208.

quae frequenter nocuit immoderatius expetita, semper autem usurpata: Evocative of the language of Cic.'s warning about military commands: *Nec vero imperia*

*expetenda, ac potius aut non accipienda interdum aut depo-
nenda nonnumquam* (*Off.* 1.68).

195. Quid horum . . . defuit . . .?: Cf. the similar question in
1.115, following the illustration of the virtues of OT characters in 1.106–14. Job is the main replacement for Cic.'s
exempla from Greek and Roman history (*Off.* 1.61, 64, 75–8,
84, 87, 90) in the discussion of courage (though A. of course
cites a good deal of other biblical, especially NT, passages as
well). On Job's tragedies, see on 1.41. Note the rhetorical
texture of the paragraph, especially the anaphora of **Quomodo** and **numquid**, and the string of rhetorical questions.
despexit salutis periculum: Cf. Cic. *Off.* 1.83–4; see also
on 1.177.
trium regum: See on 1.41.
servorum contumelia: Cf. Job 19: 15–16.
**qui imprecabatur gravia sibi si umquam . . . eam in
conspectu omnium:** Cf. Job 31: 33–4.
consentaneae: Cic. uses *consentaneus* in *Off.* 1.68 (and often
elsewhere: e.g. *Off.* 1.6; 3.20, 117; etc.; it is a favourite
Ciceronian word).

CHAPTER 40: MILITARY COURAGE EXEMPLIFIED

**196. Sed fortasse aliquos bellica defixos gloria tenet . . .
quia illa nostris deforet:** Cf. Cic. *Off.* 1.74: *Sed cum
plerique arbitrentur res bellicas maiores esse quam urbanas.*
Despite his claim that military courage is not germane to
his readers (1.175), A. continues to show enthusiasm for the
martial achievements of OT saints (cf. 1.175–7); 1.196–201
dwells on this theme. On the popularity of accounts of
bravery in war; cf. 3.5. For other anticipated objections to
the arrangement or focusing of material, cf. 1.47, 116, 231–2.
Quam fortis Iesus Nave . . . cum populis suis!: Joshua
defeated five Amorite kings, Adonizedek of Jerusalem and
his allies, in a surprise attack at Gibeon; having imprisoned
them in a cave at Makkedah, he slew them and the people of
Makkedah (Josh. 10: 1–28). The kings' armies were slain in
the battle, not at Makkedah; A. compresses his account
somewhat.

**Deinde, cum adversum Gabaonitas surgeret proelium
. . . et stetit donec victoria consummaretur:** Not, in fact,
after the defeat of the five kings, but before it—though
Deinde is possibly just A. adding another of Joshua's
exploits, without injecting the sense of chronological
sequence. More seriously, Joshua was not fighting the
Gibeonites, since he had earlier been deceived into making
a non-aggression pact with them (Josh. 9): he was fighting *for*
the Gibeonites, whom the five kings had attacked. On the
sun 'standing still', see Josh. 10: 1–15.

**Gedeon in trecentis viris . . . acerbo hoste revexit
triumphum:** See Judg. 7: 1–25.

Ionatha adulescens virtutem fecit in magno proelio:
Jonathan led a successful attack on the Philistine outpost at
Michmash, which was the prelude to an Israelite rout (1 Ki.
14: 1–15).

Quid de Machabaeis loquar?: The family of Judas ben
Mattathias, who led the heroic revolt against the Seleucids in
Judaea, first under Mattathias himself (168–166 BC), then
under his third son, Judas (166–160 BC), and then his
brothers, Jonathan (160–143 BC) and Simeon, who negotiated
independence in 142 BC. Judas was the major figure, who led
the uprising in its period of most momentous success; see
Bar-Kochva, *passim*. The remainder of A.'s illustration of
military courage (1.197–201) and the first section of his
exposition of the courage of the martyrs (1.202–4) are taken
up with the exploits of these heroes. He is fond of this
narrative; on his presentation of it elsewhere as well, see the
important study by G. Nauroy, 'Les Frères Maccabées dans
l'exégèse d'Ambroise de Milan, ou la conversion de la sagesse
judéo-hellénique aux valeurs du martyre chrétien', in *Figures
de l'Ancien Testament chez les Pères* (Strasbourg and Turnhout, 1989), 215–45; also id. 'Du combat de la piété à la
confession du sang: Ambroise de Milan lecteur critique du
IVe livre des Maccabées', *RHPhR* 70 (1990), 49–68.

97. de populo . . . patrum: See Introduction IV.4.

**qui, cum essent parati ad repugnandum . . . ne
violarent sabbatum:** See 1 Macc. 2: 29–38; cf. 2 Macc. 6:
11. Up to 1,000 men, women, and children were slaughtered
by the forces of Antiochus IV Epiphanes (167 BC).

**Sed Machabaei considerantes . . . ulti sunt innocen-
tium necem fratrum suorum: [sabbato etiam: P²**, E,
CO: *sabbatum etiam* P¹VM, Testard] See 1 Macc. 2: 39–48;
the reference in **Machabaei** is to Mattathias and his
company.

**Unde postea stimulatus rex Antiochus . . . a tribus
milibus prosternerentur:** See 1 Macc. 3: 27–4: 25 (and cf.
2 Macc. 8: 8–36). **Postea** brings us into the time of Judas
Maccabaeus, in 165 BC; **rex Antiochus** is Antiochus IV
Epiphanes. The reference is to the defeat of the Seleucid
army at Ammaus in the late summer of 165 BC.

quadraginta et octo milia: According to 1 Macc. 3: 39, the
Seleucid force consisted of 40,000 infantry and 7,000
cavalry, and 1 Macc. 3: 41 mentions some Syrian and
Philistine troops in addition; hence, presumably, the round
total of 48,000. Jos. *AJ* 12.7.3 follows these figures. 2 Macc.
8: 9 gives a Seleucid force of 'not less than 20,000'. Bar-
Kochva, 240, maintains that 1 Macc. 3: 39 gives 'an extremely inflated estimate', and considers a royal force of
under 10,000 likely, giving a total complement, including
auxiliaries, of about 20,000.

a tribus milibus: So 1 Macc. 4: 6, while 2 Macc. 8: 1, 16,
21–2 say 6,000; 3,000 is the number left after the screening of
the troops at Mizpah (1 Macc. 3: 46–60) (Bar-Kochva, 264).

198. Namque Eleazarus . . . interemit eam: See 1 Macc.
6: 43–6 (also Jos. *BJ* 1.1.5; *AJ* 12.9.4). Eleazar Avaran is
Judas' brother (1 Macc. 2: 5), though A. introduces him
simply as **de uno eius milite**; on the incident, see Bar-
Kochva, 334–7. A. paints a striking picture of Eleazar's
daring, piling clause on clause to build up the tension;
using a vivid present participle (**cadens**) to describe the
beast's demise; and summing up Eleazar's fate as being
'buried by his own triumph'.

cursu concitus: Cf. Verg. *Aen.* 12.902.

abiecto clipeo: There is no mention of this in 1 Macc. 6 o:
in Jos.; A. augments Eleazar's courage with a fictitiou·
embellishment. The words are repeated below.

utraque manu interficiebat bestiam: A. does not repro·
duce the text of the account accurately: Eleazar is said t·
have killed *men* to the right and left and *then* gone under

neath the elephant (1 Macc. 6: 45–6); A. says that he tried
(**interficiebat** is a conative imperfect) to kill *the beast* with
both hands (again with **utraque manu vulneratae molem
bestiae**, below).

**Primo, ut mortem non timeret . . . contempta morte
ferocior:** See on 1.177. On **contempta morte ferocior**, cf.
Hor. *Od.* 1.37.29: (of Cleopatra) *deliberata morte ferocior.*
quo: M, E, C: *quod* PV, O, Testard.

199. Nec fefellit opinio virum: Cf. 1.72, *nec fefellit sententia.*

**Tanto enim virtutis spectaculo defixi hostes inermem
. . . unius virtuti arbitrarentur:** A. seems to misinterpret 1
Macc. 6: 47: *Et videntes virtutem regis et impetum exercitus
eius, deverterunt ab eis*; the Jews, not the Seleucid forces, fell
back. 1 Macc. 6 says nothing about the significance of
Eleazar's action as far as the Seleucid army's psychology
was concerned. **Inermem:** Without a shield, as A. thinks;
see on 1.198.

rex Antiochus, Lysiae filius: Antiochus V Eupator, who
was brought up by the regent of Antiochus IV Epiphanes,
Lysias, as his adopted son (1 Macc. 3: 32–3; 6: 17). Eupator
succeeded his father at the age of nine in late 164 or early 163
BC, though the real power was exercised by Lysias. He was
put to death by the army in 162 BC, on the arrival in Syria of
his cousin Demetrius I Soter, the younger son of Seleucus
IV and the rightful successor of Epiphanes.

**qui centum viginti hominum milibus armatus venerat
et cum triginta duobus elephantis:** So 1 Macc. 6: 30,
detailing 100,000 infantry, 20,000 cavalry, and 32 elephants
(similarly, Jos. *AJ* 12.9.3). All of these figures are probably
exaggerated (Bar-Kochva, 306–7). 2 Macc. 13: 2 has 110,000
infantry, 5,300 cavalry, 22 elephants, and 300 scythe-bearing
chariots; Jos. *BJ* 1.1.5 says 50,000 infantry and 5,000
cavalry. Jos.'s *BJ* statistics may be nearer the mark.

**ita ut ab ortu solis . . . tamquam lampadibus ar-
dentibus refulgerent:** Cf. 1 Macc. 6: 39, loosely para-
phrased by A.

unius territus fortitudine pacem rogaret: Again, A. is
taking liberties with the story. 1 Macc. 6: 49 speaks of the
king making peace with the people of Beth Zur, but they had

surrendered prior to the battle (Bar-Kochva, 308–9). Lysias advised the king to sue for peace only when he heard that Philip had returned from the East with designs on the government: Lysias saw the danger of pressing on with an inconclusive siege of Jerusalem, with provisions running short, while a rival threatened to take control behind his back at Antioch (1 Macc. 6: 55–61; 2 Macc. 13: 23–6). (The peace was broken temporarily when the king discovered the strength of the Jewish fortification of Zion and ordered the defences to be demolished: 1 Macc. 6: 62–3.) A. puts a more romantic gloss on the narrative: Lysias and Eupator pulled back out of fear of the Jews' courage, not because of political circumstances.

CHAPTER 41: COURAGE IN ADVERSITY: THE MARTYRS

200. non solum secundis rebus sed etiam adversis: Cic. *Off.* 1.90–1 speaks of *secundae res* and *adversae res* (also *secundae res* in *Off.* 3.47); cf. A. 3.129–30. A. presents the military achievements of 1.196–9 as examples of courage in favourable or successful circumstances (in 1.198–9 we might well expect the incidents to be classified as *adversae res*, though it all depends upon perspective; to A., *haec triumphorum sint*, 1.199). In 1.200–7, he seeks to portray the courage of the faithful in situations of tragedy as well, both in war and in times of persecution.

Is enim, post victum Nicanorem, regis Demetrii ducem: Demetrius I Soter, Syrian king, 162–150 BC. On the defeat and death of his general Nicanor at the hands of the Jews at the battle of Adasa in March 161 BC, see 1 Macc. 7: 39–50; 2 Macc. 15: 1–36; also Jos. *AJ* 12.10.4–5.

securior adversus viginti milia exercitus regis: According to 1 Macc. 9: 4, the Seleucid force at the battle of Elasa in April 160 BC numbered 20,000 infantry and 2,000 cavalry (similarly, Jos. *AJ* 12.11.1), figures which are probably broadly correct (Bar-Kochva, 386).

cum nongentis viris bellum adorsus: CO give the figure of 1 Macc. 9: 6, *octingentis*, the remainder of an original force of 3,000 having fled (1 Macc. 9: 5–6). Jos. *AJ* 12.11.1 has an original force of 1,000, by scribal error for 3,000, with 800 remaining. The figure of 800 is so drastically reduced as to be worthless for historical reconstruction (Bar-Kochva, 388–9); the author of 1 Macc. wants to highlight the bravery of the Jews by vastly lengthening the odds against them.

volentibus his cedere . . . turpem fugam suasit: See 1 Macc. 9: 8–10; cf. Jos. *AJ* 12.11.1. The **gloriosam . . . turpem** antithesis again reflects A.'s esteem for martial courage depicted in traditional Stoic terminology; see on 1.177.

Ne crimen, **inquit,** *nostrae relinquamus gloriae:* 1 Macc. 9: 10; cf. Jos. *AJ* 12.11.1.

cum a primo ortu diei . . . adgressus facile avertit: See 1 Macc. 9: 13–22; cf. Jos. *AJ* 12.11.2.

ita gloriosiorem triumphis locum mortis invenit: A. shares his source's admiration for Judas' heroic death. On the deaths of heroes and martyrs, cf. *Exc. fr.* 2.44–5; on death as a good thing, cf. *Bon. mort., passim*; *Exc. fr.* 2.39–49. A. shares the Stoic perspective of brave contempt for danger to life (see on 1.177), but he moves beyond that to see death as something which for the Christian is to be welcomed, as the gateway to heavenly reward.

201. Quid Ionatham fratrem eius adtexam?: Jonathan was the youngest of the Maccabaeus brothers, leading their cause after Judas' death, 160–143 BC.

Qui cum parva manu . . . ad societatem revocavit triumphi: Jonathan was ambushed by a large force of Demetrius' troops in the plain of Asor; his men fled when they saw the scale of the Syrian opposition, and only a small band remained, but with them he was able to rout the enemy (1 Macc. 11: 67–74; cf. Jos. *AJ* 13.5.7). 1 Macc. 11: 70 says that only two of Jonathan's officers remained; Jos. *AJ* 13.5.7 adds that about 50 men stayed with them. 1 Macc. 11: 74 claims that about 3,000 Gentiles were slain; Jos. *AJ* 13.5.8 says 2,000.

202. fortitudinem bellicam: Cf. the Ciceronian division in 1.175 above.

quod mortem servituti praeferat ac turpitudini: Cf. Cic. *Off.* 1.81: *sed cum tempus necessitasque postulat,*

decertandum manu est et mors servituti turpitudinique ante-
ponenda. On A.'s attitude to slavery, see on 1.20.

Quid autem de martyrum dicam passionibus?: 1.202–7
proceeds to develop this, drawing on both biblical and more
recent *exempla.* The martyrs clearly demonstrate the ideal of
spiritual courage, but A. can honour their physical bravery as
well. The spiritual ideals of the martyrs mattered a great deal
to A., and he did much to promote a martyr-cult both in
Milan and throughout the sphere of his influence, drawing
on and greatly developing an existing fervour for his own
ends, by sponsoring the veneration of new saints and the
transference of sacred relics which brought increased prestige to his see (P. Brown, *The Cult of the Saints* (Chicago,
1981), 36–7; Humphries, 54–6, 148–9). His stage-managed
inventio of the relics of Gervasius and Protasius at the
dedication of the Basilica Ambrosiana in the aftermath of
the crisis of 386 (*Ep.* 77 [22]; Paul. *VA* 14; Aug. *Conf.* 9.7.16;
CD 22.8.2; *Serm.* 276.5) will be a recent memory for his
readers here: J. Doignon, 'Perspectives ambrosiennes: SS.
Gervais et Protais, génies de Milan', *REAug* 2 (1956), 313–
34; E. Dassmann, 'Ambrosius und die Märtyrer', *JbAC* 18
(1975), 49–68, especially 52–7; Vermeulen, 76–80, 99–100;
V. Zangara, 'L'*inventio* dei martiri Gervasio e Protasio:
Testimonianze di Agostino su un fenomeno di religiosità
popolare', *Augustinianum* 21 (1981), 119–33; McLynn, 209–
19; Williams, 219–23. Further discoveries (of still more
doubtful authenticity) would be made in Bologna in 393
(Agricola and Vitalis; cf. *Exh. virg.* 1–8; Paul. *VA* 29.1), and
again in Milan in 395 (Nazarius; cf. Paul. *VA* 32.3–33.4) (I
follow McLynn, 363–4: the reference in Paul. to the tomb of
Celsus does not, *pace* Palanque, 313; Homes Dudden i. 318–
19, mean that A. discovered *two* martyrs, Nazarius and
Celsus: A. prayed at the tomb after Nazarius' body had
been exhumed). For A. the martyrs are about far more than
the exhortation to spiritual perseverance; they are a way of
borrowing vital authority for a particular style of ecclesiastical leadership. Here, they serve as stellar exemplars of what
true fortitude is all about.

**num minorem de superbo rege . . . sicut clamavit in
Abel:** See 2 Macc. 7: 1–42. A. paints a vivid picture of the

tragic scene, with short clauses in asyndeton, tricolon, repetition of **defecerunt**, chiasmus, and so on. **Cohors** suggests that the boys are a little troop of faithful soldiers, physically unarmed in the face of the vast hordes of the wicked (on **sine armis vicerunt**, and conquering by piety alone, cf. *Iac.* 2.58; *Expl. Ps. 43.9*; *Hymn* 10.21–2; Sulp. Sev. *VM* 4.5): see generally F. Heim, 'Le thème de la "victoire sans combat" chez Ambroise', in *Ambroise de Milan*, 267–81; J. Fontaine, 'Le Culte des martyrs militaires et son expression poétique au IVe siècle: l'idéal évangelique de la non-violence dans le christianisme théodosien', in *Etudes sur la poésie latine tardive d'Ausone à Prudence. Recueil de travaux* (Paris, 1981), 351–61. The story of the seven Maccabaean boys martyred along with their mother is told at length in *Iac.* 2.45–58 (note also *Iac.* 2.42): it is quite likely that both there and here A. repeats language from an earlier panegyric; see G. Nauroy, 'La Méthode de composition d'Ambroise de Milan et la structure du *De Iacob et vita beata*', in *Ambroise de Milan*, 115–53, at 137–8.

Alius corium capitis exutus ... virtutem auxerat: This treatment was meted out to the first two brothers, at least (2 Macc. 7: 4, 7).

alius linguam iussus amputandum promere respondit: 'Non solum Dominus audit loquentes ... sicut clamavit in Abel': The defiant words here are not precisely those of the third son, whose tongue is amputated (2 Macc. 7: 10–11). Moses is mentioned by the mother and six of the boys in mutual encouragement after the death of the first (2 Macc. 7: 6), and by the last son as he defies Antiochus (2 Macc. 7: 30). But the speech here is composed by A. himself, echoing other OT verses and language used earlier in the work; cf. also *Ep.* 7 [37].37; Prud. *Perist.* 10.751–90.

qui audiebat Moysen tacentem: Cf. Ex. 14: 14–15.

Plus audit tacitas cogitationes suorum quam voces omnium: Cf. 1.9 above; on the Stoic background on the theme of an eloquent testimony through endurance, see M. Spanneut, 'Patience et martyre chez les Pères de l'Eglise', *Compostellanum* 35 (1990), 545–60; on silence especially, cf. Max. Taur. *Serm.* 16. Gregory the Great speaks in another context of the miraculous witness of speech produced without a tongue: *Dial.* 3.32.

Linguae flagellum times, flagellum sanguinis non times?: Cf. Job 5: 21; and 1.6 above.

Habet et sanguis vocem suam qua clamat ad Deum, sicut clamavit in Abel: Cf. Gen. 4: 10 (cf. also Heb. 12: 24). Cf. *Abr.* 1.47; *Cain* 2.31; *Iac.* 2.48; *Hymn* 11.7–8.

203. Quid de matre loquar . . . omni lyrae numero dulciorem?: See 2 Macc. 7: 20–3, 25–9.

tropaea: Used here, as often, for the bodies of martyrs, which are pictured as the trophies of victory in a spiritual warfare; see Mohrmann iii. 331–50.

et morientium vocibus . . . omni lyrae numero dulciorem: The seven sons are like the seven strings of the *cithara*, the perfect number producing the perfect melody. The seven-stringed instrument is said to have been introduced by Terpander in the mid-seventh century BC, as an advance on the four-stringed lyre (*New Oxford History of Music* i: *Ancient and Oriental Music*, ed. E. Wellesz (London, 1957), 250–1, 381–2); cf. Prud. *Perist.* 10.778. On some aspects of the imagery of the *cithara*, see J. Fontaine, 'Les symbolismes de la cithare dans la poésie de Paulin de Nole', in W. Den Boer, P. G. Van Der Nat, *et. al.* (eds.), *Romanitas et Christianitas: Studia Iano Henrico Waszink* (Amsterdam and London, 1973), 123–43; on Christian use of musical symbolism more generally, see G. Wille, *Musica Romana. Die Bedeutung der Musik im Leben der Römer* (Amsterdam, 1967), 400–5. In A., cf. *Iac.* 1.39; *Interp.* 4.36 (from Plot. *Enn.* 1.4.16.20–4); *Bon. mort.* 27. On the influence of Verg. *Aen.* 6.646 (Orpheus), see P. Courcelle, 'Les Pères devant les enfers Virgiliens', *Archives d'histoire doctrinal* 30 (1955), 5–74, at 32–3 and n. 8. On seven *interiora viscera*, cf. *Ep.* 31 [44].15; on spiritual numerics generally, see on 1.206. Cf. here the description in *Iac.* 2.56: *Quae cithara dulciores edere cantus quam morientes filii in tam gravibus suppliciis ediderant? Erumpebat enim naturae gemitus et invitis. Spectares per ordinem peremptorum cadavera sicut fila cordarum. Audire heptachordum psalterium triumphalibus gemitibus resultare . . isti moriebantur amore pietatis.*

204. Quid de bimulis loquar . . . quam sensum naturae?

The 'Holy Innocents', the male children of two years and under in Bethlehem and its vicinity slaughtered by Herod the Great (Mt. 2: 16–18). From an early date they were regarded as the first Christian martyrs: e.g. Iren. *Adv. Haer.* 3.16.4; Prud. *Cath.* 12.93–140; *Perist.* 10.736–45; A. *Ep.* 18 [70].9; *Expl. Ps. 37.*10; Caes. Arel. *Serm.* 222.1–2; Aug. *Serm.* 373.3; 375. Augustine speaks of the *felix ignorantia* of the infants: *illi pro Christo potuerunt pati, quem nondum poterant confiteri* (*Serm.* 199.2; cf. *En. Ps.* 47.5). Their feast is celebrated in the West on 28 December. See *AA.SS.*, Dec., 604–6; H. Leclercq, 'Innocents (Massacre des)', *DACL* vii/ 1. 608–16; P. A. Hayward, 'Suffering and Innocence in Latin Sermons for the Feast of the Holy Innocents, *c.*400–800', in D. Wood (ed.), *The Church and Childhood* (Oxford, 1994), 67–80.

palmam victoriae: The prize won by those who have faithfully completed the contest of faith (cf. especially Cypr. *Ep.* 10).

Quid de sancta Agne . . . salutem cum immortalitate commutavit?: Agnes, Rome's most celebrated virgin martyr, slain at the age of twelve. Accounts of her martyrdom vary considerably, agreeing only on her youth and her virginity; we cannot be sure when or how she died (though the Great Persecution of 303–4 is the likeliest context). Cf. *Virg.* 1.5–9; *Hymn* 8; *Ep.* 7 [37].36; Prud. *Perist.* 14; Damas. *Epig. Dam.* [ed. Ferrua], 176. The *Acts* are late and confused. PL 17 attributes to A. a sermon (48 = Max. Taur. *Serm.* 56) and a spurious *passio*. A basilica was erected to her *c.*350 on the Via Nomentana, near her tomb; her feast is celebrated in the West on 21 January. See *AA.SS.*, Jan. ii. 714–28. P. F. de' Cavalieri, 'Sant' Agnese nella tradizione e nella leggenda', *Scritti Agiografici (1893–1900)* i (*Studi e Testi*, 221, Vatican City, 1962), 293–381, compares the presentation in *Virg.* to Ovid's portrayal of the noble deaths of Polyxena in *Met.* 13.449–80 and Lucretia in *Fast.* 833–4; an oral tradition is clearly elaborated under the influence of classical models. V. Burrus, 'Reading Agnes: The Rhetoric of Gender in Ambrose and Prudentius', *JECS* 3 (1995), 25–46, attempts a modern feminist reading of the patristic portrayals.

castitatis et salutis: Cf. 2.70, 136, 138; 3.82–5; on *salus*, cf. also 3.56.

205. sanctum Laurentium qui cum videret Xistum . . . sed suam remansionem: The martyrdoms of St Lawrence and Pope Sixtus II (pope, 31 August 257–6 August 258) are among the most famous in the martyrologies. Sixtus was arrested during the persecution of Valerian, while celebrating the liturgy in a cemetery at Rome, and was beheaded along with several of his deacons. His death is mentioned by Cyprian in *Ep.* 80.1.4. Damasus wrote an epitaph for him (*Epig. Dam.* [ed. Ferrua], 123–6); cf. also *LP* i. 155. His feast is 7 (formerly 6) August. See *AA.SS.*, Aug. ii. 124–42; on the thorny questions of the identity of the Roman cemetery and of whether Sixtus was executed along with six deacons (*LP*) or four (Cyprian), see G. W. Clarke, 'Prosopographical Notes on the Epistles of Cyprian—III. Rome in August 258', *Latomus* 34 (1975), 437–48. Lawrence was Sixtus' chief deacon or archdeacon. He was ordered by the urban prefect of Rome, P. Cornelius Saecularis (*PLRE* i. 795), to hand over the treasures of the church within three days. He duly presented the poor of the city, saying that these were the church's true treasures (cf. 2.140–1; Prud. *Perist.* 2.37–312). For this act of defiance he is said to have been burned to death on a gridiron, on 10 August 258; consensus scholarship considers it far more likely that he was beheaded. A basilica was erected to him by Constantine on the site of his burial in the catacomb of Cyriaca on the Via Tiburtina, later linked with the modern San Lorenzo fuori le Mura. His feast is 10 August. See *AA.SS*, Aug. ii. 485–532; on the gridiron tradition and its numerous artistic depictions, see de' Cavalieri, *Scritti Agiografici* i. 383–9; H. Leclercq, 'Gril', *DACL* vi/2. 1827–31. Cf. Prud. *Perist.* 2; Max. Taur. *Serm.* 4; 24.3 Aug. *Serm.* 302–5; 13; *Ev. Ioh.* 27.12.2; Leo, *Serm.* 85; *LP* i 155–6. A. wrote at least one hymn to Lawrence (*Apostolorum supparem* [13]); he mentions him also in *Ep.* 7 [37].37, and attests that vows were made to him by the pious (*Exc. fr.* 1.1; (Satyrus); *Exh. virg.* 15). The dramatic account which follows of the exchange between the dying Sixtus and Lawrence and the narrative of Lawrence's death (1.205–7 reflect a lost *passio Laurentii* tradition of the mid- to late fourth century (the earliest surviving *passio* is not earlier than the second half of the fifth century): see H. Delehaye, 'Recherches sur le légendier romain,' *AB* 51 (1933), 34–98, especially 43–9. This presentation, also evident in A.'s *Hymn* 13 (cf. e.g. the legal terminology used in 1.206 (*hereditas . . . successio*) with *Hymn* 13, str. 3–4), influences the accounts of Prudentius and Augustine: see G. Nauroy, 'Le martyre de Laurent dans l'hymnodie et la prédication des IVe et Ve siècles, et l'authenticité ambrosienne de l'hymne "Apostolorum supparem"', *REAug* 35 (1989), 44–82.

Cui commisisti dominici sanguinis consecrationem . . . huic sanguinis tui consortium negas?: A. presumably does not mean that the deacon had shared in the *celebration* of the eucharist, since that was the function of the priest alone; the deacon's task was to *distribute* the sacrament. **consecrationem** must refer not to the act of consecration but to the element consecrated. By distributing this, the deacon shares in the celebration (Gryson, *Prêtre*, 143 n. 51, comparing *Luc.* 6.67, *qui* [Peter] . . . *caelestis consortium consecrationis emeruit*; Testard i. 268–9 n. 14, thinks A. is suggesting that the deacon consecrates *part* of the bread and wine (citing J. A. Jungmann, *Missarum solemnia: explication génétique de la messe romaine*, 3 vols. (Paris, 1956–8), iii. 315–16; 237–48), but this is difficult to sustain contextually). The plural **sacramentorum** is used, though only the eucharist is in mind; cf. 2.138. **huic sanguinis tui consortium negas** links the shedding of the martyr's blood with the consecrated blood of Christ in the sacramental chalice. For the common idea that the martyr drinks the cup of Christ's blood, shed for him, and then sheds his own blood for Christ in conformity to his Master's example, cf. e.g. Cypr. *Epp.* 57.2.2; 58.1.2; 63.15.2 (and see G. W. Clarke's comments in ACW 46, 220 n. 14; E. Dassmann, 'Ambrosius und die Märtyrer', *JbAC* 18 (1975), 45–68, at 61 ff.); also Aug. *Serm.* 304.1, on Lawrence: *Ibi sacrum Christi sanguinem ministravit, ibi pro Christi nomine suum sanguinem fudit.*

Abraham filium obtulit: See Gen. 22: 1–19.

Petrus Stephanum praemisit: On the stoning of Stephen, the first Christian martyr after the resurrection of Jesus, in *c.*35, see Acts 7: 1–8: 1, especially 7: 54 ff. There is no indication whatsoever in Acts that Peter 'sent Stephen on' before himself to martyrdom. According to the second-century Latin *Acts of Peter* 37–9, and Euseb. Caes. *HE* 3.1.2, Peter was crucified upside down at Rome (cf. Jn. 21: 18–19; also Tert. *Scorp*. 15). Almost certainly he perished in the Neronian persecution in 64; but the crucifixion tradition is doubtfully reliable, and the manner of his death remains uncertain (1 Clem. 5: 4, written in 95/6, does not specify). On a possible influence of A.'s depiction of Sixtus' fatherly love for Lawrence, see C. Callewaert, 'Un passo di s. Ambrogio e le lettura di una stazione quaresimale', *Ambrosius* 15 (1939), 63–4.

coronam: The crown received by the faithful Christian: cf. e.g. 2 Tim. 4: 8; Jas. 1: 12; 1 Pt. 5: 4; Apoc. 2: 10; see generally Z. Stewart, 'Greek Crowns and Christian Martyrs', in E. Lucchesi and H. D. Saffrey (eds.), *Mémorial André-Jean Festugière. Antiquité païenne et chrétienne* (Geneva, 1984), 119–24.

206.   tyranno: This could refer to the emperor Valerian, or to the executioner, perhaps the urban prefect: in 1.207, A. has this *tyrannus* present at Lawrence's death, and in Prud. *Perist*. 2, it is the prefect who speaks the cruel words A. records; cf. *Hymn* 10.27; *Iac*. 2.45–6, 58.

Mox venies, flere desiste: Very similar to the language used in the accounts of Prud. *Perist*. 2.21–8 and Aug. *Ev. Ioh.* 27.12.2. On grief at being left behind, cf. Pont. *Vita Cypr.* 19.

post triduum me sequeris. Sacerdotem et Levitam hic medius numerus decet: The interval of three days is obviously significant in a Christian context (cf. Mt. 12: 40; 26: 61; 27: 40, 63; Mk. 8: 31; 14: 58; 15: 29; Jn. 2: 19; Acts 9: 9; etc.), though the 'third day' of Christ's resurrection is by inclusive reckoning, while here three full days elapse between Sixtus' death on 6 August and Lawrence's martyrdom on 10 August. The three days correspond to the three senior grades of cleric: bishop (*sacerdos*), priest/presbyter, and deacon (*Levita*—see on 1.246). On the importance of spiritual numerics to A., see Pizzolato, 279–81.

consortium passionis meae: Cf. the 'fellowship' of Christ's sufferings in 2 Cor. 1: 7; Phil. 3: 10; 1 Pt. 4: 13.

Sic et Elias Eliseum reliquit: See 4 Ki. 2: 1–18.

207. quis prior pateretur pro Christi nomine: Cf. Acts 5: 41; 9: 16; 1 Pt. 4: 14.

In fabulis ferunt tragicis excitatos theatri . . . pro se pateretur necari: ferunt is an another oblique reference to Cic., this time to *Amic.* 24: (Laelius speaks) *Qui clamores tota cavea nuper in hospitis et amici mei M. Pacuvi nova fabula! Cum ignorante rege uter Orestes esset, Pylades Orestem se esse diceret ut pro illo necaretur, Orestes autem, ita ut erat, Orestem se esse perseveraret. Stantes plaudebant in re ficta*; cf. further *Fin.* 5.63 (and *Fin.* 2.79). The play of Pacuvius (219–129 BC) to which Laelius refers, perhaps called *Chryses*, seems to have related the sequel to the situation portrayed in Euripides' *Iphigenia in Tauris*. The devoted friendship of Pylades and Orestes was one of the most celebrated in antiquity. In this part of the tradition, Iphigenia was miraculously saved by Artemis from slaughter, and escaped along with Orestes and Pylades, pursued by Thoas, king of the Taurians (cf. Hyg. *Fab.* 121). Thoas catches up with them at the house of Chryses, son of Agamemnon and Chryseis, but is deceived by them and killed. Laelius' argument is that people approve in others what they could not do themselves, and so the crowd admired the altruism of both Orestes and Pylades. A. brings in the story to compare the friendship of the classical pair (on which cf. e.g. Aug. *Conf.* 4.6.11) with that of Sixtus and Lawrence. He immediately stresses the superiority of the Christian case: note the antithesis of **Sed illis . . . . Hic . . . .** Lawrence was motivated only by **amor devotionis**; unlike Orestes and Pylades, who had murdered Clytemnestra, he had committed no crime.

tyranno: See on 1.206.

craticulam: On the gridiron tradition, see on 1.205.

'Assum est', inquit, 'versa et manduca': Again, the phrase belongs to a common tradition.

CHAPTER 42: PERSECUTION SHOULD NOT BE
INCITED; NOR SHOULD FLATTERY BE SOUGHT

208.   Cavendum etiam reor . . . ducuntur cupiditate: Cf.
Cic. *Off.* 1.68: *Cavenda etiam est gloriae cupiditas, ut supra
dixi* (also *Off.* 1.65, 74).

in studia persecutionis excitent: A. turns Cic.'s point
about the dangers of *gloriae cupiditas* to the theme of
Christian persecution. While in 1.187 he affirms the principle that martyrdom should not be rashly sought, here he
warns of a further danger (**quantos perire faciunt**): personal bravado may lead to the deaths of others; you yourself
may survive your punishments, while others perish as a
result of the trouble you stir up. Testard i. 269–70 n. 1,
notes a similar defence of the legitimacy of flight in the pre-
Montanist Tertullian (*Pat.* 13.6; *Uxor.* 1.3.4; cf. also Cypr.
Epp. 5; 7.1); for Tertullian's later perspective, cf. his *Fuga*
(e.g. 9.4). In reality, the chances of 'perishing' for most of
A.'s addressees were slim (though Vigilius of Trent managed
to get himself martyred in *c*.405 (and there were other deaths
already among his clerical agents in the Alpine Val di Non in
397; see Lizzi, 59–96; Humphries, 146–7, 181–3) for an
excessively zealous application of the sort of philosophy
A. had proposed to him in *Ep.* 62 [19] on distancing the
Christian community from the pagan world around it—A.
had urged him only to discourage intermarriage, not to stir
up wars). More stable political circumstances produced a
different logic: it is possible to serve as Christ's martyr,
A. could argue, without necessarily being put to death in the
body (*Expos. Ps. 118*.20.46–7).

plerumque aversos a nobis: The powers that be are not to
be provoked, when they are generally antagonistic towards
the church in any case: as so often, the church is portrayed as
surrounded by a hostile world. The truth was, A. found
himself honoured by some such *potestates* (Aug. *Conf.* 6.3.3),
and he has no wish to be socially embarrassed thanks to
careless language from subordinates. The bishop who has
influence in high places is happy to cultivate a siege mental-
ity, so long as this does not lead to uncouth behaviour within

his *presbyterium*. On the error of behaving **insolentius**, cf.
1.72; also 3.134.

iracundiam: Perhaps suggested by Cic.'s warning against
the display of anger in the administration of public justice in
Off. 1.89 (cf. also *Off.* 1.69).

**209. Prospiciendum etiam ne adulantibus aperiamus
aurem . . . sed etiam ignaviae videtur:** Cf. Cic. *Off.* 1.91:
*Isdemque temporibus cavendum est ne adsentatoribus patefacia-
mus aures neve adulari nos sinamus, in quo falli facile est. Tales
enim nos esse putamus ut iure laudemur.* On **ignaviae**, cf.
propter ignaviam in Cic. *Off.* 1.73.

On flattery, cf. 1.88, 226; 2.66, 112–20; 3.58, 89, 134–5. The
Wisdom literature contains numerous warnings against the
flatterer: e.g. generally Prov. 2: 16; 6: 24; 7: 5, 21; 26: 28;
28: 23; 29: 5; and classical authorities say the same: e.g.
Arist. *EN* 1108a26–30; Thphr. *Char.* 2; fr. 532–46, 547–8
[Fortenbaugh]; Plu. *Mor.* 48e–74e; Cic. *Amic.* 89–104. No
doubt A. himself had no shortage of potential courtiers,
from new arrivals like Augustine to those who sought his
influence over civil appointments, and churchmen who
craved preferment through social climbing; see McLynn,
256–75. To heed obsequious language is to betray *fortitudo*
with a vengeance.

CHAPTER 43: TEMPERANCE: MAINTAINING A
REALISTIC ORDER IN LIFE

1.210–51 covers temperance, echoing Cic. *Off.* 1.93–151. From
1.231 onwards, the Ciceronian evocation is patchy, though still
detectable; most of the material is biblical (on Testard's
mistaken idea that the account of *temperantia* is over at the
end of 1.245, see on 1.246–51). There are some overlaps with
1.65–114: e.g. cf. 1.212 with 1.65; 1.213 with 1.81; 1.228–9
with 1.97–8; 1.231–8 with 1.13–22 (deliberately picked up; cf.
also, to a lesser extent, 1.90–7); 1.226 with 1.99–104; and 1.221
with 1.30; 1.225 with 1.82, 89, 99, 115. Many of these are
inevitable, given the length of the earlier arguments on modesty. Cic. himself repeats some of his ideas in this area, either
for emphasis or because he is attempting to combine the

Panaetian perspective on σωφροσύνη with his own understanding of propriety in social relations (Dyck, 238–49). For
instance, he too speaks twice of reason controlling impulse
(*Off.* 1.101–3 and 1.132). A.'s argument may be discursive, but
this does not mean that 1.65–114 and 1.210–51 stem from
separate layers of composition (at least, not from separate
sermons or editions of the text, at any rate; it is entirely
possible, of course, that A. *writes/dictates* the two sections on
different days, and thus offers some repeated echoes of the
same Ciceronian passages). The importance of the *decorum* is
fundamental to the ethic of book 1, and it is quite understandable that it dominates two blocks of the argument: first, in
1.28, 30, 78, 82, 89, 98–9, 105, then in 1.219–25, 230 here
(besides the references elsewhere in the book: 1.122, 140, 182,
202, 206, 253, 256). 1.219–25 explains the distinction between
the *decorum* and the *honestum*, and shows how the *decorum*
functions in both the totality and the individual parts of
creation and human life. Visible propriety, determined by
context (1.211–18) and evidenced both in the whole of life
and in its every constituent element (1.222–5), lies close to the
heart of the ideal A. is seeking to cultivate for his church. The
blend of Ciceronian respectability with scriptural authority as
the pattern for clerical modesty bears repetition. H. North,
*Sophrosyne: Self-Knowledge and Self-Restraint in Greek Liter-
ature* (Ithaca, NY, 1966), 360–70, especially 360–2, understates
the ongoing importance of human approbation in A.'s picture;
for better appraisals, see Steidle, 'Beobachtungen', 43–57, and
especially Becker, 161–212.

**210. restat ut de quarta virtute dicamus . . . spectatur et
quaeritur:** Cf. Cic. *Off.* 1.93: *Sequitur ut de una reliqua parte
honestatis dicendum sit, in qua verecundia et quasi quidam
ornatus vitae, temperantia et modestia omnisque sedatio pertur-
bationum animi et rerum modus cernitur.*
tranquillitas animi: See on 1.90.
studium mansuetudinis: Cic. mentions *mansuetudo* in *Off.*
1.88.
moderationis gratia: Cf. Cic. *Off.* 1.96, 98.
honesti cura, decoris consideratio: Cf. Cic. *Off.* 1.93–4;
also *Off.* 1.79.

211. Ordo igitur quidam vitae nobis tenendus est: Testard i. 270 n. 2 draws attention to the logical continuity between 1.210–11 and 1.219, and suggests that 1.219 may have followed 1.211 in an earlier version of the text. His argument is that 1.209–10 is based on Cic. *Off.* 1.91 and 1.93, and 1.219 ff. continues on the theme of Cic. *Off.* 1.93–5 and 1.97, whereas 1.212–18 echoes other Ciceronian passages, not *Off.* 1.93 ff. The contention that A. evokes different sections of Cic.'s text is, however, worthless: A.'s allusions are invariably piecemeal. 1.212–18 does look slightly strange if we read it as a block sandwiched between 1.211 and 1.219: 1.219, mentioning *verecundia* and *ordo*, might seem to follow 1.211 better than 1.212 does. But it is quite unnecessary to posit different origins for the two sections. 1.212–18 is all about how best to preserve a modesty appropriate to one's age, status, and abilities, and so it explains what the *ordo* mentioned in 1.211 means in practice. The reference to the benefits of older company in 1.212 follows on from the idea in 1.211 that *verecundia* is a basic foundation: in 1.65 and 1.67 A. has spoken of *verecundia* as an introductory grace—in other words, it is a virtue of particular relevance to the young—so the mention of *verecundia* in 1.211 could well be a trigger for similar reflection here. The sequence of thought is no weaker than it often is in A. On **ordo**, see on 1.82.

ut a verecundia prima quaedam fundamenta ducantur: Cf. 1.67; on **fundamenta**, cf. also 1.23.

ab omni aliena luxu: Cic. *Off.* 1.106 and 1.123 condemn *luxuria*.

sobrietatem diligit: See on 1.12. Cic. *Off.* 1.106, has *sobrie*.

212. Sequatur conversationis electio: See on 1.85.

ut adiungamur probatissimis quibusque senioribus: Cf. Cic. *Off.* 1.122: *Est igitur adulescentis maiores natu vereri, exque iis deligere optimos et probatissimos quorum consilio atque auctoritate nitatur; ineuntis enim aetatis inscitia senum constituenda et regenda prudentia est* (also *Off.* 2.46); on older company, cf. 1.87; 2.97–101.

colorat mores adulescentium et velut murice probatis inficit: Seneca uses the image of wool-dying to illustrate the way in which virtue as the sole good must be soaked in many times; those who have only been slightly tinged cannot be expected to be as wise as those who have been well steeped (*Ep.* 71.31). (Perhaps the metaphor stems from the practice of the old wearing purple; cf. also Quint. *Inst.* 1.1.5, of speech.) A. has a similar picture in mind: the orderliness of life and the probity of older men soak into the character of the young by familiarity. Cf. *imbuti* in Cic. *Off.* 1.118.

iter vitae: On being influenced to follow the right path of life (*recta vitae . . . via*), cf. Cic. *Off.* 1.118.

213. Quaerendum etiam in omni actu quid personis, temporibus conveniat atque aetatibus: Cf. Cic. *Off.* 1.125: *Ita fere officia reperientur cum quaeretur quid deceat et quid aptum sit personis temporibus aetatibus* (also *Off.* 1.117: *cum quaerimus quid deceat*); and see on 1.174. On the different *personae* of each respective age, see on 1.65.

quid etiam singulorum . . . alterum non decet: Cf. Cic. *Off.* 1.107–14, especially 110, 114, and 113: *id enim maxime quemque decet quod est cuiusque maxime*; *Off.* 1.100 has *accommodatum* and *accommodati sunt*; 1.115 has *accommodamus*. Cic. follows the Panaetian theory of adopting a realistic *persona*: each person must know his own character and behave in a way that is suited to it. This is a middle Stoic expansion of the principle of living according to nature, to take account of individual character, assessing one's gifts, faults, background, and potential. A. takes the same approach: cf. 1.187, 213–16; 2.134.

Aliud iuveni aptum, aliud seni: Cf. Cic. *Off.* 1.122: *Et quoniam officia non eadem disparibus aetatibus tribuuntur aliaque sunt iuvenum, alia seniorum, aliquid etiam de hac distinctione dicendum est* (and in general *Off.* 1.122–3).

periculis . . . rebus secundis: See on 1.200.

214. The Ciceronian argument is illustrated with OT examples:

Saltavit ante arcam Domini David . . . sed magis iste laudatus: [**nec:** PVMA, W, Testard: *nec id* E[1]: *nec ob id* E[2]: *nec ideo* COB] See 2 Ki. 6: 12–23 (cf. 1 Chr. 15: 25–16: 3).

Mutavit vultum contra regem cui nomen Achis . . . reprehensione carere potuisset: David feigned insanity

before King Achish of Gath in order to escape detection as
he fled from Saul: 1 Ki. 21: 10–15.

Saul quoque vallatus choro prophetarum . . .: *Et Saul
inter prophetas?*: See 1 Ki. 19: 18–24.

CHAPTER 44: DOING THAT TO WHICH ONE IS
SUITED

215. **Unusquisque igitur suum ingenium noverit . . . ut
bonis intendat, vitia declinet:** Cf. Cic. *Off.* 1.114: *Suum
quisque igitur noscat ingenium, acremque se et bonorum et
vitiorum suorum iudicem praebeat* (also *Off.* 1.110, 113); *nec
tam est enitendum ut bona quae nobis data non sint sequamur
quam ut vitia fugiamus.* On this pragmatic self-knowledge
principle, cf. Sen. *Tranq. an.* 6.2. In A., cf. generally *Expos.
Ps. 118*.2.13; 10.10; *Ex.* 6.39–43, 50–3; *Exh. virg.* 68; *Exc. fr.*
1.45; and see P. Courcelle, *Connais-toi toi-même de Socrate à
saint Bernard*, 2 vols. (Paris, 1974), i. 117–25.

aptum: Cic. *Off.* 1.114, has *aptissimum*.

216. **Alius distinguendae lectioni aptior . . . alius
sacrario opportunior habetur:** The Ciceronian idea is
applied directly to the ecclesiastical context. The reader
and psalm-leader performed obvious liturgical roles (probably often the same young man would do both tasks, though
A. envisages division of labour according to ability; H. Leeb,
Die Psalmodie bei Ambrosius (Vienna, 1967), especially 41–
52); the exorcist prepared catechumens for baptism and
ministered to those deemed to be suffering from demon
possession (cf. e.g. *Ep.* 77 [22]; Paul. *VA* 28; and Homes
Dudden i. 130). The deacon, among other responsibilities,
looked after the sanctuary or sacristy; cf. 1.256 (Gryson,
Prêtre, 143 n. 49). The roles of reader, psalm-leader, and
exorcist were not formally systematized like those of the
superiores ordinis, deacons, presbyters, and bishops (Gryson,
Prêtre, 144–5, *pace* Homes Dudden i. 129–31, and, to a lesser
extent, Monachino, 20–44).

Haec omnia spectet sacerdos . . . id officii deputet: The
bishop must allocate functions according to the abilities of
his clerics; cf. 2.134. Cf. the image of the bishop as ship's

commander with other clerics as crew (and the laity as passengers), in *Const. Apost.* 2.57; also Jer. *Ep.* 125.15.2.

217. Sed id, cum in omni vita difficile, tum in nostro actu difficillimum est: Cic. *Off.* 1.115–21 explains the general difficulties of determining the right career; *Off.* 1.117 has *difficillima*. For A. the calling of the church is so demanding that these problems are all the more acute.

Amat enim unusquisque sequi vitam parentum ... alii ad actiones diversas: Cf. Cic. *Off.* 1.116: *Quorum vero patres aut maiores aliqua gloria praestiterunt, ii student plerumque eodem in genere laudis excellere, ut ... in re militari* (Cic. goes on to illustrate this with examples of sons who emulated their father's military distinctions); 1.118: *Plerumque autem parentium praeceptis imbuti ad eorum consuetudinem moremque deducimur* (and cf. *Off.* 1.121); *sequi* is used in *Off.* 1.114, 119. On **plerique ... alii**, cf. *alii ... alii ... alii ...* in Cic. *Off.* 1.115. Cic. has *actiones* in *Off.* 1.111.

218. In ecclesiastico vero officio nihil rarius invenias: Cf. Cic. *Off.* 1.65: *quod vix invenitur qui ...* ; 1.119: *Illud autem maxime rarum genus est.*

qui sequatur institutum patris: Cf. Cic. *Off.* 1.116: *Fit autem interdum ut nonnulli omissa imitatione maiorum suum quoddam institutum consequantur.* A. stresses the particularly hard nature of this calling where, unlike in secular fields, sons hardly ever wish to follow in their fathers' footsteps. The reference must be to sons of clerics born before their fathers entered the church, since 1.248–9 below prescribes priestly celibacy. *Pace* De Romestin, 36 n. 2, it is unlikely that it alludes to sons of fathers in the lower orders of the church, of whom celibacy was not required, for A. goes on to say that part of what puts young men off is the difficulty of observing **abstinentia**, which is surely (in context) a sexual virtue practised by their fathers. As De Romestin rightly says, it is even more improbable that **patris** refers to a *spiritual* father.

in lubrica aetate: Cic. *Off.* 1.65 refers to *locus ... sane lubricus*; for *aetas*, cf. *Off.* 1.122. One is reminded also of Cic.'s description of young men being deterred from a legal career by the prospect of the hard work and self-denial involved, set as they are on the slippery paths of pleasure

(*Cael.* 41–3); cf. also Cic. *Flacc.* 105; *Rep.* 1.44; *Verr.* 2.5.137; Sen. *Contr.* 2.6.4; Plin. *Ep.* 3.3.4; Jer. *Ep.* 7.4.1. In A., cf. e.g. *Expl. Ps. 48*.9; *Ob. Val.* 13, 46; *Expos. Ps. 118*.16.6; *Elia* 46. On different sins besetting each respective age, cf. *Noe* 81; on the passions of youth, cf. *Paen.* 1.74; *Cain* 1.11.

abstinentia: Sexual abstinence, not just restraint in general. The celibacy demanded of priests (1.248–9), is a deterrent to young men from pursuing the same vocation; cf. 1.256–7. Augustine initially thought A.'s own celibacy the one difficult aspect of his life—and so, subliminally, it seemed to disqualify A. from the role of becoming Augustine's spiritual 'father' (*Conf.* 6.3.3; see O'Donnell ii. 343–4). Such self-restraint is only possible for the few (3.10). An essential motive in the polemic against the anti-ascetic Jovinian (a former Milanese monk) was the realization that his logic invalidated the role of the clergy as the spiritual superiors of other believers: the principle of hierarchy consolidated by sexual distinction was considered vital (cf. *Ep. extra coll.* 15 [42].2; and see D. G. Hunter, 'Resistance to the Virginal Ideal in Late-Fourth-Century Rome: The Case of Jovinian', *ThS* 48 (1987), 45–64.

alacri adulescentiae: Cf. 1.65.

vita obscurior: Cic. has *obscuris* in *Off.* 1.116; and in *Off.* 2.45 he speaks of young men seeking to escape the *obscuritas* of a lowly background by achieving great things, such as military feats.

studia: Cic. has the word in *Off.* 1.118; cf. also *Off.* 1.110.

Illi autem praesentibus, nos futuris militamus: A.'s other-worldly preoccupation is again dominant; the soldiers of Christ are serving a different *imperator* (1.185–6), and their interest, then, is in the age to come, not the semblance of reality that they see around them in the present life; cf. 1.28. A. contrasts the military service of which Cic. speaks with the *militia fidei*; cf. generally 1.185–6. On the more difficult path as more glorious, cf. Cic. *Off.* 1.64.

cura: Cic. has the word in *Off.* 1.114.

CHAPTER 45: THE SEEMLY AND THE
HONOURABLE

1.219–25 is on the *decorum*, the principle which controls a right understanding of *temperantia*. A. explains the fine distinction between the *decorum* and the *honestum*, and differentiates the *decorum generale* from the *decorum speciale*. The inspiration is Ciceronian, though the evocation is inaccurate in 1.222–4. A biblical theology of creation and redemption is fundamental as well, as A. spells out both macrocosmic and microcosmic dimensions to the *decorum* in the light of the divine purpose and divine grace. One point particularly worth noting is the stress on the *visibility* of seemliness: Cic. makes quite a bit of this in *Off.* 1.93–6, 98, 102, and A. picks up the theme: cf. 1.219, *praelucet*; 220, *videtur . . . videatur . . . species . . . emicat*; 221, *bona habitu . . . bona specie . . . speciem . . . forma . . . specie . . . adsumpsit decorem*; 222, *praeeminet . . . spectatur . . . enitet . . . praeeminentem*; 223, *speciem*; 224, *elucebat . . . resplenduit . . . gratia . . . delectat . . . videantur*; 225, *excellit et quasi in quodam speculo elucet*; cf. also 1.245, 247.

219. Teneamus igitur verecundiam et . . . modestiam: See on 1.210, on Cic. *Off.* 1.93.

illud quod decorum dicitur . . . ut magis in sermone distinctio sit quam in virtute discretio: Cf. Cic. *Off.* 1.93–4: *Hoc loco continetur id quod dici Latine decorum potest, Graece enim πρέπον dicitur [decorum]. Huius vis ea est, ut ab honesto non queat separari; nam et quod decet honestum est et quod honestum est decet.* Also *Off.* 1.95: *Est enim quiddam, idque intellegitur in omni virtute, quod deceat; quod cogitatione magis a virtute potest quam re separari.*

Differre enim ea inter se intellegi potest, explicari non potest: Cf. Cic. *Off.* 1.94: *Qualis autem differentia sit honesti et decori, facilius intellegi quam explanari potest*; also *Off.* 2.9; *Fin.* 2.35.

220. Et ut conemur aliquid eruere distinctionis . . . tamquam venustas et pulchritudo: Cf. Cic. *Off.* 1.95: *Ut venustas et pulchritudo corporis secerni non potest a valetudine, sic hoc de quo loquimur decorum totum illud* *quidem est cum virtute confusum, sed mente et cogitatione distinguitur.* While Cic. gives the Stoic simile (Dyck, 253) and then passes on, A. sees fit to explain it below. On the beauty of the human body, cf. *Ex.* 6.47, 54; *Expos. Ps. 118.*10.6; 16.6; *Inst. virg.* 20.

excellere: Cf. Cic.'s use of *excellentia* in *Off.* 1.96–7.

tamen in radice est honestatis . . . in ea floreat: A. adds a further illustration of his own. *Decorum* is the flower, *honestas* the root. Just as, in the Ciceronian picture, the *decorum* of physical *venustas et pulchritudo* cannot exist without the *honestas* of good health and soundness of body, so here the flower needs a healthy root in order to flourish. For some similar language, cf. *Is.* 60; on the beauty of flowers, cf. *Ex.* 3.36. For a survey of such imagery, see M. T. Springer, *Nature-Imagery in the Works of St Ambrose* (Washington, DC, 1931), especially 71–84, though the author does not say enough about the biblical inspiration for many of the images she lists.

Quid est enim honestas nisi quae turpitudinem quasi mortem fugiat?: The root is defined in negative terms, as the fleeing of *turpitudo*. Just as seemliness is attractive, anything that conflicts with *honestas* is repulsive.

quia radix salva est: On the quality of the flower depending on the nature of the root, cf. Mt. 7: 16–20; 12: 33; Lk. 6: 44; Jas. 3: 12.

221. Habes hoc in nostris aliquanto expressius: 'Our' Scriptures make the distinction clearer than the Ciceronian illustration does. A. traces the philosophical vocabulary in the Bible's language (cf. 1.25, 30, 36–7, 223; 2.23–7; and Introduction IV.1) and in the Christian narrative of creation–fall–redemption; cf. 1.224 below.

Dominus regnavit, decorem induit: Ps. 92: 1. *Decor* here means 'splendour', but A. harks back to the root, 'seemliness'. English cannot succinctly capture the word-play; the gloss given in the translation's 'a robe of seemly splendour' is the only way of bringing out both elements.

Sicut in die honeste ambulate: Rom. 13: 13.

Quod Graece dicunt εὐσχήμως**: [**εὐσχήμως**: Testard: *eusche-mos* Zell: *eustomos* OB Gering: εὐσχημόνως Amerbach]** A. again airs his knowledge of the Greek text; cf. 1.30.

hoc autem proprie significat: bono habitu, bona specie: *Honestas* covers the visual dimensions as well. Honourable behaviour is God's order in nature (cf. 1.77–8), and so we should be seen to live that way. *Species* appears in Cic. *Off.* 1.96.

primum hominem: An allusion to the Pauline typology of the first and the second Man, or the first and the Last Adam (Rom. 5: 12–21; 1 Cor. 15: 45–9).

bona membrorum compositione: Cf. Cic. *Off.* 1.98: *Ut enim pulchritudo corporis apta compositione membrorum movet oculos et delectat hoc ipso, quod inter se omnes partes cum quodam lepore consentiunt.*

formavit: The verb is used in the second creation narrative, in Gen. 2: 7.

Remissionem . . . peccatorum: Cf. Mt. 26: 28; Mk. 1: 4; Lk. 1: 77; 3: 3; 24: 47; Acts 2: 38; 10: 43; etc.

renovavit eum Spiritu et infudit ei gratiam: Perhaps a reference to the baptism of Jesus (Mt. 3: 16; Mk. 1: 10; Lk. 3: 22; Jn. 1: 32): the Spirit's anointing of Christ for his mediatorial service has transformative significance for humanity as a whole. On the Spirit's role at Christ's baptism, cf. *Spir.* 1.44, 100, 103; 3.65. A. sees all humanity as incorporated redemptively into the human nature of Christ (e.g. *Inc.* 54, 56; *Expos. Ps. 118*.10.14), which is divinely anointed at his baptism. Alternatively, it is possible that A. is thinking of the resurrection of Christ (cf. 1 Tim. 3: 16; note also Acts 2: 33), which guarantees the reality of *redemptio humana* (Testard i. 272 n. 8.). But the grace given to Christ and its significance for human nature were surely already in evidence prior to his resurrection (cf. Jn. 1: 14, 16–17), so the second suggestion seems less likely. (On the resurrection, cf. *Expl. Ps. 36*.36; *Expos. Ps. 118*.20.19; *Abr.* 2.80; *Exc. fr.* 2.6.) A. could well be alluding to Eph. 4: 23–4: *renovamini autem spiritu mentis vestrae, et induite novum hominem, qui secundum Deum creatus est in iustitia et sanctitas veritatis*, though properly construed these verses are of course not referring to the Holy Spirit but to believers being sanctified 'in spirit'. It would make little sense of the Latin to give **Spiritu** here a lower case 's-' and take it as a reference to the human spirit ('he renewed him in spirit'), but this does not mean that

A. cannot be subconsciously echoing the language of Eph. 4: 23–4 while referring to the Holy Spirit, especially since the idea of 'putting on' is in his mind (Tit. 3: 5–6 is quite similar, but lacks the 'putting on' language). The translation of De Romestin treats **qui venerat in servi forma et in hominis specie** (Christ, in an allusion to Phil. 2: 7) as the subject of the sentence after **sed posteaquam**, but the relative clause comes so late that to take it this way is to assume a very awkward shift of subject between **non dederat** (God) and the surely parallel **renovavit**. Whatever we say, however, there is a slight bumpiness in **eum . . . ei**: the first refers back to the **primum hominem** of the previous sentence, the second is the antecedent of **qui venerat in servi forma et in hominis specie**, Christ (and so different from the **ei** at the end of the previous sentence).

The theology of the sentence (assuming the translation given) is at any rate noteworthy. The first man possesses *honestas* according to God's design in creation; the second Man, the incarnate Christ, puts on *decor* and so elevates the first, adding (?) grace to nature. The work of redemption, the granting of the forgiveness of sins, gives an extra glory to humanity (on the potential redemption of the whole human race, cf. *Expl. Ps. 39*.6; *Expos. Ps. 118*.8.57—universal mercy); the excellence of human nature is increased (*Luc.* 2.41; *Ep.* 34 [45].15) as a result of Christ's representative achievement; cf. *Expos. Ps. 118*.10.14; 20.19; *Iac.* 1.21; *Inst. virg.* 104; *Expl. Ps. 39*.20 (the *felix ruina* idea of the Fall).

Te decet hymnus, Deus, in Sion: Ps. 64: 2; see on 1.30. **hoc est dicere: Honestum est ut . . . te honorificemus**: The distinction between the *decorum* and the *honestum* has disappeared: **decet** in Ps. 64: 2 *is* the **honestum**. A. is so concerned to find both terms in the Scriptures that he evidently forgets that he is supposed to be explaining the difference between them.

Omnia vestra honeste fiant: 1 Cor. 14: 40.

Hoc tamquam excellentius ceteris credere est decorum: The fourth virtue, like the other three, is bound up with the believer's relationship with God; here is the supreme dimension of the *decorum*. Cf. 1.9, 30, 35, 70, 122, 126–7 for similar emphases.

Mulierum quoque *in habitu ornato* orare convenit: [***ornato***: A, OB, Testard: *ornatu* PVM, E¹W, C: *et ornatu* E²: *ordinato* Monte Alto] Cf. 1 Tim. 2: 9–10.

eam decet orare velatam: Cf. 1 Cor. 11: 4–16, especially 11: 5–6. On the subject, cf. e.g. *Paen.* 1.69; Tert. *De Orat.* 20–3; *Cult. fem.* 2.7; *Virg. vel.*; Cypr. *Hab. virg.*

promittentem castitatem cum bona conversatione: A conflation of 1 Tim. 2: 10 and 1 Pt. 3: 2, 16 (cf., too, Jas. 3: 13). On prayer, see on 1.88.

CHAPTER 46: SEEMLINESS—GENERAL AND PARTICULAR

222. Est igitur decorum quod praeeminet, cuius divisio gemina est. Nam est decorum quasi generale . . . est etiam speciale quod in parte aliqua enitet: Cf. Cic. *Off.* 1.96: *Est autem eius descriptio duplex; nam et generale quoddam decorum intellegimus, quod in omni honestate versatur, et aliud huic subiectum, quod pertinet ad singulas partes honestatis.* On **spectatur**, cf. Cic. *Off.* 1.98: *et hoc quod spectatur in uno quoque genere virtutis.* Cic., however, is distinguishing the seemliness of *honestas* as a whole (of all four virtues together) from the seemliness of the fourth virtue in particular, whereas A. takes general *decorum* as something that is seen in general behaviour, and particular *decorum* as that which is observed in an individual action (Steidle, 'Beobachtungen', 47). He confuses this Ciceronian sentiment with another one, on consistency of life and behaviour in the individual person:

ac si aequabilem formam atque universitatem honestatis . . . in suis habet virtutibus praeeminentem: Cf Cic. *Off.* 1.111: *Omnino si quicquam est decorum, nihil est profecto magis quam aequabilitas universae vitae, tum singularum actionum*; cf. 1.225 below. A.'s conflation of the two passages of Cic. means that for him the *decorum generale* assumes greater importance (cf. 1.225). It is vital that people see regularity in the whole of one's life; on this basic Stoic logic, aesthetically slanted by Panaetius–Cic. to depict life a

a work of art (an idea evoked here in **concinentem**), see on
1.85.

**223. quod et decorum est secundum naturam vivere . . .
contra naturam:** The fundamental Stoic principle, probably suggested by Cic.'s references to nature in *Off.* 1.96, just
after the words echoed in 1.222 above; in *Off.* 1.98, and
especially in *Off.* 1.100: *Officium autem quod ab eo* [sc.
decorum] *ducitur hanc primum habet viam, quae deducit ad
convenientiam conservationemque naturae; quam si sequemur
ducem, numquam aberrabimus.* But A. goes on to cite a
scriptural appeal to nature's authority (albeit one that
evokes Stoic thought), and to add a Christian nuance to
the concept of nature:
*Decet mulierum non velatam orare Deum? . . . igno-
minia est illi?*: 1 Cor. 11: 13–14.
Mulier vero si capillos habeat . . . pro velamine sunt:
1 Cor. 11: 15.
Personam . . . dispensat: Cf. Cic. *Off.* 1.97: *nobis autem
personam imposuit ipsa natura magna cum excellentia prae-
stantiaque animantium reliquarum*; also *Off.* 1.98, 107.
servare: Cic. uses the verb in *Off.* 1.97.
**utinamque et innocentiam custodire possemus nec
acceptam nostra malitia mutaret!:** Cf. Cic.'s wish
about civil law as a semblance of natural law in *Off.* 3.69:
*umbra et imaginibus utimur. Eas ipsas utinam sequeremur!
Feruntur enim ex optimis naturae et veritatis exemplis.* For
A. nature is the state of innocence in which humanity is
found prior to the corruption of sin (cf. *Parad.* 63; *Apol. alt.*
41; *Ep.* 63 [73].5); Maes, 113–20. On universal corruption,
affecting even a day-old child, cf. *Noe* 81; *Expl. Ps. 1.22*;
Bon. mort. 49; also *Interp. 1.22*; *Luc.* 1.17.

224. quia fecit Deus mundi istius pulchritudinem: Cic.
has *pulchritudo* in *Off.* 1.95, 98. As in 1.222, it is clear that
A. misapplies Cic.'s distinction between general and particular *decorum*: here, one is to be seen in the creation of the
world in general, and the other in the creation of certain of
the world's features. The biblical theology of creation and
Fall (cf. 1.221, 223; also 3.13–28) shapes A.'s interpretation
of the Stoic ethical principles. Unseemly behaviour is contrary to nature, but that is because nature in its entirety and

in its individual constituents reflects the mind and purpose
of a good creator.

cum faceret Deus lucem . . . probavit singula: See Gen.
1: 1–31. Cic. has *approbationem* in *Off.* 1.98 and *probandi* in
Off. 1.100; cf. also *Fin.* 5.62.

elucebat: See on *elucet* in 1.225.

Ego eram cui applaudebat . . . cum laetaretur orbe
perfecto: Prov. 8: 30–1 (VL).

Similiter: Cic. *Off.* 1.94, has *similis*.

in fabrica humani corporis . . . convenire videantur:
[**grata:** V², COB: *gratia* PV¹MA, EW, Testard] Cf. Cic. *Off.*
1.98: *Ut enim pulchritudo corporis apta compositione mem-*
brorum movet oculos et delectat hoc ipso, quod inter se omnes
partes cum quodam lepore consentiunt, sic hoc decorum. On
fabrica, cf. also Cic. *Off.* 1.127; A. 1.76–8.

sibi quadrare: Cf. 1.82.

CHAPTER 47: CONSISTENCY OF LIFE

225. Si quis igitur aequabilitatem universae vitae et
singularum actionum modos servet: Cf. Cic. *Off.*
1.111: *Omnino si quicquam est decorum, nihil est profecto*
magis quam aequabilitas universae vitae, tum singularum
actionum, quam conservare non possis si aliorum naturam
imitans omittas tuam. Cf. also A. 1.82, 89, 115; 2.7.

ordinem quoque et constantiam dictorum atque
operum moderationemque custodiat: Cf. Cic. *Off.*
1.98: *sic hoc decorum quod elucet in vita movet approbationem*
eorum quibuscum vivitur ordine et constantia et moderatione
dictorum omnium atque factorum.

in eius vita decorum illud excellit et . . . elucet: Cf. Cic.
Off. 1.98: *sic hoc decorum quod elucet in vita movet approba-*
tionem eorum quibuscum vivitur ordine et constantia et modera-
tione dictorum omnium atque factorum; 1.102: *ex quo elucebit*
omnis constantia omnisque moderatio. On **excellit**, see on
excellere in 1.220.

226. tamen: Signals the return to the theme of temperance
proper, after the discussion of the *decorum* in 1.219–25.

suavis sermo: Cf. 1.99–104, evoking Cic. *Off.* 1.132–7 and

1.103–4; cf. also A. 1.67; 2.29–30, 96. *Suavitas* (on which cf. Cic. *Or.* 69) is the quality that Augustine noted in A.'s preaching (*Conf.* 5.13.23) and in his hymns (*Conf.* 9.6.14).

vel familiaribus vel civibus vel, si fieri potest, omnibus: Friends deserve the greatest effort, followed by citizens; the world at large should be spoken to kindly *if possible*. Cf. Cic.'s reference to *reliqui* in *Off.* 1.99; perhaps something of the same social prejudice lingers on even in such apparently casual sequences; cf. on 1.227 below.

Neque adulantem se neque adulandum cuiquam exhibeat: On not allowing oneself to be flattered, cf. 1.209 and see ad loc.; 2.66; on avoiding flattering language oneself, cf. 2.96, 112–20; 3.58, 89, 134–5.

calliditatis: Cic. *Off.* 1.108 has *callidum*.

227. Non despiciat quid de se unusquisque et maxime vir optimus sentiat . . . alterum superbiae ascribitur, alterum neglegentiae: Cf. Cic. *Off.* 1.99: *Adhibenda est igitur quaedam reverentia adversus homines, et optimi cuiusque et reliquorum. Nam neglegere quid de se quisque sentiat non solum adrogantis est sed etiam omnino dissoluti.* A. fully endorses Cic.'s preoccupation with social image, derived from the Panaetian focus on *approbatio*; cf. also Cic. *Off.* 2.43. The cleric ought to pay especial attention to the impression he makes on *viri optimi*. The opinions of those who are morally 'right' or superior (**bonorum iudicia**; cf. 1.18) are tacitly equated with the views of people of a certain class (for Cic., of course, *boni* are the optimates dedicated to the retention of the Roman Republic). On the importance of a sound reputation, cf. 1.247; 2.29 ff., 122. On arrogance, see on 1.1.

neglegentiae: Cic. uses the word in *Off.* 1.101; note also *neglegere* in *Off.* 1.98–9 (cited above), and *neglegenter* in *Off.* 1.103.

228. Sunt enim motus in quibus est appetitus ille . . . ut bonae domitrici obtemperet: Cf. Cic. *Off.* 1.100: *Sed maxima vis decori in hac inest parte de qua disputamus; neque enim solum corporis qui ad naturam apti sunt, sed multo etiam magis animi motus probandi qui item ad naturam accommodati sunt*; *Off.* 1.101: *Duplex est enim vis animorum atque natura: una pars in appetitu posita est, quae est ὁρμή*

Graece, quae hominem huc et illuc rapit, altera in ratione, quae docet et explanat quid faciendum fugiendumque sit. Ita fit ut ratio praesit, appetitus obtemperet (cf. also *Off.* 1.132); and see on 1.98.

quasi quodam . . . impetu . . . se repente: [COB's *se repente* (also Gering): *serpente* PVMA, EW, Lignamine, Testard: *se ipse te* Zell is supported by Cic.'s *repentino* next to *quodam quasi . . . impetu*] Cf. Cic. *Off.* 1.49: *Multi enim faciunt multa temeritate quadam sine iudicio, †vel morbo in omnes vel† repentino quodam quasi vento impetu animi incitati.* Cic.'s context is different (he is talking about giving and returning favours; cf. Sen. *VB* 24.1), and his text is not certain, but the language is clearly lodged in A.'s mind. Cic. also speaks of animals being carried towards pleasure *omni impetu* in *Off.* 1.105; and cf. *Off.* 1.27, *ea quae repentino aliquo motu accidunt.*

domitrici: *Pace* Testard i. 272 n. 5, the inspiration for the horse-taming image here is not so much Cic. *Off.* 1.90 as Cic. *Off.* 1.102: *Efficiendum autem est ut appetitus rationi oboediant, eamque neque praecurrant nec propter pigritiam aut ignaviam deserant* (cf. also *Off.* 1.103), which A. exploits further in 1.229. For the personification of *ratio*, cf. *misericordia* in 1.40.

229. Solliciti enim debemus esse ne quid temere aut incuriose geramus: Cf. Cic. *Off.* 1.101: *Omnis autem actio vacare debet temeritate et neglegentia*; *Off.* 1.103: *ut ne quid temere ac fortuito, inconsiderate neglegenterque agamus.*

aut quidquam omnino cuius probabilem non possimus rationem reddere: Cf. Cic. *Off.* 1.101: *nec vero agere* [sc. *debet*] *quicquam cuius non possit causam probabilem reddere; haec est enim fere descriptio officii*; *Off.* 1.8: the *medium officium* is that for which a *ratio probabilis* can be given (also *Fin.* 3.58). Several of Cic.'s editors have argued that *Off.* 1.101 is an interpolation, based upon *Fin.* 3.58 (see Dyck, 261–3). If so, it is quite an old one, given the clear evocation by A. here. Cic.'s use of *probabilis* evokes the Academic doctrine that one should act on the basis of probability (argued in *Acad.*). The idea was introduced by Philo of Larissa, who sought to relate Carneades' strict agnosticism to a workable ethic. Judgement cannot be indefinitely suspended: life involves action, and action involves judgements, so behaviour must be based on the judgement of what is probably right. A.'s knowledge of Cic.'s philosophical *œuvre* makes it highly likely that he knows the philosophical baggage which the word carries, but it is less probable that he intends to convey such specific overtones here. The classical notion of social and intellectual accountability can be elided with a NT principle that the believer must be ready to answer not only to God at the last day but also to other people in this life (e.g. 1 Pt. 3: 15; Col. 4: 6).

Actus enim nostri causa . . . in quo possimus nos excusare: We are watched, whether we like it or not, so we must be prepared to give a good account of ourselves. For A.'s obsession with what people see, cf. 1.87, 219–25. Cic. *Off.* 1.137 speaks of the need to win the approval of those *qui adsunt*.

tamen idem appetitus rationi subiectus est lege naturae ipsius et oboedit ei: Cf. Cic. *Off.* 1.102: *nec* [sc. *appetitus*] *rationi parent, cui sunt subiecti lege naturae.* On the submission of impulse to reason by nature's law, see Maes, 33–7.

Unde boni speculatoris est . . . nec ulla sentit aurigae moderamina quibus possit reflecti: Cf. Cic. *Off.* 1.102: *Efficiendum autem est ut appetitus rationi oboediant, eamque neque praecurrant nec propter pigritiam aut ignaviam deserant, sintque tranquilli atque omni animi perturbatione careant; ex quo elucebit omnis constantia omnisque moderatio. Nam qui appetitus longius evagantur et tamquam exsultantes sive cupiendo sive fugiendo non satis a ratione retinentur, ii sine dubio finem et modum transeunt.* Cic. deploys not only the metaphor of horse-taming but also language suggestive of undisciplined soldiers (*praecurrant . . . deserant*); A. evokes the image of a watchman who diligently looks out to anticipate trouble. For some similar language, cf. 1.69; on the eyes as *speculatores*, cf. *Ex.* 6.55; also 6.60. On avoiding *perturbationes* by rational control, cf. also Cic. *Off.* 1.131–2, 136. On **efferato impetu**, see on 1.228.

Unde plerumque non solum animus exagitatur . . . et nimia gestit laetitia: Cf. Cic. *Off.* 1.102: *a quibus* [sc.

appetitibus] *non modo animi perturbantur, sed etiam corpora.*
Licet ora ipsa cernere iratorum aut eorum qui aut libidine aliqua
aut metu commoti sunt aut voluptate nimia gestiunt; quorum
omnium vultus voces motus statusque mutantur. On body-
language, see on 1.71.

230. Haec cum fiunt, abicitur illa naturalis quaedam
censura gravitasque morum: Cf. Cic. *Off.* 1.103: *ita*
generati a natura sumus ut . . . ad severitatem . . . et ad
quaedam studia graviora atque maiora [sc. *facti esse videamur*].
nec teneri potest illa . . . constantia: constantia is
emphatically placed at the end of the sentence. Cf. Cic.
Off. 1.125: *Nihil est autem quod tam deceat quam in omni re*
gerenda consilioque capiendo servare constantiam. On consistency, cf. Cic. *Off.* 1.111, exploited in 1.225 above; on the
antithesis of *perturbatio* (1.229) and *constantia*, cf. Cic. *Off.*
1.137.

231. In 1.97–8, A. moves from the control of anger to the
gemini motus of the soul; here he takes the reverse direction,
going from passion versus reason to the checking of anger.
The inspiration comes from Cic. *Off.* 1.101–2 and 1.132,
136–7, but the substance of the treatment of anger which
follows in 1.233–8 is largely biblical, albeit influenced by
some philosophical assumptions (see on 1.233); Ciceronian
material reappears in 1.240. Nevertheless, key classical
vocabulary is not forgotten in 1.233–8: cf. 1.237. 1.239,
developing a three-stage conception of salvation-history, is
a bridge between the explanation of the three kinds of
response to anger in 1.233–8 and the synthesis of scriptural
and classical sentiments on *imagines* in 1.240–5.

The whole of 1.233–45 exploits Ps. 38, the text that has
evidently led A. to write on duties in the first place (1.23);
A. resumes the exposition which occupied the heart of 1.5–
22. 1.231–2 introduces this return to the Ps. He broke off his
earlier treatment, he says, because he did not wish the
introduction to the work to become too lengthy; now
under the heading of temperance, he feels it is appropriate
to go back to the later verses of the Ps., which he commended
generally in 1.23. 1.5–22 covered Ps. 38: 1–3, and now 1.233–
45 looks at these subsequent verses, especially 38: 4–7. Both
sections are similar to *Expl. Ps. 38*.1–27, which draw:

considerably on Orig. *Hom. Ps. 38*.1–2. Both, however, also
evoke Cic., so if A. uses previous exegetical material he
manages to work it into the *officia* theme in some significant
measure: despite the rhetorical colouring in these passages
(cf. here 1.233–9; in the earlier section, cf. especially 1.17–
20) we certainly cannot say that 1.1–22 (or 1.5–22) and
1.233–45 are just scraps of an early exegetical exercise loosely
inserted into the Ciceronian framework (see on 1.1–22; and
generally Introduction V). We should not read too much into
A.'s efforts to explain the relevance of the Ps. 38 material in
1.23 and 1.231–2. These passages cannot simply be trying to
cover up the joints where a sermon has been inserted, *pace*
Testard, 'Etude', 171–2; 'Recherches', 88–9, 96. A. *is* sensitive about the flow of his argument, and not surprisingly so,
given the informality of his style. But all he is doing is
anticipating surprise from readers who expect closer adherence to Cic. and so he is seeking to explain why he writes as
he does. Explanation bespeaks sensitivity; it does not necessarily imply deception or a weak effort to paste over cracks.
A. starts with Ps. 38 rather than Cic., so in 1.23 he wants to
stress why Scripture has been his starting-point. In 1.231–2,
the same Ps. has occurred to him again, so he decides to
continue with the exposition left off earlier. If the structure
seems loose here, it is no looser than in many other places.
Becker, 204–5, justly challenges Testard's view that 1.231–
45 is a series of digressions. (Steidle, 'Beobachtungen', 49–
54, seems to overstate the case when he argues that A. uses
Ps. 38 as a device to unify book 1. Nevertheless, he is right to
highlight the importance of the Ps. to the modesty motif, and
to say that the Ps. is presented as a particular focus for the
elevation of scriptural authority over classical thought.) On
anger, see on 1.90.

quam acceptae plerumque accendit iniuriae dolor:
Revenge of personal injury is forbidden (1.131); we must
turn the other cheek, and not allow *indignatio* to fester within
us (1.17–22). Cic. also urges that *gravitas* be maintained by
repressing anger, even when bitter enemies treat one out-
rageously (*Off.* 1.137).

**De quo satis nos psalmi, quem in praefatione posui-
mus, praecepta instruunt:** Cf. 1.5–22.

Pulchre autem et hoc accidit ut . . . ea praefationis nostrae adsertione uteremur: Cf. 1.23, on the inspiration of the subject of duties from Ps. 38; **pulchre** here parallels *neque improvide* there. On **scripturi**, see Introduction V.

232. supra: Especially 1.17–22.

ut oportebat, perstrinximus . . . verentes ne praefatio prolixior fieret: According to literary convention, the author did not wish his preface to be too lengthy, so he merely 'touched upon' the subject of response to injury; bear in mind the warning on verbosity in 1.100. For **prolixior**, cf. 3.110.

nunc de eo uberius disputandum arbitror: Testard, 'Etude', 171 n. 32, is confused unnecessarily by these words. He assumes that the earlier passage to which A. refers is 1.13–22, and this leaves a problem with **uberius**, since 1.233–8 (or even 1.231–8) is obviously shorter than it, not longer. Steidle, 'Beobachtungen', 64 n. 161, suggests that **uberius** does not necessarily imply a *longer* treatment of the subject here, so 1.233–8 can still be set against 1.13–22. However, 'more fully' (cf. Cic. *ND* 2.20; *Div.* 2.1.3; *Fam.* 3.11.1; Plin. *Ep.* 4.17.11) naturally does suggest 'at greater length'. In the first place, it is possible that A. simply forgets his promise, and so the passage turns out to be slightly briefer than he suggests it will. Given the general informality of his style, this is hardly out of the question (perhaps especially if the text is dictated rather than written by A.'s own hand). Alternatively, he may be referring back not to 1.13–22, but to 1.17–22. 1.17–22 is specifically on how to respond to a sinner's *iniuria*, whereas 1.13–16 is on the restraint of speech and the wiles of Satan, and does not mention *iniuria*. 1.233–8 *is* slightly longer than 1.17–22. Either way, there is little reason to stumble over **uberius**.

CHAPTER 48: THREE WAYS OF RESPONDING TO
INJURY

233. Tria itaque genera esse hominum . . . demonstrare volumus, si possumus: This task occupies 1.233–8. The three types are: (i) the *infirmus*, who repays injury with injury

(1.233); (ii) the person who has made some moral progress, who keeps quiet when insulted and does not retaliate (1.234); and (iii) the perfect man, who actually blesses the one who curses him (1.235–8). The logic of the scheme turns out to be poor. A. does not, in fact, cite a scriptural example of the first type (Testard, *'Conscientia'*, 233–4; 'Etude', 171 n. 33); he simply evokes the NT idea of the *infirmus* (see on 1.42), and quotes the OT *lex talionis* principle. There is no scriptural citation of any kind for the second stage, not even an allusion to a 'type'. In the third category, A. implies that the NT ethic is more complete than the OT standard. But then, since Ps. 38 is at the heart of the argument in this section, he is concerned not to depreciate David, whom he holds up so often as a moral paragon, so he immediately adds that David was the equal of Paul, his main exemplar in the third case (1.236–8). The problem is that, on the basis of 1.21–2, David's silence when abused by Shimei ought to place him in the second, not the third, category. A. attempts to set David on a par with Paul because David believed that the Lord had told Shimei to curse him, and because he later forgave his enemy (but see on 1.237). David, a *praedicator ecclesiae congregandae* (*Expl. Ps. 38*.37), reveals a moral prowess which straddles the two dispensations of salvation-history and anticipates the superiority of the Christian ethic. (On the logical tensions between the idea that (i) the antiquity of OT *exempla* renders them intrinsically superior to the later stories of paganism, and (ii) the NT offers a fuller revelation than the OT, see Introduction IV.5.)

The idea of moral or spiritual progress (προκοπή) is a common motif in middle Stoicism, where the focus is no longer on an ideal which only the perfect sage can attain, but on ordinary people's endeavour to make progress in and towards virtue. A framework of moral and spiritual ascent is also to be found in the Platonist tradition, very often in a three-stage scheme (e.g. in Plotinus' three stages of the soul's purification as it returns to the One: *Enn.* 1.2). The Platonist concept comes over into Judaeo-Christian thought, especially in the Alexandrians and in Gregory of Nyssa (H. Merki, Ὁμοίωσις Θεῷ *von der platonischen Angleichung an Gott zur Gottähnlichkeit bei Gregor von Nyssa* (Fribourg,

1952)); A. inherits it from this Greek tradition, particularly
from Philo (cf. e.g. the influences in *Is.* and *Fug.*, especially
Fug. 11, which describes three stages of: fear of God, love for
God, and resemblance to God). He merges it with the Stoic
idea, which he derives from Cic. (*Off.* 3.17). On the Stoic
background in particular, see A.-J. Voelke, *L'Idée de volunté
dans le stoïcisme* (Paris, 1973), 168–71; O. Luschnat , 'Das
Problem des ethischen Fortschritts in der alten Stoa',
Philologus 102 (1958), 178–214; on Cic., see Dyck, 17, 511;
on A.'s evocation of it, see Schmidt, 37; Sauer, 88–90;
Steidle, 'Beobachtungen', 49–50; Becker, 197 n. 177. In
the present passage, as in *Expl. Ps. 38.*10, the inspiration
comes directly from Orig. *Hom. Ps. 38.*1.4–5 and 1.8 (cf. also
*Hom. Ps. 36.*5.1; *Princ.* 2.11.5.7; *Hom. Num.* 28.2–3)—a fact
which commentators have, remarkably, failed to note.
A. speaks elsewhere of a *virtutis profectus* (2.113), and of a
gradual ascent towards perfection (*Expos. Ps. 118.*16.19;
*Expl. Ps. 1.*18), though the perfection attained in this
world is only a shadow of the perfection of God and of the
world to come (1.239; 3.11; *Expos. Ps. 118.*5.35). Naturally,
no one can attain perfection except by the grace of God
(*Paen.* 2.11).

**Unum est eorum quibus peccator insultat, convi-
ciatur, inequitat:** Cf. 1.17–20. The last verb suggests that
the sinner 'rides roughshod over' his victim.

de meo ordine, de meo numero: [meo: A, EW, CO: *eo*
PVM, B] Some scholars have been uncertain as to whether
A. is referring to his fellow-bishops, or to his social peers
(Gryson, *Prêtre*, 122–3): it must surely be the former
(Testard i. 273 n. 1; 'Observations', 25). The phrase *homo
ordinis mei* is often used by Christian authors to refer to an
ecclesiastic of similar rank (e.g. Jer. *Ep.* 22.28.3), as Gryson,
Prêtre, 122 n. 73, himself notes; and *ecclesiasticus ordo* in 3.58
obviously designates the clergy. Doubtless A. has some
specific target here, but there is no means of identifying it
He certainly knew what it was to be vigorously attacked
himself. Palladius of Ratiaria, Demophilus of Constantin-
ople, and Auxentius of Durostorum are mentioned as Arian
opponents in *Fid.* 1.45, all of them of episcopal rank; see also
on 1.144. And by the late 380s, of course, the redoubtable

Jerome had become an enemy of a different kind, attacking A. anonymously for what he saw as his meagre literary and theological talents.

infirmo . . . infirmus: See on 1.42. On A. as weak, cf. 1.235.

⟨non⟩ donem: Winterbottom's emendation (563) must be right. The least perfect type *does* retaliate: 'The chances are I shall *not* forgive him for it . . .'.

contentus conscientia mea: Cf. 1.6, 9, 18, 21. The conscience theme is not systematically applied to the three types (Testard, '*Conscientia*', 232–4). The first person is not content with his good conscience, so we might expect to be told that the second is (cf. especially 1.18, 21), but no mention is made of this in 1.234. Conscience reappears with David in the third category, in 1.236.

oculum pro oculo et dentem pro dente: Ex. 21: 24; Lev. 24: 20; Dt. 19: 21. A. is hinting at the superiority of the NT ethic of forgiveness to the OT principle of strict justice; cf. Mt. 5: 38–48. Retaliation is for the *infirmus*, who has not yet reached the standard set by Christ; cf. 1.235.

234. ego taceo et nihil respondeo: Cf. 1.17–22. David did this when cursed by Shimei (1.21), but A. puts him in the third category (1.236–8) rather than the second (though in 1.236 David is *primo* in the second and *deinde* in the third).

235. verbi gratia loquor, nam veritate infirmus sum: A. modest touch: A. has no wish to claim perfection for himself; cf. generally 1.1–4.

Maledicimur et benedicimus: 1 Cor. 4: 12.

Audierat enim dicentem: *Diligite inimicos vestros . . . et persequentibus vos*: Paul knew Jesus' words: Mt. 5: 44 (also Lk. 6: 27–8, 35; cf. Rom. 12: 14). Again, we have implicitly the advance of the NT ideal over the OT standard; the mature or 'perfect' Christian blesses his enemy, rather than paying him back in kind or even ignoring him. Cf. the ideal of imitating divine mercy in 1.37–8.

sustinebat . . . propositae mercedis gratia: Cf. Heb. 12: 2: (of Jesus himself) *qui pro proposito sibi gaudio sustinuit crucem*. Jesus not only prescribed, he exemplified; and Paul followed this example. The merit theology is strong in these paragraphs, though of course A. assumes that the ability to progress in virtue comes ultimately from divine grace. For the reward promised to the obedient, cf. Mt. 5: 12, 43–8; Lk. 6: 23, 35.

ut filius Dei fieret si dilexisset inimicum: Cf. Mt. 5: 45; Lk. 6: 35.

236.   **Tamen et sanctum David . . . edocere possumus:** Instead of comparing OT and NT morality, A. now wishes to show that David was no less spiritual than Paul (cf. 1.238; *Expl. Ps. 38*.10–14; *Apol.* 30–2).

filius Semei: See on 1.21.

silebat a bonis suis: Cf. Ps. 38: 3; cf. also 1.18.

quia maledicto illo divinam acquirebat misericordiam: See 2 Ki. 16: 12. The notion of divine reward is not mentioned in 1.21 (Steidle, 'Beobachtungen', 51), but is brought in here because of the comparison with Paul, who in 1.235 receives reward from God in accordance with Jesus' promise.

237.   **humilitatem et iustitiam et prudentiam:** These three qualities are identified below. A. adds his own favourite emphasis on *humilitas* (see on 1.1) to the classical terminology. *Ideo maledicit mihi quia Dominus dixit illi ut maledicat*: 2 Ki. 16: 10.

quasi servulus: David was as humble as a servant before the will of his divine Master (cf. *Ep.* 27 [58].7; *Ob. Val.* 58; also *Cain* 1.4; *Bon. mort.* 7); he showed the spirit of Christ; cf. e.g. Phil. 2: 7. On the condition of *servuli*, cf. e.g. *Abr.* 1.81–3; on clerics as humble *servuli*, cf. 1.247.

Ecce filius meus . . . quaerit animam meam: 2 Ki. 16: 11. David refers to Absalom, from whom he is fleeing. If his own son is seeking his life, why should he be surprised to find this Benjamite cursing and abusing him?

Habes iustitiam: David's logic reflects his sense of *iustitia*. Further, he did not attack his own son, but fled from him, and he treated Shimei with the same justice, ignoring rather than punishing him.

Dimitte illum ut maledicat . . . et retribuet mihi Dominus pro maledicto hoc: 2 Ki. 16: 11–12. Here is David's *prudentia*: he sought his reward from the Lord. Note the equation once more of prudence with quiet trust in God

lapidantem et sequentem illaesum reliquit: See 2 Ki 16: 6, 13.

post victoriam petenti veniam libenter ignovit: After Absalom's defeat and death, when David returned to Jerusalem, he granted pardon (again contrary to Abishai's advice) to the penitent Shimei (2 Ki. 19: 18–23). A. neglects to mention the sequel, however. On his deathbed, David charged Solomon to deal with Shimei (3 Ki. 2: 8–9), and Shimei was ultimately executed by Solomon for failing to keep his promise not to leave Jerusalem (3 Ki. 2: 36–46). David's pardon of his enemy was a personal and temporary thing; it did not stop him ordering the death of Shimei at the hands of his son.

238. evangelico spiritu: David did the Christlike thing: he blessed his enemy. On David as one who showed the *evangelicus spiritus*, cf. *Expl. Ps. 38*.37.

gratum . . . et delectatum: An exaggeration, as far as the text of 2 Ki. goes.

quasi bonus miles: Cf. 2 Tim. 2: 3, and see on 1.185.

quasi athleta fortis: See on 1.59.

A. is returning to ideas which he dealt with under the third virtue (1.182–7). The Stoics traditionally treated patience as part of courage; Gauthier, 137–41; M. Spanneut, 'Le Stoïcisme dans l'histoire de la patience chrétienne', *MSR* 39 (1982), 101–30; Sauer, 150–4. The synthesis of Stoic endurance with Christian self-denial and eschatological hope is found similarly in Tert. *Pat.* (especially 6.1ff; 8.1 ff.), used by Cyprian in *Bon. pat.* (especially 5 ff.), though Cyprian lays considerably more stress upon the idea that patience consists in the imitation of Christ. Cf. A. in 1.9, 20; *Expl. Ps. 38*.1–2, 7, and see Gauthier, 251 ff. A.'s treatment of patience is biblically illustrated, but it evinces clear Stoic preconceptions.

Notum mihi fac, Domine, finem meum . . . ut sciam quid desit mihi: Ps. 38: 5. On perfection as the state where nothing is lacking, cf. 1.37–8; *Iac.* 2.21.

finem meum . . . Finem illum: A. plays with the two senses of *finis*: 'goal/object/ destiny' and 'end'; cf. Orig. *Hom. Ps. 38*.1.8; Aug. *En. Ps. 38*.8–13; and A. *Interp.* 3.20; *Exc fr.* 2.32; *Expos. Ps. 118*.5.23.

quando *unusquisque surgit in suo ordine . . . deinde finis*: 1 Cor. 15: 23–4; cf. also *Expos. Ps. 118*.12.46; *Expl. Ps. 38*.16.

Hic ergo impedimentum, hic infirmitas etiam perfectorum, illic plena perfectio: Full perfection is reserved for heaven; cf. 3.11. On relative perfection as a kind of ἀπάθεια, cf. *Is.* 59; *Iac.* 1.32, 36. On **hic . . . illic**, cf. 1.29, 58, 103, 147; 3.11, 36.

quae terra sit repromissionis: The *terra repromissionis* of Canaan (Heb. 11: 9), used as a type of the eschatological promised land, or the *terra nova* (Apoc. 21: 1); cf. Orig. *Hom. Ps. 38.*1.8.

quae prima apud patrem mansio, quae secunda et tertia, in quibus . . . unusquisque requiescit: Cf. Jn. 14: 2: *In domo Patris mei mansiones multae sunt.* To A. paradise, the state to which the souls of most of the redeemed go at death, contains a gradation of seven *habitacula* or *mansiones*, each affording a particular degree of joy (*Bon. mort.* 45–57 (note especially 48), based upon 4 Ezr. 7: 91–9). Heaven, a higher realm to which the greatest saints go automatically at death but which most can only attain via a spell in paradise, also contains a *processus . . . mansionum* (*Luc.* 5.61), involving a progression from *consolatio* to *delectatio*, with each level allocated according to merit (*Expl. Ps. 38.*17; *Expl. Ps. 47.*23; *Is.* 71) or the degree of perfection attained during earthly life (the sequence of resurrection is also according to merit: *Exc. fr.* 2.116). So, the *infirmus* has one *mansio*; the person who has progressed somewhat has another; and the one who is 'perfect' another, presumably closest to the place 'above the heaven of heavens' where God himself is; cf. Orig. *Hom. Ps. 38.*1.8 (A. *Expl. Ps. 38.*17 enumerates seven stages here as well; it is not clear how the three grades of perfection correlate with these). Biblical eschatology is read through a Neoplatonist grid, where there are three stages in the soul's journey to God; the result is a dynamic, progressive vision of eternal fulfilment and reward; B. E. Daley, *The Hope of the Early Church: A Handbook of Patristic Eschatology* (Cambridge, 1991), 97–101, at 100; Niederhuber, *Eschatologie*, 64–99.

239. The theme of moral progress and heavenly reward is expanded into a sequential perspective on salvation-history in general. The twofold *hic . . . illic* scheme of 1.238 is extended into a threefold sequence of *umbra–imago–veritas*.

in which the *umbra* and the *imago*, equated with the first two stages in the preceding picture, are both *hic*, and the *veritas*, the place of completeness in virtue and truth, is *illic*. The reference-point for these temporal gradations is the sacrifice of Christ, which is visualized in shadowy form in the OT (in the type of the cultus), in image in the gospel, or NT/church age (in the eucharist), and in reality in heaven (in the perfect offering of the ascended Christ who intercedes with God as an advocate for believers). The inspiration here, as in *Expl. Ps. 38.25–6*, comes from Orig. *Hom. Ps. 38.2.2*.

Hic umbra, hic imago, illic veritas: umbra in lege, imago in evangelio, veritas in caelestibus: Cf. Heb. 10: 1: *Umbram enim habens lex bonorum futurorum, non ipsam imaginem rerum*; 8: 4–5: *Si ergo [pontifex] esset super terram, nec esset sacerdos, cum essent qui offerrent secundum legem munera, qui exemplari et umbrae deserviunt caelestium* (also Col. 2: 17). NT scholars debate whether the author of Heb. uses the *imago–umbra* language in a largely Platonist fashion, heavily indebted to Philonic thinking, or in a more specifically salvation-historical sense (see D. Peterson, *Hebrews and Perfection: An Examination of the Concept of Perfection in the 'Epistle to the Hebrews'* (Cambridge, 1982); on Philo, see also L. Goppelt, *Typos: The Typological Interpretation of the Old Testament in the New* (Grand Rapids, MI, 1982), 50–3, 161–78). A. clearly intends the latter idea in particular (cf. **ante . . . nunc** and **hic . . . ibi/illic**, below), but this obviously does not rule out Platonist influences. His main source, Origen, was of course deeply influenced by Platonism, and the progress theme of 1.233–8 embraces Platonist as well as Stoic assumptions. Levels of disclosure or apprehension of the truth are easily connected with stages of salvation-history; the two are not alternatives (Becker, 199–200); cf. e.g. *Expos. Ps. 118*.5.10; 18.37–8; *Expl. Ps. 1*.31, 33; *Expl. Ps. 38*.25–6; *Expl. Ps. 61*.33–4. See Hahn, 207–27 (especially 215–17), 259–75, 425–8; also Toscani, 413–53; Pizzolato, 79–83; A. Luneau, *L'Histoire du salut chez les Pères de l'Eglise* (Paris, 1964), 247–61, especially 253–4; Morgan, 163–4, 205–8. Cf. Cic. *Off.* 3.69: *Sed non veri iuris germanaeque iustitiae solidam et expressam effigiem nullam tenemus, umbra et imaginibus utimur*—probably evoking Plato's famous cave simile in

Rep. 514a ff. (cf. also Cic. *Or.* 9–10). A. follows a strong patristic tradition of interpreting *bonorum futurorum* (Heb. 10: 1) as a reference to the sacraments of the Christian church, and to the eucharist in particular; see B. F. Westcott, *The Epistle to the Hebrews*, 2nd edn. (London, 1892), 304; on the background in Origen's typology, see generally R. A. Greer, *The Captain of our Salvation: A Study in the Patristic Exegesis of Hebrews* (Tübingen, 1973), 8–18. The passover is the shadow of Christ's sacrifice (in the law); the eucharist is the image (in the gospel); and the perpetual ministry of Christ the exalted High Priest is the truth (in heaven). The eucharist is a progression from the OT rite, but it is only an anticipation of the perfect liturgy of heaven; cf. *Exc. fr.* 2.109. See further Johanny, 135–60, 253–69; Morgan, 243–5.

Ante agnus offerebatur, offerebatur vitulus; nunc Christus offertur: See Heb. 9: 13–14; 10: 3–10.

quasi recipiens passionem: See Heb. 2: 9–10.

offert se ipse quasi sacerdos: See Heb. 7: 27; 9: 14, 23–8; 10: 1–25; on A.'s use of the image, see Fenger, 75–8; Toscani, 326–32.

ubi apud Patrem pro nobis quasi advocatus intervenit: Cf. 1 Jn. 2: 1–2: *sed et si quis peccaverit, advocatum habemus apud Patrem, Iesum Christum iustum; et ipse est propitiatio pro peccatis nostris*; also Heb. 9: 24: *ut appareat nunc vultui Dei pro nobis*; and see Gryson, *Prêtre*, 61 n. 5, on e.g. *Expl. Ps. 38*.26.

Hic ergo in imagine ambulamus: Cf. 2 Cor. 5: 7: *per fidem enim ambulamus, et non per speciem.*

in imagine videmus; illic *facie ad faciem*: Cf. 1 Cor. 13 12: *Videmus nunc per speculum in enigmate; tunc autem facie ad faciem.* On the imitation of God, and the true image, cf *Fug.* 17; also 22.

CHAPTER 49: THE IMAGE OF CHRIST AND THE IMAGE OF SATAN

The references to *imago* in 1.239 signal a comparison of two lifestyles. One is the lifestyle of those who live by and display the image of Christ, and so evidence wisdom, justice, faith, an contempt for material things; the other is the lifestyle of those who live by and display the image of Satan, and so evidence greed, desire, and a futile passion for gain (1.240–5). A. follows Orig. *Hom. Ps. 38*.2 and Origen's citation of NT verses, but he also evokes Cic.: there is a convenient overlap in his sources' use of words like *imago . . . simulacra . . . umbra . . . sapientia . . . iustitia . . . vanitas*. On the psychologizing of the *imago* theme by A. within a creation-eschatological framework, see Becker, 208–12.

240. Ergo dum hic sumus, servemus imaginem: Cf. Orig. *Hom. Ps. 38.2*.

imago iustitiae . . . imago sapientiae: Cf. the scriptural language about the image of Christ (e.g. 1 Cor. 15: 49; 2 Cor. 3: 18; Col. 3: 10), but also Cic.'s slant on the middle-Stoic assertion that most people attain only a relative level of virtue; cf. Cic. *Off*. 1.46: *Quoniam autem vivitur non cum perfectis hominibus planeque sapientibus, sed cum iis in quibus praeclare agitur si sunt simulacra virtutis*; *Off*. 3.13: *In iis autem in quibus sapientia perfecta non est, ipsum illud quidem perfectum honestum nullo modo, similitudines honesti esse possunt* (also *Fin*. 5.43). Cic. says that *non veri iuris germanaeque iustitiae solidam et expressam effigiem nullam tenemus, umbra et imaginibus utimur* (*Off*. 3.69). A. adopts from Cic. and middle Stoicism the idea that perfect justice and perfect wisdom are impossible in this world, but he links this with the biblical doctrine of the *imago Dei*: to bear the image of justice and the image of wisdom is to bear the image of God. We shall be judged according to whether we have evinced the divine or the satanic image.

241. Adversarius enim diabolus . . . quem devoret: 1 Pt. 5: 8; cf. also *Expl. Ps. 38.27*.

auri cupiditatem . . . argenti acervos: As justice and wisdom are part of the image of God, so greed for money (like *rabies* and *furor*, above) is the hallmark of the **imago nequitiae**, the image of Satan.

vitiorum simulacra: The opposite of the *simulacra virtutis* mentioned by Cic. in *Off*. 1.46.

vocem libertatis: The voice of a free conscience.

Veniet huius mundi princeps et in me inveniet nihil:

The words of Jesus in Jn. 14: 30. The sinless one (cf. *Expl.*
Ps. 37.34) can be imitated; cf. Orig. *Hom. Ps. 36.*5.7; A. *Expl.*
*Ps. 38.*27; *Is.* 55; *Iac.* 2.24–5; *Bon. mort.* 16; *Ep.* 1 [7].17
(presenting Jacob as a type of Christ).

cum venerit perscrutari: Cf. Satan's insidious methods in
1.15–16.

Cognosce si quid tuorum est apud me: Gen. 31: 32.

**Merito beatus Iacob . . . simulacra deorum eius aurea
et argentea:** Rachel had stolen Laban's household gods
(Gen. 31: 19) without Jacob's knowledge (Gen. 31: 32),
and she hid them from Laban when he searched their tents
(Gen. 31: 33–5). Had the idols been found, Rachel would
have had to be put to death, according to Jacob's oath (Gen.
31: 32). Jacob's claim, quoted here, was therefore based on
his ignorance of Rachel's crime, and came from his own good
conscience. Her ploy to hide the images was the salvation of
the situation. Reading the story a different way, of course,
A. could just as readily accuse Rachel of showing Satan's
image for having stolen the idols in the first place.

242.   si sapientia, si fides: As ever, wisdom and faith are set
together; cf. 1.117, 122–9, 252–3.

**beatus eris, quia non respicis in vanitates et in insanias
falsas:** Cf. Ps. 39: 5: *Beatus vir cuius est nomen Domini spes
ipsius, et non respexit in vanitates et insanias falsas.*

ut arguendi te non possit habere auctoritatem: Satan is
classically cast as accuser (cf. Apoc. 12: 10).

**Itaque qui non respicit in vanitates, non conturbatur . . .
qui scias an possidere liceat tibi?:** Cf. Ps. 38: 5–7:
*Verumtamen universa vanitas omnis homo vivens. Verumtamen
in imagine pertransit homo: sed et frustra conturbatur. The-
saurizat et ignorat cui congregabit ea.* Cf. Orig. *Hom. Ps*
*38.*1.11; A. *Expl. Ps. 38.*27; also *Ex.* 6.51.

**243.   Nonne vanum est ut mercator . . . naufragium
impatiens morae incidat?:** The references to *vanitates* in
1.242 seem to trigger another memory of Cic., who speaks of
mercatores and *vanitas* in *Off.* 1.150–1 (for *vanitas*, cf. also
Off. 1.44; 3.58). The translation attempts to preserve the
'futility' motif as it echoes throughout the following paragraphs. A. evokes a classical *topos*, basic especially to Stoic
diatribe and to poetry influenced by it, of the merchant

working frantically and at absurd risk to heap up wealth
which then brings with it only uncertainty and worry. The
perils of storms and piracy are standard motifs: e.g. Hor. *Od.*
1.1.15–18; 1.31.10–15; 3.24.35–44; *Sat.* 1.1.29–32 (note also
1.1.37–40); 1.4.29–32; *Ep.* 1.1.42–6; Tib. 1.3.39–40; 1.9.9–
10; Prop. 3.7; Plaut. *Merc.* 80–97; Colum. *Agr.*, praef. 8; Juv.
12; 14.265–83. For other Christian descriptions of the
enormous risks taken by the seafaring merchant, cf. e.g.
Tert. *Pat.* 7.11–12; Greg. Naz. *Apol.* 100. On trade and
greed generally, cf. Arnob. *Adv. Nat.* 2.40. For A.'s own
assessment, cf. especially *Elia* 70–2: *Mare non ad navigandum
Deus facit, sed propter elementi pulchritudinem* (70); merchants who sail in any weather to make a profit, on account
of their *inexplebilis avaritia* (71), weary the elements with
their unceasing activity; also *Ex.* 4.19; 5.30–5; *Cain* 1.21
(though *Ex.* 3.21; 5.33–4 speak of the beauty of the sea, and
Ex. 3.22 extols the opportunities that it offers for commerce
and intercourse among peoples). See also on 1.185 above. On
latrones, see on 1.158.

**244. An non conturbatur etiam ille vane . . . quod
nesciat cui heredi relinquat?:** Cf. Ps. 38: 7.

**praecipiti effusione dilacerat heres luxuriosus . . .
quadam absorbet voragine:** One is reminded of the
descriptions of prodigal young men in Roman comedy (e.g.
in Ter. *Ad.*) and the greed of heirs in satire (see on 3.57). Cf.
Cic. *Sest.* 111: *Tu meo periculo, gurges et vorago patrimonii,
helluabare . . .?*; also *Verr.* 2.3.23; *Pis.* 41; *De Or.* 3.163; Val.
Max. 9.4. The use of *vorago* is apt after the allusion to storms
at sea in 1.243. On wicked heirs, cf. Cic. *Off.* 2.28; on their
spendthrift tendencies, cf. A. 1.168 above; *Nab.* 3, 17.

**speratus successor invidiam partae acquirit heredita-
tis et . . . transcribit compendia:** The successor attracts
such envy of his acquired wealth that he worries himself into
an early grave, and strangers get to enjoy the riches you had
meant him to have. A. is probably thinking of Eccl. 6: 2: *Vir
cui dedit Deus divitias et substantiam et honorem et nihil deest
animae suae ex omnibus, quae desiderat: nec tribuit ei potestatem Deus ut comedat ex eo, sed homo extraneus vorabit illud:
hoc vanitas, et miseria magna est*; the ability to enjoy one's
wealth is no less the gift of God than the wealth itself, and

when this is forgotten, God may allow a stranger to benefit instead. Cf. also *Ep.* 10 [38].6: *Ubi enim nullus cupiditati modus, qui fructus divitiarum? Nemo est dives qui quod habet secum hinc auferre non potest; quod enim hic relinquitur non nostrum sed alienum est.*

245. Quid ergo vane araneam texis . . . suspendis inutiles divitiarum copias?: Cf. Ps. 38: 12: *in increpationibus propter iniquitatem corripuisti hominem, et tabescere fecisti sicut araneam animam eius*; and Is. 59: 5–6: *Ova aspidum ruperunt, et telas araneae texuerunt. . . . Telas eorum non erunt in vestimentum, neque operientur operibus suis: opera eorum opera inutilia* (for another use of the spider's web as an image of fragility, cf. Job 8: 14–15).
Cf. also Verg. *Georg.* 4.246–7: *aut invisa Minervae, | laxos in foribus suspendit aranea cassis.* A. quotes Is. 59: 5 in *Expl. Ps. 38.*35, where he is also following Origen; L. F. Pizzolato, *La "Explanatio Psalmorum XII". Studio letterario sulla esegesi di sant'Ambrogio* (Milan, 1965), 40. For a parallel citation of Is. 59: 5 in *Ex.* 4.18, indebted to Basil, see Madec, 74 n. 275, 102 n. 10. Cf. also Orig. *Hom. Ps. 38.*2.8–9; A. *Ex.* 1.7; 4.18; Jer. *Ep. adv. Ruf.* 20; *Ep.* 125.6.2.

Quae, etsi fluant, nihil prosunt: Cf. 1.28–9; 2.15–16: wealth is, in fact, a hindrance to happiness.

exuunt . . . induunt: Cf. Eph. 4: 22–4; Col. 3: 8–17.

imaginem Dei: See on 1.164.

terreni imaginem: Cf. 1 Cor. 15: 45–9, especially 15: 49: *Igitur sicut portavimus imaginem terreni, portemus et imaginem caelestis.* Paul is referring to the first Adam and the last Adam, but A., following Orig. *Hom. Ps. 38.*2.1, takes the *terreni imago* to refer to Satan (see Löpfe, 16–19). Note the play on **terreni . . . tyranni** (also in *Expl. Ps. 38.*27). Fallen humanity has lost the *imago caelestis* (*Ex.* 6.42) through sin (*Is.* 4), and bears instead the image of Satan, the tyrant usurper. Christ paid to the devil the debt incurred by Adam, and so restored the divine image.

deponis . . . erigis: The outward, visual appearance of virtue is crucial, as always: this is what the image-language is really all about.

aeterni imperatoris: Cf. 1.186.

de civitate animae tuae: The soul is the true substance, or which the true image of God was originally impressed (*Ex.* 6.43). It is a state (equated, below, with spiritual Jerusalem), whose true *imperator* is Christ (cf. Orig. *Hom. Ps. 38*.2.2; A. *Expl. Ps. 38*.27); Christ's standard must be raised at the heart of the city, obscuring the images of sin, death, and Satan.

Haec in te fulgeat, in tua civitate . . . resplendeat: Continues the stress on visible virtue.

Domine, in civitate tua . . . deduces imagines eorum: Ps. 72: 20.

Cum enim pinxerit . . . ad imaginem suam: Cf. Is. 49: 16–17; the Lord will restore Jerusalem according to his will, and the images of idols will be removed. Cf. *Bon. mort.* 17; *Fug.* 17. On spiritual Jerusalem, see Toscani, 173–5.

tunc adversariorum omnis imago deletur: For similar exploitation of Orig. *Hom. Ps. 38*.2.1–2, cf. *Ex.* 6.42; *Interp.* 3.24. In *Interp.* 3.24, A. appends an example *de saeculo: Vide quemadmodum in civitatibus bonorum principum imagines perseverent, deleantur imagines tyrannorum.* Scholars have thought that A. is in that passage contrasting the statues of the usurper Maximus, which were overthrown after his defeat and death in 388, with the statues of Gratian, which were faithfully preserved by the people after his murder at the hands of one Maximus' subordinates in 383 (see G. Rauschen, *Jahrbücher der christlichen Kirche unter dem Kaiser Theodosius dem Grossen* (Freiburg, 1897), 293, 310; Ihm, 25; Palanque, 521; Homes Dudden ii. 687). Then again, *Expl. Ps. 38*.27 says this: *Hic si quis tyranni imagines habeat, qui iam victus interiit, iure damnatur.* This too has been taken as an identifiable allusion, most probably to the removal of the statues of Eugenius in 394 (M. Petschenig in CSEL 64, 204 n.; Ihm, 21; Palanque, 552; Homes Dudden ii. 687 n. 4). Because the present passage is so similar to these texts, Palanque, 526, imagines that it offers a clue to the dating of *Off.* For some reason, he has taken the parallel with *Interp.* 3.24. as the decisive one (despite the other obvious overlaps between *Off.* 1.233–45 and *Expl. Ps. 38*): A. is alluding to the statues of Maximus here as well, he says, so *Off.* cannot be earlier than the autumn of 388. The truth is, not one of these texts affords a specific reference. In every case, A. is following Orig. *Hom. Ps. 38*.2.2, which speaks of people being charged with a criminal offence for possessing the *imagines* of tyrants. Imperial statues came and went with the fortunes of their subjects, not least in these volatile latter years of the fourth century. The *cause célèbre* was the mutilation of the statues of Theodosius and Flaccilla in the sedition at Antioch on 4 March 387 (see John Chrysostom's famous series of twenty-one homilies *De statuis*, preached in the midst of the crisis: F. van de Paverd, *St John Chrysostom: The Homilies on the Statues* (Rome, 1991); Brown, *Power*, 104–8; *Expl. Ps. 38*.27 certainly cannot be alluding to the sedition at Antioch, since A. speaks there of a dead emperor: *Hic si quis tyranni imagines habeat, qui iam victus interiit, iure damnatur*). There is no clear evidence here to assist with the dating of *Off.*; see Homes Dudden ii. 695 n. 3 (despite his views on the parallel texts); Testard i. 46–8, 276 n. 12 (Banterle, 16–17, thinks that A. is thinking of the statues of Maximus and of Theodosius and Flaccilla *in particular*, but this remains conjectural, and is frankly unnecessary). A. is alluding in general terms to a well-known contemporary phenomenon: if you venerate (or even possess: **Si . . . aliquis . . . habeat**) the image of a tyrant who has fallen from favour, you will find yourself in trouble. He is not pointing to any case in particular. On the seriousness of defacing the *right* images, cf. *Expos. Ps. 118*.10.25.

CHAPTER 50: THE DUTIES OF CLERICS, ESPECIALLY DEACONS

1.246–51 rounds off the treatment of temperance, but the word itself is not mentioned, and there is little or no substantive Ciceronian evocation prior to the summary of the cardinal virtues at the end of 1.251 (aside from the odd fragmentary allusion, such as *decet* in 1.247). A. addresses his remarks directly to the obligations of clerics, and especially to 'Levites', or deacons. This tone continues in the final paragraphs of the book (1.252–9). Testard, 'Etude', 171–2, thinks that the temperance section is over at the end of 1.245, but this cannot be right, for 1.246–51 continues with the theme of the unimportance of wealth (cf. 1.241–5) and with the values of sobriety and chastity, and A. specifically refers to continence and sobriety when he describes the role of temperance in 1.251. The commencement of the address to *vos Levitae* (1.246), which carries on into 1.252–9, does not mean that the whole of 1.246–59 is one integral piece, separate from 1.210–45. The clerical focus is there throughout 1.246–59, but the last section of the book does not begin properly until the passage on temperance comes to an end in 1.251. The *imago sapientiae* (1.240) or *imago Christi* (1.245) of which A. has spoken is displayed when the clergy are seen to despise riches and lead sober and chaste lives. They have a high and lofty calling, and must never trivialize it by settling for less than the highest moral ideals; their real motivation is that they belong to God (1.246–7, 250–1, 257–8).

246. evangelio: E.g. Mt. 13: 22; Mk. 4: 19; Lk. 8: 14; especially Mt. 19: 23–4; Mk. 10: 23–5; Lk. 18: 24–5; Mt. 6: 24; Lk. 6: 24; 16: 13, 19–31. The preceding warnings against the pursuit of wealth are not in fact drawn from the gospels. It is possible that A. simply makes a slip, or that he uses 'in the gospel' very loosely to stand for something like 'in our Christian Scriptures'; more probably, he is not referring back to these warnings in particular but making a new point: the gospel also calls us to despise wealth. On **ad despicientiam opum**, see on 1.23.

populus ipse . . . quanto magis vos: The typical assumption that clerics have to exceed ordinary people in moral and spiritual attainment; cf. 1.249, and see on 1.184.

informatus atque institutus est: Cf. 1.107, *informatus et instructus est.*

Levitas: The OT Levitical priests are associated with Christian deacons above all, especially in *Sacr.* and *Myst.*; R. Gryson, 'Les Degrés du clergé et leurs dénominations chez saint Ambroise de Milan', *RBén* 76 (1966), 119–27, at 125–6; id. *Prêtre*, 142. On the Levites as a type of the Christian cleric, cf. *Cain* 2.7–17; *Fuga* 5–8; note also *Expos. Ps. 118*.8.2–15; *Patr.* 3–16; *Exh. virg.* 32–44; *Ep.* 17 [81].13–14; also *Ep.* 14 [33].4–5; and see Gryson, 'Typologie', 104–223, especially 207–21; some of this research is reproduced in Gryson's article, 'Les Lévites, figure du sacerdoce véritable, selon saint Ambroise', *EThL* 56/1

(1980), 89–112, especially 106–12 (see 89 n. 1 for additional references to the Levites as priests); A. Bonato, 'L'idea del sacerdozio in s. Ambrogio', *Augustinianum* 27 (1987), 423–64, especially 449–61.

quorum Deus portio est: Cf. Ps. 141: 6.

Nam cum divideretur a Moyse possessio terrena . . . aeternae possessionis consortio: [aeternae: PVMA, Testard: *a terrenae* EW, COB] See Num. 18: 20–4; this is the Lord's word to Aaron, not to Moses; Moses is instructed to tell the Levites to sacrifice to the Lord a tenth of the tithes they received in lieu of an earthly inheritance: Num. 18: 25–32.

quod ipse illis esset funiculus hereditatis: Cf. Num. 18: 20; Dt. 10: 9. **funiculus**, literally a portion of land marked out with a *funis* or rope-measure, may be in A.'s mind by conflation with Dt. 32: 9, where Jacob is said to be the Lord's *funiculus hereditatis*; cf. Jer. *Ep.* 52.5.1–2.

Dominus pars hereditatis meae et calicis mei: Ps. 15: 5. On the Lord as the clerics' portion, cf. *Ep. extra coll.* 14 [63].93–4; Paul. *VA* 41.2.

Denique sic appellatur Levita: 'Ipse meus' vel 'Ipse pro me': Similar etymologies of *Levita/Levi* (cf. Gen. 29: 34; Num. 3: 12, 45; 8: 14) are given in *Cain* 2.11, *Susceptus pro me . . . Ipse mihi Levi*, and *Expos. Ps. 118*.8.2–15, especially 8.4, *Ipse mihi adsumptus . . . Ipse meus . . . Adsumptus . . . Adsumptus mihi ipse . . . mihi Levi . . . Pro me*. On the variety of meanings which A. has culled from the *Onomastica* in his library, see R. Gryson, 'L'Interprétation du nom de Lévi (Lévite) chez saint Ambroise', *SEJG* 17 (1966), 217–29. Bonato, 'L'idea del sacerdozio', argues that A. is clearly following Philo, especially *Plant.* 64; *Sacrif.* 118–35, but Gryson convincingly shows that he is more eclectic, particularly at *Expos. Ps. 118*.8.4. For other relevant texts of Philo and Origen, see Gryson, 'Typologie', 164 ff.; cf. also Jer. *Interpr. Heb. nom.* 8.7; 13.30; 65.5; 78.8; 80.24.

Magnum ergo munus eius: Think highly of your office, and you will act accordingly—and the reputation of the church will be promoted; cf. 1.247, 250–1. The strategy is to think of yourself as special, with the Lord as your portion.

vel quemadmodum Petro dixit de statere . . . : *Dabis*

his pro me et pro te: Mt. 17: 27. The silver stater, worth four drachmae, was to pay the two-drachma temple-tax for both Peter and Jesus. A more logical application of this would be to say that Jesus supernaturally supplied the money since Peter did not have the means, and so Jesus was the 'portion' of his servant. The attempt to use the verse to illustrate the *'pro me'* etymology of *Levi/Levita* is obviously contrived. For developed mystical exegesis of the verse, cf. *Ep.* 1 [7] (reference also in *Expl. Ps. 48*.14).

cum episcopum dixisset debere esse sobrium . . . domui suae bene praepositum: 1 Tim. 3: 1–7.

Diaconos similiter oportet esse graves . . . nullum crimen habentes: 1 Tim. 3: 8–10. A. leaves out 1 Tim. 3: 6, *non neophytum, ne in superbia elatus in iudicium incidat diaboli*, though he quotes all the surrounding verses (Gryson, 'Typologie', 208 n. 5). Is this a telling omission by a bishop whose election as a neophyte contravened the church regulations based upon that principle? (His ordination *process* had, however, been formally correct: Paul. *VA* 9.3.)

247. Advertimus quanta in nobis requirantur: A. begins to pick up some of the points made in 1 Tim. 3 above: the exposition continues in the ensuing paragraphs, which amount to a loosely structured commentary on this passage. His stress throughout is on the direct relationship between the arduousness of the office and its spiritual grandeur; cf. generally 1.185–6, 217–18, 257–8. In 1.251, the scheme is synthesized with the cardinal virtues.

ut abstinens sit a vino minister Domini: Cf. 1 Tim. 3: 3, 8; also Tit. 1: 7; A. is spelling out the references to *sobrium* and *non multo vino deditos* in 1.246. On the dangers of excessive wine, cf. 1.86; *Paen.* 1.76; *Vid.* 68; the cleric should do without it if possible (*Ep. extra coll.* 14 [63].27), though for medicinal use (ibid.) a moderate intake may be beneficial (*Ex.* 3.72; *Noe* 111).

ut testimonio bono fulciatur non solum fidelium sed etiam ab his qui foris sunt: Cf. 1 Tim. 3: 7, and the *probentur* reference in 1.246. On 'outsiders', cf. also Mk. 4: 11; 1 Cor. 5: 12–13; Col. 4: 5; 1 Thess. 4: 12; for A.'s use of the idea, cf. 1.86 and 1.252; more generally, cf. 2.29 ff. Cic.

refers to the importance of earning the approval of those with
whom we live in *Off.* 1.143.

Decet enim . . . ne derogetur muneri: A.'s obsession
with image is evidenced once more; cf. 1.227; 2.29–39, 56–67
(and the dangers of this strategy, in 2.112–35). Loss of
reputation is on a par with a *vitium animi* for seriousness
(3.24).

qui videt: The cleric must be *seen* to be full of virtue; cf.
1.87, 219–25, 249.

ministrum altaris: Cf. 1.88.

auctorem praedicet et Dominum veneretur: The
reasons are lofty, naturally: to adorn the office is to encourage
others to worship the church's God; cf. 2.122, *Gratia enim
ecclesiae laus doctoris est.*

servulos: Cf. David in 1.237. These noble paragons are
ultimately lowly servants, who embody the all-important
humilitas commended from the start of the argument (cf.
1.1).

familiae: See on 1.24.

248. De castimonia: Picking up the apostolic insistence on
the need to be *pudicus* from 1.246.

quando una tantum nec repetita permittitur copula:
Cf. 1 Tim. 3: 2: *Oportet ergo episcopum irreprehensibilem esse,
unius uxoris virum*; 3: 12: *Diacones sint unius uxoris viri*; Tit.
1: 6: *Si quis . . . unius uxoris vir*. These injunctions are taken
to be a prohibition of the ordination of a man who has
remarried. The rule was interpreted differently by the Eastern and Western churches. In the East, it was held that a
marriage contracted prior to baptism did not count, so if a
man had remarried after baptism he remained eligible for
ordination, since in the eyes of the church this was his only
marriage (e.g. *Const. Apost.* 6.17; *Apost. Can.* 17; Theod.
Mops. *Comm. 1 Tim., ad* 3.2; John Chrys. *Hom. in 1 Tim.*
10.1). In the West, however, the general feeling was that it
made no difference whether the first union had taken place
before or after baptism: the ordination of a twice-married
man was forbidden either way, and strict continence was
essential after ordination (e.g. Con. Elv. (*c.*306), *can.* 33;
Con. Val. (374), *can.* 1; Siric. *Ep.* 1.18; Innoc. I, *Ep.* 2.5;
Leo, *Epp.* 4.3; 6.3; 12.3). A. insists that although baptism

washes away all sin, it cannot abrogate the law about a second marriage (**baptismo culpa dimitti potest, lex aboleri non potest**). The same line is taken in *Ep. extra coll.* 14 [63].62–4, where he claims that the Nicene canons forbid the admission of any twice-married cleric (an apparent misunderstanding of the third canon, which forbade any woman other than a mother, sister, or aunt to reside under a cleric's roof): *Quomodo enim potest consolari viduam, honorare, cohortari ad custodiendam viduitatem, servandam marito fidem, quam ipse priori coniugio non reservaverit?* (64). Jerome disputes this view, upholding the Eastern interpretation instead (*Ep.* 69; *Comm. in Tit.* 1.6; *Adv. Ruf.* 1.32): the NT prohibits polygamy, not remarriage, he argues, and the alternative reading would incriminate a large number of bishops who had already been remarried when they were ordained. Jer. *Ep.* 69, probably alludes to this passage of *Off.* in criticism of the stricter view (A. Paredi, 'S. Girolamo e s. Ambrogio', in *Mélanges Eugène Tisserant*, 5 (*Studi e Testi*, 235, Vatican City, 1964), 183–98, at 193, *pace* the scepticism of G. Nauroy, 'Jérome, lecteur et censeur de l'exégèse d'Ambroise', in Y.-M. Duval (ed.), *Jérôme entre l'Occident et l'Orient* (Paris, 1988), 173–203, at 175–6 n. 7; for a far less positive view of second marriage, cf. *Adv. Iov.* 1.13–15; also *Ep.* 123.6–7). A.'s stricter position is upheld by Augustine (*Bon. coniug.* 21). For earlier tirades against remarriage, cf. Tert. *Uxor.* 1.5–8; *Exh. cast.* 2–7; *Monog.* 10–12 (with strong Montanist input). The differences between East and West reflect fundamental soteriological distinctives: mystical grace, forgiveness, and divinization over against a more juridical framework of moral obedience; B. Kötting, 'Digamus', *RAC* iii. 1016–24, especially 1022–3.

quod culpae est igitur in baptismate relaxatur: A. sees baptism as remitting actual sin (*culpa*): cf. 3.108–9; *Spir.* 3.138; *Myst.* 11–12; *Luc.* 1.37; 8.24; *Expos. Ps. 118*.3.14; 6.2; 16.29; *Elia* 82–5; *Paen.* 1.36; 2.7–12; *Ep. extra coll.* 14 [63].11, 63; *Abr.* 2.78–81; *Is.* 76; *Ob. Theod.* 40; *Expl. Ps. 36*.63; *Apol.* 49; *Epp.* 28 [50].10; 69 [72].18 (in *Myst.* 32 (but not *Sacr.* 3.7); cf. also *Expl. Ps. 48*.8–9; *Spir.* 1.16; and a fragment of his lost *Expositio Isaiae prophetae* quoted by Aug., *Contr. duas epist. Pelag.* 4.11.29, A. distinguishes

between the remission of actual or personal sins in baptism
and the removal of original sin in the ceremony of foot-
washing, but this is exceptional, and evidently an exaggeration of the virtues of this North Italian and African, but
non-Roman, practice). See generally A. Lenox-Conyngham,
'Sin in St Ambrose', *SP* 18/4 (1990), 173–7.

**Quomodo autem potest hortator esse viduitatis qui
ipse coniugia frequentaverit?:** On moral impediment to
duty, cf. 1.138. On **hortator . . . viduitatis**, cf. Jer. *Ep.*
52.16.1: *qui de monogamia sacerdos est, quare viduam hortatur,
ut* δίγαμος sit? An 'order' of elderly widows (aged over 60)
had existed in many churches from an early date (cf. 1 Tim.
5: 3–16; also A., 2.72). A large number of these women were
destitute old ladies maintained by the clergy's benefactions.
No figures are available for Milan, but the church of Antioch
supported 3,000 widows and virgins (John Chrys. *Hom. 66 in
Matt.* 3: Brown, *Body*, 147–8), and the Milanese situation is
likely to have been in the same range. It is not these widows,
however, that A. has in mind. He is thinking rather of
younger women, especially those of high social class and
significant means, whose full-time commitment to the life
and resources of the church meant a great deal. He was all
too aware of the practical advantages to be gained by
ensuring that they did not abandon this calling, or surrender
their precious resources to fraudsters (*Expos. Ps. 118*.8.58),
or lose them through litigation (*Expos. Ps. 118*.16.6–7). He is
persistent in his exhortation to such women not to remarry
but to remain continent in absolute devotion to Christ; cf.
Vid., *passim* (note also 2.27 below, on the seemliness of
keeping faith with a dead husband). (Sometimes he spoke
rather too plainly: *Virgt.* 46 amounts to an apology for the
language of *Vid.* 52–9 (especially 58), as McLynn, 65, points
out.) See generally R. Gryson, *The Ministry of Women in the
Early Church* (Collegeville, MN, 1976), 8–10, 35–41; B. B.
Thurston, *The Widows: A Woman's Ministry in the Early
Church* (Minneapolis, MN, 1989).

**249. Inoffensum autem exhibendum . . . cognoscitis,
qui integri corpore . . . sacri ministerii gratiam re-
cepistis:** Another indication that many of the clerical addressees are young men, who have been devoted to the

church and dedicated to chastity from an early age. But A. makes sure that they, and any clerics who have not known the privilege of his tutelage in asceticism, are in no doubt as to what is required: even men who *have* had only one wife must abstain from sexual relations after ordination. Sexual intercourse incurs an impurity which vitiates the ministry of men who administer the sacraments (cf. Lev. 15: 18; 1 Ki. 21: 4–5). On the ideal of *integritas*, cf. 2.27; A. insists that a standard of ascetic purity traditionally applied to women (in devotion to the virgin-born Christ: *Virg.* 1.21) is equally essential for the new 'public man'; see Introduction VII (ii).

quia in plerisque abditioribus locis . . . quando per intervalla dierum sacrificium deferebatur: In the Eastern church, it was generally held that married clerics could legitimately cohabit with their wives at intervals between the celebration of the sacrament, so long as a voluntary 'cultic abstinence' was observed at the time of the sacrament. At Milan, as in most Italian churches of this time, the eucharist was celebrated either daily or at least in a daily sequence over periods punctuated by only brief intervals (Johanny, 73–83), and A. insists on total continence—however off-putting to potential clerical candidates such a stipulation might be (cf. 1.218). There are reports of a legendary protest at Nicaea by the Egyptian ascetic Paphnutius against enforced continence for legitimately married bishops, presbyters, and deacons (Socr. *HE* 1.11; Soz. *HE* 1.23; cf. Rufin. *HE* 10.4; see C. Cocchini, *Origines apostoliques du célibat sacerdotale* (Paris, 1981), 166–7), and even in the West it is clear that there was widespread toleration of ritual rather than mandatory abstinence, particularly in rural areas of Gaul and Spain (despite the claim of Socr., *HE* 5.22, that continence was general in Gaul, Spain, Africa, Thessaly, Macedonia, and Achaea). This evoked some hardline responses. Siricius' famous *Ep.* 1, to Himerius of Tarragona, written in 385, is uncompromising: those who serve at the altar must no longer sleep with their wives at all. A. suggests here that dissenters appealed to an earlier practice of celebrating the eucharist less regularly, which allowed for sexual relations most of the time, with a ritual two- or three-day period of abstinence prior to the sacrament. Such infrequent communication is, however,

unworthy: cf. *Sacr.* 5.25; also *Sacr.* 4.28; *Ex.* 5.90; *Patr.* 38;
Expl. Ps. 43.37; *Expos. Ps. 118*.18.26, 28; 21.14; *Ep.* 76
[20].15; Aug. *Serm. Dom. in mont.* 2.26; *Ep.* 64.2; and see
R. Gryson, *Les Origines du célibat ecclésiastique, du premier au
septième siècle* (Gembloux, 1970), 87–93. A. is resolutely
opposed to any dilution of the standard of clerical 'purity':
his criticism implicitly suggests that he considers *any* **ministerium**, not just **sacerdotium**, to be a calling to renounce
sexual activity. See Gryson, *Les Origines du célibat ecclésiastique*, especially 84 ff., 127 ff., 144 ff., 171–4; Gaudemet, 140–
1, 159–63; P. H. Lafontaine, *Les Conditions positives de
l'accession aux ordres dans la première législation ecclésiastique
(300–492)* (Ottawa, 1963), 176–81, especially 179 n. 66; J. P.
Audet, *Mariage et célibat dans le service pastoral de l'Eglise:
Histoire et orientations* (Paris, 1967), 130–3; Cocchini, *Origines apostoliques du célibat sacerdotale*, 184–94; D. Callam,
'Clerical Continence in the Fourth Century: Three Papal
Decretals', *ThS* 41 (1980), 3–50. On the eucharist as a
sacrificium, cf. e.g. *Luc.* 1.28; *Expos. Ps. 118*.8.48; *Ep.* 76
[20].15; and see Johanny, 135–60.

et lavat vestimenta sua: Ex. 19: 10 (cf. 19: 10–15). The
Israelites purified themselves over a three-day period before
the giving of the law to Moses on Sinai.

Si in figura tanta observantia, quanta in veritate!:
[**quanta**: P^2V^2, E, CO: *quanto* P^1V^1M, Testard] The relative
veritas of the Christian era as compared with the OT *umbra*;
still not the full *veritas* of heaven: cf 1.239; *Sacr.* 2.13.

sacerdos atque Levita: The priest consecrates the eucharist, the deacon distributes it, so both need to be pure. On the
necessity of a pure body for administering the sacraments, cf.
Vid. 65; *Ep. extra coll.* 14 [63].62–3; and see Johanny,
188–90.

**quid sit lavare vestimenta tua, ut mundum corpus
celebrandis exhibeas sacramentis**: The cleric's 'garments' are his body, the flesh which covers his soul; cf.
Cain 2.36; *Abr.* 2.63; *Is.* 3, 79; *Inst. virg.* 18; *Ex.* 6.39; *Luc.*
7.123; *Paen.* 1.68; the Platonist presuppositions are obvious;
see Madec, 318–23. On the defilement of the body, cf. *Bon.
mort.* 10–57. The choice of verb, **exhibeas**, is not accidental:
the *display* of purity is of the essence.

Si populus . . . tu: Cf. 1.246, and see on 1.184.

illotus mente pariter et corpore: Both the inner and the outer man need to be washed; cf. Heb. 10: 22: *accedamus cum vero corde in plenitudine fidei, aspersi corda a conscientia mala et abluti corpus aqua munda.* A. thinks of the cleansing of baptism, which means putting on *innocentiae casta velamina* (*Myst.* 34), symbolized by actual white garments. After this washing of the body, there must be no 'defilement' through sexual intercourse.

pro aliis supplicare . . . aliis ministrare: Possibly a distinction of the roles of priest and deacon at the eucharist: the priest prays on behalf of the people, the deacon administers the sacrament. But probably the statement is looser: the clerics in general intercede for and minister to the people.

250. Non mediocre officium Levitarum: Again (cf. 1.246–7), A. hammers home the message of the privilege and the corresponding responsibility which devolves upon the clerical élite. The bishop's select corps (1.24) are also the Lord's chosen ones:

Ecce eligo Levitas . . . in terra Aegypti: Num. 3: 12–13.

ut primogenita fructuum . . . in quibus est votorum solutio et redemptio peccatorum: The ancient Levites substituted for the first-born males in each family of the other Israelite tribes, to whom the Lord was entitled because he had spared them at the Passover (Ex. 13: 1–16). Where the number of Israelites exceeded the number of Levites, the Israelite families paid a tax. By this system of representation, the entire Israelite people was 'redeemed' (Num. 3: 39–51). Cf. *Ep.* 14 [33].4–8.

Non accipies, inquit, *eos inter filios Israel . . . morte moriatur:* Num. 1: 49–51; the Lord is speaking to Moses, referring in the opening words to the census of the Israelite tribes, in which the Levites were not to be included.

251. primogenitus: P^2V^2, E, CO: *primogenitos* P^1V^1M, Testard.

ut operias arcam testamenti: The ark of the covenant, kept in the tabernacle as a symbol of the divine presence (Ex. 25: 10–22), containing the two tablets of the Decalogue (Ex. 25: 16, 21; 40: 18; Dt. 10: 1–5) and the book of the law (Dt. 31: 9), was guarded by the Levites (Num. 4: 1–20). This charge is seen by A. as a foreshadowing of the Christian clergy's responsibility for the Scriptures and the sacraments. A. is now explaining the allusion to *mysterium fidei* in 1.246. The idea of 'covering' the mysteries from the eyes of the uninitiated (the unbaptized) is very common in the Fathers. **Non enim omnes vident alta mysteriorum . . . et sumant qui servare non possunt**. The *disciplina arcani* (the name dates from the seventeenth century), a conceptual amalgam of elements of the OT cultus with assumptions drawn from the mystery religions, was deemed to be an essential part of the priest's role until the late fifth century (and continued to be discussed into modern times): it meant the concealing of religious mysteries from both pagans and catechumens. The premiss was that finite and sinful minds could only plumb the depths of divine truth in a gradual fashion, as they were spiritually enlightened, and these profundities needed to be kept from the prying eyes of the unworthy. The practical consequence, of course, was an added mystique surrounding the few who hold the power. They are privileged to look into things which few people get to see (cf. Tert. *Praescr. haer.* 41.1–8); cf. *Abr.* 1.38; *Expos. Ps.* *118*.2.26–8; 4.18; *Sacr.* 1.1; *Myst.* 2, 55–6; also *Luc.* 7.43, 231. See O. Perler, 'Arkandisziplin', *RAC* i. 667–76; on A., Homes Dudden ii. 453–4; Jacob, especially 121–38, 197–280 (though Jacob exaggerates the hermeneutical significance); V. Ferrua, 'Ancora sulla "Disciplina dell'Arcano"', *Salesianum* 55 (1993), 471–83. For an example of unholy *curiositas* (see on 1.122), cf. 3.102. A. may be thinking here of the practice where the celebrant stood at the altar with his arms extended in the shape of the cross partly to hide the mystery of the consecration even from the baptized (cf. *Sacr.* 6.18; also *Virg.* 1.7; 2.27; Paul. *VA* 47) With **ad quae si alienigena accesserit, morte morietu** [**ad quae:** C, Gering, Testard: *ad quem* OB: *atque* PVMA EW, Zell] an almost preposterous degree of solemnit seems to be introduced in the Christian context: th transference of the OT principle is rhetorical, of course but the urge to instil awe and maintain control is genuin enough. The people typically came forward to communicat (*Elia* 34; Paul. *VA* 44). On **ne videant qui videre no**

debent, cf. Is. 6: 9–10 (and Mt. 13: 13–17; Mk. 4: 12; Jn. 12: 39–41; Acts 28: 24–7).

Moyses denique circumcisionem vidit spiritalem . . . ut in signo circumcisionem praescriberet: On 'spiritual' circumcision (Rom. 2: 25–9) or true circumcision as faith manifested in new works (circumcision of the flesh being unimportant), cf. Rom. 3: 30; 1 Cor. 7: 18–19; Gal. 5: 2–6; 6: 15; Phil. 3: 3; Col. 2: 11; 3: 11. A. says here that Moses prescribed circumcision, though the NT writers argue that the rite goes back to Abraham in Gen. 17 (Jn. 7: 22; Rom. 4: 9–12; 15: 8), and that the Jews had overstated the Mosaic background (Acts 15: 1, 5; 21: 21; Gal. 5: 2–12; 6: 15–16). A.'s claim that Moses was fully aware of the deeper meaning of the rite is of course classic hermeneutical posturing. He may be following Orig. *Hom. Num.* 5.1 (Gryson, 'Typologie', 219 n. 1; id. 'Les Lévites, figure du sacerdoce véritable, selon saint Ambroise', *EThL* 56/1 (1980), 89–112, at 108–9 and n. 100). For a developed exposition of spiritual circumcision, cf. *Ep.* 69 [72]; also *Abr.* 2.78–84.

azyma veritatis et sinceritatis: Cf. 1 Cor. 5: 8.

operuit passionem Domini agni vel vituli immolatione: Moses instituted the Feast of Unleavened Bread, the week-long festival which began with the Passover meal (Ex. 12: 14–20). The Passover is seen as a type of the sacrifice of Christ (1 Cor. 5: 7–8). Moses saw in advance the death of Christ, but he 'concealed' the mystery under the Passover rite, just as he 'concealed' spiritual circumcision under the physical rite. Cf. Heb. 11: 28: (of Moses) *Fide celebravit Pascha*, looking on to the sacrifice of the true Lamb.

mysterium fidei: Cf. 1 Tim. 3: 9.

Et tu mediocre putas quod commissum est tibi?: Cf. 1.246–7, 250.

Primum, ut alta Dei videas, quod est sapientiae; deinde . . . quod est temperantiae: The duties of the ecclesiastics are summed up under the scheme of the cardinal virtues; for a similar effort at synthesis, cf. 1.115–21. A. winds up his account of temperance, and particularly the loose exposition of 1 Tim. 3 in the preceding paragraphs, by bringing us back, artificially, to the tetrad as a whole. The definitions of the virtues here are heavily biblical, as we might expect in the context of OT priestly typologies (on the typology of the tabernacle or synagogue and church generally, see Toscani, 193–208; Hahn, 230–1; G. Figueroa, *The Church and the Synagogue in Saint Ambrose* (Washington, DC, 1949)). *Sapientia* is the knowledge of the *alta Dei* (cf. 1 Cor. 2: 6–16); the other three virtues are related to clerical tasks in the light of this knowledge of the mysteries (1.251): justice means keeping watch on behalf of the people (1.250–1); courage means defending the tabernacle (church) (1.250–1); and, as we have seen throughout this last section, temperance is all about maintaining continence and sobriety (1.246–9; **continentem ac sobrium** again echoes motifs from 1 Tim. 3 as evoked in 1.246).

1.252–9 rounds off book 1, continuing the direct address to clerics begun in the midst of the temperance material in 1.246, but moving on from the analysis of the fourth virtue. The passage appears to be a very rough attempt to parallel Cic.'s calculus of *honesta* in *Off.* 1.152–61. A. certainly does not dwell on the philosophical categories. Wisdom comes first, as it has consistently: duty towards God is the sum of the ethic, and everything else flows from this (1.252–3). In 1.253–5, we have examples of the kind of practical judgement which the cleric needs (and which implicitly follows from a right focus on responsibility towards God) as he serves other people. A. draws on Cic. in 1.254–5, but only from sections on justice in *Off.* 1 and 3, after mentioning yet again the link between wisdom and justice in 1.252–3. Presumably this is all done from memory; the effect is certainly artificial to any reader who expects proper conformity with a classical calculus of virtues. When A. does speak of *duo honesta*, he says simply that *id quod honestius est* should be put first (1.258). As 1.256–9 shows, the preoccupation is with extolling the dignity of the clerical office and the closing note is an invocation of divine blessing upon those who faithfully fulfil this unique calling. A.'s adherence to a Ciceronian structure is weak, but this ought to cause the reader no surprise by now. Book 1 ends as it began: *officia* are only rightly understood and rightly practised when they are determined with reference to God, and it is the clergy more than any other class of people who can and must get thi straight, so that the church can be the ideal embodiment of the morality that is pleasing to God and impressive for the watching world.

252. Haec virtutum genera principalia: On the terminology for the virtues, see on 1.115.

hi qui foris sunt: See on 1.247. The NT phrase is used to allude to Cic. and his comparison of the virtues in *Off.* 1.152–61. *Pace* Testard, 'Etude', 172–3; 'Recherches', 97, there is no profound significance in the fact that Cic. compares *honesta* (*Off.* 1.152) whereas A. here refers to the *virtutes*. The *virtutes* are simply the subsets or expressions of the *honestum*. A. mentions the comparison of *honesta* in 1.27 and 1.258, and it is equally clear from Cic. *Off.* 1.152–61 that when Cic. speaks of the comparison of *honesta* he means the comparison of the virtues; *Off.* 1.153 speaks explicitly of *virtutes*.

sed communitatis superiorem ordinem quam sapientiae iudicaverunt: *Communitas* is Cic.'s word for *iustitia* in *Off.* 1.152–61, where it epitomizes his habitual emphasis on the societal. Cic. compares justice and wisdom in *Off.* 1.153–8 and 1.160. In *Off.* 1.153 he says that *sapientia* is *princeps* among the virtues, but then goes on to claim, illogically, that since *sapientia* includes *communitas et societas* among gods and men, the duty based upon *communitas* must therefore be the most important duty (I follow the translation of Griffin and Atkins, 60 n. 1, that the subject of Cic.'s *ea si maxima est* is *communitas et societas*, not *sapientia*. Cic. is concerned to downplay speculative enquiry in comparison with practical wisdom, as in *Off.* 1.18–19. W. Miller, in his translation, *Cicero: De Officiis*, Loeb Classical Library (Cambridge, MA, and London, 1913), 156–7, tries to make sense of the traditional rendering; see also Dyck, 341–2). Cic. esteems wisdom as the first of the *virtutes*, but—apparently illogically—ranks justice as the most important *duty*; he never precisely defines what he means by saying that wisdom is *princeps*. The force of A.'s criticism thus depends on exactly what we understand by **superiorem ordinem**. He himself consistently defines wisdom or prudence as faith or the knowledge of God, and as the first virtue *or* first duty.

cum sapientia fundamentum sit iustitiae opus sit . . . nisi fundamentum habeat: [iustitiae: PVMA, EW: *iustitia* COB] Cf. 1.126–7 and 1.142. On the connection between wisdom and justice, cf. 1.126–9; 2.41–55; 3.14.

Fundamentum autem Christus est: Cf. 1 Cor. 3: 11.

253. **Prima ergo fides, quae est sapientiae:** Cf. 1.142.

ut Salomon dicit, secutus patrem: *Initium sapientiae timor Domini*: Prov. 1: 7; 9: 10 (Solomon); Ps. 110: 10 (his father David). A. returns to a favourite axiom: cf. 1.1, 117, 126.

Et lex dicit: *Diliges Dominum tuum, diliges proximum tuum*: This is Jesus' summary of the law, quoting Dt. 6: 5 and Lev. 19: 18 (Mt. 22: 37–40; Mk. 12: 29–31; Lk. 10: 27).

Pulchrum est enim ut gratiam tuam . . . Deo deputes: Cic.'s emphasis on *societas* is commendable, but it must be secondary to devotion to God. Justice and wisdom are together in the summary of the law, but wisdom (faith) is supreme; this is where the *decorum* lies first and foremost (cf. 1.221). Good works follow faith. A.'s examples of social action in 1.254–5 are drawn from Cic.'s discussions of justice. On the preciousness of the soul (**quod habes pretiosissimum**), cf. *Abr.* 2.44; the mind is the rational element of the soul (*Noe* 92; *Bon. mort.* 44, *quia mens animae principale est et virtus animae est*; *Ep.* 29 [43].14).

Cum solveris auctori debitum: A revealing phrase: duty is first of all the fulfilment of a basic human obligation: the creature must obey the creator.

pecunia, ut subvenias—debito obligatum liberes—officio: As the punctuation given in the text conveys, **debito** is ablative with **obligatum**, not dative with **subvenias** (Gryson, 'Typologie', 212 n. 3), or, even less likely, a parallel ablative with **pecunia** and **officio** (so the Maurists and Krabinger; the *ut* printed in their texts after **debito** is Valdarfer's interpolation: Banterle recognizes the problem with Krabinger's punctuation, yet retains the *ut*, as do Gryson and De Romestin; Testard gets it right). Freeing a debtor is an example of helping someone with money.

deponenda: The guarding of deposits is mentioned by Cic in *Off.* 1.31 and 3.95; see on 1.254 below. Vulnerabl individuals such as widows had long used the church as a bank to keep their money and valuables safe from predators. Clerical misappropriation or failure to look after such trusts was recognized as a very serious offence: e.g. Cypr. *Epp.* 50.1.2; 52.2.5; 59.1.2; on the earlier background (e.g. Plin. *Ep.* 10.96.7; Hippol. *Philos.* 9.12.1), see R. Bogaert, 'Changeurs et banquiers chez les Pères de l'Eglise', *AncSoc* 4 (1973), 239–70; R. M. Grant, 'Early Christian Banking', *SP* 15 (1975), 217–20 (also J. A. Crook, *Law and Life of Rome* (London, 1967), 209–10). For defiance of imperial pressure to surrender a widow's property, cf. 2.150–1 (and the biblical illustration in 2.144–9). On the oppression of *potentes*, cf. 1.63; 2.102; *Expos. Ps. 118.16.6–7*.

254. Officium est igitur depositum servare ac reddere . . . ut non sit officium reddere quod acceperis: Cf. Cic. *Off.* 1.31: *Sed incidunt saepe tempora cum ea quae maxime videntur digna esse iusto homine eoque quem virum bonum dicimus commutantur fiuntque contraria, ut reddere depositum [etiamne furioso], facere promissum. . . . Ea* [sc. *fundamenta iustitiae*] *cum tempore commutantur, commutatur officium et non semper est idem* (and *Off.* 1.32) (on the textual problem, despite A.'s evocation—Cic. does not specify exactly *why* it is wrong to return a madman's deposit—see Dyck, 127–8); *Off.* 3.95:

Ergo et promissa non facienda nonnumquam, neque semper deposita reddenda. Si gladium quis apud te sana mente deposuerit, repetat insaniens, reddere peccatum sit, officium non reddere. Quid? si is qui apud te pecuniam deposuerit bellum inferat patriae, reddasne depositum? Non credo. . . . Sic multa, quae honesta natura videntur esse, temporibus fiunt non honesta. Facere promissa, stare conventis, reddere deposita commutata utilitate fiunt non honesta. (also *Off.* 3.92–6; *Fin.* 3.59)

A. fully endorses this casuistry. He has already warned against giving to treasonous men and other unworthy seekers (1.144): cf. **ut si quis contra patriam opem barbaris ferens.** The example of the madman demanding his sword back (**si insanienti gladium depositum non neges, quo se ille interimat**) is given by Plato in *Rep.* 331c; cf. generally Plaut. *Trin.* 129; Pub. Syr. 157; Sen. *Ira* 1.19.8;

Ben. 4.10.1; Columb. 39; Phil. *Cher.* 14–15; Tert. *Fug.* 13; Dio 52.14.2.

apertus: A, CB, most editors: *apertos* PVM, EW, O.

hostis: PMA, E¹W¹, CO¹B, most editors: *hostes* V, E²W², O².

255. Est etiam contra officium nonnumquam promissum solvere, sacramentum custodire: Cf. Cic. *Off.* 1.32; 3.92–5; and A. 3.76–81, which also gives the examples of Herod and Jephthah.

ut Herodes . . . ne promissum negaret: Herod Antipas promised to give Salome, the daughter of his consort Herodias (his brother Philip's wife), whatever she asked, having been charmed by her dancing; at her mother's instigation, Salome asked for the head of John the Baptist (Mt. 14: 1–12; Mk. 6: 14–29); on John's boldness, cf. also *Virgt.* 11.

Nam de Iephte quid dicam . . . offerret Deo?: Jephthah swore to sacrifice to the Lord whatever first met him on his return home, if he defeated the Ammonites; he ended up slaying his daughter (Jdg. 11: 29–40). Jephthah's vow was a solemn oath, while Herod's promise was less official, but both men committed murder rather than break their word, foolish though they had been to give it. The story of Jephthah is often used to illustrate the dangers of rash oaths: cf. *Apol.* 16; *Exh. virg.* 51; Jer. *Adv. Iov.* 1.23; John Chrys. *Hom. Stat.* 14.7; and the discussion in Thom. Aq. *ST* 2a2ae, 88.2 (A. *Virgt.* 5–10 is somewhat more positive); it is exploited widely in European literature—often synthesized, as in George Buchanan's *Iephthes*, with the narrative of Agamemnon and Iphigenia (cf. **immolavit filiam** with *immolavit Iphigeniam* in Cicero, *Off.* 3.95); see W. O. Sypherd, *Jephthah and his Daughter: A Study in Comparative Literature* (Newark, DE, 1948).

256. Et ideo eligitur Levita qui sacrarium custodiat . . fortuitus violet occursus: Having given some practical examples of the Levite's/deacon's duties (1.253–5), A. sums up the weighty responsibilities for which he has been chosen. In 1.251, these responsibilities were expressed in the language of the cardinal virtues, and A. seems to hint at similar qualities here, though without mentioning the scheme a such; he is also still thinking of some of the qualities high-lighted in 1 Tim. 3 in 1.246, such as chastity and *gravitas*. On **sacrarium**, see on 1.216; on **ne fidem deserat**, see on 1.72,188; 3.126; on **ne mortem timeat**, see on 1.177.

qui viderit mulierem . . . adulteravit eam in corde suo: Mt. 5: 28; on this adultery of the eye, cf. e.g. *Expos. Ps. 118*.16.3; *Apol. alt.* 17; *Paen.* 1.70; *Vid.* 76; *Luc.* 6.91; 8.4.

257. Magna haec videntur ac nimis severa sed in magno munere non superflua: Again, the highest calling demands these standards, however severe they may appear; cf. 1.217–18.

in benedictionibus: When Moses, dying, blessed the twelve tribes.

Date Levi viros eius . . . hic custodit verba tua et testamentum tuum observavit: Dt. 33: 8–9. For a comprehensive analysis of the text which A. quotes here, and of Dt. 33: 10–11 as cited in 1.259, see Gryson, 'Typologie', 128–49, comparing the Ambrosian citations of these verses in *Expos. Ps. 118*. 7.5; *Patr.* 15; *Epp.* 51 [15].11, 13; 17 [81].13; *Exh. virg.* 31–45.

viros eius . . . manifestos eius: The Hebrew text refers to the Urim and Thummim, which are thought to have been stones from the high priest's breastplate which were used as lots (cf. Ex. 28: 30; Lev. 8: 8; 1 Ki. 14: 41); see I. Mendelsohn, 'Urim and Thummim', in G. A. Buttrick *et al.* (eds.), *The Interpreter's Dictionary of the Bible* iv (New York and Nashville, 1962), 739–40. But A. takes the words to refer to the faithful men of the tribe of Israel, that is, its distinguished priests, who are 'manifestly' God's devoted servants (though note *sortem suffragii sui*); the Hebrew text of the verse is itself much disputed, and the LXX translators were confused. The references in **tempta-tionibus** and **super aquam contradictionis** are to the events of 'Massah and Meribah', narrated in Ex. 17: 1–7 and Num. 20: 1–13. Dt. 33: 9 alludes to the Levites putting their duty to the Lord before all family ties; cf. also Mt. 10: 37; Lk. 14: 26. For a clerical example of such an individual, cf. *Ep.* 51 [15].11–13.

58. qui nihil in corde doli habeant: Cf. Ps. 31: 2; Jn. 1: 47.

sed verba eius custodiant: Perhaps A. is still thinking of
the *disciplina arcani* from 1.251.

in corde suo conferant, sicut conferebat et Maria: Cf.
Lk. 2: 19, 51.

**qui suos parentes officio suo non noverint praeferen-
dos:** See on 1.257; and cf. e.g. *Epp.* 48 [66].7–8; 51 [15].13;
Virg. 1.63; *Exh. virg.* 2; *Vid.* 6; *Luc.* 7.146. Note, however,
the responsibility to family mentioned in 1.150.

**qui violatores oderint castitatis, pudicitiae ulciscantur
iniuriam:** Strong language, perhaps, from one who has so
much to say about charity and forgiveness, but typical of A.'s
zeal for chastity. Perhaps Gen. 34 is in his mind; cf 1.120.
Revenge for outrage to someone else's purity is evidently
permissible, unlike personal vengeance; cf. 1.131; and 1.17–
22, 233–8. For the principle illustrated, cf. 3.117.

**noverint officiorum tempora, quod maius sit, quod cui
aptum tempori est:** On this casuistry, cf. 1.174, 213–16; on
the application to *decorum*, cf. 1.105–14. The Ciceronian
motifs are artificially worked in to the summary of the
clerical character.

**et ut id solum sequantur . . . id quod honestius est
praeponendum putent: [sequantur:** A², COB: *sequatur*
PVMA¹, EW, Testard; **putent:** A², COB: *putet* PVMA¹,
EW, Testard] An allusion to the Ciceronian *calculus of
honesta*; see on 1.27 and 1.252. The spiritual blessing spoken
of by Moses (1.257) belongs to those who can discern what
their duty is in a particular situation. The more honourable
course is the one which puts God before man, others before
self, church before family, purity before pleasure, and so on.
When faith in God is the sure point of reference (1.252–3),
officium will be right in every area, and it is the clergy who can
and must see that this is so. The Ciceronian ideal is transmuted into the spiritual and ecclesiastical paradigm.

**259. Si quis ergo manifestet iustitias Dei, incensum
imponat:** Cf. Dt. 33: 10; **iustitias** translates the Greek
plural, τὰ δικαιώματα; on the text of Dt. see Grysor
'Typologie', 128–49. **Incensum** is figurative (e.g. Ps. 140:
2; Apoc. 8: 3–4): 'to offer incense' is to please God.

**Benedic, Domine, virtutem ipsius, opera manuum
eius suscipe:** Dt. 33: 11.

ut gratiam propheticae benedictionis inveniat: The majority of MSS [PMA, EW, COB] end with **inveniat**; Zell adds *Amen*, while Amerbach and most of the other older editors add *apud eum qui vivit et regnat in saecula saeculorum. Amen.* The phrase is a typical medieval liturgicist's embellishment; it is not original to the text, which is a quotation of a prayer for divine blessing, and does not need further adornment (Testard i. 282–3 n. 37). To act so as to please God by fulfilling his righteous requirements, and thus offering him spiritual 'incense', is to live a life which deserves divine favour: A. invokes the blessing promised prophetically to all Levites, ancient and Christian, by Moses.

Book 2

2.1–21 introduces book 2. Taking the *honestum* of book 1 as the key to the blessed life, or happiness (*vita beata* or εὐδαιμονία) (2.1), A. sets out to explore the *utile* by way of a discussion of what makes for a happy life. The subject is not dealt with at any length by Cic. in *Off.*, but A. probably takes his cue from Cic.'s brief reference in *Off.* 2.6 to the constant quest of the philosophers to investigate *aliquid . . . quod spectet et valeat ad bene beateque vivendum* (note too the references to life and living in *Off.* 2.1 and 2.7; Cic. had of course already discussed the theme of happiness at a popular level in *Parad.* 6–19, and much more thoroughly in *Fin.* and *Tusc.* 5). Cic. *Off.* 2 embarks on a discussion of the kinds of duties *quae pertinent ad vitae cultum et ad earum rerum quibus utuntur homines facultatem, ad opes, ad copias* (*Off.* 2.1), but digresses to clarify the author's own attitude towards philosophy and his reasons for writing (*Off.* 2.2–8). A. has already rejected an equation of what is beneficial with external advantages, and has maintained that the true *utile* is to do with winning eternal life (1.27–9). Cic.'s praise of philosophy is replaced with an extended demonstration of the differences between philosophical or popular conceptions of happiness and happiness as defined by Scripture. The ultimate *vita beata* is the *vita aeterna*. A. thus signals the elision of the *honestum* and the *utile*: the virtue advocated in book 1 is beneficial because it is God-centred and aims at eternal reward. But because the attainment of this goal is neither furthered by external advantages nor hindered by privations—indeed, the contrary is true—A. also pictures earthly happiness in terms which assume (a) a quasi-Stoic ideal of detachment or superiority and (b) a quasi-Platonist vision of release from the world via purificatory suffering and spiritual ascent. The *beatus vir* of the Psalms (2.6 and 2.8) and the Beatitudes (2.9 and 2.15), or the biblical hero of faith (2.10–21) is invested with some of the obvious characteristics of the sage: he is preoccupied with virtuous conduct; he is content with his own good conscience, whatever others may think of him; and he learns both to rise above his circumstances and to grow through his experience of them. Yet all the while the eschatological destiny of the Christian conqueror looms large on the horizion. A. wishes to distance himself from Cic.'s and the philosophers' approach to the *utile*, but significant assumptions from the classical traditions colour his reading of the biblical narrative of self-denial, suffering, and final victory over the world. 2.1–21 offers a striking vignette of the dual influences that are always operative in A.'s mind, and of the pervasive combination of firm polemic and subtle assimilation to be found in the work as a whole.

See I. J. Davidson, 'The *Vita Beata*: Ambrose, *De Officiis* 2.1–21 and the Synthesis of Classical and Christian Thought in the Late Fourth Century', *RecTh* 63 (1996), 189–209 (though I now reject the suggestion made there that 2.1–21 may stem from an independent text). The most detailed earlier study is P. J. Couvée, *Vita beata en vita aeterna. Een onderzoek naar de ontwikkeling van het begrip 'vita beata' naast en tegenover 'vita aeterna' bij Lactantius, Ambrosius en Augustinus, onder invloed van de romeinsche Stoa* (Baarn, 1947), 131–73, especially 155 ff. Couvée's treatment is far from comprehensive, however, and in particular fails to notice the Platonist perspectives which coexist with the Stoicism. Some details are also noted in Niederhuber, *Reiche Gottes*, 143–59 and especially 191–204; Homes Dudden ii. 514–19 (again missing the Platonism). R. Holte, *Béatitude et sagesse: saint Augustin et le problème de la fin de l'homme dans la philosophie ancienne* (Paris, 1962), 63–70, 165–76, 193–201; and Dassmann, 261–7, also shed some light, the latter with better reference to Platonist influences. For other notable Christian accounts of the *vita beata*, cf. Lact. *Inst.* 3.7 ff.; 7.1 ff.; especially A.'s *Iac.*, which contains many similarities to *Off.* 2.1–21 in its synthesis of Scripture, Stoic, and Platonist ideas; and Aug.'s *VB* (quite probably influenced by the sermons which went into A.'s *Iac.*).

CHAPTER 1: HAPPINESS AS KNOWING AND
PLEASING GOD

1. **Superiore libro . . . quae convenire honestati arbitraremur:** Cf. Cic. *Off.* 2.1: *Quemadmodum officia ducerentur ab honestate, Marce fili, atque ab omni genere virtutis, satis explicatum arbitror libro superiore.* In *Off.* 2.9, Cic. adds that he wishes the treatment of what is honourable to be the part of his work with which Marcus is most familiar. On A.'s adherence to the Ciceronian arrangement of material, see Introduction III (ii) and V.

vitam beatam . . . quam scriptura appellat vitam aeternam: As ever, A. seeks scriptural authentication of classical terminology, and scriptural prescription of its meaning. On the combinations of 'realized' and 'futurist' eschatology in the characterizations of eternal life in the gospels and the epistles (eternal life as both present reality of kingdom existence and a state qualitatively different in an age to come), see R. Bultmann in *TDNT* ii. 832–75. A. concentrates on the *vita aeterna* as eternal reward (e.g. *Ep.* 51 [15].2; *Expl. Ps.* *1*.13; *Virg.* 1.64; *Expos. Ps.* *118*.15.28; 21.18; *Bon. mort.* 52–7), but he also sees the *beatitudo* of this future state as something that is realized embryonically in the believer's earthly life as well; see on 2.18. On all *beatitudo* as coming from God, cf. *Expos. Ps.* *118*.5.32; *Is.* 78–9; *Fug.* 36; *Bon. mort.* 55; *Iac.* 1.30–2.

Tantus enim splendor honestatis est . . . securitas innocentiae: Happiness in this life, in the maintenance of a good conscience. Whereas in 2.8–12 innocence is given a strong Christian force and a good conscience is the knowledge that one is guiltless in God's sight, A.'s picture here (cf. 2.2, 19, 21; also 2.10) seems very close to the classical Stoic ideal of αὐτάρκεια (Testard, 'Conscientia', 235–6).

Et ideo, sicut exortus sol . . . obumbrat: Cic. uses a similar image of the radiance of the sun over that of the star to contrast the splendour of the virtues over bodily goods in *Fin.* 5.71 and 5.90, close to a passage (*Fin.* 5.73) which A. evokes in 2.4 below; cf. also *Ex.* 4.9. Cf. also Cic. *Off.* 3.47: *Tanta vis est honesti ut speciem utilitatis obscuret.* O sun, moon, and stars, cf. especially 1 Cor. 15: 40–1. On the imagery of light and darkness in A., see on 1.54.

decore: On the intimate association with *honestas*, cf. 1.219–21.

cetera quae putantur bona: Pleasures and external goods (as the Stoics argued) are irrelevant to happiness. In 2.15–18 A. goes on to insist that *bona* such as riches are in fact an impediment to the happy life.

voluptatem corporis: A swipe at Epicurean ethical theory in particular; see on 1.50, and cf. 2.4, 12.

2. **quae non alienis . . . domesticis percipitur sensibus:** The opinions of other people do not matter; the criterion of happiness is internal. Again, the similarity to the Stoic ideal of self-sufficiency is clear.

tamquam sui iudex: On conscience as a *iudex*, cf. 3.24 (cf. also 3.29, 31).

quo minus sequitur gloriam . . . super eam eminet: Cf. Sall. *Cat.* 54.6 (of M. Porcius Cato): *ita quo minus petebat gloriam, eo magis illum sequebatur* (quoted by Aug. in *CD* 5.12); Plin. *Ep.* 1.8.14: *Praeterea meminimus quanto maiore animo honestatis fructus in conscientia quam in fama reponatur. Sequi enim gloria, non appeti debet, nec, si casu aliquo non sequatur, idcirco quod gloriam meruit minus pulchrum est*; and Liv. 20.39.20 (Fabius Cunctator speaks): *gloriam qui spreverit, veram habebit*; on the idea as a political principle, see D. C. Earl, *The Moral and Political Tradition of Rome* (London, 1967), 11–43.

umbra futurorum: Cf. Col. 2: 17; and 1.239 above; here, the obtaining of the reward of glory in this world is a shadow of the 'reward' of punishment in the life to come. For this contrast of present *merces* and eternal *remuneratio*, cf. 1.147.

Amen . . . perceperunt mercedem suam: Mt. 6: 2.

de his scilicet qui velut tuba canenti . . . gestiunt: Cf. Jesus' condemnation of ostentatious giving in Mt. 6: 2: *Cum ergo facies elemosynam, noli tuba canere ante te, sicut hypocritae faciunt in synagogis et in vicis, ut honorificentur ab hominibus*. On avoiding such false motives in charity, cf. 1.147; 2.76, 102, 109–11; and *Luc.* 1.18.

Similiter et de ieiunio . . . : *Habent*, inquit, *mercedem suam*: Mt. 6: 16.

3. **in abscondito . . . a solo Deo tuo quaerere:** Cf. Mt. 6: 4,
18. A. adds the Christian slant to the emphasis on a good
conscience in 2.2: happiness is the reward of virtue unob-
served by human eyes but witnessed by God. But **videaris**
is telling: for all the emphasis on self-effacement, it is
important that you are *seen* to be behaving in the right way.
auctor aeternitatis: Christ, who no less than God the
Father is quintessentially eternal being; cf. e.g. *Fid.* 1.48–
61; *Ep.* 55 [8].8.
Amen, amen . . . hodie mecum eris in paradiso: Lk. 23:
43, the dying Christ's words to the penitent thief.
**Unde expressius scriptura . . . divino iudicio com-
mitteretur:** [**aestimanda:** E²: *aestimandum* MSS] **hominum opinionibus** picks up *populares opiniones* in 2.2, and
contrasts the natural human estimation of happiness with the
divine perspective disclosed in Scripture. Human opinions
do not ultimately matter; what matters is that God sees your
good behaviour. God will reward secret virtue with eternal
life.

CHAPTER 2: HAPPINESS ACCORDING TO THE PHILOSOPHERS AND ACCORDING TO THE SCRIPTURES

4. **Itaque philosophi:** The focus on the philosophers is
probably suggested by Cic.'s praise of philosophy in *Off.*
2.2–6; the determined contrast of philosophical and biblical
wisdom is of course typical. **Itaque** implies a link between
the views of the philosophers and the *hominum opiniones* of
2.3: philosophers and popular judgement are equally astray.
The review of Greek philosophical definitions of the *summum
bonum* is based on details gleaned from Cic., not from *Off.*
(though *Off.* 1.5–6; 3.116–19 are informative; note especially
the echo of Cic. *Off.* 1.6, *explosa est*, in 2.8 below), but from
Fin. 5.73 (the source is identified by Madec, 171–2, and 13?
n. 240; cf. also Lact. *Inst.* 3.7–8; for other 'doxographies' ir
A., see Madec, 171–4):

Saepe ab Aristotele, a Theophrasto mirabiliter est laudata per se ipsa rerum scientia; hoc uno captus Erillus scientiam summum bonum esse defendit nec rem ullam aliam per se expetendam. Multa sunt dicta ab antiquis de contemnendis ac despiciendis rebus humanis; hoc unum Aristo tenuit: praeter vitia atque virtutes negavit rem esse ullam aut fugiendam aut expetendam. Positum est a nostris in iis esse rebus quae secundum naturam essent non dolere; hoc Hieronymus summum bonum esse dixit. At vero Callipho et post eum Diodorus, cum alter voluptatem adamavisset, alter vacuitatem doloris, neuter honestate carere potuit, quae est a nostris laudata maxime.

The views of Epicurus and Zeno the Stoic which A. cites are not mentioned explicitly in this passage, but they are alluded to by Cic. in the surrounding context in *Fin.* 5.74–5, and would in any case be well known to A. from his general knowledge of Cic.'s philosophical texts. A. here shows the same hostility to the ethics of the philosophers as he does to their physics in *Ex.* 1.1–4 (Madec, 84); on which see J. Pépin, *Théologie cosmique et théologie chrétienne (Ambroise, Exam. I.1.1–4)* (Paris, 1964). No distinction is made between those philosophers who emphasized bodily pleasure or temporal goods and those who rejected them: it is a straight contrast between the philosophers *en bloc* and Scripture. On the following details on each philosopher, consult A. A. Long and D. N. Sedley, *The Hellenistic Philosophers*, 2 vols. (Cambridge, 1987), where other key Greek and Latin sources besides Cic. can be found; Cic. is obviously A.'s predominant, if not exclusive, source. See also the relevant articles in *OCD*.

alii in non dolendo posuerunt, ut Hieronymus: Hieronymus of Rhodes, a Peripatetic philosopher and literary historian who lived at Athens *c*.290–230 BC. None of his writings is extant, but we know from Cic. that he held the supreme good to be the absence of pain: *Acad.* 2.131; *Fin.* 2.8, 16, 19, 32, 35, 41; 5.14, 20, 73; *Tusc.* 2.15; 5.84, 87–8.

alii in rerum scientia, ut Herillus: (H)erillus of Carthage, *fl. c*.260 BC, a disciple of Zeno the Stoic, and the founder of a separate, strict Stoic sect which does not appear to have survived beyond the end of the third century BC; there are, again, no extant texts. He held that knowledge is the highest good, and virtue is only a subordinate end, which differs according to circumstances: Cic. *Acad.* 2.129; *Fin.* 2.43; 4.36, 40; 5.23, 73 (cf. also *Tusc.* 5.85; *Off.* 1.6); see A. M. Ioppolo, 'Lo Stoicismo di Erillo', *Phronesis* 30 (1985), 58–78.

qui audiens ab Aristotele et Theophrasto . . . non quasi solum bonum laudaverint: A very close echo of Cic. *Fin.* 5.73. On Aristotle and Theophrastus, see below.

Alii voluptatem dixerunt, ut Epicurus: See on 1.50.

alii, ut Callipho et post eum Diodorus . . . quod sine ea non possit esse beata vita: Again, very similar to Cic. *Fin.* 5.73. Callipho, *fl.* probably early-third century BC, was a Cyrenaic or an Epicurean disciple who believed that the highest end is pleasure *and* virtue; he emphasized pleasure of the mind, whereas the founder of the Cyrenaics, the hedonist Aristippus, concentrated on bodily pleasure: Cic. *Acad.* 2.131, 139; *Fin.* 2.19, 34–5; 4.50; 5.21; *Tusc.* 5.85. He is sometimes linked with one Dinomachus. Cic. rejects the linking of *voluptas* to *honestas* as an impossible attempt to connect opposites (*Off.* 3.119–20; cf. also Sen. *Ep.* 66). Diodorus was the successor to Critolaus as the leader of the Peripatetic school, *c.*110 BC. He held that the *summum bonum* is virtue plus freedom from pain: Cic. *Acad.* 2.131; *Fin.* 2.19, 34–5; 4.50; 5.14, 21; *Tusc.* 5.85.

Zenon Stoicus solum et summum bonum quod honestum est: Zeno of Citium in Cyprus (335–262 BC), the founder of Stoicism, who taught in the Stoa Poikile at Athens from 313/2 BC. He taught that the sole, supreme good is virtue, and that this is sufficient for a happy life, which consists in living according to nature's norm: in Cic. cf. *Acad.* 1.35; 2.131; *Fin.* 3 (especially 3.50, 58); 5 (especially 5.79 ff.); *Tusc.* 5 (especially 5.33); *Off.* 3.35. A. names Zeno in only one other place (*Abr.* 2.37), where he calls him simply *Stoicorum magister atque auctor sectae ipsius*, and claims that Solomon discerned truth long before him.

Aristoteles autem vel Theophrastus . . . externis bonis adseruerunt: The view of Aristotle (see on 1.31) was that the highest good is virtue, but that external advantages are also of genuine, albeit lesser, value (especially *EN* 1099ᵃ31–ᵇ8; 1153ᵇ16–24; also Cic. *Acad.* 2.131; *Fin.* 2.19; 4.14–15). Aristotle and the Peripatetics, following Plato distinguished three types of *bona*: those of the soul, of the body, and of fortune/the externals (*EN* 1098^{b}12 ff.), noted by A. in *Abr.* 2.68–70 (cf. also *Abr.* 2.33), drawing on Philo, *Quaest. Gen.* 3.16. Theophrastus of Eresus in Lesbos (*c*.372–288/7 BC), was a pupil of, collaborator with, and, from 322, the successor of Aristotle. His interests lay particularly in natural science, chiefly botany, though little of his work survives; he was also an accomplished orator and prose-stylist. In ethics, he followed his mentor in arguing for a combination of virtue plus prosperity; virtue is the highest good, but not the only one—a position clearly repugnant to the Stoics; cf. especially Cic. *Acad.* 1.33, 35; 2.134; *Fin.* 5.12, 77, 85–6; *Tusc.* 5.24–5. The association of Aristotle and Theophrastus here is under the direct influence of Cic. *Fin.* 5.73. Throughout 2.1–21, A. is directing his fire at a Peripatetic view of happiness in particular (Testard, 'Etude', 174 n. 39; note Cic.'s tactful reference to Cratippus, Marcus' mentor, in *Off.* 2.7–8 (also *Off.* 1.2; 3.20)). He is not opposed to the Stoic conviction that virtue is sufficient (on the contrary: cf. 2.18), but he repudiates the idea held by Aristotle and his heirs that physical or external goods need to be added to virtue for a person to be truly happy, and that something might be beneficial without necessarily being honourable in itself (cf. 2.1, 8, 15, 16, 18).

5. **Scriptura autem divina:** The standard sharp antithesis of Scripture and philosophy.

vitam aeternam: Here clearly synonymous with *vitam beatam* in 2.4, in accordance with the definition given in 2.1.

in cognitione . . . divinitatis et fructu bonae operationis: Faith plus good works is the Christian prescription. The knowledge of which Scripture speaks is not the *scientia* so esteemed by Aristotle, Theophrastus, and Herillus: it is the knowledge of God. We are reminded of the formulation of the first cardinal virtue: prudence is the knowledge of God, not the pursuit of human learning (1.117–29). For *beatitudo* as the possession of goodness and truth, cf. *Iac.* 1.32; for eternal life as the vision of God, cf. *Bon. mort.* 49; *Is.* 78; *Ep.* 22 [35].13.

Haec est autem vita aeterna . . . et quem misisti Iesum Christum: Jn. 17: 3.

Omnis qui reliquerit domum . . . vitam aeternam possidebit: Mt. 19: 29.

6. **Sed ne aestimetur hoc recens esse . . . aperte videatur expressum:** The usual search for biblical anteriority (Introduction IV.2). A. obviously cannot claim that the philosophers of Hellenistic Greece developed their ideas later than Christ (in 2.5), so he goes back to the 'prophet' David (see on 1.31). It is interesting that Cic. also emphasizes ancient authority in *Off.* 2.5 and 2.8; **quam longe antequam philosophorum nomen audiretur** is probably echoing Cic. *Off.* 2.5, on the pursuit of wisdom: *Hanc igitur qui expetunt philosophi nominantur* (note also *philosophiae nomen* in *Off.* 2.2). No matter how venerable the tradition of the philosophers, the Bible has—somewhere, we may be sure—spoken long before the pursuit of these thinkers was even heard of.

Beatus quem tu erudieris . . . de lege tua docueris eum: Ps. 93: 12.

Beatus vir qui timet Dominum . . . cupiet nimis: Ps. 111: 1.

Docuimus de cognitione: By quoting these verses of David's, the first constituent of happiness, the knowledge of God, is demonstrated to be essential.

propheta, adiciens: V²'s transposition of the MSS' *adiciens propheta* makes some sense; Winterbottom's proposed deletion of **propheta** (563–4) is perhaps too drastic: **memoravit** is the better for an expressed subject.

in domo huius timentis Dominum . . . *manet in saeculum saeculi*: Ps. 111: 3.

De operibus quoque: The second element of happiness.

Beatus vir qui miseretur . . . . In memoria aeterna erit iustus: Ps. 111: 5–7.

Dispersit, dedit . . . manet in aeternum: Ps. 111: 9.

7. **quia fundamentum est bonum:** Cf. 1.126, 142, 252–3.

prudentiam suam factis repellit: Faith must be proved by good works (cf. *Exh. virg.* 43); without them, it is seen to be a sham; cf. 1.126–9, 142, 145, drawing on Jas. 2: 14–26 and:

et gravius est scire . . . quod faciendum cognoveris With knowledge comes responsibility: cf. Jas. 4: 17: *Scient* *igitur bonum facere, et non facienti, peccatum est illi* (also generally Rom. 3: 21–5: 11).

ita est ac si vitioso fundamento . . . plus corruit: Cf. Jesus' illustration in Mt. 7: 24–7; Lk. 6: 47–9.

Infida statio: Reminiscent of Verg. *Aen.* 2.23: *nunc tantum sinus et statio male fida carinis*; the same image appears in *Iac.* 2.28, where A. also evokes Lucr. 2.1–4; and in *Luc.* 4.3; cf. too *Iac.* 1.24: [*vita beata*] *nescit naufragia, qui semper in portu tranquillitatis est.* The well-known harbour image (C. Bonner, 'Desired Haven', *HThR* 34 (1941), 49–67) is used here of faith as a safe haven in which good works may be done. As faith is the *fundamentum* and *munimentum*, so it is a *fida statio* (cf. *Expl. Ps. 48*.9; also *Cain* 1.11).

aequalitas sobrietatis: Alongside prudence (faith) and justice (charity—good works) comes temperance; on *sobrietas*, see on 1.12.

CHAPTER 3: HAPPINESS IS UNRELATED TO
OUTWARD CIRCUMSTANCES

8. **explosa est:** Cic. uses this verb in rejection of the tenets of philosophers in *Off.* 1.6 and *Fin.* 5.23.

secundum philosophiae disputationes superfluas: A reference to the philosophical perspectives mentioned in 2.4. Cic. uses *disputari/disputare* in *Off.* 1.5–7; 2.6–8; *disputatio philosophorum* appears in *Off.* 3.73.

vel quasi semiperfecta sententia: As incomplete without works of virtue. Cic. uses *sententia* in *Off.* 2.7.

tam multiplices et implicatas . . . quaestiones esse philosophiae: Cic. *Off.* 1.5–7; 3.50 speaks of *quaestiones* to refer neutrally to philosopher's questions; but for A. the connotations of the word are firmly negative; cf. 2.49; 3.38, 97, 126 (see further Madec, 92 n. 392). The complicated debates of philosophy contrast with the simple and authoritative delineation of truth in **scriptura divina**. Perhaps he thinks of the surveys presented in treatises like Cic.'s *Fin.* and *Tusc.* Christians could with some justification regard traditional moral teleology as a labyrinthine subject: Augustine notes that Varro's *De philosophia* (now lost) enumerated

288 possible schools of thought *de finibus bonorum et malorum* (*CD* 19.1).

Nihil enim bonum scriptura . . . neque minuatur adversis: The classic Stoic belief that virtue alone is sufficient for the happy life, and external circumstances are irrelevant (cf. Cic. *Parad.* 2 and especially *Tusc.* 5), is attributed to the teaching of the Scriptures.

nisi quod a peccato alienum sit . . . repletum gratia Dei: The Stoic sentiment is combined with the Christian ideas of being innocent of sin and being the recipient of divine grace. Happiness is the knowledge that one is pure in God's eyes (cf. *Noe* 2). Scriptural verses follow:

Beatus vir qui non abiit . . . in lege Domini fuit voluntas eius: Ps. 1: 1–2.

Beati immaculati . . . in lege Domini: Ps. 118: 1.

9. **Innocentia igitur et scientia beatum faciunt:** In 2.5–7, happiness is said to consist of the knowledge of God plus good works; in 2.8–9, it is a combination of the knowledge of God plus innocence. Freedom from sin is a prerequisite for meritorious good works.

superius advertimus: Cf. 2.5–7.

Restat igitur ut . . . vitam beatam eminere demonstret: Scripture can prove the points made by the philosophers.

voluptatis: See on 2.4.

doloris: On the unimportance of *dolor*, cf. Cic. *Tusc.* 2, especially 2.31 ff. For similar language about *dolor* and the externals, cf. *Iac.* 1.27–39 (and *Iac.* 2.36–58).

infractum et molliculum . . . quasi eviratum et infirmum: See on 1.84, 138; and Introduction VII (ii).

in ipsis doloribus vitam beatam eminere demonstret: A. goes on to argue (2.10–21) that pain, sorrow, and loss in fact promote ultimate happiness. He parts company with Stoicism here, for the Stoics in general regarded physical troubles as ἀδιάφορα, morally neutral (though Epictetus and Seneca recognized some value in suffering). His influence, rather, is Platonist: the world is a place of purificatory trial, where the soul is increasingly purged via suffering (borne with suitably muscular fortitude—the overlaps with 1.180–95 are strong) in its progress towards final perfection. He combines this perspective with the Christian view of sanctification and eschatological hope. God brings his people to glory through suffering, so there is happiness of a kind to be known on the training-ground of divine improvement. This measure of happiness is the precursor to the perfect bliss of the eternal life to come. This points to the presentation of the *utile* in the main body of book 2: the beneficial is that which promotes the practice of faith and virtue, and so aids in the quest to gain eternal life. Cf. the typically 'Irenaean' theodicy in 1.40–64.

Beati estis cum vobis maledicent . . . et prophetas qui erant ante vos: Mt. 5: 11–12.

Qui vult venire post me . . . sequatur me: Mt. 16: 24; Mk. 8: 34; Lk. 9: 23, omitting the words 'let him deny himself'.

CHAPTER 4: HAPPINESS IN SUFFERING

10. **in doloribus**: With the examples which follow, A. thinks of a variety of forms of suffering.

   vel ad conscientiam vel ad gratiam: Virtue brings a good conscience (classical), and grace (Christian): Testard, '*Conscientia*', 237–8.

   Moyses, cum Aegyptiorum vallatus populis . . . piis meritis invenisset: See Ex. 14: 1–31.

   Quando autem fortior quam . . . exigebat triumphum?: Happiness in *dolor* is synonymous with, or dependent upon, serious courage; cf. 1.196–201.

11. **Quid Aaron? . . . a cadaveribus mortuorum?**: See Num. 16: 1–50, especially 16: 41–50; on A.'s exegesis of the passage elsewhere, see R. Gryson, 'La Médiation d'Aaron d'après saint Ambroise', *RecTh* 47 (1980), 5–15 (from Gryson, 'Typologie', 46–58).

   Quid de puero Daniele loquar . . . exemplo sui feras provocaret?: [**loquar**: P², E, CO: *loquor* P¹VM, Testard] See Dan. 14: 23–42. Daniel is **sapiens** because he knows and obeys God; his courage, too, stems from this.

12. **quae sibi bonae suavitatem exhibeat conscientiae**: Daniel was innocent in the trial mentioned in 2.11.

   virtutis voluptatem: *Voluptas* here is obviously positive: a good conscience is the satisfying reward of virtue in this life, just as eternal happiness is its remuneration in the life to come.

per voluptatem corporis aut commodorum gratiam: [**gratiam:** V², E, COB, Zell: *gratia* PV¹MA, W, Gering, Testard] This time, as in 2.1 and 2.4, *voluptas* is pejorative, and *gratia* signifies the superficial charm of outward benefits, not divine grace.

Quae mihi lucra fuerunt . . . detrimenta esse: Phil. 3: 7. *Propter quem omnia damna duxi . . . ut Christum lucrifaciam*: Phil. 3: 8.

13. **Moyses damnum suum credidit . . . opprobrium dominicae crucis praetulit:** Cf. Heb. 11: 24–6, drawing on Ps. 88: 51–2: *Fide Moses grandis factus negavit se esse filium filiae Pharaonis; magis eligens affligi cum populo Dei quam temporalis peccati habere iucunditatem, maiores divitias aestimans thesauro Aegyptiorum improperium Christi: aspiciebat enim in remunerationem.* Here, unlike in 1.123, A. takes the treasures of the Egyptians as literal wealth. On **opprobrium dominicae crucis**, cf. Gal. 5: 11, *scandalum crucis*.

cum abundaret pecunia: During his youth, as an adopted child at the court of Pharaoh (Ex. 2: 1–10).

cum egeret alimento: When leading the Israelites through the wilderness (Ex. 16: 1–36; Num. 11: 4–35).

manna ei, hoc est *panis angelorum*, ministrabatur e caelo: See Ex. 16: 13–36; Num. 11: 7–9. The manna is called *panis angelorum* in Ps. 77: 25; cf. also e.g. *Myst.* 47–8; *Expl. Ps. 36*.61; *Expos. Ps. 118.16.29.*

carnis quoque cotidiana pluvia . . . redundabat: On the supply of quail-flesh, see Ex. 16: 11–13; Num. 11: 31–3.

14. **Eliae quoque . . . caro ad vesperam deferebatur:** See 3 Ki. 17: 1–6. A.'s memory of the story is not totally accurate: in fact, *both* bread and meat were brought in the morning and again in the evening (3 Ki. 17: 6).

quia erat Deo dives: Cf. Lk. 12: 21, where, by contrast, the rich fool *non est in Deum dives*.

Aliis enim esse quam sibi divitem praestat: The riches of Elijah's faith redounded to the benefit of others; his outward poverty, like Christ's, was for others' enrichment.

qui tempore famis . . . sufficeret ac ministraret: See 3 Ki. 17: 7–24, especially 17: 7–16.

per triennium et sex menses: A. follows the NT''s chronology of a 3½-year drought (Lk. 4: 25; Jas. 5: 17), whereas 3 Ki. 18: 1 speaks of the drought ending 'in the third year'. The longer figure is probably a round number, signifying half of the seven-year period that was common for a drought (cf. Gen. 41: 27; 4 Ki. 8: 1), and thus indicating that this one was cut short. A. gives the longer figure again in 3.4, and in *Elia* 84; *Vid.* 14.

Merito ibi volebat Petrus esse . . . cum Christo in gloria apparuerunt: At the transfiguration of Jesus, when Moses and Elijah (2.13–14) appeared and talked with him: see Mt. 17: 1–9 (especially 17: 4); Mk. 9: 1–8 (especially 9: 4); Lk. 9: 28–36 (especially 9: 33).

et ipse pauper factus est cum dives esset: Cf. 2 Cor. 8: 9; see also on 1.151.

15. **Nullum ergo adminiculum . . . ad vitam beatam:** The mention of the true riches possessed by Moses, Elijah, and Jesus (2.13–14) leads to an attack on earthly riches as an impediment to happiness, a theme which recurs throughout book 2 (cf. also 1.28–9, 59, 241–5; and *Iac.* 1.35); see in general G. D. Gordini, 'La ricchezza secondo s. Ambrogio', *Ambrosius* 3 (1957), 102–23.

Beati pauperes . . . regnum Dei: Lk. 6: 20; see also on 1.59.

Beati qui nunc esuriunt . . . saturabuntur: A mélange of the versions given in Lk. 6: 21 and Mt. 5: 6.

Beati qui nunc fletis . . . ridebitis: Lk. 6: 21.

non solum impedimento . . . sed etiam adiumento: Things popularly considered to be evils or disadvantages to happiness bring the righteous sufferer to the ultimate bliss of eternal life.

CHAPTER 5: SUPPOSED ADVANTAGES ARE
A HINDRANCE, SUPPOSED EVILS A HELP

16. *Vae vobis divitibus . . . quia esurietis!*: Lk. 6: 24–5.
Et illis qui rident . . . lugebunt: Cf. Lk. 6: 25. On the reversal envisaged here, cf. 1.28–9, 59–62.

Sic: E²W²?, OB, most editors: *si* PVMA, E¹W¹, C, Testard.
Winterbottom, 564, suspects a lacuna, assuming that *si* is
correct and that the apodosis of the sentence has dropped
out, but the sense may work all right with **sic**.

sed etiam dispendio sunt: Cf. 1.28, 154.

17. **Inde enim beatus Nabuthe . . . ut eius possideret
vineam:** Naboth refused to hand over his inherited vineyard
to king Ahab of Samaria (the **dives**); the queen, Jezebel,
instigated a false trial and had Naboth condemned to death
by stoning for having cursed God and the king: 3 Ki. 21: 1–
29. A.'s *Nab.* is the only extant patristic work devoted to
Naboth: see Vasey, 21–104; M. G. Mara, *Ambrogio, La storia
di Naboth* (Aquila, 1985); for other references, including
3.63–4, see Vasey, 22, and the next note here; note the
striking portrayal of Valentinian II as Ahab, Justina as
Jezebel, and A. himself as Naboth, in the basilica crisis, in
Ep. 75a [*C. Aux.*].17–18. In *Ep.* 10 [38].8, Naboth is said to
be rich and Ahab to be in reality poor. A. says that the theme
is an old story, but the oppression of the weak by the
powerful is one that is repeated every day (*Nab.* 1).

**quia sanguine proprio defenderet iura maiorum
suorum:** With typical Roman conviction (e.g. Cic. *Off.*
1.21, 51), and in accordance with OT law (Lev. 25: 23–5),
A. evinces a traditional regard for the sanctity of family
property: Naboth was quite right not to surrender his
inheritance, and he suffered as a martyr for heredity; cf.
3.63; *Nab.* 13; *Expl. Ps.* 36.19; *Exh. virg.* 30; *Ep.* 75a
[*C. Aux.*].17–18; also *Exc. fr.* 1.59.

miser Achab suo iudicio: See 3 Ki. 21: 27; Ahab's remorse
was instilled by Elijah's prophecy of retribution on the king,
his queen, and the nation.

18. **Certum est solum et summum bonum virtutem
esse:** Thoroughly Stoic; see on Zeno in 2.4. A. nowhere
defines *virtus* (Löpfe, 71), but in this section it is obviously
synonymous with both the Stoic *honestum* (cf. 2.10, 12) and
Christian good works (cf. 2.7–8).

**eamque abundare solam ad vitae fructum beatae . . .
per quam vita aeterna acquiritur:** Next to the notorious
sentence on private property in 1.132, these are the most
disputed words in *Off.* The difficulty lies in the ambiguity of

A.'s Latin: what is the antecedent of **per quam vitam beatam**, or **virtute sola**? Is eternal life obtained by the happy life, or by virtue alone? Those who argue that **per quam** should be taken with **vitam beatam** stress the fact that earlier in the sentence A. speaks of the *fructus* of the *vita beata*, and they infer from this that it would be logical for him to go on to say that this *fructus* is *vita aeterna*. The happy life in this world, characterized by virtue, is the way to the future reward of eternal life. Supporters of this interpretation are uneasy with the alternative that **per quam** picks up **virtute sola**, for on that reading A. omits any mention of faith as a prerequisite for *vita aeterna*, and pins everything on virtue. See Niederhuber, *Reiche Gottes*, 192; id. translation, 5 n. 2 and text ad loc.; M. Badura, *Die leitenden Grundsätze der Morallehre des hl. Ambrosius* (Prague, 1921), 17; De Romestin, translation ad loc.; Dassmann, 264 n. 314; Homes Dudden ii. 516; Testard, 'Etude', 175; id. '*Conscientia*', 238; id. translation ad loc. and cf. Testard ii. 153 n. 7; Crouter, 253; also the comments of H. H. Scullard, *Early Christian Ethics in the West, from Clement to Ambrose* (London, 1907), 183–7; L. Visconti, 'Il primo trattato di filosofia morale cristiana (Il De officiis di s. Ambrogio e di Cicerone)', *Atti della Reale Accademia d'Archeologia, Lettere e Belle Arte di Napoli* 25/2 (1908), 54–7. As the translation seeks to bring out, however, the latter interpretation is more persuasive, and it has rightly won wider support: see D. Leitmeir, *Apologie der christlichen Moral. Darstellung des Verhältnisses der heidnischen und christlichen Ethik, zunächst nach einer Vergleichung des ciceronischen buches 'De officiis' und dem gleichnamigen des heiligen Ambrosius* (Augsburg, 1866), 65; Ewald, 26 n. 1; Schmidt, 18–19; Thamin, 220 n. 3; F. Wagner, *Der Sittlichkeitsbegriff in der hl. Schrift und in der altchristlichen Ethik* (Münster, 1931), 220; Stelzenberger, 335–40; Cavasin, translation ad loc.; Muckle, 68, 73; P. J. Couvée, *Vita beata en vita aeterna. Een onderzoek naar de ontwikkeling van het begrip 'vita beata' naast en tegenover 'vita aeterna' bij Lactantius, Ambrosius en Augustinus, onder invloed van de romeinsche Stoa* (Baarn, 1947), 172–3; M. Pohlenz, *Die Stoa* i (Göttingen, 1948), 446; Coyle, 233; Banterle, transl. ad loc.;

Sauer, 39–41. At the beginning of the paragraph, A. stresses
that virtue is the **solum et summum bonum**, which
uniquely redounds towards the *fructus* of the happy life. In
the sentence which concludes the paragraph, he clearly
distinguishes the happy life and eternal life (as Testard ii.
153 n. 8, has to admit): the happy life is the **fructus
praesentium**, while eternal life is the **spes futurorum**.
There is no hint that the latter is gained by the former.
There is thus in any case a clear difference between the
language here and in 2.1, 3–5, where *vita beata* and *vita
aeterna* are portrayed as synonymous, and we cannot allow
our exegesis of the present paragraph to be controlled by the
idiom of these earlier sections. Still less is it appropriate to
let our analysis be swayed by a personal doctrinal distaste for
A.'s failure to mention the role of faith at this point. *Vita
beata* here describes an earthly state which is obtained by
virtue. What A. is saying here, then, is this: virtue secures
one level of happiness in this life, and another, the complete
happiness of *vita aeterna*, in the world to come. This idea of
degrees of reward is in accordance with the notion of
progress towards eschatological perfection in 1.233–45, and
with the distinction between the kinds of perfection possible
in this world and in the next in 3.11 (cf. also the *virtutis
profectus* mentioned in 2.113). Whether certain critics like it
or not, the appeal of the Stoic ethic has here penetrated A.'s
formulation to a remarkably obvious degree. Virtue is the
'hope and cause of heaven' (Muckle, 72–3; cf. also *Fug.* 37,
where eternal life is said to be acquired *virtute*; and *Off.*
1.125, where the biblical reference to entering the *regnum
caelorum* at last comes after an allusion to Cic. *Off.* 1.19 on
thinking about how to live *beate honesteque*, an ideal which
may be approached *operibus*). It is the prerequisite for
earthly happiness *and* for eschatological bliss (Sauer, 35–
47; cf. Niederhuber, *Reiche Gottes*, 191–204). To those
troubled by the lack of reference to faith, an overall account
of A.'s moral theology would have to say that the virtue is
only possible with divine grace, and in the end only purpose-
ful when directed towards eternal destiny. But it is virtue
that is emphasized here.

19.   in hoc corpore tam infirmo, tam fragili: Reminiscen of biblical (e.g. Mt. 26: 41; Mk. 14: 38; 2 Cor. 5: 1–10; Phil. 3: 21; 2 Pt. 1: 13–14) stress on the frailty of the body; A.'s general perspective is also of course influenced by Platonist assumptions. See M. Bartelink, '"Fragilitas humana" chez saint Ambroise', in *AmbrEpisc* ii. 130–42; A. Loiselle, *'Nature' de l'homme et histoire du salut. Etude sur l'anthropologie d'Ambroise de Milan*, Diss. (Lyons, 1970), 27–34.

in altitudine sapientiae . . . virtutis sublimitate: Close to Stoic ideals of ἀπάθεια and αὐτάρκεια (cf. 2.10, 12), but biblical examples of the ideals follow.

victorem esse passionis beatum est: Cf. the NT pictures of eternal triumph as reward for earthly suffering (Rom. 8: 18, 31–9, especially 8: 37; 1 Cor. 15: 57; Jas. 1: 12); also 1.59–62, 178–95 above.

20. **caecitatem exsilium famem:** In *Tusc.* 5, Cic. records the Stoic argument that these supposed evils cannot undermine the happiness of the sage (blindness: 5.110–5; exile: 5.106–9; simplicity of food: 5.97–102); blindness, exile, need, childlessness, and other afflictions are also mentioned by Cic. in *Fin.* 5.84–6, where he criticizes the Stoic position. A. thus evokes standard classical examples of worldly misfortunes; but he is closer to Platonist–Christian sensibilities than to the Stoics in seeing redemptive value in such troubles. He appends scriptural examples:

Isaac, qui . . . suis benedictionibus conferebat: See Gen. 27: 1–40. A. omits to mention that Isaac's blindness allowed him to be duped by Jacob into giving him the blessing of the first-born, rightly Esau's, the incident which marked the beginning of the open conflict between his sons. Jacob was again blessed by Isaac when he left home (Gen. 28: 1–5).

beatus Iacob, qui . . . exsilium sustinuit: Jacob fled from Esau's revenge and served his uncle, Laban, in Haran as a shepherd: Gen. 27: 41–5; 28: 5; 29: 1–30: 43.

filiae pudicitiam ingemuit esse temeratam: See Gen. 34: 1–31 on the rape of Dinah, and the severe vengeance wrought by her brothers, though not by Jacob himself.

famem pertulit: There is no mention of this in the Gen. record, but it is perhaps implied in the vow made by Jacob at Bethel to worship the Lord if protection, food, and clothing are granted to him in his exile (Gen. 28: 20–2), and his later testimony that the Lord provided for him in hardship (Gen. 31: 40–2).

quorum fide: Cf. the emphasis on the faith of Isaac and Jacob in Heb. 11: 20–1. The reference to faith lacking in the formula in 2.18 is now brought in.

Deus Abraham, Deus Isaac, Deus Iacob: Ex. 3: 6, 15–16; 4: 5; cf. also Mt. 22: 32; Mk. 12: 26; Lk. 20: 37; Acts 3: 13; 7: 32.

Misera est servitus . . . in servitute positus coerceret: Joseph's brothers sold him to some Midianites/Ishmaelites (Gen. 37: 23–8), who in turn sold him to the Egyptian court-official, Potiphar (Gen. 39: 1), though Joseph hardly became a menial in Potiphar's house (Gen. 39: 4–6). He resisted the attempt of Potiphar's wife to seduce him (Gen. 39: 6–12), but was then imprisoned on a false charge of attempted rape (Gen. 39: 13–20). However, even in prison he again found favour and subsequent preferment (Gen. 39: 20—41: 57). On the miserable state of slavery, see Klein, 27–32.

David . . . qui trium filiorum deploravit obitum: David lost the first son Bathsheba bore him (as a punishment for his adultery with her: 2 Ki. 12: 13–23); Amnon, his eldest surviving son, was killed by Absalom for having committed incest with his sister Tamar (2 Ki. 13: 1–34); and the rebel Absalom himself was killed, contrary to David's orders, by Joab (2 Ki. 18: 1–19: 4).

et, quod his durius, incestum filiae: Tamar, raped by Amnon (2 Ki. 13: 1–34). Typically, A. sees the violation of virginity as a fate worse than death: cf. 1.68; 2.136.

de cuius successione beatitudinis auctor exortus est: The promised Messiah was of course of the house of David: Mt. 1: 6–17; Lk. 1: 26–33, 69; 2: 4; etc. He is the giver of quintessential *beatitudo*.

Beati* enim *qui non viderunt et crediderunt: Jn. 20: 29.

sensu: E²W, COB, most editors: *sensum* PVMA, E¹.

infirmitatis: PVMA, E², COB: *humilitatis* E¹W.

sed evaluerunt de infirmitate fortes: Cf. Heb. 11: 34; see also on 1.178.

sancto Iob vel in domus incendio: Job lost his servants and his vast flocks of sheep in a fire caused by lightning (Job 1: 16).

vel filiorum decem interitu momentario: Job's seven sons and three daughters (Job 1: 2) were all killed when a great wind made the oldest son's house collapse (Job 1: 18–19). Testard ii. 154 n. 19 implies that A. conflates Job 1: 16 and Job 1: 18–19 in this sentence; he fails to notice that A. differentiates the two allusions with **vel . . . vel . . .**

beatus . . . in quibus magis probatus est: Cf. Jas. 1: 12: *Beatus vir qui suffert temptationem, quia cum probatus fuerit, accipiet coronam vitae quam repromisit Deus diligentibus se*; cf. also Jas. 5: 11 on Job, and see on 1.40.

21. This paragraph contains a cluster of classical, and especially Vergilian, phrases for nature. Why we should have this particular literary flourish here we can only guess, but A. certainly demonstrates his fondness for poetic *color*.

vadosa litora: Cf. Val. Max. 8.7. ext. 1: *vadosis litoribus*. The image also occurs (*litora vadosa*) in *Luc.* 4.3.

caelum . . . obtexitur: Cf. Verg. *Aen.* 11.610–11: *fundunt simul undique tela | crebra nivis ritu caelumque obtexitur umbra.* Cf. also Plin. *NH* 2.104: *subinde per nubes caelum aliud atque aliud obtexens.* 3.100 below has *caelum intextum nubibus*; and cf. *Ex.* 1.35; 4.30.

ieiuna glarea: Cf. Verg. *Georg.* 2.212–13: *nam ieiuna quidem clivosi glarea ruris | vix humilis apibus casias roremque ministrat.*

laetas segetes: Cf. Verg. *Georg.* 1.1: *Quid faciat laetas segetes.* The metaphor is commended by Cic. in *De Or.* 3.155; in A., cf. *Ex.* 1.28; *Expos. Ps. 118.2.2.*

sterilem avenam: Cf. Verg. *Ecl.* 5.36–7: *grandia saepe quibus mandavimus hordea sulcis, | infelix lolium et steriles nascuntur avenae.* Also Verg. *Georg.* 1.153–4: *interque nitentia culta | infelix lolium et steriles dominantur avenae.* Cf. also Ov. *Fast.* 1.692.

Given the evocation of Cic. *Fin.* 5.73 in 2.4, it is quite possible that A.'s echo of these words is prompted by Cic. *Fin.* 5.91: *At enim qua in vita est aliquid mali, ea beata esse non potest. Ne seges quidem igitur spicis uberibus et crebris si avenam uspiam videris.* A little trouble does not destroy the overall happiness of life.

beatae messem conscientiae: *Messis* in this sense is a late usage (*TLL* viii. 859–60), probably in Christian authors under the influence of biblical language about the fruit of righteousness (e.g. Heb. 12: 11; Jas. 3: 18) (*pace* Testard, '*Conscientia*', 241, who detects in this instance an allusion to the parable of the sower), though A. says nothing here about eternal reward. On good conscience, cf. generally Acts 23: 1; 1 Tim. 1: 5, 19; Heb. 13: 18; 1 Pt. 3: 21.

acerbo: The reading of PMA, E², C, and most editors is correct, *pace* V, E¹W, OB's *acervo*, adopted by Banterle: the arguments are summarized in A. V. Nazzaro, 'Ambrosiana II. Note di critica testuale e d'esegesi', *Vichiana* 8 (1979), 203–10. Testard, '*Conscientia*', 240 n. 5, reads *acervo*, but his text and comment in Testard ii (154–5 n. 26) signal a change of mind.

Sed iam ad proposita pergamus: Closely reminiscent of Cic.'s comment at the end of his introduction in *Off.* 2: *Sed iam ad instituta pergamus* (*Off.* 2.8); cf. also *Off.* 1.161: *Sed iam ad reliqua pergamus*; 2.35: *Sed ad propositum revertamur*; 3.39: *Sed iam ad propositum revertamur* (echoed by A. in 3.32).

CHAPTER 6: THE BENEFICIAL IS NOT WEALTH
OR BODILY GOOD, BUT PIETY

2.22–7 introduces the real theme of book 2, the *utile*, citing scriptural authority for the use of the *utile* and the *utilitas* word-group. The preceding characterization of happiness has underlined the dangers of earthly prosperity, and A. makes it clear at once that the *utile* is not material gain but the *acquisitio pietatis* (2.23) which wins eternal reward in the presence of God. Whatever promotes the virtue that leads to the bliss of the *vita aeterna* (2.18) is *utile*. These paragraphs thus point to the assumption which lies at the heart of book 3: the *honestum* and the *utile* are in fact the same thing. This is expressly stated in 2.28. The inspiration for the passage comes from Cic. *Off.* 2.9–11, but the point of reference is biblical.

22. Superiore libro . . . secundo loco quid utile: Cf. 1.27, echoing Cic. *Off.* 1.9–10; Cic. *Off.* 1.10 speaks of a *divisio.*

Cic. *Off.* 2.9 also refers to the programme set out in book 1, and explicitly links *decus* with the *honestum*.

inter honestum et decorum est . . . quae magis intellegi quam explicari: Cf. 1.219–21, especially the evocation of Cic. *Off.* 1.94 in 1.219.

sic et cum utile tractamus, considerandum videtur quid utilius: Not a faithful résumé of the *divisio* given in 1.27 (Testard, 'Etude', 175 n. 42). In 1.27, A. adumbrates reliably the three Panaetian subjects: the honourable, the beneficial, and the relationship of the two, and alludes to Cic.'s two further topics, the calculus of *honesta* and the calculus of *utilia*. Here, he implies that the comparison of *utilia* in book 2 forms the parallel section to the distinction between the *honestum* and the *decorum* in book 1, rather than, as it should be, the corresponding piece to the comparison of *honesta*. The confusion is probably due to a vague recollection of the theme of Cic. *Off.* 2.11–22, which identifies various kinds of animate and inanimate assistance for human life, and asserts the supreme value of mutual human support, without grading these benefits in a hierarchy of *utilia* as *Off.* 2.88–9 does; cf. 2.28 below.

23. Utilitatem autem . . . acquisitione pietatis: Cf. 1.28–9; 2.15–16, 25–6; 3.9, 37, 56, 63, 90 on real *utilitas* versus popular ideas of it. Cic. *Off.* 2.9 speaks of the corruption of the word *utile*, but only with respect to its separation from *honestum* in sense. In *Off.* 2.11, he mentions gold and silver as things which may help to preserve human life (cf. *Off.* 2.88), but also speaks of the gods, and how they are placated by *pietas et sanctitas*. A. may be alluding to this in his rejection of financial gain and his esteem for Christian *pietas*. But his sentiment is equally biblical: on the superiority of *pietas* over treacherous riches, cf. 1 Tim. 6: 6–10 (2.26 below); also:

Pietas autem . . . promissionem habens vitae praesentis et futurae: 1 Tim. 4: 8.

in scripturis divinis, si diligenter quaeramus, saepe invenimus: Cf. Lk. 15: 8, of the woman who loses a coin: *quaerit diligenter, donec inveniat.*

Omnia mihi licent sed non omnia sunt utilia: 1 Cor. 6: 12. The Christian is free in his behaviour, Paul says, but this

does not mean that everything is helpful or 'beneficial' for
him, since it may ensnare him and so destroy the freedom
that he enjoys. For A. this is tantamount to saying that
utilitas equals *honestas*. For the attempt to substantiate the
philosophical terminology in the Bible, cf. 1.25, 30, 36–7,
221, 223 (Introduction IV.1).

Supra de vitiis loquebatur: In 1 Cor. 6: 9–10, Paul
condemns a catalogue of vices, including idolatry, various
sexual evils, theft, avarice, slander, and drunkenness.

Non enim Deo esca, sed ventri colligitur: Cf. 1 Cor. 6:
13: *Esca ventri, et venter escis; Deus autem et hunc et haec
destruet.*

24.   **Ergo quia quod utile, id etiam iustum:** This equation
of what is beneficial and what is just is suggested by Cic. *Off.*
2.10 (of *summa quidem auctoritate philosophi*): *quidquid enim
iustum sit, id etiam utile esse censent, itemque quod honestum,
idem iustum, ex quo efficitur ut quidquid honestum sit, idem sit
utile*. But for A. the true measure of what is just is Christ-
centred devotion:

ut serviamus Christo: Cf. Col. 3: 24: *Domino Christo
servite.*

qui nos redemit: Cf. Gal. 3: 13: *Christus nos redemit de
maledicto legis.*

ideo iusti . . . iniusti, qui declinaverunt: On suffering for
the name of Christ, cf. Acts 5: 41; 1 Pt. 4: 14. The opportunity for a glorious death must be eagerly seized (2.153); those
who decline to suffer are **iniusti**.

Quae utilitas in sanguine meo?: Ps. 29: 10. A. interprets
the psalm messianically; cf. *Iac.* 1.26. Christ is said to be
asking why he is to shed his blood in order to redeem people
who are not prepared to shed their blood for his name. In the
original context, however, the psalmist is recalling how he
pleaded for the Lord's deliverance in a situation of danger
and is asking what gain there would be in his destruction.

Adligemus iustum quia inutilis est nobis: Wisd. 2: 12;
Is. 3: 10 (LXX).

qui nos arguit condemnat corripit: Christ, the *iustus* (cf
1 Jn. 2: 1) makes these *iniusti* feel uncomfortable in their
unwillingness to suffer, and so they seek to 'bind' (get rid of
this one who is 'of no benefit' to them in their wickedness.

**sicut in Iuda proditore legimus . . . pecuniae cupidi-
tate:** See Mt. 26: 14–16, 47–50; Mk. 14: 10–11, 43–6; Lk. 22:
3–6, 47–8; Jn. 18: 1–8; Judas was also a dishonest keeper of
the disciples' common purse, according to Jn. 12: 6. The
reference to dishonesty and wickedness is possibly prompted
by Cic.'s comments in *Off.* 2.10: those who cannot see the
connection between what is honourable and what is beneficial have mistaken wickedness for wisdom, and have shown
misplaced admiration for those who achieve their ends by
fraudulent and crafty means.

laqueum proditionis incurrit atque incidit: A deliberate
pun on the manner of Judas' death (cf. *Spir.* 3.123): see Mt.
27: 3–10; cf. Acts 1: 18–19.

25. **ipsis verbis:** A particularly conscious effort to anchor the
Ciceronian language in the Bible.

*Hoc autem ad utilitatem vestram dico . . . sed ad id
quod honestum est:* 1 Cor. 7: 35. The mention of Judas'
laqueus in 2.24 reminds A. of a verse which speaks of both
utilitas and a *laqueus*.

**Liquet igitur quod honestum est utile esse; et quod
utile, honestum:** The basic Stoic and Ciceronian assumption: cf. Cic. *Off.* 2.9–10; 3.11, 34.

ad mercatores lucri cupidine avaros: On the attitude to
trade, see on 1.185, 243; cf. also 3.57, 65. On the distinction
between the greedy trader and the godly man, cf. 2.67; 3.37.

sed ad filios sermo est, et sermo de officiis: See
Introduction V–VI. Cic. refers to his *oratio* in *Off.* 2.20.

quos elegi in ministerium Domini: See on 1.24.

**inculcare gestio atque infundere . . . etiam sermone
ac disciplina aperiantur:** A comprehensive confession of
the immediate didactic aims of the work: A. wishes to
inform and shape the whole character of his clerics' conduct, their speech and behaviour. For the prescriptions, cf.
especially 1.65–114. On **usu atque institutione**, cf. 1.2, *usu
. . . atque exemplo*; for **inolita atque impressa sunt**, cf.
2.37.

26. *Declina cor meum in testimonia tua et non in
avaritiam:* Ps. 118: 36; cf. *Fug.* 1.

Denique aliqui habent: *Declina cor meum . . . non ad
utilitatem:* Cf. *Expos. Ps. 118.5.27:*

'Utilitatem' alii habent et puto, quod ideo mutatum sit, quia utilitas bonae rei videtur esse expetenda potius quam declinanda. Sed quia plerique lucrum pecuniarum utilitatem suam putant esse, ideo, si legimus 'utilitatem', non animae utilitatem accipere debemus prophetam declinare, sed utilitatem pecuniae. Sanctus enim lucra ista non novit, sed omnia haec detrimentum arbitratur, ut Christum lucretur. Et recte; quod enim putamus lucrum esse pecuniae, damnum est animae, quia virtutis est detrimentum. Ergo secundum eos, qui ita acceperunt, ut optet propheta inclinari cor suum in testimonia, et non in avaritiam, et nos congruimus ad sensum.

The similarity between the two passages is noted by W. Wilbrand, 'Zur Chronologie einiger Schriften des hl. Ambrosius', *HJ* 41 (1921), 1–19, at 14–15, but his conclusion that this must date *Off.* later than *Expos. Ps. 118* is unwarranted. Cf. also Hilar. *Tract. Ps. 118*.5.13; and especially the discussion in Aug. *En. Ps. 118*.11.6. The LXX reads πλεονεξία, and the Vulg. *avaritia*; Sabatier's VL cites the present passage as authority for the *versio antiqua*. On warnings against desires for riches, cf. also Cic. *Off.* 2.71, 77.

Vulgo enim hoc solum dicunt utile . . . nos autem de ea tractamus utilitate: The distinction between the popular and the Christian conceptions of *utilitas* is partly suggested by the Panaetian dichotomy between genuine and apparent *utilitas* which is central to Cic.'s equation of the *honestum* and the *utile* in *Off.* 3, but it is also typical of A.'s frequent antitheses of pagan and Christian conceptions of worth; cf. 1.28–9; 2.15–16, 23, 66–7; 3.9, 37, 56, 63, 90; see on 3.37.

quae damnis quaeritur, ut Christum lucremur: Cf. Phil. 3: 7–8.

cuius *quaestus est pietas cum sufficientia*: Cf. 1 Tim. 6: 6.

quae apud Deum dives est: See on 2.14.

non caducis facultatibus sed muneribus aeternis: On the contrast of perishable and imperishable riches, cf. Mt. 6 19–21. Poverty is to be embraced in order to win heavenly riches; see Gryson, *Prêtre*, 301–5.

27. *Corporalis enim exercitatio ad modicum . . . pietas autem ad omnia est utilis*: 1 Tim. 4: 8.

immaculatum servare corpus: A typical stress on sexual purity; A. is thinking of chastity generally. On 'purity' o body, cf. 1.249. More generally, cf. Jas. 1: 27: *immaculatum se custodire ab hoc saeculo.*

ut vidua uxor defuncto coniugi fidem servet: On the calling of widows, see on 1.248.

Quid etiam hoc utilius, quo regnum caeleste acquir-itur?: [**quo:** EW, COB, most editors: *quod* PVMA, Zell, Lignamine, Monte Alto] As well as introducing the next quotation, the phrase effectively sums up the characterization of the *utile* which will follow.

Sunt **enim** *qui se castraverunt propter regnum caelorum*: Mt. 19: 12.

CHAPTER 7: THE HONOURABLE AND THE
BENEFICIAL ARE IDENTICAL; NOTHING IS MORE
BENEFICIAL THAN TO BE LOVED

28. This paragraph sums up the argument of 2.22–7 on what the *utile* is all about, and leads into the substance of the book, the classification of differing sorts of *utilia*, which begins in 2.29.

qui regnum caelorum volebat omnibus aperire: Curiously reminiscent of l. 17 of the *Te Deum*, a hymn once wrongly attributed to A. (see *ODCC*, 1581–2): *aperuisti credentibus te regna caelorum.*

Unde ordo quidam nobis et gradus faciendus est . . . ut ex pluribus utilitatis colligamus profectum: A. is thinking of Cic.'s reference to different kinds of advantages to human life, and to the supreme value of human support, in *Off.* 2.11–22. As in 2.22, he seems to equate this with the kind of actual classification of *utilia* which Cic. makes later, in *Off.* 2.88–9; on the Stoic background, see A. A. Long and D. L. Sedley, *The Hellenistic Philosophers*, 2 vols. (Cambridge, 1987), i. 355–9; ii. 352–5. He picks up Cic. *Off.* 2.11–22, but he never goes on to develop a parallel section to *Off.* 2.88–9. The key point here, however, is A.'s emphasis on doing what is beneficial to the greatest possible number. He upholds Cic.'s stress on the social dimensions of virtue, but replaces debates about health versus wealth with the basic argument that it is better to benefit many than to benefit only oneself. If the *utile* is ultimately all about winning the kingdom of heaven—not just attaining it oneself, but bringing it closer to others—the value of an action must be gauged by the extent to which it reflects conformity with the example of Christ, who came to bring the supreme *utile* by *opening* that kingdom to all. In Cic., *Off.* 2.11–22 is followed by a lengthy argument (*Off.* 2.23–85) on how to acquire the support of others, which is said to be the greatest *utile* of all. A. similarly goes on to explore the various ways in which the dutiful cleric can attain the benefit of popular support and esteem. The paradigm of Christlike service is supposed to invest his ethic with a loftier significance. His pragmatism, nevertheless, is obvious: social *utilitas* is all about respectability, about behaving in a fashion that will ensure a good reputation with the widest possible constituency. The appeal to self-interest and the appeal for ecclesiastical decorum merge neatly. The virtue that merits eschatological reward is also the virtue that promotes the image of the church.

The structure of the argument as it unfolds from this point on in book 2 is confused and confusing. 2.29–39 presents the first of the *utilia*, according to the *ordo* and *gradus* spoken of in 2.28. It is that there is nothing more beneficial than to be loved. The inspiration for this passage comes in the first instance from Cic. *Off.* 2.23–9, where Cic. argues that it is far better to win people's genuine love than to try to control them by the use of fear (*Off.* 2.23–9). For Cic., that love can be gained in three ways: (i) by acting in a way that wins glory (*Off.* 2.30–51); (ii) by financial generosity (*Off.* 2.52–64); and (iii) by generosity in performing services to individuals and to the community at large (*Off.* 2.65–85). A., however, conflates this threefold scheme ('A') with another one ('B') which appears in Cic. *Off.* 2.31–8, where Cic. argues that there are three ways to win glory, all of which derive from justice: (i) by earning people's love or goodwill (*Off.* 2.32); (ii) by winning and maintaining people's faith (*Off.* 2.33–4); and (iii) by earning their honour and admiration (*Off* 2.36–8). In 2.29–39, A. confuses the first of these ways to attain glory with the theme of love versus fear, thus mixing up the argument of Cic. *Off.* 2.32 with that of Cic. *Off.* 2.23–9. The confusion is clear in 2.40, where the love spoken of is scheme 'A' and the faith spoken of in scheme 'B' are treated as points (i) and (ii) of a single series, with the *admiratio* spoken of only in scheme 'B' as point (iii). From 2.41 onwards, 'A' and 'B' are fudged completely (Testard, 'Etude', 176–9). A. attempts in 2.41–55 to discuss point (ii) of 'B', on gaining glory by winning and maintaining faith (though the word *fides* appears only in 2.41–2 and 2.55), but he confuses what Cic. says about faith in 'B', at *Off.* 2.33–4, with what he says about faith in 'A', at *Off.* 2.23–9.[1] Point (iii) of 'B', on the value of possessing qualities which are counted worthy of honour and *admiratio*, follows in 2.56–67. In 2.68–85, however, A. reverts to plan 'A', and starts to talk about generosity, but he does not differentiate point (ii) of 'A', the financial generosity outlined in Cic. *Off.* 2.52–64, from point (iii) of 'A', on generosity of services, discussed in Cic. *Off.* 2.65–85 (see on 2.68). This means that from 2.86 onwards the Ciceronian divisions have gone out of the window altogether: 2.86–151 amounts to a fairly haphazard series of other *utilia*, which draws at random on various passages of Cic.[2]

A. clearly works from memory of Cic.'s material, and it is difficult to avoid the conclusion that his fidelity to Cic.'s arrangement of themes is particularly weak in this book. The attempt of Steidle, 'Beobachtungen 2', to defend the coherence of his organizational structure is a shade too ambitious. Nevertheless, Steidle is right to say that the whole argument is dominated by one key theme—that of being approved. For A., the logical and even theological importance of the *utile* of being loved extends far beyond the parameters of just 2.29–39 and the Ciceronian arguments which lie behind it (cf. e.g. 2.68 and 2.78). His confusion of the theme of being loved rather than feared with the theme of winning glory reflects not just a faulty memory of Cic.'s text, but a strategic preoccupation with a

[1] Just to make matters worse, 2.41–55, following Cic. *Off.* 2.33–4, makes a great deal of the importance of being seen to give reliable *consilium*, but that motif then continues well beyond this section, and affects the argument significantly at later points as well, such as 2.86–9, 93–4; see on 2.40.

[2] The goodwill spoken of by Cic. in 'B', at *Off.* 2.32, also appears at various unexpected points in the Ambrosian 'A'–'B' *mélange*, such as at 2.60, 95, 134.

single overriding principle—self-commendation. The ideal of *commendatio* is partly Ciceronian (*Off.* 2.45–6), but, significantly, it is also a key motif in Paul's argument in 2 Cor. (3: 1; 4: 2; 5: 12; 10: 12, 18). It directly replaces the Ciceronian *gloria* in 2.40, and it dominates the argument right to the end of the book (in 2.134, the horizon is extended beyond the human field, and A. speaks of his readers commending themselves to God). Whatever patchiness may characterize his evocation of Cic., then, the thrust of A.'s concern is abundantly clear: winning and keeping a good reputation is everything, both in human society and with eschatological *approbatio* in mind; cf. 1.227, 247; 2.56–67; 3.23–4.

29. **nihil tam utile quam diligi, nihil tam inutile quam non amari:** Cf. Cic. *Off.* 2.23: *Omnium autem rerum nec aptius est quicquam ad opes tuendas ac tenendas quam diligi nec alienius quam timeri.* Cic. is discussing motives for people to support others' causes, especially in the political field; authority is better maintained by popular love than by intimidation. On the maxim of being loved more than feared, quoted by Benedict at *Reg.* 64, see K. Gross, 'Plus amari quam timeri. Eine antike politische Maxime in der Benediktinerregel', *VChr* 27 (1973), 218–29. At *Conf.* 10.36.59, Augustine laments the fact that the desire to be loved *or* feared by other people for the sheer pleasure of it is a temptation which is still with him as a bishop. For him, both are bad, and they are used by the devil to divert a bishop's attention away from God; the enemy wants him to enjoy being loved and feared by others not because of God, but instead of God, to whom such emotions are truly due. To Augustine, episcopal office is always something of a burden, and the eminence it brings is always a danger; A., by contrast, has a far greater natural affinity, even thirst, for social prominence, and to him the importance of being loved is therefore self-evident.

nam odio haberi exitiale ac nimis capitale arbitror: Cic. *Off.* 2.23 quotes Ennius (probably a fragment of the *Thyestes*): *quem metuunt oderunt, quem quisque odit periisse expetit* (quoted by Jerome at *Ep.* 82.3.2). The last words of the line explain A.'s strong **exitiale** and **capitale**.

influamus in adfectum hominum: Cf. Cic. *Off.* 2.31: *Sed est alius quoque quidam aditus ad multitudinem, ut in universorum animos tamquam influere possimus.*

Ea si mansuetudine morum ac facilitate . . . procedit ad cumulum dilectionis: Cf. Cic. *Off.* 2.32: *Vehementer autem amor multitudinis commovetur ipsa fama et opinione liberalitatis beneficentiae iustitiae fidei omniumque earum virtutum quae pertinent ad mansuetudinem morum ac facilitatem.*

adfabilitate sermonis . . . adiuvetur gratia: Cf. Cic. *Off.* 2.48: *sed tamen difficile dictu est quantopere conciliet animos comitas adfabilitasque sermonis*; cf. also *Amic.* 66. On the *adfabilitas sermonis*, cf. 2.96; and 1.99–100 (also 1.67). The commendation of *modestia* is also suggested by Cic., *Off.* 2.48, where *mixta modestia gravitas* in speech is said to inspire admiration.

30. **Legimus enim non solum in privatis sed etiam in ipsis regibus . . . et potestatem solveret:** An oblique reference to Cic. *Off.* 2.48: *Exstant epistolae et Philippi ad Alexandrum et Antipatri ad Cassandrum et Antigoni ad Philippum filium, trium prudentissimorum (sic enim accepimus), quibus praecipiunt ut oratione benigna multitudinis animos ad benevolentiam adliciant militesque blande appellando sermone deleniant.* Cic. is speaking of a forged correspondence (produced by the rhetorical schools) between Philip II of Macedon (r. 359–336 BC) and his son, Alexander the Great (r. 336–323 BC); and (now lost) letters between Antipater (397–319 BC, created regent of Macedonia by Alexander in 334 BC) and his son, Cassander (358–297 BC), and between Alexander's general, Antigonus (*c.*382–301 BC) and his son, Philip (cf. also Cic. *Off.* 2.53–4). This is the allusion in **regibus**. **Legimus** clearly presupposes a knowledge of the Ciceronian text. With **ut regna ipsa labefactaret et potestatem solveret**, Cic. *Off.* 2.23–9 is in A.'s mind. Thinking especially of his enemy Julius Caesar, whose oppression has brought the Roman Republic to its state of precariousness (*Off.* 2.23, 27–9), Cic. demonstrates how tyrants who secure influence by intimidation end up destroying themselves by incurring the hatred of the masses.

officiis: Cic. has the word in *Off.* 2.43.

si quis periculum suum . . . ut populus salutem eius et

gratiam sibi praeferat: A. doubtless thinks of his own experience in this quasi-contractual business of winning praise as the pay-off for taking risks. The bishop who had stuck his neck out in the crisis of 386 had certainly managed to increase his reputation in the aftermath. A.'s standing among his supporters grew thanks to his brilliant exploitation of the situation at the height of the dispute and his show of strength afterwards, in the consecration of his own new imposing basilica and the ensuing *inventio* of the relics of Gervasius and Protasius in the Hortus Philippi nearby (McLynn, 181–219). On the glories of such activism, cf. 3.23; also 1.135, 177; 3.82–5.

31. **Quantas Moyses . . . absorbebat contumelias!:** [**absorbebat:** EW, COB, most editors: *absolvebat* PVMA, Zell, Lignamine, Valdarfer, Scinzenzeler, Marchand] See e.g. Ex. 14: 10–12; 15: 22–5; 16: 2–3; 17: 1–4; Num. 11: 1–3, 10–15; 14: 1–45; 20: 2–13.

se tamen . . . ut indignationi divinae plebem subduceret: See Ex. 32: 7–14, 30–2.

deliniebat oraculis: See e.g. Ex. 14: 13–14. **deliniebat** and **appellatione** are further echoes of Cic. *Off*. 2.48 (see above); A.'s *delinio* and Cic.'s *delenio* are alternative forms of the same verb.

fovebat operibus: Such as in the provision of food and water; see on 2.13. (These words are omitted from Banterle's text, though he translates them.)

Merito aestimatus est supra homines: Cf. Dt. 34: 10.

et vultum eius non possent intendere: See Ex. 34: 29–35 and cf. 2 Cor. 3: 7–18.

et sepulturam eius non repertam crederent: Cf. Dt 34: 6.

32. **Eius imitator sanctus David:** David imitated the modest and kindly behaviour of Moses towards his people On his humility, cf. 1.1, 21, 236–8.

electus ex omnibus ad plebem regendam: On the choosing and anointing of David by Samuel, see 1 Ki. 16 1–13.

Ante regnum se pro omnibus offerebat: In his duel with Goliath (1 Ki. 17; cf. 19: 5).

rex cum omnibus . . . fortis in proelio: See e.g. 2 Ki.

17–25; 8: 1–14; 10: 17–19; 21: 15–17; 1 Chr. 14: 8–17; 18: 1–13.

patiens in convicio: Cf. 1.21, 236–8 and see ad locc.

ut iuvenis . . . resistens cogeretur: David was a *parvulus/puer/adulescens* when chosen by Samuel (1 Ki. 16: 11; 17: 33, 55–8); he became king at the age of thirty (2 Ki. 5: 4). The OT narratives do not say that he was forced to become king against his will, though the account of his early years at the court of Saul certainly suggests that he did not have pretensions to the throne. David is once again the implicit role model of A. himself, the reluctant bishop; cf. 1.1–4. On the authority that such an approach ensures, cf. 3.60.

senex ne proelio interesset a suis rogaretur . . . quam illum pro omnibus: David's life was narrowly saved by Abishai in a battle with the Philistines; his men subsequently made him swear that he would not go into battle with them again (2 Ki. 21: 15–17). David is not actually said to have been a **senex** at the time of this incident; A. presumably infers it from the fact that the incident occurs towards the latter stages of the narrative of David in 2 Ki. (perhaps also from the detail that David was exhausted in the battle).

33. **in discordiis populi:** In the war between the houses of Saul and David (1 Ki. 19–2 Ki. 4).

exsulare in Hebron . . . regnare in Hierusalem: See 2 Ki. 2: 1–4.

iustitiam etiam his . . . suis praestandum putaret: When he spared the lives of Saul and his men (1 Ki. 24; 26).

fortissimum adversae partis propugnatorem Abner . . . quo suam mortem doleret: David made peace with Abner, Saul's general, in return for the hand of Saul's daughter Michal, who had earlier been betrothed to David (2 Ki. 3: 6–21). A feast was given for Abner and twenty of his men at Hebron (2 Ki. 3: 20). Not long afterwards, Abner was deceitfully killed by Joab in vengeance for the death of Joab's brother Asahel. David mourned Abner's death as an innocent man (2 Ki. 3: 22–39).

34. **alieno periculo cibum non quaerere:** When the child borne to David by Bathsheba was dying, David refused to eat while he pleaded with the Lord for the child's life to be spared, ultimately without success (2 Ki. 12: 15–23).

potum recusare: This probably refers to the time when David refused to drink water from the well of Bethlehem, brought for him at the risk of his chief warriors' lives (2 Ki. 23: 13–17). If so, A. runs together two incidents here (Testard ii. 158 n. 17). Alternatively, he gratuitously adds the detail of David's not drinking to the account of his not eating when praying for his child.

peccatum fateri . . . offerens se diceret: When he had sinned by commissioning a census of his fighting men, and had brought a plague on Jerusalem as punishment, David was confronted by the Angel of the Lord standing with a drawn sword; he prayed for mercy, asking that he and his household be destroyed rather than his people (2 Ki. 24: 1–25; 1 Chr. 21: 1–30).

Ecce sum, ego peccavi. . . . Fiat manus tua in me: 2 Ki. 24: 17; 1 Chr. 21: 17.

35. **dolum meditantibus non aperiebat os suum:** Cf. Pss. 37: 13–15; 38: 3, 9–12.

non respondebat conviciis . . . cum malediceretur, benedicebat: Cf. 1.21, 236–8.

Ambulans in simplicitate: Cf. Prov. 19: 1: *Melior est pauper qui ambulat in simplicitate sua quam torquens labia insipiens*; 20: 7: *Iustus qui ambulat in simplicitate sua beatos post se filios derelinquet.*

sector immaculatorum: Ambulans above triggers a memory of Ps. 118: 1: *Beati immaculati in via, qui ambulant in lege Domini.*

qui cinerem miscebat alimentis suis . . . et potum suum temperabat fletibus: Cf. Ps. 101: 10: *Quia cinerem tamquam panem manducabam, et potum meum cum fletu miscebam.*

Merito sic expetitus est ab universo populo . . . Tu pasces populum meum: 2 Ki. 5: 1–2; 1 Chr. 11: 1–2. The shepherding terminology is apt: David is the ideal pastor.

Inveni David secundum cor meum: Acts 13: 22, a mélange of Ps. 88: 21 and 1 Ki. 13: 14.

Quis enim in sanctitate cordis et iustitia sicut iste ambulavit: Cf. 3 Ki. 3: 6 (Solomon prays): *sicut [David ambulavit in conspectu tuo in veritate, et iustitia, et recto corde tecum*; also 3 Ki. 9: 4.

propter quem . . . praerogativa est reservata heredibus:
Cf. 3 Ki. 11: 9–13; in accordance with the Lord's promise to
David (2 Ki. 7: 12–16), the tribe of Judah remained the
chosen line from which the Messiah ultimately came, despite
the sins of David's descendants.

36. **Quis igitur non diligeret eum . . .? Denique parentes
eum filiis suis:** Probably an allusion to Saul's initial
fondness for David, as noted in 1 Ki. 16: 21: *at ille* [Saul]
dilexit eum nimis; though the OT narrative does not actually
say that Saul preferred David to his son Jonathan. The
references to friendship here and in 2.37 are suggested by
Cic.'s mention of it in *Off.* 2.30–1.

**filii praeferebant parentibus. Unde graviter indignatus
Saul . . . quam vel pietatem vel auctoritatem pater-
nam:** On the affection of Saul's son Jonathan for David, see
1 Ki. 18: 1–4; 20; for Saul's jealous attempt to kill Jonathan
with his spear, see 1 Ki. 20: 24–34.

37. **si quis vicem amantibus reddat . . . quam ipse
amatur:** In 1.160–8, drawing on Cic. *Off.* 1.47–9,
A. advises people to display greater generosity in repaying
a kindness than they were shown when they received it, and
he praises goodwill for its ability to return gratitude even
when the means for material repayment are lacking (cf. Cic.
Off. 2.32). The same idea is present here: return still greater
affection to those who have shown affection to you. The
Ciceronian *amor* and the biblical *caritas* are elided. For
redamare, cf. Cic. *Amic.* 49.

faciat: PMA, Zell, Testard: *fiat* V, Valdarfer: *pateat* E²,
COB, Maurists: *patet* Erasmus (1527): *patent* W.

**Quid tam insitum naturae quam ut diligentem dili-
gas?:** A. goes on to cite Scripture, but he is thinking
particularly of Cic. *Off.* 2.30–2, on forging relationships
with those who love you and esteem your good qualities:
cf. especially *Off.* 2.32: *a natura ipsa diligere cogimur*. Jesus
teaches that to love those who love you is natural and basic
even to 'sinners'; Christians must love their enemies as well:
cf. Lk. 6: 32: *Et si diligitis eos qui vos diligunt, quae vobis est
gratia? Nam et peccatores diligentes se diligunt* (also Mt. 5: 46).
Throughout these paragraphs, A. uses *amari*, *caritas*, and
diligere as synonyms, without making the distinctions often

found in Christian authors; on the dominance of the classical background, see Sauer, 179–83; Pétré, 72–8; and R. T. Otten, '*Amor, caritas,* and *dilectio*: Some Observations on the Vocabulary of Love in the Exegetical Works of St Ambrose', in L. J. Engels *et al.* (eds.), *Mélanges offerts à Mlle. Christine Mohrmann* (Utrecht, 1963), 73–83. On charity as an essential clerical virtue, see Gryson, *Prêtre*, 297–301.

tam inolitum atque impressum: Cf. 2.25, *inolita atque impressa.*

sapiens: Jesus ben Sirach.

Perde pecuniam propter fratrem et amicum: Eccli. 29: 10 (13).

Amicum salutare non erubescam et . . . non me abscondam: Eccli. 22: 25 (31).

Siquidem vitae et immortalitatis medicamentum . . . Ecclesiasticus sermo testatur: Cf. Eccli. 6: 16: *Amicus fidelis medicamentum vitae et immortalitatis*; A. cites the longer Latin version.

in caritate . . . cum apostolus dicat: *Omnia suffert . . . caritas numquam cadit*: 1 Cor. 13: 7–8. On the sentiments here, cf. 3.129.

38. **Ideo David non cecidit quia . . . diligi a subiectis quam timeri maluit:** Cf. Cic. *Off.* 2.29: *Atque in has clades incidimus . . . dum metui quam cari esse et diligi malumus.* Julius Caesar fell and brought the Roman Republic down after him (even if, despite his gloomy language, Cic. in *Off.* still dreamt of its salvation) because power was maintained by intimidation; David survived because he was loved by his subjects.

Timor enim temporalis tutaminis servat excubias, nescit diuturnitatis custodiam: Cf. Cic. *Off.* 2.23: *Malus enim est custos diuturnitatis metus, contraque benevolentia fidelis vel ad perpetuitatem*; 2.25: *Nec vero ulla vis imperii tanta est quae premente metu possit esse diuturna*; also *Phil.* 2.90: *timor non diuturnus magister officii*; and *Phil* 2.112; Sen. *Ep.* 47.18 (Dyck, 394).

Itaque ubi timor decesserit, audacia obrepit: Cf. Cic.' examples of this in 2.25–9.

fidem: Here, and in 2.39 below, the sense is obviousl

Ciceronian. *Fides* is mentioned in the precise context of love versus intimidation in *Off.* 2.23–30; it is also the second of the three ways of winning glory in *Off.* 2.33–4.

39.   ad commendationem . . . caritas . . . fides: Cf. Cic. *Off.* 2.29: *sequitur ut disseramus quibus rebus facillime possimus eam quam volumus adipisci cum honore et fide caritatem*; 2.30: *Certum igitur hoc sit, idque et primum et maxime necessarium, familiaritates habere fidas amantium nos amicorum et nostra mirantium.* Cic. speaks of *caritas* in *Off.* 2.24 and 2.29, and A. is of course treating love as the theme of 2.29–39. Cic. uses the word *commendatio* in *Off.* 2.45–6; A. makes it a substitute for *gloria* in 2.40. On the Pauline overtone, see on 2.29–39.

ut committere se . . . quem pluribus carum adverterint: quem refers grammatically to **adfectui**, but in sense looks back to **tuo**: people naturally commit themselves to *you*, rather than to the quality of your love or affection (Banterle, 205 n. 13).

tamquam influat in animos universorum: Cf. Cic. *Off.* 2.31, cited on 2.29 above.

CHAPTER 8: PRUDENCE AND JUSTICE WIN
POPULAR RESPECT

40.   Duo igitur haec ad commendationem . . . et tertium hoc . . . et iure honorandum putent: Cf. Cic. *Off.* 2.31: *Summa igitur et perfecta gloria constat ex tribus his: si diligit multitudo, si fidem habet, si cum admiratione quadam honore dignos putat.* A. replaces Cic.'s *gloria* with the less presumptuous *commendatio*, which is biblical (see introductory comment on 2.29–39; for another substitution for *gloria*, cf. 2.112) as well as Ciceronian (cf. *Off.* 2.45–6). The classical ideal of social esteem nevertheless remains vitally important. On the three ways to win glory outlined by Cic. in *Off.* 2.31–8, see on 2.29–39. The present paragraph, setting out the three points of (i) *caritas*; (ii) *fides*; and (iii) *admiratio* implies that 2.29–39 has dealt with *both* (i) *and* (ii), but the argument which ensues assumes that *only* (i) has been explained: (ii) follows in 2.41–55, and (iii) in 2.56–67. On the confusion of plans, see on 2.29–39. The pairing of *caritas* and *fides* by Cic. in *Off.* 2.29 (echoed by A. in 2.39), and the references to faith in the context of love elsewhere in Cic. *Off.* 2.23–9, may be partly to blame for A.'s confusion of *Off.* 2.23–9 (from scheme 'B') with *Off.* 2.31–8 (from scheme 'A'). He replaces Cic.'s *benevolentia* (*Off.* 2.32, 38) with *caritas* (from *Off.* 2.24, 29) and mixes up the place of faith in Cic. *Off.* 2.23–9, with the separate point about faith as a way to glory in Cic. *Off.* 2.33–4. The exposition of *fides* occupies 2.41–55 (the word *fides* itself occurs only in 2.41–2 and 2.55); the value of possessing qualities which are counted worthy of *admiratio* is discussed in 2.56–67. Like Cic., A. structures the *fides* theme around the values of prudence and justice. He puts much more stress than Cic. does on the importance of giving reliable advice; doubtless he has an eye to the pastoral realities faced by a clerical body who, like their leader (cf. Aug. *Conf.* 6.3.3), will be continually asked for practical counsel. The significance of *consilium* extends far beyond 2.41–55, in fact. It not only pervades the next main section of the book, on generosity (2.68–85); it also introduces (2.86–9) the ensuing account of other qualities which can be called *utilia*, such as humility, justice, affability, and so on (2.86–151), and affects that account as well (cf. e.g. 2.93–4). The *commendatio* motif continues to appear to the end of the book; it is clearly the controlling idea in the author's mind (see on 2.29–39).

41.   consiliorum usus: Cf. Cic. *Off.* 2.33: *Nam et iis fidem habemus quos plus intellegere quam nos arbitramur quosque et futura prospicere credimus et, cum res agatur in discrimenque ventum sit, expedire rem et consilium ex tempore capere posse; hanc enim utilem homines existimant veramque prudentiam.* The value of *practical* wisdom is again central to A., as it is to Cic. and his predecessors; cf. 1.122–5.

ideo prudentia et iustitia . . . utile consilium ac fidele desideranti dare: [**ea:** MSS and most editors: *eo* Testard; **exspectatur:** PVM, E¹, Testard: *exspectantur* E², Zell *spectatur* CO: *spectantur* Valdarfer] Cf. Cic. *Off.* 2.33 *Fides autem ut habeatur duabus rebus effici potest, si existimabimur adepti coniunctam cum iustitia prudentiam;* 2.34: *prudentia sine iustitia nihil valeat ad faciendam fidem* [etc.]. Or the interdependence of prudence and justice, cf. 1.126–9, 252–3; 3.14; but here *fides* is used in the classical sense.

se committat: Cf. Cic. *Off.* 2.33: *Itaque his salutem nostram, his fortunas, his liberos rectissime committi arbitramur.*

quem non putet plus sapere . . . qui quaerit consilium: See above on Cic. *Off.* 2.33.

42. **auctoritate:** Cic. uses the word in *Off.* 2.34, though differently; see in general Ring, 153–9.

prospiciat futura . . . expediat . . . in tempore . . . ita fides habetur: All close echoes of Cic. *Off.* 2.33; **argumentum expediat** is also reminiscent of Cic.'s *expedire rem* (*Off.* 2.33). Such (typically Roman) intellectual foresight is said to be a mark of courage in 1.188–92; the overlapping character of the virtues is again implicitly in view.

Et si mala mihi evenerint per illum, sustineo: Eccli. 22: 26 [31]; cf. the use of the saying in 1.172; 3.130.

43. **salutem nostram . . . committimus:** Cf. Cic. *Off.* 2.33: *Itaque his* [sc. *iustis et fidis hominibus*] *salutem nostram . . . rectissime committi arbitramur.*

Facit enim iustitia . . . ut nulla erroris suspicio sit: Cf. Cic. *Off.* 2.33: *Iustis autem [et fidis] hominibus, id est bonis viris, ita fides habetur ut nulla sit in iis fraudis iniuriaeque suspicio.* This precise separation of the roles of justice and prudence is Ambrosian, not Ciceronian; but see below on Cic. *Off.* 2.35.

Promptius tamen nos . . . committimus: Cf. Cic. *Off.* 2.34: *Harum igitur duarum ad fidem faciendam iustitia plus pollet, quippe cum ea sine prudentia satis habeat auctoritatis.*

ut secundum usum vulgi loquar: Cf. Cic. *Off.* 2.35: *cum ad opinionem communem omnis accommodatur oratio. Quam ob rem, ut vulgus, ita nos hoc loco loquimur. . . . cum loquimur de opinione populari.* Both Cic. and A. maintain the Stoic principle of the inseparability of the virtues (see on 1.115), but Cic. claims to be following Panaetius (*Off.* 2.35)—who was himself following the lead of Chrysippus (Dyck, 415)— in making a concession to the popular belief that a person might be just without being prudent, or *vice versa*. This is the nuance A. is evoking here.

Denique sapientum definitione . . . nec potest sine iustitia esse prudentia: Cf. Cic. *Off.* 2.35, where it is said that the unity of the virtues is agreed upon *inter omnes philosophos*.

Quod etiam in nostris invenimus: The wisdom of the *sapientes* was, as ever, anticipated in the OT (Introduction IV.2).

Iustus miseretur et fenerat: Ps. 36: 21.

Iucundus vir qui miseretur et fenerat: Ps. 111: 5.

44. Ipsum illud nobile Salomonis iudicium: The 'judgement' of the OT's most celebrated sage (cf. *Luc.* 10.30: *Salomonis illud sublime iudicium*; *Virgt.* 1–3) demonstrates the concurrence of prudence and justice in the giving of advice (2.44–7). A. relates the story accurately from 3 Ki. 3: 16–28. On this paragraph, see 3 Ki. 3: 16–22. Testard, 'Recherches', 99, suggests that here and in 2.51–3 A. incorporates a separate treatment of the episode. However, as in other passages where A. expounds scriptural texts at some length, it is probably better to say that he is repeating familiar interpretative ideas, rather than formally importing independent expository material.

45. See 3 Ki. 3: 22–7.

vindicaret: V², EW, COB: *vindicarent* PV¹MA, Testard.

negaret: V², EW, COB: *negarent* PV¹MA, Testard.

46. Itaque non immerito aestimatus est intellectus Dei in eo esse: Cf. 3 Ki. 3: 28, quoted in 2.47.

Quoniam quae occulta sunt Deo?: Heb. 4: 13, *omnia autem nuda et aperta sunt oculis eius*, is very probably in A.'s mind, since in 2.47 he also echoes Heb. 4: 12.

qua: PVMA, EW, OB, Gering, Testard: *quam* C, Zell: *quia* Valdarfer.

patuit: MA, EW, COB, most editors: *pavit* PV, Testard.

47. et, velut quadam machaera . . . animae et mentis viscera: Solomon's blade is a type of the sword of the Spirit (which is the *verbum Dei*: Eph. 6: 17): cf. Heb. 4: 12: *Vivu est enim Dei sermo, et efficax, et penetrabilior omni gladi ancipiti; et pertingens usque ad divisionem animae ac spiritus compagum quoque et medullarum, et discretor cogitationum e intentionum cordis.* On A.'s spiritual exegesis, see Introduc tion IV.5; for this example, cf. *Spir.* 3.36–8; *Virgt.* 3; *Interp* 4.15. The typology of Solomon-Christ (*verus Salomon*: 2.52 is motivated by Christ's own words in Lk. 11: 31, and is c course very common in Christian preaching, particularly in allegorical interpretations of Ct. (especially Orig. *Comm. Ct.*, influencing A. *Is.*); cf. also e.g. *Apol.* 13; *Apol. alt.* 22–5; *Luc.* 7.96.

Audivit, inquit, omnis Israel hoc iudicium . . . ut faceret iustitiam: 3 Ki. 3: 28.

Denique et ipse Salomon ita poposcit sapientiam . . . et iudicare cum iustitia: See 3 Ki. 3: 9–12; cf. 2 Chr. 1: 7–12; Wisd. 7: 7–15; 8: 17–9: 12.

The emphasis here is consonant with the argument in 1.117, 122–9, 252–3, and throughout: the key to true wisdom is the knowledge of God.

CHAPTER 9: PRUDENCE AND JUSTICE ARE
LINKED

48. **scripturam divinam, quae antiquior est:** The usual stress on the anteriority of the Bible to secular wisdom— albeit the point is the same in both authorities.

quia ubi una earum virtutum, ibi utraque est: Cf. 2.43.

Daniel quoque, quam sapienter . . . innocentem subducere: Daniel saw through the elders' fraudulent charge of adultery against Susanna; her sentence of death was repealed, and the deceivers were put to death: Dan. 13, especially 13: 44–64.

49. **sed vulgi usu dividitur una quaedam forma virtutum:** Cf. Cic. *Off.* 2.35, cited above on 2.43.

ut temperantia sit in despiciendis voluptatibus . . . suum cuique conservans: The definitions of the virtues here are essentially classical, according to the context of the *vulgi usus* or *communis opinio*; cf. 1.115 and see ad loc.

custos . . . et vindex: The words are often paired classically: e.g. Cic. *Agr.* 2.24; *Sest.* 144; *Verr.* 2.5.126; Liv. 2.1.8.

communis opinionis gratia: Cf. Cic. *Off.* 2.35: *cum ad opinionem communem omnis accommodatur oratio.*

ut ab illa subtili disputatione philosophiae . . . quasi ex adyto quodam eruitur: Cf. Cic. *Off.* 2.35: *alia est illa cum veritas ipsa limatur in disputatione subtilitas* (Dyck, 415, reads *subtili* in Cicero, from MS c and from A.). Cic. says that in

popular parlance (which he, like Panaetius, is here imitating)
one person is said to be brave while another is called good or
wise, while the philosophers argue that whoever possesses
one virtue possesses them all. A. implies that the whole
fourfold *divisio* of virtue is a popular rather than a technical
idea. This is a deft move. First, it amounts to a justification
for his discussion of each of the cardinal virtues in turn as a
framework for the *honestum*: he is speaking in ordinary
language (cf. 1.29, 116; 2.8). Secondly, it constitutes another
swipe at pagan wisdom: he can contrast the common-sense
approach of Christian morality with the subtleties of secular
philosophy; cf. 2.8; 3.97, 126. The irony is, of course, that
the *divisio* remains a classical one. *adytum* is a common
Vergilian word (e.g. *Aen*. 2.115, 297, 351, 404, 764; 3.92;
6.98; 7.269); the figurative use is exemplified by Lucr. 1.737,
ex adyto tamquam cordis responsa dedere. A. is fond of it: e.g.
Ex. 6.68; *Noe* 17; *Interp*. 3.19.

retrahentes pedem: Cf. Verg. *Aen*. 10.307: *retrahitque
pedem*.

Hac: V²M, EW, COB, most editors: *haec* PV¹A, Testard.

revertamur ad propositum: [**revertamur:** E¹W, Amerbach: *ut revertamur* PVMA, E², COB, Zell, Testard: ⟨sequi-
tur/decet⟩ *ut revertamur* Winterbottom, 564] Cf. Cic. *Off*.
2.35: *Sed ad propositum revertamur*; *Off*. 3.39: *Sed iam ad
propositum revertamur*).

CHAPTER 10: THE PRUDENT AND JUST GIVER
OF ADVICE

50. Prudentissimo cuique . . . frequenter praeponderat:
Cf. Cic. *Off*. 2.33–4, cited above on 2.43.

Utilia **enim** *vulnera amici quam aliorum oscula*: Prov.
27: 6.

iusti iudicium est: Cf. Prov. 12: 5 (LXX).

calliditas: Cic. uses the comparative adjective *callidior* in
Off. 2.34, but he warns that the quality must be combined
with integrity (cf. also *Off*. 1.62–3; 2.10). The just person has
a certain moral intuition which enables him to give advice
appropriate to the situation; the wise person has the intellec-

tual dexterity to formulate strategies. But a concern to do what is right carries more weight than mere cleverness. Note the use of the technical vocabulary of rhetoric: **iudicium ... argumentum ... disceptationis ... inventionis**.

51.   admiratione: This seems to anticipate the third of the Ciceronian ways to glory listed in 2.40; the discussion proper does not begin until 2.56.

sicut quaerebant omnes reges terrae . . . audire sapientiam eius: Cf. 3 Ki. 10: 24; 2 Chr. 9: 23. A. himself knew a similar fame, according to Paulinus, who tells of learned Persians coming to consult his wisdom (*VA* 25, clearly in evocation of Solomon's example), though his *captatio benevolentiae* to Gratian in *Fid.* 1.1 insists that he is no Solomon, to be consulted by his imperial majesty.

ita ut Saba regina veniret ad eum . . . *nec ullum verbum praeterivit eam*: Cf. 3 Ki. 10: 1–3 (and the whole section 10: 1–13); 2 Chr. 9: 1–2 (and 9: 1–12). The last words of the quotation, ***nec ullum verbum praeterivit eam***, and the explanation of them which follows at the beginning of 2.52, reverse the sense of 3 Ki. 10: 3; 2 Chr. 9: 2 given in the LXX and the Vulg., which is that 'no word eluded *the king*' (hence O¹'s *eum*), not that the queen of Sheba did not miss one of his words. As Testard ii. 161 n. 4, says, Sabatier's VL cites *eam* solely on the basis of A. here.

52.   o homo: Cf. 1.156; also 3.16 (*homo*).

Verus est*, inquit, *sermo quem audivi . . . qui audiunt omnem prudentiam tuam*:** 3 Ki. 10: 6–8; 2 Chr. 9: 5–7. The words ***et viderunt oculi mei are echoed by Simeon in the *Nunc dimittis*: *quia viderunt oculi mei salutare tuum* (Lk. 2: 30), further evidence of an early association of Solomon and Christ. A. mentions Simeon in 2.53.

convivium veri Salomonis: Cf. 1.162–5 for different treatments of the feast of Solomon. Here, Christ is the true Solomon, whose fame stretches even further than the king's, to the ends of the earth.

contemplantibus. . . . Quoniam *quae videntur temporalia sunt, quae autem non videntur aeterna*: 2 Cor. 4: 18.

53.   mulieres, nisi illae: EW, COB, several editors: *mulieres* PVMA¹, Zell, Lignamine, Testard: *mulieres nisi* A².

quia multae verbum Dei audiunt et faciunt: [**faciunt:** Davidson: *pariunt* MSS; Testard i. 161–2 n. 9, tries to defend *pariunt* with reference to A.'s language in *Luc.* 2.26, evoking Lk. 1: 45 (*Et beata quae credidit*): *Sed et vos beati, qui audistis et credidistis: quaecumque enim crediderit anima et concipit et generat Dei verbum et opera eius agnoscit*; but the parallel is not very helpful; the case for emending in the light of Lk. 8: 21 (and the quotation which follows: cf. next note) seems compelling] Cf. Lk. 11: 28: (Jesus speaks): *Quippini beati qui audiunt verbum Dei, et custodiunt*; 8: 21: *Mater mea et fratres mei hi sunt, qui verbum Dei audiunt et faciunt.*

Quicumque enim fecerit . . . et mater est: Mt. 12: 50; also Mk. 3: 35; Lk. 8: 21.

Usque in hunc diem . . . minori ac maiori: Acts 26: 22.

Simeon qui . . . ut videret consolationem Israel: Cf. Lk. 2: 25.

Quomodo enim dimitti posceret . . . nisi voluntatem Domini adeptus esset?: See Lk. 2: 29–32. On being subject to such royal command, cf. *Bon. mort.* 7.

54. **Ioseph quoque . . . quominus de rebus incertis consuleretur:** See Gen. 40–1.

ut non sentiret . . . levaret ieiunio: See Gen. 41: 54–7. Among the 'other peoples' who came to Egypt to buy grain were of course Joseph's brothers.

55. **Daniel . . . adnuntiavit futura:** [**regalium:** V²M², EW, COB, most editors: *gregalium* PV¹?M¹A, Testard] See Dan., *passim*, on the elevation of Daniel from Hebrew captive to interpreter of the dreams of kings Nebuchadnezzar, Belshazzar, and Darius. On **adnuntiavit futura**, see on *prospiciat futura* in 2.42.

vere: PVM, B, Zell, Testard: *vera* A: *veri* EW, CO, Amerbach.

adnuntiatum: PVMA, Zell, Gering, Lignamine, Paderborn, Testard: *adnuntium* EW, COB, other editors.

CHAPTER 11: ADVICE THAT WINS ADMIRATION

56. **Sed etiam tertius locus . . . exemplo decursus videtur:** This is the third Ciceronian way to win glory

(*Off.* 2.36–8), echoed in 2.40 above. It occupies 2.56–67. Cf. Cic. *Off.* 2.36: *Erat igitur ex iis tribus, quae ad gloriam pertinerent, hoc tertium, ut cum admiratione hominum honore ab iis digni iudicaremur.* The illustrations are inevitably biblical: Joseph, Solomon, and Daniel are carried over from the preceding paragraphs, and are joined by Moses.

Nam quid de Moyse loquar . . . consilia praestolabatur?: See especially Ex. 18: 13–16.

Quorum vita . . . admirationemque eius augebat: [**faciebat** (EW, COB) is better than PVMA's *sciebat*, retained by Testard, in view of Cic. *Off.* 2.34: *ad faciendam fidem* (Winterbottom, 564); the reading of editors such as Zell and Valdarfer (*et al.*), *sociabat*, makes little sense] A combination of the second and the third Ciceronian points mentioned by A. in 2.40: *fides* and *admiratio*. These further haphazard allusions to the Ciceronian headings indicate the patchy recollection with which A. is working. **Quorum** is loose: it is Moses who is in view, but the connecting relative also embraces the other heroes just mentioned.

cui seniores . . . diiudicanda servabant: See Ex. 18: 13–27, especially 18: 26. The illustration is biblical; the language is suggested by Cic. *Off.* 2.33: *Nam et iis fidem habemus, quos plus intellegere quam nos arbitramur*; 2.37: *Admiratione autem afficiuntur ii, qui anteire ceteris virtute putantur.*

57. **Quis Daniele sapientior?:** Ezek. 28: 3; the precise relationship between the Daniel of this verse (cf. also Ezek. 14: 14) and the hero of Dan. is in fact somewhat unclear, but to A. his identity is straightforward.

eorum: The biblical characters in 2.56.

Moysi consilio bella conficiebantur: See e.g. Ex. 17: 8–16; Num. 31: 1–54; and cf. Cic. *Off.* 1.79: *in quo non minorem utilitatem afferunt, qui togati rei publicae praesunt, quam qui bellum gerunt. Itaque eorum consilio saepe aut non suscepta aut confecta bella sunt, non numquam etiam illata*: Cic.'s comments about the worth of advice from *togati* (those in civilian politics as opposed to military life) are applied to Moses.

de caelo adfluebat alimonia: See on 2.13.

potus e petra: See Ex. 17: 1–7; cf. also Num. 20: 2–13.

58. **Quam purus Danielis animus, ut . . . mitigaret**

leones!: Daniel twice escaped the mouths of lions: Dan. 6: 1–28; 14: 23–42.

Quae in illo temperantia . . . continentia: See e.g. Dan. 1: 8–16.

Nec immerito mirabilis . . . nec delatum sibi honorem plus faciebat quam fidem: See e.g. Dan. 6: 3–5; in this case, Daniel enjoyed the favour of Darius.

vehementer: Cic., *Off*. 2.37, uses *vehentissime*, though negatively.

aurum non quaerebat: See Dan. 6: 4–5.

honorem: Cic. uses the word in this context in *Off*. 2.29, 31, 36.

fidem: The sense of the word here is religious, rather than the Ciceronian 'good faith' which has been dominant in recent paragraphs, since A. goes on to say that Daniel was ready to endanger himself **pro lege Domini**. He was thrown into the lions' den for worshipping the Lord only (Dan. 6: 5; 14: 24); note also his scruple about eating pagan food (Dan. 1: 8). Daniel exemplified the very virtues highlighted by Cic. in *Off*. 2.36–8: he was free from sensual *voluptates*; he was a man of integrity; he looked down on riches; and he had no fear of death. All of these are the kind of qualities which win *admiratio*. His motivation for being prepared to endanger himself was not, however, the winning of human esteem: it was devotion to God's law.

59. **castimonia et iustitia quid dicam? Quarum . . . refutavit praemia:** [**Quarum:** V²A, EW, COB, most editors: *quam* PV¹M, Testard] On Joseph's resistance of the wiles of Potiphar's wife, see on 2.20. As with Daniel in 2.58, A. is careful to mention Joseph's sexual purity. He is thinking particularly of Cic.'s language about the rejection of *voluptates* in *Off*. 2.37—and, of course, of his own ideal of chastity.

altera mortem contempsit . . . carcerem praeoptavit: Cic. says that contempt for death elicits admiration (*Off*. 2.37), and the man who is just has no fear of death, pain, exile, or need (*Off*. 2.38). The character that attracts *admiratio* epitomizes all the cardinal virtues. His prudence and justice are obvious; his rejection of sensual pleasures requires temperance; and his contempt for monetary gain and for death itself reflects courage. We are back with the Stoic snapshot of 2.49; see also on 1.200. For another such summary of Joseph, cf. 2.84.

temporis sterilitatem . . . fecundavit: See on 2.54; the agricultural language is aptly transferred to the description of the effects of Joseph's advice.

CHAPTER 12: THE GIVER OF ADVICE MUST BE
BOTH UPRIGHT AND APPROACHABLE

60.   vitae probitas: Cic. refers to *probitas* in *Off.* 2.34; on the necessity for integrity generally, cf. *Off.* 2.36–8. On the character of the giver of advice in 2.60–7, cf. 2.86–92 below.
virtutum praerogativa: Cf. Cic. *Off.* 2.36: *Itaque eos viros suscipiunt maximisque efferunt laudibus, in quibus existimant se excellentes quasdam et singulares perspicere virtutes*; 2.37: *Admiratione autem afficiuntur ii, qui anteire ceteris virtute putantur.*
benevolentiae usus: *Benevolentia* is Cic.'s first means of acquiring glory (*Off.* 2.32, 38), which A. conflates with the theme of love versus fear in 2.29–39.
Quis enim in caeno fontem requirat? . . . Quis non despiciat morum colluvionem?: Cic. uses the image of a *fons* in a different context in *Off.* 2.52, *fontem ipsum benignitatis exhaurit*, but the imagery is fundamentally scriptural: e.g. Prov. 10: 11; 13: 14; 14: 27; 16: 22; 25: 26; Eccli. 21: 16 (*Scientia sapientis tamquam inundatio abundabit, et consilium illius sicut fons vitae permanet*); Jas. 3: 11–12. Note the rhetorical texture of this and the following paragraphs.
luxuria . . . vitiorum confusio: Cf. Cic.'s warning against sensual *vitia* in *Off.* 2.37.
Quis utilem . . . quem videt inutilem suae vitae?: Cf. Cic. *Off.* 2.36: *contemnuntur ii, qui 'nec sibi nec alteri', ut dicitur* (alluding to Hes. *Op.* 293–7, especially 296–7).
Quis iterum improbum . . . omni studio declinet?: Cf. Cic. *Off.* 2.36: *Nam quos improbos, maledicos, fraudulentos putant et ad faciendam iniuriam instructos, eos contemnunt quidem neutiquam, sed de iis male existimant.*

61.   Quis vero, quamvis instructum . . . difficili tamen accessu ambiat?: On A.'s own accessibility, see on 1.88. His advice in 1.85–9 is that the clergy must show their modesty and integrity by keeping away from dangerous company and letting those who require their presence come to them (especially 1.88), but this must not mean that they hide themselves from people who need their counsel.

The water-imagery is continued from 2.60: **in quo sit illud tamquam si qui aquae fontem praecludat . . . Si consulendi intercludas copiam . . . clausisti fontem, ut nec aliis influat nec tibi prosit:** Cf. Cic. *Off.* 2.36, cited above on 2.60.

62.   commaculat eam vitiorum sordibus: Cf. Cic. *Off.* 2.37.

eo quod aquae exitum contaminet: Further water-imagery.

Degeneres animos vita arguit: An adaptation of Verg. *Aen.* 4.13: *degeneres animos timor arguit.* Cf. also Tac. *Ann.* 4.38.4.

Quomodo enim potes eum iudicare . . . quem videas inferiorem moribus?: The whole argument here is similar to that of Cic. in *Off.* 2.36–8, though Cic. does not relate the *admiratio* theme to the subject of *consilium.*

cuius animum voluptates occupent, libido devincat: Cf. Cic. *Off.* 2.37, on *voluptates, blandissimae dominae* (and cf., on Epicureanism, *Off.* 3.117).

avaritia subiuget, cupiditas perturbet: On freedom from greed, cf. Cic. *Off.* 2.37–8.

quatiat metus: Cic. mentions fear of *dolorum . . . faces* in *Off.* 2.37, and in *Off.* 2.38 he speaks of fear of death, pain, exile, and need.

consilio: C: *consilii* most MSS and editors.

ubi nullus quieti: In effect, a sort of Stoic ἀπάθεια is prescribed; see on *tranquillitas* in 1.90; and cf. *Iac.* 2.28–9.

63.   Admirandus mihi . . . offensus abstulit: [suspiciendus: P¹V¹M, E¹W², COB, Amerbach, Testard: *suscipiendus* P²V²A, E²W¹, Zell] Cf. Is. 3: 1–3. The removal of men who could give sound advice was a sign of God's judgement upon his people; when they were available, it was a mark of his favour. **Admirandus** bridges the Ciceronian theme with the scriptural language. On **patribus**, see Introduction IV.4.

nihil inquinatum in illam incurrit: Wisd. 7: 25.

CHAPTER 13: THE BEAUTY OF WISDOM

64. Quis igitur tamquam vultu speciem praeferat pulchritudinis . . . et specialiter pulchritudo sapientiae?: Cf. Cic. *Off.* 2.37: *tum quis non admiretur splendorem pulchritudinemque virtutis?* The language is also somewhat similar to that of Cic. *Off.* 3.32 (on 'amputating' or expelling diseased or tyrannical members from the 'body' of humanity): *sic ista in figura hominis feritas et immanitas beluae a communi tamquam humanitate corporis segreganda est* (cf. also *Rep.* 2.48). Combining the beauty of a human face with the lower parts of an animal, as in hybrid mythological creatures like the sirens, centaurs, scyllas, or Triton, is ridiculous and grotesque, because it lacks verisimilitude; cf. especially Hor. *AP* 1–5 (with C. O. Brink, *Horace on Poetry: The 'Ars Poetica'* (Cambridge, 1971), 85–6). On the superiority of the human body (*forma*) to the bodies of beasts, cf. *Ex.* 6.54; *Inst. virg.* 20; *Expos. Ps. 118.*10.6; on the absurdity of humans adopting bestial ways (by following an Epicurean *voluptas* ideal), cf. *Ep. extra coll.* 14 [63].23.

et specialiter pulchritudo sapientiae: Wisdom, as supreme among the virtues (1.252–3), is pre-eminent in beauty (contrast the primacy of justice in Cic. *Off.* 2.38). As Testard ii. 165 n. 3 says, A. assumes in these paragraphs the biblical tradition's own synthesis between divine Wisdom personified and human moral Wisdom personified. This link is of course basic to the refrain that the knowledge of God is the way to wisdom.

series scripturae: Cf. 3.139, on the treatise as a *series . . . vetustatis*, drawn from biblical *exempla*.

Est enim haec speciosior sole . . . sapientiam autem non vincit malitia: Wisd. 7: 29–30.

65. scripturae testimonio comprobavimus. Superest ut doceamus scripturae auctoritate: A typical appeal to

scriptural authority; cf. 1.151, and see generally Introduction
IV.5.

Cuius spiritus est disertus . . . omnia prospiciens:
Wisd. 7: 22–3.

Sobrietatem docet et iustitiam et virtutem: Wisd. 8: 7,
a famous evocation of the cardinal virtues in the Wisdom
tradition.

CHAPTER 14: PRUDENCE IS LINKED TO ALL
OTHER VIRTUES, ESPECIALLY TO THE
DESPISING OF RICHES

66. **prudentia:** A. returns to the usual Ciceronian term, after
the biblical quotations speaking of *sapientia* in 2.65.
Nam quomodo potest utile . . . nisi habeat iustitiam:
Cf. Cic. *Off.* 2.34, on the essential link between prudence
and justice here.
**ut . . . mortem non reformidet . . . nullo revocetur
metu:** Cf. Cic. *Off.* 2.38: *nemo enim iustus esse potest qui
mortem, qui dolorem, qui exsilium, qui egestatem timet.*
nulla adulatione a vero deflectendum putet: See on
1.209.
exsilium non refugiat . . . egestatem non timeat: Cf.
Cic. *Off.* 2.38, above.
quae noverit sapienti patriam mundum esse: A celebrated Stoic maxim, on the wise man as 'cosmopolitan'; it is
attributed first to Socrates (Plu. *Exil.* 600e–601b; Cic. *Tusc.*
5.108): cf. e.g. Sen. *Ep.* 28.4; *Helv.* 9.7; in A., *Ep.* 34 [45].16.
cui totus mundus divitiarum est: See on 1.118; and cf.
3.7.
**qui auro moveri nesciat, contemptum habeat pecu-
niarum:** Cf. Cic. *Off.* 2.38: *Maximeque admirantur eum qui
pecunia non movetur* (also *Off.* 2.37); see also on 1.23.
**et velut ex arce quadam despiciat hominum cupidi-
tates:** See on 1.192, and cf. Cic. *Off.* 2.37: *Quae qui in
utramque partem excelso animo magnoque despiciunt*; 2.38:
haec animi despicientia. See also on 1.23.
Quod qui fecerit . . . supra hominem esse arbitrantur:
Cf. Cic. *Off.* 2.38: *quod in quo viro perspectum sit, hunc ign.*

spectatum arbitrantur. Note also *Expos. Ps. 118.8.15*: *Quam magnum contemnere divitias; sed quam rarum hoc ipsum est!* The characterization of justice throughout this paragraph is strongly reminiscent of aspects of the presentation of courage in book 1; cf. 1.181–95. The influence is directly Ciceronian: the role of justice in *Off*. 2.37–8 evokes that of courage in *Off*. 1. A.'s ideal is undeniably Stoic in colour: the cleric is to pattern himself on this virtually superhuman model of detachment and self-sufficiency; there is no mention here of the dynamic of grace which might make such feats possible; cf. 2.10–21.

Quis est, inquit, et laudabimus eum? Fecit enim mirabilia in vita sua: Eccli. 31: 9.

qui divitias spernit, quas plerique saluti propriae praetulerunt: A Christian slant is given to the Stoic language. Cf. Cic. *Off*. 2.38: [sc. *admiratio*] *quod eas res spernit et neglegit ad quas plerique inflammati aviditate rapiuntur*. To Cic., most people are preoccupied with external attractions such as wealth, and so do not attain the sage's inner contentment in his virtue. To A., the majority are taken up with the pursuit of riches at the expense of their eternal salvation; cf. 1.28–9, 59, 241–5; 2.15–16, 26.

67. qui honore praestet: See on 2.58.

et pecuniis serviat qui praeest liberis: Slavery to money is seen as a real possibility. The idea that the ostensibly free person can be morally enslaved is biblical (e.g. Jn. 8: 34; Rom. 6: 14–23; 2 Pt. 2: 19); A. also espouses the Stoic principle that the wise man is free, regardless of his circumstances, whereas the fool is in bondage to his vices: e.g. *Abr*. 2.79; *Iac*. 2.12; *Ios*. 20; *Nab*. 28; *Expl. Ps. 36*.16; *Expl. Ps. 45*.16–17; and especially *Ep*. 7 [37]. On the synthesis of the two ideas, see Klein, 17–27; also Faust, 25–30, 52–5, 82–97, 120–9. **qui praeest liberis** seems at first more suited to a political than an ecclesiastical readership, more Ciceronian than Ambrosian. But of course a very real measure of power is invested in the church's officials, in teaching authority and in the exercise of discipline, as well as in the settling of civil disputes (see Ring, 196–220), and essentially A. sees his clerical readers as a new class of governors, charged with giving direction and wise counsel to a free society which looks to them for moral and social guidance.

primario viro: A classical élitism intrudes, albeit in the context of Christian *humilitas*; the criteria of classical *admiratio* may be inverted, but A. no less than Cic. is envisaging the formation of a select corps who can take their place on the foremost social stage.

cum Tyriis negotiatoribus et Galaaditis mercatoribus: Traders from two of the most renowned mercantile centres of antiquity. Phoenician Tyre was famed as a financial centre and for trade in textiles (above all, the purple cloth stained with dye extracted from local shellfish), slaves, and white marble (cf. e.g. Is. 23: 2, 8; Ezek. 26–8; Hor. *Od.* 3.29.60; and see generally H. J. Katzenstein, *The History of Tyre* (Jerusalem, 1973)). On the mores of Tyrian merchants, cf. *Elia* 69–76. Gilead, in Transjordan, provided spices, balm, myrrh, and other medicinal plants; it was well known also for its goats and its timber (cf. e.g. Gen. 37: 25; and A. *Ios.* 17; see generally M. Ottosson, 'Gilead', *ABD* ii. 1020–2).

turpis lucri cupidinem: Cf. Tit. 1: 7; also 1 Tim. 3: 8; Tit. 1: 11; 1 Pt. 5: 2; and 3.72 below.

et tamquam mercenario munere . . . calculari compendia: See on 1.185; 1.243; and cf. 2.25–6; 3.37, 57, 65 for the typically scathing depiction of commercial activities.

CHAPTER 15: GENEROSITY AS A WAY TO
POPULARITY: THE RANSOM OF PRISONERS

2.68–85 is on another of Cic.'s *utilia*: obtaining the support and esteem of others through generosity (*Off.* 2.52–85). Cic. divides this into generosity of a financial kind (*Off.* 2.52–64) and generosity demonstrated by service to individuals and to the community at large (*Off.* 2.65–85). A. does not observe this clear-cut distinction, but covers various types of generosity both in this section and later (such as hospitality in 2.103–8, and kindness versus prodigality in 2.109–11); 2.69–75 describes some of these. 2.76–85 argues that it is necessary to maintain measure in giving so as to avoid both miserliness and prodigality that are alike *inutilis*. A. is applying the classical emphases on casuistry and on observing the golden mean to the realities of the social circumstances faced by his addressees. Church officials were continually plagued by the requests of charlatans (2.76–7), but, on the other hand, people were loath to give their money to *dispensatores* if these men appeared so careful that they could be suspected of keeping funds for their own use (2.78). The shining exemplar of wise generosity is Joseph (2.79–85).

68. quanto illud praestantius, si . . . liberalitate acquiras: Cf. Cic. *Off.* 2.32: *quae* [sc. *benevolentia*] *quidem capitur beneficiis maxime. Vehementer autem amor multitudinis commovetur ipsa fama et opinione liberalitatis beneficentiae.* A. is again conflating Ciceronian sections: this language comes from Cic.'s description of the first of the three ways to win popularity by glory (see on 2.40), not from his discussion of generosity.

neque superflua . . . neque restricta: Cf. Cic. *Off.* 2.55: *Quam ob rem nec ita claudenda est res familiaris ut eam benignitas aperire non possit, nec ita reseranda ut pateat omnibus.* On **importunos**, see on 1.159, and cf. 2.77.

69. verum etiam his, qui publice egere verecundantur . . . non exhauriatur: See on 1.148; and cf. 1.158; 2.77. In *Off.* 2.61–3 and 2.69–71, Cic. argues that individual cases calling for financial help must be treated differently. The unfortunate, and people who are of good character but not necessarily of any means, must come first, unless they deserve their misfortune. In *Off.* 2.54 he speaks of the needy who are *idonei homines* to receive aid. Cic. *Off.* 2.52 has *exhaurit*.

ut si officium sacerdotis gerat . . . ad inopiae necessitatem redactum: A priest or archdeacon (the *dispensator* was directly appointed by the bishop to oversee local administrative business, and especially to act as almoner: cf. 2.78; and generally Jer. *Ep.* 125.15.2; Isid. Pelus. *Ep.* 1.29; Con. Carth. (398), *can.* 17; Leo *Ep.* 111.2: see Gryson, *Prêtre*, 143 n. 56) should bring to the attention of his bishop the names of people who have fallen into need through some calamity such as robbery or the loss of an inheritance, when these people are too embarrassed to seek assistance openly; cf. *Const Apost.* 2.32.

maxime si non effusione adulescentiae: In *Off.* 2.54,
Cic. speaks of those who *effuderunt* their inheritance, though
as a result of indiscriminate giving, not through luxury (cf.
also *Phil.* 3.3). The equation of extravagance with youth is
reminiscent of the spendthrift young men of Roman comedy,
such as in Ter. *Ad.*; and A. goes on to echo this genre; cf. also
on 1.244.

sumptum exercere: Cf. Ter. *Heaut.* 143: *sumptum exer-
cirent suom*, also alluded to in *Nab.* 15; *Ep.* 17 [81].2; *Interp.*
1.6.

70. **Summa etiam liberalitas captos redimere:** Cf. Cic.
Off. 2.55: *liberales autem qui suis facultatibus . . . captos a
praedonibus redimunt*; 2.63: *Atque haec benignitas etiam reipublicae est utilis, redimi e servitute captos.* The ransom of
prisoners of war was a very real issue in an empire continually troubled by barbarian incursions: cf. e.g. Cypr. *Ep.*
62; Lact. *Inst.* 6.12.16, 39; *Const. Apost.* 4.2 [*Didasc.* 18];
5.1–2; Aug. *Enchir.* 72; Possid. *Vita Aug.* 24; and see further
C. Osiek, 'The Ransom of Captives: Evolution of a Tradition', *HThR* 74 (1981), 365–86. A. sees no need to justify it
scripturally (cf. indirectly, Lk. 4: 18–19, quoting Is. 61: 1–2),
since there is already an established Christian tradition; he
simply urges it upon his clerics as an important work of
Christian charity; cf. *Expos. Ps. 118*.8.41: *Redime captivos, et
solvisti vincula tua*; also *Epp.* 68 [26].6; 73 [18].16; Paul. *VA*
38 (M. Pavan, 'Sant'Ambrogio e il problema dei barbarici',
Romano-barbarica 3 (1978), 167–87, at 170–3). He does
however go on to defend his own controversial disposal of
sacred vessels as currency, in response to criticism from
homoian opponents (2.136–43). Over the fifth and sixth
centuries, the practice was recognized in law as an ecclesiastical right; see Jones iii. n. 73 on 854; Biondi ii. 241–9, and on
2.136 below). Beneath it all lay the engrained assumptions of
a patronal society: the conferring of this charitable *beneficium*
(like every other) brought the recipients under the social
patronage of their episcopal benefactor (see generally R. P.
Saller, *Personal Patronage under the Early Empire* (Cambridge, 1982), 22–39).

et maxime feminas turpitudini: A Christian moral point
is added: the salvation of women's virginity is a prominent

objective in the ransom of prisoners: cf. 2.136, 138; Aug. *CD* 1.16 ff.; *Ep.* 111.7, 9 (other texts in H. Leclercq, 'Captifs', *DACL* ii/2. 2112–27). Such females were often reduced to *lupanaria*: cf. e.g. Tert. *Apol.* 50.12; *Pudic.* 1.14; Cypr. *Ep.* 62.2.3; *Mort.* 15; Hippol. *In Dan.* 4.51; Greg. Thaum. *Ep. can.* 1; Euseb. Caes. *HE* 8.12.3 ff.; 8.14.14 ff. (F. Augar, *Die Frau in römischen Christenprocess* (Leipzig and Berlin, 1905)). Very probably a number of the virgins brought to the church of Milan from areas such as North Africa (*Virg.* 1.59) were just such prisoners (McLynn, 67–8).

redimere parentibus liberos, parentes liberis: Children often sought themselves to buy back their parents, according to *Ep.* 7 [37].13.

Nota sunt haec nimis Illyrici vastitate et Thraciae: Following the rout of the Eastern Roman forces and the death of Valens at Adrianople on 9 August 378, the Goths swiftly ravaged Thrace, Moesia, and Illyricum, and conducted raids right up to the foot of the Julian Alps, causing considerable destruction and much loss of life. Many Illyrian refugees reached Italy (*Ep.* 36 [2].27–8); if Valentinian II and his mother Justina arrived in Milan late in 378, as most scholars have believed, they were fugitives themselves (McLynn, 122, disputes this, and dates their arrival to the winter of 380–1, arguing that they would have been unlikely to leave Sirmium so long as the Western army was there to offer them protection; it is possible, however, that they were moved at Gratian's instigation as a temporary precautionary measure: Williams, 139). A. presents the devastation as a divine judgement on the Arian (homoian) faith that was so entrenched in the Danubian provinces; Italy had been spared because of her orthodoxy (*Fid.* 2.139–43; cf. *Ep.* 36 [2].28). Cf. also *Luc.* 10.10; Jer. *Ep.* 60.16; *Comm. Ezech.* 2, praef. On Adrianople and its aftermath, cf. Amm. 31.12–17; Zos. 4.24.1–2; Socr. *HE* 4.38; 5.2; Soz. *HE* 6.39–40; 7.2.1; Theod. *HE* 4.33–7; and see T. S. Burns, *Barbarians within the Gates of Rome: A Study of Roman Military Policy and the Barbarians, ca. 375–425 AD* (Bloomington and Indianapolis, IN, 1994), 1–42. McLynn, 55 n. 11, maintains that the ravages referred to need not have *followed* Adrianople, since there were prisoners to be ransomed in Illyricum from at least 374. This is true (and so caution is necessary in using the present passage as a firm cue for dating *Off.*); nevertheless, Adrianople made the situation far worse, so it remains likely that the bulk of A.'s 'purchases' were made after the battle.

unius provinciae numerum explere non possint?: Clearly several thousand individuals are in view, but the context is in any case exaggerated, with **toto . . . orbe,** above. **Fuerunt tamen qui . . . inviderent alienam misericordiam:** The homoian community at Milan, which strongly criticized A. for breaking up and selling church plate in order to redeem some of the captives; cf. 2.136–43. The detail confirms the open hostility faced by A. in the late 370s, and his reference to it indicates his determination to respond to lingering criticism. According to 2.136, the homoians were not really opposed to the bishop's action in principle; they simply wanted an excuse to attack him—and still, in the late 380s, he sees a need (or an opportunity) to justify his behaviour. A great deal of A.'s anti-Arian polemic involved the claim that Arianism was synonymous with barbarism— an argument obviously designed to appeal to instinctive racial prejudices. The Goths had been in contact with Christian influences since at least the 250s (when they had taken clergy and other believers prisoner in their raids on Cappadocia: Philost. *HE* 2.5). In addition to the impact of a half-century and more of missionary activity, pioneered most famously by the veteran bishop Ulfila (see E. A. Thompson, *The Visigoths in the Time of Ulfila* (Oxford, 1966), 94–132 P. J. Heather and J. F. Matthews, *The Goths in the Fourth Century* (Liverpool, 1991), 133–53), Gothic Christianity was extended when the Tervingi formally embraced the faith as part of their admission to Thrace by Valens in 376 (see P. J Heather, 'The Crossing of the Danube and the Gothic Conversion', *GRBS* 27 (1986), 289–318). In both cases the influences were firmly homoian, and homoian Arianism would in time become intrinsic to the Goths' ethnic character. A. can refer to the gospel's expansion into Gothic territory (*Luc.* 10.14; cf. 2.37); nevertheless, his habit is t paint the ravages of the 370s as the work of the worst pagan brutes (2.71,136), and as the crimes of the wicked Gog c

Ezek. 38–9 and Apoc. 20: 8 (*Fid.* 2.137–8), whose atrocities may signal the final tribulation before the end of the world (*Luc.* 10.10; cf. 10.14); cf. C. Corbellini, 'Ambrogio e i barbari: giudizio o pregiudizio?', *RSCI* 31 (1977), 343–53.

Part of the Arian argument in criticism of A.'s lavish expenditure on the captives had perhaps been that the Gothic troops would treat their prisoners humanely, because of the spread of Christianity among them (cf. Aug. *CD* 1.1–7, exaggeratedly praising the clemency shown later by Alaric's troops at the sack of Rome). Such a claim had clearly not been borne out by the Goths' actual behaviour, and it suits A. to associate his homoian accusers with the evils of these barbarian forces: so much for the Arians' Christianity, when they begrudge mercy even to innocent sufferers (cf. 2.137). A further vital twist to the innuendo here and in 2.136–43 is that there were Goths *among* A.'s homoian opponents in Milan. After the Gothic peace with Theodosius in 382 (see P. J. Heather, *Goths and Romans 332–489* (Oxford, 1991), 157–65) some of the Goths performed military service for Rome, both as individual recruits and as *foederati*. Milan had a number of Gothic officers; some were doubtless attracted westwards by the financial incentives of service for Valentinian; others may well have been part of a bodyguard which Justina had brought with her from Pannonia. A. had made no attempt to convert them, but had left them to their homoian beliefs; they met in a 'wagon' (*plaustrum*) for their church, apparently in the company of other settlers (*Ep.* 76 [20].12, referring to people formerly living in wagons); cf. A.'s advice to Constantius of Claterna (in early 379) to inoculate his congregation against the heresy of Arian refugees who had settled in his area, and his warning against automatic acceptance of their professions of faith: *Ep.* 36 [2].27–9. After the passing of the infamous law of 23 January 386 granting freedom of worship to homoians (*CTh* 16.1.4), probably drafted by Auxentius of Durostorum, a former protégé of Ulfila's, Gothic *tribuni* are mentioned as being among the forces ranged against A. in Milan during the Easter crisis (cf. *Ep.* 76 [20].9; cf. 16, 20–1, where they are described as worse than heathen). A. has now emerged from this *débâcle*, but as well as defending his own actions in disposing of church property he is also taking a swipe at some of his most troublesome opponents: the local homoians, reinforced by Gothic incomers, represent, together with the barbarians, an evil alliance of foes ranged against the gospel. The local Arians' hostility to the display of episcopal charity to the needy confirms that they are as wicked as the marauding thugs to the East.

Ipsi si in captivitatem venissent, servirent liberi? Si venditi fuissent, servitutis ministerium non recusarent?: The sense is rather obscure. The translation tentatively adopts the suggestion of Winterbottom, 564, that the clauses should be punctuated as questions (though the Latin is still fairly peculiar): 'If they had ended up in slavery themselves, would they be happy to behave like slaves, free men that they are? If they had been sold, would they not be refusing to serve as slaves too?' A. is then challenging his critics: if *they* had been taken prisoner themselves, would they be willing to submit to it meekly? Surely not; yet this is what they expect others to do.

A. says in 2.137 that he 'put the matter to the people' at the time (a measure of how controversial his behaviour apparently was—episcopal demagoguery was deployed to justify it): the rhetoric here, as in 2.136–43, may well amount to a paraphrase of some of the language of his address.

Et volunt alienam libertatem rescindere . . . sed redimitur: Even more opaque. The idea may be that the homoians are themselves spiritually enslaved, and are unable (at least while they persist in their wilful opposition to the bishop and his theology?) to do anything about it. The ironical (?) concession from **nisi forte** onwards is extremely obscure, especially since it is an *emptor* who is said to receive the potential payment, rather than a *vendor*, as we might surely expect. I suspect a possible 'in' joke at the homoians' expense. Is their devotion pictured as something that is potentially 'for sale' to the highest bidder (patronage a court?); and if so, is the point then that such prostitution implies only a change of masters, not an end to their servile condition (they would simply be 'redeemed' from one state of slavery to enter another)? Our inability to pin down th actual chronological context of the dispute frustrates the task of guessing at the sense more closely. Most translators have chosen to pass over the problem in silence. The puzzle of what A. means may well persist.

71. et maxime . . . qui nihil deferat humanitatis ad misericordiam: See on 1.144; 2.136; 3.84; and cf. *Ex.* 2.12 (*ferae gentes*); 3.22 (*barbaricus furor*).

nisi quod avaritia reservaverit ad redemptionem: The Latin is again quite compressed, but the sense seems to be that the barbarians spare some of their prisoners from further atrocities only out of **avaritia**, in that they have a view to the profit they might make from the receipt of ransom-money for (more or less unscathed?) captives (**ad redemptionem**).

aes alienum subire, si debitor solvendo non sit: Cf. Cic. *Off.* 2.55: *aes alienum suscipiunt amicorum*. Cic. speaks of helping out friends who are in debt; A. does not confine the practice to friends (cf. 1.253).

pupillos tueri: See on 1.63.

72. Sunt etiam qui virgines orbatas parentibus . . . sumptu adiuvent: Cf. Cic. *Off.* 2.55: *in filiarum conlocatione adiuvant*. Cic. commends those who help to provide dowries for the daughters of impoverished friends; A. is more concerned to safeguard the chastity of young women who have been orphaned. Since it is better for them to be married than debauched, money may be used for this end.

Est etiam illud genus liberalitatis: Cf. Cic.'s use of *genera* in *Off.* 2.55, and of *genere* in *Off.* 2.72.

Si quis fidelis habet viduas . . . sufficiat: 1 Tim. 5: 16; and see on 1.248.

73. viri boni: Cf. Cic. *Off.* 1.20; 2.38, 63; 3.70, 75–7, on the importance of the quality of justice to the description of a person as 'good'.

tenues: Cic. uses the word in *Off.* 2.63 and 2.70.

idonei: The word appears, though in different contexts, in Cic. *Off.* 2.54 and 2.62.

Est enim duplex liberalitas . . . quae operum collatione impenditur: Cf. Cic. *Off.* 2.52: *cuius* [sc. *beneficentiae ac liberalitatis*] *est ratio duplex; nam aut opera benigne fit indigentibus aut pecunia*; and see on 2.68–85.

multo frequenter splendidior multoque clarior: Cf. Cic. *Off.* 2.52: *sed illa lautior ac splendidior et viro forti claroque dignior.* A. shares Cic.'s greater esteem for personal service compared with financial help. Cic. argues that monetary assistance is easier, especially for a rich man, whereas personal service costs *virtus* as well as money (*Off.* 2.52). A.'s preference for *opera* is doubtless motivated particularly by Christian ideas of good works, and fits with his general depreciation of money.

74. **Quanto illustrius Abraham . . . quam si redemisset!:** See Gen. 14, especially 14: 12–16. Abraham took up arms rather than agreeing to hand over money for Lot. The point here is obviously different from that in 2.70–1. On **armis victricibus**, cf. Verg. *Aen.* 3.54: *victriciaque arma.*

   Quanto utilius regem Pharaonem sanctus Ioseph . . . quam si contulisset pecuniam!: See on 2.54.

   per quinquennium: Gen. 41 says that the famine lasted for seven, not five, years, and some editors, like Banterle, have quite reasonably emended the text to *per septennium*, supported by E. The Maurist editors defend the MSS' reading on the basis of Gen. 41: 53–6, which states that the Egyptians survived the first two years of the seven-year famine by living on grain privately stored up in the preceding fruitful period, only seeking the help of Joseph and his granaries once the famine had begun to take hold (PL 16. 130 n. 77). **per quinquennium** might be better defended on the basis of Gen. 45: 6, where Joseph says to his brothers that two years of famine have now passed but *five years* of dearth are still to come (Testard ii. 167 n. 16). In 2.54 and 2.83, A. correctly states that Joseph staved off seven years of famine in all.

75. **Facile autem pecunia consumitur, consilia exhauriri nesciunt:** Cf. Cic. *Off.* 2.52: *largitioque, quae fit ex re familiari, fontem ipsum benignitatis exhaurit.* On **consilia**, see on 2.40.

   atque ipsam destituit benignitatem, ut . . . pauciores adiuves: Cf. Cic. *Off.* 2.52: *Ita benignitate benignitas tollitur qua quo in plures usus sis, eo minus in multos uti possis.* Jerome also evokes this phrase in *Ep.* 58.7.1. Lact. *Inst.* 6.11.9–10 misunderstands Cic., taking him to be against generosity, and strongly criticizes him.

alii: PVMA: *aliis* EW, COB.

Consilii autem operisque collatio . . . et in suum fontem recurrit: Cf. Cic. *Off.* 2.53: *At qui opera, id est virtute et industria, benefici et liberales erunt, . . . quo pluribus profuerint, eo plures ad benigne faciendum adiutores habebunt.* Cic. has *fontem* in *Off.* 2.52, above.

et quo pluribus fluxerit, eo exercitius fit omne quod remanet: Cf. Cic. *Off.* 2.53: *dein consuetudine beneficentiae paratiores erunt et tamquam exercitatiores ad bene de multis promerendum.*

A. extends the water image of Cic.'s *fontem . . . exhaurit* with **diffunditur . . . redundantior . . . refluit . . . fluxerit** (and perhaps **ubertas** as well—'abundance' suggesting the fecundity of a well-watered piece of land).

CHAPTER 16: MAINTAINING DUE MEASURE IN
THE DISPLAY OF GENEROSITY

76. Liquet igitur debere esse liberalitatis modum ne fiat inutilis largitas: Cf. Cic. *Off.* 2.55: *Quam ob rem nec ita claudenda est res familiaris ut eam benignitas aperire non possit, nec ita reseranda ut pateat omnibus; modus adhibeatur, isque referatur ad facultates.*

Sobrietas tenenda est: See on 1.12.

maxime a sacerdotibus: As ever, the highest standards are incumbent upon priests.

ut non pro iactantia sed pro iustitia dispensent: Cic. *Off.* 2.55–60 disapproves of extravagant expenditure on public shows by aediles courting popularity; money is better spent on public building programmes. Overall, the golden mean must be observed where public benefaction is concerned. A. applies this principle to almsgiving: the temptation to give for the sake of display must be resisted; cf. 1.147; 2.2–3, 102, 109–11.

Veniunt validi, veniunt nullam causam nisi vagandi habentes: Professional wandering beggars, who seek to usurp the right of the genuinely poor of a locality by feigning poverty; cf. 1.149. The problem was likely to have been particularly bad in Milan, given the importance of the city and its place as a crossroads for so many journeys. For the need of discernment in receiving visitors, cf. *Did.* 11–12; Lucian, 55.10–13; *Const. Apost.* 7.28–9; A. *Ep.* 68 [26].5; Jer. *Ep.* 58.7.1 (citing Cic. *Off.* 2.52); Bened. *Reg.* 1.10; for some of their dubious practices, cf. Paul. Nol. *Carm.* 24.323–32. For a classic account of such an *ordo vagandi* in medieval times, see H. Waddell, *The Wandering Scholars*, 7th edn. (London, 1934), 161–94.

ambitu vestium: They parade their rags as 'proof' of their poverty.

natalium simulatione: They profess noble birth, which may earn them special attention (cf. 1.158).

77. **Plerique simulant debita: sit veri examen:** Having recommended charity towards debtors (2.71), A. adds the warning that there are charlatans about, whose claims are not genuine.

Exutos se per latrocinia deplorant . . . quo propensius iuvetur: Those who have really been robbed deserve help (1.158; see ad loc. on *latrocinia*); relatives (1.150) and fellow-Christians (1.148) should take priority.

propensius: Cic. has *propensior* in *Off.* 2.62.

Ab ecclesia relegatis . . . si desit eis alendi copia: The condition of the *relegati* is somewhat unclear, since, as Testard ii. 167–8 n. 5 notes, there is no evidence for the legal vocabulary of *relegatio* as regular ecclesiastical terminology. They are perhaps people who have been temporarily debarred from the rites of the church because they are performing public penance (so the Maurist editors at PL 16, 131 n. 81), rather than those who have been definitively excommunicated, *pace* Gryson, *Prêtre*, 300–1; Banterle, ad loc.; on the latter, cf. 2.135, and on the obligations of public penance (confession, exclusion from the eucharist, fasting and works of charity), see Gryson, *Prêtre*, 275–90; and Gryson's edition of *Paen.*, SCh 179 (Paris, 1971), 31–50. If this is right, A.'s point is that individuals undergoing such a process may be under formal discipline, but this does not mean that they should be ignored if they are in hardship.

importunitas vociferantum: Cf. 2.68; and see on 1.159.

ille qui erubescit videri: See on 1.148; and cf. 2.69.

Ille etiam clausus in carcere occurrat tibi . . . qui aures non potest: 'Corporal works of mercy', including visiting the imprisoned and the sick, were designated as prime duties of Christian charity from earliest times, in accordance with Mt. 25: 31–46: e.g. Heb. 10: 34; 1 Clem. 59: 4; Arist. *Apol.* 15; Tert. *Apol.* 39.5–6; *Const. Apost.* 4.1–3; Aug. *Enchir.* 72; on the traditional sevenfold scheme, see *ODCC*, 419–20.

78. **Quo plus te operari viderit populus, magis diliget:** [**diliget:** M, CO, Testard: *diligit* P?V?, E] Harks back to the Ciceronian language from *Off.* 2.31–2; cf. especially *Off.* 2.31: *si diligit multitudo.* Cf. 2.68, and see on 2.29–39.

Scio plerosque sacerdotes . . . nemo enim vult nisi pauperi proficere suam collationem: People will give more generously if they see that a priest desires to help the needy rather than to fill his own pockets; in the process, the cleric himself benefits with a greater return of favour for his greater charity. Cypr. *Op. et el.* 9–13 urges believers to go so far as to exhaust their patrimonies through giving; God always provides for those who are generous in almsgiving, and is never anyone's debtor; cf. A. *Expos. Ps. 118.*8.10–11.

dispensatorem: See on 2.69.

ut quod benefacis . . . ne subtrahas necessitati quod indulseris effusioni: Cf. Cic. *Off.* 2.54: *Quid autem est stultius quam, quod libenter facias, curare ut id diutius facere non possis?* Cic. also has *effuderunt* earlier in *Off.* 2.54.

Cave ne intra loculos tuos includas . . . in tumulis sepelias vitam pauperum: Money is not to be sought for personal gain, but for the salvation of the poor. Cf. *Nab.* 39: *Quanto melius est liberalem esse dispensatorem quam sollicitum custodem! Quantum tibi prodesset ad gratiam multorum pupillorum patrem nominari quam innumeras stateras in sacculo obsignatas habere!*

79. 2.79–85 presents Joseph's generosity as a model (cf. the *consilium* of Joseph in 2.74). The substance is essentially biblical, but into it A. weaves various Ciceronian motifs (more than Testard, 'Recherches', 100, seems to notice). The synthesis is not altogether successful; cf. below on 2.79. On Joseph as a model of priestly charity, see A. M. Piredda,

'La tipologia sacerdotale del patriarcha Giuseppe in Ambrogio', *Sandalion* 10–11 (1987–8), 153–63.

Potuit donare Ioseph . . . quam donare esurientibus:
Joseph sold rather than gave away the grain stored up for the
seven years of famine in Egypt (Gen. 41: 56–7; 42: 3, 5, 6, 10;
43: 20).

quia si paucis donasset, plurimis defuisset: Cf. Cic. *Off.*
2.52: *Ita benignitate benignitas tollitur, qua quo in plures usus
sis, eo minus in multos uti possis.* The Ciceronian point about
the danger of exhausting resources is not at all obvious,
however, from the Gen. narrative. By selling the grain and
by acquiring the Egyptians' livestock, land, and finally their
freedom itself (Gen. 47: 13–26), Joseph astutely enriched his
master, Pharaoh. Quite how he provided grain for more
people through selling it rather than giving it away is
unclear, since the famine is said to have been so severe
throughout the ancient world (Gen. 41: 57) that Joseph
presumably could not have used the proceeds to buy extra
grain for the others from elsewhere. The implication that the
system of buying grain ensured that the Egyptians continued
to cultivate their own land (**ne gratis accipiendo cultus
terrarum relinquerent**) is equally weak. If the drought
was so severe, their fields presumably did not yield much in
any case, no matter how assiduously they were cared for.
A. seems to think that the Egyptians continued to tend and
harvest their own crops, and perhaps just supplemented
these with the grain bought from Joseph, but there is no
clue to this effect in Gen.

Patefacit horrea . . . subsidium frumentarium: Cf. Gen
41: 56–7.

80. **Itaque primo . . . quo sua tutius habere possent**
Joseph collected all the Egyptians' money, then their live
stock, then their land, and finally bought their own freedom
from them, in return for grain (Gen. 47: 13–26). Seed wa
given to the Egyptians on condition that they would give
fifth of the crop to Pharaoh (Gen. 47: 23–4, 26). Cic. speak
of the moderate corn dole inaugurated by M. Octavius in
c.120 BC, which, unlike the large-scale distribution of ver
cheap corn arranged by C. Gracchus in 123 BC, benefited th
state as well as the people (*Off.* 2.72); M. Octavius raised th

price of corn, and perhaps reduced the number of recipients, so that the state could bear the cost. Cic. also says that *tributum* should not be levied unless it is absolutely necessary, and *danda erit opera ut omnes intellegant, si salvi esse velint, necessitati esse parendum* (*Off.* 2.74). Joseph's policy fulfilled both conditions: both state and people benefited, and the people realized that the measure was their salvation. Careful generosity won Joseph lasting gratitude (cf. Cic. *Off.* 2.63). The ideology reflects where A.'s political affiliations might lie in a modern context: he praises Joseph for helping people to help themselves.

Sanasti nos, invenimus gratiam in conspectu domini nostri: Gen. 47: 25.

81. **O virum magnum, qui . . . perpetuam commoditatem constituit providentiae!:** Cf. Cic. *Off.* 2.83: *O virum magnum dignumque qui in republica nostra natus esset!* Cic. is eulogizing Aratus of Sicyon (271–213 BC), who, having returned to his native city from Argos, banished tyranny, brought back 600 wealthy exiles, and gained generous financial help from his friend Ptolemy II Philadelphus of Egypt in order to deal with the problem of the Sicyonians' lands. Some who had taken land unjustly were persuaded to relinquish it in return for money, while others who had lost their land were reimbursed with its cash value (Cic. *Off.* 2.81–2; cf. Plu. *Arat.* 9.3, 12–14). Aratus exemplifies the taking of money for the good of the public, rather than the seizure of property rights.

nec . . . aliena subsidia desiderarent: Joseph effectively outstripped Aratus, since he did not have to go elsewhere for money; the people provided it themselves.

Quintam portionem collationis statuit: See on 2.80.

82. **Somnium regis primum hoc fuit . . . illas quae praestabant et forma et gratia:** See Gen. 41: 1–4.

in ipso riparum toro: Cf. Verg. *Aen.* 6.674–5: *riparumque toros et prata recentia rivis | incolimus.* These lines are also evoked in *Ex.* 1.28; 3.65 (cf. too Stat. *Theb.* 4.819–20).

Et somnium secundum hoc fuit . . . steriles et tenues devoraverunt: See Gen. 41: 5–7. On **laetas**, see on 2.21.

83. **Hoc somnium ita aperuit sanctus Ioseph . . . annum consummat integrum:** See Gen. 41: 26–36.

Quae ideo ascendebant de flumine . . . et cursim labuntur: The explanation is not given in Gen. 41, but *fluere* and *labi* are both very commonly used classically of time: cf. Ov. *Met.* 10.519–20: *Labitur occulte fallitque volabilis aetas,* | *et nihil est annis velocius* (cf. *Am.* 1.8.49). Cf. also e.g. Verg. *Aen.* 1.283; 2.14; *Georg.* 1.6; Ov. *Fast.* 6.771; *Trist.* 3.3.11; 4.10.27; *AA.* 3.65; *Met.* 15.179; Hor. *Od.* 2.14.1–2; *Ep.* 1.1.23.

84. **in ipsum . . . cubile:** [**ipsum:** A, E², COB: *ipso* PVM, E¹W, Testard] Cf. e.g. Cic. *Verr.* 2.2.190; *Clu.* 82; Amm. 30.4.8; Claud. 22.214.

This paragraph perhaps implicitly offers another summarizing list of the cardinal virtues: Joseph showed wisdom (**ingenium**) in discerning the truth; justice (**vigilantiam atque iustitiam**) in maintaining due equity in all his provisions for the people; courage (**de magnanimitate**) in enduring the hardship of slavery; and temperance (**de suavitate**) in sparing and helping his brothers who had treated him so badly; cf. 2.59.

quarum: most editors: *quorum* MSS.

altera imposito: V²A, E²W, COB: *alteram imposito* PV¹, E¹: *alterum imposito* M.

altera aequalitatem: Winterbottom, 564: *alteraque aequalitatem* V, Testard: *altera quae aequalitatem* PMA, E¹W, O: *altera qua aequalitatem* E², CB.

Quod venditus a fratribus in servitutem: See on 2.20.

non retulit iniuriam sed famem depulit: See Gen. 42–50.

Quod dilecti fratris praesentiam . . . ut obsidem teneret gratiae: See Gen. 44, especially 44: 1–17.

85. **ei a patre dicitur:** Jacob's dying blessing to Joseph.

Filius ampliatus meus Ioseph . . . zelotes filius meus adulescentior: Gen. 49: 22 (LXX/VL).

Adiuvit te Deus meus . . . et desideria collium aeternorum: Gen. 49: 25–6 (again, closer to the LXX than to the Vulg.).

Qui visus est, inquit, *in rubo. . . . et ipsi milia Manasses*: [*unicornui*: EW, COB: *unicornus* PMA: *unicornis* V; *in ipsis*: EW, COB, several editors: *in ipsius cornuc* PVMA, Zell, Lignamine, Maurists, Testard] Dt. 33: 16–17 For an exposition of these verses, cf. *Patr.* 46–56.

CHAPTER 17: THE VIRTUES OF AN EXEMPLARY
GIVER OF ADVICE

2.86–151 surveys a range of further qualities which can be
called *utilia*, all of them relating to the character of the person
who lives in the public eye. The praise of Joseph's generosity in
2.79–85 also amounts to praise of his *consilium* (cf. 2.74), so
A. naturally continues with a list of the qualities required in
one who gives advice to others (2.86–92). Among these are
contentment and humility. A. then thinks of Rehoboam, a man
who took the wrong advice, and so was responsible for great
injustice, which led to political disaster rather than stability
and personal popularity (2.93–5). It is kindness or goodwill
that promotes social cohesion (2.95); this must be manifested
through affability (2.96). Rehoboam's folly had also been the
result of the advice of young men (2.93), and so A. again extols
the virtues of older company for *adulescentes* (2.97–101). He
then sets out a series of *utilia* which win a good reputation:
rescuing the needy (2.102); showing hospitality (2.103–7);
displaying the right kinds of practical generosity (2.108–11);
being sincere (2.112–20); and behaving generally in a way that
will preserve unity within the ecclesial body, avoiding greed
and a love of money (2.121–35). Examples of services follow:
the redemption of prisoners of war (2.136–43), and the guarding of deposits (2.144–51). In both cases, A. is seeking to justify
his own conduct in controversial incidents.

The structural flow of the whole of this section is quite poor,
and the thematic divisions are not very easy to trace. A. evokes a
number of points from Cic. *Off.* 2.23–87, but in no particular
sequence, and indeed with some repetition (cf. e.g. 2.108–11
with 2.68–9, 76–8; 2.29–30 with 2.96; 2.60–7 with 2.86–92;
2.70–1 with 2.136–43). The overriding concern, as from 2.29
onwards, is with image, popularity, *commendatio*. The *utile*, for
the cleric, is all to do with gaining eternal life through the
practice of faithful virtue, and the practice of that virtue equally
means the presentation of a specific ecclesiastical character.

86. **ut se ipsum formam aliis praebeat . . . ut sit eius
sermo salubris atque irreprehensibilis:** Cf. Tit. 2: 7–8:

In omnibus te ipsum praebe exemplum bonorum operum, in doctrina, in integritate, in gravitate; verbum sanum, irreprehensibile.

consilium utile, vita honesta, sententia decora: As so often, the Ciceronian terminology is appended artificially to the scriptural quotation.

87. **Talis erat Paulus, qui consilium dabat virginibus:** See 1 Cor. 7: 25–40, especially 7: 25–8.

magisterium sacerdotibus: A. is thinking of the Pastoral Epistles; cf. especially 1 Tim. 3–4; 6: 11–21; 2 Tim., *passim*; Tit. 2–3. No doubt we are again meant to see A.'s own example as a clear imitation of the Pauline model: the devoted instructor of virgins and clerics is following the apostolic pattern; cf. 1.3–4, 183–4. Cf. also *Ep. extra coll.* 14 [63].61–5.

ut primum se ipsum formam nobis praeberet ad imitandum: Cf. 1 Cor. 11: 1, *Imitatores mei estote*; Phil. 3: 17, *Imitatores mei estote, fratres*; 1 Thess. 1: 6, *Et vos imitatores nostri facti estis et Domini*; 2 Thess. 3: 7, *Ipsi enim scitis quemadmodum oporteat imitari nos*; also 1 Cor. 4: 6; Phil. 4: 9.

Ideo et humiliari sciebat: Cf. Phil. 4: 12: *Scio et humiliari*.

Ioseph, qui summo ortus patriarcharum genere: The line of Abraham, Isaac, and Jacob.

non dedignatus degenerem servitutem: See on 2.20.

et dominum appellabat eum: In view of the quotation which follows, the earthly, visible *dominus* is contrasted with the divine, invisible *Dominus* of whose higher imperatives Joseph was mindful (Testard ii. 170 n. 6):

Si dominus meus . . . et peccabo coram Domino?: Joseph's words to Potiphar's wife: Gen. 39: 8–9.

88. **qui nihil nebulosum habeat. . . . Alia sunt enim quae fugiuntur, alia quae contemnuntur:** Cf. Cic. *Off.* 2.36: *despiciunt autem eos et contemnunt in quibus nihil virtutis, nihil animi, nihil nervorum putant. Non enim omnes eos contemnunt de quibus male existimant. Nam quos improbos maledicos fraudulentos putant et ad faciendam iniuriam instructos, eos contemnunt quidem neutiquam, sed de iis male existimant.* Cf also *Off.* 3.68: *Ratio ergo hoc postulat, ne quid insidiose, ne quid simulate, ne quid fallaciter.* The sentiments here are similar to those in 2.60–7.

ut si is qui consulitur . . . hic fugitur ac declinatur:
Cf. 2.58, 60, 62, 66–7, and see ad locc. on Cic. *Off.* 2.36–8.
voluptarius: Cic. *Off.* 2.37 has *voluptates.* [**voluptarius,
intemperans:** EW, COB, Amerbach, Testard: *voluntarius
interpretans* PVMA, Zell: *voluntarius intemperans* Gering.]
cupidior lucri turpis: See on 2.67.

89. *Ego enim didici in quibus sim sufficiens esse:* Phil.
4: 11.

Sciebat enim *omnium malorum radicem esse avaritiam:* 1 Tim. 6: 10; for other references, cf. *Exc. fr.* 1.55;
*Expl. Ps. 1.*28; *Expl. Ps. 61.*31; *Paen.* 2.75; *Elia* 69; *Ep.* 36
[2].15. For similar language in classical sources, cf. *Auct. ad
Her.* 2.22.34; Quint. *Inst.* 9.3.89; Rutil. Lup. 2.6; DL, 6.50.
On A.'s hatred of greed in the lives of clerics, cf. Paul. *VA*
41; see generally Vasey, 176–81; Dassmann, 247–50.

Expressius aliquid dicendum videtur: An informal
touch.

Sufficit: E², several editors: *efficit* PVMA, EW, COB, Zell,
Lignamine, Valdarfer, Scinzenzeler, Marchand.

Hoc de pecunia: Paul is talking about a sufficiency of
material goods in Phil. 4: 11. *Pace* Testard, 'Recherches',
101, there is no need to see **pecunia** here as an attempt to
link this paragraph to the generosity theme of 2.68–85, since
financial greed has already been mentioned in 2.88, under
the influence of Cic. *Off.* 2.36–8.

90. **sufficiebant:** E², several editors: *efficiebant* PVMA, E¹W,
OB, Zell, Lignamine, Valdarfer, Scinzenzeler, Marchand:
efficiebat C.

**sed debiti finem certaminis . . . securus meriti prae-
stolabatur:** Cf. 2 Tim. 4: 7–8; also Phil. 3: 13–14. On
patiens laboris, cf. 2 Cor. 6: 4–10; 11: 21–33.

Scio, inquit, *et humiliari:* Phil. 4: 12.

Et humiles spiritu salvabit: Ps. 33: 19.

quo in loco . . . in quo munere: Introduces the classical
casuistry.

Nescivit Pharisaeus . . . iustificatus est: See Lk. 18: 9–14.

91. **Sciebat et abundare Paulus:** Cf. Phil. 4: 12.

*Os nostrum patet ad vos . . . cor nostrum dilatatum
est:* 2 Cor. 6: 11.

92. **In omnibus erat imbutus et saturari et esurire:** Cf. Phil. 4: 12.

    Beatus qui sciebat saturari in Christo: Cf. Mt. 5: 6, *Beati qui esuriunt et sitiunt iustitiam, quoniam ipsi saturabuntur*, and Lk. 6: 21, *Beati, qui nunc esuritis, quia saturabimini.*

    scientiae: PV¹MA, Valdarfer, Scinzenzeler, Marchand, Testard: *scientia* EW, COB, other editors.

    non in pane solo . . . sed in omni verbo Dei: Dt. 8: 3, quoted by Jesus at his temptation in Mt. 4: 4; Lk. 4: 4.

    qui sciebat quia esurientes manducabunt: Paul knew the truth expressed in the Beatitude.

    qui nihil habebat et possidebat omnia: Cf. 2 Cor. 6: 10.

CHAPTER 18: JUSTICE BENEFICIAL TO LEADERS

93. **itaque:** At first glance, the link with the preceding paragraphs is unclear, since justice has not been mentioned since 2.84. However, the intellectual connection is the subject of *consilium*. The *in*justice of Rehoboam stemmed from his rejection of the right advice, offered by his elders, and his adoption of the foolish suggestions of the young.
    praesidentes muneri may possibly be picking up Cic. *Off.* 2.77, where it is said that *avaritia* is particularly offensive in those who hold political office. A. perhaps thinks of this in the context of Paul's contentment and hatred of *avaritia* (2.89). The importance of justice as a way to glory in any activity (even a disreputable one) is stressed by Cic. in *Off.* 2.38–43; A. also exploits *Off.* 2.23–9, thus implicitly merging once more the material on love versus fear.
    cum populus Israel . . . et leviora gravioribus suppliciis mutaret: See 3 Ki. 12: 1–16; 2 Chr. 10: 1–16.

94. ***Non est nobis portio cum David . . . in tabernacula tua, Israel:*** 3 Ki. 12: 16; 2 Chr. 10: 16.
    ducem erit nobis: Several editors: ⟨*ducem*⟩ *est eligendus* A²: *ducem* PVMA¹, EW, COB, Zell, Lignamine, Valdarfer, Scinzenzeler, Marchand.
    vix duarum tribuum . . . habere potuit societatem: The folly of Rehoboam precipitated the division of Israel and Judah in 930 BC: Judah remained loyal to the house of David.

in accordance with the Lord's promise, for the sake of the merits of David (3 Ki. 11: 12–13; 12: 20; 2 Chr. 10: 19), while Israel elected Jeroboam (I) as her new king.

CHAPTER 19: JUSTICE, GOODWILL, AND AN AFFABLE MANNER

95. Claret ergo . . . iniustitia dissolvat: On the necessity of political justice, cf. Cic. *Off.* 2.29 and 2.40. The example of Rehoboam in 2.93–4 replaces Cic.'s references to Julius Caesar and other figures from classical history in *Off.* 2.23–9.

Nam quomodo potest malitia . . . ne unam quidem privatam potest regere familiam?: Cf. Cic. *Off.* 2.29: *Quae si populo Romano iniuste imperanti accidere potuerunt, quid debent putare singuli?*

ut non solum publica gubernacula . . . privata iura tueamur: Cic., *Off.* 2.24, says that the use of love rather than fear brings success *et privatis in rebus et in republica.*

96. Adfabilitatem quoque sermonis diximus . . . valere plurimum: Cf. 2.29–30 and see on 2.29; cf. also 1.67.

Sed hanc volumus esse: Prescriptive.

sine ulla adulatione, ne . . . dedeceat sermonis adulatio: Cf. 1.226; 2.112–20; 3.58, 76, 89, 134; and see on 1.209. Cf. generally Cic. *Off.* 2.43, 63.

Forma enim esse debemus ceteris . . . in castitate ac fide: Cf. 2.86–7, and 1 Tim. 4: 12: *sed exemplum esto fidelium, in verbo, in conversatione, in caritate, in fide, in castitate.* For the exemplarism, cf. 1.142; 2.124.

Quales haberi volumus . . . talem aperiamus: Cf. Cic. *Off.* 2.43: *Quamquam praeclare Socrates hanc viam ad gloriam proximam et quasi compendiariam dicebat esse, si quis id ageret, ut qualis haberi vellet, talis esset.* On the saying of Socrates (fr. IC 483), cf. Plat. *Rep.* 361b–c; Aesch. *Th.* 592; also Xen. *Mem.* 2.6.39; Val. Max. 7.2 ext. 1; Plu. *Arist.* 3.3–4.

Neque dicamus in corde nostro verbum iniquum: dicamus in corde nostro is reminiscent of such verses as Dt. 9: 4; Is. 14: 13; 47: 8; 49: 21; Rom. 10: 6.

quia audit in occulto dicta: Probably an allusion to Cic. *Off.* 2.44: the young man who is born into an illustrious family (such as Marcus) lives in the public gaze, *ita nullum obscurum potest nec dictum eius esse nec factum.* But the idea is here elided with the biblical thought of living in the sight of God, from whom nothing can be hidden (cf. 1.9, 53–6).

et cognoscit secreta viscerum: Cf. Ps. 43: 22: *Ipse enim novit abscondita cordis.*

tamquam sub oculis constituti iudicis: On this motivation, cf. 1.124, 188.

quidquid gerimus . . . ut omnibus manifestetur: Cf. Mt. 10: 26–7; Mk. 4: 22; Lk. 8: 17; 12: 2–3.

CHAPTER 20: YOUTH BENEFITS FROM OLDER COMPANY

2.97–101 is on the benefits of older company for young men, a theme of particular relevance to the younger clerics whom A. is particularly addressing (cf. 1.65, 81, 87, 212). Early Christianity faced a potential tension between (*a*) the emergent conviction that people of every age are equal in the sight of God, hence age is irrelevant, and (*b*) a traditional Semitic and classical esteem for the old. The resulting consensus was the belief that the young can acquire a maturity of spirit far beyond their years, not least by associating with wise elders (see generally C. Gnilka, *Aetas spiritalis: Die Überwindung der natürlichen Altersstufen als Ideal frühchristlichen Lebens* (Bonn, 1972)). The present passage is linked to the preceding paragraphs in two ways. First, the story of Rehoboam in 2.93 shows the folly of ignoring the counsel of elders and heeding the advice of *adulescentes*, so the subject of older company is already in A.'s mind. Secondly, 2.96 evokes Cic. *Off.* 2.43–4 and in *Off.* 2.44–51 Cic. goes on to suggest various ways in which a young man of obscure birth may make a name for himself; among these, he lists the value of associating with distinguished elders (*Off.* 2.46–7).

97. Adulescentibus quoque . . . sequantur: Cf. Cic. *Off.* 2.46: *Facillime autem et in optimam partem cognoscuntur adulescentes qui se ad claros et sapientes viros bene consulentes reipublicae contulerunt.* Cic. thinks of men of distinction in politics (and, in *Off.* 2.47, of eminent lawyers and orators); A. has the counsel of spiritual sages in mind.

qui congreditur sapientibus, sapiens est: Cf. Prov. 13: 20: *Qui cum sapientibus graditur, sapiens erit; amicus stultorum efficietur similis.* As so often, scriptural language is appended to the Ciceronian idea.

Ostendunt enim ... quibus adhaerent: Cf. Cic. *Off.* 2.46: *quibuscum si frequentes sunt, opinionem adferunt populo eorum fore se similes quos sibi ipsi delegerint ad imitandum.*

convalescit opinio: Cf. 2.102, *egregiae convalescit opinionis testimonium.*

98. Biblical illustration follows, replacing Cic.'s example of the influence of the jurist P. Mucius Scaevola (consul in 133 BC) on the young P. Rutilius Rufus (consul in 105 BC).

Inde tantus Iesus Nave ... sanctificavit ad gratiam: From an early age, Joshua was Moses' *minister* (Ex. 24: 13; 33: 11; Num. 11: 28; Dt. 1: 38), and it was in fact Moses who gave him the name 'Joshua' (Num. 13: 17) (originally he was Hosea, 'salvation'; the prefix of the divine name made this more specific: 'the Lord is salvation'). As Moses' successor he knew the Lord's presence in the same way as his mentor (Dt. 31: 7–8; 34: 9; Josh. 1: 5), and was shown equal reverence by the Israelites (Josh. 4: 14).

Denique cum in eius tabernaculo ... solus erat in tabernaculo Iesus Nave: [**in eius tabernaculo:** COB: *in eius tabernaculum* PVMA, EW, Testard] See Ex. 33: 11.

Moyses cum Deo loquebatur ... nube sacra tegebatur: See Ex. 33: 7–11.

Presbyteri ... ascendebat: See Ex. 24: 13–14. A. runs together two incidents: the presence of the Lord with Moses and Joshua (cf. Ex. 33: 11) in the tent of meeting, and the giving of the Law on Sinai. Joshua set out with Moses to climb Sinai (Ex. 24: 13), and was there when Moses descended to the Israelite camp (Ex. 32: 17), but the Ex. narrative makes no mention of his being with Moses when the Lord spoke from the cloud (Ex. 24: 15–31: 18). A. thinks that Joshua was there, though in 3.2 he says that Moses was alone. The conflation of the two passages (Sinai and the tent of meeting) is perhaps because both speak of the other Israelites standing back while Moses and Joshua go to the sacred place (Ex. 24: 13–14 and Ex. 33: 7–11). For an application of the idea that God's servants are set apart from the rest of the *populus Dei*, cf. *Ep.* 6 [28].1–2.

Omnis populus . . . in tabernaculo testimonii: See Ex. 33: 7–11.

quasi fidus adstabat minister . . . iuvenis: Cf. Ex. 33: 11; Joshua is there called a *puer* (LXX: νέος), though he had already led in battle (Ex. 17: 8–13).

99.   **reveranda secreta:** On the secrecy of spiritual things, see on 1.251.

fieret successor potestatis: See Dt. 1: 38; 3: 28; 34: 9; etc.

Merito vir . . . ut sisteret fluminum cursus: See Josh. 3: 5–17.

diceret: *Stet sol, et staret sol:* See Josh. 10: 1–15, especially 10: 12–13; and cf. 1.196; 2.130.

ille mari: See Ex. 14: 13–31.

100.   **Pulchra itaque copula seniorum atque adulescentium:** On the sentiment, cf. Cic. *Sen.* 20, 26 (especially), 28–9.

Omitto quod Abrahae adhaesit Loth adulescentulus etiam proficiscenti: See Gen. 12: 4–5.

propinquitatis: EW, COB: *propinquitas* PVMA.

aestimetur: PVMA, OB: *existimetur* EW, C.

Licet . . . iuniorem fuisse: A. is right to say that Scripture does not call Elisha a young man, though it is a fair assumption from 3 Ki. 19: 19–21.

Barnabas Marcum adsumpsit, Paulus Silam: See Acts 15: 39–40. John Mark's youth is perhaps inferred from his return to Jerusalem in Acts 13: 13, which is taken by Paul to be desertion from the cause in Acts 15: 38: was his departure due to youthful fickleness? (The young man mentioned in Mk. 14: 51 has generally been taken as a reference by the author to himself, but A. and some others think differently: see on 2.101 below.) Mark and Barnabas, the Levite from Cyprus who sold his property for the common good of the early Christians (Acts 4: 36–7; 'a good man': Acts 11: 24), were cousins (Col. 4: 10). There is no indication in Acts that Silas was younger than Paul. Silas is described as a leader (Acts 15: 22) and a prophet (Acts 15: 32) in the church at Jerusalem, and he shared with Paul in the evangelizing of

Syria, Asia Minor, Macedonia, Thessalonica, and Corinth (Acts 16–18); but unlike Barnabas (Acts 14: 14), he is not called an apostle, and, like Mark before him (Acts 13: 5), he seems to have held a subordinate function (cf. his literary role in 1 Pt. 5: 12). Cf. generally 2 Cor. 1: 19; 1 Thess. 1: 1; 2 Thess. 1: 1.

Paulus Timotheum: See Acts 16: 1–3. Timothy clearly *was* a young man: 1 Tim. 1: 2, 18; 4: 12; 2 Tim. 1: 2; 2: 22; cf. 1 Cor. 4: 17; Phil. 2: 19–23.

Paulus Titum: See Gal. 2: 1 (cf. also 2 Cor. 2: 13; 7: 13). Like Timothy, Titus is described as Paul's 'son' (Tit. 1: 4). Titus does not in fact appear in Acts.

101. sicut delectabantur Petrus et Iohannes: See Lk. 22: 8; Jn. 20: 2–9; Acts 3–5; 8: 14.

Nam adulescentem legimus in evangelio Iohannem et sua voce: John is not specifically said anywhere in the gospels to have been a young man (nor is Peter said to have been older), but A. thinks that he was: **et sua voce** (which has caused problems for some editors) may allude to the action, described in the Fourth Gospel, of 'the disciple whom Jesus loved' (Jn. 13: 23; 19: 26; 20: 2; 21: 7, 20), traditionally thought to have been John, leaning on Jesus' breast in Jn. 13: 23–5, as the intimate gesture of a young man. John's youth might also be inferred from Jn. 20: 1–9: John outstrips Peter in running to Jesus' tomb (youthful vigour?), but waits outside until Peter arrives (youthful timidity?). Jer., *Adv. Iov.* 1.26, speaks of John as almost a *puer*. A. takes John to be the unnamed young man who flees at Jesus' arrest, in Mk. 14: 51–2: cf. *Expl. Ps. 36.53*: *Novit [Scriptura] et Iohannem adulescentem in Christi pectore recumbentem. . . . Hic est puer qui patrem genitalem reliquit, secutus est patrem eum quem cognovit aeternum, adulescens amictus sindone, Dominum sequebatur tempore passionis, qui sua omnia derelinquerat.* The identification of John as the figure of Mk. 14: 51–2 is made also by Greg. Magn. *Moral.* 14.57; Bede, *In Marc.* 4.950–91.

erat enim in eo senectus venerabilis . . . stipem pendit: Cf. Wisd. 4: 8–9. An unblemished life brings the reward of venerable longevity. John, though a young man, showed the prudence of an older man; his life was as unblemished as the lives of those who have reached old age. In support of Testard's persuasive suggestion of **stipem pendit** in lieu of PVMA's *stipendio* or the reading *stipendium est* offered by EW, COB and preferred by most editors (Testard ii. 173–4 n. 23), cf. the references to Wisd. 4: 8–9 in *Epp.* 20 [77].9; 52 [16].5; 73 [18].7; *Expl. Ps. 36.*59; *Expl. Ps. 43.*5; *Expos. Ps. 118.*2.17; 6.20, 30; 13.13; 16.6; *Iac.* 2.35; *Ios.* 43. On abstinence and discipline as particular keys to acquiring maturity at an early age, cf. *Ep. extra coll.* 14 [63].26, 98.

CHAPTER 21: INTERCESSION, HOSPITALITY, AND KINDNESS

102. **Adiuvat hoc quoque . . . si de potentis manibus eripias inopem:** A synthesis of a biblical verse with a Ciceronian statement: cf. Ps. 81: 4: *Eripite pauperem, et egenum de manu peccatoris liberate* (also Prov. 24: 11; Eccli. 4: 9; Jer. 21: 12), and Cic. *Off.* 2.51 (on advocacy): *Maxime autem et gloria paritur et gratia defensionibus, eoque maior si quando accidit ut ei subveniatur qui potentis alicuius opibus circumveneri urgerique videatur.* For the oppressive behaviour of the *potens,* cf. 1.63.

de morte damnatum eruas: Cf. Prov. 24: 11: *Erue eos qui ducuntur ad mortem.* A. quotes this verse also in *Expos. Ps. 118.*8.41: *Eripe eum qui ducitur ad mortem, hoc est: eripe eum intercessione, eripe gratia tu, sacerdos, aut tu, imperator, eripe subscriptione indulgentiae, et soluisti peccata tua, exuisti te e vinculis tuis.* Both there and here, he is thinking of episcopal *intercessio,* an *ex officio* duty enshrined by the Council of Sardica (343), *can.* 7–9 [Greek]; 8–10 [Latin], and a responsibility that was taken seriously in the late fourth and early fifth centuries; e.g. Jer. *Ep.* 52.11; Aug. *Epp.* 113–16, 133–4, 139.2, 151–3; *Serm.* 302.17; *Ev. Ioh.* 25.10 (see A. Ducloux, Ad ecclesiam confugere: *Naissance du droit d'asile dans les églises (IVe–milieu du Ve s.)* (Paris, 1994); Homes Dudden i. 121–2 and 122 n. 1; Gaudemet, 282–7, 351). So successful were some clerical appeals that civil legislation in the 390s moved to curtail the church's power on behalf of convicted criminals (*CTh* 9.10.15 forbade *intercessio* if the condemna tion was for a very serious crime, and *CTh* 11.36.31 prohibited it if the criminal had made a frank confession; cf. also *CTh* 9.45.1–2; 9.14.3.2; 9.40.16; 11.30.57; 9.45.3).

A. was sometimes forced to go to extreme lengths to press his case. Soz., *HE* 7.25.10–13, says that on one occasion he had to interrupt a private hunting expedition at Gratian's palace in order to secure the repeal of the death sentence passed against a senator who had insulted the emperor (Palanque, 113–15; the senator was a pagan who had apparently criticized Gratian's anti-pagan legislation; the case shows that A. did not restrict his appeals for clemency to just Christian victims); and Paul., *VA* 37, speaks of his being refused an audience by Gratian's *magister officiorum* Macedonius (his firm opponent in the Priscillianist affair: H. Chadwick, *Priscillian of Avila: The Occult and the Charismatic in the Early Church* (Oxford, 1976), 40–4) on another intercessory visit (Paul. *VA* 37, also records that the roles were later reversed, in accordance with a prophecy from A.: when Macedonius himself sought refuge in a church after the demise of Gratian, he was unable to get in, even though the doors were open). Such incidents show the influence that A. could wield in court circles, yet also highlight the difficulty he faced in sustaining that influence consistently. The power of his connections did serve his clients well, though: *Ep.* 26 [54].1 recalls his successful appeal to the praetorian prefect of Milan on behalf of an *apparitor praefecturae* who faced confiscation of his property; he acted at the request of his friend, Eusebius of Bologna (it is Palanque, 470, who identifies the Eusebius of *Epp.* 26 [54]and 38 [55] with Eusebius of Bologna; he is followed by McLynn, 66, 261, though Ihm, 53; Homes Dudden ii. 696 n. 7; *et al.* disagree). A. could claim success, too, with Theodosius himself (*Ep.* 74 [40].25). Both in writing and in person, he pleaded for mercy for the supporters of Eugenius who sought asylum in his church after the usurper's death (*Epp. extra coll.* 2–3 [61–2]; Paul. *VA* 31).

Sometimes episcopal histrionics were followed by providential intervention which brought tyrannical officials to their senses and made them commute sentences. Paul., *VA* 34, describes A. lying weeping in front of his altar when

Stilicho's soldiers forcibly removed one Cresconius, an asylum-seeker, to be thrown to the beasts in the amphitheatre. When the soldiers arrived at the games, the leopards promptly broke loose and mauled them. Stilicho came to repentance, and Cresconius' sentence was reduced to exile. The dynamics of these confrontations were subtle. The idea was that the bishop's virtues were great enough to cover the crimes of the worst defendants, and that his motives were solely compassionate. Compassion there may have been; but in reality his successes added to the impression of a churchman whose word carried weight in high places, and in cases like his defence of Eugenius' supporters it also guaranteed him the undying gratitude of officials who might be able to help his cause in future delicate situations. This is where the real *utile* of *intercessio* is uncovered. A. can counsel discretion with good reason; a cleric who intercedes only out of a desire to make a name for himself may do more harm than good (cf. *Expos. Ps. 118*.8.25–6). The value of this right of appeal lay precisely in the purchase it secured in the right circles; but it needed cautious handling, for the church as much as for the defendant. Cf. also 3.59. Augustine took a more circumspect course: he refused to intercede on behalf of his friends (Possid. *Vita Aug.* 20).

ne videamur iactantiae magis causa facere quam misericordiae: Cf. 1.147; 2.2–3, 76, 109–11.

et graviora inferre vulnera dum levioribus mederi desideramus: The language here appears to be reminiscent of two passages in the letters of Novatian to Cyprian preserved in Cyprian's collection: *Ep.* 30.3.3 and *Ep.* 31.6.2–3 (C. Curti, 'Una reminiscenza di Novaziano nel *De officiis ministrorum* di Ambrogio', in *Mnemosynum. Studi in onore di Alfredo Ghiselli* (Bologna, 1989), 149–53). If A. is echoing these passages, it is presumably subconsciously: it is easy to see how the image might be replicated.

Iam si oppressum opibus potentis . . . liberaveris: See above on Cic. *Off.* 2.51.

egregiae convalescit opinionis testimonium: *convalesci opinio* has already appeared in 2.97; the phrase seems to be lodged in A.'s mind.

103. Commendat plerosque etiam hospitalitas: 2.103–8

is on hospitality, a subject mentioned by Cic. in *Off*. 2.64. Cic. treats hospitality as a means towards a political end (cf. Lact. *Inst*. 6.12.5–14): by entertaining foreign guests Rome builds up a network of valuable links with other peoples. The support of visiting Christians and *tuitio* of the needy and the oppressed were from earliest times regarded as important Christian duties (cf. Rom. 12: 13; 1 Tim. 3: 2; 5: 10; Tit. 1: 8; Heb. 13: 2; 1 Pt. 4: 9; 3 Jn. 8), and at first sight, A. dwells less on self-interest and more on charitable generosity to strangers, particularly fellow-believers (2.107). His exhortations must, however, be read in the light of his whole argument on the *utile*. **Commendat** is significant: hospitality is a public duty, which furthers one's popular esteem (2.103); it brings advantages in terms of *amicitia*, with all its attendant boons (2.106), and it earns an eternal reward (2.107). Pragmatic interests are never too far away. A.'s own hospitality certainly involved looking after men of influence (see on 1.86); and such opportunities were jealously guarded against usurpation by wealthy laymen; cf. Jer. *In Ep. Tit*. 1.8–9. Cf. generally 1.39, 86, 167; *Ex*. 5.54; *Luc*. 6.66; 7.64 (also 5.35); *Ep*. 62 [19].6; *Ep. extra coll*. 14 [63].105; for a useful survey, see O. Hiltbrunner, D. Gorce, and H. Wehr, 'Gastfreundschaft', *RAC* viii. 1061–1123.

publica species humanitatis: The vital thing is to be *seen* to be beneficent. Cic. *Off*. 2.64 says that hospitality *rei-publicae est ornamento*.

ut peregrinus hospitio non egeat: Cf. Cic. *Off*. 2.64: *homines externos hoc liberalitatis genere in urbe nostra non egere*.

pateat advenienti ianua: Cf. Job 31: 32, quoted in a similar context in 1.167.

Valde id decorum totius est orbis existimationi . . . explorari adventus hospitum: Cf. Cic. *Off*. 2.64: *Recte etiam a Theophrasto est laudata hospitalitas* [in his lost Περὶ Πλούτου; cf. *Off*. 2.56]. *Est enim, ut mihi quidem videtur, valde decorum patere domus hominum inlustrium hospitibus inlustribus.*

104. Quod Abrahae laudi est datum . . . ne transiret hospes: For Abraham's hospitality to three strangers, at least two of whom were angels (Gen. 19: 1), see Gen. 18:

1–22. The story is often cited as a model of charitable behaviour (cf. 2.104, 107; *Abr.* 1.32 ff.; and e.g. Paul. Nol. *Epp.* 13.21; 23.40). Patristic exegetes regularly treat the three strangers as a theophany of the Trinity: cf. 2.107; also *Epp. extra coll.* 12 [1].3; 14 [63].105; *Fid.* 1.80.

Domine . . . ne praeterieris puerum tuum: Gen. 18: 3.

105. Loth quoque nepos eius . . . supplicia detorsit: For Lot's hospitality to the two angels: Gen. 19: 1–3.

106. Decet igitur hospitalem esse . . . et tranquillitatis gratiam: Cf. Cic. *Off.* 2.64:

> Conveniet autem cum in dando munificum esse, tum in exigendo non acerbum, in omnique re contrahenda, vendendo emendo, conducendo locando, vicinitatibus et confiniis aequum facilem, multa multis de suo iure cedentem, a litibus vero, quantum liceat et nescio an paulo plus etiam quam liceat, abhorrentem. Est enim non modo liberale paulum nonnumquam de suo iure decedere, sed interdum etiam fructuosum.

For **non alieni cupidum**, cf. 1 Tim. 3: 3. For **fugitantem litium**, cf. Ter. *Phorm.* 623: *fugitans litium*; and see on 1.185.

quod: COB: *quo* PVMA, EW, Testard.

amicitia, ex qua oriuntur plurimae commoditates: Cf. Cic. *Amic.* 23: *Cumque plurimas et maximas commoditates amicitia contineat*. On the advantages (and responsibilities), cf. 3.125–38.

fructuosa: Cic. *Off.* 2.64 has *fructuosum* (and *fructus*).

107. In officiis autem hospitalibus omnibus . . . uberior deferenda honorificentia: Cic. argues that good character is more important than wealth as a criterion for deserving kindness (*Off.* 2.69–71). A. probably elides this with the NT principle that fellow-believers have first claim on our generosity (Gal. 6: 10); cf. 1.148.

Quicumque enim iustum receperit . . . mercedem iusti accipiet: Mt. 10: 41.

ut ne potus quidem aquae frigidae . . . immunis sit: Cf. Mt. 10: 42; Mk. 9: 41.

Vides quia Abraham . . . dum hospites quaerit: See on 2.104.

Vides quia Loth angelos recepit: See on 2.105.

The author of Heb. is probably thinking of these stories when he says: *Hospitalitatem nolite oblivisci, per hanc enim latuerunt quidam angelis hospitio receptis* (Heb. 13: 2).

Unde scis ne . . . suscipias Christum? . . . quia Christus in paupere est: For the principle, see on 1.39; see also Y. Frot, 'Le Pauvre, Autre Christ, dans quelques lettres de saint Ambroise', in *L'etica cristiana nei secoli III e IV: eredità e confronti* (Rome, 1996), 299–304.

In carcere eram . . . et operuistis me: Mt. 25: 36.

108. Verum hoc malum iamdudum humanis influxit mentibus: On the significance of original sin to the introduction of greed and private property, cf. 1.132, 137; 2.129–33. Cic. refers to both hospitality and greed in *Off.* 2.64, and inveighs against avarice in *Off.* 2.58, 75, 77.

ut pecunia honori sit: Cic. laments this in *Off.* 2.69–71 (and 2.37–8); cf. also Sall. *Cat.* 12.1.

et animi hominum divitiarum admiratione capiantur: Cf. Cic. *Off.* 2.71: *Sed corrupti mores depravatique sunt admiratione divitiarum.* Dyck, 457, cites the evocation of these words by Vincent of Beauvais, *Spec. Doctr.* 4.50.

ut homines damnum putent quidquid praeter morem impenditur: People become parsimonious, considering anything more than a token gift as money wasted.

Melior est hospitalitas cum oleribus . . . : Prov. 15: 17.

Melior est panis in suavitate cum pace: Prov. 17: 1.

The verses, lifted out of context, carry us from the theme of generous hospitality to that of extravagance:

Non enim prodigos nos docet esse scriptura, sed liberales: The terminology of *prodigi* and *liberales* is Ciceronian (*Off.* 2.55). A. adopts the classical language and sentiment, but attributes the teaching to Scripture.

109. Largitatis enim duo sunt genera: unum liberalitatis, alterum prodigae effusionis: Cf. Cic. *Off.* 2.55: *Omnino duo sunt genera largorum, quorum alteri prodigi, alteri liberales* (the language is of course Aristotelian at heart: *EN* 1119^{b}22–1122^{a}17). On maintaining measure, cf. above, 2.76–85.

nudum vestire: Cf. Mt. 25: 36, quoted in 2.107.

redimere captivos: See on 2.70; it is a practice of the *liberales* in Cic. *Off.* 2.55.

non habentes sumptu iuvare: Cf. Cic. *Off.* 2.61–3, on helping the needy.

prodigum est sumptuosis effluescere conviviis et vino plurimo: Cf. Cic. *Off.* 2.55: *prodigi, qui epulis . . . pecunias profundunt.* On such excess, see on 1.86; and cf. 3.10. **effluescere** is an Ambrosian coinage, apparently unique (*TLL* v/2. 192).

Prodigum est vinum et contumeliosa ebrietas: Prov. 20: 1.

Prodigum est . . . exinanire proprias opes: Cf. Cic. *Off.* 2.54, 64 on not wasting one's wealth (and so squandering one's resources for doing good).

quod faciunt qui ludis circensibus . . . patrimonium dilapidant suum: Cf. Cic. *Off.* 2.55: *prodigi, qui . . . gladiatorum muneribus, ludorum venationumque apparatu pecunias profundunt.* Cic. is condemning the extravagant public entertainment laid on by aediles in their bid for popularity (his own political advancement, courtesy of his oratorical skills more than his wealth, was, however, hardly typical). A.'s allusion can have little direct bearing on the *modus operandi* of most of his addressees; it is simply a general shaft at the kind of excess that is an enduring feature of popular electoral systems.

ut vincant superiorum celebritates: Cf. Cic. *Off.* 2.57: *Omnes autem P. Lentulus* [P. Cornelius Lentulus Spinther] *me consule* [63 BC] *vicit superiores*; for a further echo of these words, cf. 2.154 below.

quandoquidem etiam bonorum operum sumptibus . . . non deceat: Cic. advises moderation in public expenditure in *Off.* 2.59–60; A. relates this to *bona opera* in general.

110. **erga ipsos quoque pauperes . . . ut abundes pluribus:** Cf. Cic. *Off.* 2.52–64, especially 2.55, *modus adhibeatur, isque referatur ad facultates*; and 2.60, *et ad facultates accommodanda et mediocritate moderanda est.* Giving with discretion and moderation ensures that resources may be stretched to help many, rather than benefiting only a few.

non conciliandi favoris gratia ultra modum fluere: Testard ii. 176 n. 24 points out that with these words A. seems to reject the very end which Cic. has most in mind in advocating generosity in services—winning favour (though cf. 2.78–80 above). What Testard fails to say is that while A. may mouth such sentiments, the whole thrust of his argument about the *utile* is every bit as pragmatic as Cic.'s. **non superfluas aedificationes adgredi nec praetermittere necessarias:** Reminiscent of Cic. *Off.* 2.60, where it is said that money is better spent on public works, such as *muri navalia portus aquarum ductus*, which endure, than on transient entertainments. 2.111 makes it clear that A. is thinking of church buildings. There is some significant self-justification at work here. A. began to construct basilicas at an early stage in his episcopacy (cf. *Exc. fr.* 1.20 for a reference to work going on in 378), and Milan can scarcely ever have been free from the evidence of building activity throughout his tenure (Augustine, by contrast, took little interest in such affairs, according to Possid. *Vita Aug.* 24). Though hastily constructed, his edifices were lavishly adorned (see R. Krautheimer, *Three Christian Capitals: Topography and Politics* (Berkeley and Los Angeles, 1983), 69–92; McLynn, 226–37; Humphries, 196–202, citing other key literature), and there is every reason to suppose that his opponents attacked the sums being spent on them, as his church's physical presence expanded ever more dominantly into the Milanese suburbs, simultaneously imposing the authority of the bishop and symbolizing the triumph of the Nicene cultus over both the traditional pagan symbolism of civic identity and the presence of rival Christian forces. Some of the money must have come from the investment of A.'s own property assets, but some evidently came too from the disposal of church assets dating from Auxentius' time: cf. 2.142. Whatever the source, the expenditure clearly invited suspicion and criticism: were not the poor being neglected in the process? The work on which he has been engaged is, he implies, 'necessary' construction, the 'appropriate' decoration of the *Dei templum* (2.111). That appropriateness was clearly directly related to the likely social impact of the projects; but A. professes that it is determined by the worthiness of the God whom he serves. Evidently, not all were convinced by his claims.

111. impensas: Cf. Cic. has *impensae* in *Off.* 2.60.

ne restrictiorem . . . aut indulgentiorem: Cf. Cic. *Off.* 2.55.

erga clericos: Perhaps clerics requesting funds for improving church buildings.

necessitati ⟨eorum⟩: E²: *necessitati eorum* most editors: *necessitati* Testard.

a sordidis negotiationis aucupiis retrahere debeas: A. is prominent among the Fathers in his polemic against the evils of commercial moneylending (the OT bases are Ex. 22: 25; Lev. 25: 35–8; Dt. 23: 19–20; Ps. 14: 5; Ezek. 18: 8, 13, 17; 22: 12). He paints vivid pictures of the cruelty and dishonesty of usurers, devoting his *Tob.* to a stylized attack on their wicked trade. Usury is contrary to divine law, contrary to nature, and invariably associated with the oppression of the poor. Cf. 3.20, 41; *Ep.* 62 [19].4–5. The trade is despised by Cic. in *Off.* 1.150 and 2.89 (the latter passage is evoked by A. in *Tob.* 46); cf. also Cato, *De agric.*, praef. 1; Colum. *Agric.*, praef. 8; Sen. *Ira* 3.33.3. On the influence of Greek authors, especially Basil, on A., see S. Giet, 'De saint Basile à saint Ambroise. La condamnation du prêt à intéret au IVe siècle', *RSR* 31 (1944), 95–128 (though Giet mistakenly thinks that A. was not proficient in Greek); S. Calafato, *La proprietà privata in s. Ambrogio* (Turin, 1958), 119–35; Homes Dudden ii. 470–4; Vasey, 165–71 (discussing the legislation of the late fourth century against some of the excesses of the money-lenders). A good general survey, citing the earlier literature, is given by R. P. Maloney, 'The Teaching of the Fathers on Usury: An Historical Study on the Development of Christian Thinking', *VChr* 27 (1973), 241–65 (251–6 on A.); see also B. Gordon, 'Lending at Interest: Some Jewish, Greek and Christian Approaches, 800 BC–AD 100', *History of Political Economy* 14 (1982), 406–26. On trade generally, see on 1.185, 243.

CHAPTER 22: INSINCERE KINDNESS DOES NOT WIN LASTING FAVOUR

2.112–35 is on the *utile* of sincere behaviour. A. cites the negative example of Absalom, whose rise to power on the strength of an obsequious cultivation of popular support brought him only short-term success (2.113–16). He draws on Cic.'s arguments against pretence in *Off.* 2.43 and against bribery in *Off.* 2.52–5. At first sight, the target is not particularly clear: it is easier to imagine Cic.'s readership of aspiring politicians more than A.'s clerics resorting to such tactics (cf. the reference to exercising *potestas* in 2.120 below). But in reality A.'s church itself was (and what church is not?) an elaborate power-structure, rife with ambitions and petty jealousies, and A. is evidently trying to nip such contention in the bud, while resolutely affirming his own authority. Officials must not seek to win preferment by courting popular opinion so as to outstrip their superiors (cf. 2.119), or by showing unfair bias towards the rich and influential, especially in judicial cases (2.124–33) (of course, A. himself knows a thing or two about populism). Nor must a bishop overlook a man for promotion whose popularity is lower than his neighbour's (2.121). Seniors must not envy juniors who enjoy success (2.122), but equally, no one should display insubordination by seeking to overshadow the merits of his bishop (2.123). Arrogance, jealousy, and injustice are all reprehensible. Deacons (*ministri*) in particular are mentioned in 2.134, where the bishop is encouraged to allocate roles according to ability. Does this suggest that there had been some particular tensions within the diaconate? The number of references to arrogance and the need to practise humility (2.119, 122, 124, 134; 3.129, 133), and the condemnation of ambitious attempts to outdo episcopal glory (2.123), do seem rather telling; cf. also the mention of extreme church discipline in 2.135.

What A. is doing is showing the incidental dangers of his constant stress on external reputation (cf. 1.247): encourage clerics to seek popularity too much, and it will only exacerbate the kind of personal tensions that are already a reality of the church's life, and so destabilize the structure of the pyramid. Appeals to cultivate the right kind of personal *existimatio* must be guarded by warnings against injustice and rivalry, and carefully qualified by references to the well-being of the church as a whole.

112. **ne aut nimia remissio videatur aut nimia sever-itas:** Cf. Cic. *Off*. 2.55.

sed nihil simulatam . . . alta fundatur radice: [**verae virtutis:** E²W², OB: *esse verae virtutis* Gering: *vere virtutis* V², E¹W¹, C: *esse vere virtutis* Paderborn: *severe virtutis* A: *esse severe virtutis* Zell: *sed verae virtutis* P²: *sed vere virtutis* P¹V¹: *severae virtutis* Testard] Cf. Cic. *Off*. 2.43: *Vera gloria radices agit atque etiam propagatur, ficta omnia celeriter tamquam flosculi decidunt, nec simulatum potest quicquam esse diuturnum.* A. speaks of 'true virtue' instead of Cic.'s 'true glory'; for a similar substitution, cf. 2.40. The fleeting beauty of flowers or grass is of course a common biblical image, too (e.g. Ps. 89: 6; Is. 40: 6–8 [and 1 Pt. 1: 24–5]; Jas. 1: 10–11). On sincerity, cf. 1.75, 93, 101, 104; 3.58, 76.

113. **Et ut exemplis adsertionis nostrae probemus . . . proferamus testimonium:** [**adsertionis:** PV, Zell, Ligna-mine, Testard: *adsertiones* A, EW, COB, other editors; **nostrae** PVA¹, Zell, Lignamine: *nostras* A², EW, COB, other editors; **decidunt:** C, several editors: *decidant* PVMA, EW, OB, Lignamine, Testard] Cf. Cic. *Off*. 2.43: *Testes sunt permulti in utramque partem, sed brevitatis causa familia contenti erimus una.* Cic. illustrates the transience of a reputation gained by feigned generosity by referring to the Gracchi family. Tiberius Sempronius Gracchus, the distin-guished consul of 177 and 163 BC and victor over the Celtiberians, has, he says, achieved lasting glory for his military and political achievements, while his sons, Tiberius (tribune of the plebs in 133 BC) and Gaius (tribune of the plebs in 123 and 122 BC), were revolutionaries who deserved to be killed and whose honour has faded. A. similarly points to one family, the illustrious house of David, and contrasts the enduring glory of David himself with the short-lived esteem enjoyed by his usurper son, Absalom. The *adsertio* is as much Cic.'s as *nostra*. On **ad virtutis profectum**, see on 1.233.

114. **Absalon erat . . . usque ad verticem immaculatus:** See 2 Ki. 14: 25. Absalom is made to sound rather like a Vergilian hero: cf. *Aen*. 5.295: *Euryalus forma insignis vir-idique iuventa*; 4.559 (of Aeneas): *membra decora iuventae.*

Is fecit sibi currus . . . . 'Et quisquis ad me veniet . . . iustificabo illum': See 2 Ki. 15: 1–4.

Talibus deliniebat singulos sermonibus: Cf. Cic. *Off.* 2.48, cited on 2.30 above.

Et cum accederent adorare eum . . . osculabatur eos: See 2 Ki. 15: 5–6.

115. honorabilia: Cf. Cic. *Sen.* 63: *Haec enim ipsa sunt honorabilia quae videntur levia atque communia, salutari adpeti decedi adsurgi deduci reduci consuli.*

Ubi parva processit dilatio . . . paulisper cedendo interponendam putavit: The **propheta** is David, who sent Hushai the Arkite to feign loyalty to Absalom and advise him to delay his attack on David's forces (2 Ki. 15: 32–7; 16: 15–19; and especially 17: 1–16); the delay enabled David to get safely away across the Jordan.

David commendabat . . . ut ei parcerent: See 2 Ki. 18: 5.

Ideoque nec proelio interesse maluit, ne . . . videretur, sed tamen filio: A somewhat idealized interpretation. In fact, David fully intended to fight, but was dissuaded by his men, who argued that the risk of losing him was too great (2 Ki. 18: 2–4).

referre: MSS: Winterbottom, 564, conjectures *inferre* instead, but this does not seem necessary.

parricidae licet: Absalom of course *attempted* parricide; he did not carry it off.

116. adsentatione: Cic. has *adsentatorum* in *Off.* 2.63.

CHAPTER 23: BRIBERY AND FLATTERY DO NOT
EARN ENDURING LOYALTY

117. Quis igitur . . . fidos sibi arbitretur?: Cic. condemns the winning of popular support through bribery: cf. *Off.* 2.21–2: *aut postremo pretio ac mercede ducuntur, quae sordissima est illa quidem ratio et inquinatissima, et iis qui ea tenentur et illis qui ad eam confugere conantur. Male enim se res habet cum quod virtute effici debet, id temptatur pecunia.* On the instability of allegiance procured this way, cf. *Off.* 2.53: *Praeclare in epistula quadam Alexandrum filium Philippus accusat* [see on 2.30 above] *quod largitione benevolentiam Macedonum consectetur: 'Quae te, malum,' inquit, 'ratio in*

istam spem induxit, ut eos tibi fideles putares fore quos pecunia
corrupisses? . . .' [etc.].

118. adulatione: See on 1.226 and 1.209; and cf. 2.96; 3.89,
134.

et ille qui obsecratione ambitus videtur, vult semper
se rogari: Obsequious treatment is an addictive drug: the
more someone is courted, the more he comes to expect it as a
right.

CHAPTER 24: HONEST GIVING RATHER THAN
RAW AMBITION

119. et maxime ecclesiasticum: As ever, ecclesiastical
standards must be the highest of all; cf. 2.124.
adrogantia: Perhaps the reader is meant to contrast the
spirit condemned here and in 2.122 with A.'s own example in
1.1–4; cf. also 2.122, 124, 134; 3.28, 36. On the dangers of
wanting to be feared and loved simply for the sheer pleasure
of it in the episcopal life, cf. Aug. *Conf.* 10.36.59.
turpis . . . indecora: The Ciceronian terms recur.
se . . . commendat: See on 2.29–39.

120. nec nimiam remissionem, ne aut potestatem exer-
cere: On maintaining a due balance between severity and
leniency in public office, cf. Cic. *Off.* 1.88 (cf. also 3.133–4
below). A. the former *consularis* no doubt knows full well the
difficulty of achieving such a balance.
aut susceptum officium nequaquam implere vide-
amur: Cf. 1.213–18, applying corresponding pragmatism
to the business of allocating clerical responsibilities. The
philosophy is nothing if not realistic: competence is what
matters.

121. Enitendum quoque . . . et collatam reservemus
gratiam: Cf. Cic. *Off.* 2.17: *proprium hoc statuo esse virtutis*
conciliare animos hominum et ad usus suos adiungere; and
especially 2.65: *Haec igitur opera grata multis et ad beneficii*
obstringendos homines accommodata; also 2.67. On **beneficii**
. . . obligemus, cf. Cic. *Off.* 1.58: *quorum beneficiis maxime*
obligati sumus; and 1.56: *Magna etiam illa communitas es*
quae conficitur ex beneficiis ultro et citro datis acceptis, quae

mutua et grata dum sunt, inter quos ea sunt firma devinciuntur societate. On winning popularity through *beneficia* generally, cf. Cic. *Off.* 2.65–85.

sacerdotem: Here, as often = 'bishop' (Gryson, *Prêtre*, 134–6). Bishops are not to antagonize their clergy by treating them unjustly, but should show deference to their priests and deacons as if to their parents; hence the father–son relationship (see on 1.24) effectively works both ways.

ministro: Probably a deacon. On the order of bishop, priest, deacon here, cf. *Expos. Ps. 118.2.23: ut sacerdos summus, ut presbyter, ut minister altaris sacri;* further references in Gryson, *Prêtre*, 134 n. 3.

122. Neque hos . . . humilitatem tenere: Those who are approved must remain humble, and bishops must not become jealous if lesser clerics win favour by their good deeds; the popularity of any cleric is to the credit of the church. Cf. generally 3.129; on *humilitas,* see on 1.1.

aut quisquam de clero: Such as a reader or an exorcist; cf. 1.216.

ieiunio: On the importance of fasting, a duty A. regarded seriously both as an ecclesiastical routine and as a personal obligation, cf. 3.10; *Elia, passim; Ep. extra coll.* 14 [63].15–31; *Ep.* 15 [42].9–11; and see Homes Dudden i. 108–10. More generally, consult R. Arbesmann, 'Fasten', *RAC* vii. 471–93; V. E. Grimm, *From Feasting to Fasting, the Evolution of a Sin: Attitudes to Food in Late Antiquity* (London and New York, 1996).

doctrina et lectione: Cf. 1 Tim. 4: 13.

Gratia enim ecclesiae laus doctoris est: The underlying motivation is typical: the whole clerical persona is directed towards the esteem of the church.

Laudent enim . . . et non suum os: Cf. Prov. 27: 2: *Laudet te alienus, et non os tuum: extraneus, et non labia tua.*

123. Ceterum si quis . . . simulata adfectatione doctrinae aut humilitatis aut misericordiae: [**oboedit:** Winterbottom, 564: *oboediat* PVM²A, EW, COB, Testard: *oboediet* M¹; ⟨**et**⟩ **extollere:** E²] The bishop has a unique authority (cf. *Acta conc. Aquil.* 51–2; *Ep.* 75 [21].4; *Ep. extra coll.* 1a [40].1–4), and no junior cleric should seek to outdo his leader by putting on a show of special spirituality. A. the

strict disciplinarian makes it clear that he will brook no
challenge to his episcopal prerogatives; obedience is
demanded within the clerical *ordo*.

**quoniam veritatis ea est regula . . . quo minor alius
fiat:** The **veritatis . . . regula** (cf. e.g. *Ex.* 2.3) qualifies the
theme of self-commendation (see on 2.29–39): there must be
no commending of self at the expense of others; cf. Cic. *Off.*
2.68.

**124. Non defendas improbum . . . cuius crimen non
deprehenderis:** Cic. *Off.* 2.51 argues that the innocent
must be spared prosecution on a capital charge (one where
their civic status is at stake); but he also advises that a guilty
person be defended, so long as he is not *nefarius impiusque*.
The principle of not committing **sancta** to an unworthy
person (cf. Mt. 7: 6) is set out by Paul in 1 Cor. 6: 1–11:
disputes among Christians should be settled within the
church and not in the secular courts. The injunction gave
rise to the tradition of the *episcopalis audientia*, outlined in
the third century in the *Didascalia* (2.37–56) and given
formal legitimacy in 318 (*CTh* 1.27.1). By A.'s time, there
had been a whole series of imperial pronouncements on the
rights of these episcopal courts, attempting to define (and
curtail) their powers, often with no great clarity (Gaudemet,
229–40; Biondi i. 435–61; W. Selb, 'Episcopalis Audientia
von der Zeit Konstantins bis zur Novelle XXXV Valentinians III', *ZRG* 84 (1967), 167–217; W. Waldstein, 'Zur
Stellung der Episcopalis Audientia im spätrömischen Prozess', in D. Medicus and H. H. Seiler (eds.), *Festschrift für
Max Kaser zum 70. Geburtstag* (Munich, 1976), 533–56; J. C
Lamoreaux, 'Episcopal Courts in Late Antiquity', *JECS*
(1995), 143–67). Many churchmen were to find the work a
severe burden: Augustine frequently had to arbitrate
between litigants from early morning till late afternoon
(Possid. *Vita Aug.* 19), and he deplored the time and
energy that this duty demanded (*Op. mon.* 37), as he settled
disputes over money, land, and cattle (*Ep.* 33.5), as well a
matters of the faith. Nevertheless, he still insists tha
Christians should take their cases before ecclesiastic
rather than civil courts (*En. Ps. 80.*21; cf. Ambros. *Comn
1 Cor.* 6) (see P. Brown, *Augustine of Hippo: A Biograph*

(London, 1967), 195–6; K. Raikas, 'St Augustine on Juridical Duties: Some Aspects of the Episcopal Office in Late
Antiquity', in J. C. Schnaubelt and F. Van Fleteren (eds.),
*Collectanea Augustiniana: Augustine: 'Second Founder of the
Faith'* (New York, 1990), 467–83). It is Augustine who tells
us how busy A. was dealing with people's problems (*Conf.*
6.3.1); these were not all formal cases for arbitration, but no
doubt A. was kept more than occupied in a community as
large and complex as Milan's. We can picture the ex-
administrator and advocate far more at home in this realm
than Augustine. In several passages, he mentions the qualities necessary in a judge (e.g. *Cain* 2.38; *Expos. Ps.
118*.20.36–58; cf. also *Expos. Ps. 118*.8.25; *Tob.* 36; see
V. R. Vasey, 'St Ambrose's Mirror for Judges', *The Jurist*
39 (1979), 437–46); on bishops judging holy/ecclesiastical
matters, cf. *Ep.* 75 [21].2, 15. Consult G. Vismara, 'Ancora
sulla episcopalis audientia. Ambrogio arbitro o giudice',
SDHI 53 (1987), 53–73; McLynn, 269–72.

tum maxime in ecclesia: On the church as a model of
justice, cf. 1.142.

aequitatem: Cf. Cic. *Off.* 2.71: *Extremum autem praeceptum
in beneficiis operaque danda ne quid contra aequitatem contendas, ne quid pro iniuria; fundamentum enim est perpetuae
commendationis et famae iustitiae, sine qua nihil potest esse
laudabile.*

potentior . . . ditior: Cic. mentions the *fortunatus et potens*
in *Off.* 2.69.

ut nihil: EW, COB: *et ut nihil* PVMA, Testard.

vindicet . . . usurpet . . . adroget . . . humiliorem: For
the language and the principle, cf. 1.1–4 and see ad loc.; cf.
also 2.134; 3.28, 36.

in Christo unum sunt: Cf. Gal. 3: 28: *omnes enim vos unum
estis in Christo Iesu* (cf. also Jn. 17: 20–3).

25. Sed nec personam alterius accipiamus in iudicio:
Cf. Jas. 2: 1–13; and 1.149 above; also *Const. Apost.* 2.5; 2.42.

fidem: Harks back to the Ciceronian point first mentioned
in 2.40.

Licet tibi silere in negotio dumtaxat pecuniario: Cf.
3.59; and *Luc.* 7.122, on Jesus' refusal to arbitrate in a
dispute over an inheritance in Lk. 12: 13–14: *Bene terrena*

declinat qui propter divina descenderat, nec iudex esse dignatur litium et arbiter facultatum vivorum habens mortuorumque iudicium arbitriumque meritorum. . . . Unde non immerito refutatur hic frater, qui dispensatorem caelestium gestiebat corruptibilibus occupare, cum inter fratres patrimonium non iudex medius, sed pietas debeat sequestra dividere, quamquam immortalitatis patrimonium, non pecuniae sit hominibus expetendum. In his *Ep.* 3.36, Symmachus seeks to dissuade A. from involvement in a suit between Caecilianus, Symmachus' relative and a *praefectus annonae* at Rome, and one Pirata (or his *procurator*), who, it was rumoured, might enjoy the bishop's favour (see P. Bruggisser, 'Orator disertissimus: A propos d'une lettre de Symmaque à Ambroise', *Hermes* 115 (1987), 106–15). McLynn, 271–2, suggests that Symmachus, concerned that A. would not be impartial in deciding Caecilianus' case, is there using *Off.* 2.125 and 3.59 against him: *Negavi solere te recipere in tuam curam pecuniarias actiones*, exploiting the theoretical limits which A. had placed upon his own activity in a bid to circumscribe his actual behaviour.

We know of at least one case of a material kind that A. did settle. A Christian widow, having been left land by her brother Marcellus, a cleric, on the condition that she bequeath it to the church after her death, was challenged by another brother, Laetus, to give up the property. The case first went before the prefect's court in Milan, and then, after the lawyers there had argued long enough to ensure that it ran out of court time, it was submitted to the bishop for judgement. A. settled the issue by ruling that the brother could have the land, but should pay an annual revenue of its produce to his sister, after whose death he would be freed from his obligation; the only loser, he says, was the church (*Ep.* 24 [82]): see F. Martroye, 'Une sentence arbitrale de saint Ambroise', *Revue historique de droit français et étranger* ser. 4/8 (1929), 300–11.

In causa autem Dei . . . etiam dissimulare peccatum est non leve: In a dispute which threatens the harmony of the church (cf. 1.170), a bishop must not turn a blind eye: to do so is a grave sin. On **causa Dei**, cf. *Ep. extra coll.* 1 [40].4; also *Ep. extra coll.* 1a [40].27, *causa religionis*; *Ep.* 7

[21].4, *causa fidei*; 3.127 below. This is the principle by which A. claims to be operating when he presents a show of defiance and challenge to the imperial powers; see generally Gryson, *Prêtre*, 253–60; also Morino, 69–72. Typically, of course, the harmony that he perceives to be jeopardized is the stability of his own Nicene cause.

CHAPTER 25: SERVING THE POOR RATHER THAN
THE RICH

126.   Quid autem tibi prodest favere diviti? . . . a quibus referendae vicem speramus gratiae: Cf. Cic. *Off.* 2.69: *sed quis est tandem qui inopis et optimi viri causae non anteponat in opera danda gratiam fortunati et potentis? A quo enim expeditior et celerior remuneratio fore videtur, in eum fere est voluntas nostra propensior* [etc.]. In 2.124–5, A. is thinking about rich litigants: favouritism must not be shown to them because of their money, in the hope of some personal return.

Sed eo magis infirmo et inopi nos studere convenit . . . remunerationem speramus a Domino Iesu: Cf. 1.166, where it is said that the grateful goodwill of a poor person may be a greater repayment for a kindness than the gold or silver of the wealthy; on divine reward for charity to the poor, cf. 1.38–9.

qui sub specie convivii generalem . . . sed pauperes invitandos: [docens: E², Maurists, Krabinger: *ducens* PMA¹, E¹W, O, Testard: *dicens* VA², CB, other editors] See Lk. 14: 12–14.

remuneratorem nobis faciunt . . . obligandum obtulit: On earning this reward, see on 1.39.

127.   Ad ipsum quoque . . . et pudet eum debitorem esse gratiae: Cf. Cic. *Off.* 2.69: *At qui se locupletes, honoratos, beatos putant, ii ne obligari quidem beneficio volunt; quin etiam beneficium se dedisse arbitrantur cum ipsi quamvis magnum aliquid acceperint, atque etiam a se aut postulari aut exspectari aliquid suspiciantur, patrocinio vero se usos aut clientes appellari mortis instar putant.*

pauper vero . . . refert gratiam: Cf. Cic. *Off.* 2.69:

Nimirum enim inops ille, si bonus est vir, etiam si referre gratiam non potest, habere certe potest. On inferiors benefiting superiors, cf. Sen. *Benef.* 3.18–28. For other advantages of giving to the poor, cf. 1.38–9.

gratia numquam exinanitur. Reddendo vacuatur pecunia; gratia . . . solvendo retinetur: Cf. Cic. *Off.* 2.69: *Commode autem quicumque dixit pecuniam qui habeat, non redidisse, qui reddiderit, non habere, gratiam autem et qui rettulerit habere et qui habeat rettulisse*; the saying is found also in *Planc.* 68; *Red. Quir.* 23.

Quanto igitur melius . . . locare beneficium!: Cf. Cic. *Off.* 2.71: *Quam ob rem melius apud bonos quam apud fortunatos beneficium conlocari puto* (also Cic. *Off.* 2.63, on the ungrateful person as the common enemy of the poor).

128. The warnings against favouring the rich lead to a general denunciation of *avaritia* (2.128–33); on Cic. on avarice, see on 2.108. The tone of the attack may be standard enough, but the fact that A. condemns greed so often in *Off.* suggests that he is countering a real problem in the clerical ranks. 3.57–8 singles out the vice of legacy-hunting, which certainly was a regular malaise at this time (3.57–8).

Nolite possidere . . . pecuniam: Mt. 10: 9.

Qua velut falce pullulantem . . . succidit avaritiam: Christ came to cut the *radix* of avarice. On its insidious growth, cf. *Paen.* 2.75: *avaritia . . . tamquam sub terra occulte in nostro serpit corpore.*

Petrus quoque claudo . . . ait: *Argentum et aurum non habeo. . . . surge et ambula:* Acts 3: 6; on the whole incident, see 3: 1–10.

Quanto melius . . . quam pecuniam sine salute!: Reminiscent of Eccli. 30: 14–16. *Salus* goes beyond the *sanitas* which was restored to the lame man: A. is thinking of spiritual salvation, which is of infinitely greater worth than *pecunia.*

Sed haec vix . . . ut divitiae contemptui sint: On despising riches, cf. 1.23.

CHAPTER 26: AVARICE, AND THE
WORTHLESSNESS OF MONEY

**129. Ceterum ita incubuerunt mores hominum admir-
ationi divitiarum:** [**admirationi:** Testard: *admiratione*
PVMA, EW, Zell: *ad admirationem* COB, Erasmus (1527)]
Cf. Cic. *Off.* 2.71: *Sed corrupti mores depravatique sunt
admiratione divitiarum.*

**Neque hic recens usus . . . inolevit hoc vitium hu-
manis mentibus:** Avarice entered at the fall; see on 1.137.
The *radix* image is continued from 2.128.

**cum Hiericho magna civitas . . . per avaritiam atque
auri cupiditatem:** See Josh. 6: 1–27.

**Nam cum de spoliis urbis incensae sustulisset Achar
. . . prodidit furtum:** See Josh. 7: 1–26, especially 7: 19 ff.
where the name is spelt *Achan*; 1 Chr. 2: 7 calls him *Achar*,
and this is the form used by the LXX and A.'s Latin Bible in
Josh. (E, O² here read *Achan*; V has *Acham*.)

oblatus Domino: When solemnly charged to tell the truth
on oath to the Lord (Josh. 7: 19).

**130. quae cum ipsis divinae legis coepit oraculis . . . lex
delata est:** Akin to the Pauline argument that the law was
given in order to check sin and to accentuate people's
perception of their need for forgiveness (Rom. 3: 19–31; 5:
12–21; Gal. 3: 19–25). A. doubtless thinks of the tenth
commandment in particular (Ex. 20: 17; Dt. 5: 21).

**Balac putavit . . . nisi Dominus maledicto eum absti-
nere iussisset:** [**abstinere:** MSS: *abstineri* Testard; **iussisset** EW, Maurists, Krabinger: *vetuisset*: PVMA, COB;
Testard's proposal of *abstineri* in order to redeem the
strongly attested but obviously awkward *vetuisset* requires
an awkward change of antecedent with **eum** from **Balaam**
to **populum patrum**, and is not very convincing] See Num.
22: 1–24: 25, especially 22: 15–20.

praecipitatus Achar: See Josh. 7: 24–6.

Iesus Nave, qui potuit solem statuere ne procederet:
See on 2.99.

ne serperet: A favourite Ciceronian trope: e.g. *Att.* 1.13.3;
Cat. 4.6; *Phil.* 1.5; *Rab. post.* 15; cf. 2.135 below.

paene amisit victoriam: The victory over Ai was jeopardized.

131. **Fortissimum omnium Samson . . . avaritia decepit?:** See Jdg. 16: 1–22, especially 16: 15 ff. *Mulier* is pejorative, as often (cf. 1.66); on the snare of this 'foreign' woman, cf. *Ep.* 62 [19].7–34.

qui rugientem leonem manibus discerpsit: See Jdg. 14: 5–6.

qui vinctus . . . mille ex his peremit viros: See Jdg. 15: 9–17.

qui funes . . . dirupit: With these Delilah had bound Samson in an earlier attempt to overpower him and deliver him to the Philistines (Jdg. 16: 6–9). Cf. also *Spir.* 2, prol. 5–16 (influencing Paul. Nol. *Ep.* 23.11–21); *Apol. alt.* 16.

gratia: In two senses: Samson's moral glory *and* his divinely endowed strength departed from him (see Jdg. 16: 19–20); cf. *Spir.* 2.13. Note the neat chiasmus of **Influxit pecunia . . . discessit gratia**.

132. **Feralis igitur avaritia:** Cf. 1 Tim. 6: 10.

quae habentes contaminat . . . custodiae periculum: [**alios, si sit:** E²: *alios sit* P²V, COB: *alius sit* P¹MA, E¹W, *alios si alius sit* Testard; **copiosior:** P²V²A¹, E², CO, several editors: *cupiosior* P¹V¹MA², E¹W, B, Lignamine: *cupidio,* Testard] Cf. Cic. *Off.* 2.71: *Illum fortasse adiuvat qui habet Ne id quidem semper; sed fac iuvare. Utentior sane sit, honestior vero quomodo?* The fallacy of imagining that riches are always a blessing is a *topos* in classical poetry: e.g. Plaut *Aul.*; Hor. *Od.* 3.24.45–52; *Sat.* 1.1; *Ep.* 1.7; Juv. 10.23 ff. 14.107 ff. On one disadvantage, cf. 3.135 below.

CHAPTER 27: JUSTICE, LOVE, UNITY, AND
HUMILITY; EXCOMMUNICATION AS A LAST
RESORT

133. **iustitiae forma:** Cf. 1.142, of the church.

ne quid faciamus umquam adversus iustitiam sed . . custodiamus eam: On the centrality of justice, cf. Ci *Off.* 2.71: *Extremum autem praeceptum in beneficiis operaq danda ne quid contra aequitatem contendas, ne quid pro iniuri* *fundamentum enim est perpetuae commendationis et famae iustitia, sine qua nihil potest esse laudabile* (also generally *Off.* 2.38–43).

134. commendare nos: See introductory note on 2.29–39; the reference is doubtless inspired by the mention of *commendatio* in Cic. *Off.* 2.71, in the passage which A. has in mind in 2.133. Here, A. aims higher, pointing to the ultimate in *utilitas* (cf. 1.28; 2.2–3, 23–7): the Christian servant's real desire is to commend himself to God. **caritatem habeamus . . . alterutrum existimantes superiorem sibi:** Cf. Phil. 2: 2–4: *implete gaudium meum, ut idem sapiatis, eandem caritatem habentes, unanimes, id ipsum sentientes; nihil per contentionem neque per inanem gloriam, sed in humilitate superiores sibi invicem arbitrantes: non quae sua sunt singuli considerantes, sed et ea quae aliorum.* **humilitas . . . adroget:** Cf. 1.1–4 and see ad loc.; perhaps A. is harking back to those prefatory remarks here; cf. 2.124. **Episcopus . . . quem cuique viderit aptum muneri, ei deputet:** Cf. 1.215–18, especially 216. One way to avoid the tensions of jealousy and resentment which can mar the image of ecclesial unity (2.121–3) is to make sure that clerics are allocated the kind of roles to which their talents best suit them. **Membris** evokes the NT image of the church as Christ's body (Rom. 12: 4–5; 1 Cor. 12: 12–31; Eph. 1: 22–3; 2: 16; 3: 6; 4: 4, 12, 16; 5: 23; Col. 1: 18, 24; 2: 19; 3: 15—the nuances vary from passage to passage); the language is continued in 2.135 (on the classical roots, see on 3.17; on the biblical side in A., see Toscani, 179–82). The *ministri* again are deacons, those who are the true sons of the bishop; cf. 1.24. The fact that A. singles out deacons here may imply that certain deacons in particular have been expressing discontent; see on 2.112–35.

135. Cum dolore amputatur . . . cum dolore abscidere: Cf. *Expos. Ps. 118*.8.26:

Medicus ipse si serpentis interius inveniat vulneris cicatricem, cum debeat resecare ulceris vitium, ne latius serpat, tamen a secandi urendique proposito lacrimis inflexus aegroti medicamentis tegat quod ferro aperiendum fuit: nonne ista inutilis misericordia est, si propter brevem incisionis vel exustionis dolorem corpus omne tabescat, vitae usus intereat? Recte igitur et sacerdos vulnus, ne latius serpat, a toto corpore ecclesiae quasi bonus medicus debet abscidere et prodere virus criminis quod latet, non fovere, ne, dum unum excludendum non putat, plures dignos faciat quos excludat ab ecclesia.

Cf. also *Expos. Ps. 118*.9.16; and on the bishop as a physician, *Ep. extra coll.* 14 [63].46–7; the wise man is a *medicus sibi* (*Expl. Ps. 38*.15). On A.'s knowledge of medicine generally, see G. Müller, 'Arzt, Kranker und Krankheit bei Ambrosius von Mailand (334–397)', *Sudhoffs Archiv für Geschichte der Medizin und der Naturwissenschaften* 51/3 (1967), 193–216; F. Meissel, *Medizin in den Werken des hl. Ambrosius*, Diss. (Karl-Franzens-Universität Graz, 1983); also Gryson, *Prêtre*, 287 nn. 157–8. Notably, the imagery is used by Cic. *Off.* 1.136, where he is talking about administering rebukes: *Sed ut ad urendum et secandum, sic ad hoc genus castigandi raro invitique veniemus, nec umquam nisi necessario, si nulla reperietur alia medicina*; and in *Off.* 3.32, where he is justifying the extermination of tyrants from society: *Etenim, ut membra quaedam amputantur si et ipsa sanguine et tamquam spiritu carere coeperunt et nocent reliquis partibus corporis, sic ista in figura hominis feritas et immanitas beluae a communi tamquam humanitate corporis segreganda est*. A. insists that only with extreme reluctance and sorrow (cf. 2 Cor. 2: 4) should the amputation of a 'sick' member of the body of the church—excommunication—be carried out, lest the contagion spread (cf. 1 Cor. 5: 6). Before this, 'medicinal' remedies should be tried: in other words, public penance should be administered (see on 2.77). All favouritism for beloved or esteemed members must be put aside. The rhetoric of such episcopal rebuke can be read in *Ep.* 72 [17] and *Ep. extra coll.* 11 [51]. On A.'s (formal) grief, cf. Paul. *VA* 39 drawing on *Paen.* 2.73; similar expressions of anguish at excommunication are to be found in many conciliar documents, as the Maurists point out (PL 16, 147 n. 47). On discipline as cauterization, cf. e.g. Jer. *Ep.* 117.2; for some other references, see A. S. Pease, 'Medical Allusions in the Works of St Jerome', *HSCPh* 25 (1914), 73–96, at 76–7). On **serpentia**, see on 2.130.

ut cogitemus . . . quae aliorum: Cf. Phil. 2: 4, quoted above on 2.134.

irati: See on 1.90.

CHAPTER 28: SHOWING MERCY TO PRISONERS;
THE POOR ARE THE CHURCH'S TRUE TREASURE

136. calamitatibus: Cic. uses the word in *Off.* 2.61–2.

quantum possumus . . . et plus interdum quam possumus: Cf. Cic. *Off.* 2.64: *quantum liceat et nescio an paulo plus etiam quam liceat*; also 2 Cor. 8: 3. These Ciceronian reminiscences are overlooked by Testard, 'Recherches', 102; Testard ii. 187–8 n. 9, when he claims that there is no evocation of Cic. in 2.136–51. Testard, 'Etude', 180–1; 'Recherches', 102, is also wrong to say that 2.136–51 is meant to correspond with the calculus of *utilia* in Cic. *Off.* 2.88–9. A. makes no mention of the theme in this section: all he does is argue that it is better to favour the poor than the rich, and better to spend resources on the needy than to retain them for the wealth of the church; these ideas have appeared earlier in the book (e.g. 2.126–32), and nowhere in 2.136–51 are they arranged in a hierarchical scheme of differing types of *utilia* (see on 2.22 and 2.28).

ut nos aliquando in invidiam incidimus . . . quod Arianis displicere potuerat: [**incidimus:** E², Valdarfer, Testard: *incidamus* PVMA, E'W, CO, Zell: *incendamus* B] Cf. 2.70. A. incurred the criticism of the Milanese homoians for having broken up and sold church plate in order to ransom some of the captives taken by the Goths. He argues that it is better to use such resources to help the needy than to preserve them simply for the wealth of the church. For similar liquidation of treasure for this end, cf. e.g. the actions of Cyril of Jerusalem (Soz. *HE* 4.25); John Chrysostom (*Hom. Mt.* 50–1.4); Exsuperius of Toulouse (Jer. *Ep.* 125.20.3–5); Acacius of Amida (Socr. *HE* 7.21); Hilary of Arles (Honor. *Vita Hilar.* 11); Deogratias of Carthage (Vict. Vit. *Hist. persec. Afr. prov.* 1.8); Caesarius of Arles (*Vita Caes.* 1.32–3); and Maroveus of Poitiers (Greg. Tur. *HF* 7.24). A.'s example in particular became cited as a precedent in the West: Possid. *Vita Aug.* 24; Luther, *WA* 6.46–7; 1.603 (*TRE* ii. 382); Calvin, *Inst.* 4.4.8. For a valuable study, illustrating an evocation of A.'s language (in rather different circumstances), see W. Klingshirn, 'Charity and Power: Caesarius of Arles and the Ransoming of Captives in Sub-Roman Gaul', *JRS* 75 (1985), 183–203.

The act of selling plate for charitable purposes, then, was not necessarily controversial in itself. In this particular case, however, there were two factors which inevitably provoked dismay. First, the vessels that A. chose were almost certainly ones which stemmed from Auxentius' time: he certainly made sure that he had never consecrated them hitherto (2.143); contrast his *refusal* to give up other church plate, in *Ep.* 75a [*C. Aux.*].5, which points up the double standards being applied. These vessels were not just perceived by many to be 'sacred' by virtue of the fact that they belonged to the church's treasury; many of them must have been inscribed with the names of homoian families, who had donated or bequeathed them in the interests of their personal salvation. A. was deliberately seizing a chance to rid his vaults of chalices that in his eyes were defiled by association (Brown, *Power*, 96), while proclaiming it a price worth paying in the interests of showing compassion to the oppressed. No wonder the homoians were upset to see this deliberate dismantling (2.142–3) of their benefactions, and with it the outrageous jeopardizing of the salvation of their forebears: 'the gesture of "smashing" the plate probably made more of an impact at Milan than did any subsequent transactions at the impromptu sales held by the Goths' (McLynn, 56, comparing a modern example of the symbolism of public sacrifice in a worthy cause: the removal of park railings in wartime Britain). Secondly, A. was not just ransoming prisoners or giving to the poor. He was also evidently using (or being suspected of using) some of the money to build cemetery basilicas (2.142). It looked as if he was furthering his own programme of church expansion at the homoians' expense all under the guise of providing burial plots for the dead in suitably pious surroundings. He was cleverly exploiting an opportunity to present himself as a great bestower o bounty, and reinforcing his own status, while getting rid of a tainted inheritance.

The criticisms of the homoians required an answer. In 2.136–43, as in 2.70, A.'s attempt to justify his actions involves paraphrasing an oral argument addressed to his people at the time (cf. 2.137: *ita in populo prosecuti sumus*). The rhetorical texture of the Latin, with its anaphora, general repetition, rhetorical questions, asyndeton, direct address to 'you' in 2.139, and imaginary rebuke by the Lord himself in 2.137–8, bears this out; the citation of the lofty *exemplum* of Lawrence in 2.140–1 may also be reminiscent of the kind of vivid illustration used in an earlier address. The interesting thing is that A. still feels the need to be so defensive these years later. Criticism of his use of funds was evidently an ongoing complaint: cf. *Ep.* 75a [*C. Aux.*].33. On the whole section, see T. Sternberg, '"Aurum utile." Zu einem Topos vom Vorrang der Caritas über Kirchenschätze seit Ambrosius', *JbAC* 39 (1996), 128–48.

Quis autem est tam durus immitis ferreus . . .?: A typically Ciceronian question: cf. e.g. *Verr.* 2.5.121: *Quis tam fuit . . . ferreus, quis tam inhumanus . . .?*; *Arch.* 17: *Quis nostrum tam animo agresti ac duro fuit, ut . . . non commoveretur?*; *Or.* 148: *quis . . . se tam durum agrestemque praeberet . . .?*

femina ab impuritatibus barbarorum, quae graviores morte sunt: The Goths have no moral scruples; see on 2.70. On barbarian *impuritates* and rape as a fate worse than death, cf. 3.83; also 1.204.

ab idolorum contagiis, quibus mortis metu inquinabantur: The 'pollution' of idols is a motif found especially in Ezek. (e.g. 20: 31, 39; 22: 4; 23: 7, 30, 37; 36: 18, 25; 37: 23; cf. also Acts 15: 20; 1 Cor. 8); in A., cf. e.g. *Abr.* 2.81. On the 'idolatry' of the Goths, cf. *Ep. extra coll.* 4 [10].9. A.'s equation of the Goths *en bloc* with murderous heathens reflects his attempt to invent a theological-racial axis between his local opponents and the barbarian hordes beyond, and thus to play on the fears of other Milanese in the interests of his own cause; see on 2.70. For sixth-century examples of Christian prisoners being martyred for refusing to defile themselves, cf. Greg. Magn. *Dial.* 3.27–8.

137.   ita in populo prosecuti sumus: See on 2.136 above.

Qui enim sine auro misit apostolos: Cf. Mt. 10: 9, quoted in 2.128; also *Ep. extra coll.* 14 [63].87.

Quid opus est custodire quod nihil adiuvat?: Cf. 2.132.

An ignoramus quantum . . . Assyrii sustulerint?: When Nebuchadnezzar's forces captured the temple at Jerusalem in 597 BC (4 Ki. 24: 13; 2 Chr. 36: 9–10).

Nonne dicturus est Dominus . . .?: A. visualizes a judgement-day scene of accusation, as the Lord asks terse, searching questions about whether the transient riches of the world have been preferred to the eternal wealth of his kingdom; for a similar picture, cf. 1.63.

vasa viventium: On the soul/person as a 'vessel', cf. Acts 9: 15; Rom. 9: 21–3; 1 Thess. 4: 4; 2 Tim. 2: 21; 1 Pt. 3: 7; and 2 Cor. 4: 7, quoted in 2.140.

138.   'Aurum sacramenta non quaerunt neque auro placent, quae auro non emuntur': The sacraments (A. means the eucharist in particular; cf. 1.205) 'are not bought with gold', but with the cost of Christ's blood, and do not require gold: i.e. cheaper vessels will do. On the antithesis of gold and Christ's blood in redemption, cf. 1 Pt. 1: 18–19.

Vere illa sunt vasa pretiosa . . . quod sanguis eius operatus est: The sacramental cup, once consecrated, contains the blood of Christ, shed to redeem souls (cf. Eph. 1: 7; Col. 1: 14; 1 Pt. 1: 18–19; and see generally Seibel, 146–52; Johanny, 89–134; Fenger, 41–59). If the cup itself is then used to redeem captives, it too is effecting a release. Both cup and contents are redemptive (**cum in utroque viderit redemptionem, ut calix ab hoste redimat quos sanguis a peccato redimit**). The sacrament is adorned with a practical demonstration of the divine ransom. This is a bold parallel, though the association of earthly, physical ransom with the eternal, spiritual redemption by Christ's blood is of course only feasible because it is the eucharistic chalice that is in mind. Another striking idea is found in Cyprian: Christ is present in our captive brethren, and tests our faith; he shed his blood to ransom us, we use our money to ransom him (*Ep.* 62.2.2). In A.'s rhetoric, the Christian owes the price Christ paid for him (*Ios.* 42). For **qu**

operatur quod sanguis eius operatus est, cf. 3.103,
*propitiationem . . . quam propitiator in sua operatus est
passione*. For **agnoscitur**, cf. the similar use of the verb in
3.103.

captivorum: EW, COB, most editors: *peccatorum* PVMA,
Zell, Gering, Lignamine, Paderborn.

**Ecce aurum quod probari potest, ecce aurum utile . . .
quo . . . servatur castitas!:** This gold, unlike most wealth,
is **utile** (cf. 1.28; 2.15–16, 23). What matters is the use to
which wealth is put (see on 1.132). On **pudicitia . . .
castitas**, see on 2.70.

**139. Huic muneri proficere debuit . . . ut redimeret
periclitantes:** The gold of the chalice and the 'gold' of the
Redeemer, the blood of Christ (the *bonum aurum*: *Expl. Ps.
35.1*), are both redemptive.

Agnosco: Cf. 3.103.

irrutilasse: An Ambrosian coinage; cf. *Is.* 60; *Apol.* 45; *Ep.*
73 [18].24; *Exc. fr.* 2.10; *Luc.* 8.29 (*TLL* vii/2. 454).

**140. Tale aurum sanctus martyr Laurentius Domino
reservavit:** See on 1.205. Lawrence had sold the treasures
of the church in order to pay the poor, and so had nothing
but the poor themselves, the church's true wealth, to present. On a recent gesture of charity which evokes something
of Lawrence's example, cf. 3.48 and see ad loc.

'Hi sunt thesauri ecclesiae': Cf. *Ep.* 73 [18].6: *Nihil
ecclesia sibi nisi fidem possidet. Hos redditus praebet, hos
fructus. Possessio ecclesiae sumptus est egenorum*; also *Ep.* 75a
[*C. Aux.*].33.

Habentes thesaurum in vasis fictilibus: 2 Cor. 4: 7; cf.
also *Spir.* 1.147.

**Esurivi, et dedistis mihi manducare . . . hospes eram,
et collegistis me:** Mt. 25: 35.

Quod enim uni horum fecistis, mihi fecistis: Mt. 25:
40.

141. et vicit: Martyrdom is true victory; See on 1.187 and
1.202.

persecutor: Valerian, or possibly the urban prefect of
Rome, P. Cornelius Saecularis (see on 1.205), before whom
Lawrence presented the poor.

Itaque Ioachim . . . et in captivitatem deduci: The

young king Jehoiachin was taken captive to Babylon, along with the treasures of the Jerusalem temple, by the forces of Nebuchadnezzar in 597 BC (4 Ki. 24: 10–16; 2 Chr. 36: 9–10).

pro singulari suae interpretationis vivacitate: Because of his bold presentation of the poor as the real *thesauri ecclesiae*. Lawrence's courageous interpretation was a sign of the *fortitudo* for which the crown of martyrdom is the ultimate prize: cf. 1.198, 200–7.

142. Nemo enim potest dicere. . . . nemo potest dolere . . . : [queri: A, B: *quaeri* PV, EW, CO] The opposition of the homoians is absurd: they are complaining that poor people are being kept alive, that captives are being ransomed, that churches are being built, and that the faithful are being given Christian burial.

templum Dei: Probably neither purely literal (cf. 2.111, 138) nor entirely spiritual (*pace* Testard ii. 188 n. 16), but deliberately ambivalent. *Vita Caes.* [CCL 104] 1.32–3, which is conscious of Ambrose, speaks of Caesarius of Arles's decoration of the *verum templum*, namely people. The bishop's church-building programme *amounts to* the building up of the spiritual temple of God (on which cf. 1 Cor. 3: 16–17; 6: 19; 2 Cor. 6: 16–7: 1; Eph. 2: 19–22; and see Toscani, 175–9).

quia humandis fidelium reliquiis . . . Christianorum requies defunctorum est: The churches in question were cemetery basilicas, built adjacent to Christian burial sites. The provision of burial for the faithful can be presented as a work of *humanitas* (e.g. Arist. *Apol.* 15; Tert. *Apol.* 39.6; Lact. *Inst.* 6.12.25; A., *Tob.* 2–5, 36–7; *Expos. Ps. 118.*21.13; Aug. *Cur. mort.*; *CD* 1.12–13) and a clerical duty (Jer. *Ep.* 1.12) (see Biondi ii. 249–61; Y. Duval, *Auprès des saints corps et âme. L'inhumation 'ad sanctos' dans la chrétienté d'Orient et d'Occident du IIIe au VIIe siècle* (Paris, 1988), 30–2), but in reality the burial grounds around such churches offered space for the interment of only the élite of court society like the Egyptian doctor Dioscorus, or Manlius Theodorus' sister Daedalia, a distinguished convert to A.'s corps of consecrated virgins (McLynn, 233–4). A.'s opponents could see the dangers perfectly well: the bishop was constructing elaborate burial chambers to show off the names of his high-ranking followers, all the while professing his charity to the unfortunate victims of violent times.

In his tribus generibus: The previous sentence has four limbs, not three, but the last two are speaking of the same *genus*, the burial of believers. The three causes for which it is permissible to dispose of church plate are therefore (i) the relief of the poor; (ii) the construction of church buildings; and (iii) the provision of burial plots for the deceased in Christian tombs.

143. **Opus est . . . ministerium transferatur:** The mystical shape of a sacred cup is vital, and restricts its use exclusively to the sacramental. The chalices were not sold for profane use as ordinary vessels; they were broken up, melted down, and sold as precious metal.

primum quaesita sunt vasa quae initiata non essent: Not just any vessels were taken, we are told: A. first looked for vessels which had not yet been consecrated. If they were homoian bequests, of course, he had no doubt carefully avoided using them in any case.

CHAPTER 29: THE GUARDING OF DEPOSITS

144. **ut deposita viduarum intemerata maneant:** On the church's function as a bank for the deposits of the vulnerable, see on 1.253, and cf. 1.253–4 generally.

maior est causa viduarum et pupillorum: See on 1.63.

145. **sicut in libris Machabaeorum legimus:** See 2 Macc. 3. A. goes on to relate accurately the story of the attempted seizure of the deposits in the treasury at Jerusalem by Heliodorus, the regent of Seleucus IV Philopator (r. 187–175 BC). However, **Antiocho regi** is a slip: the king is Seleucus, not Antiochus IV Epiphanes (r. 175–164 BC), his brother who succeeded him. On this paragraph, see 2 Macc. 3: 1–9.

summo sacerdoti: Onias.

146. See 2 Macc. 3: 10–22.

praestare: PVMA, EW: *praestaret* COB.

accinctaeque mulieres pectus . . . per fenestras alii prospectabant: The details are elaborated, as A. turns a biblical scene into a typical classical one (Banterle, 267 n. 4; Testard ii. 190 n. 5). In 2 Macc. 3: 19, the virgins, who are normally confined, run outside, some to the gates, some to the walls, while others look out through the windows (LXX); or they run to Onias or to the walls, or look out of the windows (Vulg.). **pulsabant ianuam** is not found in either the LXX or the Vulg.

147. See 2 Macc. 3: 23–31.

armis praefulgens aureis: Cf. Aeneas' special horse in Verg. *Aen.* 8.552–3: *quem fulva leonis | pellis obit totum praefulgens unguibus aureis.* 2 Macc. 3: 25 has *videbatur arma habere aurea.*

Oborta est laetitia: Cf. Ter. *Heaut.* 680: *tanta haec laetitia obortast.* 2 Macc. 3: 30 has *laetitia impletum est.*

148. See 2 Macc. 3: 32–9.

149. Servanda est igitur . . . adhibenda diligentia: Cf. 1.253–4.

impressio potentis: An example of such an assault follows in 2.150–1.

150. Meministis: An incident in recent history; cf. 1.72.

Recens exemplum ecclesiae Ticinensis proferam: The date of the incident is impossible to pin down. 386 may be the likeliest setting, since Valentinian II was resident at Ticinum (Pavia) on 15 February of that year (*CTh* 12.12.11): Homes Dudden i. 119–20; ii. 694–5; followed (apparently) by Testard i. 46 (though at ii. 190 n. 6, Testard seems less sure). The Maurists (PL 16, 25–6); Cavasin, 549; F. Savio, *Gli antichi vescovi d'Italia, dalle origini al 1300: Milano* (Bologna, 1913, repr. 1975), 135, also suggest 386 (the time of the crisis with Justina). Others have thought that a more appropriate context can be found in the arbitrary confiscations of Italian property by the invading force of the usurper Maximus in the spring of 388 (Palanque, 192–3, 526–7, accepted by L. Cracco Ruggini, 'Ambrogio di fronte alla compagine sociale del suo tempo', in *AmbrEpisc* i. 230–65, at 248 n. 45; Cracco Ruggini, 199 n. 626; and (tentatively) by Paredi, 297; Banterle, 16 (though in 269 n. 9 Banterle appears less decisive), but the references to **praeceptis imperatoris** here and *imperator* in 2.151 rule this out (McLynn, 286 n. 139). For an analysis of the legal context see M. Sargenti and R. B. Bruno Siola, *Normativa imperiale e diritto Romano negli scritti di s. Ambrogio* (Milan, 1991), 19–28. The episode is striking as much for its rather proud depiction of the author's authoritarian manner and belligerence in the face of (ostensibly legitimate) civil claims as it is for its illustration of a basic point about looking after trusts.

quae viduae depositum quod susceperat, amittere periclitabatur: The deposit in question was most likely a sum of money, though it may conceivably have been some other valuable; it was lodged in *conclavia* (2.151). Presumably the widow had incurred some kind of debt which had led her creditor (**qui sibi . . . vindicare cupiebat**) to take legal action. It is not difficult to see why the authorities would have seen the case as straightforward (**Legebatur rescripti forma directior**).

imperiali rescripto: An authoritative imperial decision (A. Honoré, *Emperors and Lawyers*, 2nd edn. (Oxford, 1994), 33–70 (up to the early fourth century); J. Gaudemet, *La Formation du droit séculier et du droit de l'Eglise aux IVe et Ve siècles*, 2nd edn. (Paris, 1979), 34–9), in this case, a legal warrant for the confiscation of the widow's property.

clerici contendebant auctoritatem: [**contendebant:** PV²MA, EW, Zell, Testard: *contendebunt* V¹: *non tenebant* COB, Valdarfer; **auctoritatem:** P¹MA, COB, most editors: *auctoritate* P²V, EW] The reading *non tenebant* is at first tempting, in view of the admission which follows (**Traditum erat**), but it may be more likely in the light of **Commune hoc vobiscum mihi** above that A. is at this point commending the courage of the local clergy: they initially sought to challenge the order by asserting their official responsibility to maintain the deposit inviolate (only to be unable to resist the weight of legal *auctoritas* invoked against the widow).

Honorati: Ex-officials, now prominent men in the local community: see A. Chastagnol, *L'Evolution politique, sociale et économique du monde romain de Dioclétien à Julien* (Paris, 1982), 287–91; Sargenti and Bruno Siola, *Normativa imperiale e diritto Romano*, 24–5.

intercessores dati: Official executors, appointed to mediate in the dispute: see Sargenti and Bruno Siola, *Normativa imperiale e diritto Romano*, 25–8.

magistri officiorum: The chief official who controlled the great imperial *scrinia;* see M. Clauss, *Der Magister Officiorum in der Spätantike (4.–6. Jahrhundert)* (Munich, 1980), 15–98. Flavius Caesarius (*PLRE* i. 171) was *magister officiorum* in 386–7, but did not take office until the late summer or autumn of 386, so even if the spring of that year is the likeliest setting he cannot be the figure in question. The chronological ambiguity of the affair tends in any case to rule out a firm identification.

agens in rebus: On the typical responsibilities of such a functionary, chiefly to act as a messenger of imperial authority, see Jones ii. 578–82; Clauss, *Der Magister Officiorum*, 23–32. For examples from this period, cf. the pious Christian Ponticianus (Aug. *Conf.* 8.6.14–15; Symm. *Epp.* 1.99; 5.32) (386–7; see *PLRE* i. 715) and his fellow-African, Evodius, another friend of Augustine (Aug. *Conf.* 9.8.17) (387; see *PLRE* i. 297). Presumably the official in this case was not friendly to the church's position: **imminebat** (though he may have been simply carrying out his duties in accordance with a plain legal directive).

151. **Tamen communicato mecum consilio:** A. was consulted on the matter—probably not because he had any official metropolitan status (*pace* Homes Dudden i. 126–9; Gryson, *Prêtre*, 155–8; G. Menis, 'Le giurisdizioni metropolitiche di Aquileia e di Milano nell'antichità', *AAAd* 4 (1973), 271–94, at 284–9), but simply out of deference to his personal authority (E. Cattaneo, 'Il governo ecclesiastico nel IV secolo nell'Italia settentrionale', *AAAd* 22 (1982), 175–87; followed by McLynn, 276). The bishop of Pavia throughout the 380s was Pompeius Eventius (Savio, *Gli antichi vescovi d'Italia, dalle origini al 1300*, 17, 20), a supporter of A. at the Council of Aquileia in 381 (*Acta conc. Aquil.* 56); A. installed his successor—and the journey to Pavia precipitated his own final illness—early in 397 (Paul. *VA* 45.1).

obsedit sanctus episcopus ea conclavia: The bishop was advised to obstruct physically the strongroom to which the deposit had been taken, so as to prevent the widow's property being actually appropriated by the creditor. *Pace* McLynn, 286, the chamber in question was not where the bishop himself had lodged the deposit: it was the one **ad quae translatum illud depositum viduae cognoverat**.

receptum sub chirographo est: A written agreement was exchanged that the deposit was being pursued by the creditor as his legal property.

ut ipse per semetipsum nos conveniret: A remarkable sign of the stand-off which had developed.

exposita divinae legis auctoritate et serie lectionis: They were apparently not content with putting their case in person; a written argument, suitably laced with biblical proof-texts, also seems to have been presented to bolster the petition (Homes Dudden i. 119–20).

vix tandem rationem imperator accepit: 'Reason' from A.'s perspective, of course; doubtless the emperor may have had other ways of describing the concession.

ut redderet viduae quod acceperat: Presumably the creditor had by now dropped his case (though A. does not say so); if not, the bishop's action can hardly have helped the widow much (McLynn, 286).

non fides: EW, COB several editors: *non est fides* PVMA¹, Lignamine: *non etiam fides* Testard.

periclitabatur: PVMA, Zell, Testard: *periclitatur* EW, COB, Amerbach, Maurists.

CHAPTER 30: CONCLUDING EXHORTATIONS

The book closes with an address specifically to A.'s 'sons' (2.152–6; note *filii* . . . *filii* at the beginning of 2.152 and 2.153); cf. the clerical section at the close of book 1 (1.246–59). These paragraphs consist of a mosaic of biblical verses, which are used to sum up the responsibility of the clergy to dwell at peace and to live a pious life. The *utile* as such is not mentioned; but implicit in the advice is the objective that persists throughout book 2: the clergy are to behave this way so as to win the benefit of a good social standing, and the higher advantage of divine reward. There is one brief Ciceronian phrase in 2.154, and a possible allusion to Cic. *Off.* 2.32, in 2.154, so even though A. makes no attempt to echo Cic.'s closing calculus of *utilia* (*Off.* 2.88–9) the classical model has not been forgotten entirely (*pace* Testard, 'Recherches', 102).

152. fugite improbos, cavete invidos: Cf. the advice of Ps. 1; Prov. 1: 10–19; 4: 14–17; etc.

153. Laudabilis mortis cum occasio datur, rapienda est illico: The opportunity for martyrdom should be seized (not shunned: cf. 2.24), but it ought not to be deliberately sought (1.187, 208; cf. generally *Virg.* 2.22–33; 3.32–8).

dilata gloria fugit, nec facile comprehenditur: Cf. Cic. *Fam.* 11.28.4: *Numquam enim honestam mortem fugiendam, saepe etiam adpetendam putavi.* See generally Faust, 120–3; Vermeulen, 53–96, especially 76–80.

154. Iosias . . . quemadmodum nemo ante eum: The reference to *amor* possibly looks back to Cic.'s argument about winning the *amor multitudinis* by goodwill and a reputation for virtues such as *fides* (*Off.* 2.32), though in the present passage *fides* clearly means religious faith. King Josiah instituted a revival of the Passover, with unprecedented grandeur, in the eighteenth year of his reign (4 Ki. 23: 21–3; 2 Chr. 35: 1–19), though A. thinks that Josiah was eighteen years old: **cum esset annorum decem et octo** (Testard ii. 192 n. 2, points out that the LXX version of 4 Ki. 22: 3 is ambiguous). The reading of PVM, **adversariis** [*universis* E, CO], is defensible if we assume that A. is following the 2 Chr. account. In 2 Chr. 35: 20–1, the Egyptian king, Neco, is unwilling to fight Josiah himself, saying that his quarrel is not with the king personally but with the house of Judah generally (since Judah was perhaps allied with Babylon at this time); in the end Josiah insisted on fighting, in disguise, and was fatally wounded (2 Chr. 35: 22–3). A. perhaps thinks that Neco's attitude was the result of a regard for Josiah's *fides et devotio*. There is also, perhaps, a point being made about Josiah's youthfulness: the young king, in showing such religious devotion, blazed a trail for young clerics.

vicit superiores: Cf. Cic. *Off.* 2.57, of the entertainment laid on by the curule aedile P. Cornelius Lentulus Spinther in 63 BC: *Omnes autem P. Lentulus me consule vicit superiores.* Cf. the evocation of these words in 2.109.

Exquisivit me zelus domus tuae: Ps. 68: 10; cf. *Expos. Ps. 118*.18.10–18.

Apostolus Christi zelotes dictus: Simon the Zealot (Lk. 6: 15; Acts 1: 13).

Zelus domus tuae comedit me: Jn. 2: 17, quoting Ps. 68: 10.

non iste humanus, invidiam generat: A. commends 'zeal' in the sense of religious fervour, not human envy or jealousy. On *invidia*, cf. Rom. 1: 29; Phil. 1: 15; 1 Tim. 6: 4; Tit. 3: 3; Jas. 4: 5.

sit inter vos pax, quae superat omnem sensum: Cf. Phil. 4: 7: *et pax Dei, quae exsuperat omnem sensum, custodiat corda vestra et intellegentias vestras in Christo Iesu.* For further injunctions to be at peace, cf. e.g. 2 Cor. 13: 11; Col. 3: 15; 1 Thess. 5: 13; 2 Thess. 3: 16; 2 Tim. 2: 22; Heb. 12: 14.

155. Amate vos invicem: Cf. Jn. 13: 34; 15: 12, 17; 1 Thess. 4: 9; Heb. 13: 1; 1 Jn. 3: 11, 23; 4: 7, 11–12; 2 Jn. 5.

Et vos ipsi scitis quod prae ceteris vos semper dilexi et diligo: Cf. 1.24.

coaluistis: Cf. the corporate growth mentioned, for example, in Eph. 4: 15; 1 Pt. 2: 2. A. implies that the young men have been given to the service of the church for some time, perhaps in some cases from an early age (cf. generally 1.24, 65, 81).

in adfectu germanitatis: Cf. Rom. 12: 10; Heb. 13: 1; 1 Pt. 2: 17; 2 Pet. 1: 7; etc.; see Pétré, 104–40, especially 129–33; cf. also 1.170.

156. *Quae bona sunt tenete*: 1 Thess. 5: 21.

et *Deus pacis et dilectionis erit vobiscum* in Domino Iesu: 2 Cor. 13: 11.

cui est honor gloria . . . in saecula saeculorum. Amen: Cf. Rom. 16: 27; also 1 Pt. 4: 11. The doxological conclusion is a fitting climax to paragraphs composed almost entirely of a series of apostolic injunctions (contrast 1.259, where the liturgical phrase which appears in the Maurists' text is a later addition). On possible reasons as to why this is the only doxology in the work, see Introduction V.

Book 3

CHAPTER I: ACTIVE LEISURE

3.1–7 introduces book 3. It is based on Cic.'s opening to his third book, *Off*. 3.1–4. There Cic. speaks of the enforced solitude and *otium* in which he has been writing, away from his political and legal career in Rome. He contrasts his own involuntary withdrawal from public life with the voluntary *otium* enjoyed intermittently by the elder Scipio Africanus (see on 3.2), and praises Scipio for the way in which he used his leisure-time productively to plan his political activities: he was never idle or alone, for he took counsel with himself in his free hours (*Off*. 3.1–4). Cic. plays with the antithesis of *otium* and *negotium*, evoking three different senses of *otium* : (i) 'leisure-time' (as taken by Scipio); (ii) 'absence from public activity' (as forced on Cic. himself): and (iii) 'political stability' (Griffin and Atkins, 101 n. 1, drawing on Holden, 349, 351; *otiosum* in *Off*. 3.1 has the first meaning, and *otiosus* the second). Classically, the commonest notion of *otium* is the image of leisure-time spent on literary pursuits, especially in a country retreat (an ideal which retained a strong appeal in the late fourth century: witness Augustine and his friends at Cassiciacum): e.g. Cic. *Tusc*. 1.3–8; Ov. *Trist*. 1.41; Plin. *Epp*. 1.9; 8.9. *Otium* can also refer to the contemplative life as opposed to political activity (e.g. Cic. *Off*. 1.69–70; Sen. *Ot. sap.*; *Brev. vit.* 14 ff.); orthodox Stoicism was nevertheless traditionally hostile to political quietism, which it associated closely with Epicurean assumptions. See J. M. André, *Recherches sur l'otium romain* (Paris, 1962); id. *L'Otium dans la vie intellectuelle et morale romaine des origines à l'époque augustéenne* (Paris, 1966); W. A. Laidlaw 'Otium', *G & R* 15 (1968), 42–52.

In his prologue, Cic. goes on to exhort Marcus to pursue his studies diligently, and to imitate his father's industry and fame (*Off.* 3.5–6), but as in book 2, A. gives no parallel to these more personal introductory remarks. He uses 3.1–7 to argue, as ever, for the superiority of biblical exemplars to classical ones, a note that will be sounded especially often in book 3. He approves of Cic.'s preference for a *negotiosum otium* (cf. also 1.9) and his emphasis on the proper use of *solitudo* (see on 1.88), but he can show that the biblical tradition in this connection is older (3.2) and superior (3.6). The kind of virtues which ought to fill out the believer's *otium* have already been implied elsewhere, in 1.85–8 (cf. also 1.9): as we might expect, spiritual activity is the key note. A. evokes the standard image of the holy man who never wastes a single hour but devotes himself to prayer and meditation at all times (e.g. Sulpic. Sev. *VM* 26). The cultivation of piety is an important part of the clerical *persona*, and one to which A. himself gave careful attention. But, as the traditional picture of A. the man of action suggests, such devotion is more than simply a private exercise. As the biblical heroes teach, he argues, communion with God and with Christ (3.2 and 3.7) leads to the achievement of great things in the real world, the channelling of divine power into amazing feats in desperate human situations (3.2–6). If the right use of *otium* has the potential to produce dazzling results, let the clergy apply themselves to it at all costs. Prayer can lead to revelations of divine guidance, and such displays, as A. well knew from his *inventio* of relics and the accompanying manifestation of their powers, did a great deal for clerical prestige (see on 1.202). *Negotiosum otium*, like everything else in the Ambrosian package, is heavily associated with the furthering of ecclesiastical image. On the section as a whole, see C. Somenzi, 'Ambrogio e Scipione l'Africano: la fondazione cristiana dell'"otium nego-tiosum"', in *Nec timeo mori*, 753–68; also R. Lizzi, 'Tra i classici e la Bibbia: l'"otium" come forma di santità episco-pale', in G. Barone *et al.* (eds.), *Modelli di santità e modelli di comportamento. Contrasti, intersezioni, complementarità* (Turin, 1994), 43–64.

1. David propheta docuit . . . cum bono contubernali: Cf. Ps. 100: 2: *Perambulabam in innocentia cordis mei, in medio domus meae.* Cf. *Spir.* 3.120–1. **in ampla domo**

deambulare strangely recalls David on the afternoon when
he caught sight of Bathsheba (2 Ki. 11: 2): *Apol.* 2; *Apol. alt.*
5 (so Moorhead, 160 n. 5).

et loqueretur secum: Cf. Cic. *Off.* 3.1 (of Scipio: see on 3.2
below): *quae declarat illum . . . in solitudine secum loqui
solitum.*

***Dixi, custodiam vias meas*:** Ps. 38: 2.

***Bibe aquam de . . . puteorum tuorum fontibus*:** Prov.
5: 15.

***Aqua enim alta, consilium in corde viri*:** Prov. 20: 5.

***Nemo*, inquit, *alienus particeps . . . confabulentur
tecum*:** Prov. 5: 17–19. The water images are confused
here. In Prov. 5, water signifies a wife: the injunction to
the *filius* is, 'Be satisfied with the "spring" of your wife's
affections and do not go after prostitutes or let other men
near your wife'. It is only in Prov. 20 that water refers to
counsel. For other references to the verses, cf. e.g. *Parad.* 13;
Is. 22–4; *Iac.* 1.29; 2.17.

2.   **Non ergo primus Scipio . . . cum otiosus esset:** Cf.
Cic. *Off.* 3.1: *P. Scipionem . . . eum qui primus Africanus
appellatus est, dicere solitum scripsit Cato . . . numquam se
minus otiosum esse quam cum otiosus, nec minus solum quam
cum solus esset.* Cic. quotes a *bon mot* preserved by the elder
Cato (234–152 BC), probably in the collection of his
Apophthegmata (*Hist. fr.* 127) mentioned in *Off.* 1.104 (and
De Or. 2.271); cf. also *Planc.* 66 (with doubtful attribution to
Cato, *Orig.*) (H. Peter (ed.), *Historicorum Romanorum reli-
quiae* 1, 2nd edn. (Leipzig, 1914), fr. 2 and fr. 127). The
elder P. Cornelius Scipio Africanus (236–184/3 BC) success-
fully oversaw the expulsion of the Carthaginians from Spain
during the Second Punic War, and invaded Africa, where he
defeated Hannibal at Zama in 202 BC. In 190 BC, he shared
with his brother Lucius the command against Antiochus in
the East, but was subsequently implicated in Lucius' trial
for financial misconduct during the war; he escaped indictment by voluntarily retiring to Liternum, where he died.
Scipio's saying is also cited by Cic. in *Rep.* 1.26–7, where it
is taken to mean that Scipio found philosophy in solitude to
be the highest intellectual activity. A. quotes it in *Ep.* 33
[49].1, describing to Sabinus his own activity in solitude; cf.

also *Iac.* 1.39; *Virg.* 2.10 (also *Ep.* 33 [49].2); Jer. *Adv. Iov.* 1.47; Paul. Nol. *Ep.* 26.1; Pasch. Radb. *Expos. Ps.44*.1; Geoff. Aux. *Vita prima S. Bern.*, 3.1; Wm. Thier. *Ep. Mont. Dei* 29–30. See further K. Gross, ' "Numquam minus otiosus quam cum otiosus." Das Weiterleben eines antiken Sprichwortes im Abendland', *A & A* 26 (1980), 122–37.

scivit ante ipsum Moyses: The usual stress on biblical anteriority.

qui cum taceret clamabat: A famous oxymoron: cf. Cic. *Cat.* 1.21: *cum tacent, clamant*; and see on 1.9. When Moses assured the Israelites at the Red Sea that the Lord would deliver them if they kept quiet, the Lord asked Moses why he was crying out to him, and instructed him to command the people to advance (Ex. 14: 14–15). Moses was silent because he was praying; cf. the case of Susanna in 1.9 and 1.68.

Adeo otiosus . . . qui dimicabant: Again, the *otium* was used for supplicatory prayer: as long as Moses' hands remained raised, the Israelites triumphed over the Amalekites; when he grew tired, Aaron and Hur supported his arms (Ex. 17: 8–16, especially 17: 11–12). The outstretched arms are often taken by Christian exegetes to be a typical sign of the cross: e.g. *Ep. Barn.* 12.2; Just. *C. Tryph.* 90; Max. Taur. *Serm.* 38.3 (see also on 1.251).

ceteri: Possibly suggested by Cic. *Off.* 3.1: *Ita duae res, quae languorem adferunt ceteris, illum acuebant, otium et solitudo.*

qui quadraginta diebus . . . complexus est: See Ex. 24: 15–31: 18.

Et in illa solitudine . . . non defuit: Cf. Cic. *Off.* 3.1 (of Scipio): *quae declarat illum . . . in solitudine secum loqui solitum, ut neque cessaret umquam et interdum conloquio alterius non egeret.* According to the Scipio legend, Africanus himself meditated daily in the Capitoline temple of Jupiter, and his mystical inspiration guided his public actions (Polyb. 10.2; Liv. 26.19.4–9; Gell. *NA* 6.1.6). Such contemplation was unusual in Roman religion, and Scipio's behaviour is regarded with scepticism by the classical historians (F. W. Walbank, 'The Scipionic Legend', *PCPhS* 13 (1967), 54–69, at 64).

Audiam quid loquatur in me Dominus Deus: Ps. 84: 9.
Et quanto plus . . . quam ipse secum: The implication is that Scipio communed with himself, whereas Moses and David had fellowship with God. Yet the legend does describe Scipio's communion with the gods, so the cogitation-versus-prayer antithesis is weak. A. might have drawn a more obvious contrast between Scipio's meditation on the pagan gods and the saints' fellowship with the true God.

3. **Transibant apostoli . . . curabat infirmos:** Peter's passing shadow cured the sick (Acts 5: 15).
   Tangebantur vestimenta . . . sanitas deferebatur: Clothing touched by Paul healed the sick (Acts 19: 11–12). Paulinus records similar miracles with A.'s own garb: *VA* 10; cf. 48.

4. **Sermonem locutus est Elias . . . et sex mensibus:** See on 2.14.
   et hydria farinae non defecit . . . non est exinanitum: See on 2.14.

5. **Et quoniam plerosque delectant bellica:** See on 1.196, on Cic. *Off.* 1.74.
   Sedebat Eliseus . . . obsidere eum: See 4 Ki. 6: 8–23.

6. **Conferamus hoc otium . . . indulgere quieti et tranquillitati:** [**Conferamus:** EW, COB: *conferimus* PVMA, Testard] Cf. Cic. *Off.* 3.2: *Sed nec hoc otium cum Africani otio nec haec solitudo cum illa comparanda est. Ille enim requiescens a reipublicae pulcherrimis muneribus otium sibi sumebat aliquando, et e coetu hominum frequentiaque interdum tamquam in portum se in solitudinem recipiebat, nostrum autem otium negotii inopia, non requiescendi studio constitutum est.* A. transforms Cic.'s contrast between his own *otium* and Scipio's into an antithesis between Elisha's *otium* and the normal secular idea of *otium*. Secular *otium* is relaxation of the mind, whereas Elisha's *otium* was used to perform mighty feats by the power of the Lord. On Elisha's spiritual warfare (prayer) in a time of physical relaxation, cf. *Ep.* 51 [15].5–7.
   in solitudine Iordanem . . . in fontem recurrat: Elisha used Elijah's cloak to repeat Elijah's miracle (4 Ki. 2: 13–14; and 2: 7–8).
   aut in Carmelo . . . sterilem conceptione fecundat

Elisha predicted the birth of a son to a Shunnamite woman married to an aged husband (4 Ki. 4: 8–17). The prediction was not given on Mt. Carmel (A. perhaps is confused by thinking of Elijah's solitude on Mt. Carmel), but the woman came to see Elisha there later on when the child died:

aut resuscitat mortuos: See 4 Ki. 4: 18–37.

aut ciborum temperat . . . admixtione dulcescere: See 4 Ki. 4: 38–41.

aut decem panibus distributis . . . plebe saturata: See 4 Ki. 4: 42–4. Twenty loaves, not ten, were in fact distributed.

aut ferrum securis excussum . . . facit supernatare: See 4 Ki. 6: 1–7.

aut emundatione leprosum: The healing of Naaman (4 Ki. 5: 1–27).

aut siccitatem imbribus: See 4 Ki. 3: 5–27, especially 3: 9, 15 ff. where, according to the prophecy of Elisha, the desert of Edom is filled with water. In 4 Ki. 3: 17, though, it is specifically said that *rain* will not be seen.

aut famem mutat fecunditate: A. seems to be thinking of Elisha's prediction, during the famine in Samaria, that grain would soon become plentiful again, as it did when the Syrians abandoned their camp, leaving their supplies behind (4 Ki. 6: 24–5; 7: 1–20). Testard ii. 197–8 n. 29 treats **aut siccitatem imbribus aut famem mutat fecunditate** as one clause, and thinks that A. is conflating the story of Elisha and the Syrian camp with the account of Elijah's prophecies about drought and famine in 3 Ki. 17–18. However, although **fecunditate** might well normally suggest fertility produced by rain, it is better to take each **aut** of the sentence as properly disjunctive, and so to identify different incidents in **siccitatem imbribus** and **famem mutat fecunditate**. Testard makes no mention of the water supplied through Elisha's prophecy in 4 Ki. 3.

7. **Quando ergo iustus solus est qui cum Deo semper est?:** On knowing the presence of the divine in and through solitude, cf. 1.88; *Ep.* 33 [49].5.

Quis nos separabit, **inquit,** *a dilectione Christi?:* Rom. 8: 35.

Confido quia neque mors neque vita neque angelus: Rom. 8: 38.

cui totus mundus divitiarum possessio est: See on 1.118; and cf. 2.66.

quasi ignoratur . . . et possideat omnia: Cf. 2 Cor. 6: 8–10.

qui non eorum quae caduca . . . censetur: Cf. 2 Cor. 4: 18; cf. also 1.28–9; 2.10–21.

3.8–28 introduces the substance of book 3, the relationship between what is honourable and what is beneficial. The inspiration comes from Cic. *Off.* 3.7–39, but material from the latter (especially the Gyges story of *Off.* 3.38–9) is echoed later on as well: the correspondence is loose. Cic. begins by commenting on Panaetius' plan, lamenting the fact that he never answered the question of how to decide between the honourable and the beneficial (*Off.* 3.7–18; cf. 3.33–4). He maintains that what is honourable and what is beneficial can only *appear* to conflict, and he proposes a *formula*, or 'rule of procedure', by which to adjudicate in such apparent cases. This *formula* is grounded in nature, as Stoicism would insist that it must be (though it is equally compatible with Peripatetic sensibilities: *Off.* 3.33). It is the principle that it is contrary to nature to secure a benefit for oneself at the expense of someone else. If something is truly honourable, it is beneficial for all; purely private benefit is dishonourable (*Off.* 3.19–32). The resolution of the apparent tension between what is honourable and what is beneficial lies in the supremacy of the social justice which behaviour that is honourable must always exemplify.

A. also begins by referring to the philosophers' arrangement of the three themes (3.8), but he immediately suggests that a conflict between the honourable and the beneficial can only appear to exist if people assume a worldly definition of the *utile*. Once it is realized that the *utile* is not a matter of personal material gain but the consideration of the interests of others (with a view to eternal reward, of course), there can be no problem (3.9, 13–15, 25–8). Cic.'s *formula* is thus recast in Christian terms (3.13–28). It is equally said to be rooted in nature, but it is nature as established by the Creator's design (3.24, 28). Cic. adduces three main arguments in support of his *formula*. Unjust gain is contrary (i) to nature, which intends humanity to live in society and to function harmoniously as a body (*Off.* 3.21–2); (ii) to the laws which individual people-groups have established for themselves (*Off.* 3.23); and (iii) to reason, which is *lex divina et humana* (*Off.* 3.23). A. evokes Cic.'s first point in 3.17–19 (adding, in 3.15–16, the example of Christ and the significance of the etymology of *homo*), and his second and third points are covered in 3.20–1 (Testard identifies four points in 3.16–24, but the divisions are weak: the text does not suggest a distinction between the point being made in 3.16 and that being made in 3.17–19; and 3.21–4 does not look like a separate point from 3.20, since law is mentioned in both cases). But for him the Christocentric pattern is crucial (3.15, 19, 27). The *formula* is not so much a principle by which to settle difficult cases as a reminder that to practice *humanitas* is to imitate Christ. His incarnation confirms and enhances human dignity; his redemptive work has universal significance; and his way was to sacrifice himself for the benefit of all (well put by Becker, 271; the classical casuistry is rejected in favour of Christ's example in 3.27; note also the interplay of *forma/formula* in 3.13, 15, 17, 20, and the idea of being 'con-formed' to Christ in 3.15).

In 3.9–12, A. draws on Cic. *Off.* 3.13–17, where Cic. talks of popular ideas of goodness and says that his focus is on 'middle' duties—standards which are widely accessible, rather than the perfect *honestas* which is found only in the wise. Like Panaetius, Cic. is interested in a realistic morality, appropriate to most people's real circumstances. 'Middle' duties are not complete in the absolute sense (despite what some may think), but the repeated practice of them increasingly makes people look wise and enables them to progress towards the true virtue that only the wise possess. For A., *perfectum officium* is for the few, but it is precisely for the few whom he is addressing. It is the way of self-denial; the repudiation of earthly pleasures and profit; the consideration of others first and foremost. It aspires to a relative (earthly) perfection, in imitation of the (heavenly) perfection of God himself (cf. .36–8). Of course, only a kind of perfection is attainable in this world; true perfection belongs to God alone. The *telos* of moral progress (cf. 1.233–45) is conformity to God's own character, which is something that will only be completed eschatologically. But the practical imperative is still clear: ordinary conceptions of duty, assuming secular ideas of *utilitas*, are to be shunned; the bishop's addressees are to aim for a standard which proves here and now that they have been set apart for higher things. Cic. concentrates on *media officia*; A.'s men are called to pursue *perfecta officia*, and *media officia* end up being implicitly equated with a popular notion of selfish gain (3.12). The middle Stoic dualism is again (as in 1.36–8), transformed into an ethical pattern in which the select few walk a higher path, but here (unlike in 1.36) anything less is not simply inadequate: it is wrong. The philosophers' accommodation of the ordinary will not do; the servants of the church, the new *sapientes*, must go further (a degree of Panaetian realism remains, of course, as 1.213–16 makes clear; it is the *psychological* importance of stressing the higher calling of the clergy that matters, especially as a contrast with the Ciceronian approach for readers who are inevitably comparing the two).

CHAPTER 2: THE HONOURABLE AND THE
BENEFICIAL ARE IDENTICAL; DIFFERING LEVELS
OF DUTY

8. Et quoniam de duobus superioribus locis diximus . . . et utile tractavimus: On the division of the topics, see on 1.27.

utrum honestum illud . . . utrum utile an inutile: A. does not specifically say in either 1.27 or 2.22 that book 1 is on the *honestum* versus the *turpe* and that book 2 is on the *utile* versus the *inutile*, but these respective themes are of course central to the two books. In any case, he is here following Cic. *Off*. 3.7, where this is the language that is used of Panaetius' plan: *uno cum dubitarent honestumne id esset de quo ageretur an turpe, altero utilene esset an inutile, tertio, si id quod speciem haberet honesti pugnaret cum eo quod inutile videretur, quomodo ea discerni oporteret.* Testard, 'Etude' 182 n. 56, makes far too much of the lack of earlier descriptions of each book in the terms used here, when h speaks of two different 'plans' for the work.

nonnulli requirendum putant: A typically vague allusio

to Panaetius and Cic. Testard ii. 198 n. 1 strangely takes it as a precise reference to Cic.'s allusion in *Off.* 3.11 to those whom Socrates used to curse for suggesting that things which were combined by nature (to the Stoics, the beneficial and the honourable) could be severed. But A. is simply describing the third stage in the argument as set out by Panaetius and explored by Cic., drawing on *Off.* 3.7.

9. **Nos autem:** An immediate antithesis with the pagan *nonnulli* in 3.8.

compugnantia: Cic. uses *pugnare* for the apparent conflict between the honourable and the beneficial in *Off.* 3.7, 9, 19; *Off.* 3.11 has *contendere*.

quae iam supra unum esse ostendimus: Cf. especially 2.22–8, and Cic. *Off.* 3.11.

quia non sequimur sapientiam carnis . . . sed sapientiam quae ex Deo est: Cf. 2 Cor. 1: 12 for *sapientia carnalis*, and 1 Cor. 1: 18–31 for the contrast of the wisdom of the world and the wisdom of God.

apud quam utilitas . . . pluris habetur: Cf. 1.28–9; 2.15–16, 23, 25–6, 66–7; 3.37, 56, 63, 90. A tension between the honourable and the beneficial is possible only if we follow 'the wisdom of the flesh' and equate what is beneficial with monetary gain. Cic., *Off.* 3.18, speaks of those who think only in terms of profits and advantages (*commoda*) when they measure what is honourable against what is beneficial. On *commoda*, cf. also *Off.* 3.21–6.

pro detrimento habentur: Cf. Phil. 3: 8.

10. **Hoc est enim κατόρθωμα:** See on 1.37 on Cic. *Off.* 1.8.

quod perfectum et absolutum officium est: Cf. Cic. *Off.* 3.14: *Illud autem officium quod rectum idem* [the Stoics] *appellant perfectum atque absolutum est.*

Cui secundum est commune officium . . . quod potest plurimis esse commune: Cf. Cic. *Off.* 3.14: *Haec enim officia, de quibus his libris disputamus, media Stoici appellant; ea communia sunt et late patent*; and especially 3.15: *Haec igitur officia, de quibus his libris disserimus, quasi secunda quaedam honesta esse dicunt, non sapientium modo propria, sed cum omni hominum genere communia.*

elegantiore convivio . . . usitatum est: See on 1.86; and cf. 2.109.

ieiunare autem . . . esse paucorum est: On fasting, see
on 2.122; **continentem** clearly means chastity; on which cf.
1.218, 248–9.

contra autem detrahere velle alteri: Cf. Cic. *Off.* 3.21:
Detrahere igitur alteri aliquid; 3.23: *et id quod alteri detraxerit*
sibi adsumat.

prima cum paucis, media cum pluribus: Perfect duty is
asceticism, a higher path on which only a few can walk; cf.
1.36–8 and see ad loc.; also 1.16, 125, 184, 246, 249. **prima** is
A.'s word, not Cic.'s. Testard ii. 199 n. 6 makes an
unnecessary fuss over this, trying to locate other possible
Ciceronian influences for this use of *primus*. By **prima**,
A. means quite simply that perfect duties are the most
important kind. Testard also notes the fact that Cic. speaks
of perfect duty in the singular, whereas A. here (though not
at the start of the paragraph, or in 1.36–7) uses the plural. It
is true that Cic. thinks of perfect duty as something which
belongs to the world of the ideal rather than the stratified
world of everyday realities. It is equally true, and more
obvious, that A. has just given a number of examples of
what he thinks of as 'middle' duty, followed by a number of
examples of the kinds of behaviour which can be classed as
perfect: it is quite right that he should then refer to both
categories of *officia* in the plural.

11. **Aliter enim bonum Deum dicimus . . . et sapientem**
Deum aliter dicimus, aliter hominem: Cf. Cic. *Off.*
3.16:

Nec vero, cum duo Decii aut duo Scipiones fortes viri commem-
orantur aut cum Fabricius aut Aristides iustus nominatur, aut ab
illis fortitudinis aut ab his iustitiae tamquam a sapiente petitur
exemplum; nemo enim horum sic sapiens ut sapientem volumus
intellegi, nec ii qui sapientes habiti et nominati, M. Cato et
C. Laelius, sapientes fuerunt, ne illi quidem septem, sed ex
mediorum officiorum frequentia similitudinem quandam gerebant
speciemque sapientium.

Cic. argues that the words *fortis*, *iustus*, and *sapiens* mean one
thing in the scale of 'middle' duties, and something quite
different from a perspective of perfect duty. The classical
heroes [Publius Decius Mus: father and son of the sam

name sacrificed themselves for Rome in battle, in *c*.340 BC (fighting the Latins) and 295 BC (against the Samnites, Umbrians, and their allies) respectively; the two Scipios: the elder Africanus (see on 3.2) and his younger namesake, Aemilianus, consul in 147 BC and destroyer of Carthage in 146 BC; Fabricius: see on 3.91; Aristides: 'The Just', Athenian statesman of the fifth century BC, general at Marathon in 490 BC, archon in 489 BC, ostracized in 482 BC after coming into conflict with Themistocles, but recalled just before the invasion of Xerxes to co-operate with Themistocles in the winning of the battle of Salamis in 480; he was the architect of the Delian League (his name is bracketed by some editors of Cic. here as a Greek intrusion into an otherwise Roman series of heroes in this limb of the sentence), cf. also 3.87 below; Marcus Porcius Cato: consul in 196 BC, famously vigorous holder of the censorship in 184 BC, and virulent opponent of Carthage, but a cultured literary figure, depicted in gentle tones in Cic.'s *Sen.*; Gaius Laelius: 'The Wise', friend and colleague of Scipio Aemilianus, consul in 140 BC, and in 132 BC involved in the senatorial commission against the supporters of Tiberius Gracchus; he is the main speaker in Cic.'s *Amic.*; the Seven Wise Men of Greek fame: Bias, Chilo, Cleobulus, Pittacus, Periander, Solon, and Thales] became exemplars of one level of courage, justice, and wisdom because they repeatedly practised 'middle' duties, but they were not perfectly courageous, just, and wise as true sages would be (cf. also *Off.* 1.46; 2.35). A. sharpens the point by speaking of the distinction between God and men: no one is good or just or wise as God is. He goes on to contrast the levels of moral distinction attainable in this world and the world to come. This theological framework is central; mention of the divergence between eminent and ordinary men comes afterwards, in 3.12 (where inevitably the examples are biblical). The reference to goodness (rather than courage) may stem from Cic.'s reference to those who are thought to be *boni* in *Off.* 3.17, or from his distinction between popular and philosophical ideas of *viri boni* in quite similar terms in *Off.* 2.35.

Estote ergo et vos perfecti sicut et Pater . . . perfectus est: Mt. 5: 48; cf. 1.37–8 for similar appeal to this passage. A

related argument is adduced by Clem. Alex. *Strom.* 6.111.3;
7.88.5–6, with reference to the true γνῶσις as human conformity to divine perfection.

Non quod iam acceperim . . . si comprehendam: Phil.
3: 12.

Quicumque ergo perfecti sumus: Phil. 3: 15.

alia plenos numeros habens: Cf. Cic. *Off.* 3.14: *Illud
autem officium . . . perfectum atque absolutum est, et, ut idem
dicunt, omnes numeros habet. . . .* The metaphor, found in a
number of Stoic sources (*SVF* iii. 136.14; iii. 20.20; iii. 4.40;
Cic. *Fin.* 3.24; Sen. *Ep.* 95.5), may stem from the Pythagorean belief that ten is the perfect number, containing within
itself all the other numbers (Dyck, 513–14; others relate the
image to musical theory).

**alia hic, alia ibi; . . . alia secundum perfectionem
futuri**: Cf. 1.238–9; also 1.29, 58, 103, 147; 3.36. Perfect
duty is eschatologically orientated, since perfection in the
true sense will only be possible in the life to come.

12. **Quis Daniele sapientior?**: Ezek. 28: 3; see on 2.57.

**Salomon, qui repletus est sapientia . . . super omnes
sapientes Aegypti**: Cf. 3 Ki. 4: 29–34.

**Aliud est enim communiter sapere, aliud sapere
perfecte**: Cf. Cic. *Off.* 3.16, cited above on 3.11.

Qui communiter sapit . . . et sibi adiungat: The logical
step is now taken: 'middle' duty is not just inadequate (as in
1.36); it is really no virtue at all. It is all about self-interest
and the acquisition of temporal goods; in short, it epitomizes
the popular understanding of advantage. By making perfection the only acceptable standard for his men, and by
presenting God and the eschaton, not the human consensus
and this world, as the real reference-points, A. ends up
obliterating the Ciceronian notion of 'middle' duty as an
appropriate measure of moral achievement for a spiritual
élite. On **ut alteri detrahat aliquid**, see on 3.10.

aliud quod aeternum est . . . sed quod omnibus: If a
large part of perfect duty is altruism, it is altruism with an
eye to the future. The philosophical vocabulary (**decorum
atque honestum . . . utile**) is brought in fairly artificially
and delineated with reference to the Christian hope. But the
point about the centrality of the *honestum* over profit and

personal gain (false views of the *utile*) in the thinking of those who are good is Ciceronian: cf. *Off.* 3.18. For **quaerens non quod sibi utile est sed quod omnibus**, cf. 1 Cor. 10: 24, quoted in 3.13 below.

13. Itaque haec sit formula . . . suum commodum augere velit: [**augere:** PVMA: *augeri* EW, COB] Cf. Cic. *Off.* 3.19: *Itaque, ut sine ullo errore diiudicare possimus, si quando cum illo quod honestum intellegimus pugnare id videbitur quod appellamus utile, formula quaedam constituenda est; quam si sequemur in comparatione rerum, ab officio numquam recedemus*; 3.20: *Erit autem haec formula Stoicorum rationi disciplinaeque maxime consentanea*; 3.21: *Detrahere igitur alteri aliquid et hominem hominis incommodo suum commodum augere magis est contra naturam quam mors, quam paupertas . . .* [etc.]. A *formula* in Roman civil law was 'a rule of procedure'. The praetor or other magistrate would detail the facts of a case which the judge would require in order to reach a decision (Holden, 392–3). For Cic., the moral *formula* sets out the facts necessary to make a correct assessment of apparent benefit. It is the principle that we must not benefit at someone else's expense. This application of legal terminology to moral analysis is typical of Cic.: it reflects his own background and that of many of his envisaged readers, and it is also germane to his desire to present justice as the key social virtue in book 3. A.'s sympathies are similar on both counts (cf. also 3.66–7, drawing on Cic. *Off.* 3.60).

Hanc formam tibi praescribit apostolus: The *formula* is taken from Cic. but authority for it is sought in a biblical *forma*; cf. 3.20 (and note the use of *forma* in 3.15, 17; it is scarcely possible to capture in translation the repeated play on the word in these paragraphs). Cic. uses *praescribit* in *Off.* 3.27.

Omnia licent sed . . . sed quod alterius: 1 Cor. 10: 23–4.

Alter alterum existimantes . . . sed quae aliorum: Phil. 2: 3–4.

14. dicente sancto per Salomonem Spiritu: On the inspiration of Scripture, see on 1.3.

Fili, si sapiens fueris . . . solus hauries mala: Prov. 9: 12.

Sapiens . . . utriusque forma virtutis: On the link between wisdom and justice, cf. 1.126–9, 252–3; 2.41–55.

15. Hoc est enim conformari Christo: Cf. Rom. 8: 29: *Nam quos praescivit et praedestinavit conformes fieri imaginis Filii eius.* On Christ's example, cf. 3.27, 36, 136.

cum esset in Dei forma . . . formam susciperet hominis: Cf. Phil. 2: 6–7.

Hoc enim agis . . . tua commoda augere expetis: Cf. Cic. *Off.* 3.21, cited above on 3.13.

Selfish gain involves robbery from others, which amounts to a dishonouring of the human condition which Christ has enriched by his incarnation. Cf. also Cic. *Off.* 3.26: *qui omnino hominem ex homine tollat.*

We are to be con-formed to the one whose work has given us the supreme *forma* (cf. 3.13, 20) of kenotic service by taking our human *forma* to himself. On the equation of material enrichment with spiritual impoverishment, see on 1.59.

16. Considera, homo, unde nomen sumpseris: ab humo utique: The standard, and correct, etymology of *homo* (on the address, cf. *o homo* in 1.156; 2.52): e.g. Quint. *Inst.* 1.6.34 (sceptical); Isid. *Orig.* 1.29.3; 11.1.4; Hyg. *Fab.* 220.3; and Tert. *Adv. Marc.* 5.10; *Apol.* 18.2; Lact. *Inst.* 2.10.3; *Ira* 10.43; Zen. Ver. *Tract.* 2.4.4 (CCL = 1.12.2 PG); Greg. Elv. *Tract. Orig.* 1.13; Ps.-Aug. *Quaest. test.* 108.1; Cassiod. *Expl. Ps. 139.2*; also Arat. *Act. Apost.* 1.373–5 (see further *TLL* vi/3. 2871). Gen. 2: 7 makes a similar word-play with *Adam* (man) and *adama* (ground), though there is no etymological connection between the Hebrew roots; cf. also Gen. 2: 19; 3: 19; Jn. 3: 31; 1 Cor. 15: 47; and the Greek myth of Prometheus, which pictures humans as formed from the earth (see I. Opelt, 'Christianisierung heidnischer Etymologien', *JbAC* 2 (1959), 70–85, at 82–5). On the earth as parent, cf. 1.161; 3.45.

quae . . . fructus ministrat: Cf. 1.132–4 for a biblical justification of the Stoic argument that the earth's productiv

ity for all is a model for human obligations to help one
another because of common humanity; also 1.38; 3.40, 45–
52. On humanity as nature's law, cf. Cic. *Off.* 3.21–8.
**Inde appellata humanitas specialis et domestica virtus
hominis:** *Humanitas* is also derived from *humus*, so it is (or
ought to be) the innate virtue of a *homo*; cf. *Ex.* 6.46. In 3.45,
A. evokes the celebrated words of Ter. *Heaut.* 77, quoted by
Cic. in *Off.* 1.30: *Homo sum: humani nil a me alienum puto.*
See ad loc.

17. **Ipsa te doceat forma . . . officia sibi vindicat . . .:** Cf.
1 Cor. 11: 14, *Nec ipsa natura docet vos . . .?* and Cic. *Off.*
3.22:

> Ut, si unum quodque membrum sensum hunc haberet, ut posse
> putaret se valere si proximi membri valetudinem ad se traduxisset,
> debilitari et interire totum corpus necesse esset, sic, si unus quisque
> nostrum ad se rapiat commoda aliorum detrahatque quod cuique
> possit emolumenti sui gratia, societas hominum et communitas
> evertatur necesse est. . . . illud natura non patitur, ut aliorum spoliis
> nostras facultates copias opes augeamus.

On **forma**, cf. 3.13, 15, 20. The metaphor of society as a
body is Greek in origin. It is taken up by Livy in the famous
parable/fable of Menenius Agrippa in the narrative of the
struggle of the orders (Liv. 2.32.8–12) (R. M. Ogilvie, *A
Commentary on Livy Books 1–5* (Oxford, 1965), 312–13;
W. Nestle, 'Die Fabel des Menenius Agrippa', *Klio* 21
(1927), 350–60, remains useful for background, though a
number of the citations are invalid), and finds natural affinity
with the Stoic view that the individual shares in the all-
pervasive cosmic spirit: the Stoic cosmopolis assumes a
universal human brotherhood which must function co-
operatively as a body; cf. Xen. *Mem.* 2.3.18; Sen. *Ep.*
95.52; *Dial.* 4.31.7; Plu. *Arat.* 24.6; Marc. Aur. 2.1; 7.13;
8.34. It is fortuitous for A. that Cic. uses the same language
to speak of human society that the NT does to picture the
church, in 1 Cor. 12: 12–31 (Paul is probably influenced by
Stoicism here; for other texts, see on 2.134), and he is able to
exploit this biblical passage in 3.18 (plus related ones in
3.18–19). But it is wrong to think that the two sources, Cic.
and Scripture, as simply juxtaposed. Rather, A. applies the

classical language with a particular slant: underneath the extension of body image to society as a whole lies his pervasive conviction that the church should be the model of how human beings ought to relate (cf. 1.142; 2.124). Damage to a member of the societal body and damage to a member of the ecclesial body are placed on a par in 3.19 (Becker, 254, speaks of a Christian transformation of the Stoic image, qualifying the otherwise still helpful analysis of Pétré, 275–93, especially 285 ff.). On the *officia/munera* of parts of the body, cf. *Ex.* 6.54–74, especially 6.60 ff.

totum hominem exuas: Cf. Cic. *Fin.* 5.35, also echoed by A. in 3.46 below.

si aut de sinistra cibum suggeras . . . nisi forte poscat necessitas: The convention of the *triclinium* (or, more likely at this time, the *sigma* couch of the *stibadium*; see K. M. D. Dunbabin, 'Triclinium and Stibadium', in W. J. Slater (ed.), *Dining in a Classical Context* (Ann Arbor, MI, 1991), 121–48) was to lie on one's left side, supporting one's head with one's left arm. This limited the availability of the left hand to do much more than wield a napkin. Food was taken with the right hand. On the suitability of the hands to their tasks, cf. generally Cic. *ND* 2.150–2; Lact. *Opif.* 10; and see K. Gross, 'Lob der Hand im klassischen und christlichen Altertum', *Gymnasium* 83 (1977), 423–40.

18.   **ut possit detrahere . . . statum dissolvet naturae?:** Cf. Cic. *Off.* 3.22, cited above on 3.17.

   Si totum corpus oculus . . .? Si totum auditus, ubi odoratus?: 1 Cor. 12: 17.

   Omnes ergo unum corpus sumus et diversa membra: Cf. 1 Cor. 12: 12, 14, 20; and Rom. 12: 4–5.

   non enim potest membrum . . . dicere: 'Non est mihi necessarium': Cf. 1 Cor. 12: 21.

   Quin etiam ipsa . . . se requirunt sollicitudinem: Cf. 1 Cor. 12: 22–3.

   Et si cui dolet . . . ei membra omnia: [cui V², Zell Valdarfer, Scinzenzeler, Marchand, Testard: *qui* PV¹M W, Lignamine: *quid* E, COB, other editors: *quid est* A] Cf. 1 Cor. 12: 26.

19.   **Haec utique lex naturae est . . . stringit humanitatem:** Throughout Cic. *Off.* 3.21–8, nature's law is said t

ordain the common rights and mutual responsibilities of all human beings. On this role of nature, cf. *Noe* 94: *Eadem enim natura omnium mater est hominum, et ideo fratres sumus omnes una atque eadem matre generati cognationis eodem iure devincti.* (See generally Maes, especially 6–8, 123–38, 151–203. M. Poirier, ' "Consors naturae" chez saint Ambroise: Copropriété de la nature ou communauté de nature?', in *AmbrEpisc* ii. 325–35, does not make enough of the Stoic input. The doctoral thesis of R. J. Hebein, 'St Ambrose and Roman Law' (St Louis University, MO, 1979) is inaccurate in a number of respects, but is doubtless right in its conclusion that A. is more interested in *ius* than *lex*, and in the theological dimensions of the higher law of God in human life (especially 58–87, 143–63, 164–7). A. Lenox-Conyngham, 'Law in St Ambrose', *SP* 23 (1989), 149–52, gives some examples of places where A. uses *lex* for *ius*, stressing the superiority of natural/divine law to positive (Mosaic/Roman) law; positive law is necessary because of human inability to keep natural/divine law. Lenox-Conyngham does not consider the possible relevance of 3.19–23 to that discussion.)

negabit: V, Winterbottom, 566: *negavit* MSS.

communio totius humanitatis solvitur: Cf. Cic. *Off.* 3.26: *dissolvetur omnis humana consortio.*

violatur natura generis humani et sanctae ecclesiae congregatio: When humanity as a whole is harmed, so is the church. The church is a microcosm of society as it should be; cf. 1.170.

quae in unum conexum corpus . . . adsurgit: Cf. Eph. 4: 16: *ex quo* [sc. *Christus*] *totum corpus, compactum et conexum per omnem iuncturam subministrationis, secundum operationem in mensuram uniuscuiusque membri, augmentum corporis facit in aedificationem sui in caritate* ; also Eph. 4: 13: *in unitatem fidei*; Eph. 4: 2: *supportantes invicem in caritate*.

Christus quoque Dominus, qui pro universis mortuus est: Cf. 2 Cor. 5: 14–15.

mercedem sanguinis sui evacuatam dolebit: When one member is damaged, the unity of the whole body is fractured. This makes Christ grieve, for he shed his blood to redeem the entire body, not just parts of it.

20. Quod etiam lex Domini . . . tui commodi servandi gratia: A. adds the authority of divine law to Cic.'s reference (*Off.* 3.23–4) to human laws (which he goes on to mention in 3.21). On *forma*, cf. 3.13, 15, 17.

Non transferas terminos . . . patres tui: Prov. 22: 28.

cum vitulum errantem . . . reducendum praecipit: See Ex. 23: 4.

cum furem mori iubet: Not strictly true. If a householder killed a thief breaking in at night, he was not guilty of bloodshed (Ex. 22: 2), though he was if the act occurred in daylight (Ex. 22: 3). In general, theft was punished not with death but with reparation (Ex. 22: 1–9).

cum vetat mercenarium debita mercede fraudari: See Lev. 19: 13; Dt. 24: 14–15. In *Ep.* 62 [19].3, A. tells Vigilius to warn the merchant who defrauds his worker that he will be denied his heavenly reward.

cum pecuniam sine usuris reddendam censuit: See Ex. 22: 25; Lev. 25: 36–7; Dt. 23: 19–20; and see on 2.111.

erat opus: Winterbottom, 565: *erit opus* PVM, Testard: *eguit* E, CO

Absolvis igitur alteri debitorem ut condemnes tibi: Cf. Cic. *Verr.* 2.2.22: *Hunc hominem Veneri absolvit, sibi condemnat.*

auctio: An apt choice of word in the context of financial dealings.

21. Hoc praestamus ceteris animantibus . . . conferre aliquid nesciunt: In 1.124, A. says that the ultimate difference between man and beast is man's possession of reason. The same idea may well be in his mind here, because Cic. argues in *Off.* 3.23 that unjust gain is contrary to *ipsa naturae ratio*. Reason causes men to share, while irrational beasts generally snatch away one another's food. For a different view of animals' habits, cf. 3.45.

ferae autem eripiunt: Winterbottom, 565, proposes *ferae enim eripiunt*; but A. need not be so precise in signalling the clause.

Iustus miseretur et tribuit: Ps. 36: 21.

et aves cibo suo pullos satiant suos: Birds at least provide for their own young; cf. Sen. *Ep.* 66.26. For a similar point with dumb animals, cf. e.g. *Abr.* 1.8. On birds and their habits generally, cf. *Ex.* 5.36–92.

Nec ipsae leges nos docent? . . . aut multa revocet: Cf.
Cic. *Off.* 3.23: *Neque vero hoc solum natura, id est iure
gentium, sed etiam legibus populorum, quibus in singulis civitatibus res publica continetur, eodem modo constitutum est, ut non
liceat sui commodi causa nocere alteri. Hoc enim spectant leges,
hoc volunt, incolumem esse civium coniunctionem; quam qui
dirimunt, eos morte, exsilio, vinculis, damno coercent.* For some
examples of the relevant *multae*, cf. Gaius, *Inst.* 3.182–225;
Isid. *Orig.* 5.27. On learning from the law, cf. 3.73 below.

22. **ut aliqui alteri detrahant:** Cf. Cic. *Off.* 3.21: *Detrahere
igitur alteri aliquid*; 3.23: *cui* [sc. *rationi*] *parere qui velit . . .
numquam committet ut alienum appetat et id quod alteri
detraxerit sibi adsumat.*

Servile hoc vitium et familiare ultimae conditioni:
Indicative of a certain snobbery about slaves and their
likely mores; cf. 1.20 and see ad loc.

adeo contra naturam . . . quam natura suadere: Cf. Cic.
Off. 3.21–2, 26.

**Servorum tamen occulta furta, divitum rapinae pub-
licae:** The petty theft of slaves remains a private matter
within a household, but the large-scale extortion of the rich
is seen by all.

23. **Quid autem tam contra naturam . . . tui commodi
causa . . .?:** Cf. Cic. *Off.* 3.26: *Deinde qui alterum violat . . .;
. . . nihil existimat se facere contra naturam . . .; Si nihil
existimat contra naturam fieri hominibus violandis*; 3.27: *certe
violare alterum naturae lege prohibemur.*

**cum pro omnibus excubandum . . . copiis functus
egisset:** Cf. Cic.'s reference to the labours of Hercules, a
hero who transcended ethnic boundaries in championing the
good of all humanity: *Off.* 3.25: *Itemque magis est secundum
naturam pro omnibus gentibus, si fieri possit, conservandis aut
iuvandis maximos labores molestiasque suscipere, imitantem
Herculem illum quem hominum fama beneficiorum memor in
concilio caelestium conlocavit, quam vivere in solitudine non
modo sine ullis molestiis sed etiam in maximis voluptatibus,
abundantem omnibus copiis, ut excellas etiam pulchritudine et
viribus*; also *Off.* 1.69–70; and *Tusc.* 1.28; *Fin.* 3.65–6.
A. inherits Cic.'s anti-Epicurean attitude to the duties of
political leadership (**quam si in otio positus tranquillam**

vitam voluptatum copiis functus egisset), and shares a traditional Stoic admiration for the person who gets involved in the hazards and glories of politics. This is a far nobler existence than a dishonourable life of selfish *otium* (for a similar description in Cic. cf. *Sest.* 139) (Vermeulen, 45–7). On A.'s patriotism, see on 1.144; and cf. 1.127, 254; 3.82–5, 127. His own style of leadership reflects a self-conscious conviction that the cleric is to be seen to spend himself and take risks in defence of the common good. It is of course the *gloria* to be won by this kind of courageous (cf. 1.177) churchmanship which matters above all: cf. 2.29–39 (especially 30, 32, 34), 56–67.

CHAPTER 4: THE CHRISTIAN MUST PUT OTHERS
BEFORE SELF

24.   Hinc ergo colligitur . . . nocere non possit alteri: Cf. Cic. *Off.* 3.25: *Ex quo efficitur hominem naturae oboedientem homini nocere non posse*. Again, nature's norm, expressed in conscience (cf. 3.29, 31), is synonymous with God's design: cf. 1.78, 135, 221, 223–4. Conscience dictates consideration for others; on the role of the inner norm in this section, see Testard, '*Conscientia*', 246.

quod, si qui nocet, naturam violet: See on 3.23.

neque tantum esse commodi . . . quod ex eo sibi accidat: The syntax is conflated: after **colligitur**, A. has **quod** with the subjective (twice); now, still with **colligitur** understood, he has an accusative and infinitive construction.

Quae enim poena gravior quam interioris vulnus conscientiae?: Cf. Cic. *Off.* 3.26: *errat in eo, quod ullum aut corporis aut fortunae vitium vitiis animi gravius existimat* (also *Off.* 3.85).

Quod severius iudicium quam domesticum . . .?: On conscience as a *iudex*, cf. 2.2; also 3.29, 31.

quod iniuriam fratri indigne fecerit: Cf. Cic. *Off.* 3.26: *facere cuiquam iniuriam*. A. changes Cic.'s *cuiquam* to **fratri**, giving a Christian tone to the expression (Testard, '*Conscientia*', 244–5 n. 5). Cf. the point of 1 Cor. 6: 8: *Sed vo iniuriam facitis, et fraudatis, et hoc fratribus*.

Ex ore stultorum baculum contumeliae: Prov. 14: 3.
**Nonne hoc magis fugiendum . . . et existimationis
dispendio?**: Cf. Cic. *Off*. 3.26: *Sin fugiendum id quidem
censet, sed multo illa peiora, mortem paupertatem dolorem,
errat in eo, quod ullum aut corporis aut fortunae vitium vitiis
animi gravius existimat.* In *Off*. 3.26 Cic. also mentions
*mortem paupertatem dolorem, amissionem etiam liberorum
propinquorum, amicorum.* With **existimationis dispendio**,
A. adds a further calamity to Cic.'s mention of *vitia animi.*
On the obsession with reputation, cf. 1.227, 247; 2.29–39,
56–67; loss of esteem is implicitly as serious as a spiritual
failing.

**25. Liquet igitur id exspectandum . . . utilitas quae sit
universorum:** Cf. Cic. *Off*. 3.26: *Ergo unum debet esse
omnibus propositum, ut eadem sit utilitas unius cuiusque et
universorum.*

Mihi certe: For the personal assertion, cf. 3.27, *Mihi
quidem.*

Etenim si una lex naturae . . . utilitas universorum:
The key principle and the nub of the whole argument in this
section: *utilitas* is always synonymous with the law of nature.

ad consulendum . . . naturae lege constringimur: Cf.
Cic. *Off*. 3.27: *Quod si ita est, una continemur omnes et eadem
lege naturae.*

Non est ergo eius . . . ei adversum legem naturae: Cf.
Cic. *Off*. 3.27: *Atque etiam, si hoc natura praescribit, ut homo
homini, quicumque sit, ob eam ipsam causam quod is homo sit,
consultum velit, necesse est secundum eandem naturam omnium
utilitatem esse communem.*

**26. Etenim hi qui stadium currunt . . . manu deicere
non ausit:** [**qui stadium currunt:** O: *qui in stadium currunt*
most MSS: *qui in stadio currunt* E] Cf. Cic. *Off*. 3.42: *Scite
Chrysippus, ut multa, 'qui stadium,' inquit, 'currit, eniti et
contendere debet quam maxime possit ut vincat, supplantare
eum quicum certet aut manu depellere nullo modo debet; sic in
vita sibi quemque petere quod pertineat ad usum non iniquum
est, alteri deripere ius non est'* [Chrysippus (250–207/6 BC),
head of the Stoa after Cleanthes, from 232 BC, was the first
systematizer of Stoic doctrines; cf. here *SVF* iii. 173.10].
feruntur keeps it vague: A. will not attribute the example to

either Cic. or Chrysippus; but of course the allusion is bound
to be identifiable to his literate readers. **hi qui stadium
currunt** also evokes 1 Cor. 9: 24, *hi qui in stadio currunt*
(which probably accounts for E's reading here). On the
clerical life as conducted *in stadio*, cf. *Ep. extra coll.* 14 [63].72.

27.   Quaerunt aliqui . . . utrum debeat?: The question is
asked by Hecato of Rhodes in his sixth book on duties,
according to Cic. *Off.* 3.89: [sc. *quaerit*] '*Si tabulam de
naufragio stultus adripuerit, extorquebitne eam sapiens, si
potuerit?*' *Negat, quia sit iniurium* (cf. also *Off.* 3.90; *Rep.*
3.30 [Lact. *Inst.* 5.16.10; 5.17.10–34]). A. again leaves the
source of the question unspecified. Cic. is exploring how the
principle of the supremacy of natural justice works out in a
problem case. In *Off.* 3.29–31, he argues that the benefit of
the sage's survival does not allow the injustice of his survival
at the cost of another's life, unless the sage is going to render
some great service to the state and to human society—in
which case nature's law entitles him to survive though an
idle, foolish person perishes. A. concedes that the survival of
the **sapiens**—who is below explicitly equated with the **vir
Christianus et iustus et sapiens**—does seem more beneficial to the common good than the survival of the fool (cf.
Lact. *Inst.* 6.16–17). But he rejects the classical situation-
ethic in the light of Christ's pacifism. Secular *humanitas* does
not go far enough. The believer must harm no one, even if
harmed himself. Satyrus, when shipwrecked, was delivered
through faith alone, and not by seizing a plank: *Exc. fr.*
1.43–4.

Mihi quidem: Cf. 3.25, *Mihi certe.*
vir Christianus: Cf. 3.58.
utpote qui . . . referire non possit: On the condemnation
of personal revenge, cf. 1.131 and see ad loc.; also 3.59;
contrast Cic. *Off.* 2.18; *Mil.* 10. On the problem of *latrones*,
see on 1.158; *CTh* 9.14.2 (391) would give civilians the right
to carry arms to protect themselves against such brigands,
but for A. such retaliation even in self-defence is evidently
less than Christian.

contaminet: Cic. uses the verb in *Off.* 3.37.
Reconde gladium tuum . . . gladio ferietur: Mt. 26: 52;
cf. Jn. 18: 11. On Christ's example, cf. 3.15, 36, 136.

latro: V²A², W², COB, Testard: *latrone* PV¹MA¹, EW¹.

qui voluit . . . omnes sanare: Cf. Is. 53: 5. Like many other early Christian writers (cf. e.g. R. Arbesmann, 'The Concept of Christus Medicus in St Augustine', *Traditio* 10 (1954), 1–28), A. often refers to Christ's work in terms of medicine and healing: e.g. 3.94; *Expl. Ps. 35*.3; *Expl. Ps. 37*.4; for further references see Gryson, *Prêtre*, 287 n. 157.

28. Cur enim te potiorem altero iudices . . .?: Cic. *Off.* 3.31 warns that the wise, good, and brave man who is preserved at the cost of the life of an idle and worthless person must not be led by excessive self-esteem and self-love to do injury to others. On the Aristotelian roots of the sentiment, on avoiding the equal dangers of failing to discern one's usefulness to society, on the one hand, and behaving entirely selfishly on the other, see Dyck, 534. A. is probably thinking also of Phil. 2: 3–4.

nihil sibi adrogare . . . adsumere . . . vindicare: On avoiding presumptuous claims, cf. 1.1–4; 2.119, 122, 124, 134; 3.36.

Deinde cur non potius . . . diripere adsuescas?: Cf. Cic. *Off.* 3.30: *suum cuique incommodum ferendum est potius quam de alterius commodis detrahendum* (also *Off.* 3.28).

non esse contentum eo quod habeas: On contentment with one's lot, cf. 1.185; and, for the philosophical and spiritual *topos*, cf. Lucr. 5.1118–19; Cic. *Off.* 1.70; *Parad.* 51; Sall. *Cat.* 2.1; Sen. *Epp.* 74.12; 110.18; 119.6; 123.3; and Phil. 4: 11–13; 1 Tim. 6: 6–10; Heb. 13: 5.

Nam si honestas secundum naturam . . . naturae lege sint: Cf. Cic. *Off.* 3.35: *Quod si nihil est tam contra naturam quam turpitudo (recta enim et convenientia et constantia natura desiderat, aspernaturque contraria) nihilque tam secundum naturam quam utilitas, certe in eadem re utilitas et turpitudo esse non potest*; also *Leg.* 1.45 (= *SVF* iii. 77.16).

omnia enim Deus fecit bona valde: Cf. Gen. 1: 31: *Viditque Deus cuncta quae fecit: et erant valde bona* (the climax to the refrain of Gen. 1: 4, 10, 18, 21, 25). The biblical phrase may well be inserted to replace Cic.'s description of the honourable as *aut solum aut summum bonum, quod autem bonum, id certe utile, ita quidquid honestum, id utile (Off.* 3.35). The *honestum* is 'very good' since it is in conformity with the good design of God's creation; its antithesis, the *turpe*, sin and injustice, is contrary to this purpose, and so, by implication, it must be contrary to the *utile* as well. On nature as God's will, cf. 1.78, 135, 223–4.

3.29–124 constitutes the heart of book 3. The core thesis is that nothing except what is honourable should be sought. This is the 'capstone' (3.29) which A. takes from Cic. *Off.* 3.33. Cic. argues that genuine *utilitas* can never conflict with the honourable course: only apparent benefit can do that (*Off.* 3.40–120). He illustrates this with reference to each of the four virtues in turn, but focuses particularly on justice. The cause of justice must judge the claims of self-interest masquerading as wisdom (*Off.* 3.40–96), and it must govern behaviour which looks courageous, like keeping oaths (*Off.* 3.97–115), or temperate, such as a definition of restraint which in fact only legitimates hedonism (*Off.* 3.116–20). Cic.'s reasoning is infused with a fascination for the application of jurisprudence to ethical conundra. He discusses examples of the kinds of conduct which may seem beneficial to the individual person or state but which in fact contradict the basic principle of what is right for human society as a whole. This approach has already been followed in *Off.* 3.29–32, 35–9, with direct reference to his *formula*.

A. adopts the same method, but typically draws his Ciceronian material at random: the story of Gyges (3.29–36), for example, comes from Cic. *Off.* 3.35–9, not from *Off.* 3.40–120. A regular motif is the superiority of biblical *exempla* to Ciceronian ones, but here A. describes the latter in greater detail (albeit dismissively, and often with *praeteritio*): cf. 3.29–36; 3.70–5; 3.76–81; 3.86–7; 3.91–5; or 3.96–7. Cic.'s enthusiasm for the *mos maiorum* is paralleled by the continuing praise for the exploits of *patres nostri*: here we see the centrality of *honestas* as nowhere else. A contrast between Christian and pagan treatments of *peregrini* in recent situations of famine makes a similar point about the justice of humanity, and shows how honourable leadership also proves beneficial to society (3.45–52). A. makes no attempt to bring the cardinal virtues into the argument, except in so far as he is sketching the perspective of the Christian *sapiens*, for whom reverence for

God and consideration for others are equally fundamental. Keeping these twin ideals in mind is what doing the honourable thing is all about; real *utilitas*, in this world and the next, follows upon it every time (3.52, 60, 84, 88–90; on spurious *utilitas*, cf. 3.37, 44, 49–51, 56, 63).

CHAPTER 5: THE WISE PERSON WILL NOT ACT
DISHONOURABLY EVEN IN SECRET

29. **Sed iam ut etiam in hoc libro ponamus fastigium . . . nisi quod honestum:** [**in quod:** E², C: *in quo* MSS: *quo* C¹; **finem:** E, C: *fine* MSS] Cf. Cic. *Off.* 3.33: *Sed quoniam operi inchoato, prope tamen absoluto, tamquam fastigium imponimus . . ., ego a te postulo, mi Cicero, ut mihi concedas, si potes, nihil praeter id quod honestum sit propter se esse expetendum* [etc.].
neque quidquam facit . . . etiamsi latere possit: Cf. Cic. *Off.* 3.37: *satis enim nobis, si modo in philosophia aliquid profecimus, persuasum esse debet, si omnes deos hominesque celare possimus, nihil tamen avare, nihil iniuste, nihil libidinose, nihil incontinenter esse faciendum* (also *Off.* 3.39).
Sibi enim est reus . . . quam conscientia est: Cic. does not mention conscience in *Off.* 3.37–9, but it is clearly assumed in his argument that the right-thinking person would never do something unjust, even if he could conceal it from the gods and men. 3.31 shows that A. is again thinking of conscience as a natural law imprinted on the human heart by the Creator; cf. 3.24.
Quod non fictis fabulis . . . docere possumus: A. goes on to relate the tale anyhow in 3.30. Cic. *Off.* 3.38 recounts Plato's story (*Rep.* 359c–360b) about Gyges, king of Lydia *c.*685–657 BC and founder of the Mermnad dynasty, who became king with the aid of a magic ring, which enabled him to murder king Candaules and take his wife (for different versions of the usurpation, cf. Herod. 1.8–12; Justin, 1.7.15–19; consult, with some caution, K. F. Smith, 'The Tale of Gyges and the King of Lydia', *AJPh* 23 (1902), 261–82, 361–87; there is also a fragmentary ancient drama on the theme, which may or may not belong to the Hellenistic period: E. Lobel, 'A Greek

Historical Drama', *PBA* 35 (1949), 207–16). Cic. has *ut
ferunt fabulae* in *Off.* 3.38 and in *Off.* 3.39 he speaks of
philosophi (the Epicureans) who criticize Plato's myth as a
ficta et commenticia fabula. Contrasting biblical *exempla*
follow in 3.33–6. The fictitious nature of the Gyges tale is
stressed repeatedly: *fictis fabulis* (3.29); *non simulabo . . .
fabulosum* (3.30); *non fabulosa pro veris, sed vera pro fabulosis
exempla . . . fingere . . . figmento* (3.32); *fabula, etsi vim non
habet veritatis* (3.36). This contrasts with the historical
veracity of the scriptural illustrations: *verissimis iustorum
virorum exemplis* (3.29); *vera exempla . . . ex rebus gestis*
(3.32); note Cic. *Off.* 3.69: *ex optimis naturae et veritatis
exemplis. Philosophi* (3.29) have invented the story in order
to illustrate their hypothesis about the honour of the sage;
Scripture proves the point with real happenings. The rhetoric loses some of its edge, however, when we note that Cic.
himself makes no claims that the story actually happened,
and freely says that it is simply designed to illustrate a moral
point (*Off.* 3.39; his words are echoed by A. in 3.36); cf. a
similar note in Cic. *Off.* 3.99, with 3.92 below.

30.   Non igitur ego simulabo: For the *praeteritio*, cf. *non ego
. . . notabo* in 3.70; A. expects the story to be known.
The whole of this paragraph follows Cic. *Off.* 3.38 very
closely:

Hinc ille Gyges inducitur a Platone, qui cum terra discessisset
magnis quibusdam imbribus, descendit in illum hiatum aeneum-
que equum, ut ferunt fabulae, animadvertit, cuius in lateribus fores
essent; quibus apertis corpus hominis mortui vidit magnitudine
invisitata anulumque aureum in digito; quem ut detraxit, ipse
induit (erat autem regius pastor), tum in concilium se pastorum
recepit. Ibi cum paleam eius anuli ad palmam converterat, a nullo
videbatur, ipse autem omnia videbat; idem rursus videbatur, cum
in locum anulum inverterat. Itaque hac opportunitate anuli usus
reginae stuprum intulit eaque adiutrice regem dominum interemit
sustulit quos obstare arbitrabatur, nec in his eum facinoribus
quisquam potuit videre. Sic repente anuli beneficio rex exortus
est Lydiae. Hunc igitur ipsum anulum si habeat sapiens, nihilo plus
sibi licere putet peccare quam si non haberet; honesta enim bonis
viris, non occulta quaeruntur.

fabulosum: E: *fabularum* other MSS.

exanimum corpus iaceret: Cf. Verg. *Aen.* 6.149: *praeterea iacet exanimum tibi corpus amici.* Cf. also Lucr. 6.705–6.

palam: E², Erasmus (1527), Testard: *paleam* PVMA, E'W, COB, Zell.

31. **Da, inquit, hunc anulum sapienti . . . quam si non possit latere:** Cf. Cic. *Off.* 3.38: *Hunc igitur ipsum anulum si habeat sapiens, nihilo plus sibi licere putet peccare quam si non haberet; honesta enim bonis viris, non occulta quaeruntur.* The subject of **inquit** is Plato rather than Cic., since in 3.30 A. says that the story *a Platone inducitur* (cf. Cic. *Off.* 3.38: *inducitur a Platone*). In *Rep.* 360b–d, Glaucon applies the tale in the way outlined here. E, C are right to omit the MSS' *enim* between **non** and **minus**: the style is idiomatic (Winterbottom, 566).

lex non iusto sed iniusto posita est: 1 Tim. 1: 9.

quia iustus legem habet . . . iustitiae suae normam: The just person is directed by his conscience. Note the shift from the earlier emphasis on nature as a universal norm to the focus here on the Christian *sapiens/iustus* as specifically attuned to this imperative.

honestatis regula: The words are used by Cic. in *Off.* 3.74.

32. **ut ad propositum redeamus:** Cf. Cic. *Off.* 3.39: *Sed iam ad propositum revertamur.* A. uses the phrase (cf. also on 2.21, *Sed iam ad proposita pergamus*) to return to his point that he can demonstrate the instinctive honesty of the *sapiens* using true rather than fictitious examples (though his references to the Gyges tale are not over). Cic. is resuming the main theme of book 3, the relationship of *honestas* to apparent *utilitas*, after speaking of the false attractions of apparent *utilitas* in cases like that of Gyges.

non fabulosa pro veris sed vera pro fabulosis: Cf. 1.122: *non falsa pro veris*; and see ad loc.

Nempe eo tendit istud . . . ad perpetrandum scelus?: [**istud:** EW, COB, several editors: *studio* PVMA, Zell, Valdarfer, Scinzenzeler, Marchand: *studium* Lignamine] Cf. Cic. *Off.* 3.39: *Haec est vis huius anuli et huius exempli: si nemo sciturus, nemo ne suspicaturus quidem sit, cum aliquid divitiarum potentiae dominationis libidinis causa feceris, si id dis hominibusque futurum sit semper ignotum, sisne facturus?* [etc.]

vir sapiens: David; the story follows in 3.33–4. Gyges' immoral usurpation contrasts with David's honourable refusal to seize power by violence. The real *vir sapiens* is an OT hero, not a character from the philosophers' tales.

33. **Denique David, cum fugeret . . . ne ab aliquo qui simul ingressus fuerat, perimeretur:** A. accurately relates the narrative from 1 Ki. 26. On this paragraph, see 1 Ki. 26: 1–11. David could have killed Saul, as Abishai suggested, and seized the throne. But, for him, unlike Gyges, even the chance to escape detection was not enough to justify regicide. The desire to remain *purus* (see the quotation below), to keep a clear conscience, regulated David; and this in turn was determined by his awareness that he was accountable to God (cf. 1.124; 2.96).

Conclusit Dominus hodie . . . et nunc occidam eum?: 1 Ki. 26: 8.

Non consumas eum . . . et purus erit?: 1 Ki. 26: 9.

Vivit Dominus . . . in christum Domini: [*in pugnam descenderit:* E, COB: *in pugnam discenderet* W: *in pugna descenderit* V: *in pugna discesserit* PM, Testard: *inpugnandis cesserit* A] 1 Ki. 26: 10–11.

34. **See 1 Ki. 26: 12–25.** Some of the language in this paragraph (**egressus de castris . . . quod nequaquam fidam adhiberet custodiam . . .**) is similar to Cic.'s in *Off.* 1.40 (a bracketed but defensible passage in most editions, relating an incident from the Second Punic War which Cic. recounts more fully in 3.113–15; see Dyck, 150–3): *exisset e castris . . . ; . . . egressus e castris . . . ; Semper autem in fide quid senseris, non quid dixeris, cogitandum est* (1.40); *egressus e castris* (3.113); for apparent Ambrosian validation of the rest of *Off.* 1.40, cf. 3.91.

Et Dominus, **inquit,** *restituat . . . in christum Domini:* 1 Ki. 26: 23.

sedem exsilio mutans: Cf. Verg. *Georg.* 2.511: *exsilio domos et dulcia limina mutant.* Cf. also Ov. *Fast.* 6.665; Curt. 3.7.11. A. also evokes the Vergilian words at *Ex.* 5.27.

35. **Ubi opus fuit Iohanni . . . non esset occisus ab Herode?:** John the Baptist was imprisoned and subsequently beheaded by Herod Antipas for having condemned the king's relationship with Herodias, the wife of his brother

Philip (Mt. 14: 1–12; Mk. 6: 14–29). For A., John had a
greater concern for right and wrong than he had for his own
life; cf. 3.89. Like David, John did the right thing in the
presence of a king. Though he was still in peril initially
(3.34), David gained personally in the end (3.60), whereas
John was executed; but no matter what the outcome, both of
these *sapientes* put Gyges to shame. In John's case, the crime
that he repudiated was someone else's, not his own, which
presumably makes his courage all the greater.

**Certe hoc negare non possunt . . . anuli beneficio
absconderetur:** Cf. Cic. *Off.* 3.39: *Negant* [sc. *philosophi
quidam*] *id fieri posse. Quamquam potest id quidem; sed quaero,
quod negant posse, id si posset, quidnam facerent. . . . Negant
enim posse et in eo perstant, hoc verbum quid valeat non vident.*
Cic. criticizes the pedantry of Epicurean philosophers who
refused to see the relevance of hypothetical moral *exempla*
and denied the possibility that Gyges' disappearing act could
have taken place. No one can deny that John the Baptist could
have kept quiet about Herod's sin: the story of what Gyges
did assumes the miraculous; John's moral boldness was for
real. But there is of course a considerable difference between
the two stories. Gyges committed a crime because he could
count on the fact that he would not be caught; John was duty-
bound by his conscience not to turn a blind eye to Herod's
sin. On the wrong kind of silence, cf. 1.9.

36. Sed fabula . . . hanc . . . rationem habet: Cf. Cic. *Off.*
3.39: *Haec est vis huius anuli et huius exempli*; Cic. does not
make any claims that the story is true, but he maintains that
it affords a useful illustration of what might happen in such a
theoretical situation.

**ut, si possit celare se vir iustus . . . quasi celare non
possit:** Cf. Cic. *Off.* 3.39: *Cum enim quaerimus, si celare
possint, quid facturi sint, non quaerimus possintne celare.*

**nec personam suam indutus . . . Christum indutus
abscondat:** The idea of 'putting on Christ' (Rom. 13: 14;
Gal. 3: 27; cf. Eph. 4: 24) or 'hiding with Christ in God'
(Col. 3: 3) is, however, entirely different from the point of
the Gyges myth. The ring was put on to escape detection in a
crime yet to be committed, in order to avoid human punishment; the believer 'puts on Christ' or 'hides with Christ in

God' in order to cover over the unworthiness he or she has on account of sins already committed, and in this spirit of humble flight from the corrupting effects of the present evil world escapes divine condemnation in the life to come.

Vita nostra abscondita est cum Christo in Deo: Col. 3: 3.

nemo sibi adroget, nemo se iactet: Cf. 1.1–4 and see ad loc.; cf. 2.119, 122, 124, 134; 3.28.

Nolebat se Christus hic cognosci . . . cum in terris versaretur: See Mt. 8: 4; 9: 30; 12: 16; 16: 20; 17: 9; Mk. 1: 44; 3: 12; 5: 43; 7: 36; 8: 26, 30; Lk. 5: 14; 8: 56; 9: 21. Again, this is a completely different matter from the invisibility of Gyges. Whatever NT scholarship may make of the so-called 'Messianic secret' (see C. M. Tuckett, 'Messianic Secret', *ABD* iv. 797–800), Christ was obviously not hiding in the doing of evil. On Christ as example, cf. 3.15, 27, 136; also 1.9.

Melius est hic esse in humilitate, ibi in gloria: The *honestum* of Christlike self-effacement **hic** brings the lasting *utile* of glorification **ibi**; on the contrast of the two states, cf. 1.29, 58, 103, 147, 238–40; 3.11. On *humilitas*, see on 1.1. The principle expressed here of being content with obscurity or anonymity needs to be measured against the considerable emphasis on self-commendation in book 2 (see on 2.29–39), and on the importance of visible propriety in the exposition of temperance in book 1 (see on 1.210–51).

Cum Christus, inquit, **apparuerit . . . apparebitis in gloria**: Col. 3: 4.

3.37–52 considers wrong conceptions of the relationship between *honestas* and *utilitas*, where *utilitas* is understood only as apparent short-term advantage. In 3.37–44, A. attacks those who go for selfish gain by capitalizing on food-shortages and selling grain at higher prices in times of need. The subject is suggested by Cic. *Off*. 3.50–3. The thesis is that while such speculation may look like a legitimate return for diligent farming and prudent storage of grain, it is really a trade in other people's suffering and a violation of nature's purpose that the earth's produce should be shared by all alike. A. pictures a rhetorical dispute between someone who takes the farmer's position and defends his right to sell his grain at a higher price in a time of famine, and an interlocutor who argues that such practice amounts to dishonourable greed (3.38–40). He follows Cic. *Off*. 3.51–3, where we read of a debate between the Stoic Diogenes of Babylon (*c*.240–152 BC) and his successor, Antipater of Tarsus (head of the Stoa in the mid-second century BC and teacher of Panaetius). Diogenes contends that the seller is justified in seeking the highest possible price for his goods so long as there is no trickery involved, while Antipater maintains that the vendor is duty-bound to reveal to his clients that other supplies are available, and so to serve the interests of society.

In 3.45–52, A. inveighs against the evil of banishing foreigners from a city during times of famine. It may look advantageous to do this, he argues, but it turns out to be both inhumane and short-sighted, for the city may lose a vital source of skilled labour in the process. Far better to share resources and help these *peregrini*: such an honourable course proves genuinely beneficial, for the workers are then retained to be of service to the community in the future. The ξενηλασία theme is inspired by Cic. *Off*. 3.47, but Cic. does not relate it to times of famine. He cites two occasions where *peregrini* were expelled and contrasts these with a notorious act of legislation from earlier in the first century BC which, he argues, was designed to circumscribe the rights of such aliens but not to oppress them (see on 3.45). A. instead offers two contrasting examples of the way in which *peregrini* were treated in recent history: the first, which happened earlier, is in 3.46–8; the second is in 3.49–51, and is a recent event (*proxime* in 3.49 clearly corresponds to *nuper* in Cic. *Off*. 3.47).

A. reverses the order in which the material appears in Cic.'s text (Testard, 'Recherches', 105), but there is nothing particularly significant about this, since he is simply working from memory. The debate in the first section is not personalized in the way that Cic.'s is. A. refers contemptuously to the kind of dispute that is typical to *controversum genus . . . dicendi* (3.38), and contrasts the clear-cut precepts and examples of Scripture on the subject of speculation, while at the same time evidently relishing the opportunity to engage in a little creative rhetoric to set off both sides of the case. So much is standard Ambrosian technique. We should not be puzzled over the relevance of this

or the following section in a work addressed to clerics (*pace*
Testard i. 27; 'Recherches', 104–6), for the material is clearly of
particular relevance to some of A.'s other potential readers
(Introduction VI–VII). There is no need at all to suppose that
a piece initially constructed for a separate audience has been
inserted into the text (besides the Ciceronian inspiration
common to 3.37–52 and the preceding paragraphs, note the
citation of Col. 3: 3–4 in 3.36 and the evocation of Col. 3: 5 in
3.37). At the same time, it would be equally wrong to imagine
that such an attack on selfish hoarding was likely to change
much in practice (for similar stylized rhetoric, cf. e.g. *Nab.* 29–
40, drawing on Basil, on Lk. 12: 16–21, also evoked in 3.43).
3.37–42 is making familiar noises on a conventional theme in
order to illustrate a standard argument about promoting the
common good.

The function of the lengthy second section, however, is more
significant. A. turns a point made in a few words by Cic. into an
argument which lasts for eight paragraphs. He sings the praises
of an unnamed Christian prefect of the city of Rome (on the
likely identification of him as Aradius Rufinus, see on 3.46)
who handled a famine the right way, making sure that needy
peregrini were not deported but were supported by senatorial
subscription (3.46–8). He then slates the cruelty and stupidity
reflected in a recent situation at Rome: this time, *peregrini* were
heartlessly deported, even though the prospects were far from
serious. Salvation was at hand if the authorities had only
sought help and waited a little longer for ships which they
were expecting to arrive with fresh supplies (3.49–51). In this
case, there is, again, no mention of the prefect's name. The
scene can, however, be dated plausibly to late 384, when the
prefect was Q. Aurelius Symmachus. The people whose interests were so disregarded by the prefect's overreaction to a
temporary problem were not the agricultural workers from
Campanian estates and perhaps displaced artisans evidently
envisaged in the first famine (3.46–8, 51): they were *corporati*
(3.50), and 'sons' of Italians (3.49), who had been engaged over
years in the feeding of the Roman populace (3.49). A. paints
them as hapless refugees (3.49), but in all probability they were
important businesspeople, members of the powerful trade
guilds licensed to provision Rome. The reference to them as

filii of Italians may contain a hint that they were relatives or agents of members of the *corpus negotiatorum* in Milan, and that they had been engaged in selling surplus produce from northern Italy on the open market in Rome. Expulsion for them was no doubt disruptive, but could hardly have involved the same hardships as it would have entailed for the *peregrini* of the earlier incident. It is quite likely that some of the victims in 384 had made for Milan, where it is easy to imagine them narrating their plight in suitably graphic terms to the bishop. No matter that their regular commercial activities may well have involved just the kind of speculation A. is so keen to condemn in the preceding paragraphs; this can be conveniently overlooked. These *peregrini* may in fact have been among those who showed A. loyal support in his hour of crisis with his local homoian opponents in 386, when the Milanese *corpus negotiatorum* had incurred a (temporary) severe fine for the actions of a small group of its members whose antipathy to Arianism had extended to the beating up of a homoian presbyter, Castulus (*Ep.* 76 [20]).

If this interpretation (for details see Cracco Ruggini, 112–46) is correct, the upshot of the section is that A. is seizing a chance to engage in thinly veiled polemic against Symmachus, and at the same time offering a spirited defence of those who may have backed him in his own domain. Modern readers must resort to guesswork, but no contemporary would have been likely to miss the edge of A.'s allusions. The gracious prudence of the Christian *sapiens* is obliquely contrasted with the callous folly of pagan officialdom, which dared to insult those whose religious allegiances (and so entire character) have been shown to be in the right place. It is easy to imagine Symmachus himself reading the work, and recognizing himself as the anonymous target of the invective (McLynn, 272–5). A. seems to be going well beyond the exigencies of clerical instruction or philosophical argument: he is scoring personal points to suit his own ends, and in the process choosing not to press charges of *avaritia* against those who had sided with his cause.

3.45–52 has elicited a good deal of scholarly discussion. The fundamental treatments are: J.-R. Palanque, 'Famines à Rome à la fin du IVe siècle', *REA* 33 (1931), 346–56 (who wrongly sees A.'s silence over the identity of the second prefect as a

piece of tact: 349–51); Cracco Ruggini, 112–46, especially
116 ff.; ead. 'Ambrogio di fronte alla compagine sociale del
suo tempo', in *AmbrEpisc* i. 230–65, especially 253 ff.; E. Faure,
'Saint Ambroise et l'expulsion des pérégrins de Rome', in
Etudes d'histoire du droit canonique dédiées à Gabriel Le Bras i
(Paris, 1965), 523–40; H. P. Kohns, *Versorgungskrisen und
Hungerrevolten im spätantiken Rom* (Bonn, 1961), 71 ff.,
145 ff., 168 ff.; J. Durliat, *De la ville antique à la ville byzantine.
Le problème des subsistences* (Rome, 1990), 518–22 (underesti-
mating the force of A.'s contextual shaft at Symmachus);
McLynn, 272–5. I adopt the basic interpretation of Cracco
Ruggini, and, with McLynn, see A.'s portrait of the grief of the
second group of *peregrini* as part of the rhetorical strategy to
exaggerate the effect of the prefect's actions, rather than (so
Faure) a description of genuine difficulties experienced by
peregrini to be identified as *navicularii* (3.50 does not imply
that the victims were involved in the work of the expected
grain-ships, only that they were *corporati*). (I have not been
able to see the unpublished work of J.-M. Salamito,
'Recherches sur les conceptions de l'agriculture chez les
chrétiens d'Italie dans l'Antiquité tardive (IIIe–VIe siècle)',
cited by Testard ii. 207 n. 1.)

CHAPTER 6: THE HONOURABLE MUST COME
BEFORE THE SUPPOSED BENEFIT OF
FINANCIAL GAIN

37. **Non vincat igitur honestatem utilitas, sed honestas
utilitatem:** Cf. Cic. *Off.* 3.19: *Vicit ergo utilitas honestatem?
Immo vero honestatem utilitas secuta est.*

secundum vulgi opinionem: Cf. Cic. *Off.* 3.84: *Non habeo
ad vulgi opinionem quae maior utilitas* (also *Off.* 3.18, 34). On
popular ideas of *utilitas*—the apparent benefit of financial
gain versus real gain—cf. 1.28–9; 2.15–16, 23, 25–6; 3.9, 56,
60, 63, 90.

Mortificetur avaritia, moriatur concupiscentia: Cf.
Col. 3: 5: *Mortificate ergo membra vestra quae sunt super
terram: concupiscentiam malam, et avaritiam.*

Sanctus in negotiationem introisse negat: The **sanctus**

is David; cf. Ps. 70: 15 (VL), which accords with the Codex Vaticanus version of the LXX: *quoniam non cognovi nego-tiationes* (πραγματείας); the standard LXX text reads γραμμα-τείας, which in the Vulg. becomes *litteraturam*: see Aug. *En. Ps. 70.*15–17. Cf. also Ps. 25: 4: *Non sedi cum concilio vanitatis: et cum iniqua gerentibus non introibo.* On trade, see on 1.185, 243; and cf. 2.25–6, 67; 3.57, 65.

alius: Solomon.

Captans pretia frumenti maledictus in plebe est: Prov. 11: 26. The text in fact refers to the hoarding of grain rather than to speculation on the price of it (Banterle, 297 n. 2).

38. Definita est sententia . . . solet dicendi esse: Cic. *Off.* 3.37 speaks of *hoc . . . deliberantium genus*; *controversia* (between philosophers) appears in *Off.* 3.92, 119; *disputatio* is used in *Off.* 3.73, and *disputare* in *Off.* 3.89 (cf. A. 2.8). A. would be familiar with such scholastic debates from his schooldays; for background see G. A. Kennedy, *The Art of Rhetoric in the Roman World, 300 BC–AD 300* (Princeton, 1972), 312–30. He may routinely deprecate the special effects of rhetorical contrivance (e.g. *Expl. Ps. 36.*28; *Luc.* 7.218; 8.13), but his own skills are obvious; cf. especially 3.39, 41.

cum alius adlegat . . . apud omnes haberi: Esteem for agriculture is a standard classical theme, not least in Stoic thought. Cic. celebrates it in *Off.* 1.151: *Omnium autem rerum ex quibus aliquid adquiritur nihil est agricultura melius, nihil uberius, nihil dulcius, nihil homine [nihil] libero dignius*, and refers to the treatment of the theme in his *Cato Maior* (*Sen.* 51–60, especially 51). He is thinking of the large-scale farming practised by senators (Colum. *Agr.*, praef. 10 ff.), rather than the labour of smallholders (on the latter, cf. Verg. *Georg.* 2.513–40, and, with some irony, Hor. *Epod.* 2). In *Off.* 2.12, he praises the effort which has made agriculture possible; cf. also *Off.* 2.87, 89. A.'s enthusiasm for the hard-working farmer (cf. *Paen.* 2.3; also *Noe* 107) is typical of Christian rhetoric: see B. Gordon, *The Economic Problem in Biblical and Patristic Thought* (Leiden, 1989), 112–20.

39. 'Aravi', inquit, 'studiosius . . .': The first speaker's defence of his (imaginary) conduct in seeking a legitimate return for his hard work continues in direct speech.

recondidi: Most editors: *recondi* MSS.

Nunc . . . vendo. . . . Quid hic fraudi est . . .?: [**pluris:** E², COB: *pluri* E¹W: *plus* PVMA, Testard] Cf. the protest of Diogenes' merchant in Cic. *Off.* 3.51: '*Advexi, exposui; vendo meum non pluris quam ceteri, fortasse etiam minoris, cum maior est copia; cui fit iniuria?*'

'Et Ioseph frumenta . . . in caritate vendidit': See Gen. 41: 47–56; and cf. 2.79–85 above. The speculator, given his words by A., can cite Scripture; but his interpretation of Joseph's action is corrected in 3.42. Cic. uses *caritas* in *Off.* 3.50.

iniuria: Cf. Cic. *Off.* 3.51, above.

40. **exsurgit alius dicens:** Cf. Cic. *Off.* 3.52: *Exoritur Antipatri ratio ex altera parte.*

quae fructus ministrat omnibus: Cf. Antipater's appeal to the interests of human society in Cic. *Off.* 3.52; cf. also A., 1.38, 132; 3.16.

tritici: Cic. mentions this in *Off.* 3.52.

Fecunda terra . . . solet restituere proventus: Cf. 1.160–1 and see ad locc. In Cic. *Off.* 3.52, Antipater argues that all human beings have an obligation to follow the *principia naturae.*

41. A.'s own words again, after the imaginary debate of 3.38–40; the style is no less rhetorical. The background lies in Cic. *Off.* 3.50. In a time of famine at Rhodes, an honest merchant who has imported grain from Alexandria discovers that other merchants have set sail from Alexandria to bring corn to Rhodes. Should he inform the Rhodians of the imminent arrival of the other resources, or should he keep quiet and sell his own stock at the highest possible price? Cic.'s verdict in *Off.* 3.57 is that the man must not conceal the truth just to boost his own profits. Strictly speaking, his point is about honesty versus concealment of the truth for selfish gain, but in making it Cic. condemns financial speculation at the expense of the needy. A. endorses his position.

uberis glaebae: Cf. Verg. *Aen.* 1.531: *terra antiqua, potens armis atque ubere glaebae.* Cf. also Sen. *Oed.* 156; Dracont. *Laud. Dei* 3.312.

sentiunt: V²A², COB, Zell: *sentiant* EW, Amerbach: *sentio* PV¹MA, Testard.

⟨propter⟩ pretium: Winterbottom, 565: *per pretium* V².

ingemiscis, fles . . . deploras, exploras: Cf. Cypr. *Ad Dem.* 10: you complain of barrenness, when greed abounds.

Votis tuis gaudes . . . ut nihil cuiquam nasceretur: The speculator has prayed that there will be a blight—a divine curse—on the crops of others, so long as his own are favoured. Cf. Augustine's condemnation of the farmer who wishes famine on the poor in order to maximize his own profits: *En. Ps. 70.*15.

et hanc tu industriam vocas, hanc diligentiam nominas: Picking up the other man's words in 3.39.

quae calliditatis versutia, quae astutia fraudis est: Cf. Cic. *Off.* 3.57 (on the nature of the man who deliberately conceals the truth for his own gain): *Certe non aperti, non simplicis, non ingenui, non iusti, non viri boni, versuti potius, obscuri astuti fallacis malitiosi callidi veteratoris vafri.*

et hoc tu remedium vocas: The first speaker does not actually use the word *remedium* in 3.39, but he claims '*subvenio esurientibus*'.

Latrocinium: See on 1.158.

acervetur: *acervatur* most MSS: *acuatur* V.

usura: See on 2.111.

quasi maior: V², preserving the sting of (somewhat odd) **quasi**-clauses: *quia maior* MSS.

Lucrum tuum damnum publicum est: Cf. again Antipater's argument in Cic. *Off.* 3.52–3.

42. **Ioseph sanctus . . . non clausit:** Cf. Gen. 41: 56, and see on 2.79–85. A. is correcting the speculator's interpretation of Joseph's behaviour given in 3.39. The example of Joseph is held up in a similar context in *Nab.* 33.

43. **hunc frumentarium . . . in evangelio Dominus Iesus:** See Lk. 12: 16–21.

Quid faciam? . . . destruam horrea et maiora faciam: Lk. 12: 17–18.

utrum sequenti nocte . . . ab eo reposceretur: Cf. Lk. 12: 20.

44. *Qui continet, . . . relinquet illud nationibus:* Prov. 11: 26 (LXX).

emolumentum: Cic. uses the word in *Off.* 3.57.

Captans annonam maledictus . . . qui participat: Prov. 11: 26, a fusion of the version found in 3.37 with the LXX

version; relying on his memory, A. imagines both versions
are included in the biblical text (**Et addidit**).

**45. Sed et illi qui peregrinos urbe prohibent, nequa-
quam probandi:** Cf. Cic. *Off.* 3.47: *Male etiam qui peregrinos urbibus uti prohibent eosque exterminant, ut Pennus apud
patres nostros, Papius nuper. . . . usu vero urbis prohibere
peregrinos, sane inhumanum est.* Marcus Iunius Pennus was
tribune of the plebs in 126 BC. He carried a law forbidding
the settling of *peregrini* in or around Rome and expelling
existing settlers. Gaius Papius was tribune in 65 BC. He
carried a similar law expelling non-Italians from Rome (Dio
37.9.5); it was aimed especially at the Transpadanes whose
citizenship cause was being supported by the censor
M. Licinius Crassus. Archias (*Arch.* 10) and Balbus (*Balb.*
38, 52) were among the clients of Cic. who were indicted
under Papius' law. Cic. also refers in *Off.* 3.47 to the consuls
L. Licinius Crassus and Q. Mucius Scaevola and their
legislation of 95 BC, the *Lex Licinia Mucia*, against aliens
who posed as citizens (particularly Latins). He carefully
distinguishes this from the cruel deportation measures of
Pennus and Papius.

On the *peregrini* A. has in mind in the two incidents which
follow, see above on 3.37–52. In the first case, they are
primarily a *plebs rusticanorum* (3.51): they include workers
with valuable skills as *cultores* (3.46–7, 51) or *agricolae* (3.46),
presumably employed on the great estates of wealthy *honorati* or senators (3.45–6, 48) (Palanque, 'Famines à Rome',
350; A. Chastagnol, *La Préfecture urbaine à Rome sous le Bas-
Empire* (Paris, 1960), 267–8; Cracco Ruggini, 140–1 n. 389).
Others are said to provide additional services, ministering to
other needs besides the physical (3.46), perhaps as teachers
or other professionals. They have *communia iura* (3.45), but
no automatic entitlement to *frumentum publicum/panis popu-
laris* in a time of crisis (Faure, 'Saint Ambroise et l'expulsion

des pérégrins', 529 ff.). For a good number of these people, an exclusion order might well have meant genuine privation. In the second case, they are *corporati* (3.50) with North Italian connections (3.49), who have spent most of their lives in the metropolis (3.49), doubtless enjoying a lucrative role in the city's food industry. The wholesale dismissal of the latter group was almost certainly accidental, the result of a panic measure intended only to remove obvious dependants, which misfired because it stipulated a deportation of all *peregrini*. On **nequaquam probandi**, cf. 1.74, 84, *nec/non probo*; 1.150, *probanda*; 1.75; 3.125, *probabilis*.

quo debent: A, Maurists, Krabinger, Winterbottom: *quo debet* PVM, Zell, Lignamine, Testard: *quo deberet* CB: *quo deberent* EW, O², other editors; the argument of Testard, 'Problèmes de critique verbale dans le *De Officiis*, III, 45, de saint Ambroise', *REL* 66 (1988), 219–28, at 227 in favour of *debet* is not very convincing: the sentence reads more naturally if the **illi** are the ones who are personally failing to carry out their moral duty.

communis parentis: [**communis:** MA, E², COB, most editors: *communes* PV, E¹, Valdarfer, Scinzenzeler, Marchand; **parentis:** M²A, E², COB, most editors: *parentes* PV, E¹W, Valdarfer, Scinzenzeler, Marchand] Though A. is speaking of famines at Rome, he is not thinking of Rome as the mother-city of the empire (*pace* the Maurist editors in PL 16, 167 n. 23; Cavasin, 443 n. 2; Banterle, 303 n. 2), but (as Niederhuber rightly renders it) of the earth as the common mother of all humanity (cf. *parentis* in 1.161, and the idea of human origins in the earth in 3.16: see Testard, 'Problèmes de critique verbale', at 224 and n. 20; and cf. e.g. *Parad.* 54; *Noe* 94; *Abr.* 2.28). To banish the *peregrini* is to prevent the common produce (1.38, 132; 3.16, 40) of the common mother from being traded and enjoyed among all her children.

inita iam consortia vivendi averruncare: A solemn disruption of relationships within extended households and estates: the *familia* (3.46; cf. 3.49) included all the workers and servile staff; cf. *Nab.* 12: *commercium vivendi*. Testard's objection ('Problèmes de critique verbale', 227; cf. also Testard ii. 210 n. 1) to **averruncare** after **vivendi** (A²,

EW, C, several editors, including Maurists, Krabinger: *vivendi avocare* OB, Gering, Valdarfer, Paderborn, Scinzenzeler, Marchand) is ill-founded: the presence of such a striking word as *averruncare* in a strong MS tradition invites more caution than Testard concedes. An ancient religious verb for averting disasters or other 'ill-fated' eventualities (cf. *Fid*. 1.73: *Deus hanc averruncet amentiam*), *averruncare* may perhaps lend a certain solemn flavour to the condemnation (*TLL* ii. 1316). The crime of those who would banish *peregrini* is an almost sacrilegious destruction of established human bonds; such people would 'avert' these ties as if *they* were the evil, rather than guarding them as they should against the sorts of violations of natural justice which inhumane behaviour produces. Cf. *Expl. Ps.* 47.8: *edomare carnis lasciviam, averruncare luxuriam* (though the word there has often been emended to *evacuare*).

Ferae non expellunt feras . . . victum quem terra ministrat: In 3.21, the human instinct to share is contrasted with the tendency of animals to snatch food for themselves. Here, man's inhumanity to man is worse than bestial: even wild animals do not prevent their own kind from eating. For similar arguments that human selfishness is lower than the ways of the animals, cf. *Nab*. 12; *Tob*. 5; *Noe* 94.

homo . . . qui nihil a se alienum debet credere quidquid humani est!: Cf. Ter. *Heaut*. 77, quoted by Cic. in *Off*. 1.30; *Leg*. 1.33 (and *Fin*. 3.63): *Homo sum humani nil a me alienum puto*. On this celebrated phrase, cf e.g. Sen. *Ep*. 95.51–3; Juv. 15.140–2; Lact. *Inst*. 6.10.4, 26 Paul. Nol. *Ep*. 13.20; Aug. *Ep*. 155.14; *C. Iul*. 4.83; *humanitas* is ironical in Ter., but it is generally injected with the sense of *misericordia* in later writers: see H. D. Jocelyn ' "Homo sum: humani nil a me alienum puto" ', *Antichthon* (1973), 14–46, especially 37 ff.; also Pétré, 200–21.

46. Quanto ille rectius qui . . . poposcit ut in medium consulerent: The urban prefect is a Christian: he i *sanctissimus* (3.48); A. makes him quote and allude t Scripture (3.46); and he wins great *commendatio apu Deum* (3.48). He is also advanced in years (3.46), a *sene* (3.48). He is very probably Aradius Rufinus, who held offic in 376 (*PLRE* i. 775–6—though he is there wrongly said t be a pagan: he was pagan in 363 (Lib. *Ep.* 1374), but was subsequently converted); cf. Symm. *Ep.* 7.126. *CTh* 1.6.7 of 13 July 376 mentions a corn dole; the shortage was probably caused by the Danubian invasion of 375 (Palanque, 'Famines à Rome', 347–9; Cracco Ruggini, 118–20 nn. 316–18; Cracco Ruggini, 'Ambrogio di fronte alla compagine sociale', 256; Chastagnol, *La Préfecture urbaine à Rome*, 267, 436–7; Kohns, *Versorgungskrisen und Hungerrevolten*, 145–53; Testard i. 45; ii. 207 n. 1, 210 n. 4). On the implausibility of other suggested identifications, such as Aemilius Magnus Arborius, a relative of the poet Ausonius (380) (Ihm, 6; cf. R. P. H. Green, *The Works of Ausonius, Edited with Introduction and Commentary* (Oxford, 1991), 280, 318); Sallustius Aventius (384) (G. Hermant, *La Vie de saint Ambroise* (Paris, 1679), 159); or Furius Maecius Gracchus (376–7) (C. Baronius, *Annales Ecclesiastici*, v (Lucca, 1739), *ad ann.* 383; cf. Faure, 'Saint Ambroise et l'expulsion des pérégrins', 527), see Cracco Ruggini, 118–19 n. 316.

ut in talibus solet: Actual expulsion of foreigners was infrequent in the fourth century, but the crowd often demanded it (Faure, 531). *Fear* of famine was a powerful element in the urban psyche, producing clamour for action even when shortages did not actually happen (P. Brown, *Religion and Society in the Age of Saint Augustine* (London, 1972), 15; see further G. Rickman, *The Corn Supply of Ancient Rome* (Oxford, 1980), 198–209; P. Garnsey, *Famine and Food Supply in the Graeco-Roman World: Responses to Risk and Crisis* (Cambridge, 1988), 218–43): on the murmurings of the *vulgus*, cf. Amm. 14.6.19; 19.10.1–4; 21.12.24; 28.4.32; Symm. *Ep.* 2.6–7; on the popular appeal of expulsion decrees, cf. Lib. *Or.* 11.174; Themist. *Orat.* 18.222a.

hominem ab homine exui: See on 3.17.

'Canes ante mensam impastos . . . et homines excludimus': Reminiscent of Mt. 15: 26–7; Mk. 7: 27–8. On the rich treating their animals better than their fellow-human beings, cf. *Nab.* 12, 56; John Chrys. *Hom. Ep. Heb.* 11.3; Gaud. Brix. *Tract.* 13; Max. Taur. *Serm.* 36.3.

Quam inutile quoque: A. is inventing what the good prefect said, and he deliberately incorporates a reference to the lack of *utilitas* in letting the *peregrini* go.

Quanta sunt quae . . . hoc ipso tempore ministrantur!: These *peregrini* cannot be supplying food; they are ministering to people's need for something more than 'bread alone'. Some of them are likely to be professionals: Amm. 14.6.19, speaks of professors of the liberal arts (such as himself) as among those victimized by deportation measures.

Non in solo pane vivit homo: Dt. 8: 3.

47. **'Primum omnium misericordia . . . adiuvatur'**: Divine providence always blesses those who seek to mirror God's own universal generosity (on which cf. 1.38).

'non alii nobis redimendi cultores videntur': The agricultural *peregrini* possessed sought-after skills; without them, it would apparently be difficult to find skilled *cultores* to employ. On the difference between a true farmer and a mere worker of the land, cf. *Noe* 107.

'Quanto vilius est pascere quam emere cultorem?': For a speculative estimate of the respective costs, see Cracco Ruggini, 125–6 n. 338.

48. **Quid plura?**: A. continues in his own words, after the direct speech of the prefect in the previous paragraph.

qui vere potuit imperatori dicere . . . hos tua curia morti abstulit: The emperor is Gratian, who visited Rome during Aradius Rufinus' prefecture in the summer of 376. The words could come from a written *relatio* (Cracco Ruggini, 118–19 n. 316, followed by Faure, 'Saint Ambroise et l'expulsion des pérégrins', 527), but it is much likelier that they are deictic and spoken in person (Palanque, 'Famines à Rome', 349). A. seems to envisage Rufinus as a second Lawrence, presenting precious human beings saved by Christian charity as the trophies of grace: cf. 2.140–1 (though in this case the pious hero is able to acknowledge the help of the secular powers, instead of having to stand up to their intimidation). The 'province' is the area of the urban prefect's jurisdiction, extending over a 100–mile radius from Rome (Palanque, 'Famines à Rome', 349 n. 3; Cracco Ruggini, 140–1 n. 389; Faure, 'Saint Ambroise et l'expulsion des pérégrins', 534). For a similar senatorial contribution in 396, cf. Symm. *Ep.* 6.12, 14, 26.

49. **Quanto hoc utilius quam illud quod proxim Romae factum est**: The Christian example turned out t

be far more beneficial in the true sense of the word (cf. 3.37, 44): others were put first, and the long-term advantages brought to the city by the presence of the *peregrini* were retained (3.51). **proxime** corresponds to *nuper* in Cic. *Off.* 3.47, introducing the more recent of the two examples of ξενηλασία. This deportation is to be dated to the end of 384. The year had been fruitful, A. says (3.49): this rules out the time of the widespread crop failure (which was particularly acute in central and southern Italy) in 383 referred to elsewhere (Symm. *Rel.* 3.15–17; *Ep.* 2.6.2; A. *Ep.* 73 [18].17–21) (*pace* Homes Dudden i. 259–60; Paredi, 218–19; Ihm, 26). The problem in this case was confined to a food-shortage at Rome itself (3.49), and the 'Italians' were in a position to help (3.49), so their crops clearly had not suffered. In late 384, there was a delay in importing the corn to Rome (apparently due to unfavourable winds: cf. 3.50), and the mob became restive. In this tense situation, the urban prefect, Q. Aurelius Symmachus (in office from the summer of 384 until January/February 385; see *PLRE* i. 865–71, especially 867–8), ordered the *peregrini* to be expelled (his *Ep.* 2.7.3 speaks of fears of a *defectus annonae* and *misera fames*, but says nothing about crop failure) (Palanque, 'Famines à Rome', 349–55; Cracco Ruggini, 140 ff.; Cracco Ruggini, 'Ambrogio di fronte alla compagine sociale', 256 ff.; Kohns, *Versorgungskrisen und Hungerrevolten*, 168–82; and (tentatively) Faure, 'Saint Ambroise et l'expulsion des pérégrins', 527–8; Chastagnol, *La Préfecture urbaine à Rome*, 268; Testard i. 45; ii. 207 n. 1). This is the same expulsion to which Ammianus indignantly refers (as one of the ejected himself) in 14.6.19. The gratuitous adjective **amplissima** is appended to the reference to the *urbs* in this case, and the mildness of the problem is underlined: **Et certe adriserat anni fecunditas** (cf. 3.50). Such precipitate action was madness: the city was throwing away the asset of its official suppliers (3.49–51). The *corporati* are depicted as refugees: **flentes cum filiis abiisse . . . direptas adfinitates**, but few if any of them could have been reduced to difficult straits. Symmachus' orders were doubtless aimed at the dispossessed poor of Campania or at popular targets such as the despised *pantapolae*, but in the

end any *peregrini* who could not muster sufficient patronage
were treated as legitimate targets. He himself expresses
personal distress at the actual outcome (Symm. *Ep.* 2.7.3),
but his original intentions and dismay at what ensued are of
no interest to A. The consequences of a mistaken strategy
can be exaggerated to contrive a bitter contrast of pagan and
Christian leadership, and to speak up for vested interests.

Et certe adriserat anni fecunditas: Cf. *Ep.* 73 [18].20.

turpius: The Ciceronian vocabulary is worked in.

50. inutile . . . utile . . . quod non decet: More of the basic
philosophical terminology.

**Quantis corporatorum subsidiis dudum Roma frau-
data est!:** On the nature of such *corporati,* see generally
Jones ii. 858–61; also 698–705 on food supply in particular.

exspectatis ventorum . . . commeatu navium: The ships
must have arrived not long after the foreigners were banished. For a similar situation of popular unrest due to the
delay, caused by bad weather, in the arrival of the grain-
ships at Ostia in 359, cf. Amm. 19.10. On the relief of seeing
ships arrive, cf. e.g. Sen. *Ep.* 77; Symm. *Rel.* 9.7.

51–2. The section is rounded off with a cluster of Ciceronian
language; cf. generally *Off.* 3.35. The charitable *collatio*
organized by the Christian prefect was a clear example of
the convergence of what was honourable and what was
beneficial. Human beings were fed, which was honourable,
and skilled workers were retained to continue the farming,
which was beneficial for the city. A. offers a macroeconomic
justification for generosity: charity and pragmatism are of a
piece.

CHAPTER 8: GOD APPROVES THOSE WHO PUT
THE HONOURABLE BEFORE APPARENT BENEFIT

A. continues to expound the centrality of the *honestum*, con
trasting the glories of this ideal with the folly of pursuing
apparent benefit (the *utile* seen from a worldly perspective
with reference to biblical incidents. In 3.53–6, the example
come from the story of the Exodus and the conquest of Canaan
The emphasis on *maiores nostri* (Introduction IV.4) parallel

the similar concern to present the ancestral tradition as a model in Cic. *Off.* 3 (e.g. *Off.* 3.44, 47, 67, 69, 99–114).

53. servitio exire: Cf. Verg. *Ecl.* 1.40. A. echoes the words often: e.g. *Ex.* 5.49; *Cain* 1.20; 2.9; *Ios.* 19; on other references (e.g. *Expos. Ps. 118.*3.27; *Expl. Ps.* 37.28; *Bon. mort.* 21; *Is.* 16; *Iac.* 2.12; *Ep.* 37.24), see A. V. Nazzaro, 'La I Ecloga virgiliana nella lettura di Ambrogio', in *AmbrEpisc* ii. 312–24, at 317–19.

nisi id non solum turpe . . . regi servire Aegyptiorum: See Ex. 2: 23–5 on the Israelites' complaint to the Lord about their slavery (cf. also Ex. 4: 31); on their deliverance, see Ex. 5–14.

54. Iesus quoque et Caleb . . . nuntiaverunt: Joshua and Caleb were among the twelve spies sent to explore Canaan, and they alone sided with Moses in urging the Israelites to invade the fertile land, confident that the Lord would give them victory over its fierce inhabitants. The people of Israel, however, threatened to stone them for their suggestion. See Num. 13: 1–14: 45; cf. Dt. 1: 19–46. On this paragraph, see Num. 14: 1–10; cf. Dt. 1: 19–33.

alii: The other spies (Num. 13: 31–3; cf. Dt. 1: 28).

proelio: EW, CNB: *proelium* PVMA, several editors.

55. Exarsit Domini indignatio, ut omnes vellet perdere: See Num. 14: 10–45; cf. Dt. 1: 34–46.

sed pueri et mulieres . . . terrae promissam hereditatem: The children are explicitly said to have been reprieved (Num. 14: 31; cf. Dt. 1: 39); A. infers that the women were as well.

56. Pars igitur melior . . . deterior salutem honestati: *Gloria* is equated with *honestas*; *salus* (in the ordinary, not the spiritual, sense) is implicitly associated with *turpitudo*. For this language, cf. Cic. *Off.* 3.84–8; and 3.88–90, 125 below. On the traditional Roman Stoic esteem for courage and the pursuit of glory at the risk of personal safety, see on 1.177; for a somewhat different perspective on *gloria*, cf. 2.2.

Divina . . . sententia: Divine approval sanctioned those who took the very course that Ciceronian logic would endorse.

ea quae videbantur . . . honestati accommoda: On apparent as opposed to real advantage, see on 3.37.

CHAPTER 9: SHUN DISHONOURABLE GAIN

57. amorem honestatis: Love for/care for/consideration for/contemplation of *honestas* is the dominant motif throughout the remainder of the argument (cf. 3.29): 3.63, 66, 84–5, 89–90, 98–9, 111, 117–18.

usu quodam degeneris mercaturae: See on 1.185 and 1.243; cf. also 2.25–6, 67; 3.37, 65. Cic. mentions *mercaturae* in *Off.* 3.83.

diebus ac noctibus hiare in alieni detrimenta patrimonii: Inheritance-hunting, described in terms evocative of a rich satirical tradition; on the literary characterization and the actual social realities in the Roman world, see A. R. Mansbach, ' "Captatio": Myth and Reality', Ph.D. Diss. (University of Princeton, 1982); K. Hopkins, *Death and Renewal: Sociological Studies in Roman History*, 2 (Cambridge, 1983), 235–47; E. Champlin, *Final Judgements: Duty and Emotion in Roman Wills, 200 BC–AD 250* (Berkeley and Los Angeles, 1991), 87–102, with textual summary at 201–2. On **hiare**, cf. Hor. *Sat.* 2.5.56, on the adventurer as a *corvus hians* (for *corvus*, cf. Petr. *Sat.* 116.9); for *hiare* of greed in general, cf. e.g. Cic. *Verr.* 2.2.134; Sen. *Benef.* 7.26.3; Tac. *Hist.* 1.12.3; cf. *inhiare* in Plaut. *Stich.* 605; *Miles* 715; Hor. *Sat.* 1.70–1. On fourth-century *captatio*, cf. e.g. Amm. 14.6.22; 28.4.22; Aus. *Ep.* 27.6–7; on the scandal of clerics as culprits, cf. Jer. *Epp.* 22.28.3–5; 52.6.4–5, 9.2; 60.11.3; for Augustine's disapproval, cf. Possid. *Vita Aug.* 24. Significantly, no churchman is on record as denying that *captatio* was going on among the clergy; the evidence in fact indicates that Christian denunciations, for all their stylized language (cf. e.g. *Expos. Ps. 118.8.54: qui ad lectum aegrotantis adsidet non ut capiendae hereditatis tendat aucupium, sed ut morbi vim sollicito mitiget ministerio, ut sedulo fessum sermone demulceat 9.21: pecuniosus, qui cotidiana emolumenta sollicito rimatur adfectu, qui cotidie opes aggerat, qui hereditatis tendit aucupia qui circa aegrotantis lectulum indefessas exercet excubias)* wer directed at a fairly widespread practice. A ruling of Valentinian I to Damasus in July 370 (*CTh* 16.2.20) had ordered ecclesiastics not to frequent the homes of widows and other women (cf. 1.87 above, though the main danger there is sexual temptation), and had declared bequests to priests to be invalid. A. refers to this law in *Ep.* 73 [18].13–14 (in 384), where he comments that it treats clergy with a severity not applied to other parties (note also his general reference to *leges publicae* against false practices in the context of inheritance in 3.73 below, evocative of Cic.; see ad loc.). In 372 the terms of *CTh* 16.2.20 had been extended to cover bishops and virgins (*CTh* 16.2.22), but it is clear from other legislation that opportunism by individual clerics continued (cf. *CTh* 16.2.27; 2.28, in 390). Jerome writes to Nepotian of *CTh* 16.2.20 in 393: *nec de lege conqueror, sed doleo cur meruerimus hanc legem* (*Ep.* 52.6.1); he admits that its prescriptions were often circumvented by the use of trusts (*fideicommissa*), which were a way of ensuring against state alienation of property by committing it for an interim period to a reliable third party who could later pass it on to the desired recipient. In the present passage, A.'s generalized condemnation of the pursuit of gains from inheritances is a predictable admonition to his charges not to be seen to engage in such unsavoury behaviour. It also perhaps hints at a deeper concern: ecclesiastics who behaved obsequiously towards potential benefactors were not only acting distastefully and incurring social opprobrium; by potentially provoking further restrictive civil legislation they might also be jeopardizing their church's right to inherit bequests obtained by subtler means (see I. J. Davidson, '*Captatio* in the Fourth-Century West', *SP* 34 (2001), 33–43).

58. Hinc nascuntur . . . gravitatis simulatione captatae: Cf. Cic. *Off.* 3.74: *Mihi quidem etiam verae hereditates non honestae videntur, si sunt malitiosis blanditiis, officiorum non veritate sed simulatione quaesitae.* On *simulatio*, cf. also Cic. *Off.* 3.60–1, 64, 68, 72, 74, 95; on the evils of pretence in general, cf. A. 2.112–20; 3.76; on flattery, cf. 1.226; 2.96; 3.134–5; see also on 1.209. Cic. speaks of *continentia* in *Off.* 3.96; on *gravitas* (mentioned by Cic. in *Off.* 3.93), see on 1.18.

Christiani viri: Cf. 3.27. A. may be thinking here of the believer as the *vir bonus* of Cic. *Off.* 3.54, 64, 75–8: he is in 3.59.

omne enim quod arte elicitum . . . caret merito simplicitatis: Cic. *Off.* 3.57 speaks of a person being (or not being) *simplex*; cf. 3.66 below. For the typical Christian contrast of *ars* and *simplicitas*, cf. generally 1.29 and 1.116.

In ipsis . . . adfectatae ambitio hereditatis: An allusion particularly to Cic.'s condemnation of fraudulent inheritance in Cic. *Off.* 3.74–5. The assumption that secular moral opinion constitutes a bare minimal standard is typical. This is the first explicit reference to the role of clerics in book 3.

in supremo fine vitae . . . quod sentiunt: Those at the end of their lives should not be put under pressure to do what they have not planned. On A.'s counsel on handling death and the dying as expressed above all in *Bon. mort.*, see generally E. Rebillard, *In hora mortis. Evolution de la pastorale chrétienne de la mort aux IVe et Ve siècles dans l'Occident latin* (Rome, 1994), 11–28.

cum vel sacerdotis . . . obesse nemini: The regular refrain: cf. Cic. *Off.* 3.64: *sive vir bonus est is qui prodest quibus potest, nocet nemini*; 3.76: *iam se ipse doceat eum virum bonum esse qui prosit quibus possit, noceat nemini nisi lacessitus iniuria*; and. A. 1.26, 131; 3.59.

59. Ideoque in causis pecuniariis intervenire non est sacerdotis: The bishop may refuse to adjudicate (see or 2.124) in a financial case, where it is impossible to avoid offending one party; cf. 2.125 and see ad loc. Cases of life and death, however, are different. The reference to episcopal adjudication is of course A.'s own contextual application of the Ciceronian argument; Cic. talks simply about fraud and cheating in general.

Proposita igitur forma . . . aliqua iniuria offensus: Cf Cic. *Off.* 3.76: *iam se ipse doceat eum virum bonum esse qu prosit quibus possit, noceat nemini nisi lacessitus iniuria* (an *Off.* 1.20, cited above on 1.131; *Off.* 3.64). As in 1.131 A. dissents from Cic.'s rule that retaliation to provocation i acceptable (though in 1.177 he implicitly concedes it wit reference to David). Once again he is emphasizing th superiority of the ethic of the *sacerdotis officium* over the *officium* prescribed by Cic.

Bonus enim est vir qui dixit: Cic. *Off.* 3.54, 64, 75–8 speaks of the *vir bonus*; A.'s **bonus vir** is David.

Si reddidi retribuentibus mihi mala: Ps. 7: 5: *Si reddidi retribuentibus mihi mala, decidam merito ab inimicis meis inanis.* Ironically, this verse in context assumes rather than rejects the principle of vengeance: the psalmist acknowledges his enemy's right to kill him if he has acted evilly.

Quae enim est gloria . . . qui nos non laeserit?: Cf. 1 Pt. 2: 20: *Quae enim gloria est, si peccantes et colaphizati suffertis?* (also Mt. 5: 38–48; Lk. 6: 27–35).

60. Quam honestum . . . maluit parcere! Quam etiam utile . . . hoc profuit . . . !: Testard, 'Recherches', 77–84; Testard ii. 213 n. 6 believes that this paragraph follows rather strangely after 3.59. 3.59 alludes to David as the *bonus vir* who speaks the words of Ps. 7: 5, but makes no mention of the incident assumed at the start of 3.60, when David spared Saul (the *rex inimicus*), or of the fact that David became Saul's *successor*. David is not actually named anywhere in 3.59–62. The OT narrative evoked in 3.60 last appeared in 3.33–4, in the midst of the discussion of Gyges and his ring. In terms of biblical theme, then, 3.60 looks as if it could follow 3.33–4. However, 3.60 also uses the basic Ciceronian terminology of the *honestum* and the *utile*, and this is not used in 3.33–4 (though *honestum* is mentioned at the start of the Gyges section in 3.29). For Testard, the upshot is that A. has made use of an earlier exposition of David in writing book 3. In this earlier text, what is now 3.60–2 followed the passage that is 3.33–4. A. splits the earlier text into two: 3.33–4 is inserted into the Gyges section, between the tale of Gyges himself (3.30–2) and the example of John the Baptist (3.35). When he alludes to David in 3.59, it occurs to him to return to the earlier treatment of David, from which he lifts the substance of 3.60–2, carefully colouring it with Ciceronian language (3.60). 3.37–59 consists of other earlier texts which are similarly reshaped into the Ciceronian perspective and inserted into *Off.* as part of the redaction process.

The conjecture is too clever by half. Testard has resorted

to drastic measures in an attempt to explain why it is that
3.60 speaks of a *rex inimicus* who has not been named in 3.59,
and why David is never actually named anywhere in 3.59–62.
It is far simpler to assume that A. expects his addressees to
know the biblical passages to which he refers. Those who
recognize Ps. 7: 5 know at once who the *bonus vir* of 3.59 is,
and they can just as readily identify the *rex inimicus* of 3.60.
nocere and **profuit** in 3.60 continue the language of 3.58–9,
and the use of the key Ciceronian philosophical terms in 3.60
is just part of A.'s habitual attempt to fit the Stoic terminology to scriptural narratives. The absence of Ciceronian
evocation in 3.61–2 does not have to mean that A. is using an
earlier text on David. It simply means that, as often, he gets a
little carried away with the biblical material.

On the biblical references in this paragraph, see on 3.33–4.
ut discerent omnes . . . sed vereri: On the right way to
consolidate authority and inspire *fides*, as demonstrated by
David, cf. 2.32–8. This proper grip on power is of course
particularly important to A. as an example.
Itaque et honestas utilitati praelata est et utilitas
secuta honestatem est: Cf. Cic. *Off.* 3.19: *Vicit ergo*
utilitas honestatem? Immo vero honestas utilitatem secuta est
(Winterbottom's retention of the transmitted text is controversial; on the case for the deletion of *secuta est*, found in
Amic. 51, *non igitur utilitatem amicitia, sed utilitas amicitiam*
secuta est, see Dyck, 519). The nuancing of *utilitas* is
obviously different in A.'s two mentions of it (unlike in
Cic.'s): when the honourable thing is put before apparent
benefit, real benefit follows from it. In context, Cic. has just
referred to the exceptional case of tyrannicide, clearly thinking of the recent murder of Julius Caesar. In A.'s mind,
David is Caesar's exact opposite (as in 2.32–8).
61. *Montes qui estis in Gelboe . . . perierunt arma*
   concupiscenda?: 2 Ki. 1: 21–7.
62. **Aruerunt montes . . . sententiam maledicentis**
   implevit: Picks up the words of David's lament in 2. Ki
   1: 21, though there is no mention in the biblical narrative of
   their fulfilment. The obvious classical parallel is the enchant-
   ment of nature by the despairing songs of Orpheus: Verg.
   Georg. 4.507–27; Ov. *Met.* 10.86–739; 11.1–66.

63. Quid vero sancto Nabuthe?: See on 2.17.

indecorum pretium: Surrender of the inheritance would have been shameful; hence the proposed compensation was **indecorum**.

Non mihi, **inquit,** *faciat Dominus . . . patrum meorum:* 3 Ki. 21: 3.

vulgarem utilitatem loquor: Financial reward and royal favour; cf. 1.28–9; 2.15–16, 23, 25–6; 3.9, 37, 56, 60, 90.

64. mulieris: Jezebel.

congruo supplicio plectendam: Her body was eaten by dogs (3 Ki. 21: 23; 4 Ki. 9: 10, 30–7).

3.65–75 attacks the dishonour, and so the false *utilitas*, of fraud in commercial agreements and contracts. The inspiration comes from Cic.'s discussion of justice and the law in *Off.* 3.50–78. A. supports the gist of the Ciceronian argument about justice in legal and financial business, speaking as a former magistrate and current episcopal adjudicator himself, well used to the everyday realities of claims of fraud. The retention of the classical themes, recollected in no particular sequence, is merely formal: commonplaces about the need for honesty and good faith in human dealings are obviously unexceptional, whether A. is thinking of his clerics or of other readers. But it is no surprise that he points to scriptural precedent for secular legislation against *dolus malus* (3.66–7), and compares notorious classical stories of fraudulent practice with the Bible's own condemnations of such wickedness.

65. Turpis itaque omnis est fraus: Cic. repudiates *fraus omnis* in *Off.* 3.71.

Denique etiam in rebus vilibus: In commerce; see on 1.185, 243; and cf. 2.25–6, 67; 3.37, 57.

exsecrabilis est staterae fallacia et fraudulenta mensura: See below on Prov. In Cic. *Off.* 3.54, Antipater says that failure to show the way to someone who is lost is something *quod Athenis exsecrationibus publicis sanctum est*.

Si in foro rerum venalium . . . inter officia virtutum?: Cf. Cic. *Off.* 3.50–74, generally. A. uses another standard *a fortiori* argument to demand the highest standards among believers (though not specifically clerics this time).

Pondus magnum . . . coram Domino: Prov. 20: 10.
Statera adultera . . . illi: Prov. 11: 1.

CHAPTER 10: FRAUD IN AGREEMENTS IS
ALWAYS WRONG

**66. de contractibus ceteris, ac maxime de coemptione
praediorum:** Cic. discusses the law concerning the sale of
praedia in *Off.* 3.65 (cf. also *Off.* 3.71); on the subject, cf.
Plin, *Ep.* 3.19. In Roman law, *coemptio* was technically the
pretended or symbolic purchase of property offered in a
mock sale in order to transfer some or all of the obligations
which devolved upon the owner; it came to signify particularly the transference of a woman from one family into the
power of her husband in marriage: cf. e.g. Cic. *Mur.* 27;
Flacc. 84; *De Or.* 1.237; Gaius *Inst.* 1.110, 113–14.

vel transactionibus atque pactis: Cic. *Off.* 3.70–1 mentions various transactions in which good faith is necessary,
and *Off.* 3.73–6 speaks of the importance of honesty with
regard to testamentary inheritance. *Pacta* are referred to in
Off. 3.92. A. maintains that these topics are irrelevant to
him—but he has already spoken of inheritance in 3.57–8, and
he comes to the question of property deals in 3.70–5.

Nonne formulae sunt dolum malum abesse . . .?: In
Off. 3.60–1, Cic. refers to the *de dolo malo formulae* of
C. Aquilius Gallus, his friend and colleague in the praetor-
ship in 66 BC. Aquilius' rules of procedure (see on 3.13)
enabled either party in a commercial contract to plead the
'bad faith' of the other, and so to claim restitution in cases of
fraudulent pretence (cf. Cic. *ND* 3.74). Cic. also mentions
laws against *dolus malus* which existed prior to Aquilius'
formulae, such as the the prescriptions about *tutela* in the
fifth-century Twelve Tables (cf. *Leg. XII. Tab.* 5.3), and a
Lex Laetoria/Plaetoria of *c.*192 BC against defrauding minors
(those under twenty-five years old) (*Off.* 3.61; cf. *ND* 3.74
Pl. *Ps.* 303; *Rud.* 1381–2). He says that there are very few
areas where *dolus malus* is not a relevant concern (*Off.* 3.64)
On **abesse**, Cic. *Off.* 3.71 has *abest*.

eumque cuius dolus . . . obnoxium fore: Cf. Cic. *Off*

3.65: *Nam cum ex duodecim tabulis* [cf. *Leg. XII. Tab.* 6.1] *satis esset ea praestari quae essent.*

dolum excludit: Cf. Cic. *Off.* 3.71: *fraus omnis excluditur.*

Nec fecit proximo suo malum: Ps. 14: 3. The verse's **malum** is obviously the trigger for the connection with *dolus malus.* It is not just secular law that proscribes bad faith.

generalem . . . sententiam indicates that A. is aware that the reference to the OT is a less-than-precise parallel. Cf. further in 3.67.

in contractibus . . . prodi iubetur: Cf. Cic. *Off.* 3.65: *Ac de iure quidem praediorum sanctum apud nos est iure civili ut in iis vendendis vitia dicerentur quae nota essent venditori. . . . a iuris consultis etiam reticentiae poena est constituta. Quidquid enim esset in praedio vitii, id statuerunt, si venditor sciret, nisi nominatim dictum esset, praestari oportere* (and generally *Off.* 3.51–68).

aperienda simplicitas: Cf. Cic. *Off.* 3.57: *Hoc autem celandi genus quale sit et cuius hominis, quis non videt? Certe non aperti, non simplicis* (also *Off.* 1.109).

veritas: Cic. uses the word in *Off.* 3.74.

67. Veterem autem istam . . . evidenter expressit: [**expressit:** EW, COB, several editors: PVMA omit: *ostendit* Zell, Gering, Lignamine, Paderborn] The familiar conceit of biblical anteriority. The illustration here is more successful than the contrived citation of the psalmist's reference to *malum* in 3.66. Cic. *Off.* 3.60 speaks of Aquilius as one who was *peritus definiendi*; and *Off.* 3.65 refers to the *iuris consulti.*

qui Iesu Nave scribitur: Cf. 3.79, *qui scribitur Numeri.*

Nam cum exisset fama per populos: Cf. Josh. 5: 1.

siccatum esse mare in Hebraeorum transitu: See Ex. 14.

fluxisse aquam de petra: See Ex. 17: 1–7; Num. 20: 1–13.

de caelo diurnam . . . abundantem: See Ex. 16: 13–36.

corruisse muros Hiericho . . . arietatos: See Josh. 6: 1-27.

Geth quoque regem . . . ad vesperam: A. mistakes the place: it is Ai, not Gath (OB read *Hai*). On the destruction of Ai, see Josh. 8: 1–29; on the king's fate, see 8: 29.

Gabaonitae metuentes . . . ut secum firmaret societatem: See Josh. 9: 3–27; on this paragraph, see 9: 3–15. Cic.

uses *versuti* in *Off.* 3.57, and *societas* in *Off.* 3.52–3, 69–70 (though obviously in different contexts).

inscius: Cic. *Off.* 3.72 has *inscitia*.

68.   Adeo sancta erat illis temporibus fides . . . suscep-tum habere quod non sunt: The gullibility of Joshua and the Israelites is presented as a holy innocence. 3.67 at least manages to mention the explanation that Josh. 9: 14 gives for their mistake: they had not sought divine guidance in the matter. This is conveniently forgotten here: A. would rather praise the innocence and good faith of *maiores nostri*. Cf. the innocence of Eve in 1.169. On **mentiri neminem putant, fallere quid sit ignorant**, Cic. uses *ignorare* a number of times in *Off.* 3.51–75 (and *ignoratio* in *Off.* 3.72), and *mentiri* in *Off.* 3.93.

Innocens credit omni verbo: Prov. 14: 15.

vituperanda: Cic. *Off.* 3.58 has *vituperandi*; 3.105 has *vituperare*.

bonitas: Cic. speaks of the *vir bonus* in *Off.* 3.54, 64, 75–8.

circumscribitur: Cic. *Off.* 3.61 has *circumscriptio*.

bene iudicat: On making wise judgements, cf. Cic. *Off.* 3.70–1. Joshua epitomizes the good man who thinks well of everyone, and even keeps his word with those who have betrayed him:

69.   On this paragraph, see Josh. 9: 15–27.

testamentum: Cic. uses the word in *Off.* 3.73, 75.

simulaverunt: See on 3.58.

religione: Cf. the references in Cic. *Off.* 3.46, 102, 104.

ne . . . suam fidem solveret: Cf. 1.139; and Cic., *Off.* 3.107–15, on keeping faith even with an enemy on the basis of a solemn oath.

perfidiam: Cic. *Off.* 3.60 has *perfidi*.

vilioris obsequio ministerii: The Gibeonites were to be woodcutters and water-carriers for the Israelites (Josh. 9: 21, 23, 27).

sententia: Cic. has the word in *Off.* 3.66.

astutiae: Cic. uses *astuti* in *Off.* 3.57, *astutos* in *Off.* 3.67, *astutias* in *Off.* 3.68, and *astutiae* in *Off.* 3.71.

in hunc diem: See Josh. 9: 27. A. relates this as if he believes that the Gibeonites are still slaves of the Israelites in his own day, not just in the time of the writer of the Josh. narrative.

CHAPTER 11: FRAUD CONDEMNED IN BIBLICAL
EXAMPLES

70. Non ego in hereditatibus adeundis . . . saltationes notabo (nam haec etiam vulgo notabilia): [saltationes: C, Monte Alto, Maurists, Krabinger, Testard: *salutationes* PVMA, EW, OB, other editors] Cf. Cic. *Off.* 3.75: *Itaque si vir bonus habeat hanc viam, ut, si digitis concrepuerit, possit in locupletium testamenta nomen eius inrepere, hac vi non utatur, ne si exploratum quidem habeat id omnino neminem umquam suspicaturum. At dares hanc vim M. Crasso, ut digitorum percussione heres posset scriptus esse, qui re vera non esset heres, in foro, mihi crede, saltaret.* M. Licinius Crassus, consul in 70 and in 55 BC, and member of the 'first triumvirate' with Caesar and Pompey in 60 BC, was famed for his vast wealth. The phrase *digitorum percussione* is also used by Cic. in *Off.* 3.78. On dancing publicly, cf. Cic. *Off.* 3.93:

Quid? si qui sapiens rogatus sit ab eo qui eum heredem faciat, cum ei testamento sestertium milies relinquatur, ut antequam hereditatem adeat luce palam in foro saltet, idque se facturum promiserit, quod aliter heredem eum scripturus ille non esset, faciat quod promiserit necne? Promisisse nollem, et id arbitror fuisse gravitatis; quoniam promisit, si saltare in foro turpe ducet, honestius mentietur si ex hereditate nihil ceperit quam si ceperit, nisi forte eam pecuniam in reipublicae magnum aliquod tempus contulerit, ut vel saltare, cum patriae consulturus sit, turpe non sit.

On the disgrace of singing *in foro*, cf. Cic. *Off.* 1.145; and on the disapproval of public dancing, cf. Ter. *Ad.* 752; Lucian, *Salt.* 1; Macr. *Sat.* 2.3.16; and above all (the *locus classicus* of social disdain) Cic. *Mur.* 13: *Nemo enim fere saltat sobrius, nisi forte insanit* (words which A. quotes in *Virg.* 3.25, attributing them to *quidam saecularium doctor*). For Christian perspectives on dancing (in A., cf. e.g. *Ep.* 27 [58]; *Paen.* 2.41–3; *Virg.* 3.25–31), see C. Andresen, 'Altchristliche Kritik am Tanz: Ein Ausschnitt aus dem Kampf der alten Kirche gegen heidnische Sitte', in H. Frohnes and U. W. Knorr (eds.), *Kirchengeschichte als Missionsgeschichte*, 1: *Die alte Kirche* (Munich, 1974), 344–76. On **non . . . notabo**, cf. *non . . . simulabo* in 3.30. On **vulgo**, cf. *vulgus hominum* in Cic. *Off.* 3.73.

non simulatae piscationis . . . emptoris illiceretur adfectus: More *praeteritio*: A. alludes to Cic.'s story about Canius and Pythius (*Off.* 3.58–60); cf. 3.71–2. On **simulatae**, see on 3.58.

repertus est: Cic. *Off.* 3.72 has *reperietur*.

71. **de Syracusano illo amoeno secretoque secessu:** A. expects the story to be identified. A sophisticated *eques* of the late second century BC, Gaius Canius, was taken in by one Pythius, a banker in Syracuse, who persuaded him to pay an extortionate price for his Sicilian estate in the belief that it was the recipient of the bounty of all the local fishermen, whereas in fact no fishing at all was done there. According to Cic. *Off.* 3.60, Canius was powerless in the face of Pythius' deception, since the event took place prior to the passing of Aquilius' *formulae de dolo malo* in 66 BC, and so Pythius was not legally obliged to reveal the truth about the property (his moral obligations were another matter).

Siculi hominis: Pythius, who was probably not a Syracusan citizen, but ran his business there (cf. Cic. *Off.* 3.58: *Pythius . . . quidam, qui argentariam faceret Syracusis*); apart from Cic.'s story, he is unknown to us.

calliditate: Cic. *Off.* 3.57 has *callidi*; *calliditas* and *callidus* appear in *Off.* 3.113.

peregrinum aliquem: C. Canius. Note that A. typically refuses to name the characters of the classical story.

ad cenam in hortos rogaverit: promisisse invitatum, postridie venisse: Cf. Cic. *Off.* 3.58: *et simul ad cenam hominem in hortos invitavit in posterum diem. Cum ille promisisset . . . et ab iis petivit ut ante suos hortulos postridie piscarentur.*

piscatorum multitudinem: Cf. Cic. *Off.* 3.58: *cumbarum . . . multitudo.*

oculos recumbentium resilientes verberabant: Cf. Cic. *Off.* 3.58: *ante oculos.*

Mirari hospes: Cf. Cic. *Off.* 3.59: *Et ille 'Quid mirum? inquit.*

tantam copiam piscium tantumque numerum cymbarum: [tantumque: EW, COB: *tantarumque* PVMA, Testard] Cf. Cic. *Off*. 3.59: '*Tantumne piscium? tantumne cumbarum?*'

Responsum quaerenti . . . innumerabiles eo pisces convenire: Cf. Cic. *Off*. 3.59: '*Hoc loco est Syracusis quidquid est piscium, hic aquatio . . .*' (W. H. Alexander's suggestion, in 'Hic aquatio: Cicero, *De officiis* III.14–59', *CJ* 36 (1941), 290–3, that *aquatio = aqua* in the sense of territorial water rather than a place from where water was drawn, is convincingly refuted by J. P. Turley, 'Hic aquatio: Cicero, *De officiis* III.14–59', *CJ* 37 (1942), 485–9). Cic. uses the adjective *innumerabilis* in *Off*. 3.72 and 3.77.

Quid multa?: Cic. has the phrase at exactly the same point in *Off*. 3.59. There is no obvious reason to infer, as Testard ii. 215 n. 6, does, that A. is necessarily betraying a stereotypical view of Sicilian greed by implying 'What do you expect of a Sicilian in such circumstances?'

vendere volens cogitur: Pythius pretended that the estate was not for sale, but his reluctance was insincere.

pretium gravatus suscipit: Cf. Cic. *Off*. 3.59: *Gravate illo primo.*

72. **Sequenti die . . . navigium nullum invenit:** Cf. Cic. *Off*. 3.59.

Percontanti num . . . die feriarum sollemnitas: Cf. Cic. *Off*. 3.59: *Quaerit . . . num feriae quaedam piscatorum essent.*

nulla nec umquam . . . piscari solitos: Cf. Cic. *Off*. 3.59: '*Nullae, quod sciam,*' inquit ille, '*sed hic piscari nulli solent. Itaque heri mirabar quid accidisset*'.

Quam hic redarguendi . . . captarit aucupium deliciarum?: Cic. in *Off*. 3.60 reserves all his condemnation for Pythius, and says how regrettable is was for Canius that the affair took place prior to the enactment of Aquilius' *formulae de dolo malo*. To A., Canius was no better than Pythius, since he had so greedily insisted on having the estate. His desire for luxurious living was as great a sin as the act of deception itself, so he had no basis of moral *auctoritas* upon which to criticize Pythius for his dishonesty. There is a certain humour in the way it is put: the estate, with all its apparent fish, seemed a great 'catch' to Canius.

Qui enim alterum . . . debet alienus esse: A scriptural
sentiment: cf. Mt. 7: 3–5; Lk. 6: 41–2; Jn. 8: 7; for classical
parallels, cf. Plaut. *Truc.* 159 (cf. *Ps.* 612); Cato, *Monost.* 41;
Dist. 1.30; Men. fr. 710 [Kock].

huiusmodi nugas: The matter is denigrated by A., but he
tells the story all the same in order to make the point that he
who casts the first stone must be without sin, and to make an
implicit comparison with the *weighty* biblical *exempla* which
follow in 3.74–5.

in hanc ecclesiasticae censionis auctoritatem: The
church condemns greed on the basis of Scripture's teaching.
It, unlike Pythius, has the moral *auctoritas* to do so; see Ring,
196–220.

lucri turpis appetentiam: See on 2.67.

brevique sermonis compendio: Cf. 3.139, *series . . .
vetustatis quodam compendio expressa.* Cic. *Off.* 3.63 uses
compendium, but differently.

versutiam: Cic., *Off.* 3.57, has *versuti.*

73. **Nam de illo quid loquar . . . hereditatem sibi aut
legatum vindicet . . .?:** Cf. Cic. *Off.* 3.73: *L. Minuci Basili
locupletis hominis falsum testamentum quidam e Graecia
Romam attulerunt. Quod quo facilius obtinerent, scripserunt
heredes secum M. Crassum et Q. Hortensium, homines eiusdem
aetatis potentissimos. Qui cum illud falsum esse suspicarentur,
sibi autem nullius essent conscii culpae, alieni facinoris munus-
culum non repudiaverunt. Quid ergo? satin est hoc, ut non
deliquisse videantur? Mihi quidem non videtur.* L. Minucius
Basilus was a *legatus* under Sulla, and a distinguished
military tribune at the battle of Orchomenus in 86 BC; he
was dead by 70 BC. On Crassus, see on 3.70. Q. Hortalus
Hortensius (114–50 BC) was the most renowned orator of his
age, until he was surpassed by Cic.; he was Cic.'s main
opponent in the famous case against Verres in 70 BC. On
vindicet, Cic. uses the verb in *Off.* 3.61, though differently.

leges publicae: Cic. mentions several *leges* against fraud in
Off. 3.65–74. See also on 3.21 above.

adstringant: Cic. uses the verb in *Off.* 3.111, 113, talking of
legal oaths.

Regula autem iustitiae manifesta est: Cf. Cic. *Off.* 3.74
nam eadem utilitatis quae honestatis regula; 3.81: *Sed omnium
una regula est.*

virum . . . bonum: See on 3.59.

Having dismissed the classical examples, A. in 3.74–5 adduces some solemn biblical instances of *fraus*.

74. Quid evidentius eo quod Ananias?: See Acts 5: 1–11.

fallaciae: Cic., *Off.* 3.57, has *fallacis*; *Off.* 3.68 has *fallaciter*.

75. *Vulpes foveas habent*: Mt. 8: 20; Lk. 9: 58. The statement is no condemnation of *dolus*, however: it is part of an argument about the cost of following the Son of Man. Jesus contrasts his homelessness with the state of the foxes which have their holes. A. thinks of the cunning of foxes, as in Aesop 10; 14; 74; 135; 147; Hor. *Ep.* 1.1.73–5; Suet. *Vesp.* 16.3; Lk. 13: 32; and Cic. *Off.* 1.41: *fraus quasi vulpeculae . . . videtur*; cf. *Ex.* 6.12; for heretics as foxes, cf. *Luc.* 7.30–1: *Fallax quippe animal et insidiis semper intentum rapinam fraudis exercet. Nihil tutum, nihil otiosum, nihil patitur esse securum, quod inter ipsa hospitia hominum praedam requirat. Haereticis autem vulpes comparat . . .* [etc.].

in simplicitate cordis: See on 3.58.

Sicut novacula acuta fecisti dolum: Ps. 51: 4.

nequitiae arguens proditorem: David condemns Doeg the Edomite (Ps. 51: 2), who informed Saul that Ahimelech the priest had shown hospitality to David during David's flight from Saul (1 Ki. 22: 9–23).

malitiae ebrius vino: Cic. uses *malitiosi* in *Off.* 3.57, 60; *malitiose* in *Off.* 3.61.

rex: Saul.

CHAPTER 12: PROMISES HONOURABLE AND DISHONOURABLE

3.76–81 picks up another of Cic.'s puzzles about justice and apparent *utilitas*: is it always right to keep agreements and promises (*Off.* 3.92–5)? Cic. argues that a promise is not binding if the consequences of fulfilling it are not beneficial to the recipient. A. agrees, but he says nothing about the *utile* as such: for him, a promise or oath should not be kept if this means doing something immoral. Promises are either honourable (in which case they are beneficial in the true sense), or they are dishonourable (in which case they cannot be beneficial at all). The supremacy of the *honestum* over the *turpe* is clear. Similar casuistry on the question of when it is right to refuse to return a deposit has already been advocated in 1.255 (drawing on Cic. *Off.* 1.31–2, as well as on *Off.* 3.94–5), where we find the same examples of Herod (3.77) and Jephthah (3.78–81). A. seems to assume a certain distinction between the obligations of Herod's promise, made at a drunken party, and Jephthah's solemn vow, made, albeit rashly, to the Lord. In the first case, the lesson is that it is better simply to break your word (3.77). In the second, the principle is to be very careful with the terms of a vow; never pledge something to God that God would not wish. In any case, A. suggests, even God himself changes his mind about things, as the case of Isaac shows (3.79). A. criticizes Jephthah for his folly in making the pledge that he did, but admits that there was a *miserabilis necessitas* (3.78) about his fulfilling it. In this religious connection, his devotion and *fides* cannot be censured. Then, instead of dwelling on Jephthah's stupidity, he ends up extolling Jephthah's daughter for her determination to keep her side of the obligation. The upshot is that A. is so keen to find a positive lesson in the OT story that he wanders off the point: having begun the chapter talking about the kind of circumstances in which it is better *not* to fulfil a promise, he then praises her precisely because she *did* keep her vow to return to her father to meet her death. He compares her *pietas* with the *amicitia* shown by two Pythagorean philosophers, Damon and Phintias, in another situation where execution was scheduled. Cic. cites this *exemplum* in *Off.* 3.45–6, but the context is different. He is speaking there not of promises, but of the demands of justice versus the apparent *utilitas* of friends. In the ordinary sort of friendships shared by those who practise 'middle' duties, the *honestum* must prevail over any apparent *utile*, and nothing should ever be demanded of a friend which involves a breach of patriotic principles, or of an oath, or of good faith (*Off.* 3.43). The Pythagoreans were 'wise and perfect men', and so this ideal was naturally a foregone conclusion with them. A.'s preoccupation with the centrality of the *honestum* leads him to conflate material from different sections of Cic. As always, he is clearly working from memory.

76. Purum igitur ac sincerum . . . simplicem sermonem proferat: Honest speech comes from a pure and sincere heart: this sums up the preceding paragraphs on the evil of *dolus*, and leads into the next passage on the avoidance of promises whose fulfilment is *turpis*. Cic. *Off.* 3.92 broaches the promises theme by speaking of agreements which have been made 'without force or *dolus malus*', citing the rubric of the praetors' *formulae* (cf. *Off.* 1.32). On sincerity, cf. 1.75, 93, 101, 104; 2.96, 112–20.

vas suum in sanctitate possideat: Cf. 1 Thess. 4: 4: *ut sciat unusquisque vestrum suum vas possidere in sanctificatione et honore.*

nec fratrem circumscriptione verborum inducat: Cf. 1 Thess. 4: 6: *ut ne quis supergrediatur neque circumveniat in negotio fratrem suum.* On **circumscriptione**, see on 3.68.

nihil promittat inhonestum . . . quam facere quod turpe sit: Cf. Cic. *Off.* 3.93 (on one who has promised to dance in public in order to inherit a fortune): *Promisisse nollem, et id arbitror fuisse gravitatis; quoniam promisit, si saltare in foro turpe ducet, honestius mentietur si ex hereditate nihil ceperit quam si ceperit.*

77. Saepe plerique constringunt . . . faciunt quod spoponderunt: Cf. generally Cic. *Off.* 3.94–5. On the solemnizing of promises with oaths, cf. *Off.* 3.43: *At neque contra rempublicam neque contra iusiurandum ac fidem amici causa vir bonus faciet* (and 3.44) (for Cic., however, a legal oath taken to a god amounts to an oath to one's own *mens*, since the divine cosmic *ratio* is immanent within human beings; see generally Dyck, 547–8); and especially *Off.* 3.97–115. Cic. uses *adstringere* (but not *constringere*) in *Off.* 3.111, 113.

sicut de Herode supra scripsimus: Cf. 1.255; 3.35. For the details, see on 1.255; on **scripsimus**, see Introduction V.

qui saltatrici praemium turpiter promisit: Cic. *Off.* 3.93, evoked in 3.76 (cf.*Off.* 3.75, evoked in 3.70), talks of dancing, so A. introduces Herod's promise to a *saltatrix*. The promise was *turpis*, and it was made in circumstances which only encouraged immorality; cf. 3.70 and see ad loc.; *Virg.* 3.25–31.

crudeliter . . . crudele: Cic. *Off.* 3.46 has *crudele* and *crudelitas*.

religione: Cic. commends this in *Off.* 3.46, in the passage
A. has in mind in 3.80–1; cf. also *Off.* 3.102, 104

**Quanto tolerabilius tali fuisset periurium sacra-
mento!:** Cf. Cic. *Off.* 3.94: *Quanto melius fuerat in hoc
promissum patris non esse servatum!* Herod's promise to his
niece replaces Sol's promise to his son Phaëthon. Sol
promised Phaëthon that he would do whatever his son
wished: Phaëthon asked to ride in his father's chariot, but
disaster struck when he was consumed by a stroke of lightning. (Cic. also mentions Neptune's promise to Theseus and
the death of Hippolytus; cf. also *Off.* 1.32.) On Herod's oath,
cf. *Virg.* 3.28: *Tolerabiliora periuria quam sacramenta sunt
tyrannorum.*

**Si tamen periurium posset dici . . . quod . . . promp-
serat:** The oath probably did not count since it was made in
a scene of drunkenness and dancing. The gospels do not
specifically say that Herod was drunk, though it is doubtless
a reasonable inference. For casuistry on **periurium**, cf. Cic.
Off. 3.106–8: oaths in certain categories, such as those made
to people outside society (like pirates) need not be kept,
unlike those made *ex animi tui sententia*. Herod's promise
was made to a *saltatrix*, a comparable socially undesirable
person.

eviratus: On A.'s ideals of masculinity, of which Herod's
debauched state is the polar opposite, cf. 1.84–5 (especially
85, on the effect of devotion to *convivium, ludus ac iocus*:
those who pursue such things *enervant gravitatem illam
virilem*), 138, and see Introduction VII (ii).

inter saltantium choros: Rhetorical exaggeration: the
gospels mention only Herodias' daughter as dancing.
Herod epitomizes all that is wrong: he is cruel, thoughtless,
a drunkard, and effeminate.

Infertur disco: On the suitability of the platter as a dish on
which the savagery of the company could be feasted, cf. *Virg.*
3.29.

fidei: Mentioned by Cic. in *Off.* 3.43, 46, 104, 106–7, 111.

amentiae: Possibly A. is thinking of Cic.'s point in *Off.* 3.95
that insanity nullifies the right of a depositor to claim his
property under the terms of an agreement (on which cf
1.255). Cic. *Off.* 3.83 has *amens*, in a different context.

78. Iephte: On the story of Jephthah's solemn vow and the tragic sacrifice of his daughter, see on 1.255. Jephthah and his daughter here replace Agamemnon's vow to Diana and the slaughter of Iphigenia in Cic. *Off.* 3.95. On this common parallel, see on 1.255.

immolaret: Cic. uses the verb in *Off.* 3.95.

Heu me! Filia, impedisti me: in stimulum doloris facta es mihi: Jdg. 11: 35.

acerbitatem: Cic. *Off.* 3.112 has *acerbe*.

durae: Cic. *Off.* 3.46 has *durius*.

Ambulabant, inquit, filiae . . . quattuor diebus in anno: Jdg. 11: 40.

Non possum accusare virum . . . sed tamen miserabilis necessitas: Jephthah's *fides* cannot be censured, but the fulfilment of his vow involved such terrible consequences that it would have been better if he had committed perjury. Cf. Cic. *Off.* 3.95 (of Agamemnon): *Promissum potius non faciendum quam tum taetrum facinus admittendum fuit.*

parricidio: Cic. uses the word (more loosely, of Caesar's attempt to 'murder' the *patria*) in *Off.* 3.83.

79. Melius est non vovere . . . cui promittitur nolit exsolvi: Cf. Eccl. 5: 4: *Multo melius est non vovere, quam post votum promissa non complere* (cf. also Prov. 20: 25).

Denique in Isaac habemus exemplum . . . immolari sibi: See Gen. 22, especially 22: 13. The Lord did not desire the sacrifice of Isaac (he was merely testing Abraham's *fides*), and a ram was provided as a substitute. But A. suggests that the Lord changed his mind when faced with the horror of the imminent slaughter of Isaac. On **immolari**, see on 3.78.

qui scribitur Numeri: Cf. 3.67: *qui Iesu Nave scribitur*.

proposuerat percutere morte . . . reconciliatus est populo suo: See Num. 16 (especially 16: 22) on the rebellion of Korah, Dathan, and Abiram, and the intercession of Moses (and Aaron) on behalf of the other Israelites. Again, the implication is that there is divine authority for changing one's mind and not fulfilling a promise if the consequences are going to be so dire. On changing circumstances, cf. Cic. *Off.* 3.95.

Dividite vos . . . et consummabo eos simul: Num. 16: 21.

80. Praecellentius et antiquius istud exemplum de filia

Iephte: The usual contrast of classical and earlier, superior biblical examples.

quam illud . . . de duobus Pythagoreis: The behaviour of the famous Pythagorean philosopher friends, Damon and Phintias, is described by Cic. in *Off.* 3.45; **apud philoso-phos** is another vague reference to Cic. in particular (who simply has *ferunt*). For **memorabile**, cf. 3.91. The tyrant is probably Dionysius the Younger of Syracuse (367–344 BC). The story circulated in two versions in antiquity: one (Aristox. fr. 31 [Wehrli]; cf. Iamb. *VP* 233) pictures Diony-sius in exile at Corinth devising a ruse to test the strength of the Pythagorean friendship; the other (Diod. Sic. 6.243; 10.4.2–6), probably Cic.'s source (cf. also *Tusc.* 5.63; *Fin.* 2.79), sees the threat of death as a real one. Cf. further Plu. *Mor.* 93e; Val. Max. 4.7. ext. 1; Lact. *Inst.* 5.17.22–4; Porph. *VP* 60–1; Hyg. *Fab.* 257; Pacat. *Paneg. Theod.* 17.1; Jer. *In Mich.* 2.7.5–7; *Comm. Matt.* 3.18.19–20. A. relates the anecdote also in *Virg.* 2.34–5, drawing equally on Cic. *Off.* 3.45 (in the paragraphs which follow in *Virg.* 2.36–8, he also exploits Cic. *ND* 3.83–5, but in that text Cic. is speaking not of the Younger Dionysius but of Dionysius I (405–367 BC); see P. Courcelle, 'Les Sources de saint Ambroise sur Denys le tyran', *RPh* 43 (1969), 204–10. In the present passage, Damon and Phintias are examples of *sapientes viri perfectique* (Cic. *Off.* 3.45), who did the right thing as friends, keeping their word. But Jephthah's daughter exemplified the capacity of the saint to go beyond the highest attainments of any pagan sages.

praescripto mortis die . . . ut commendaret suos: Cf. Cic. *Off.* 3.45: *cum . . . paucos sibi dies commendandorum suorum causa postulavisset.*

ac, ne revertendi nutaret fides . . . pro eo moriendum agnosceret: Cf. Cic. *Off.* 3.45: *ut . . . vas factus sit alter eius sistendi, ut, si ille non revertisset, moriendum esset ipsi.*

alter ad diem recepit: Cf. Cic. *Off.* 3.45: *Qui cum ad diem se recepisset.*

Quod eo usque . . . quorum urgebat periculum: Cf. Cic. *Off.* 3.45: *admiratus eorum fidem tyrannus petivit ut se ad amicitiam tertium adscriberent.* Cic. uses *mirabilis* in *Off.* 3.110–11.

81. in spectatis et eruditis viris: Pagan thinkers like Cic. Perhaps A. also thinks of Cic.'s reference to *sapientes viri perfectique* in *Off.* 3.45.

in virgine: Jephthah's daughter (Jdg. 11: 37–9).

***Fac mihi ut exivit de ore tuo*:** Jdg. 11: 36.

nec fefellit hora: The portrayal of Jephthah's daughter's faithful piety is somewhat similar to A.'s description of the dutiful behaviour of the Virgin Mary in *Luc.* 2.19–21, on the visitation scene in Lk. 1: 39–56, where Mary also spends a period of seclusion *in montana* (Testard ii. 218 n. 18).

quasi ad votum rediret: The presentation is subtle: what began as a denunciation of Jephthah's careless vow has become a celebration of his daughter's obedience in consecrating her virginity.

CHAPTER 13: PUTTING THE HONOURABLE
FIRST: THE EXAMPLE OF JUDITH

3.82–90 returns to the theme of the convergence of the *honestum* and the *utile*, citing scriptural narratives to demonstrate how a concern to do the honourable thing always produces genuine benefit, whereas an attempt to seek specious *utilitas,* such as personal safety, is *turpis.* There is a particular emphasis on the *honestum* as courage, drawing on Cic. *Off.* 3.97–115.

82. Ecce tibi Iudith . . . virum Holophernem adit: [**tibi:** EW, COB, most editors: *ibi* PVMA, Zell, Lignamine] On Judith's visit to and murder of Holophernes, Nebuchadnezzar's commander-in-chief, see Jdth. 8 ff. **mirabilis** picks up *mirabile* in 3.80, since A. goes on in 3.83 to compare Judith's courage with that of the two Pythagoreans: here is another biblical story that really is *mirabilis.*

Quem primo . . . circumscripsit elegantia: See Jdth. 10: 20–13: 20. On **circumscripsit**, see on 3.61; this time, the process is a good thing.

Primus triumphus eius . . . de tabernaculo hostis revexit: Holophernes desired to seduce Judith, but became too drunk (Jdth. 12: 16–13: 3). She affirmed

subsequently that her honour was intact (Jdth. 13: 20). On
Holophernes as another enervated character, like Herod in
3.77, cf. *Ep. extra coll.* 14 [63].29.

fugavit populos consilio suo: Judith's killing of Holophernes so intimidated the Assyrians that they fled, pursued
by the Israelites (Jdth. 15: 1–8).

83. **Horruerunt Persae audaciam eius:** See Jdth. 15: 1–8.
**Utique quod in illis Pythagoreis duobus . . . nec totius
exercitus tela trepidavit:** Damon and Phintias (3.80) are
surpassed by Judith as well as by Jephthah's daughter (3.81).
**non expavit mortis periculum, sed nec pudoris, quod
est gravius bonis feminis:** On the concern for virginity; cf.
1.204; 2.70, 136, 138; for other portrayals of Judith as a
model, cf. *Virg.* 2.24 (with J. Doignon, 'La Première
Exposition ambrosienne de l'*exemplum* de Judith (*De virginibus*, 2, 4, 24)', in *Ambroise de Milan*, 219–28); *Vid.* 37–42;
Ep. extra coll. 14 [63].29. Judith put her religion before her
chastity and her country, and succeeded in saving both. On
courage which overcomes the fear of death, cf. 1.177, 188,
196–209; also 3.56, 89–90, 124–5.
inter victricia arma: Cf. Verg. *Aen.* 3.54: *res Agamemno-
nias victriciaque arma secutus.*
quantum ad fidem, dimicatura: On the fight of faith, cf. 1
Tim. 6: 12; 2 Tim. 4: 7.

84. **Honestatem igitur secuta est Iudith et . . . utilitatem
invenit:** By pursuing the honourable course, Judith won the
benefit of deliverance for her people; cf. 3.88. Cic. uses *sequi*
similarly in *Off.* 3.48; cf. also 3.125 below.
Honestatis enim fuit: The key elements of *honestas* are
similar here to those mentioned in 2.70 and 2.136: deliverance from the evil of false religion; preservation of virginity;
and self-sacrifice.
ne ritus patrios et sacramenta proderet: Cf. 3.98–110
for further illustration of this vital concern; on ancestral
property more generally, cf. the case of Naboth in 2.17;
3.63.
sacras virgines, viduas graves, pudicas matronas: The
usual hierarchy of feminine sexual virtue: see on 1.69.
barbaricae . . . impuritati: Cf. 2.136.
se malle pro omnibus periclitari ut omnes eximeret a

periculo: See on 3.23; and cf. the example of Regulus in Cic. *Off.* 3.115.

85. **honestatis auctoritas:** Cic. uses the phrase in *Off.* 3.109; see generally Ring, 143–51.

ut consilium de summis rebus femina . . . nec principibus populi committeret: A curious mixture of typical ancient prejudice about the suitability of women to lead and admiration that Judith had the courage of her convictions to transcend convention. Cic. speaks of Regulus as a *princeps populi Romani* in *Off.* 3.105. At *Vid.* 41 (cf. also *Ep. extra coll.* 14 [63].29), Judith is said to have taught *men* real courage. In A.'s mind, women are normally suited more to domestic duties than to the public realm (*Parad.* 50; *Noe* 43), but Judith was a conspicuous exception of a strong woman whose public activities were excellent.

ut Deum adiutorem praesumeret: Cf. Pss. 29: 11; 53: 6; 117: 6; Heb. 13: 6; and see Judith's prayers for divine help in Judith 9 and 13: 9, and her assurance of God's presence in Judith 13: 13 (cf. also Judith 16).

CHAPTER 14: BIBLICAL EXAMPLES OF CONCERN
FOR THE HONOURABLE

86. **cum exercitum Syriae . . . cuius oculos caecitate obduxerat:** See 4 Ki. 6: 8–23. On the standards of justice maintained by Elisha, cf. 1.139–40 and see ad loc.

Domine, aperi oculos eorum ut videant: 4 Ki. 6: 20.

piratae: Cic. refers to them in *Off.* 3.49, 87, 107.

87. **Quanto hoc sublimius quam illud Graecorum . . . de gloria imperioque decertarent:** Again, a biblical *exemplum* is superior to a classical one: cf. Cic. *Off.* 3.49. The **duo populi** are the Athenians and the Spartans, and the story relates to their power-struggle following the defeat of Persia in 479 BC. Cic. tells how Themistocles announced to the Athenian assembly that he had a plan which would benefit their city, and that he wished to discuss it with someone confidentially. The people appointed Aristides, and Themistocles confided in him concerning his plan to set fire secretly to the Spartan fleet at Gytheum, and thus to

decimate the Spartan war-machine. Aristides did not disclose the details of the scheme to the assembly, but said only
that the idea was *minime honestum.* This alone was enough to
make the Athenians reject it: *quod honestum non esset, id ne
utile quidem putaverunt.* For the story, cf. Plu. *Them.* 20.1–2,
where it is said that the plan was to burn the whole Greek
fleet, not just the Spartan ships, and that the ships were
stationed at Pagasae, not Gytheum (Cic. confuses the reference to Tolmides' action in Thuc. 1.108.5); also Plu. *Arist.*
22.2–4; Val. Max. 6.5, ext. 2 (also Gytheum, following Cic.).
On fighting **de gloria imperioque**, cf. Cic. *Off.* 1.38; 3.86–
8 (and Dyck, 148–9); and especially Liv. 28.19.7. On
decertarent, cf. Cic.'s use of the verb in *Off.* 3.116. Cic.
says in *Off.* 3.49 that the Athenians acted better than the
Romans, for Rome allows pirates to get off scot-free
(Pompey settled them in Cilicia free of taxes) while levying
taxes on her allies (reimposing tribute obligations in the 70s
BC on states formerly released from such burdens by Sulla:
Off. 3.87). A. presents Elisha's behaviour as superior to the
Athenian example:

Et isti quidem . . . non possent tamen non erubescere:
Elisha had the opportunity to bring about the death of *hostes*
who had been ambushed, whereas the Athenians rejected a
stratagem to harm former *socii.* Furthermore, the Athenians
shrank only from burning *ships*; Elisha spared the Syrians'
lives. Cic. uses *flagitium* in *Off.* 3.86.

Elisaeus autem . . . nisi pepercisset: [E², followed by
Winterbottom, 566, deletes **licet**, but it can probably stand]
Elisha's case had nothing to do with *fraus*; the Syrians were
struck blind by the Lord's power. Even so, Elisha wished to
save them.

88. **quod decorum est, semper esse utile:** Typically,
decorum = *honestum.*

Iudith sancta: Cf. 3.84.

Elisaeus: Elisha granted a reprieve to the Syrian enemy,
rather than allowing them to be slaughtered, and so he did the
honourable thing. By treating the Syrians as guests, he won
the long-term benefit of an end to raids on Israelite territory.

89. **Quid autem aliud Iohannes . . . consideravit . . .?:**
See on 3.35.

Non tibi licet illam uxorem habere: Mk. 6: 18 (cf. Mt. 14: 4). Herod's relationship contravened Lev. 18: 16; 20: 21.
inclinare regi propheticam auctoritatem: John exercised a prophet's authority in speaking against the moral evil, and could have chosen to keep silent if he had valued his own life above what was right (he resisted the temptation to adopt the *wrong* kind of silence: cf. 1.9). His prophetic authority was in this instance grounded, of course, in the OT prohibitions of the behaviour of which the king was guilty.
adulatione: Cf. 1.226; 2.96, 112–20; 3.58, 134–5; see also on 1.209.
Et tamen quid utilius . . . advexit gloriam?: By putting the honourable ideal first and acting with courage, John gained the ultimate benefit: the glory of martyrdom and eternal reward.

90. Sancta quoque Susanna: See Dan. 13, especially 13: 23.
dum honestati intendit, etiam vitam reservavit: By refusing to yield to the elders' advances, even though the alternative was the public disgrace of a false indictment and the sentence of death, Susanna obtained *utilitas*: she received justice and her life was spared (through Daniel's intervention). If she had consented to the elders' desires, she would have forfeited the glory of *honestas and* lost the *utilitas* of her salvation. The language of *vita . . . salus . . . gloria* is used by Cic. in *Off.* 3.84–8; cf. also A. *Off.* 3.56, 125. On *turpitudo* as the antithesis of *utilitas*, cf. Cic. *Off.* 3.85.
utilitatis: A², E², C, most editors: *utilitati* PVMA¹, E¹W, OB, Lignamine, Testard.

CHAPTER 15: MOSES SUPERIOR TO A CLASSICAL
GENERAL

91. Memorabile ferunt rhetores . . . eum ad hostem miserit: rhetores means Cic. in particular: cf. *Off.* 3.86:

Quamquam id quidem cum saepe alias [that nothing is beneficial that is not honourable], tum Pyrrhi bello a C. Fabricio consule iterum et a senatu nostro iudicatum est. Cum enim rex Pyrrhus populo Romano bellum ultro intulisset cumque de imperio certamen esset cum rege generoso ac potente, perfuga ab eo venit in castra Fabrici eique est pollicitus, si praemium sibi proposuisset, se, ut clam venisset, sic clam in Pyrrhi castra rediturum, et eum veneno necaturum. Hunc Fabricius reducendum curavit ad Pyrrhum, idque eius factum laudatum a senatu est. Atqui si speciem utilitatis opinionemque quaerimus, magnum illud bellum perfuga unus et gravem adversarium imperii sustulisset; sed magnum dedecus et flagitium quicum laudis certamen fuisset, eum non virtute sed scelere superatum.

C. Fabricius Luscinus was consul in 282 and 278 BC and successful general in Rome's war with Pyrrhus of Epirus (280–275 BC); he was famed for his integrity. Cf. also Cic. *Off*. 1.40: *Maximum autem exemplum est iustitiae in hostem a maioribus nostris constitutum, cum a Pyrrho perfuga senatui est pollicitus se venenum regi daturum et eum necaturum. Senatus eum et C. Fabricius consul Pyrrho dedit: ita ne hostis quidem et potentis et bellum ultro inferentis interitum cum scelere approbavit.* The deserter was an Ambracian, variously called in the sources Timochares or Nicias; Cic. does not name him. For varying versions of the story, cf. Liv. 39.51.11; Val. Max. 6.5.1; Sen. *Ep*. 120.6; Tac. *Ann*. 2.88.1; Flor. 1.13.21; Gell. *NA* 3.8; Val. Ant. *Hist*. 21; Claud. Quadr. *Hist*. 40–1; Plu. *Pyrrh*. 21.1–3 (cf. *Flam*. 20.6); Dio, fr. 40.44; Amm. 30.1.22. A. perhaps knows it from other sources besides Cic.: Cic. does not call the deserter a *medicus* (Florus (like Seneca) does, though he confuses Fabricius with M. Curius Dentatus, consul in 290 BC); nor does he say that the man was sent back to the enemy camp *vinctus*. The disputed text of Cic. *Off*. 1.40 appears once again to be authenticated by A., as in 3.34 above: cf. *senatui est pollicitus se venenum regi daturum et eum necaturum* in *Off*. 1.40 with A.'s **pollicens daturum se regi venenum**, while in *Off*. 3.86 Cic. has *ei est pollicitus . . . se, ut clam venisset, sic clam in Pyrrhi castra rediturum, et eum veneno necaturum.* Cic. *Off*. 1.40 also speaks of *fraus*. For **memorabile**, cf. 3.80.

praeclarum: Cic. *Off*. 3.104 has *praeclare*.

92. **Redeamus ad nostrum Moysen . . . ut quanto praestantiora tanto antiquiora promamus:** As well as making his standard contrast between pagan exemplar and 'our' biblical hero (on the principle so neatly summed up

here, see Introduction IV.2), A. is thinking of Cic. *Off.* 3.99, where Cic. turns away from mythological and foreign illustrations to tell the story of M. Atilius Regulus: *Sed omittamus et fabulas et externa; ad rem factam nostramque veniamus*; cf. also *Off.* 3.110: *Quare ex multis mirabilibus exemplis haud facile quis dixerit hoc exemplo aut laudabilius aut praestantius.*

Nolebat Aegypti rex populum dimittere patrum: See Ex. 5: 1–18.

Dixit Moyses . . . super omnes aquas Aegypti: See Ex. 7: 19–21.

sincera autem fluenta patribus abundabant: The scriptural account does not specifically say that the Israelites escaped the effects of the plague of blood, though it is a reasonable inference from the fact that they were spared during the plagues of flies (Ex. 8: 20–4), murrain (Ex. 9: 1–7), hail (Ex. 9: 22–6), and darkness (Ex. 10: 21–3), and at the destruction of the first-born (Ex. 11: 1–12: 30).

Iactaverunt favillam . . . in hominibus et quadrupedibus: [**candentes:** B, Lignamine, Monte Alto, Maurists, Krabinger, Testard: *cadentes* PVMA¹, E¹W, O, several editors: *scatentes* E², Erasmus-Gelen-Coster: *scatientes* C] See Ex. 9: 8–12.

Deduxerunt grandinem . . . supra terram omnia: See Ex. 9: 13–35, especially 9: 22 ff.

93. **Iterum caligantibus tenebris . . . tenebras infuderat:** See Ex. 10: 21–3.

Moriebatur omne primogenitum . . . inoffensa progenies: See Ex. 11: 1–12: 30.

Rogatus Moyses . . . oravit et impetravit: See Ex. 8: 8–15, 28–32; 9: 27–35; 10: 16–20.

In illo: In the case of the *dux Romanorum* of 3.91, Fabricius.

in hoc mirabile . . . etiam ab hoste detorserit: [**supplicia virtute** COB: *supplicia et virtute* MSS] Fabricius refused to *overcome* his enemy by *fraus*, Moses actually *brought relief to* his enemy by interceding for him. On **mirabile**, see on 3.80; on **virtute propria**, cf. Cic. *Off.* 3.100: *Harum enim est virtutum proprium.*

vere nimium . . . mansuetus et mitis: Cf. Num. 12: 3: *Erat enim Moses vir mitissimus super omnes homines qui morabantur in terra.*

Sciebat quod fidem rex non servaret promissi: Moses
knew that his enemy Pharaoh could not be trusted to keep
faith, that his promises were worthless, yet still he did the
honourable thing in response. On keeping promises, cf. Cic.
Off. 3.92–5.

laesus benediceret: See on 1.235.

The Moses narrative is interpreted typologically in 3.94–5:
Christ is to be seen in these ancient events.

94. **Proiecit virgam . . . serpentes Aegyptiorum:** See Ex.
7: 8–13; the staff is Aaron's.

significans quod Verbum caro fieret: Cf. Jn. 1: 14.

**quae serpentis diri venena vacuaret . . . et indulgen-
tiam peccatorum:** Christ, the incarnate Word, took away
the poisons of the serpent Satan, the pollution of sin which
has affected humanity since the wound was inflicted by the
devil in Adam's heel (cf. *Expl. Ps. 48*.8); on Christ's
redemptive work as a healing process, see on 3.27. Possibly
we are also meant to pick up the reference to *venenum* in 3.91:
Fabricius refused to use (literal) poison; Christ, typified by
Moses, dealt with the terrible effects of (spiritual) poisons
(plural).

Virga est enim Verbum . . . insigne imperii: On the rod
as a symbol of the word of God, cf. *Sacr.* 5.3; on its power,
cf. *Myst.* 50–4; also *Ep. extra coll.* 1 [41].2–4; *Ep.* 5 [4].4–5.
The transformed rod was variously seen by patristic exegetes
as a type of the cross (e.g. Orig. *Hom. Ex.* 4.6); as a symbol of
God's power to raise the dead (Epiph. *Ancor.* 96); or as a
type of Christ's healing work (e.g. Cyr. Jerus. *Catech.* 18.12;
Aug. *En. Ps. 73*.5; *Trin.* 3.20). For some related themes, see
M. Dulaey, 'Le Symbole de la baguette dans l'art paléochrétien', *REAug* 19 (1973), 3–38. On **insigne imperii**, cf. Ps.
44: 7.

qui erat Filius Dei . . . Filius hominis factus est: On the
details of A.'s Christology, consult Homes Dudden ii. 591–
605; P. K. Schwerdt, *Studien zur Lehre des Heiligen Ambrosius von der Person Christi* (Bückeburg, 1937), especially 41–
119.

natus ex Virgine: The word-play of *virga–virgo* assists the
contrived typology: as the *virga* became a serpent, so the Son
of God became the Son of Man by being born of the *Virgo*

qui quasi serpens . . . vulneribus infudit humanis: The **serpens** which came from Moses's *virga* typifies Christ; the *serpentes Aegyptiorum* symbolize Satan, whom Christ overcomes.

Sicut Moyses exaltavit . . . ita exaltari oportet Filium hominis: Jn. 3: 14, alluding to Num. 21: 8–9. This statement is the basis for the standard equation (e.g. Tert. *Adv. Marc.* 3.18.7; *Adv. Iud.* 10; *Idol.* 5) of the serpent with the Son of Man. Moses raised a bronze serpent on a pole in order that those who had been bitten by the venomous snakes could look at it and be healed. Christ was raised on the cross so that those who look to him might be healed of the deadly disease of sin which was inflicted by the serpent Satan at the Fall; cf. e.g. *Spir.* 3.50; Aug. *En Ps. 118*.122; Caes. Arel. *Serm.* 112.

95. **Misit manum suam . . . sicut carnis humanae species:** Ex. 4: 6–7.

primum fulgorem divinitatis: Cf. generally Heb. 1: 3; 2 Cor. 4: 4; Col. 1: 15. On Christ's divinity as light in A., see Morgan, especially 84–8, 126–31, 137–49, 171–250.

in qua fide . . . oporteret: Cf. Jn. 3: 36; Rom. 1: 5, etc. As we might expect, A. presents a strongly exclusivist line on faith and salvation; see generally J. Eger, *Salus gentium. Eine patristische Studie zur Volkstheologie des Ambrosius von Mailand*, Diss. (Munich, 1947); Fenger, 97 ff.

quia dextera Dei Christus est: Cf. Acts 2: 33; 5: 31; Rom. 8: 34; Eph. 1: 20; Col. 3: 1; Heb. 1: 3; 8: 1; 10: 12; 12: 2; etc.

in cuius divinitate . . . quasi reprobus flagellatur: On the punishment of unbelievers, cf. e.g. *Expl. Ps. 1*.51–6; and see generally Niederhuber, *Eschatologie*, 99–126.

iste rex: Pharaoh.

honestatis adfectus: The exegesis is linked to the philosophical theme.

et eo maxime . . . de libro viventium se deleret: See Ex. 32: 31–2; Moses' intercession is taken as a type of Christ's vicarious suffering.

CHAPTER 16: HONESTY IN THE DISCLOSURE OF
DEFECTS

96. Tobias quoque ... invitaret inopes: See Tob. 2: 1–8;
cf. 1: 17. **evidentius** is not an admission that the preceding
section is weak, *pace* Testard, 'Recherches', 108–9; the
comparative form is simply emphatic, hence the translation
'very clearly'. On **formam ... honestatis**, see on 1.62

**Raguel praecipue ... cum rogaretur ut filiam suam in
coniugium daret:** Raguel's daughter Sarah was sought by
her kinsman Tobias, son of Tobit, with the help of Azarias,
the angel Raphael. Raguel revealed that she had already been
married to seven husbands (not six, as A. says), all of whom
had been slain by a demon on their wedding-night (Tob. 7
especially 7: 11). Tobias still married her, and the demon was
repelled, as Raphael advised, by burning the heart and liver
of a fish on ashes of incense in the wedding-chamber, and
subsequently caught and bound by the angel (Tob. 8: 1).

vitia ... non tacebat: The theme discussed by Cic. in *Off.*
3.51–68.

**malebat innuptam sibi manere filiam quam ... extra-
neos periclitari:** This is going beyond what Tob. 7 says;
A.'s enthusiasm for Raguel's *contemplatio honestatis* runs
away with him. Still, Raguel did dig a grave for Tobias
during the night, in the expectation that he too would be
killed by the demon (Tob. 8: 10–18).

97. Quam breviter absolvit ... arbitratus est: Cic. *Off.*
3.50 speaks of *quaestiones* concerning cases where the *utile*
seems to conflict with the *honestum*, and he goes on to
describe some philosophical opinions on these with regard
to justice (*Off.* 3.50–96; cf. *quaestiones* in *Off.* 3.89). For A.'s
contrast between the complicated questions of the philosophers and the clarity of Scripture, cf. 2.8, 49; 3.126. In
this case, the *quaestio* is raised by Cic. in *Off.* 3.54: *Vendat
aedes vir bonus propter aliqua vitia quae ipse norit, ceteri
ignorent ... quaero, si haec emptoribus venditor non dixerit
aedesque vendiderit pluris multo quam se venditurum putarit
num id iniuste aut improbe fecerit?* The Stoic Antipater felt
that there was a moral obligation for the seller to disclose

everything; his mentor Diogenes argued that only such faults as civil law required ought to be mentioned, since the seller was entitled to seek the best possible price (*Off.* 3.51–5; possibly the debate draws upon Hecato, though Cic. may have read of it elsewhere). Cic.'s own judgement (*Off.* 3.57) is that if a vendor stays silent with deliberate intent to profit at the expense of someone else, then, and only then, is his action wrong. This is in accordance with the *formula* laid down in *Off.* 3.21. Merely keeping quiet is not dishonourable concealment. For the suggestion that Cic. misconstrues Diogenes' argument, see J. Annas, 'Cicero on Stoic Moral Philosophy and Private Property', in M. Griffin and J. Barnes (eds.), *Philosophia Togata: Essays on Philosophy and Roman Society* (Oxford, 1989), 151–73, with a pertinent response from Dyck, 556–64.

celanda: Cic. uses the verb throughout *Off.* 3.50–7.

si conferamus quanto praestantior . . . quam rei venalis pecunia: The *philosophi* are discussing revenues from property sales—mere trivialities. Raguel (**noster**) was dealing with his daughter's marriage. The biblical *exemplum* not only settles the matter: it shows a superior concern for the *honestum* since the individual in question was handling far weightier matters. Cic. has *praestantius* in *Off.* 3.110.

CHAPTER 17: CONCERN FOR THE HONOURABLE:
THE EXAMPLE OF THE FATHERS ON GOING INTO
EXILE

3.98–110 tells of another 'ancestral' feat which evinces a determination to do the honourable thing: the preservation of the divine mysteries in the time of the Babylonian captivity. A similar theme has already been signalled in connection with Judith in 3.84. The section is very probably intended to replace Cic.'s celebration of the virtues of the quintessential Roman patriot, M. Atilius Regulus, in *Off.* 3.99–111. Regulus illustrates courage above all, and there are echoes of this in the depiction of *maiores nostri* here (some similar language has already been used of Judith, Elisha, John the Baptist, and Susanna in 3.82–90). A.'s repeated stress on the captive status

of the spiritual ancestors may well be intended to evoke the
centrality of the *captivi* in the Regulus story.

98.   in captivitate: [V, E, O: *in captivitatem* PM, C, Testard]
During the Babylonian captivity under Nebuchadnezzar
(604–562 BC). A large proportion of the population of
Judah was deported in two waves, first after the fall of
Jerusalem in 597 BC (4 Ki. 24: 10–17), and then again
following the sack of the city in *c.*586 BC (4 Ki. 25: 1–21).
After the capture of Babylon by Cyrus the Great of Persia
(559–530 BC) in *c.*539, some of the exiles were allowed to
return to Jerusalem (Ezr. 1–2), but the majority did not go
back until at least a hundred years later, starting with the
time of Artaxerxes I (see below).
    Nullis enim adversis . . . quam in prosperis: Courage is
fundamental: cf. 1.200. For the language generally, cf. 1.167;
2.10–21; 3.129–38.
    vincula: Cic. uses *vinculum* in *Off.* 3.111.
    servitutem, quae liberis omni supplicio gravior est:
See on 1.20. Cic. *Off.* 3.100 has *supplicia*; *cum liberis* appears
in *Off.* 3.99.
    patriae cineres: Cf. Verg. *Aen.* 10.59; Auct. Her. 4.8.12;
Cic. *Sull.* 19; Sen. *Troad.* 29. Cic. speaks of Regulus' *patria*
in *Off.* 3.99–100, 110.
99.   Dei omnipotentis: Cf. Gen. 17: 1; 35: 11; etc.
    acceptum ignem . . . occulte in valle absconderunt:
See 2 Macc. 1: 19. The priests sought to obey the divine
injunction that the sacred fire on the altar must never be
allowed to go out (Lev. 6: 13).
    silentio: Important to the spiritual mysticism; cf. 3.108.
    Non illis studio . . . quod servarent posteris suis: The
priests were concerned to preserve the purity of divine
worship, not to ensure the material enrichment of their
descendants.
    deformium: Cic. *Off.* 3.105 has *deformitate*.
100.   sola religione liberi: Their spiritual freedom was
unassailable, despite their physical bondage; see generally
Faust, 62–81, 120–9.
    regi Persarum: Artaxerxes I (465–424 BC).
    legitimos: Cic. uses the word in *Off.* 3.108.

Nehemiam: Artaxerxes' cupbearer. He was granted permission to return to Jerusalem on a mission of mercy, and he arrived in Jerusalem as governor in March–April, 445/4 BC (Neh. 1 ff.), where, despite intense opposition, he supervised the rebuilding of the city walls in a period of just fifty-two days (Neh. 6: 15). He returned to the Persian court, but made a second trip to Jerusalem some time later, probably around 432 BC, when he introduced some significant moral and religious reforms (Neh. 13: 6–31). Artaxerxes was continuing the policy of restoration begun under Cyrus, when a number of exiles were permitted to return to Jerusalem with the treasures of the Temple and to commence the rebuilding of the Temple, which was dedicated in the reign of Darius I (522–486 BC) (Ezr. 1–6). A. follows 2 Macc. 1: 18 in suggesting that the Temple was completed in the time of Nehemiah and Artaxerxes; it was in fact finished in 516 BC. On the narrative in this paragraph, see 2 Macc. 1: 20–32.

qui profecturi ... ignem absconderunt: One is reminded of the way in which Aeneas and his men took with them their Trojan *penates* (Verg. *Aen.* 1.68). Cic. uses *proficisci* in *Off.* 3.100.

adolerent altaria: Cf. Lucr. 4.1237; Verg. *Aen.* 1.704; 7.71; *Georg.* 4.379; Tac. *Hist.* 2.3.2; *Ann.* 14.30.3.

visu mirabile: Cf. Verg. *Aen.* 7.78; 10.637. The classical phrase replaces *ita ut omnes mirarentur* in 2 Macc. 1: 22.

caelum intextum nubibus: See on 2.21.

101. See 2 Macc. 1: 33–6.

Appellaverunt autem illud ... 'Epathar' ... a plurimis 'Nepthe' vocatur: Cf. 2 Macc. 1: 36. The author of 2 Macc. thinks that the name is related to the Hebrew *nephtar/niphtar*, which literally means 'released, free from obligation', and hence, by tenuous extension, 'purified'. He is attempting to find authority for the Feast of Purification in the mysterious event recorded here. In fact, the root of the word is the Akkadian *naptu*, which in Hebrew becomes *nepht*, and in Aramaic *nephta/naphta*, and hence the Greek νάφθα (LXX: νέφθαρ); the Greek world probably heard of it from Aramaic-speaking Syrians. The pitch-like naphtha was known to the ancients to come from Babylonia/Assyria (Str.

Geog. 16.1.4, 15, 24; Plin. *NH* 2.235; 24.158; 35.179; Amm.
23.6.16, 38). The first name which A. gives it, **Epathar**
(PM), is odd, since the initial *n-* is missing (as it is in all the
many variants in the MSS: *epathar/ephata/phatur/ephitar*).
He cannot be thinking of some other Hebrew derivation, for
he does not know Hebrew, and a Greek etymology appears
inconceivable; he must simply be relying on his memory of
the text of 2 Macc. He correctly speaks of *naphtha* in *Elia* 19.
**Invenitur autem in descriptionibus Ieremiae proph-
etae:** See 2 Macc. 2: 1–8. The author of 2 Macc. draws on
texts such as the Epistle of Jeremiah.

Hic est ignis qui . . . consumpsit illud: Cf. 2 Macc. 2: 10.
Exivit ignis a Domino . . . super altare holocausta: Lev.
9: 24.

**ideoque filios Aaron . . . ut mortui extra castra proicer-
entur:** Nadab and Abihu were destroyed for offering
unauthorized fire to the Lord (Lev. 10: 1–5).

102. See 2 Macc. 2: 5–8.

curiosius: They sought to pry into sacred things; see on
1.122; cf. also 1.251.
Ignotus erit locus . . . et apparebit maiestas Domini: 2
Macc. 2: 7–8.

A. conflates two different episodes in 3.101–2: (i) the dis-
covery of the sacred fire (2 Macc. 1: 19–2: 1), and (ii)
Jeremiah's hiding of the sacred objects of the tabernacle,
the ark, and the altar of incense in a cave (2 Macc. 2: 4–8)
(Testard, 'Etude', 188 n. 70; Testard ii. 223 n. 12). The
stories are adjacent in the narrative of 2 Macc., and fire is
mentioned again after the second incident in 2 Macc. 2: 10,
so it is easy to see how confusion could arise when working
from memory of the text.

CHAPTER 18: TYPES OF CHRISTIAN BAPTISM IN
THE OLD TESTAMENT

3.103–10 is an *excursus* (3.110), explaining the typologica
significance of the OT references to fire and water: th
coming of the Holy Spirit, baptism, and penance are a
foreshadowed in these scriptural events. A. cites other text

in addition to the 2 Macc. narratives exploited in 3.98–102: he identifies baptismal types in the sacrifice of Elijah (3.107–8), the crossing of the Red Sea (3.108), and the Flood (3.109). The philosophical theme disappears until 3.110.

103. Congregationem populi tenemus, propitiationem . . . agnoscimus: Picking up 2 Macc. 2: 7 in 3.102. *Maiores nostri* (3.98)/*patres nostri* (3.99) have their spiritual offspring in the Christian church (Introduction IV.4; see also Toscani, 164–70). These forebears knew in shadow (1.239) the mysteries that are now appreciated in the age of Christ and the Spirit, and the lineaments of the same sacramental grace can be traced in their spiritual experiences. For **agnoscimus**, cf. the similar language in another piece of spiritual interpretation in 2.138–9.

propitiator: On the model, cf. 1 Jn. 2: 2.

cum legerimus quia baptizat Dominus Iesus . . . sicut in evangelio dixit Iohannes: The words of John the Baptist: Mt. 3: 11; Lk. 3: 16; cf. also Jn. 1: 33.

sacrificium . . . pro peccato: See on 3.108. On Christ's death as a sacrifice, see Jn. 1: 29, 36; Rom. 8: 3; 1 Cor. 5: 7; Eph. 5: 2; Heb. 9: 11–10: 18; 1 Pt. 1: 19; Apoc. 5: 6–10; 13: 8.

typus: See generally Introduction IV.5.

Et factum est in corde meo . . . et ferre non possum: Jer. 20: 9.

Sed et in Actibus Apostolorum . . . legimus: Cf. Acts 2: 3–4.

Denique sic vaporabatur . . . musto repleti esse aestimarentur: Cf. Acts 2: 13. E[2]'s transposition of **aestimarentur** to follow **esse** rather than **acceperant** (so MSS) is persuasive (Winterbottom, 566).

104. spiritalis gratia . . . peccata nostra: The mysterious transformation of the water into fire in 2 Macc. 1, and the references to fire in connection with the baptism administered by Christ and the Holy Spirit, suggest the purging of baptism. The fire symbolizes the Holy Spirit, who appears as fire at Pentecost, and descends on the baptismal font when the priest invokes the Triune name (e.g. *Spir.* 3.137–8; *Luc.* 2.79; *Sacr.* 2.11, 14–15; *Myst.* 26–7); it is the power of the Spirit's presence which effects the work of regeneration,

'burning up' the subject's *culpa* (*Elia* 83). Elsewhere (e.g. *Expos. Ps. 118.*3.14–17; 20.12–15; cf. *Expl. Ps. 1.*38), A. explains a verse such as Ps. 65: 12 (*Transivimus per ignem et aquam*) as teaching a twofold purging of sins: first, by the water of baptism in this world, and second, by purgatorial fire at the entrance to paradise (see Homes Dudden ii. 660 n. 4; Niederhuber, *Eschatologie*, 28–42). The verses from 1 Cor. 3 which he quotes below were also traditionally cited in support of the doctrine of purgatory. It is unlikely, however, that he is thinking of purgatorial fire here. *Elia* 83, a passage that is very similar to 3.107–8, takes the fire as that of the Holy Spirit, and the *locus* is baptism.
Uniuscuiusque opus . . . ignis probabit: 1 Cor. 3: 13.
Si cuius opus . . . quasi per ignem: 1 Cor. 3: 15.

105. Notum est ergo . . . descendit super sacrificium: Cf. 3.100–2.

106. Hic igitur ignis . . . tempore autem libertatis promitur: In 3.100, the period of the Babylonian captivity is visualized as a time when *patres nostri* remained free in religious terms despite their physical slavery. The hermeneutic here is different: the captivity symbolizes the time of spiritual bondage, when the rite is hidden; in an age of liberty and grace, the significance of baptism is revealed (on this tension more generally in A.'s use of OT exemplars, see Introduction IV.4). A. is probably thinking of Rom. 5: 14, 17, 21; 6: 12, on the contrast of the reigns of sin, death and of grace.
Ego sum ignis consumens: Dt. 4: 24 (cf. Dt. 9: 3).
Me dereliquerunt fontem aquae vivae: Jer. 2: 13.
nam ipse in evangelio suo dicit . . . ut ignem in terras mitteret: Cf. Lk. 12: 49.
et potum sitientibus . . . ministraret: Cf. Jn. 7: 37–8 (also Jn. 4: 13–14).

107. Eliae quoque tempore . . . sine igne accenderent: See 3 Ki. 18: 20–40: the prophets of Baal could not invoke fire on their sacrifice, but Elijah called down fire from the Lord even when the altar had been drenched with water. A. also pictures this incident as a type of baptism in *Elia* 83. *Si quis autem non est baptizatus, securior convertatur remissionem accipiens peccatorum. Siquidem baptismus velut ign* *quidam peccata consumit, quia Christus in igne et Spiritu baptizat. Denique hunc typum legis in Regnorum libris, ubi Elias super altare ligna imposuit* (the narrative from 3 Ki. 18 then follows). Elijah's sacrifice is not commonly taken as a type of baptism, but cf. *Sacr.* 2.11; and Greg. Nyss. *In bapt. Chr.*, PG 46, 592 B–D (J. Daniélou, *The Bible and the Liturgy* (London, 1960), 106–7). The typology is fostered by the NT's link between Elijah and John the Baptist (Mt. 11: 14; 17: 10–13), drawing on the prophecy of a revival of Elijah's ministry before the coming of the Day of the Lord (Mal. 4: 5–6).

108. Hostia illa tu es. Considera tacitus singula: Cf. *Elia* 83 again: *Tu es homo super altare, qui ablueris aqua, cuius exuritur culpa ut vita renovetur; lignum enim et stipulam consumit ignis. Noli timere ignem per quem illuminaris . . .* (etc. and 84–5). **tacitus:** An important element of the humility necessary when handling holy things, and an obvious way of building up and preserving the sense of mystery surrounding the sacramental rite; cf. 1.35. Cf. also *Luc.* 10.4: *Vide ergo singula.*

Denique quod consumptum est . . . sacrificium pro peccato erat: On the sin-offering, see Lev. 4: 1–5: 13; 6: 24–30; 8: 14–17; 16: 3–22.

eo quod non sit manducatum . . . consumptum est: 2 Macc. 2: 11.

homo . . . exterior: Cf. 2 Cor. 4: 16.

Vetus homo noster . . . apostolus clamat: A conflation of Rom. 6: 6, *quia vetus homo noster simul crucifixus est*, and Gal. 2: 20, *Christo crucifixus sum cruci.*

Illic . . . ubi baptizati sunt patres sub nube et in mari: Cf. 1 Cor. 10: 1–2: *quoniam patres nostri omnes sub nube fuerunt, et omnes mare transierunt, et omnes in Mose baptizati sunt in nube et in mari.* Paul is referring to the cloud of the divine presence (Ex. 13: 21–2; 14: 19, 24; etc.). A. seems to connect this with the reference to the clouds which preceded the sunshine and the fire in the case of Nehemiah's sacrifice (2 Macc. 1: 22), though he does not make the association explicit (in *Sacr.* 1.22 he sees the cloud of 1 Cor. 10 as a 'shadow' of the Holy Spirit). The crossing of the Red Sea as a type of baptism is very common in early Christian exegesis:

among many examples, cf. Tert. *Bapt.* 9; Orig. *Hom. in Ex.*
5.5; Hil. *In Ps. 134.*19; Didym. *Trin.* 2.14; Bas. *Spir.* 31; Jer.
Epp. 10.1.2; 69.6.3; Aug. *Catech.* 34; *Fid. op.* 17; *En. Ps.*
*80.*8; *En. Ps. 106.*3; in A., *Ex.* 1.14 (also 5.17); *Epp.* 62 [19].2;
Sacr. 1.12, 20–2; 2.9; *Myst.* 12; *Expos. Ps. 118.*16.29. The
Egyptian is generally taken to represent the old, sinful, outer
man who perishes in the baptismal font, and the Hebrew as
the new man, the believer who emerges safely from the
waters. See F. J. Dölger, 'Der Durchzug durch das Rote
Meer als Sinnbild der christlichen Taufe', *AC* 2 (1930),
63–9; J. Daniélou, 'Traversée de la Mer Rouge et baptême
aux premiers siècles', *RSR* 33 (1946), 402–30; P. Lundberg,
La Typologie baptismale dans l'ancienne Eglise (Leipzig and
Uppsala, 1942), 116–45; J. P. Lewis, *A Study of the*
Interpretation of Noah and the Flood in Jewish and Christian
Literature (Leiden, 1968), 167–73.

109. In diluvio quoque . . . caro omnis: Cf. Gen. 7: 21.

iustus tamen cum sua progenie servatus est: See Gen.
7: 23; 8: 15–18.

Denique exterior corrumpitur, sed renovatur interior:
Cf. 2 Cor. 4: 16; on the *homo interior*, see on 1.11.

Nec solum in baptismate: On the Flood as a type of
baptism, cf. 1 Pt. 3: 20–1. This becomes another standard
image, often associated with the idea of the church as the ark
of salvation. Examples include Tert. *Bapt.* 8; Cypr. *Epp.*
69.2.2–3; 74.11.3; Didym. *Trin.* 2.14; Aug. *Catech.* 32; in A.,
Sacr. 1.23; 2.1, 9; *Myst.* 10–11; see Lundberg, *La Typologie*
baptismale dans l'ancienne Eglise, 73–116; J. Daniélou, *Sacra-*
mentum Futuri: Etudes sur les origines de la typologie biblique
(Paris, 1950), 69–85.

sed etiam in paenitentia: See on 2.77.

Iudicavi ut praesens . . . in die Domini nostri Iesu
Christi: 1 Cor. 5: 3, 5.

110. Prolixior excursus . . . factus videtur: A. admits that
his enthusiasm for the spiritual heroism of the ancestors has
run away with him, and he calls the argument back to the
concern for the *honestum*. Testard, 'Recherches', 108–9
Testard ii. 224 n. 24, imagines that the Ciceronian vocabulary here (and in 3.98–9) reflects a redaction process. He fails
to catch the subtle echoes of Cic.'s Regulus story at variou

points throughout 3.98–102. The sparse references to the *honestum*, and the confession of prolixity in 3.110, are best taken at face value: once again, A. sets out to illustrate a philosophical motif with scriptural *exempla*, and becomes carried away with the details of the scriptural narrative. For **prolixior**, cf. 1.232; for another **excursus**, cf. 1.47 on 1.41–6.

admirandi gratia mysterii . . . revelatum . . . sacramentum: On the revelation of the mystery to the faithful (and its corresponding hiddenness to the unworthy) see on 1.251; even for initiates, of course, a fuller degree of disclosure awaits: cf. 1.239.

quod eo usque . . . ut sit plenum religionis: A telling clue to A.'s overall perspective: *honestas* and *religio* are never ultimately far apart. Virtue is truly performed by those who have experienced the grace of God, the death of the old man, and the regeneration of Christian baptism (Löpfe, 46–52; Seibel, 161–9).

CHAPTER 19: CONCERN FOR THE HONOURABLE:
THE FATHERS' REVENGE ON THE BENJAMITES

111. Quanta autem honestatis cura maioribus fuit: CO's **fuit** makes better sense than the other MSS' *fuerit*, retained by Testard. One other possibility is to adopt E²'s *in hoc evidentissime claruit* before **ut** (Winterbottom, 565), but I opt for the more economical course.

ut unius mulieris iniuriam . . . bello persequerentur: The concubine of a Levite was raped by the men of Gibeah, who were Benjamites; the Israelites *en masse* avenged the crime with war against all the Benjamites, who had refused to hand over the guilty party (Jdg. 19–20). The Israelites also swore not to give their daughters in marriage to the Benjamites; but, to save the tribe of Benjamin from extinction, they allowed the Benjamites to take women from Jabesh Gilead and Shiloh (Jdg. 21). The style of A.'s account combines the narrative literalism of the OT's Latin with numerous echoes of Ciceronian language. For a considerable expansion of the narrative, cf. *Ep.* 57 [6].

Remanserat: Cic. *Off.* 3.100 has *remansisset*; *remanere* appears in *Off.* 3.115.

fraudis necessariae: Brings in the Ciceronian language of *fraus* again (cf. *Off.* 3.107, 115); Cic. uses *necessarius* in *Off.* 3.101.

indulgentia: Cic. *Off.* 3.112 has *perindulgens*.

intemperantiae: Cic. *Off.* 3.116–20 discusses apparent *utilitas* and *temperantia*.

supplicio: See on 3.98.

ut rapto inirent coniugia: By the seizure of the girls of Shiloh (Jdg. 21: 15–23).

non connubii sacramento: *Coniugium* is physical union; *conubium* is marriage properly constituted in law. For A., marriage is an indissoluble *sacramentum*, akin to the union of Christ and the church (cf. Eph. 5: 22–3): see Monachino, 175–8.

Et revera dignum fuit: A. sanctions the principle of judgement and vengeance on evil-doers; see on 1.176.

112. See Jdg. 19: 1–3.

Quam plena autem miserationis historia!: Cf. Cic. *Off.* 3.117: *Quam miser . . .!* Cic. uses the word *historia* in *Off.* 3.115.

iugalem (quam a concubitu concubinam appellatam arbitror): A. is slightly coy about the woman's status (though he goes on to praise her in 3.115); cf. *Ep.* 57 [6].3). The Vulg. calls her both *uxor* (Jdg. 19: 1, 9, 29; 20: 5) and *concubina* (Jdg. 19: 10, 24, 25, 27); the LXX says γυνή and παλλακή. A. is again keen on etymology (Introduction IX); both *concubina* and *concubitus* stem from *concumbere*, which in turn is from *cubare*: cf. Eutych. *Gramm.* 5.454.22 for the derivation of *concubina* from *cubare*.

offensa rebus: In *Ep.* 57 [6].3, she is said to leave because he has criticized her for looking down on him.

Exsurrexit: Cic. *Off.* 3.112 has *surrexit*.

in domum patris sui: Cic. *Off.* 3.112 speaks of an encounter in a *domus* between an *adulescens* and a man who was bringing charges against his *pater*.

113. See Jdg. 19: 3–10.

adulescentulae: Cic. *Off.* 3.112 speaks of an *adulescens*.

surrexit: See above on 3.112.

diluculo: Cic. *Off.* 3.112 has *primo luci.*

retentus est: Cic. *Off.* 3.100 has *retinuit*; *Off.* 3.105 has *retinendi.*

proficisci: Cic. has the word in *Off.* 3.100 (and cf. *Off.* 3.110).

die septimo: Not so: the man left on the evening of the fifth day (Jdg. 19: 5–10). A. is relating the story from memory, and the seventh day doubtless seems the significant one in terms of the usual spiritual numerics; *Ep.* 57 [6].4 is closer to the truth.

114. See Jdg. 19: 10–22.

ad urbem Iebusaeorum: The ancient name for Jerusalem (Jdg. 19: 10). The party had travelled only about nine kilometres north from Bethlehem.

vir peregrinus: An Ephraimite (Jdg. 19: 16).

115. See Jdg. 19: 22–6.

mensae remotae: Cf. Verg. *Aen.* 1.216: *Postquam exempta fames epulis mensaeque remotae.* Cic. *Off.* 3.112 has *remotisque arbitris.*

irruerunt pestilentes viri, circumierunt domum: A. discreetly does not record the specific demand of the **pestilentes viri** to the old man in Jdg. 19: 22: *Educ virum qui ingressus est domum tuam, ut abutamur eo.* In *Ep.* 57 [6].7–8, it is the woman who is demanded.

coaequalem eius, cum qua cubitare solita esset: A. evidently conflates the story with the similar incident in Gen. 19, when Lot offers the men of Sodom his two virgin daughters (Gen. 19: 4–8). In Jdg. 19: 24, the old man offers one daughter plus the Levite's concubine. In *Ep.* 57 [6].8, he offers only his daughter.

ratio . . . vis praevaluit: Cic. uses both *vis* and *valere* a number of times in *Off.* 3.99–114; cf. also *Off.* 3.104: *Haec quidem ratio non . . . valet.*

supremo licet vitae munere . . . marito reservaret: Such devotion to duty even in death is of a piece with her innocent virtue; she is a typical female martyr in A.'s eyes.

116. See Jdg. 20, especially 20: 8 ff.

condemnatus quoque . . . iurisiurandi sacramento est: See Jdg. 21: 1. Cic. uses *ex . . . numero* in *Off.* 3.107. The force of *iusiurandi* is central to Cic. *Off.* 3.99–114.

quod tam acerbam . . . temperaverunt: Cic. *Off.* 3.112 has *acerbe severus.*

ut orbatas parentum virgines . . . pro delicto perempti forent: [Banterle's **quarum**, adopted also by Testard, is obviously preferable to the MSS' *quorum*] The men and married women of Jabesh Gilead were put to the sword for having failed to assemble with the other Israelites at Mizpah, but 400 virgins were saved to be wives for some of the Benjamites (Jdg. 21: 6–14).

vel rapto copulam sociarent: The Benjamites hid in vineyards and seized the girls of Shiloh who had come out to dance (Jdg. 21: 20–3).

turpis . . . fraudis: The Ciceronian language is woven in.

exhibuere: Cic. uses the verb in *Off.* 3.112.

indulta est: See on 3.111.

coniventia: most editors: *cohibentia* MSS, Zell, Valdarfer, Scinzenzeler, Marchand, Testard; Testard's attempt to defend the MSS' reading (Testard ii. 226 n. 11) is not very persuasive: *coniventia* is post-classical and rather rare (*TLL* iv. 319–20), but the substantive *cohibentia* in the sense needed would be very peculiar indeed (cf. *TLL* vii/2. 624–5).

117. **quadraginta milia virorum:** A slip: Jdg. 20: 2, 17 say *quadringenta*, which appears as a gloss in some MSS (P², E², C); cf. *Ep.* 57[6].11.

stringerent gladium: Cic. *Off.* 3.112 has *gladium destrinxit.*

dum ulcisci volunt iniuriam pudicitiae . . . temeratores castitatis non sufferebantur: The Israelites *en masse* showed the kind of spirit described as a hallmark of the spiritual élite in 1.258.

sexaginta quinque milia: This is the total if the figures of Jdg. 20: 21, 25, and 46 are added together. The precise figure, if Jdg. 20: 21, 25, 31/39, and 35 are totalled, is 65,130.

exustae urbes: Gibeah itself was burnt (Jdg. 20: 38), as were the other Benjamite towns (Jdg. 20: 48).

Et cum inferior primo fuisset populus Israel: The Israelites lost 40,000 men in the first two engagements (Jdg. 20: 19–25).

CHAPTER 20: CONCERN FOR THE HONOURABLE: THE LEPERS OF SAMARIA

118. quando etiam leprosis . . . honestatis non defuit consideratio: The lepers felt that it was not right to keep to themselves the plunder of the Syrian camp, and they informed the starving people of Samaria that the enemy had fled (4 Ki. 7: 3–20).

119. Fames erat magna . . . Syrorum exercitus: See 4 Ki. 6: 24–31; and cf. 1.139–40; 3.86 above.

Rex: Probably Joram. On **Regnorum**, see on 1.141.

vel quia non permiserat regi . . . quos caecitate perfuderat: See 4 Ki. 6: 18–23.

120. Sedebat Eliseus . . . in Bethel: See 4 Ki. 6: 32–7: 2. Elisha was not in Bethel, in fact, but in his own house in Samaria.

121. See 4 Ki. 7: 6–7.

multa equitum: E^2, CNB, Valdarfer: *multae quantum* PV^1M, W, Zell: *multa quantum* V^2A, E^1, Gering: *multa quam tum* Paderborn: *multitudinis* Amerbach: *multa equitantum* Testard.

possent: P^3V^2, E^3, N: *possint* C: *possit* P^1M, E^1: *posset* P^2V^1, E^2.

nec praetendere audebant: This is not mentioned in the biblical text, though perhaps it is a fair inference from the description of the dejection in Samaria.

122. Erant autem leprosi quattuor ad portam civitatis: See 4 Ki. 7: 3–9.

mori lucrum: Cf. Phil. 1: 21.

123. Quo indicio egressus est populus . . . abundantiam fecit: A. does not mention the party sent out by the king to reconnoitre first (4 Ki. 7: 10–20).

nuntius ille . . . mortuus est: See 4 Ki. 7: 17–20.

CHAPTER 21: THE HONOURABLE COMES FIRST IN TRUE FRIENDSHIP

24. Quid Esther regina . . . nec immitis regis trepidavit furorem?: See Esth. 4 ff. (note especially 4: 16). The king is generally thought to be Xerxes I (486/5–465 BC). Esther revealed to him the plot of his favourite official Haman (uncovered by her cousin Mordecai) to massacre the Jews. On Esther's courage, cf. the similar example of Judith in 3.82–5, 88.

ei qui: Haman.

suasisset: Cic. *Off.* 3.109 has *suasor* and *suasit*.

Denique quem . . . cruci tradidit: Haman was hanged on the gallows he had had prepared for Mordecai (Esth. 7).

125. **Ea enim amicitia probabilis . . . praeferenda sane opibus honoribus potestatibus:** Cf. Cic. *Off.* 3.43: *Quae enim videntur utilia, honores divitiae voluptates, cetera generis eiusdem, haec amicitiae numquam anteponenda sunt* (also Cic. *Off.* 3.46; *Amic.* 63). On **probabilis**, cf. 1.75, 144; also 1.74, 84, *nec/non probo*; 1.150, *probanda*; 3.45, *nequaquam probandi*. Haman's friendship was the wrong kind, because he put his own interests above *honestas* and advised the king to do *tam indecora* (3.124). Xerxes himself had the proper approach: what is right must come before everything else.

sequi: See on 3.84.

Qualis fuit Ionathae . . . nec salutis periculum refugiebat: See 1 Ki. 20, especially 20: 30 ff. For the language, 3.56, 88–90 above.

Qualis fuit Ahimelech . . . fugientis amici subeundam arbitrabatur: Ahimelech the priest showed hospitality to the fugitive David and his men, and provided David with Goliath's sword (1 Ki. 21: 1–9). He incurred the wrath of Saul when Doeg the Edomite informed the king of his action, and Ahimelech and the other priests of the Lord were put to death (1 Ki. 22: 9–23). On the duties of hospitality, cf. 1.167; 2.103–8. Cic. *Off.* 3.43 speaks of *officii in amicitiis*.

3.125–38

A. evokes Cic.'s discussion in *Off.* 3.43–6 of the apparent *utilitas* of friends versus the demands of justice. This provides a cue for a lengthy exposition of the virtues and obligations of *amicitia*, which occupies almost all of the rest of the work (3.125–38). Friendship is an important ideal for A.: it has already been mentioned or implied several times (1.167, 171–4, and 2.36–7, drawing on Cic. *Off.* 1.55–6 and 2.30–1; cf. also A. *Off.* 1.207; 2.103–8 (hospitality); 3.80–1). Cic.'s *Off.* remains significant to the ensuing passage, and there is evocation of it in 3.127, 134–5; there are no good grounds, then, for picturing 3.125–38 as stemming from an originally independent homily. But A.'s enthusiasm (and the practical realities which drive it; see below) takes him far beyond the bounds of *Off.* 3.43–6, to draw extensively on another of Cic.'s works, the celebrated *Laelius* (De Amicitia). *Amic.* embraces elements of orthodox Stoic thought, which saw friendship as based on wisdom or virtue, and upon shared interests rather than *utilitas* in the first instance (*pace* Epicurean perspectives); the spokesman, Gaius Laelius, epitomizes the proverbially virtuous Stoic gentleman enjoying an unselfish friendship with someone more distinguished than himself, the great Scipio Aemilianus. The work also reflects an Aristotelian ideal that friendship is a bond between those who are one in goodness and virtue (*EN* 1155^{a}3–1172^{a}15; see Guthrie vi. 384–90); the principle is evidence of Cic.'s reading in Peripatetic sources, above all Theophrastus. Its most famous statement is the capsule definition of friendship in *Amic.* 20: *Est enim amicitia nihil aliud nisi omnium divinarum humanarumque rerum cum benevolentia et caritate consensio.* Strangely enough, A. (unlike Augustine: *C. Acad.* 3.13; *Ep.* 258.1) never mentions this phrase. As in his use of Cic.'s *Off.*, he works from memory, and his reminiscences are *ad hoc* rather than organized. On the classical background generally, see D. Konstan, *Friendship in the Classical World* (Cambridge, 1997); J.-C. Fraisse, *Philia: La notion d'amitié dans la philosophie antique* (Paris, 1974); on *amicitia* in Cic.'s time especially, see P. A. Brunt, ' "Amicitia" in the Late Roman Republic', *PCPhS* 191 (1965), 1–20, especially 1–8 (also in R. Seager, *The Crisis of the Roman Republic* (Cambridge, 1969) and in Brunt's *The Fall of the Roman Republic* (Oxford, 1988)); on *Amic.*, see M. Seyffert and C. F. W. Müller (eds.), *Laelius: De amicitia dialogus* (Hildesheim, 1965).

Christian ideals of friendship have been much studied. The fourth century appears to be something of a golden age for seeing how good these ideals looked in practice: the famous relationships of Basil and Gregory of Nazianzus, Paulinus of

Nola and Sanctus and Amandus, or Augustine and Alypius all seem to provide differing models of Christian *amicitia* in action. Our access to these figures is nevertheless conditioned by the literary conventions within which their relationships are presented, and by the varying intellectual and moral strategies of the writers: it is not necessarily possible to 'read off' straightforward construals of the dynamics of such friendships from the carefully controlled *personae* of letters, poems, or reflective journals. Christian authors tend to work with some fairly standard themes. They typically contrast the intimacy of love shared by believers with the shallower feeling which they take to characterize non-Christian friendships (e.g. A. *Ep.* 17 [81].7). Christians are said to love one another in accordance with God's electing grace; their *caritas* is seen as a reflection of the ἀγάπη of God himself—so much so that their active benevolence extends even to their enemies (cf. such passages as Aug. *Conf.* 4.4–9; Paul. Nol. *Epp.* 3.1; 40.2). In reading of Christian friendship, we are thus dealing with a tantalizing combination of the real and the idealized: the realities of human relationships with all their emotional flux are refracted through categories drawn variously from the classical past and from Scripture, all combined to celebrate the profundity of the Christian life as superior to every alternative. On the Christian context generally, see K. Treu, 'Freundschaft', *RAC* viii. 418–34 (with, amazingly, just a fleeting reference to *Off.*); G. Vansteenberghe, 'Amitié', *DSp* i. 500–29, especially 501–18. The most accessible survey is White; see also L. F. Pizzolato, *L'idea di amicizia nel mundo antico classico e cristiano* (Turin, 1993), 269–75; Konstan, *Friendship in the Classical World*, 149–73. E. Carmichael, 'Friendship: A Way of Interpreting Christian Love. A Study of the Western Christian Tradition', D.Phil. Diss. (Oxford, 1990), is also useful for the bigger picture. A helpful anthology of some of the key Western patristic passages can be found in L. F. Pizzolato, *L' amicizia cristiana. Antologia dalle opere di Agostino di Ippona, e altri testi di Ambrogio di Milano, Gerolamo e Paulino di Nola* (Turin, 1973 with *Off.* at 129–42). Paulinus of Nola is discussed by P. Fabre *Saint Paulin de Nole et l'amitié chrétienne* (Paris, 1949), 137–54 on Augustine, see M. A. McNamara, *Friendship in Saint Augustine* (Fribourg, 1958), especially 193–225.

A.'s correspondence illustrates the challenges of interpreting *amicitia* in this context. On the one hand, there is plenty of evidence which suggests that he enjoyed genuinely close fellowship with a number of Christian associates. One relationship at least, with a man called Priscus, who served as a trustworthy go-between and deliverer of the bishop's correspondence to and from Rome, had evidently survived from childhood (*Epp.* 41–2 [86, 88]). His letters to Sabinus of Piacenza in particular are couched in warm and intimate tones, and speak of his gratitude for his friend's help as a proofreader and critic of his written work (cf. *Epp.* 34, 39, 37, 32–3 [45–9], 27 [58]). Sabinus proved a loyal ally in critical moments, serving A. well at the Council of Aquileia in 381. Felix of Como can be thanked for a gift of truffles (*Ep.* 43 [3]; cf. *Ep.* 5 [4].1), and Eusebius of Bologna (probably not an aristocratic layman, *pace* Ihm, 53; Homes Dudden ii. 696 n. 7, but the bishop referred to in *Virgt.* 129, and another staunch supporter at Aquileia: Palanque, 470; McLynn, 66 n. 46) entrusted his three grandchildren to A.'s care while they were being schooled in Milan (*Epp.* 26, 38 [54–5]—with perhaps a predictable outcome: one of them, a girl called Ambrosia, ended up taking the veil in 392: cf. *Inst. virg.* 1–15). A. also maintained an obvious affection for his erstwhile tutor and ultimate successor, Simplicianus (cf. *Epp.* 7 [37], 10 [38], 2 [65], 3 [67]; Aug. *Conf.* 8.2.3; Paul. *VA* 46), and it is no surprise to see him on respectful terms with the distinguished Paulinus of Nola (cf. Paulinus' *Ep.* 3.4, and A.'s *Ep.* 27 [58]; none of their correspondence, however, survives).[1]

On the other hand, there are other examples of apparent closeness which need to be treated with caution. Some of A.'s language, like that of his obituary letter for Acholius of Thessalonica (*Ep.* 51 [15]) is essentially formal, a deliberate attempt to claim a special bond with a spiritual leader whom he had, in fact, met only once (at the council of Rome in 382, when A., confined to a sickbed at the house of his sister Marcellina, was visited by Acholius, and shared a tearful session with him

---

[1] His relationship with Satyrus as pictured in *Exc. fr.* 1 also seems to have been close, even allowing for the formalities of funereal grief in the style of his rhetoric.

in sombre reflection on the evils of the age: *Ep.* 51 [15].10). In
the case of non-Christian correspondents in particular, courtesy of style is no indication of true intimacy. A.'s relations
with Symmachus, for example, were based firmly on the
civilities of mutual self-interest rather than any clear affection:
each could use the other to serve the causes of his respective
acquaintances and clients in Milan and Rome (McLynn,
263–9). Letter-writing offered a way of claiming friendships
with quite casual acquaintances, while avoiding the potential
embarrassments of genuine self-revelation (Fabre, *Saint Paulin
de Nole et l'amitié chrétienne*, 387–90; P. Brown, *Augustine of
Hippo: A Biography* (London, 1967), 160–1).

It is not always easy, then, to gauge from A.'s language of
amicitia how much is genuine affinity and how much is stylized
epistolary convention, the technique of a leader who knows that
his ends are best met by impressionable satellites and useful
associates when presented as tender brotherly counsel. As with
many powerful public figures in every age, the sheer pace of
A.'s life, and his need to differentiate true friends from false,
perhaps left him a slightly lonelier figure than his rhetoric
might imply. Not all of those who did his bidding or solicited
his advice can have counted him as a true confidant, however
affectionately he addressed them. Supporters, admirers, and
attendants were never necessarily boon-companions. In the
end, the prosaic reality doubtless is that A., like most people,
possessed bonds of varying intensity: a few friends, it seems, to
whom he was truly close; many more with whom his relations
were formally polite and pleasant, but essentially shallow. The
depth of the cordiality he expresses can only be determined
according to context.

The paragraphs which follow here are among the best known
of the work, and have often been anthologized as an example of
early Christian delight in the glories of friendship. Their
immediate literary and historical setting has, however, too
often been ignored. A. is not interested in sketching an
intellectual analysis of *amicitia* as a philosophical entity or a
social phenomenon. Ostensibly, he does set out to prove that
the scriptural portrayal of friendship and the scriptural insistence on the primacy of the *honestum* settle all the debates of the
philosophical casuists about the relative status of circumstan-

tial advantages *vis-à-vis* essential goodness. He is concerned with what should and should not be done in the interests of 'true' (or honourable) friendship; the temptations to elevate friendship over the *honestum* are seen to stem from a false conception of what friendship really is: when the honourable comes first and friendship second, friendship itself is right. But the substance of the argument is a typical combination of the piecemeal and the platitudinous, of secular and sacred authorities evoked side by side. No overall definition of friendship is offered at all, and much of what A. does say is not distinctively Christian in any strict sense. In rejecting any sort of utilitarian or contractual basis for friendship (3.134), he agrees with Peripatetic and Stoic sentiments; in exhorting his addressees to pursue the ideal of being one in both joy and sorrow (3.129–32), he is developing an argument which goes back to Plato (cf. the cohesion of society as the result of a ἡδονῆς τε καὶ λύπης κοινωνία in *Rep.* 462b). The sharing of secrets (3.129, 132, 136), the altruistic correction of a friend's faults (3.128, 133–4), the avoidance of flattery (3.134–5), and the necessity for faithfulness (3.128, 129–31,137) are all *topoi*, obligations which Cic. likewise commends in *Amic.* Other than the quotation from Eccli. 6: 16 in 3.129 (*'Fidelis' enim 'amicus medicamentum est vitae', immortalitatis gratia*), the closest we get to a summary delineation of what it means to call someone a friend may be the words of 3.134: *Qui est enim amicus nisi consors amoris, ad quem animum tuum adiungas atque applices et ita misceas ut unum velis fieri ex duobus, cui te alteri tibi committas, a quo nihil timeas, nihil ipse commodi tui causa inhonestum petas?* Once again, however, the formula simply evokes Ciceronian phrases (see ad loc.). Unlike Augustine or Paulinus of Nola, A. makes no overt distinction between natural human *amicitia* and the unity of believers who have come to share in God's grace. In short, to say that A. 'speaks of friendship with something of the old pre-Christian enthusiasm' (Homes Dudden ii. 532–3; also Thamin, 229–30; Fabre, *Saint Paulin de Nole et l'amitié chrétienne*, 152–4) is to put it mildly.

There is, of course, a Christian texture to his presentation, but it consists largely in the piling up of texts and stock illustrations of scriptural *amicitia*, rather than in a thoroughgoing Christianizing of the characterization of friendship as such. It comes as no surprise to read of the friendship of Jonathan and of Ahimelech for David (3.125); of the relations of Saul and Jonathan, and of the three Hebrew youths in Daniel (3.132); of the failure of Job's friends (3.131, 138); of the treachery of Judas Iscariot (3.137); and of the intimacy between Jesus and his disciples (3.136). We expect the usual attempts to validate Ciceronian sentiments in the Wisdom literature, the Psalms, and the gospels. A. does claim that *fides* towards God is indispensable to showing *fides* towards fellow-men (3.133), and he claims that *qui facit mandata Dei amicus est, et hoc honoratur nomine* (3.137). 3.136 speaks of friendship as shared by angels and men, and 3.137 of Christ setting the example of friendship for his followers. Friendship with God through Christ is naturally said to be the ultimate dimension (3.136: *forma amicitiae quam sequamur*). This paradigm clearly offers a potentially more profound exploration of the theme (see ad loc.), but it is not developed very far. On the whole, A. simply elides classical and Christian registers. For example, *consors amoris* in 3.134 (cf. also *amor* in 3.132) uses a common Ciceronian word for love, while under biblical influence *amor* is elsewhere a virtual synonym for Christian *caritas* (Pétré, 81–5). Or again, the insincerity of the friendship typically shown to the rich is compared in 3.135 with the genuine love bestowed on the poor (from whom no material reward can be expected). The point is made by Laelius, but A.'s reproduction of it is probably infused by his habitual association of physical poverty and spiritual worth, in contrast to the spiritual bankruptcy of those who enjoy affluence in this world (cf. 1.59). A. never works out the respective claims or the relative merits of the secular and the Christian ideals; he simply slides from one world to the other, and does not seize the chance to assess the relationship between them.

His concern is, in fact, highly practical, and to that end, typically, the philosophical principles are assumed rather than explored. His clerical 'sons' are exhorted to maintain the *initam cum fratribus amicitiam, qua nihil est in rebus humanis pulchrius* (3.132). The primary focus is on promoting the cohesion of the ecclesiastical brotherhood. It is this, far more than any real appeal to idealized familiarity, which shapes the argument (D. Konstan, 'Problems in the History of Christian Friendship', *JECS* 4 (1996), 87–113, at 106 ff.). The alert reader will detect the cumulative import of the references to deserting *fides* (3.126—albeit with reference to the philosophers' *quaestiones*); to testifying against a friend in a *Dei causa* (3.127); to putting *religio* first (3.127); to encouraging one another *in persecutionibus* (3.132); to the evils of *perfidia* (3.137); to infidelity towards God (3.133); and to the need for constancy, not least in adversity (3.128–31). A. knew all about pressure, and about clerics deserting their *ordo* (cf. 1.72, 188, 256). No doubt he had experienced problems with clergy stabbing one another in the back or abandoning the cause in search of alternative preferments elsewhere. His pleas for honesty and openness, for humility and concord; his denunciations of those who betray their brethren; his insistence that friends may have to endure transferred *opprobrium*—all imply a determination to lay down firm parameters for a *presbyterium* still affected by some lingering personal tensions. Certainly A. had been able to implement significant changes within his hierarchy, and he is able in *Off.* to address young clerics who have been part of his staff through their formative years (or who are still at such a stage) [Introduction VII (ii)]. The overall loyalty of his men may be reasonably secure; nevertheless, there is doubtless still plenty of scope for internecine rivalries, petty jealousies, and quests for one-upmanship among them (cf. 2.119–23).

It is no accident, then, that A. chooses to round off his treatise with a direct and sustained appeal for unity. As with his earlier emphases on corporate harmony, his concern is to mould his clergy into an integrated force. Many conventional classical maxims about companionship remain, to his mind, perspicuously true; in the interests of pragmatism, they are merged with Christian principles about the importance of mutual love and cooperation within the believing community. Here we find *in nuce* the vision of a clerical body living and working as one, determined to do what is right, and (A. hopes) then finding that the benefit of added social impact and secular esteem follows. For all the attractiveness of much of what A. commends, the pattern of *amicitia* here is not primarily to do with a pleasant world of small-scale intimacy: it is a lifestyle objective for a church leadership that is being called to show the world what it is about.

From the considerable body of literature, the following are pertinent: E. Boularand, 'L'amitié d'après saint Ambroise, dans le De officiis ministrorum, Lib. III, Cap. XXI–XXII', *BLE* 73 (1972), 103–23; M. D. Diederich, 'Cicero and Saint Ambrose on Friendship', *CJ* 43 (1948), 219–22; C. Peroni, 'Amicizia e mistero cristiano in s. Ambrogio', *La Scuola Cattolica* 102 (1974), 429–50 (part of the fruit of Peroni's dissertation, 'L'amicizia in sant'Ambrogio', Università Cattolicà del Sacro Cuore, Milan, Anno Accad. 1970–1); L. F. Pizzolato, 'L'amicizia nel *De officiis* di sant'Ambrogio e il *Laelius* di Cicerone: tradizione lessicale e originalità ideologica', in *Ricerche storiche sulla Chiesa ambrosiana, nel XVI centenario del l'episcopato di s. Ambrogio* iv (Milan, 1974), 53–67; id. *L'idea di amicizia nel mondo antico classico e cristiano* (Turin, 1993), 269–75; Sauer, 184–91; Carmichael, 'Friendship', 97–122; White, 111–28. Pizzolato and Boularand argue that A. subtly transforms the classical nuances, but White is essentially persuasive in her argument that A.'s perspective remains close to Cic.'s.

CHAPTER 22: THE RESPONSIBILITIES AND
DELIGHTS OF FRIENDSHIP; CONCLUSION TO
THE WORK

126. **scriptura admonet:** E², CNB: *scriptura admonet de amicitia* most MSS and editors; *de amicitia* is redundant in the wake of **amicitiae studio** just previously.
**Sunt enim pleraeque philosophorum quaestiones . . .
dum indulget atque intendit amici commoditatibus:** *quaestiones* are mentioned by Cic. in *Off.* 3.50 and 3.89; A. is thinking particularly of *Off.* 3.43: *At neque contra rempublicam neque contra iusiurandum ac fidem amici causa vir bonus faciet.* On *fides,* cf. 3.133 below. In *Amic.* 36–7, Laelius argues that it would have been wrong for friends to help (say) Coriolanus in his attack on his own land, or to assist other aspiring despots of the fifth century BC; it was right that the tribune Tiberius Gracchus was deserted by his friends in 133 BC. For A., such *quaestiones* (cf. *Off.* 3.43–6 generally) are implicitly settled by **scriptura** (cf. 3.127 as

well); for the point, cf. 2.8; 3.97. On **fidem deserat**, cf. 1.72
and see ad loc.; 1.188, 256.

127. *Clava et gladius . . . adversus amicum suum*: Prov.
25: 18.

**Quid enim si Dei causa . . . aliquis dicere testimo-
nium?**: Responsibility to God and responsibility to one's
country must come before the claims of friendship; cf. 1.127
(and see ad loc.), where the order of priority is: *Deus, patria,
parentes, omnes.* A. brackets the cause of God and patriotism
together on the scale of important responsibilities here; cf.
1.144; and, on patriotism generally, 1.254; 3.23, 82–5. On
Dei causa, see on 2.125.

**Numquid praeponderare debet amicitia . . . caritati
civium?**: Cf. Cic. *Off.* 3.46: *Cum autem in amicitia quae
honesta non sunt postulabuntur, religio et fides anteponatur
amicitiae.* For A., **religioni** clearly means 'religion', not
'scruple', in the light of **Dei causa** above: the Ciceronian
sense is altered. Cic. speaks of Regulus' *caritas patriae* in *Off.*
3.100.

neque innocenti insidiari: Cf. such verses as Prov. 1: 11
and 24: 15.

128. **si quid in amico vitii cognoverit . . . corripere
palam**: Cf. Mt. 18: 15–17: *Si autem peccaverit in te frater
tuus, vade et corripe eum inter te et ipsum solum: si te audierit,
lucratus es fratrem tuum. Si autem non te audierit, adhibe
tecum adhuc unum vel duos, ut in ore duorum testium vel trium
stet omne verbum. Quod si non audierit, dic ecclesiae. Si autem
et ecclesiam non audierit, sit tibi sicut ethnicus et publicanus.*
(Cf. Lk. 17: 3.) On the administering of rebukes in friendship, cf. Cic. *Off.* 1.58; *Amic.* 44, and especially 88–91; A.
1.173; 3.133–4. On the value of correction generally, cf.
Prov. 10: 17; 12: 1; 13: 18; 15: 5, 10, 31–2; 17: 10; 28: 23.

Tolerabiliora sunt . . . quam adulantum oscula: Prov.
27: 6.

**Constans enim debet esse amicitia, perseverare in
adfectu**: On *constantia* in friendship, cf. Cic. *Amic.* 33,
and especially 62–5.

non puerili modo . . . debemus sententia: Cf. Cic. *Amic.*
33–4 (also 74), where it is said that the friendships of *pueri*
(33) often do not last beyond the age of taking the *toga*

praetexta, i.e. sixteen. Instability in friendship is a mark of youthful immaturity. In Cic. *Amic.* 67–8, Laelius says that it may sometimes be right to prefer new friends to older ones, but only if the new ones are worthy. On the fickleness of *pueri*, cf. 1.93 above.

129.   **Aperi pectus tuum amico, ut fidelis sit tibi:** Cf. Cic. *Amic.* 97: *In qua nisi, ut dicitur, apertum pectus videas tuumque ostendas, nihil fidum, nihil exploratum habeas, ne amare quidem aut amari, cum id quam vere fiat ignores.* For the proverbial *apertum pectus videas*, cf. Sen. *Ep.* 59.9; Plin. *Ep.* 6.12.3.

Fidelis enim amicus medicamentum est vitae, immortalitatis gratia: Cf. Eccli. 6: 16.

Defer amico ut aequali . . . amicitia enim nescit superbiam: In Cic. *Amic.* 64, it is said that one who prefers his friend's *honor* to his own is hard to find, and that it is also rare for people to lower themselves to associate with the unsuccessful; cf. also 3.133 below. A.'s stress on avoiding pride and resentment may again suggest that he is addressing a particular tension within the ranks of his clergy; cf. 2.119–23.

Amicum salutare non erubescas: Eccli. 22: 25 (31).

Nec deseras amicum . . . neque destituas: Cf. Cic. *Amic.* 64, on those who *in malis deserunt* their friends; on the advantages of sharing troubles, cf. *Amic.* 22. Cf. also 2.37 above.

Ideo in ea onera portamus, sicut apostolus docuit: [**in ea onera**: P²V, EW, Amerbach, Testard: *ea onera* P¹A: *onera* CNB, Zell: *in eius onera ut* Valdarfer; **portamus** PVA, EW, Zell, Lignamine, Testard: *portemus* CNB, other editors] Cf. Gal. 6: 2.

eiusdem . . . caritas: The friendship of Paul's addressees and the friendship of the Milanese clergy are of a piece: A. again evokes the continuity theme (cf. 1.184, and Introduction IV.4).

secundae res . . . in adversis . . . rebus: See on 1.200; Cic. has *in adversis rebus* in *Amic.* 22.

consilio: Cf. Cic. *Off.* 1.58.

130.   *Et si mala mihi evenerint . . . sustineo:* Eccli. 22: 26 (31).

In adversis enim amicus probatur; nam in prosperis amici omnes videntur: Cf. Cic. *Amic.* 64, on those who *aut si in bonis rebus contemnunt aut in malis deserunt.* A. may well also be thinking of Prov. 17: 17: *Omni tempore diligit qui amicus est, et frater in angustiis comprobatur* (cf. too Eccli. 12: 8–9).

auctoritas: Cicero uses the word in *Amic.* 44.

131. **Miseremini mei, amici, miseremini:** Job 19: 21.
Job's friends ought to have shown him compassion in his sufferings, instead of rebuking him. Rather than imploring their pity, he criticizes them for their failure to behave as friends should.

132. **Servate igitur, filii, initam cum fratribus amicitiam:** Vital to understanding the point of the whole development: the *amicitia* A. has in mind is precisely the cohesion of the clerical body; cf. generally 2.155.

qua nihil est in rebus humanis pulchrius: Cf. Cic. *Off.* 1.55–6; *Fin.* 1.65; and especially *Amic.* 47: [sc. *amicitia*] *qua nihil a dis immortalibus melius habemus, nihil iucundius*; 20: *qua quidem haud scio an excepta sapientia nihil melius homini sit a dis immortalibus datum*; cf. also 104.

ut habeas cui pectus aperias tuum: See on 3.129.

cum quo arcana participes, cui committas secretum pectoris tui: Cf. Cic. *Amic.* 22: *Quid dulcius quam habere quicum omnia audeas sic loqui ut tecum?* (also Cic. *Tusc.* 5.72; *Fin.* 2.85; Sen. *Ep.* 3.2; Plin. *Ep.* 5.1.12).

qui in prosperis gratuletur tibi . . . in persecutionibus adhortetur: Cf. Cic. *Amic.* 22: *Qui esset tantus fructus in prosperis rebus nisi haberes qui illis aeque ac tu ipse gauderet? Adversas vero ferre difficile esset sine eo qui illas gravius etiam quam tu ferret. . . . nam et secundas res splendidiores facit amicitia, et adversas partiens communicansque leviores.* **in persecutionibus** adds a Christian dimension to the Ciceronian *adversae res*, and suggests one of the reasons why A. is so keen to encourage unity.

Quam boni amici Hebraei pueri . . . nec fornacis ardentis flamma divisit!: On Shadrach, Meshach, and Abednego, see Dan. 3.

De quo loco superius diximus: Not so. Most probably, A. simply makes a mistake. On the rough edges in his composition generally, see Introduction V.

Saul et Ionatha . . . in morte non sunt separati: 2 Ki. 1: 23.

133. non ut fides propter amicitiam destruatur: Cf. 3.126; and Cic. *Off.* 3.43–4, 46; *Amic.* 65: *Firmamentum autem stabilitatis constantiaeque est, eius quam in amicitia quaerimus, fides: nihil est enim stabile quod infidum est.*

Non potest enim homini amicus esse, qui Deo fuerit infidus: *Fides* in and towards God is the prerequisite for true *fides* among human beings. In *Off.* 3.43–4, Cic. says that a person who is sitting as a judge in his friend's case must remember his oath of integrity, since a god is his witness. For Cic., the god is the person's own *mens*, in which the immanent cosmic *ratio* is present. A.'s idea of divinity is of course radically different. Human reliability is linked to Christian faith—and more than: it is linked to fidelity to the Nicene position. Abandoning friends and abandoning the true faith are all of a piece.

ut superior inferiori . . . inferior superiori: Cf. Cic. *Amic.* 69: *Sed maximum est in amicitia parem esse inferiori;* 71: *Ut igitur ei qui sunt in amicitiae coniunctionisque necessitudine superiores exaequare se cum inferioribus debent, sic inferiores non dolere se a suis aut ingenio aut fortuna aut dignitate superari;* 72: *Quamobrem ut ei, qui superiores sunt, submittere se debent in amicitia, sic quodam modo inferiores extollere.* Cf. 2.119–23; also the example of Mary, the *magistra humilitatis*, in *Luc.* 2.22, coming to Elizabeth.

Inter dispares enim mores non potest esse amicitia: Cf. Cic. *Amic.* 74: *dispares enim mores disparia studia sequuntur, quorum dissimilitudo dissociat amicitias* (also 20, 48, 50, 82); *Off.* 1.56: *Nihil autem est amabilius nec copulatius quam morum similitudo bonorum . . .* [etc.].

nec auctoritas desit inferiori, si res poposcerit: Cf. Cic. *Amic.* 44: *plurimum in amicitia amicorum bene suadentium valeat auctoritas; eaque et adhibeatur ad monendum, non modo aperte sed etiam acriter, si res postulabit, et adhibitae pareatur.*

humilitas: The habitual *desideratum*; see on 1.1.

et ille quasi amicus moneat, obiurget: See on 3.134.

non iactantiae studio: Cf. generally 1.147; 2.2–3, 76, 102, 109–11.

134. Neque monitio aspera sit neque obiurgatio contu-

meliosa: Cf. Cic. *Off.* 1.137: *ut et severitas adhibeatur et contumelia repellatur, atque etiam illud ipsum quod acerbitatis habet obiurgatio, significandum est ipsius id causa qui obiurgetur esse susceptum*; and *Amic.* 88–91, especially 89: *Omni igitur hac in re habenda ratio [et] diligentia est, primum ut monitio acerbitate, deinde ut obiurgatio contumelia careat.*

sicut enim adulationis fugitans amicitia debet esse: On the importance of avoiding flattery, cf. Cic. *Amic.* 89–100; see on 1.209 above, and cf. 1.226; 2.66, 96, 112–20; 3.58, 89.

Qui est enim amicus nisi . . . cui te alteri tibi committas: Cf. Cic. *Amic.* 48: *ad quam se similis animus applicet et adiungat*; 81: *qui et se ipse diligit et alterum anquirit cuius animum ita cum suo misceat ut efficiat paene unum ex duobus*; 80: *verus amicus . . . qui est tamquam alter idem*; 92: *Nam cum amicitiae vis sit in eo ut unus quasi animus fiat ex pluribus.* The idea that a friend is 'another self' is both Aristotelian (*EN* 1166ᵃ; 1170ᵇ6; *EE* 1245ᵃ; *MM* 1213ᵃ; cf. also DL 5.20: a single soul in two bodies) and Stoic (DL 7.23). A. quotes it also in *Spir.* 2.154, where he argues from the unity of friends to the oneness of the Trinity. According to Cic. *Off.* 1.56, *ut unus fiat ex pluribus* is Pythagorean; cf. also *Att.* 3.15.4; 4.1.7; *Fam.* 2.15.4; Plin. *Ep.* 2.9.1.

Non enim vectigalis amicitia est: On friendship not being based on utilitarian greed, cf. Cic. *Amic.* 30–1, 51, 58, attacking an Epicurean idea in particular.

quia non pecunia paritur, sed gratia: Cf. Sall. *Iug.* 10.4. On the shallowness of relationships procured with money, cf. 2.117–18.

sed concertatione benevolentiae: On goodwill as the basis of friendship, see on 1.167; 1.171–4.

135. et frequenter divites sine amicis sunt quibus abundant pauperes: Cf. Cic. *Amic.* 52–5, especially 54: *sic multorum opes praepotentium excludunt amicitias fideles*; also Cic. *Off.* 2.69–71; and see on 2.132 above.

ubi est fallax adulatio: Cf. 3.134.

136. quae angelis communis et hominibus est: Angels and men are linked in 1 Cor. 13: 1, and it is quite likely that the famous celebration of *caritas* in that passage is in A.'s mind in these paragraphs (Boularand, 'L'Amitié d'après saint Ambroise', 122). A. believes in guardian angels (*Ep.* 75a [*C. Aux.*].11; *Expl. Ps. 37.43*; *Expl. Ps. 38.32*; *Expos. Ps. 118.7.36*; also *Spir.* 1.83) and apparently also in prayer to angels (*Ep.* 75a [*C. Aux.*].11; *Vid.* 55). He argues elsewhere that believers should strive to please and befriend angels (*Luc.* 7.210), not least by giving to the poor (*Luc.* 7.245, on Lk. 16: 9, quoted below). Augustine suggests there is a community between Christians and the good angels in their worship of the true God, even though the human worship requires stronger faith (*CD* 8.25). On A.'s angelology, see Homes Dudden ii. 586–9; more generally, G. Bareille, 'Angélologie d'après les Pères', *DTC* i/1. 1192–1222.

Facite vobis amicos . . . qui recipiant vos in aeterna tabernacula sua: Lk. 16: 9.
Ipse nos Deus amicos . . ., sicut ipse ait: Iam vos . . . quae ego praecipio vobis: Cf. Jn. 15: 14–15: *Vos amici mei estis, si feceritis quae ego praecipio vobis. Iam non dico vos servos, quia servus nescit quid facit dominus eius; vos autem dixi amicos, quia omnia quaecumque audivi a Patre meo, nota feci vobis.* Jesus' words are cited as the words of **Ipse . . . Deus**.
Dedit formam amicitiae quam sequamur: On Christ giving his followers an example, cf. Jn. 13: 15; 1 Pt. 2: 21; and 3.15, 27, 36 above. A. may simply be recalling random verses on friendship, but in the process he perhaps hints at a more overt Christocentric foundation for friendship here and in 3.137 than is developed elsewhere in the section. Human intimacy is modelled on the divine self-disclosure of the incarnation. The beneficiaries of incarnational revelation are Christ's friends; yet Christ also knew betrayal by one to whom he had opened his heart. A. encourages closeness within the brotherhood, and underscores the seriousness of deserting the cause; he warns his readers to remember the perfidy of Judas (3.137). He also implicitly reassures his men that if they experience treachery, so did Christ himself. Testard, 'Recherches', 113–14, rightly points out the significance of Jn. 13–17 for A.'s thought in these two paragraphs, but he seems to overstate the spiritual profundity of the ensuing synthesis: given the obvious theological possibilities of the theme, A. does not explore it very far.

ut aperiamus secreta nostra . . . et illius arcana non ignoremus: See on 3.132.

Ostendamus illi . . . et ille nobis aperiat suum: See on 3.129; the practice advocated by Laelius was exemplified by Christ.

Ideo, **inquit,** *vos dixi amicos . . . nota feci vobis:* Jn. 15: 15.

effundit animum suum: On 'pouring out' the heart or soul, cf. Ps. 41: 5, and especially Ps. 61: 9.

sicut effundebat mysteria Patris Dominus Iesus: Cf. Jn. 15: 15, above, and Jn. 1: 18: *Deum nemo vidit umquam; unigenitus Filius, qui est in sinu Patris, ipse enarravit.* On the revelation given by the divine Son, cf. e.g. *Spir.* 2.130; *Expl. Ps. 43.87.*

137. **Ergo qui facit mandata Dei . . . honoratur nomine:** [**mandata:** CNB, Maurists, Krabinger: *mandatum* VA, EW, other editors; **et:** A², E²] Probably A. is thinking of Jn. 14: 15, 21, where Jesus says that the disciple who loves him keeps his commandments. The friend of God in Christ keeps the divine commandments; so too, by implication, does the true friend of man.

Unde in proditorem . . . conviviis amicitiae venenum malitiae miscuerit: [**proditorem:** VA, E¹W, Valdarfer, Scinzenzeler, Marchand, Testard: *proditore* E², CNB, other editors] See Mt. 26: 14–16, 20–5, 47–50; Mk. 14: 10–11, 17–21, 43–6; Lk. 22: 1–6, 21–3, 47–8; Jn. 13: 2, 18–30; 18: 1–11.

conviviis amicitiae of course refers especially to the Last Supper. Judas mixed the *venenum malitiae* with the *dulces cibi* which he shared with Christ:

Tu vero, homo unanimis meus . . . qui semper mecum dulces capiebas cibos: Ps. 54: 14.

Nam si inimicus meus maledixisset mihi . . . qui me oderat, absconderem me: Ps. 54: 13. The interpretation of these verses as referring to Judas is traditional (e.g. Hilar. *Tract. Ps. 54.*13–4; Cassiod. *Expl. Ps. 54.*13–24). Jesus himself applies the similar sentiment of Ps. 40: 10 in this way in Jn. 13: 18.

38. **a tribus regibus:** See on 1.41.

rogavit Iob, et Dominus ignovit: See Job 42: 7–10. Job's

friends failed him (3.131), yet his gracious prayer for them
proved efficacious.

139. The closing paragraph comes abruptly. There is no
indication that the friendship section is over, nor is there
any mention of the *honestum* or the *utile* (contrast Cic. *Off.*
3.118–20). The *honestum* is last mentioned in 3.125–6; the
utile disappears after 3.90. A. rounds off his work hurriedly,
more interested in its practical import than in establishing a
sustained conclusion to a philosophical argument. His last
words are, however, revealing. There are three main features
to notice:

First of all (although, incredibly, commentators appear
not to have noticed it), A. is clearly evoking Cic.'s final
paragraph, *Off.* 3.121: *Habes a patre munus, Marce fili, mea
quidem sententia magnum, sed perinde erit ut acceperis. Quamquam hi tibi tres libri inter Cratippi commentarios tamquam
hospites erunt recipiendi.* The bishop's *filii* again replace Cic.'s
filius, Marcus (cf. 1.24). The *tres libri* are mentioned by both
authors. A.'s estimation of the merits of his work is different,
however: while Cic. calls his treatise a *munus . . . magnum*,
A. returns to the self-depreciation which we find in 1.1–4,
29, 116, with **si sermo nihil deferat gratiae**. This may
reflect a degree of conventional modesty (not to say a candid
awareness that structurally the work is hardly all that it
might be: Testard, 'Etude', 191), but, as in the *praefatio*,
the main aim is to provide a contrast with Cic.'s self-
assurance, and to make a specific statement about what the
treatise is intended to be. The literate reader will appreciate
just how different the text is from its classical ancestor, and
needs to understand that he or she is seeing the *humilitas* of
Christian morality in action. As A. began, so he ends.

Secondly, A. adopts a quasi-apostolic *persona*. While Cic.
describes his work as a *munus* to his son, A. thinks of his as a
deposit to be guarded. This is reminiscent of Paul's words to
his 'son' Timothy; cf. 1 Tim. 6: 20: *O Timothee, depositum
custodi*; 2 Tim. 1: 14: *Bonum depositum custodi.* Like a deposit
of the mysteries of the faith, A.'s counsel is entrusted to his
faithful family, so that they may learn from its spiritual
instruction. This biblical teaching is 'handed down' or
'passed on' to them to be faithfully kept (cf. 1.2–3). **Custo**

diatis also chimes in with the language of the introduction (cf. 1.6–7, 9–11, 14, 19).

Thirdly, A.'s parting shot is on the importance of biblical *exempla*, and their value as a pattern from the ancient past—the same emphasis which has been at the core of his didactic approach throughout (cf. 1.116, and see Introduction IV.4); cf. Rom. 15: 4. Having put together a **series . . . vetustatis** (cf. *Expos. Ps. 118*.7.15; on **quodam compendio**, cf. 3.72) of the words and deeds of characters, good and bad, from almost every part of Scripture, he wishes these to be the abiding study of those who desire to please God by their *officia*. The closing sentiment is, as Testard, 'Etude', 190–1, rightly says, much less banal than it may appear: the moral lessons to be learned from the scriptural figures are presented as the bishop's ultimate concern. Cic. urges Marcus to study his father's work in tandem with his notes from the lectures of his mentor Cratippus; A. asserts that the worth of *his* three books lies in their presentation of biblical illustrations, which have the weight of greater antiquity on their side than pagan wisdom can muster. It is to Scripture that A. has sought to direct his readers from the start, and it is Scripture that is meant to triumph over Cic. in the end.

SELECT BIBLIOGRAPHY

AA. VV., *Sant'Ambrogio nel XVI centenario della nascita*, Pubblicazioni dell'Universita Cattolica del S. Cuore, ser. 5, Scienze Storiche, 18 (Milan, 1940).

AA. VV., *L'etica cristiana nei secoli III e IV: eredità e confronti. XXIV Incontro di studiosi dell'antichità cristiana, Roma, 4–6 maggio 1995*, Studia Ephemeridis Augustinianum, 53 (Rome, 1996).

AA. VV., *Vescovi e pastori in epoca teodosiana. In occasione del XVI centenario della consacrazione episcopale di s. Agostino, 396–1996. XXV Incontro di studiosi dell'antichità cristiana, Roma, 8–11 maggio 1996*, Studia Ephemeridis Augustinianum, 58, 2 vols. (Rome, 1997).

ADKIN, N., 'A Problem in the Early Church: Noise during Sermon and Lesson', *Mnemosyne*, 38 (1985), 161–3.

—— 'Jerome, Ambrose and Gregory Nazianzen (Jerome, *Epist.* 52, 7–8)', *Vichiana*, 4 (1993), 294–300.

ALEXANDER, W. H., 'Hic aquatio: Cicero, *De officiis* III.14–59', *Classical Journal*, 36 (1941), 290–3.

ALFONSI, L., 'Ambrogio "Ciceronianus"', *Vigiliae Christianae*, 20 (1966), 83–5.

AMATI, A., 'Nuovi studi su s. Ambrogio: La proprietà', *Rendiconti del R. Istituto Lombardo di Scienze e Lettere* 2nd ser. 30 (1897), 764–85.

ANDRÉ, J.-M., *Recherches sur l'otium romain*, Annales littéraires de l'Université de Besançon, 62 (Paris, 1962).

—— *L'otium dans la vie intellectuelle et morale romaine, des origines à l'époque augustéenne*, Publications de la faculté des lettres et sciences humaines de Paris, série 'recherches', 30 (Paris, 1966).

ANDRESEN, C., 'Altchristliche Kritik am Tanz. Ein Ausschnitt aus dem Kampf der alten Kirche gegen heidnische Sitte', in H. Frohnes and U. W. Knorr (eds.), *Kirchengeschichte als Missionsgechichte*, 1: *Die alte Kirche* (Munich, 1974), 344–76.

ANNAS, J., 'Cicero on Stoic Moral Philosophy and Private Property', in M. Griffin and J. Barnes (eds.), *Philosophia Togata: Essays on Philosophy and Roman Society* (Oxford, 1989), 151–73.

ARBESMANN, R., 'The Concept of Christus Medicus in St Augustine', *Traditio*, 10 (1954), 1–28.

—— 'Fasten', *Reallexikon für Antike und Christentum*, vii (1969), 471–93.

ARNHEIM, M. T. W., *The Senatorial Aristocracy in the Later Roman Empire* (Oxford, 1972).

ARNS, E. P., *La Technique du livre d'après saint Jérôme* (Paris, 1953).

AUDET, J.-P., *Mariage et célibat dans le service pastorale de l'Eglise. Histoire et orientations* (Paris, 1967).

AUGAR, F., *Die Frau in römischen Christenprocess*, Texte und Untersuchungen zur Geschichte der altchristlichen Literatur, N.F. 13/4 (Leipzig and Berlin, 1905).

AVILA, C., *Ownership: Early Christian Teaching* (Maryknoll, NY and London, 1983).

AYMARD, J., *Essai sur les chasses romaines, des origines à la fin du siècle des Antonins (Cynégetica)*, Bibliotheque des écoles françaises d'Athènes et de Rome, 171 (Paris, 1951).

BACONSKY, T., *Le Rire des Pères. Essai sur le rire dans la patristique grecque*, Théophanie (Paris, 1996).

BADURA, M., *Die leitenden Grundsätze der Morallehre des hl. Ambrosius* (Prague, 1921).

BANKERT, D. A., WEGMANN, J., and WRIGHT, C. D., *Ambrose in Anglo-Saxon England, with Pseudo-Ambrose and Ambrosiaster*, Old English Newsletter, Subsidia, 25 (1997).

BANNIARD, M., Viva voce. *Communication écrite et communication orale du IVe au IXe siècle en Occident Latin*, Collection des études augustiniennes, série Moyen Âge et Temps modernes, 25 (Paris, 1992).

—— 'Niveaux de langue et communication latinophone d'après et chez Ambroise', in L. F. Pizzolato and M. Rizzi (eds.), *Nec timeo mori* (Milan, 1998), 513–36.

BANTERLE, G., *Sant'Ambrogio: Opere Morali I—I Doveri: Introduzione, traduzione e note*, Sancti Ambrosii Episcopi Mediolanensis Opera, 13 (Milan and Rome, 1977).

BARDENHEWER, O., *Geschichte der altchristlichen Literatur*, iii: *Das vierte Jahrhundert mit Ausschluss der Schriftsteller syrischer Zunge* (Freiburg, 1923).

BARDY, G., 'Traducteurs et adaptateurs au quatrième siècle', *Recherches de science religieuse*, 30 (1940), 257–306.

BAREILLE, G., 'Angélologie d'après les Pères', *Dictionnaire de théologie catholique* i/1 (1909), 1192–1222.

Bar-Kochva, B., *Judas Maccabaeus: The Jewish Struggle against the Seleucids* (Cambridge, 1989).

BARNES, M. R., and WILLIAMS, D. H. (eds.), *Arianism after Arius Essays on the Development of the Fourth-Century Trinitarian Conflicts* (Edinburgh, 1993).

BARONIUS, C., *Annales Ecclesiastici*, v (Lucca, 1739).

BARRY, M. F., *The Vocabulary of the Moral-Ascetical Works of Saint Ambrose: A Study in Latin Lexicography*, Catholic University of America Patristic Studies, 10 (Washington, DC, 1926).

BARTELINK, G., 'Sprachliche und stilistische Bemerkungen in Ambrosius' Schriften', *Wiener Studien*, 92 (1979), 175–202.

—— 'Quelques observations sur les dénominations du diable et des démons chez saint Ambroise et Jérôme', in G. Bartelink, A. Hilhorst, and C. H. Kneepkens (eds.), *Eulogia: Mélanges offerts à Antoon A. R. Bastiaensen*, Instrumenta Patristica, 24 (The Hague, 1991), 1–10.

BARTELINK, G. J. M., ' "Fragilitas humana" chez saint Ambroise', in G Lazzati (ed.), *Ambrosius Episcopus*, 2 vols. (Milan, 1976), ii. 130–42.

BARTON, T. S., *Power and Knowledge: Astrology, Physiognomics, and Medicine under the Roman Empire*, The Body, in Theory: Histories of Cultural Materialism (Ann Arbor, MI, 1994).

BASKIN, J. R., 'Job as Moral Exemplar in Ambrose', *Vigiliae Christianae*, 35 (1981), 222–31.

BAUNARD, L., *Histoire de saint Ambroise*, 2nd edn. (Paris, 1872).

BAUS, K., *Das Gebet zu Christus beim hl. Ambrosius: Eine frömmig-keitsgeschichtliche Untersuchung* (Trier, 1952).

CANTALAMESSA, R. *et al.* (eds.), *Cento Anni di Bibliografia Ambrosiana (1874–1974)*, Studia Patristica Mediolanensia, 11 (Milan, 1981).

BECKER, M., *Die Kardinaltugenden bei Cicero und Ambrosius: De officiis*, Chrêsis: Die Methode der Kirchenväter im Umgang mit der antiken Kultur, 4 (Basle, 1994).

BERTON, R., 'Abraham dans le *De officiis ministrorum* d'Ambroise', *Revue des sciences religieuses*, 54 (1980), 311–22.

BEUGNET, A., 'Aumône', *Dictionnaire de Théologie Catholique*, i/2 (1909), 2561–71.

BIERMANN, M., *Die Leichenreden des Ambrosius von Mailand. Rhetorik, Predigt, Politik*, Hermes Einzelschriften, Heft 70 (Stuttgart, 1995).

BIONDI, B., *Il diritto romano cristiano*, 3 vols. (Milan, 1952–4).

BITTNER, F., *De Ciceronianis et Ambrosianis officiorum libris commentatio* (Braunsberg, 1849).

BLACKMAN, E. C., *Marcion and his Influence* (London, 1948).

BLUM, H., *Die antike Mnemotechnik* (Hildesheim, 1969).

BOGAERT, R., 'Changeurs et banquiers chez les Pères de l'Eglise', *Ancient Society*, 4 (1973), 239–70.

BONATO, A., 'L'idea del sacerdozio in s. Ambrogio', *Augustinianum*, 27 (1987), 423–64.

BONNER, C., 'Desired Haven', *Harvard Theological Review*, 34 (1941), 49–67.

BOTTOMLEY, F., *Attitudes to the Body in Western Christendom* (London, 1979).

BOULARAND, E., 'L'amitié d'après saint Ambroise, dans le De officiis ministrorum, Lib. III, Cap. XXI–XXII (P.L. t.16, col. 179B-184A)', *Bulletin de littérature ecclésiastique*, 73 (1972), 103–23.

BOWERSOCK, G. W., 'From Emperor to Bishop: The Self-Conscious Transformation of Political Power in the Fourth Century AD', *Classical Philology*, 81 (1986), 298–307.

BREMMER, J. and RODDENBURG, H., *A Cultural History of Gesture, from Antiquity to the Present Day* (Cambridge, 1991).

BRINK, C. O., *Horace on Poetry: The 'Ars Poetica'* (Cambridge, 1971).

BROWN, P., *Augustine of Hippo: A Biography* (London, 1967).

—— *Religion and Society in the Age of Saint Augustine* (London, 1972).

—— *The Cult of the Saints: Its Rise and Function in Latin Christianity* (Chicago, 1981).

—— *The Body and Society: Men, Women and Sexual Renunciation in Early Christianity* (New York, 1988).

—— *Power and Persuasion in Late Antiquity: Towards a Christian Empire*, The Curti Lectures, 1988 (Madison, WI, 1992).

—— *Authority and the Sacred: Aspects of the Christianisation of the Roman World* (Cambridge, 1995).

—— 'Christianization and Religious Conflict', in A. Cameron and P. Garnsey (eds.), *The Cambridge Ancient History*, xiii: *The Late Empire, AD 337–425* (Cambridge, 1998), 632–64.

BRUGGISSER, P., 'Orator disertissimus: A propos d'une lettre de Symmaque à Ambroise', *Hermes*, 115 (1987), 106–15.

BRUNT, P. A., '"Amicitia" in the Late Roman Republic', *Proceedings of the Cambridge Philological Society*, 191 (1965), 1–20.

BÜRGI, E., 'Prolegomena quaedam ad S. Ambrosii episcopi Mediolanensis libros de officiis tres', in *75 Jahre Stella Matutina*, i (Feldkirch, 1931), 43–68.

BURGHARDT, W. J., 'Cyril of Alexandria on "Wool and Linen"', *Traditio*, 2 (1944), 484–6.

BURNS, T. S., *Barbarians within the Gates of Rome: A Study of Roman Military Policy and the Barbarians, ca. 375–425 AD* (Bloomington and Indianapolis, IN, 1994).

BURROW, J. A., *The Ages of Man: A Study in Medieval Writing and Thought* (Oxford, 1986).

BURRUS, V., *The Making of a Heretic: Gender, Authority and the Priscillianist Controversy*, Transformation of the Classical Heritage 24 (Berkeley and Los Angeles, 1995).

—— 'Reading Agnes: The Rhetoric of Gender in Ambrose and Prudentius', *Journal of Early Christian Studies*, 3 (1995), 25–46.

—— '"Equipped for Victory": Ambrose and the Gendering of Orthodoxy', *Journal of Early Christian Studies*, 4 (1996), 461–75.

—— '"In the Theater of this Life": The Performance of Orthodoxy in Late Antiquity', in W. E. Klingshirn and M. Vessey (eds.), *The Limits of Ancient Christianity: Essays on Late Antique Thought and Culture in Honor of R. A. Markus*, Recentiores: Later Latin Texts and Contexts (Ann Arbor, MI, 1999), 80–96.

BUZZI, F., 'La recezione di Ambrogio a Wittenberg', in L. F. Pizzolato and M. Rizzi (eds.), *Nec timeo mori* (Milan, 1998), 569–83.

CALAFATO, S., *La proprietà privata in s. Ambrogio*, Scrinium Theologicum, 6 (Turin, 1958).

CALLAM, D., 'Clerical Continence in the Fourth Century: Three Papal Decretals', *Theological Studies*, 41 (1980), 3–50.

CALLEWAERT, C., 'Un passo di s. Ambrogio e le letture di una stazione quaresimale', *Ambrosius*, 15 (1939), 63–4.

CAMERON, A., *Christianity and the Rhetoric of Empire: The Development of Christian Discourse*, Sather Classical Lectures, 55 (Berkeley and Los Angeles, 1991).

CAMPENHAUSEN, H. VON, *Ambrosius von Mailand als Kirchenpolitiker*, Arbeiten zur Kirchengeschichte, 12 (Berlin and Leipzig, 1929).

—— *The Fathers of the Latin Church*, ET (London, 1964).

CANATA, P., *De S. Ambrosii libris qui inscribuntur 'De officiis ministrorum' quaestiones* (Modena, 1909).

—— *De syntaxi ambrosiana in libris qui inscribuntur 'De officiis ministrorum'* (Modena, 1911).

CARMICHAEL, E., 'Friendship: A Way of Interpreting Christian Love', D.Phil. Diss. (Oxford, 1990).

CARPANETO, G. M., 'Le opere oratorie di s. Ambrogio', *Didaskaleion*, 8 (1930), 35–156.

CATTANEO, E., 'Il governo ecclesiastico nel IV secolo nell'Italia settentrionale', *Antichità altoadriatiche*, 22 (1982), 175–87.

CAVALLERA, F., *Saint Jérôme: Sa vie et son œuvre*, 2 vols. (Louvain and Paris, 1922).

CAVASIN, A., *Sant'Ambrogio, Dei Doveri degli Ecclesiastici: Testo, introduzione, versione e note*, Corona Patrum Salesiana, ser. lat. 5 (Turin, 1938).

CHADWICK, H., *Early Christian Thought and the Classical Tradition: Studies in Justin, Clement, and Origen* (Oxford, 1966).

—— *Priscillian of Avila: The Occult and the Charismatic in the Early Church* (Oxford, 1976).

CHADWICK, H., 'The Role of the Christian Bishop in Ancient Society', in H. C. Hobbs and W. Wuellner (eds.), *The Role of the Christian Bishop in Ancient Society*, Protocol of the 35th Colloquy, Center for Hermeneutical Studies, Berkeley (Berkeley and Los Angeles, 1980), 1–14.

CHAMPLIN, E., *Final Judgements: Duty and Emotion in Roman Wills, 200 BC–AD 250* (Berkeley and Los Angeles, 1991).

CHASTAGNOL, A., *La Préfecture urbaine à Rome sous le Bas-Empire* (Paris, 1960).

——*L'Evolution politique, sociale et économique du monde romain de Dioclétien à Julien* (Paris, 1982).

CHERUBELLI, P., 'Sant'Ambrogio e la rinascita: fonti manoscritte, edizioni a stampa e iconografia del santo nel secoli XIV, XV e XVI—Saggio', in *Sant'Ambrogio nel XVI centenario della nascita* (Milan, 1940), 571–91.

CHRISTOPHE, P., *L'Usage chrétien du droit de proprieté dans l'Ecriture et la tradition patristique* (Paris, 1964).

CIRCIS, P., *The Ennoblement of the Pagan Virtues: A Comparative Treatise on Virtues in Cicero's Book De Officiis and in St Ambrose's Book De Officiis Ministrorum* (Rome, 1955).

CITTERIO, B., 'Spiritualità sacerdotale nel "De officiis" di s. Ambrogio', *Ambrosius*, 32 (1956), 157–65; 33 (1957), 71–80.

CLARK, E., 'Sex, Shame and Rhetoric: En-Gendering Early Christian Ethics', *Journal of the American Academy of Religion*, 59 (1991), 719–45.

CLARKE, G. W., 'Prosopographical Notes on the Epistles of Cyprian—III. Rome in August 258', *Latomus*, 34 (1975), 437–48.

——(tr./ed.), *Cyprian, Letters*, 4 vols., Ancient Christian Writers vols. 43–4, 46–7 (Westminster, MD and London, 1984–9).

CLASSEN, C. J., 'Der platonisch-stoische Kanon der Kardinaltugenden bei Philon, Clemens Alexandrinus und Origenes' in A. M Ritter (ed.), *Kerygma und Logos: Beiträge zu den geistesgeschichtli chen Beziehungen zwischen Antike und Christentum. Festschrift fü Carl Andresen zum 70. Geburtstag* (Göttingen, 1979), 68–88.

CLAUS, F., 'De opvatting van Ambrosius over de navolging in de "D officiis"', *Handelingen XXVI der Koninklijke Zuidernederlands Maatschappij voor Taal-en Letterkunde en Geschiedenis* (1972), 63 72.

CLAUSS, M., *Der Magister Officiorum in der Spätantike (4.–6. Jahr hundert). Das Amt und sein Einfluß auf die kaiserliche Politi* Vestigia, 32 (Munich, 1980).

COCCHINI, C., *Origines apostoliques du célibat sacerdotale* (Pari 1981).

COCHRANE, C. N., *Christianity and Classical Culture: A Study of Thought and Action from Augustus to Augustine* (Oxford, 1940).

COLISH, M. L., *The Stoic Tradition from Antiquity to the Early Middle Ages*, 2 vols: (i) *Stoicism in Classical Latin Literature*; (ii) *Stoicism in Christian Latin Thought through the Sixth Century*, Studies in the History of Christian Thought, 34 (Leiden, 1985).

—— 'Cicero, Ambrose, and Stoic Ethics: Transmission or Transformation?', in A. Bernardo and S. Levin (eds.), *The Classics in the Middle Ages*, Papers of the Twentieth Annual Conference of the Center for Medieval and Early Renaissance Studies (Binghamton, NY, 1990), 95–112.

COLLIN, L. P., *Ciceronis et Ambrosii scripta 'De officiis'* (n.p., 1835).

CONSOLINO, F. E., *Ascesi e mondanità nella Gallia tardoantica: Studi sulla figura del vescovo nei secoli IV–VI* (Naples, 1979).

—— 'Gli *exempla maiorum* nel *De officiis* di Ambrogio e la duplice eredità dei cristiani', in *La tradizione: forme e modi. XVIII Incontro di studiosi dell'antichità cristiana, Roma, 7–9 maggio 1989*, Studia Ephemeridis Augustinianum, 31 (Rome, 1990), 351–69.

COPPA, G., 'Istanze formative e pastorali del presbitero nella vita e nelle opere di sant'Ambrogio', in F. Sergio (ed.), *La formazione al sacerdozio ministeriale nella catechesi e nella testimonianza di vita dei Padri* (Rome, 1992), 95–132.

CORBELLINI, C., 'Sesto Petronio Probo e l'elezione episcopale di Ambrogio', *Rendiconti del Istituto Lombardo*, 109 (1975), 181–9.

—— 'Ambrogio e i barbari: giudizio o pregiudizio?', *Rivista di storia della chiesa in Italia*, 31 (1977), 343–53.

—— 'Il problema della militia in sant'Ambrogio', *Historia*, 27 (1978), 630–6.

CORBETT, P., *The Scurra* (Edinburgh, 1986).

COURCELLE, P., *Les lettres grecques en Occident de Macrobe à Cassiodore* (Paris, 1948).

—— 'Les Pères devant les enfers Virgiliens', *Archives d'histoire doctrinal*, 30 (1955), 5–74.

—— 'L'Humanisme chrétien de saint Ambroise', *Orpheus*, 9 (1962), 21–34.

—— *Les Confessions de saint Augustin dans la tradition littéraire. Antécédents et postérité* (Paris, 1963).

—— 'Anti-Christian Arguments and Christian Platonism: From Arnobius to Ambrose', in A. Momigliano (ed.), *The Conflict between Paganism and Christianity in the Fourth Century* (Oxford, 1963), 151–92.

—— 'Deux grands courants de pensée dans la littérature latine tardive: Stoïcisme et néo-Platonisme', *Revue des études latines*, 42 (1964), 122–40.

COURCELLE, P., 'Virgile et l'immanence divine chez Minucius Félix', in A. Stuiber and A. Hermann (eds.), *Mullus: Festschrift Theodor Klauser* (Münster, 1964), 34–42.

——*La Consolation de la philosophie* (Paris, 1967).

——*Recherches sur les Confessions de saint Augustin*, 2nd edn. (Paris, 1968).

——'Le Visage de Philosophie', *Revue des études anciennes*, 70 (1968), 110–20.

——'Les Sources de saint Ambroise sur Denys le tyran', *Revue de philologie*, 43 (1969), 204–10.

——*Recherches sur saint Ambroise: 'Vies' anciennes, culture, icono-graphie* (Paris, 1973).

——*Connais-toi toi-même de Socrate à saint Bernard*, 2 vols. (Paris, 1974).

COUVÉE, P. J., *Vita beata en vita aeterna. Een onderzoek naar de ontwikkeling van het begrip 'vita beata' naast en tegenover 'vita aeterna' bij Lactantius, Ambrosius en Augustinus, onder invloed van de romeinsche Stoa* (Baarn, 1947).

COX, P., *Biography in Late Antiquity: A Quest for the Holy Man* (Berkeley and Los Angeles, 1983).

COYLE, A. F., 'Cicero's "De Officiis" and the "De Officiis Minis-trorum" of St Ambrose', *Franciscan Studies*, 15 (1955), 224–56.

CRACCO RUGGINI, L., *Economia e società nell' 'Italia Annonaria': Rapporti fra agricoltura e commercio dal IV al Vi secolo d. C.* Fondazione Gugliemo Castelli, 30 (Milan, 1961).

——'Ambrogio e le opposizioni anticattoliche fra il 383 e il 390', *Augustinianum*, 14 (1974), 409–49.

——'Ambrogio di fronte alla compagine sociale del suo tempo', in G. Lazzati (ed.), *Ambrosius Episcopus*, 2 vols. (Milan, 1976), i. 230–65.

CROOK, J. A., *Law and Life of Rome* (London, 1967).

CROUSE, R., '"Summae auctoritatis magister": The Influence of St Ambrose in Medieval Theology', in L. F. Pizzolato and M. Rizzi (eds.), *Nec timeo mori* (Milan, 1998), 463–71.

CROUTER, R. E., 'Ambrose's "On the Duties of the Clergy": A Study of its Setting, Content, and Significance in the Light of its Stoic and Ciceronian Sources', Th.D. Diss. (Union Theological Seminary, New York, 1968).

CURTI, C., 'Una reminiscenza di Novaziano nel *De officiis ministrorum* di Ambrogio', in *Mnemosynum. Studi in onore di Alfredo Ghisell* (Bologna, 1989), 149–53.

D'Agostino, V., 'I concetti di "pudore" e "pudicizia" negli scrittori antichi', *Rivista di studi classici*, 17 (1969), 320–9.

Daley, B. E., *The Hope of the Early Church: A Handbook of Patristic Eschatology* (Cambridge, 1991).

Daniélou, J., 'Traversée de la Mer Rouge et baptême aux premiers siècles', *Recherches de science religieuse*, 33 (1946), 402–30.

—— *Sacramentum Futuri: Etudes sur les origines de la typologie biblique* (Paris, 1950).

—— *The Bible and the Liturgy*, ET (London, 1960).

Dantu, C., *La Place et le rôle de l'Ecriture dans le De Officiis Ministrorum de saint Ambroise* (Dijon, 1970).

Dassmann, E., *Die Frömmigkeit des Kirchenvaters Ambrosius von Mailand: Quellen und Entfaltung*, Münsterische Beiträge zur Theologie, 29 (Münster, 1965).

—— *La sobria ebrezza dello Spirito: la spiritualità di sant'Ambrogio vescovo di Milano* (Varese, 1975).

—— 'Ambrosius und die Märtyrer', *Jahrbuch für Antike und Christentum*, 18 (1975), 49–68.

—— 'Ambrosius', *Theologische Realenzyklopädie*, ii (1978), 362–86.

—— 'Pastorale Anliegen bei Ambrosius von Mailand', in L. F. Pizzolato and M. Rizzi (eds.), *Nec timeo mori* (Milan, 1998), 181–206.

Davidson, I. J., 'Ambrose's *De Officiis* and the Intellectual Climate of the Late Fourth Century', *Vigiliae Christianae*, 49 (1995), 313–33.

—— 'The *Vita Beata*: Ambrose, *De Officiis* 2.1–21 and the Synthesis of Classical and Christian Thought in the Late Fourth Century', *Recherches de théologie ancienne et médiévale*, 63 (1996), 189–209.

—— 'Pastoral Theology at the End of the Fourth Century: Ambrose and Jerome', *Studia Patristica*, 33 (1997), 295–301.

—— 'Ambrose', in P. F. Esler (ed.), *The Early Christian World*, 2 vols. (London and New York, 2000), ii. 1175–1204.

—— 'Staging the Church? Theology as Theater', *Journal of Early Christian Studies* 8 (2000), 413–51.

—— 'A Tale of Two Approaches: Ambrose, *De Officiis* 1.1–22 and Cicero, *De Officiis* 1.1–6', *Journal of Theological Studies*, NS 52 (2001), 61–83.

—— '*Captatio* in the Fourth-Century West', *Studia Patristica*, 34 (2001), 33–43.

—— 'Social Construction and the Rhetoric of Ecclesial Presence: Ambrose's Milan', *Studia Patristica*, 38 (2001), 385–93.

De Capitani, F., 'Studi su sant'Ambrogio e il Manichei: I. Occasioni di un incontro', *Rivista di filosofia neoscolastica*, 74 (1982), 596–610;

'II. Spunti antimanichei nell' Exameron ambrosiano', *Rivista di filosofia neoscolastica*, 75 (1983), 3–29.

DE' CAVALIERI, P. F., *Sancti Agiografici 1 (1893–1900)*, Studi e Testi, 221 (Vatican City, 1962).

DEFERRARI, R. J., 'St Augustine's Method of Composing and Delivering Sermons', *American Journal of Philology*, 43 (1922), 97–123, 193–219.

DEKKERS, E., *Clavis Patrum Latinorum*, 3rd edn. with A. Gaar, *Corpus Christianorum, series latina* (Turnhout and Steenbrugge, 1995).

DE LACY, P. H., 'The Four Stoic *Personae*', *Illinois Classical Studies*, 2 (1977), 163–72.

DELANEY, M. R., *A Study of the Clausulae in the Works of St Ambrose*, Catholic University of America Patristic Studies, 40 (Washington, DC, 1934).

DELEHAYE, H., *Sanctus. Essai sur le culte des saints dans l'antiquité*, Subsidia Hagiographica, 17 (Brussels, 1927).

—— *Les Origines du culte des martyrs*, Subsidia Hagiographica, 20, 2nd edn. (Brussels, 1933).

—— 'Recherches sur le légendier romain', *Analecta Bollandiana*, 51 (1933), 34–98.

DEMAN, TH., 'Le "De officiis" de saint Ambroise dans l'histoire de la théologie morale', *Revue des sciences philosophiques et théologiques*, 37 (1953), 409–24.

DEN BOEFT, J., 'Ambrosius Lyricus', in J. den Boeft and A. Hilhorst (eds.), *Early Christian Poetry: A Collection of Essays*, suppl. to *Vigiliae Christianae*, 22 (Leiden, 1993), 77–89.

DE ROMESTIN, H., 'Ambrose, *De Officiis Ministrorum*' translation in H. Wace and P. Schaff (eds.), *A Select Library of Nicene and Post-Nicene Fathers of the Christian Church*, 2nd ser., x (repr. Grand Rapids, MI and Edinburgh, 1980), 1–89.

DE STE CROIX, G. E. M., 'Early Christian Attitudes to Property and Slavery', in D. Baker (ed.), *Church, Society and Politics*, Studies in Church History, 12 (Oxford, 1975), 1–38.

DI BERARDINO, A. (ed.), *Patrology* iv: *The Golden Age of Latin Patristic Literature, from the Council of Nicaea to the Council of Chalcedon* (= J. Quasten, *Patrology* 4) Augustinian Patristic Institute, Rome, ET (Westminster, MD, 1986).

DIEDERICH, M. D., *Vergil in the Works of St Ambrose*, Catholic University of America Patristic Studies, 29 (Washington, DC 1931).

—— 'Cicero and Saint Ambrose on Friendship', *Classical Journal*, 43 (1948), 219–22.

DIHLE, A., 'Demut', *Reallexikon für Antike und Christentum*, iii (1957), 735–78.

D'IZARNY, R., 'La Virginité selon saint Ambroise', Th.D. thesis, 2 vols. (Institut Catholique de Lyon, 1952).

DÖRRIE, H., 'Das fünffach gestufte Mysterium. Der Aufstieg der Seele bei Porphyrios und Ambrosius', in A. Stuiber and A. Hermann (eds.), *Mullus: Festschrift Theodor Klauser, Jahrbuch für Antike und Christentum*, Ergänzungsband 1 (Münster, 1964), 79–92.

DOIGNON, J., 'Perspectives ambrosiennes: SS. Gervais et Protais, génies de Milan', *Revue des études augustiniennes*, 2 (1956), 313–34.

—— 'La Première exposition ambrosienne de l'*exemplum* de Judith (*De virginibus*, 2, 4, 24)', in Y.-M. Duval (ed.), *Ambroise de Milan. XVIe Centenaire de son élection épiscopale. Dix études* (Paris, 1974), 219–28.

—— 'La Tradition latine (Cicéron, Sénèque) de l'episode des Sirènes entre les mains d'Ambroise de Milan', in *Hommages à Jean Cousin: Rencontres avec l'antiquité classique*, Annales Littéraires de l'Université de Besançon, 273 (Paris, 1983), 271–8.

DOOLEY, W. J., *Marriage according to St Ambrose*, Catholic University of America Studies in Christian Antiquity, 11 (Washington, DC, 1948).

DRAESEKE, J., 'M. Tulli Ciceronis et Ambrosii episcopi Mediolanensis De officiis libri III inter se comparantur', *Rivista di filologia e d'istruzione classica*, 4 (1876), 121–64.

DROGE, A. J., *Homer or Moses? Early Christian Interpretations of the History of Culture*, Hermeneutische Untersuchungen zur Theologie, 26 (Tübingen, 1989).

DUCLOUX, A., Ad ecclesiam confugere: *Naissance du droit d'asile dans les églises (IVe–milieu du Ve s.)*, De l'archéologie à l'histoire (Paris, 1994).

DULAEY, M., 'Le Symbole de la baguette dans l'art paléochrétien', *Revue des études augustiniennes*, 19 (1973), 3–38.

DUNBABIN, K. M. D., 'Triclinium and Stibadium', in W. J. Slater (ed.), *Dining in a Classical Context* (Ann Arbor, MI, 1991), 121–48.

DUNN, J. D. G., *Christology in the Making: A New Testament Inquiry into the Origins of the Doctrine of the Incarnation*, 2nd edn. (London, 1989).

DUPLACY, J., 'Citations patristiques et critique textuelle du Nouveau Testament: A propos d'un livre récent', *Recherches des sciences religieuses*, 47 (1959), 391–400.

DUPONT, F., *Daily Life in Ancient Rome*, ET (Oxford and Cambridge, MA, 1993).

DURLIAT, J., *De la ville antique à la ville byzantine. Le problème des subsistences*, Collection de l'école français de Rome, 136 (Rome, 1990).

DUVAL, Y., *Auprès des saints corps et âme. L'inhumation 'ad sanctos' dans la chrétienté d'Orient et d'Occident du IIIe au VIIe siècle* (Paris, 1988).

DUVAL, Y.-M., 'Sur une page de saint Cyprien chez saint Ambroise. Hexameron 6, 8, 47 et De habitu virginum 15–17', *Revue des etudes augustiniennes*, 16 (1970), 25–34.

——(ed.), *Ambroise de Milan. XVIe Centenaire de son élection épiscopale. Dix études* (Paris, 1974).

——L'Originalité du De virginibus dans le mouvement ascétique occidental: Ambroise, Cyprien, Athanase', in *Ambroise de Milan. XVIe Centenaire de son élection épiscopale. Dix études* (Paris, 1974), 9–66.

—— 'Ambroise, de son élection à sa consécration', in G. Lazzati (ed.), *Ambrosius Episcopus*, 2 vols. (Milan, 1976), ii. 243–83.

—— 'Formes profanes et formes bibliques dans les oraisons funèbres de saint Ambroise', in M. Fuhrmann (ed.), *Christianisme et formes littéraires de l'Antiquité tardive en Occident*, Fondation Hardt, Entretiens sur l'Antiquité Classique, 23 (Geneva, 1977), 235–301.

——(ed.), *Jérome entre l'Occident et l'Orient. XVIe centenaire du départ de saint Jérome de Rome et de son installation à Bethléem. Actes du Colloque de Chantilly, Septembre, 1986* (Paris, 1988).

DYCK, A. R., *A Commentary on Cicero, De Officiis* (Ann Arbor, MI, 1996).

EARL, D. C., *The Moral and Political Tradition of Rome* (London, 1967).

EBERT, A., *Allgemeine Geschichte der Literatur des Mittelalters im Abendlande*, 2nd edn., i (Leipzig, 1889).

ECK, W., 'Der Einfluss der konstantinischen Wende auf die Auswahl der Bischöfe im 4. und 5. Jahrhundert', *Chiron*, 8 (1978), 561–85.

EDWARDS, C., *The Politics of Immorality in Ancient Rome* (Cambridge, 1993).

EGER, J., *Salus Gentium. Eine patristische Studie zur Volkstheologie des Ambrosius von Mailand*, Diss. (Munich, 1947).

ELLSPERMANN, G. L., *The Attitude of the Early Christian Latin Writers toward Pagan Literature and Learning*, Catholic University of America Patristic Studies, 82 (Washington, DC, 1949).

ELM, S., *Virgins of God: The Making of Asceticism in Late Antiquity*, Oxford Classical Monographs (Oxford, 1994).

EMENEAU, M. B., 'Ambrose and Cicero', *The Classical Weekly*, 24/7 (1930), 49–53.

ERNOUT, A. and MEILLET, A., *Dictionnaire etymologique de la langue latine: histoire des mots*, 4th edn. (Paris, 1959).

ERSKINE, A., 'Cicero and the Expression of Grief', in S. Morton Braund and C. Gill (eds.), *The Passions in Roman Thought and Literature* (Cambridge, 1997), 36–47.

EVANS, E. C., *Physiognomics in the Ancient World* (Philadelphia, 1969).

EWALD, P., *Der Einfluss der stoisch-ciceronianischen Moral auf die Darstellung der Ethik bei Ambrosius* (Leipzig, 1881).

EYBEN, E., 'Young Priests in Early Christianity', in M. Wacht (ed.), *Panchaia: Festschrift für Klaus Thraede, Jahrbuch für Antike und Christentum*, Ergänzungsband 22 (Münster, 1995), 102–20.

FABRE, P., *Saint Paulin de Nole et l'amitié chrétienne*, Bibliothèque des Ecoles Françaises d'Athènes et de Rome, 167 (Paris, 1949).

FALLER, O., 'La data della consacrazione vescovile di sant'Ambrogio', in G. Galbiati *et al.* (eds.), *Ambrosiana: Scritti di storia, archeologia ed arte pubblicati nel XVI centenario della nascita di sant'Ambrogio, CCCXL–MCMXL* (Milan, 1942), 97–112.

FAURE, E., 'Saint Ambroise et l'expulsion des pérégrins de Rome', in *Etudes d'histoire du droit canonique dédiées à Gabriel le Bras*, i (Paris, 1965), 523–40.

FAUST, U., *'Christo servire libertas est': Zum Freiheitsbegriff des Ambrosius von Mailand*, Salzburger Patristische Studien, 3 (Salzburg, 1983).

FENGER, A.-L., *Aspekte der Soteriologie und Ekklesiologie bei Ambrosius von Mailand*, Europäische Hochschulschriften, ser. 23, Theol. 149 (Frankfurt and Berlin, 1981).

FERGUSON, J., *Moral Values in the Ancient World* (London, 1958).

FERRUA, V., 'Ancora sulla "Disciplina dell'Arcano"', *Salesianum*, 55 (1993), 471–83.

FESTUGIÈRE, A. J., *Epicurus and his Gods*, ET (Oxford, 1955).

—— *L'Idéal religieux des Grecs et l'Evangile* (Paris, 1932).

FEUVRIER-PRÉVOTAT, C., 'Donner et recevoir: remarques sur les pratiques d'échanges dans le De officiis de Cicéron', *Dialogues d'histoire ancienne*, 11 (1985), 257–90.

FIELD, F., *Origenis Hexaplorum quae supersunt; sive Veterum Interpretum Graecorum in totum Vetus Testamentum Fragmenta*, 2 vols., 2nd edn. (Oxford, 1874).

FIGUEROA, G., *The Church and the Synagogue in Saint Ambrose*, Catholic University of America Studies in Sacred Theology, 2nd ser., 25 (Washington, DC, 1949).

FISCHER, B., 'Hat Ambrosius von Mailand in der Woche zwischen seiner Taufe und seiner Bischofskonsekration andere Weihen empfangen?' in P. Granfield and J. A. Jungmann (eds.), *Kyriakon: Festschrift Johannes Quasten*, 2 vols. (Münster, 1970), ii. 527–31.

FLÜCKIGER, F., *Geschichte des Naturrechtes* i: *Altertum und Frühmittelalter* (Zurich, 1954).

FÖRSTER, R. (ed.), *Scriptores physiognomici Graeci et Latini*, 2 vols. (Leipzig, 1893).

FÖRSTER, TH., *Von den Pflichten der Geistlichen (De Off. Min.): Ein Beitrag zur Pastoraltheologie von Ambrosius, Bischofs von Mailand* (Halle, 1879).

——*Ambrosius, Bischof von Mailand: Eine Darstellung seines Lebens und Wirkens* (Halle, 1884).

FOLEY, D. M., 'The Religious Significance of the Human Body in the Writings of Ambrose of Milan', Ph.D. Diss. (University of Saint Paul, Ottawa, 1996).

FONSECA, C. D., 'Gli "Excerpta Ambrosii" nelle sillogi canonicali dei secoli XI e XII', in G. Lazzati (ed.), *Ambrosius Episcopus*, 2 vols. (Milan, 1976), ii, 48–68.

FONTAINE, J., 'Les Symbolismes de la cithare dans la poésie de Paulin de Nole', in W. DEN BOER *et al.* (eds.), *Romanitas et Christianitas: Studia Iano Henrico Waszink A.D. VI KAL. NOV. A. MCMLXXIII. XIII lustra completi oblata* (Amsterdam and London, 1973), 123–43.

——'Prose et poésie: l'interférence des genres et styles dans la création littéraire d'Ambroise de Milan', in G. Lazzati (ed.), *Ambrosius Episcopus*, 2 vols. (Milan, 1976), i. 124–70.

——'Le Culte des martyrs militaires et son expression poétique au IVe siècle: l'idéal évangelique de la non-violence dans le christianisme théodosien', in *Etudes sur la poésie latine tardive d'Ausone à Prudence. Recueil de travaux* (Paris, 1981), 351–61.

——'En quel sens peut-on parler d'un "classicisme" ambrosien?', in L. F. Pizzolato and M. Rizzi (eds.), *Nec timeo mori* (Milan, 1998), 501–10.

FRAISSE, J.-C., *Philia: la notion d'amitié dans la philosophie antique* (Paris, 1974).

FRATTINI, E., 'Proprietà e ricchezza nel pensiero di s. Ambrogio' *Rivista internazionale di filosofia del diritto*, 39 (1962), 745–66.

FREDE, H. J., 'Probleme des ambrosianischen Bibeltextes', in G. Lazzati (ed.), *Ambrosius Episcopus*, 2 vols. (Milan, 1976), i 365–92.

FREDOUILLE, J.-C., *Tertullien et la conversion de la culture antiqu* (Paris, 1972).

FREND, W. H. C., 'St Ambrose and other Churches (except Rome)' in L. F. Pizzolato and M. Rizzi (eds.), *Nec timeo mori* (Milan, 1998), 161–80.

FREYBURGER, G., *Fides. Etude sémantique et religieuse depuis les origines jusqu'à l'époque augustéenne*, Collection des études anciennes (Paris, 1986).

FROT, Y., 'Le Pauvre, autre Christ, dans quelques lettres de saint Ambroise', in *L'etica cristiana nei secoli III e IV: Eredità e confronti* (Rome, 1996), 299–304.

FUHRMANN, M., 'Persona, ein römischer Rollenbegriff', in O. Marquard and K. Stierle (eds.), *Identität* (Munich, 1979), 83–106.

GAFFNEY, J., 'Comparative Religious Ethics in the Service of Historical Interpretation: Ambrose's Use of Cicero', *Journal of Religious Ethics*, 9 (1981), 35–47.

GALBIATI, G. *et al.* (eds.), *Ambrosiana: Scritti di storia, archeologia ed arte pubblicati nel XVI centenario della nascita di sant'Ambrogio, CCCXL–MCMXL*, Biblioteca Ambrosiana, 20 (Milan, 1942).

GAMBLE, H. Y., *Books and Readers in the Early Church: A History of Early Christian Texts* (New Haven, CT and London, 1995).

GARNSEY, P., *Famine and Food Supply in the Graeco-Roman World: Responses to Risk and Crisis* (Cambridge, 1988).

GARRISON, R., *Redemptive Almsgiving in Early Christianity*, suppl. to *Journal for the Study of the New Testament*, 77 (Sheffield, 1993).

GAUDEMET, J., *L'Eglise dans l'empire romain (IVe–Ve siècles): Histoire du droit et des institutions de l'Eglise en Occident*, iii (Paris, 1958).

—— 'Droit séculier et droit de l'Eglise chez Ambroise', in G. Lazzati (ed.), *Ambrosius Episcopus*, 2 vols. (Milan, 1976), i. 286–315.

—— *Le Droit romain dans la littérature chrétienne occidentale du IIIe au Ve siècle*, Ius Romanum Medii Aevi, I, 3, b (Milan, 1978).

—— *La Formation du droit séculier et du droit de l'Eglise aux IVe et Ve siècles*, Institut de droit romain de l'Université de Paris, 15, 2nd edn. (Paris, 1979).

GAUTHIER, R.-A., *Magnanimité: Idéal de la grandeur dans la philosophie païenne et dans la théologie chrétienne* (Paris, 1951).

GIBBON, E., *The History of the Decline and Fall of the Roman Empire*, 3 vols., ed. D. Womersley (London, 1994).

GIET, S., 'De saint Basile à saint Ambroise. La condamnation du prêt à intéret au IVe siècle', *Recherches de science religieuse*, 31 (1944), 95–128.

—— 'La Doctrine de l'appropriation des biens chez quelques-uns des Pères. Peut-on parler de communisme?', *Recherches de science religieuse*, 35 (1948), 55–91.

GILBERT, R. O., *Sancti Ambrosii episcopi Mediolanensis de officiis clericorum libri tres, ad manuscriptorum et optimorum librorum fidem emendavit et selectam lectionum varietatem adiecit*, Bibliotheca Patrum Ecclesiasticorum Latinorum selecta, 8/1 (Leipzig, 1839).

GILL, C., 'Personhood and Personality: The Four-*Personae* Theory in Cicero, *De Officiis* I', *Oxford Studies in Ancient Philosophy*, 6 (1988), 169–99.

GILLIARD, F. D., 'Senatorial Bishops in the Fourth Century', *Harvard Theological Review*, 77 (1984), 153–75.

GLEASON, M. W., 'The Semiotics of Gender: Physiognomy and Self-Fashioning', in D. M. Halperin, J. J. Winkler, and F. I. Zeitlin (eds.), *Before Sexuality: The Construction of Erotic Experience in the Ancient Greek World* (Princeton, NJ, 1990), 389–415.

——*Making Men: Sophists and Self-Presentation in Ancient Rome* (Princeton, NJ, 1995).

GNILKA, C., *Chrêsis. Die Methode der Kirchenväter im Umgang mit der antiken Kultur*, i: *Der Begriff des 'rechten Gebrauchs'* (Basle, 1984).

——*Aetas spiritalis: Die Überwindung der natürlichen Altersstufen als Ideal frühchristlichen Lebens* (Bonn, 1972).

GONZÁLEZ, J. L., *Faith and Wealth: A History of Early Christian Ideas on the Origin, Significance and Use of Money* (San Francisco, 1990).

GOPPELT, L., *Typos: The Typological Interpretation of the Old Testament in the New*, ET (Grand Rapids, MI, 1982).

GORDINI, G. D., 'La ricchezza secondo s. Ambrogio', *Ambrosius*, 3 (1957), 102–23.

GORDON, B., 'Lending at Interest: Some Jewish, Greek and Christian Approaches, 800 BC–AD 100', *History of Political Economy*, 14 (1982), 406–26.

——*The Economic Problem in Biblical and Patristic Thought*, suppl. to *Vigiliae Christianae*, 9 (Leiden, 1989).

GORMAN, P., *Pythagoras: A Life* (London and Boston, 1979).

GOSSEL, W., *Quibus ex fontibus Ambrosius in describendo corpore humano hauserit (Ambros. Exaem. VI.54–74)*, Diss. (Leipzig, 1908).

GOTTLIEB, G., *Ambrosius von Mailand und Kaiser Gratian*, Hypomnemata: Untersuchungen zur Antike und zu ihrem Nachleben, 40 (Göttingen, 1973).

——'Der Mailänder Kirchenstreit von 385/386: Datierung, Verlauf, Deutung', *Museum Helveticum*, 52 (1985), 37–55.

GRANGER TAYLOR, H., 'The Two Dalmatics of Saint Ambrose', *Bulletin de Liaison, Centre Internationale d'Etude des Textiles Anciens*, 57–8 (1983), 127–73.

GRANT, R. M., 'Early Christian Banking', *Studia Patristica*, 15 (1975), 217–20.

—— *Early Christianity and Society* (London, 1978).

GRASMÜCK, E. L., 'Der Bischof und sein Klerus. Ambrosius von Mailand: De officiis ministrorum', in A. E. Hierold, V. Eid, *et al.* (eds.), *Die Kraft der Hoffnung. Gemeinde und Evangelium. Festschrift für Alterzbischof DDr. J. Schneider zum 80. Geburtstag* (Bamberg, 1986), 84–97.

GRAUMANN, T., *Christus Interpres: Die Einheit von Auslegung und Verkündigung in der Lukaserklärung des Ambrosius von Mailand*, Patristische Texte und Studien, 41 (Berlin and New York, 1994).

—— 'St Ambrose on the Art of Preaching', in *Vescovi e pastori in epoca teodosiana*, 2 vols. (Rome, 1997), ii. 587–600.

GREEN, R. P. H., *The Works of Ausonius, Edited with Introduction and Commentary* (Oxford, 1991).

—— *Augustine, De Doctrina Christiana, Edited with an Introduction, Translation, and Notes*, Oxford Early Christian Texts (Oxford, 1995).

GREEN, W. M., 'A Fourth-Century Manuscript of Saint Augustine?', *Revue Bénédictine*, 69 (1959), 191–7.

GREER, R. A., *The Captain of our Salvation: A Study in the Patristic Exegesis of Hebrews*, Beiträge zur Geschichte der biblischen Exegese, 15 (Tübingen, 1973).

—— 'Cicero's Sketch and Lactantius's Plan', in A. J. Malherbe, F. W. Norris, and J. W. Thompson (eds.), *The Early Church in its Context: Essays in Honor of Everett Ferguson* (Leiden, 1998), 155–74.

GRIFFIN, M. T. and ATKINS, E. M. (eds.), *Cicero: On Duties*, Cambridge Texts in the History of Political Thought (Cambridge, 1991).

GRIMM, V. E., *From Feasting to Fasting, the Evolution of a Sin: Attitudes to Food in Late Antiquity* (London and New York, 1996).

GROSS, K., 'Plus amari quam timeri. Eine antike politische Maxime in der Benediktinerregel', *Vigiliae Christianae*, 27 (1973), 218–29.

—— 'Lob der Hand im klassischen und christlichen Altertum', *Gymnasium*, 83 (1977), 423–40.

—— '"Numquam minus otiosus quam cum otiosus." Das Weiterleben eines antiken Sprichwortes im Abendland', *Antike und Abendland*, 26 (1980), 122–37.

GRYSON, R., 'La Typologie sacerdotale de saint Ambroise et ses sources', Th.D. Diss. (Université Catholique de Louvain, 1966).

—— 'Les Degrés du clergé et leurs denominations chez saint Ambroise de Milan', *Revue Bénédictine*, 66 (1966), 119–27.

GRYSON, R., 'L'Interprétation du nom de Lévi (Lévite) chez saint Ambroise', *Sacris Erudiri*, 17 (1966), 217–29.

—— *Le Prêtre selon saint Ambroise* (Louvain, 1968).

—— *Les Origines du célibat ecclésiastique, du premier au septième siècle*, Recherches et synthèses, section d'histoire, 2 (Gembloux, 1970).

—— *The Ministry of Women in the Early Church*, ET (Collegeville, MN, 1976).

—— 'Les Elections épiscopales en Occident au IVe siècle', *Revue d'histoire ecclésiastique*, 75 (1980), 275–83.

—— 'La Médiation d'Aaron d'après saint Ambroise', *Recherches de théologie ancienne et médiévale*, 47 (1980), 5–15.

—— 'Le Thème du baton d'Aaron dans l'œuvre de saint Ambroise', *Revue des etudes augustiniennes*, 26 (1980), 29–44.

—— 'Les Lévites, figure du sacerdoce véritable, selon saint Ambroise', *Ephemerides theologicae Lovanienses*, 56/1 (1980), 89–112.

GUALANDRI, I., 'Il lessico di Ambrogio: problemi e prospettive di ricerca', in L. F. Pizzolato and M. Rizzi (eds.), *Nec timeo mori* (Milan, 1998), 267–311.

GUNDEL, W., 'Astrologie', *Reallexikon für Antike und Christentum*, i (1950), 817–31.

GUNDERSON, E., 'Contested Subjects: Oratorical Theory and the Body', Ph.D. Diss. (University of California, Berkeley, 1996).

GUTHRIE, W. K. C., *A History of Greek Philosophy*, 6 vols. (Cambridge, 1962–81).

HADOT, P., 'Platon et Plotin dans trois sermons de saint Ambroise', *Revue des études latines*, 34 (1956), 202–20.

HAGENDAHL, H., 'Methods of Citation in Post-Classical Latin Prose', *Eranos*, 45 (1947), 114–28.

—— *Latin Fathers and the Classics: A Study on the Apologists, Jerome, and other Christian Writers*, Studia Graeca et Latina Gothoburgensia, 6 (Gothenburg, 1958).

—— 'Die Bedeutung der Stenographie für die spätlateinische christliche Literatur', *Jahrbuch für Antike und Christentum*, 14 (1971), 24–38.

HAHN, V., *Das wahre Gesetz: Eine Untersuchung der Aufassung des Ambrosius von Mailand vom Verhältnis der beiden Testamente*, Münsterische Beiträge zur Theologie, 33 (Münster, 1969).

HALKIN, FR., Review of J.-R. Palanque, *Saint Ambroise et l'empire romain*, *Analecta Bollandiana*, 52 (1934), 399–400.

HALLIWELL, S., 'The Uses of Laughter in Greek Culture', *Classical Quarterly*, 85 (1991), 279–96.

HAMMAN, A. G., 'La Formation du clergé latin, dans les quatres premiers siècles', *Studia Patristica*, 20 (1989), 238–49.

HANSON, R. P. C., *The Search for the Christian Doctrine of God: The Arian Controversy 318–381* (Edinburgh, 1988).

HARNACK, A., *History of Dogma*, v, ET (London, 1898).

——*Militia Christi: The Christian Religion and the Military in the First Three Centuries*, ET (Philadelphia, 1981).

HARRIS, H. A., *Greek Athletes and Athletics* (London, 1964).

HASLER, F., *Über das Verhältnis der heidnischen und christlichen Ethik auf Grund einer Vergleichung des ciceronianischen Buches 'De officiis' mit dem gleichnamigen des heiligen Ambrosius* (Munich, 1866).

HATCH, E., *The Influence of Greek Ideas and Usages upon the Christian Church*, Hibbert Lectures, 1888, 7th edn. (London, 1888).

HAYWARD, P. A., 'Suffering and Innocence in Latin Sermons for the Feast of the Holy Innocents, *c.* 400–800', in D. Wood (ed.), *The Church and Childhood*, Studies in Church History, 31 (Oxford, 1994), 67–80.

HEATHER, P. J., 'The Crossing of the Danube and the Gothic Conversion', *Greek, Roman, and Byzantine Studies*, 27 (1986), 289–318.

——*Goths and Romans 332–489*, Oxford Historical Monographs (Oxford, 1991).

——and MATTHEWS, J. F., *The Goths in the Fourth Century*, Translated Texts for Historians, 11 (Liverpool, 1991).

HEBEIN, R. J., 'St Ambrose and Roman Law', Ph.D. Diss. (St Louis University, MO, 1970).

HEIM, F., 'Le Thème de la "victoire sans combat" chez Ambroise', in Y.-M. Duval (ed.), *Ambroise de Milan. XVIᵉ Centenaire de son élection épiscopale. Dix études* (Paris, 1974), 267–81.

——*La Théologie de la victoire, de Constantin à Théodose*, Theologie historique, 89 (Paris, 1992).

HELLEMAN, W. E. (ed.), *Christianity and the Classics: The Acceptance of a Heritage* (Lanham, MD, 1990).

HENGEL, M., *Property and Riches in the Early Church: Aspects of a Social History of Early Christianity*, ET (London, 1974).

HENNECKE, E. and SCHNEEMELCHER, W., *New Testament Apocrypha*, 2 vols., ET 5th edn. (London, 1987–9).

HERMANT, G., *La Vie de saint Ambroise* (Paris, 1679).

HERRMANN, J., '"Fundamentum est iustitae fides." Vergleichende Betrachtung zu Cicero (De officiis 1,20 ff.) und Ambrosius (De officiis ministrorum 1,139 ff.)', in G. Schiemann (ed.), *Kleine Schriften zur Rechtsgeschichte*, Münchener Beiträge zur Papyrusforschung und Antiken Rechtsgeschichte, 83 (Munich, 1990), 315–20.

HILL, C., 'Classical and Christian Traditions in Some Writings of

Saint Ambrose of Milan', D.Phil. Diss. (University of Oxford, 1979).

HILTBRUNNER, O., 'Die Schrift "De officiis ministrorum" des hl. Ambrosius und ihr ciceronisches Vorbild', *Gymnasium*, 71 (1964), 174–89.

——GORCE, D., and WEHR, H., 'Gastfreundschaft', *Reallexikon für Antike und Christentum*, viii (1969), 1061–1123.

HOLDEN, H. A., *M. Tulli Ciceronis De Officiis Libri Tres, with Introduction, Analysis, and Commentary*, 3rd edn. (Cambridge, 1899).

HOLTE, R., *Béatitude et sagesse: Saint Augustin et le problème de la fin de l'homme dans la philosophie ancienne* (Paris, 1962).

HOMES DUDDEN, F., *The Life and Times of St Ambrose*, 2 vols. (Oxford, 1935).

HONORÉ, A., *Emperors and Lawyers*, 2nd edn. (Oxford, 1994).

HOPKINS, K., *Death and Renewal: Sociological Studies in Roman History*, 2 (Cambridge, 1983).

HÜBNER, W., *Die Begriffe 'Astrologie' und 'Astronomie' in der Antike. Wortgeschichte und Wissenschaftssytematik mit einer Hypothese zum Terminus 'Quadrivium'* (Stuttgart and Wiesbaden, 1990).

HUHN, J., *Ambrosius von Mailand, ein sozialer Bischof: Das Vorbild unserer Zeit* (Fulda, 1946).

——*Das Geheimnis der Jungfrau-Mutter Maria nach dem Kirchenvater Ambrosius* (Würzburg, 1954).

——'Der Kirchenvater Ambrosius im Lichte der Pfarrseelsorge', *Anima*, 10 (1955), 136–50.

——'Bewertung und Gebrauch der heiligen Schrift durch den Kirchenvater Ambrosius', *Historisches Jahrbuch*, 77 (1958), 387–96.

HUMPHRIES, M., *Communities of the Blessed: Social Environment and Religious Change in Northern Italy, AD 200–400*, Oxford Early Christian Studies (Oxford, 1999).

HUNT, H. A. K., *The Humanism of Cicero* (Melbourne, 1954).

HUNTER, D. G., 'Resistance to the Virginal Ideal in Late-Fourth-Century Rome: The Case of Jovinian', *Theological Studies*, 48 (1987), 45–64.

IHM, M., *Studia Ambrosiana*, in *Neue Jahrbücher für klassische Philologie*, suppl. bd. 17 (1890), 1–124.

——'Philon und Ambrosius', *Neue Jahrbücher für klassische Philologie*, 141 (1890), 282–8.

INGLEBERT, H., *Les Romains chrétiens face à l'histoire de Rome. Histoire, christianisme et romanités en Occident dans l'Antiquité tardive (IIIe–Ve siècles)*, Collection des études augustiniennes, série antiquité, 145 (Paris, 1996).

IOPPOLO, A. M., 'Lo Stoicismo di Erillo', *Phronesis*, 30 (1985), 58–78.

IRMSCHER, J., 'Ambrogio nel giudizio dei riformatori tedeschi', in L. F. Pizzolato and M. Rizzi (eds.), *Nec timeo mori* (Milan, 1998), 633–8.

JACOB, C., *'Arkandisziplin', Allegorese, Mystagogie: Ein neuer Zugang zur Theologie des Ambrosius von Mailand*, Athenäum Monografien: Theologie Bd. 32: Theophaneia (Frankfurt, 1990).

JANES, D., *God and Gold in Late Antiquity* (Cambridge, 1998).

JANSON, T., *Latin Prose Prefaces: Studies in Literary Conventions*, Studia Latina Stockholmiensia, 13 (Stockholm, 1964).

JANSSENS, J., 'La verecundia nel comportamento dei chierici secondo il De officiis ministrorum di sant'Ambrogio', in F. Sergio (ed.), *La formazione al sacerdozio ministeriale nella catechesi e nella testimonianza di vita dei Padri* (Rome, 1992), 133–43.

JELLICOE, S., *The Septuagint and Modern Study* (Oxford, 1966).

JOCELYN, H. D., '"Homo sum: humani nil a me alienum puto"', *Antichthon*, 7 (1973), 14–46.

JOHANNY, R., *L'Eucharistie, centre de l'histoire du salut chez saint Ambroise de Milan*, Théologie historique, 9 (Paris, 1968).

JONES, A. H. M., *The Later Roman Empire, 284–602: A Social, Economic, and Administrative Survey*, 3 vols. + maps (Oxford, 1964).

JONES, H., *The Epicurean Tradition* (London and New York, 1989).

JÜRGENS, H., *Pompa Diaboli. Die lateinischen Kirchenväter und das antike Theater*, Tübingener Beiträge zum Altertumswissenschaft, 46 (Stuttgart, 1972).

JUNGMANN, J. A., *Missarum solemnia: explication génétique de la messe romaine*, 3 vols. (Paris, 1956–8).

KASTER, R. A., *Guardians of Language: The Grammarian and Society in Late Antiquity*, Transformation of the Classical Heritage, 11 (Berkeley and Los Angeles, 1988).

KATZENSTEIN, H. J., *The History of Tyre* (Jerusalem, 1973).

KAUFMAN, P. I., *Church, Book, and Bishop: Conflict and Authority in Early Latin Christianity*, Explorations (Boulder, CO, and Oxford, 1996).

—— 'Diehard Homoians and the Election of Ambrose', *Journal of Early Christian Studies*, 5 (1997), 421–40.

KELLNER, J. B., *Der heilige Ambrosius, Bischof von Mailand, als Erklärer des alten Testaments. Ein Beitrag zur Geschichte der biblischen Exegese* (Regensburg, 1893).

KELLY, J. N. D., *Jerome: His Life, Writings and Controversies* (London, 1975).

KENNEDY, G. A., *The Art of Rhetoric in the Roman World, 300 BC–AD 300* (Princeton, NJ, 1972).

KESELING, P., 'Familiensinn und Vaterlandsliebe in der Pflichten-lehre des hl. Ambrosius (Max Pohlenz zum 80. Geburtstag)', *Zeitschrift für Religions- und Geistesgeschichte*, 5 (1953), 367–72.

KILLIAN, C., 'Saint Aurelius Ambrose: Orator Catholicus', *Classical Bulletin*, 46 (1970), 38–40, 46.

KLEIN, R., *Der Streit um den Victoriaaltar: Die dritte Relatio des Symmachus und die Briefe 17, 18 und 57 des Mailänder Bischofs Ambrosius*, Texte zur Forschung, 7 (Darmstadt, 1972).

——*Die Sklaverei in der Sicht der Bischöfe Ambrosius und Augustinus*, Forschungen zur antiken Sklaverei, 20 (Stuttgart, 1988).

KLINGSHIRN, W., 'Charity and Power: Caesarius of Arles and the Ransoming of Captives in Sub-Roman Gaul', *Journal of Roman Studies*, 75 (1985), 183–203.

KÖTTING, B., 'Digamus', *Reallexikon für Antike und Christentum*, iii (1957), 1016–24.

KOHNS, H. P., *Versorgungskrisen und Hungerrevolten im spätantiken Rom*, Antiquitas 1/6 (Bonn, 1961).

KONSTAN, D., 'Problems in the History of Christian Friendship', *Journal of Early Christian Studies*, 4 (1996), 87–113.

——*Friendship in the Classical World*, Key Themes in Ancient History (Cambridge, 1997).

KOPECEK, T. A., *A History of Neo-Arianism*, 2 vols., Philadelphia Patristic Foundation Patristic Monograph series, 8 (Cambridge, MA, 1979).

KRABINGER, J. G. (ed.), *S. Ambrosii episcopi Mediolanensis De Officiis Ministrorum* (Tübingen, 1857).

KRAUTHEIMER, R., *Three Christian Capitals: Topography and Politics*, Una's Lectures, 4 (Berkeley and Los Angeles, 1983).

KRESTAN, L. (ed.), *Wortindex zu den Schriften des hl. Ambrosius, nach der Sammlung von Otto Faller: Vorarbeiten zu einem Lexicon Ambrosianum*, Corpus Scriptorum Ecclesiasticorum Latinorum, suppl. 4 (Vienna, 1979).

LABHART, A., 'Curiositas. Notes sur l'histoire d'un mot et d'une notion', *Museum Helveticum*, 17 (1960), 206–24.

LABRIOLLE, P. DE, 'Le "De officiis ministrorum" de saint Ambroise et le "De officiis" de Cicéron', *Revue des cours et conférences*, 16/2 (1907–8), 177–86.

——'Saint Ambroise et l'exégèse allégorique', *Annales de philosophie chrétienne*, 155 (1908), 591–603.

——*The Life and Times of St Ambrose*, ET (St Louis, MO and London, 1928).

LAFONTAINE, P. H., *Les Conditions positives de l'accession aux ordres dans la première législation ecclésiastique (300–492)* (Ottawa, 1963).

LAFFRANQUE, M., *Poseidonios d'Apamée. Essai de mise au point*, Publications de la faculté des lettres et sciences humaines de Paris, série recherches, 13 (Paris, 1964).

LAIDLAW, W. A., 'Otium', *Greece and Rome*, 15 (1968), 42–52.

LAISTNER, M. L. W., 'The Western Church and Astrology during the Early Middle Ages', *Harvard Theological Review*, 34 (1941), 251–75.

LAKE, K., *Landmarks in the History of Early Christianity* (London, 1920).

LAMIRANDE, E., 'La Datation de la 'Vita Ambrosii' de Paulin de Milan', *Revues des études augustiniennes*, 27 (1981), 44–55.

——*Paulin de Milan et la 'Vita Ambrosii'. Aspects de la religion sous le Bas-Empire*, Recherches 30, Théologie (Paris and Montreal, 1983).

LAMOREAUX, J. C., 'Episcopal Courts in Late Antiquity', *Journal of Early Christian Studies*, 3 (1995), 143–67.

LAUSBERG, H., *Handbuch der literarischen Rhetorik*, 2 vols. (Munich, 1960).

LAWSON, A. C., 'The Sources of the "De ecclesiasticis officiis" of St Isidore of Seville', *Revue bénédictine*, 50 (1938), 26–36.

LAZZATI, G., 'Esegesi e poesia in sant'Ambrogio', *Annuario della Università Cattolica del Sacro Cuore* (1958), 75–91.

——*Il valore letterario della esegesi ambrosiana*, Archivio Ambrosiano, 11 (Milan, 1960).

——(ed.), *Ambrosius episcopus. Atti del congresso internazionale di studi ambrosiani nel XVI centenario della elevazione di sant'Ambrogio alla cattedra episcopale, Milano, 2–7 Decembre, 1974*, 2 vols. Studia Patristica Mediolanensia, 6–7 (Milan, 1976).

LECLERCQ, H., 'Captifs', *Dictionnaire d'archéologie chrétienne et de liturgie*, ii/2 (1910), 2112–27.

——'Gril', *Dictionnaire d'archéologie chrétienne et de liturgie*, vi/2 (1925), 1827–31.

——'Innocents (Massacre des)', *Dictionnaire d'archéologie chrétienne et de liturgie*, vii/1 (1926), 608–16.

——'Janvier (Calendes de)', *Dictionnaire d'archéologie chrétienne et de liturgie*, vii/2 (1927), 2147–53.

LÉCUYER, J., 'Le Sacerdoce chrétien selon saint Ambroise', *Revue de l'Université d'Ottawa*, 22 (1952), 104*–126*.

LEEB, H., *Die Psalmodie bei Ambrosius*, Wiener Beiträge zur Theologie, 18 (Vienna, 1967).

LEITMEIR, D., *Apologie der christlichen Moral. Darstellung des Verhältnisses der heidnischen und christlichen Ethik, zunächst nach einer Vergleichung des ciceronianischen Buches 'De officiis' und dem gleichnamigen des heiligen Ambrosius* (Augsburg, 1866).

LENOX-CONYNGHAM, A., 'The Judgement of Ambrose the Bishop on Ambrose the Roman Governor', *Studia Patristica*, 17 (1982), 62–5.

——'The Topography of the Basilica Conflict of AD 385/6 in Milan', *Historia*, 31 (1982), 353–63.

——'Juristic and Religious Aspects of the Basilica Conflict of AD 386', *Studia Patristica*, 18/1 (1985), 55–8.

——'Law in St Ambrose', *Studia Patristica*, 23 (1989), 149–52.

——'Sin in St Ambrose', *Studia Patristica*, 18/4 (1990), 173–7.

——'Ambrose and Philosophy', in L. R. Wickham and C. P. Bammel (eds.), *Christian Faith and Greek Philosophy in Late Antiquity: Essays in Tribute to George Christopher Stead*, suppl to *Vigiliae Christianae*, 19 (Leiden, 1993), 112–28.

LEQUES, N., *Conferuntur T. Ciceronis et s. Ambrosii de officiis libri* (Toulouse, 1849).

LEWIS, J. P., *A Study of the Interpretation of Noah and the Flood in Jewish and Christian Literature* (Leiden, 1968).

LEWY, H., *Sobria ebrietas: Untersuchungen zur Geschichte der antiken Mystik*. Beihefte zur Zeitschrift für die Neutestamentliche Wissenschaft, 9 (Giessen, 1929).

LIEBESCHUETZ, J. H. W. G., *Barbarians and Bishops: Army, Church, and State in the Age of Arcadius and Chrysostom* (Oxford, 1990).

LIEU, S. N. C., *Manichaeism in the Later Roman Empire and Medieval China: A Historical Survey*, 2nd edn., Wissenschaftliche Untersuchungen zum Neuen Testament, 63 (Tübingen, 1992).

LIZZI, R., *Vescovi e strutture ecclesiastiche nella città tardoantica (L' 'Italia Annonaria' nel IV–V secolo d. C.)*, Biblioteca di Athenaeum, 9 (Como, 1989).

——'Ambrose's Contemporaries and the Christianization of Northern Italy', *Journal of Roman Studies*, 80 (1990), 156–73.

——'Tra i classici e la Bibbia: l'"otium" come forma di santità episcopale', in G. BARONE *et al.* (eds.), *Modelli di santità e modelli di comportamento. Contrasti, intersezioni, complementerità* (Turin, 1994), 43–64.

LOBEL, E., 'A Greek Historical Drama', *Proceedings of the British Academy*, 35 (1949), 207–16.

LÖPFE, D., *Die Tugendlehre des heiligen Ambrosius* (Sarnen, 1951).

LOISELLE, A., *'Nature' de l'homme et histoire du salut. Etude sur l'anthropologie d'Ambroise de Milan*, Diss. (Lyons, 1970).

LONG, A. A., *Hellenistic Philosophy (Stoics, Epicureans, Sceptics)* (London, 1974).

——and SEDLEY, D. N., *The Hellenistic Philosophers*, 2 vols. (Cambridge, 1987).

LOVEJOY, A. O., 'The Communism of Saint Ambrose', *Journal of the*

History of Ideas, 3 (1942), 458–68. [= *Essays in the History of Ideas* (Baltimore, MD, 1948), ch. 15.]

LUCCHESI, E., *L'Usage de Philon dans l'œuvre exégètique de saint Ambroise: Une 'Quellenforschung' relative aux commentaires d'Ambroise sur la Genèse*, Arbeiten zur Literatur und Geschichte des hellenistischen Judentums, 9 (Leiden, 1977).

LUNDBERG, P., *La Typologie baptismale dans l'ancienne église*, Acta Seminarii Neotestamentici Upsaliensis, 10 (Leipzig and Uppsala, 1942).

LUNEAU, A., *L'Histoire du salut chez les Pères de l'Eglise. La doctrine des âges du monde*. Théologie historique, 2 (Paris, 1964).

LUSCHNAT, O., 'Das Problem des ethischen Fortschnitts in der alten Stoa', *Philologus*, 102 (1958), 178–214.

McHUGH, M. P., 'Satan and Saint Ambrose', *Classical Folia*, 26/1 (1972), 94–106.

—— 'Linen, Wool and Colour—Their Appearance in Saint Ambrose', *Bulletin of the Institute of Classical Studies*, 23 (1976), 99–101.

—— 'The Demonology of Saint Ambrose in Light of the Tradition', *Wiener Studien*, 91 (1978), 205–31.

MACKENDRICK, P., *The Philosophical Books of Cicero* (London, 1989).

McLYNN, N. B., *Ambrose of Milan: Church and Court in a Christian Capital*, The Transformation of the Classical Heritage, 22 (Berkeley and Los Angeles, 1994).

—— 'Diehards: A Response', *Journal of Early Christian Studies*, 5 (1997), 446–50.

MACMULLEN, R., *Enemies of the Roman Order: Treason, Unrest and Alienation in the Empire* (Cambridge, MA, 1966).

—— 'The Preacher's Audience (AD 350–400)', *Journal of Theological Studies*, NS 40 (1989), 503–11.

McNAMARA, M. A., *Friendship in Saint Augustine*, Studia Friburgensia, NS 20 (Fribourg, 1958).

MADEC, G., *Saint Ambroise et la philosophie* (Paris, 1974).

—— 'L'homme intérieur selon saint Ambroise', in Y.-M. Duval (ed.), *Ambroise de Milan. XVIᵉ Centenaire de son élection épiscopale. Dix études* (Paris, 1974), 283–308.

—— ' "Verus philosophus est amator Dei." S. Ambroise, s. Augustin et la philosophie', *Revue des sciences philosophiques et théologiques*, 61 (1977), 549–66.

MÄHL, S., *Quadriga Virtutum: Die Kardinaltugenden in der Geistesgeschichte der Karolingerzeit* (Cologne, 1969).

MAES, B., *La Loi naturelle selon saint Ambroise de Milan*, Analecta Gregoriana, 162, Facultatis Theologicae, B52 (Rome, 1967).

MAIER, H. O., 'Private Space as the Social Context of Arianism in Ambrose's Milan', *Journal of Theological Studies*, NS 45 (1994), 72–93.

MALDEN, R. H., 'Saint Ambrose as an Interpreter of Holy Scripture', *Journal of Theological Studies*, 16 (1915), 509–22.

MALONEY, R. P., 'The Teaching of the Fathers on Usury: An Historical Study on the Development of Christian Thinking', *Vigiliae Christianae*, 27 (1973), 241–65.

MANSBACH, A. R., '"Captatio": Myth and Reality', Ph.D. Diss. (University of Princeton, 1982).

MARA, J. A., *The Notion of Solidarity in St Ambrose's Teaching on Creation, Sin, and Redemption* (Rome, 1970).

MARA, M. G., *Ambrogio, La storia di Naboth* (Aquila, 1985).

MARKSCHIES, C., *Ambrosius von Mailand und die Trinitätstheologie: Kirchen- und theologiegeschichtliche Studie zu Antiarianismus und Neunizänismus bei Ambrosius und im lateinischen Westen (364–381 n. Chr.)*, Beiträge zur historischen Theologie, 90 (Tübingen 1995).

MARKUS, R. A., *Christianity in the Roman World* (London, 1974).

—— 'Paganism, Christianity and the Latin Classics in the Fourth Century', in J. W. Binns (ed.), *Latin Literature of the Fourth Century* (London, 1974), 1–21.

MARROU, H. I., *A History of Education in Antiquity*, ET of 3rd edn. (London, 1956).

—— *Saint Augustin et la fin de la culture antique*, 2nd edn. (Paris, 1949).

MARTIN, J.-P., *Providentia deorum: Recherches sur certains aspects réligieux du pouvoir impérial romain* (Rome, 1982).

MARTROYE, M., 'Une sentence arbitrale de saint Ambroise', *Revue historique de droit français et étranger*, ser. 4/8 (1929), 300–11.

MATTHEWS, J., *Western Aristocracies and Imperial Court, AD 364–425* (Oxford, 1975).

MAUR, H. J., Auf der, *Das Psalmenverständnis des Ambrosius von Mailand: Ein Beitrag zum Deutungshintergrund der Psalmenverwendung im Gottesdienst der alten Kirche* (Leiden, 1977).

MAZZARINO, S., *Storia sociale del vescovo Ambrogio*, Problemi e ricerche di storia antica, 4 (Rome, 1989).

MEISSEL, F., *Medizin in den Werken des hl. Ambrosius*, Diss. (Karl-Franzens-Universität Graz, 1983).

MENDELSOHN, I., 'Urim and Thummim', in *The Interpreter's Dictionary of the Bible*, iv (New York and Nashville, 1962), 739–40.

MENIS, G., 'Le giurisdizioni metropolitiche di Aquileia e di Milano nell'antichità', *Antichità altoadriatiche*, 4 (1973), 271–94.

MERKI, H., *Ὁμοίωσις Θεῷ von der platonischen Angleichung an Gott zur Gottähnlichkeit bei Gregor von Nyssa* (Fribourg, 1952).

MERTEN, E. W., *Bäder und Badegepflogenheiten in der Darstellung der Historia Augusta*, Antiquitas, Reihe 4: Beiträge zur Historia-Augusta-Forschung, Bd. 16 (Bonn, 1983).

MESLIN, M., 'Nationalisme, état, et religions à la fin du IVe siècle', *Archives de sociologie des religions*, 18 (1964), 3–20.

—— *Les Ariens d'Occident, 335–430*, Patristica Sorbonensia, 8 (Paris, 1967).

MESOT, J., *Die Heidenbekehrung bei Ambrosius von Mailand*, suppl. to *Neue Zeitschrift für Missionswissenschaft*, 7 (Schöneck-Beckenried, 1958).

MICHEL, A., 'Les Lois de la guerre et les problèmes de l'impérialisme romain dans la philosophie de Cicéron', in J.-P. Brisson (ed.), *Problèmes de la guerre à Rome* (Paris, 1969), 171–83.

—— 'Du De officiis de Cicéron à saint Ambroise: la théorie des devoirs', in *L'etica cristiana nei secoli III e IV: eredità e confronti* (Rome, 1996), 39–46.

MILLER, W. (ed./tr.), *Cicero: De officiis*, Loeb Classical Library (Cambridge, MA and London, 1913).

MIRABELLA ROBERTI, M., *Milano Romana* (Milan, 1984).

MITCHELL, T. N., *Cicero the Senior Statesman* (New Haven, CT, and London, 1991).

MOHRMANN, C., *Etudes sur le Latin des chrétiens*, 4 vols. (Rome, 1961–77).

MOHRMANN, M. E., 'Wisdom and the Moral Life: The Teachings of Ambrose of Milan', Ph.D. Diss. (University of Virginia, 1995).

MOMIGLIANO, A. (ed.), *The Conflict between Paganism and Christianity in the Fourth Century* (Oxford, 1963).

MONACHINO, V., *S. Ambrogio e la cura pastorale a Milano nel secolo IV* (Milan, 1973).

MOORHEAD, J., *Ambrose: Church and Society in the Late Roman World*, The Medieval World (London and New York, 1999).

MORGAN, R., *The Imagery of Light in St Ambrose's Theology* (Melbourne, 1998).

MORINO, C., *Church and State in the Teaching of St Ambrose*, ET (Washington, DC, 1969).

MUCKLE, J. T., 'The De Officiis Ministrorum of Saint Ambrose: An Example of the Process of Christianization of the Latin Language', *Mediaeval Studies*, 1 (1939), 63–80.

—— 'The Influence of Cicero in the Formation of Christian Culture', *Transactions of the Royal Society of Canada*, ser. 3, 42/2 (1948), 107–25.

MÜLLER, G., 'Arzt, Kranker und Krankheit bei Ambrosius von Mailand (334–397)', *Sudhoffs Archiv für Geschichte der Medizin und Naturwissenschaften*, 51/3 (1967), 193–216.

MÜLLER, D. H., 'Die Deutungen der hebräischen Buchstaben bei Ambrosius', *Sitzungsberichte der Kaiserlichen Akademie der Wissenschaften in Wien, Phil.-hist. Klasse*, 167/2 (1911).

MUNCEY, R. W., *The New Testament Text of Saint Ambrose*, Texts and Studies, 4 (Cambridge, 1959).

NAUROY, G., 'La Méthode de composition d'Ambroise de Milan et la structure du *De Iacob et vita beata*', in Y.-M. Duval (ed.), *Ambroise de Milan. XVIᵉ Centenaire de son élection épiscopale. Dix études* (Paris, 1974), 115–53.

—— 'La structure du *De Isaac vel de anima* et la cohérence de l'allégorèse d'Ambroise de Milan', *Revue des études latines*, 63 (1985), 210–36.

—— 'L'Ecriture dans la pastorale d'Ambroise de Milan', in J. Fontaine and C. Pietri (eds.), *Le Monde latin antique et la Bible*, Bible de tous les temps, 2 (Paris, 1985), 371–408.

—— 'Jérôme, lecteur et censeur de l'exégèse d'Ambroise', in Y.-M. Duval (ed.), *Jérôme entre l'Occident et l'Orient* (Paris, 1988), 173–203.

—— 'Le Fouet et le miel. Le combat d'Ambroise en 386 contre l'Arianisme milanais', *Recherches augustiniennes*, 23 (1988), 3–86.

—— 'Les Frères Maccabées dans l'exégèse d'Ambroise de Milan, ou la conversion de la sagesse judéo-hellénique aux valeurs du martyre chrétien', in *Figures de l'Ancien Testament chez les Pères*, Cahiers de Biblia Patristica, 2 (Strasbourg and Turnhout, 1989), 215–45.

—— 'Le Martyre de Laurent dans l'hymnodie et la prédication des IVe et Ve siècles, et l'authenticité ambrosienne de l'hymne "Apostolorum supparem"', *Revue des études augustiniennes*, 35 (1989), 44–82.

—— 'Du combat de la piété à la confession du sang: Ambroise de Milan lecteur critique du IVe livre des Maccabées', *Revue d'histoire et philosophie religieuse*, 70 (1990), 49–68.

NAUTIN, P., 'Etudes de chronologie hiéronymienne (393–397)', *Revues des études augustiniennes*, 20 (1974), 251–84.

NAWROCKA, A., 'L'Etat d'études concernant l'influence de l'éthique de Cicéron sur l'éthique de saint Ambroise', *Helikon*, 28 (1988), 315–24.

NAZZARO, A. V., 'La I Ecloga virgiliana nella lettura di Ambrogio', in G. Lazzati (ed.), *Ambrosius Episcopus*, 2 vols. (Milan, 1976), ii. 312–24.

—— 'Ambrosiana I. Note di critica testuale e d'esegesi', in

R. Cantalamessa and L. F. Pizzolato (eds.), *Paradoxos Politeia. Studi patristici in onore di Giuseppe Lazzati*, Studia Patristica Mediolanensia, 10 (Milan, 1979), 436–9.

—— 'Ambrosiana II. Note di critica testuale e d'esegesi', *Vichiana*, 8 (1979), 203–10.

NDOLELA, L., 'Original Communism in the "De Officiis" of Ambrose of Milan', *World Justice*, 12 (1970), 216–37.

NELSON, N. E., 'Cicero's De Officiis in Christian Thought: 300–1300', in *Essays and Studies in English and Comparative Literature*, University of Michigan Publications in Language and Literature, 10 (Ann Arbor, MI, 1933), 59–160.

NESTLE, W., 'Die Fabel des Menenius Agrippa', *Klio*, 21 (1927), 350–60.

NEUMANN, C. W., *The Virgin Mary in the Works of Saint Ambrose*, Paradosis, 17 (Fribourg, 1962).

NIEDERHUBER, J. E., *Die Lehre des hl. Ambrosius vom Reiche Gottes auf Erden: Eine patristische Studie*, Forschungen zur christlichen Literatur- und Dogmengeschichte, 4/3–4 (Mainz, 1904).

—— *Die Eschatologie des heiligen Ambrosius: Eine patristische Studie*, Forschungen zur christlichen Literatur- und Dogmengeschichte, 6/3 (Paderborn, 1907).

—— *Des heiligen Kirchenlehrers Ambrosius von Mailand, Pflichtenlehre und ausgewählte Kleinereschriften*, Bibliothek der Kirchenväter, 3/32 (Kempten and Munich, 1917).

NORTH, H., *Sophrosyne: Self-Knowledge and Self-Restraint in Greek Literature*, Cornell Studies in Classical Philology, 35 (Ithaca, NY, 1966).

—— 'Canons and Hierarchies of the Cardinal Virtues in Greek and Latin Literature', in L. Wallach (ed.), *The Classical Tradition: Literary and Historical Studies in Honor of Harry Caplan* (Ithaca, NY, 1966), 165–83.

NOSARI, G., *Del preteso stoicismo ciceroniano nei libri 'De officiis' di s. Ambrogio* (Parma, 1911).

OBERHELMAN, S. M., *Rhetoric and Homiletics in Fourth-Century Christian Literature: Prose Rhythm, Oratorical Style, and Preaching in the Works of Ambrose, Jerome, and Augustine*, American Philological Association: American Classical Studies, 26 (Atlanta, GA, 1991).

OBERTI SOBRERO, M., *L'etica sociale in Ambrogio di Milano: Ricostruzione delle fonti ambrosiane nel De iustitia di san Tommaso, II, II, qq. 57–122* (Turin, 1970).

O'DONNELL, J. J., 'The Demise of Paganism', *Traditio*, 35 (1979), 45–88.

O'Donnell, J. J., Augustine, Confessions: *Introduction, Text, &*
Commentary, 3 vols. (Oxford, 1992).

Ogilvie, R. M., *A Commentary on Livy Books 1–5* (Oxford, 1965).

Ogle, M. B., 'Molle atque facetum', *American Journal of Philology*,
37 (1916), 327–32.

O'Meara, J., 'Augustine and Neo-Platonism', *Recherches augusti-*
niennes, 1 (1958), 91–111.

Opelt, I., 'Christianisierung heidnischer Etymologien', *Jahrbuch für*
Antike und Christentum, ii (1959), 70–85.

—— 'Ciceros Schrift *De natura deorum* bei den lateinischen Kirch-
envätern', *Antike und Abendland*, 12 (1966), 141–55.

—— 'Etymologie', *Reallexikon für Antike und Christentum*, vi (1966),
797–844.

Orabona, L., 'L' "usurpatio" in un passo di s. Ambrogio (De off.
I.28) parallelo a Cicerone (De off. I.7) su "ius commune" e "ius
privatum"', *Aevum*, 33 (1959), 495–504.

Osiek, C., 'The Ramsom of Captives: Evolution of a Tradition',
Harvard Theological Review, 74 (1981), 365–86.

Otten, R. T., '*Amor, Caritas*, and *Dilectio*: Some Observations on
the Vocabulary of Love in the Exegetical Works of St Ambrose', in
E. J. Engels *et al.* (eds.), *Mélanges offerts à Mlle. Christine*
Mohrmann (Utrecht, 1963), 73–83.

Ottosson, M., 'Gilead', *Anchor Bible Dictionary*, ii (1992), 1020–2.

Pace, N., 'Il canto delle Sirene in Ambrogio, Gerolamo e altri Padri
della Chiesa', in L. F. Pizzolato and M. Rizzi (eds.), *Nec timeo mori*
(Milan, 1998), 673–95.

Palanque, J.-R., 'Famines à Rome à la fin du IVe siècle', *Revue des*
études anciennes, 33 (1931), 346–56.

—— *Saint Ambroise et l'empire romain. Contribution à l'histoire des*
rapports de l'Eglise et de l'Etat a la fin du quatrième siècle (Paris,
1933).

—— 'Les Préfets du prétoire sous les fils de Constantin', *Historia*, 4
(1955), 257–63.

Paredi, A., 'La liturgia di sant'Ambrogio', in *Sant'Ambrogio nel XV*
centenario della nascita (Milan, 1940), 69–157.

—— *Saint Ambrose: His Life and Times*, ET (Notre Dame, IN
1964).

—— 'S. Gerolamo e s. Ambrogio' in *Mélanges Eugene Tisserant*, 5
Studi e Testi, 235 (Vatican City, 1964), 183–98.

Pasini, C., *Ambrogio di Milano: Azione e pensiero di un vescov*
(Milan, 1996).

Pastè, R., 'Il sacerdozio negli scritti di tre Padri della chiesa', *L*
Scuola Cattolica, 54 (1926), 81–106, 271–85, 334–59.

PASTORINO, A., 'La filosofia antica in sant'Ambrogio (Rassegna bibliografica)', *Bollettino di studi latini*, 7 (1977), 88–104.

PAVAN, M., 'Sant'Ambrogio e il problema dei barbari', *Romano-barbarica*, 3 (1978), 167–87.

PEASE, A. S., 'Medical Allusions in the Works of St Jerome', *Harvard Studies in Classical Philology*, 25 (1914), 73–96.

PELLEGRINO, M., *Paulino di Milano: Vita di s. Ambrogio*, Verba seniorum, NS 1 (Rome, 1961).

——'"Mutus . . . loquar Christum." Pensieri di sant'Ambrogio su parola e silenzio', in R. Cantalamessa and L. F. Pizzolato (eds.), *Paradoxos Politeia: Studi patristici in onore di Giuseppe Lazzati*, Studia Patristica Mediolanensia, 10 (Milan, 1979), 447–57.

PÉPIN, J., *Théologie cosmique et théologie chrétienne (Ambroise, Exam. I.1.1–4)*, Bibliothèque de philosophie contemporaine (Paris, 1964).

——*Mythe et allégorie. Les origines grecques et les contestations judéo-chrétiennes*, 2nd edn. (Paris, 1976).

PERINI, C., 'Il celibato ecclesiastico nel pensiero di s. Ambrogio', *Divus Thomas*, 66 (1963), 432–50.

PERKINS, J., *The Suffering Self: Pain and Narrative Representation in the Early Christian Era* (London and New York, 1995).

PERLER, O., 'Arkandisziplin', *Reallexikon für Antike und Christentum*, i (1950), 667–76.

PERONI, C., 'Amicizia e mistero cristiano in s. Ambrogio', *La Scuola Cattolica*, 102 (1974), 429–50.

PETERSON, D., *Hebrews and Perfection: An Examination of the Concept of Perfection in the 'Epistle to the Hebrews'*, Society for New Testament Studies monograph series, 47 (Cambridge, 1982).

PETERSON, E., 'Das jugendliche Alter der Lektoren', *Ephemerides liturgicae*, 48 (1934), 437–42.

PÉTRÉ, H., '"Misericordia": Histoire du mot et de l'idée du paganisme au Christianisme', *Revue des études latines*, 12 (1934), 376–89.

——*Caritas: Etude sur le vocabulaire latin de la charité chrétien*, Spicilegium Sacrum Lovaniense, Etudes et Documents, 22 (Louvain, 1948).

PFITZNER, V. C., *Paul and the Agon Motif: Traditional Athletic Imagery in the Pauline Literature*, Suppl. to *Novum Testamentum*, 16 (Leiden, 1967).

PHAN, P. C. (ed.), *Social Thought*, Message of the Fathers of the Church, 20 (Wilmington, DE, 1984).

PICASSO, G. G., 'Gli "Excerpta Ambrosii" nelle collezioni canoniche dei secoli XI e XII', in G. Lazzati (ed.), *Ambrosius Episcopus*, 2 vols. (Milan, 1976), ii. 69–93.

PIEPER, J., *Das Viergespann. Klugheit, Gerechtigkeit, Tapferkeit, Mass* (Munich, 1964).

PIETRI, C., 'Les Pauvres et la pauvreté dans l'Italie de l'Empire chrétien', in *Miscellanea Historiae Ecclesiasticae*, 6, Bibliothèque de la *Revue d'histoire ecclésiastique*, 67 (Brussels, 1983), 267–300.

PIGANIOL, A., *L'empire chrétien (325–395)*, 2nd edn. (Paris, 1972).

PILHOFER, P., *Presbyteron Kreitton. Der Altersbeweis der jüdischen und christlichen Apologeten und seine Vorgeschichte*, Wissenschaftliche Untersuchungen zum Neuen Testament, 2. Reihe (Tübingen, 1990).

PIREDDA, A. M., 'La tipologia sacerdotale del patriarcha Giuseppe in Ambrogio', *Sandalion*, 10–11 (1987–8), 153–63.

—— 'Susanna e il silenzio: l'interpretazione di Ambrogio', *Sandalion*, 14 (1991), 169–92.

—— 'Il tema dell'ascolto negli scritti di Ambrogio di Milano', in *Dizionario di spiritualità biblica e patristica*, v (Rome, 1993), 292–9.

—— 'Aspetti del βίος pitagorico nell'etica cristiana di Ambrogio', in *L'etica cristiana neci secoli III e IV: eredità e confronti* (Rome, 1996), 305–16.

PIZZOLATO, L. F., *La 'Explanatio Psalmorum XII'. Studi letterario sulla esegesi di sant'Ambrogio*, Archivio Ambrosiano, 17 (Milan, 1965).

—— *L'amicizia cristiana. Antologia delle opere di Agostino di Ippona, e altri testi di Ambrogio di Milano, Gerolamo e Paulino di Nola*, Civiltà Letteraria di Grecia e di Roma, ser. lat. 31 (Turin, 1973).

—— 'L'amicizia nel *De officiis* di sant'Ambrogio e il *Laelius* di Cicerone: tradizione lessicale e originalità ideologica', in *Ricerche storiche sulla Chiesa ambrosiana, nel XVI centenario del l'episcopato di s. Ambrogio*, 4, Archivio Ambrosiano, 27 (Milan, 1974), 53–67.

—— *La dottrina esegetica di sant'Ambrogio*, Studia Patristica Mediolanensia, 9 (Milan, 1978).

—— *L'idea di amicizia nel mondo antico classico e cristiano* (Turin, 1993).

—— and Rizzi, M. (eds.), *Nec timeo mori: Atti del Congresso internazionale di studi ambrosiani nel XVI centenario della morte di sant'Ambrogio, Milano, 4–11 aprile 1997* (Milan, 1998).

—— 'Ambrogio e la retorica: le finalità del discorso', in *Nec timeo mori*, 235–65.

POHLENZ, M., *Die Stoa: Geschichte einer geistigen Bewegung*, 2 vols (Göttingen, 1948–9).

POHLSANDER, H. A., 'Victory: The Story of a Statue', *Historia*, 18 (1969), 588–97.

POIRIER, M., '"Consors naturae" chez saint Ambroise: Copropiété d la nature ou communauté de nature?', in G. Lazzati (ed.), *Ambrosius Episcopus*, 2 vols. (Milan, 1976), ii. 325–35.

—— '"Christus pauper factus est" chez saint Ambroise', *Rivista di Storia e letteratura religiosa*, 15 (1979), 250–7.

POWELL, J. G. F. (ed.), *Cicero the Philosopher: Twelve Papers* (Oxford, 1995).

PRÉAUX, J., 'Les Quatres Vertus païennes et chrétiennes. Apothéose et ascension', in J. Bibauw (ed.), *Hommages à Marcel Renard*, 3 vols. Collection Latomus, 101 (Brussels, 1969), i. 639–57.

PRINZIVALLI, E. (ed.), *Origène, Homélies sur les Psaumes 36 à 38*, with intro. transl. and notes by H. Crouzel and L. Brésard, Sources Chrétiennes, 411 (Paris, 1995).

RAHNER, H., *Symbole der Kirche. Die Ekklesiologie der Väter* (Salzburg, 1964).

RAIKAS, K., 'St Augustine on Juridical Duties: Some Aspects of the Episcopal Office in Late Antiquity', in J. C. Schnaubelt and F. Van Fleteren (eds.), *Collectanea Augustiniana: Augustine: 'Second Founder of the Faith'* (New York, 1990), 467–83.

RAMAGE, E. S., Urbanitas: *Ancient Sophistication and Refinement*, University of Cincinnati Classical Studies, 3 (Norman, OK, 1973).

RAMSEY, B., 'Almsgiving in the Latin Church: The Late Fourth and Early Fifth Centuries', *Theological Studies*, 43 (1982), 226–59.

——*Ambrose*, The Early Church Fathers (London and New York, 1997).

RAND, E. K., *Founders of the Middle Ages* (Cambridge, MA, 1928).

RAUSCHEN, G., *Jahrbücher der christlichen Kirche unter dem Kaiser Theodosius dem Grossen* (Freiburg, 1897).

REBENICH, S., *Hieronymus und sein Kreis: Prosopographische und sozialgeschichtliche Untersuchungen*, Historia Einzelschriften, Heft 72 (Stuttgart, 1992).

REBILLARD, E., *In hora mortis. Evolution de la pastorale chrétienne de la mort aux IVe et Ve siècles dans l'Occident latin*, Bibliothèque des écoles françaises d'Athènes et de Rome, fasc. 283 (Rome, 1994).

——and SOTINEL, C. (eds.), *L'Evêque dans la cité du IVe au Ve siècle. Image et authorité*. Actes de la table ronde organisée par l'Istituto patristico Augustinianum et l'Ecole Française de Rome (Rome, Ier et 2 décembre 1995), Collection de l'école Française de Rome, 248 (Rome, 1998).

REEB, J., *Über die Grundlagen des Sittlichen nach Cicero und Ambrosius: Vergleichung ihrer Schriften De officiis. Ein Beitrag zur Bestimmung des Verhältnisses zwischen heidnisch-philosophischer und christlicher Ethik* (Zweibrücken, 1876).

REYNOLDS, L. D., *M. Tulli Ciceronis De finibus bonorum et malorum libri quinque recognovit brevique adnotatione critica instruxit*, Oxford Classical Texts (Oxford, 1998).

RICCI, M. L., 'Fortuna di una formula ciceroniana presso sant'Ambrogio (a proposito di *iustitia*)', *Studi italiani di filologia classica*, 43 (1971), 222–45.

RICHLIN, A., 'Gender and Rhetoric: Producing Manhood in the Schools', in W. J. Dominik (ed.), *Roman Eloquence: Rhetoric in Society and Literature* (London and New York, 1997), 90–110.

RICKMAN, G., *The Corn Supply of Ancient Rome* (Oxford, 1980).

RIDINGS, D., *The Attic Moses: The Dependency Theme in Some Early Christian Writers*, Studia Graeca et Latina Gothoburgensia, 59 (Gothenburg, 1995).

RIGGI, C., 'L'"Auxesis" del Salmo XXXVIII nel "De officiis" di s. Ambrogio', *Salesianum*, 29 (1967), 623–68.

——'La verginità nel pensiero di s. Ambrogio', *Salesianum*, 42 (1980), 789–806.

RING, T. G., *Auctoritas bei Tertullian, Cyprian und Ambrosius*, Cassiciacum, 29 (Würzburg, 1975).

RIST, J. M., *Stoic Philosophy* (Cambridge, 1969).

——*Augustine: Ancient Thought Baptized* (Cambridge, 1994).

ROBERTS, B. J., *The Old Testament Text and Versions: The Hebrew Text in Transmission and the History of the Ancient Versions* (Cardiff, 1951).

ROSEN, K., 'Fides contra dissimulationem: Ambrosius und Symmachus im Kampf um den Victoriaaltar', *Jahrbuch für Antike und Christentum*, 37 (1994), 29–36.

ROSSI, C., 'Il De officiis di Cicerone e il De officiis di Ambrogio: rapporti di contenuto e forma', in F. Sergio (ed.), '*Humanitas*' *classica e 'sapientia' cristiana: scritti offerti a Roberto Iacoangeli* (Rome, 1992), 145–62.

ROUECHÉ, C., 'Acclamations in the Later Roman Empire: New Evidence from Aphrodisias', *Journal of Roman Studies*, 74 (1984), 181–99.

ROUSSELLE, A., 'Parole et inspiration: le travail de la voix dans le monde romain', *History and Philosophy of the Life Sciences*, 5 (1983), 129–57.

RUNIA, D. T., *Philo in Early Christian Literature: A Survey*, Jewish Traditions in Early Christian Literature, 3 (Assen and Minneapolis, MN, 1993).

RUSCH, W. G., *The Later Latin Fathers* (London, 1977).

RUSSELL, D. A., 'De Imitatione', in D. West and A. J. Woodman (eds.), *Creative Imitation and Latin Literature* (Cambridge, 1979), 1–16.

RYAN, J. A., *Alleged Socialism of the Church Fathers* (St Louis, MO, 1913).

SACHMATA, R., *La concezione della virtù nel 'De officiis ministrorum' di sant'Ambrogio* (Rome, 1993).

SALLER, R. P., *Personal Patronage under the Early Empire* (Cambridge, 1982).

SALLMANN, K., 'Christen von dem Theater', in J. Blänsdorf (ed.), *Theater und Gesellschaft im Imperium Romanum* (Tübingen, 1990), 243–60.

SANDERS, G. and VAN UYTFANGHE, M. (eds.), *Bibliographie signalétique du latin des chrétiens*, Corpus Christianorum, series Latina, Lingua Patrum, 1 (Turnhout, 1989).

SARGENTI, M. and BRUNO SIOLA, R. B., *Normativa imperiale e diritto Romano negli scritti di s. Ambrogio: Epistulae—De officiis—Orationes funebres*, Accademia Romanistica Costantiniana: Materiali per una palingenesi delle costituzioni tardo-imperiali, 4 (Milan, 1991).

SAUER, R., *Studien zur Pflichtenlehre des Ambrosius von Mailand*, Diss. (Würzburg, 1981).

SAVIO, F., *Gli antichi vescovi d'Italia, dalle origini al 1300: Milano* (Bologna, 1913, repr. 1975).

SAVON, H., 'Quelques remarques sur la chronologie des œuvres de saint Ambroise', *Studia Patristica*, 10 (1970), 156–60.

—— 'Maniérisme et allégorie dans l'œuvre d'Ambroise de Milan', *Revue des études latines*, 55 (1977), 203–21.

—— *Saint Ambroise devant l'exégèse de Philon le Juif* (Paris, 1977).

—— 'Saint Ambroise et la philosophie à propos d'une étude récente', *Revue d'histoire des religions*, 191 (1977), 173–196.

—— La Première Oraison funèbre de saint Ambroise (*De excessu fratris* 1) et les deux sources de la consolation chrétienne', *Revue des études latines*, 58 (1980), 370–402.

—— 'Un modèle de sainteté à la fin du IVe siècle: la virginité dans l'œuvre de saint Ambroise', in J. Marx (ed.), *Sainteté et martyre dans les religions du Livre*, Problèmes d'histoire du christianisme, 19 (Brussels, 1989), 21–31.

—— 'Les Intentions de saint Ambroise dans la préface du *De officiis*', in M. Soetard (ed.), *Valeurs dans le stoïcisme, du portique à nos jours: Textes rassemblés en hommage à Michel Spanneut* (Lille, 1993), 155–69.

—— 'Les Recherches sur saint Ambroise en Allemagne et en France de 1870 à 1930', in J. Fontaine, R. Herzog, and K. Pollmann (eds.), *Patristique et Antiquité tardive en Allemagne et en France de 1870 à 1930: influences et échanges: Actes du colloque franco-allemand de Chantilly (25–27 octobre 1991)* (Paris, 1993), 111–28.

SAVON, H., 'Saint Ambroise a-t-il imité le recueil de lettres de Pline le Jeune?', *Revue des études augustiniennes*, 41 (1995), 3–17.
—— *Ambroise de Milan (340–397)* (Paris, 1997).
SCHANZ, M., *Geschichte der römischen Literatur bis zum Gesetz-gebungswerk des Kaisers Justinian*, 4/1 (Munich, 1914).
SCHILLING, O., *Reichtum und Eigentum in der altchristlichen Literatur* (Freiburg, 1908).
—— 'Der Kollektivismus der Kirchenväter', *Theologische Quartal-schrift*, 114 (1933), 481–92.
SCHMID, D., *Der Erbschleicher in der antiken Satire*, Diss. (Tübingen, 1951).
SCHMID, W., 'Epikur', in *Reallexikon für Antike und Christentum*, v, 681–819.
SCHMIDT, TH., *Ambrosius, sein Werk De officiis libri III und die Stoa* (Augsburg, 1897).
SCHNUSENBERG, C., *Das Verhältnis von Kirche und Theater. Dar-gestellt an ausgewählten Schriften der Kirchenväter und liturgischen Texte bis auf Amalarius von Metz (a.d. 775–852)*, Europaïsche Hochschulschriften, 141 (Frankfurt, 1981).
SCHOFIELD, M., *The Stoic Idea of the City* (Cambridge, 1991).
SCHULTE, F. X., *Ausgewählte Schriften des heiligen Ambrosius, Bischofs von Mailand*, Bibliothek der Kirchenväter, 2 (Kempten, 1877).
SCHWERDT, P. K., *Studien zur Lehre des heiligen Ambrosius von der Person Christi* (Bückeburg, 1937).
SCULLARD, H. H., *Early Christian Ethics in the West, from Clement to Ambrose* (London, 1907).
SEIBEL, W., *Fleisch und Geist beim heiligen Ambrosius*, Münchener Theologische Studien, 2/14 (Munich, 1958).
SEIPEL, I., *Die wirtschaftsethischen Lehren der Kirchenväter* (Vienna, 1907).
SELB, W., 'Episcopalis Audientia von der Zeit Konstantins bis zur Novelle XXXV Valentinians III.', *Zeitschrift der Savigny-Stiftung für Rechtsgeschichte* (Romanistische Abteilung), 84 (1967), 162–217.
SEVENSTER, J. N., *Paul and Seneca* (Leiden, 1961).
SEYFFERT, M. and MÜLLER, C. F. W. (eds.), *Cicero, Laelius: De amicitia dialogus* (Hildesheim, 1965).
SHERIDAN, J. J., 'The Altar of Victory—Paganism's Last Battle', *L'antiquité classique*, 35 (1966), 186–206.
SIMBECK, K. (ed.), *M. Tulli Ciceronis scripta quae manserunt omnia. Cato Maior; Laelius* (with O. Plasberg (ed.), *De gloria*), Bibliotheca Scriptorum Graecorum et Romanorum Teubneriana, fasc. 47 (Stuttgart, 1961).

Simonetti, M., *La crisi Ariana nel IV secolo*, Studia Ephemeridis Augustinianum, 11 (Rome, 1975).

Smith, K. F., 'The Tale of Gyges and the King of Lydia', *American Journal of Philology*, 23 (1902), 261–82, 361–87.

Sörries, R., *Auxentius und Ambrosius. Ein Beitrag zur frühchristlichen Kunst Mailands zwischen Häresie und Rechtgläubigkeit*, Christliche Archäologie, 1 (Dettelbach, 1996).

Solignac, A., 'Nouveaux parallèles entre saint Ambroise et Plotin: le "De Iacob et vita beata" et le Περὶ Εὐδαιμονίας (*Ennéade* I, 4)', *Archives de philosophie*, 20 (1956), 148–56.

Somenzi, C., 'Ambrogio e Scipione l'Africano: la fondazione cristiana dell' "otium negotiosum"', in L. F. Pizzolato and M. Rizzi (eds.), *Nec timeo mori* (Milan, 1998), 753–68.

Sordi, M., 'La concezione politica di Ambrogio', in *I Cristiani e l'Impero nel IV secolo. Atti del convegno di Macerata (17–18 decembro 1987)* (Macerata, 1988), 143–54.

Spach, F., *Etude sur le traité de saint Ambroise, 'De officiis ministrorum'* (Strasbourg, 1859).

Spanneut, M., *Le Stoïcisme des Pères de l'Eglise, de Clément de Rome à Clément d'Alexandrie*, Patristica Sorbonensia, 1 (Paris, 1957).

—— *Permanence du stoïcisme, de Zénon à Malraux* (Gembloux, 1973).

—— 'La Notion de nature, des stoïciens aux Pères de l'Eglise', *Recherches de théologie ancienne et médiévale*, 37 (1970), 165–73.

—— 'Les Normes morales du stoïcisme chez les Pères de l'Eglise', *Studia Moralia*, 19 (1981), 153–75.

—— 'Le Stoïcisme dans l'histoire de la patience chrétienne', *Mélanges science religieuse*, 39 (1982), 101–30.

—— 'Patience et martyre chez les Pères de l'Eglise', *Compostellanum*, 35 (1990), 545–60.

Spedalieri, F., 'S. Ambrogio e l'eccellenza del sacerdozio', *La civiltà cattolica*, 91/4 (1940), 321–31.

Springer, M. T., *Nature-Imagery in the Works of St Ambrose*, Catholic University of America Patristic Studies, 30 (Washington, DC, 1931).

Squire, A., *Ælred of Rievaulx: A Study* (London, 1969).

Squitieri, G., *Il preteso communismo di s. Ambrogio* (Sarno, 1946).

Steidle, W., 'Beobachtungen zu des Ambrosius Schrift, De Officiis', *Vigiliae Christianae*, 38 (1984), 18–66.

—— 'Beobachtungen zum Gedankengang im 2. Buch von Ambrosius, De Officiis', *Vigiliae Christianae*, 39 (1985), 280–98.

Stelzenberger, J., *Die Beziehungen der frühchristlichen Sittenlehre zur Ethik der Stoa: Eine moralgeschichtliche Studie* (Munich, 1933).

Sternberg, T., ' "Aurum utile." Zu einem Topos vom Vorrang der

Caritas über Kirchenschätze seit Ambrosius', *Jahrbuch für Antike und Christentum*, 39 (1996), 128–48.

STEWART, Z., 'Greek Crowns and Christian Martyrs', in E. Lucchesi and H. D. Saffrey (eds.), *Mémorial André-Jean Festugière. Antiquité païenne et chrétienne*, Cahiers d'Orientalisme, 10 (Geneva, 1984), 119–24.

STOWERS, S. K., *The Diatribe and Paul's Letter to the Romans* (Chico, CA, 1981).

STUDER, B., 'Il sacerdozio dei fedeli in sant'Ambrogio di Milano (Rassegna bibliografica 1960–1970)', *Vetera Christianorum*, 7 (1970), 325–40.

SWIFT, L. J., 'St Ambrose on Violence and War', *Transactions and Proceedings of the American Philological Association*, 101 (1970), 533–43.

—— '*Iustitia* and *Ius privatum*: Ambrose on Private Property', *American Journal of Philology*, 100 (1979), 176–87.

—— *The Early Fathers on War and Military Service*, Message of the Fathers of the Church, 19 (Wilmington, DE, 1983).

SWOBODA, A., 'Projęcie beneficentia i benevolentia w "De officiis ministrorum" św. Ambrożego i w "De officiis" Cycerona', *Vox Patrum*, 8 (1988), 767–85.

SYME, R., *The Roman Revolution* (Oxford, 1939).

SYPHERD, W. O., *Jephthah and his Daughter: A Study in Comparative Literature* (Newark, DE, 1948).

SZYDZIK, S.-E., *'Ad imaginem Dei': Die Lehre von der Gottebenbildlichkeit des Menschen bei Ambrosius von Mailand*, Diss. (Freie Universität, Berlin, 1961).

—— 'Die geistigen Ursprünge der Imago-Dei-Lehre bei Ambrosius von Mailand', *Theologie und Glaube*, 53 (1963), 161–76.

TANZOLA, V. T., 'A Comparative Study of the Cardinal Virtues in Cicero's De Officiis and in St Ambrose's De Officiis Ministrorum', Ph.D. Diss. (Catholic University of America, 1975).

TAORMINA, L., 'Sant'Ambrogio e Plotino', *Miscellanea di studi di letteratura cristiana antica*, 4 (1953), 41–85.

TARDIEU, M., *Le Manichéisme* (Paris, 1983).

TESTARD, M., *Saint Augustin et Cicéron*, 2 vols. (Paris 1958).

—— 'Le Fils de Cicéron, destinataire du De officiis', *Bulletin de l'Association Guillaume Budé* (1962), 198–213.

—— (ed.), *Cicéron, Les Devoirs: Texte établi et traduit*, 2 vols. (Paris 1965–70).

—— 'Observations sur le thème de la *conscientia* dans le *De officiis ministrorum* de saint Ambroise', *Revue des études latines*, 51 (1973) 219–61.

—— 'Etude sur la composition dans le *De officiis ministrorum* de saint Ambroise', in Y.-M. Duval (ed.), *Ambroise de Milan. XVIe Centenaire de son élection épiscopale. Dix études* (Paris, 1974), 155–97.

—— *Saint Ambroise: Les Devoirs: Texte établi, traduit et annoté*, 2 vols. (Paris, 1984–92).

—— 'Saint Ambroise et son modèle cicéronien dans le *De officiis*', in R. Chevallier (ed.), *Présence de Cicéron: Actes du colloque des 25, 26 Septembre 1982, hommage au R.P.M. Testard, Caesarodunum*, 19 bis (Paris, 1984), 103–6.

—— 'Observations sur le rhétorique d'une harangue au peuple dans le Sermo contra Auxentium de saint Ambroise', *Revue des études latines*, 63 (1985), 193–209.

—— 'Jérôme et Ambroise. Sur un "aveu" du *De officiis* de l'évêque de Milan', in Y.-M. Duval (ed.), *Jérôme entre l'Occident et l'Orient* (Paris, 1988), 227–54.

—— 'Problèmes de critique verbale dans le *De Officiis*, III, 45, de saint Ambroise', *Revue des études latines*, 66 (1988), 219–28.

—— 'Recherches sur quelques méthodes de travail de saint Ambroise dans le *De Officiis*', *Recherches augustiniennes*, 24 (1989), 65–122.

—— 'Le *De officiis* de saint Ambroise. Observations philologiques et historiques sur le sens et le contexte du traité', *Recherches augustiniennes*, 28 (1995), 3–35.

THAMIN, R., *Saint Ambroise et la morale chrétienne au IVe siècle: Etude comparée des traités 'Des Devoirs' de Cicéron et de saint Ambroise*, Annales de l'Université de Lyon, 18 (Paris, 1895).

THOMPSON, E. A., *The Visigoths in the Time of Ulfila* (Oxford, 1966).

THURMAIR, M., 'Das Decorum als zentraler Begriff in Ciceros Schrift de Officiis', in E. Hora and E. Kessler (eds.), *Studia humanitatis: Ernesto Grassi zum 70. Geburtstag* (Munich, 1973), 63–78.

THURSTON, B. B., *The Widows: A Woman's Ministry in the Early Church* (Minneapolis, MN, 1989).

TIBILETTI, C., 'Stoicism and the Fathers', in A. di Berardino (ed.), *Encyclopedia of the Early Church*, 2 vols., ET (Cambridge, 1992), ii. 795–7.

TOSCANI, G., *Teologia della Chiesa in sant'Ambrogio*, Studia Patristica Mediolanensia, 3 (Milan, 1974).

TREU, K., 'Freundschaft', *Reallexikon für Antike und Christentum*, viii (1970), 418–34.

TSCHANG, B. IN-SAN, *Octo Beatitudines: Die Acht Seligspreisungen als Stufenleiter der Seele bei Ambrosius*, Diss. (Rheinische Friedrich-Wilhelms-Universität, Bonn, 1986).

TUCKETT, C. M., 'Messianic Secret', in *Anchor Bible Dictionary*, iv (1992), 797–800.

TURLEY, J. P., 'Hic aquatio: Cicero, *De officiis* III.14–59', *Classical Journal*, 37 (1942), 485–9.

VAGGIONE, R. P., *Eunomius: The Extant Works*, Oxford Early Christian Texts (Oxford, 1987).

VAN DE PAVERD, *St John Chrysostom: The Homilies on the Statues* (Rome, 1991).

VAN HAERINGEN, J. H., 'De Valentiniano II et Ambrosio: Illustrantur et digeruntur res anno 386 gestae', *Mnemosyne*, 5 (1937): (1) 'Valentinianus II basilicam adornitur (de Ambrosii epistula XX)', 152–8; (2) 'De Ambrosii epistula XXI', 28–33; (3) 'De Ambrosii epistulis XX et XXI: temporum descriptio', 229–40.

VANSTEENBERGHE, G., 'Amitié', *Dictionnaire de spiritualité*, i (1937), 500–29.

VAN STRAATEN, M., *Panétius, sa vie, ses écrits et sa doctrine, avec une édition des fragments* (Amsterdam and Paris, 1946).

VASEY, V. R., 'Proverbs 17.6b (LXX) and St Ambrose's Man of Faith', *Augustinianum*, 14 (1974), 259–76.

—— 'St Ambrose's Mirror for Judges', *The Jurist*, 39 (1979), 437–46.

—— *The Social Ideas in the Works of St Ambrose: A Study on De Nabuthe*, Studia Ephemeridis Augustinianum, 17 (Rome, 1982).

VERBEKE, G., *The Presence of Stoicism in Medieval Thought* (Washington, DC, 1983).

VERMEULEN, A. J. *The Semantic Development of* Gloria *in Early-Christian Latin*, Latinitas Christianorum Primaeva, 12 (Nijmegen, 1956).

VESSEY, M., 'English Translations of the Latin Fathers, 1517–1611', in I. Backus (ed.), *The Reception of the Church Fathers in the West, from the Carolingians to the Maurists*, 2 vols. (Leiden, 1997), ii. 775–835.

VEYNE, P. *Bread and Circuses*, ET (London, 1990).

VISCONTI, L., 'Il primo trattato di filosofia morale cristiana (Il De officiis di s. Ambrogio e di Cicerone)', *Atti della Reale Accademia d'Archeologia, Lettere e Belle Arte di Napoli*, 25/2 (1908), 41–61.

VISMARA, G., 'Ancora sulla episcopalis audientia. Ambrogio arbitro o guidice', *Studia et documenta historiae et iuris*, 53 (1987), 53–73.

VOELKE, A.-J., *L'Idée de volunté dans le stoïcisme* (Paris, 1973).

VOGEL, C., *Medieval Liturgy: An Introduction to the Sources*, ET (Washington, DC, 1986).

WACHT, M., 'Privateigentum bei Cicero und Ambrosius', *Jahrbuch für Antike und Christentum*, 25 (1982), 28–64.

WADDELL, H., *The Wandering Scholars*, 7th edn. (London, 1934).

WAGNER, F., *Der Sittlichkeitsbegriff in der hl. Schrift und in de altchristlichen Ethik*, Münsterische Beiträge zur Theologie, 19 (Münster, 1931).

WALBANK, F. W., 'The Scipionic Legend', *Proceedings of the Cambridge Philological Society*, 13 (1967), 54–69.

WALDSTEIN, W., 'Zur Stellung der Episcopalis Audientia im spätrömischen Prozess', in D. Medicus and H. H. Seiler (eds.), *Festschrift für Max Kaser zum 70. Geburtstag* (Munich, 1976), 533–56.

WALSH, P. G. (tr./ed.), *Letters of St. Paulinus of Nola*, 2 vols., Ancient Christian Writers, 35–6 (Westminster, MD, and London, 1967).

—— 'Paulinus of Nola and the Conflict of Ideologies in the Fourth Century', in P. Granfield and J. A. Jungmann (eds.), *Kyriakon: Festschrift Johannes Quasten*, 2 vols. (Münster, 1970), ii. 565–71.

—— 'The Rights and Wrongs of Curiosity (Plutarch to Augustine)', *Greece and Rome*, 35 (1988), 73–85.

—— and WALSH, J., *Divine Providence and Human Suffering*, Message of the Fathers of the Church, 17 (Wilmington, DE, 1985).

WAND, J. W. C., *The Latin Doctors* (London, 1948).

WEISMANN, W., *Kirche und Schauspiele. Die Schauspiele im Urteil der lateinischen Kirchenväter unter besonderer Berücksichtigung von Augustin*, Cassiciacum, 27 (Würzburg, 1972).

WEISS, F., 'Der hl. Ambrosius an die Priester', *Schweizerische Kirchenzeitung*, 126 (1958), 310–12.

WEISSENGRUBER, F., 'Benützung des Ambrosius durch Cassiodorus', in G. Lazzati (ed.), *Ambrosius Episcopus*, 2 vols. (Milan, 1976), ii. 378–98.

WELTIN, E. G., *Athens and Jerusalem: An Interpretative Essay on Christianity and Classical Culture*, American Academy of Religion Studies in Religion, 49 (Atlanta, GA, 1987).

WENGST, K., *Humility: Solidarity of the Humiliated* (London, 1988).

WESTCOTT, B. F., *The Epistle to the Hebrews*, 2nd edn. (London, 1892).

WHITE, C., *Christian Friendship in the Fourth Century* (Cambridge, 1992).

WIESEN, D. S., *St Jerome as a Satirist: A Study in Christian Latin Thought and Letters* (Ithaca, NY, 1964).

WILBRAND, W., 'Ambrosius und Plato', *Römische Quartalschrift für christliche Altertumskunde*, 25 (1911), 42*–49*.

—— 'Die Deutungen der biblischen Eigennamen beim hl. Ambrosius', *Biblische Zeitschrift*, 10 (1912), 337–50.

—— 'Zur Chronologie einiger Schriften des hl. Ambrosius', *Historisches Jahrbuch*, 41 (1921), 1–19.

—— 'Heidentum und Heidenmission bei Ambrosius von Mailand',

Zeitschrift für Missionswissenschaft und Religionswissenschaft, 1 (1938), 193–202.

WILBRAND, W., 'Ambrosius von Mailand als Bischof', *Theologie und Glaube*, 33 (1941), 190–5.

WILES, M., 'Eunomius: Hair-Splitting Dialectician or Defender of the Accessibility of Salvation?', in R. Williams (ed.), *The Making of Orthodoxy: Essays in Honour of Henry Chadwick* (Cambridge, 1989), 157–72.

WILLE, G., *Musica Romana. Die Bedeutung der Musik im Leben der Römer* (Amsterdam, 1967).

WILLIAMS, D. H., 'When did the Emperor Gratian Return the Basilica to the Pro-Nicenes in Milan?' *Studia Patristica*, 24 (1994), 208–15.

—— *Ambrose of Milan and the End of the Nicene–Arian Conflicts*, Oxford Early Christian Studies (Oxford, 1995).

—— 'Politically Correct in Milan: A Reply to "Diehard Homoians and the Election of Ambrose"', *Journal of Early Christian Studies*, 5 (1997), 441–6.

WILLIAMS, R., *Arius: Heresy and Tradition* (London, 1987).

WILLIS, G. G., review of R. W. Muncey, *The New Testament Text of Saint Ambrose*, in *Journal of Theological Studies*, NS 11 (1960), 172–6.

WINTERBOTTOM, M., *M. Tulli Ciceronis, De Officiis, recognovit brevique adnotatione critica instruxit*, Oxford Classical Texts (Oxford, 1994).

—— 'The Text of Ambrose's *De Officiis*', *Journal of Theological Studies*, NS 46 (1995), 559–66.

WOMER, J. L. (ed.), *Morality and Ethics in Early Christianity*, Sources of Early Christian Thought (Philadelphia, 1987).

YEGÜL, F. K., *Baths and Bathing in Classical Antiquity* (New York, 1992).

YOUNG, F., *Biblical Exegesis and the Formation of Christian Culture* (Cambridge, 1997).

ZANGARA, V., 'L'*inventio* dei martiri Gervasio e Protasio: Testimonianze di Agostino su un fenomeno di religiosità popolare', *Augustinianum*, 21 (1981), 119–33.

ZELZER, K., 'Zur Beurteilung der Cicero-Imitatio bei Ambrosius, De officiis', *Wiener Studien*, 90 (1977), 168–91.

—— 'Randbemerkungen zu Absicht und Arbeitsweise des Ambrosius in De officiis', *Wiener Studien*, 107/8 (1994–5), 481–93.

—— 'L'etica di sant'Ambrogio e la tradizione storica delle virtù', in *L'etica cristiana nei secoli III e IV: eredità e confronti* (Rome, 1996), 47–56.

ZELZER, M., 'Ambrosius von Mailand und das Erbe der klassischen Tradition', *Wiener Studien*, 100 (1987), 201–26.

—— '*Plinius Christianus*: Ambrosius als Epistolograph', *Studia Patristica*, 23 (1989), 203–8.

—— 'Vescovi e pastori alla luce delle lettere ambrosiane', in *Vescovi e pastori in epoca teodosiana*, 2 vols. (Rome, 1997), ii. 559–68.

—— 'Zur Chronologie der Werke des Ambrosius: Überblick über die Forschung von 1974 bis 1997', in L. F. Pizzolato and M. Rizzi (eds.), *Nec timeo mori* (Milan, 1998), 73–92.

ZIELINSKI, TH., *Cicero im Wandel der Jahrhunderte*, 2nd edn. (Leipzig and Berlin, 1908).

INDEXES

References are for the most part to clear or possible evocations of sources, rather than to citations of general parallels or other comments in notes. Figures relate to sections of Ambrose's text.

I. Cicero

II. Other Ancient Authors

III. Biblical

Index

IV. General

Index